THE
THIRD
COAST

WHEN CHICAGO BUILT

the

AMERICAN DREAM

THOMAS DYJA

The Penguin Press

New York

2013

THE PENGUIN PRESS
Published by the Penguin Group
Penguin Group (USA) Inc., 375 Hudson Street,
New York, New York 10014, USA

USA • Canada • UK • Ireland • Australia
New Zealand • India • South Africa • China

Penguin Books Ltd, Registered Offices:
80 Strand, London WC2R 0RL, England
For more information about the Penguin Group visit penguin.com

Permission credits appear on pages 507–8.

All maps by Marty Schnure.

Library of Congress Cataloging-in-Publication Data
Dyja, Tom.
The third coast : when Chicago built the American dream /
Thomas Dyja.
pages cm
Includes bibliographical references and index.
ISBN 978-1-59420-432-6
1. Chicago (Ill.)—History—20th century.   2. Chicago (Ill.)—Social
conditions—20th century.   3. Chicago (Ill.)—Intellectual life—20th
century.   4. Chicago (Ill.)—Relations—United States.   5. United
States—Relations—Illinois—Chicago.   I. Title.
F548.52.D95 2013
977.3'11043—dc23   2012039710

Printed in the United States of America
1   3   5   7   9   10   8   6   4   2

Book design by Marysarah Quinn

FOR KAYE

"There may be unknown dreamers here!"

Louis Sullivan

CONTENTS

CHICAGOLAND

Lake

DOWNTOWN
& TOWERTOWN

BRONZEV

Caldwell's Lily Pool

STANISLAWOWO

JEFFERSON PARK

Cicero,

McDonald's No. 1

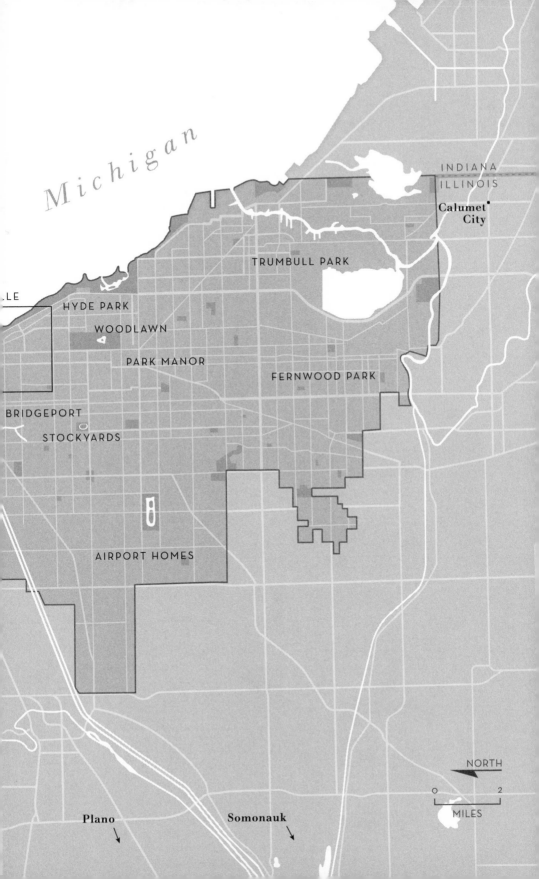

BRONZEVILLE

NORTH

0   1/2

MILES

DOWNTOWN

and

TOWERTOWN

LAKE SHORE DRIVE

RUSH ST.

DIVISION ST.

CHICAGO AVE.

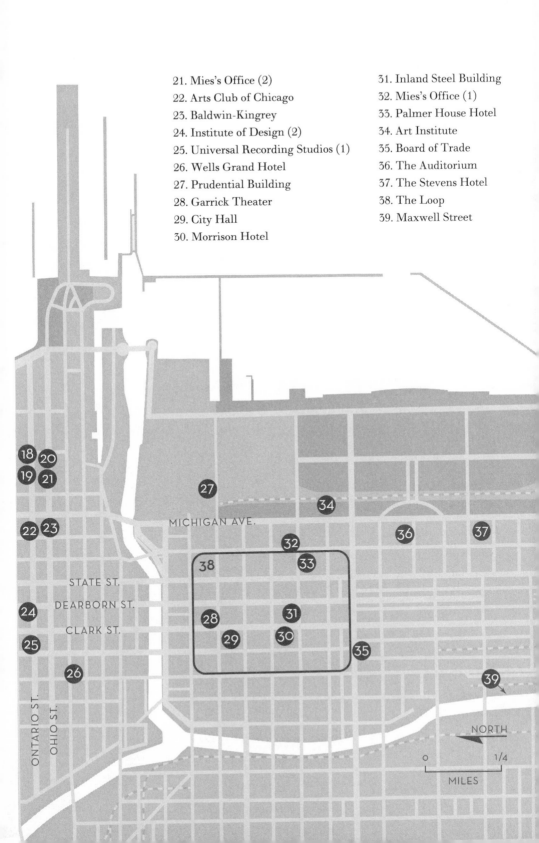

MICHIGAN AVE.

STATE ST.

DEARBORN ST.

CLARK ST.

ONTARIO ST.

OHIO ST.

NORTH

0   1/4

MILES

THE THIRD COAST

PREFACE

UNDER THE LIGHT of a single bulb, the old drunk slipped into a coma. Louis Sullivan, the greatest architect in a city of great architecture, lay dying of kidney disease at the Warner Hotel on 33rd and Cottage Grove, five years after the White Sox had met there to fix the 1919 World Series. His last designs had been a series of extravagant little banks in midwestern hamlets, jewel boxes cascading with his glorious ornament, but they'd paid nothing, so old friends like his former protégé Frank Lloyd Wright had chipped in for this dingy room. As the bulb swung and his breathing shallowed, Chicagoans went on shopping in his department stores, cooking dinner in his homes, shuffling papers in his offices, dozing off in his theaters, and praying in the churches he'd created. Few had any clue how Sullivan had given form to the functions of their lives.

He'd come to Chicago in 1873, chased west by the year's financial panic to a city whose purpose was to be in the middle. Before Marquette and Joliet came through in the late 1600s, centuries of Potawatomi Indians had portaged here between Lake Michigan and the Des Plaines River, paddling on to the Mississippi. French fur traders set up shop in the 1700s, and as the railroads pushed west in the next century, the frontier outpost named Fort Dearborn grew into Chicago, hub of the expanding nation. From every direction, people, resources, and products moved through its muddy plains, soon the site of the world's biggest, wildest boomtown, and when the fire of 1871 scoured most of the city away, America willed it back into existence, this time even bigger and wilder. Between 1870 and 1890, the city's population grew from just under 300,000 to more than a million souls densely packed and separate, every person there to do, to make, to somehow get theirs. Grain and livestock mattered as much as pig iron; labor confronted capital; new sciences were explored amid back-alley violence. "Having seen it, I urgently desire never to see it again," said an uncharacteristically prim Rudyard Kipling after an 1890 visit. "It is inhabited by savages." Historian William Cronon has called it "the grandest, most spectacular country fair the world has ever seen." You could probably find fifty just like it now in China, but Chicago was the first of its kind, and Louis Sullivan had loved it at first sight. "Here . . . was power," he wrote, "naked power, naked as the prairies, greater than the mountains."

After a short stint at the École des Beaux-Arts in Paris, Sullivan teamed up with Dankmar Adler to design scores of buildings that expressed the extremes of the city that gave America its meat, steel, and the Wizard of Oz. Together Sullivan and Adler refined the idea of what a skyscraper should be. They pushed the limits of technology in buildings such as the Auditorium and the Schiller Theater, while Sullivan developed his distinctive ornamentation, an intricate, organic system that wound around the straight lines of modern industry, exploring the aesthetic possibilities of a grain of wheat the way Bach explored music. Sullivan's florid yet rational ornament mediated between Chicagoans and their buildings. It captured the creative tension between rural and urban, past and present, the individual man and the democratic nation that fueled the city. Sullivan gave form to the idea of Chicago as a crossroads, where all of America's impulses met to converse and trade, battle and build, each structure a message about how technology and man could thrive together. The Columbian Exposition of 1893 ended all that, though. Grand as Daniel Burnham's fair was, it pushed the first generation of Chicago skyscraper builders out of fashion, and the city's progress stumbled. Adler and Sullivan split, and as Sullivan took to the bottle, he warned—or cursed—that it would be fifty years before American architecture recovered. He was off by only five or so.

When Sullivan died that night in 1924, he died forgotten. Chicago was no longer his city, as much as it ever had been. In the 1920s virtually everyone went on the take—not just Al Capone but union bosses and corporate heads, aldermen and corner cops; even a few priests were mobsters under the Roman collar. Five years later the stock market crash would drag the city to the brink of collapse.

Out of those ashes, Chicago did rise again. It was a slow, often painful progress infused with creativity and greed, overshadowed by the two glamorous cities on the other coasts, but central in all ways to the mass-market America we know today. Beginning in the late 1930s and rolling on through the 1950s, Chicagoans produced much of what the world now calls "American": the liberated, leering sexuality of *Playboy;* glass and steel modern architecture; rock and roll and the urban blues; McDonald's and the spread of the fast-food nation; the improvisational sketch comedy that's trained everyone from Joan Rivers and John Belushi to Steve Carell and Tina Fey; *Ebony* magazine and Emmett Till, whose murder catalyzed the civil rights movement; geodesic domes; avant-garde jazz and gospel music; the Nation of Islam; modern photography; the atom bomb and the Great Books; *Kukla, Fran and Ollie;* and the last great political machine.

The Third Coast is the history of Chicago's greatest—and final—period as the nation's primary meeting place, market, workshop, and lab, but it is also the story of how America's uniform culture came to be. As New York positioned itself on the global stage and Hollywood polished the nation's fantasies, the most profound aspects of American modernity grew up out of the flat, prairie land next to Lake Michigan. The real struggle for America's future—whether it would be directed by its people or its institutions—took place in postwar Chicago.

THE LATE-1930S double-dip of the Depression, when *The Third Coast* begins, saw Chicagoans fearing a return to days that had been especially brutal to them. In 1926 Chicago had put up a robust $367 million worth of new construction; by 1933 that amount had plummeted to $3.7

million. Teetering on bankruptcy, the city had laid off police and firemen, paid teachers with promissory notes; its business community all but seized up. Unlike the big East Coast fortunes, old money here was young, no silver sets buried in backyards, so out of 25,000 American suicides in 1930, more took place in Chicago than in New York, home of Wall Street.

Chicago's remaining wealth retreated into enclaves north and west: Glencoe and Barrington; Winnetka and Lake Forest. Republican, Protestant, and lockstep followers of Colonel Robert McCormick and his arch-conservative *Chicago Tribune*, they aped the English with fox hunts, hosted lavish costume parties and charity teas, packed the boards of the beloved orchestra and the just-daring-enough Art Institute. Those with mansions in the Gold Coast north of the Loop or along Lake Shore Drive held some interest in the city proper, even if it was just to get a table at the new Pump Room, where turbaned waiters presented entrées on flaming swords. "The customers seem to like it," said owner Ernie Byfield, "and it doesn't hurt the food much."

But average Chicagoans enjoyed few flaming swords at their dinner tables. This was America's biggest labor town, the birthplace of May Day, the eight-hour day, the Industrial Workers of the World, and the American Communist Party, and these were tense years. In August 1931, 100,000 demonstrators had hit the streets to protest the shooting of three activists; the 1933 Century of Progress fair could distract only so much from unemployment rates above 40 percent. On Memorial Day 1937 police killed ten strikers at the Republic Steel plant. The CIO began unionizing packinghouses, while sociologist Saul Alinsky, with money and support from the archdiocese and from his friend Bishop Bernard Sheil, founder of the Catholic Youth Organization, pulled together the first community organization.

The Left was in vogue culturally too with the Spanish Civil War a cause célèbre, and Picasso's *Guernica* on its way for a visit to the Arts Club. *Esquire* magazine, housed in the Palmolive Building, premiered an antifascist, anti-Communist magazine bearing maybe the worst name in publishing history—*Ken*. Polo-playing department store heir Marshall Field

III had been transformed by psychoanalysis into a liberal philanthropist, while at the University of Chicago, president Robert Maynard Hutchins faced down right-wing censorship in his classrooms. Carl Sandburg, plugging the second volume of his Lincoln biography, sang old labor songs to packed houses and tended the flames of the city's two recently deceased Progressive saints: Hull House's Jane Addams, winner of the Nobel Peace Prize, and Clarence Darrow, known in Chicago at least as much for his labor advocacy as for the Scopes Monkey Trial. "Lost causes," he supposedly once said, "are the only ones worth fighting for."

Separated by their skin colors, forms of worship, ethnicities, and wealth, Chicagoans lived in a patchwork whose central point was the intersection of State and Madison—all the city's street numbers radiated from in front of Sullivan's gorgeous rotunda entrance to Carson Pirie Scott department store in the Loop. The main business district and Chicago's old heart, the Loop got its name from the ring of elevated tracks that cast their shadows through the canyons. In here were the department stores along State Street and the banks and Board of Trade on LaSalle, Chicago's Wall Street. Just north of the Loop, across the Chicago River, was an expanse of landfill slowly developing east of Michigan Avenue, and on the other side Towertown, a mix of mansions, high-rises, and seedy storefronts. The lakeshore belonged to the rich, from the tony Edgewater Beach Hotel up north down to where the steel mills began near the lake's southern tip.

Circling this core was the city's next ring, where older buildings were sinking into decrepit neighborhoods of factories and tenements dominated by the Poles, Irish, and Germans who hadn't yet moved to outlying areas. West of the Loop, the old Jewish and Italian ghettoes were giving way to blacks; to the southwest were the Stockyards, and northwest of the Loop was *Stanislawowo*, the huge Polish ghetto. Beyond was a band of new bungalows pushing further into the prairie, farther away from the lake in every direction but east. Ethnicity still mattered in these long streets of small homes, each with its front and backyard, but what mattered most here was owning, stability, ascent.

Sociologist Ernest Burgess based his Concentric Zone Theory on Chicago's apparently neat progress of radiating growth, but he didn't account for the wide gash of slums down State Street and Michigan south of the Loop—the vast black ghetto of the South Side. The chosen destination of southern migrants, the South Side was now, through custom and violence, where White Chicago forced most of the black population to live. Various as it was—mansions of doctors and lawyers lined some streets, but elsewhere rats were boss—White Chicago considered it all a problem. One of the major themes of *The Third Coast* is how the city's leadership tried to address the racial wound Chicago had inflicted on itself.

As serious thinkers asked whether America would work better as a dictatorship than a democracy, what was coming next was on everyone's mind. The first section of *The Third Coast* looks at how the city confronted the chaos of the Depression and the war and how its approaches, plans, and reactions planted the seeds of what would emerge artistically, commercially, and politically in the postwar era.

Some Chicagoans gave Communism a look, especially blacks attracted by the party's support for evicted tenants and the Scottsboro Boys. The party-sponsored John Reed Clubs gave black writers and artists a rare chance to meet like-minded whites. By 1936 and the advent of the Works Progress Administration (WPA), a gingerly interracial arts community of leftist writers, artists, and performers moved among theater, radio, print, and the fine arts. "These were the days of 'black and white, unite and fight,'" said one artist. Most everyone involved was employed by the WPA, whose primary subject matter—the folklore and folkways of common Americans—connected naturally to Chicago traditions of realism, Prairie Style Arts and Crafts, and labor. The Illinois Writers' Project drew ex–John Reed Club members Nelson Algren and his friend Richard Wright, as well as Saul Bellow, Margaret Walker, Willard Motley, Arna Bontemps, and Jack Conroy.

Race informed virtually every aspect of life in Chicago, as much if not more than it did in Birmingham or in Selma, and it proved a rich theme for the city's artists. For poet Walker, the WPA ended "the long isolation of the Negro artist" and led Chicago's African American artists to a confrontation with the political and cultural realities of black life in Depression-era America. There was nothing formal about the Chicago Black Renaissance—that was the point. "Chicago reenacted [Harlem] without finger bowls and with increased power," wrote Bontemps. "The important audience," said artist Margaret Taylor, "are the little people, the street people." Up from Mississippi, Richard Wright was the central figure. Difficult years on the South Side finally brought him into the John Reed Clubs and the Communist Party. At the same time, Wright started his own circle, the South Side Writers' Group, which nurtured what scholar Lawrence P. Jackson calls "a luxurious collection of talent": the vigorous, street-smart poetry of Margaret Walker anticipates Maya Angelou and Alice Walker, and Frank Marshall Davis's strident, chest-pounding verse clearly foreshadows the Black Arts Movement. "By contrast with the raw, savage strength of Chicago," wrote Davis, "I looked upon New York as a slick sissy although I had never been there." (After the war, Davis moved to Hawaii, where he occasionally gave avuncular advice, tinged with old Chicago leftism, to the young Barack Obama, thus planting the seeds of a thousand crackpot blogs.) Other members included playwright Ted Ward and critic Edward Bland, both strict Marxists, as well as Fern Gayden and Bontemps, who collaborated with Jack Conroy on the first study of the Great Migration, *Anyplace But Here*. Wright's manifesto "Blueprint for Negro Writing" was another signal product of the group.

Geography bonded Chicagoans, though; its overwhelming flatness stranded everyone. The city has no hills, and in those years, away from the lake, few things other than chimneys or steeples rose taller than five stories. From the beaches through the killing floors and slums way out to the western fringes of that third residential ring, the city's grid ordered it all. In the same way, towering success mattered less to the vast majority of Chicagoans than just being "regular": a house and a lawn in a parish full of *your* kind of people; kids safe and in line, and same with the wife; your nose out of other people's business and theirs out of yours. "Beyond being regular," wrote novelist Nelson Algren, "there was nothing expected of a man. To give more wasn't regular. To give less wasn't straight." Being "regular" bridged ethnicities usually at war with one another and had implications for the nation as a whole. Wrapped on all sides by a thousand miles, living in America's meeting place, Chicagoans developed a unique understanding of what their fellow citizens had in common, and made the most of it.

The city's three most powerful institutions—the Cook County Democratic Party, the Catholic Church, and the Mob—all promoted themselves as advocates and servants for the "regular guy," their gangsters, priests, and politicians all drawn from the same immigrant well. The Irish went toward politics, the Mob attracted Italians and Jews, and the archdiocese was patched together out of various ethnic "national" parishes. In the 1930s, leaders of all three tried to consolidate their power. Al Capone took control of the Mob, George Cardinal Mundelein challenged the big national parishes, and Bohemian mayor Anton Cermak forced the Irish to share the Democratic machine.

Cermak's Machine offered regular guys who couldn't crack LaSalle Street a shot at power, but it stole as much out of Chicago as it gave. The mayor's inadvertent martyrdom in 1933—he took a fatal bullet for president-elect Roosevelt in Miami—seemed to save the city, as a grateful (and canny) FDR sent bags of New Deal money for the extension of Lake Shore Drive, new bridges over the river, and other public works. As long as the Machine continued to deliver votes, the money and jobs would keep coming. But Machine money and Machine jobs brought Machine corruption. Cermak had let the Mob run off the leash, and his successor, Big Ed Kelly, saw no reason to change things. Raised just upwind of the Stockyards, he'd dropped out of school at twelve, at which point his mother had told him, "Always keep neat and never drink out of somebody else's beer can"—sensible, if limited, advice that had somehow taken him as far as chief engineer of the Sanitary District until the City Council elected him mayor in 1933 after Cermak's death. Since then he'd made no pretense of transparency, accountability, or responsibility, flashing a fatherly smile as he lined his bank account with a thick slice of the $20 million or so that the Mob paid out annually in bribes to city officials. Meanwhile the schools stayed terrible, the police corrupt, and the garbage uncollected. Chicago's government had never had much relation to the will and well-being of the people, but as long as Kelly was in City Hall, anything went—policy and slots, whores and kickbacks, bribes big and small.

Without the Machine, though, Chicago would have lacked a skeleton. The fourth-largest city in the world at that point had no legal autonomy— the statehouse in Springfield controlled what and how much it could tax, and how much of the revenue it sent downstate came back. Worst yet, Chicago wasn't run by one central government but seven separate agencies, all of which had to work things out with the mayor. In the absence of meaningful civic coordination, the Machine, the Church, and the Mob provided structure even as they bled into one another, corrupted one another, and protected their power above the needs of the people they served. The game was rigged. Most regular guys knew that and just tried to get theirs.

But the Machine's hold on Chicago only appeared solid. It had full control of only eleven scruffy, industrial wards downtown and along the river—the "Automatic Eleven," packed with the stiffest of the working stiffs who hadn't made it out. The Mob ran the Loop, so that went to the Machine too. But Hyde Park and the Lakefront voted against it no matter what, and the huge sections northwest and southwest in the third ring could go either way. So for purely political reasons, Mayor Kelly followed FDR's lead and reached across the color line to name Bill Dawson the Democratic committeeman for the Second Ward; next election, the Second and Third voted in their first Democratic aldermen. Since then, the Machine's power had relied on black votes.

Cynicism was probably never worse than in the late 1930s. Yet as Sullivan once wrote, "There can be no new New York, but there may be a new Chicago." At the turn of the century, the city's business community had invited Daniel Burnham to create the *Plan of Chicago*, and as the Depression lingered on, it looked for ways once again to reinvigorate the economy and to some degree repair its profound social tears. For expertise, they turned not to the University of Chicago but to Germany, in particular to the Bauhaus design school, famous for its pioneering attempt to merge technology and industry with modernist aesthetics until the Nazis closed it. In 1937 former Bauhaus instructor László Moholy-Nagy came over at the invitation of a group of Chicago businessmen to restart the school on the South Side. Then a year later, the Armour Institute of Technology hired a former Bauhaus director, architect Ludwig Mies van der Rohe, to run its architecture department and design a new campus as part of an expansion plan.

Chicago's location and industrial base identified it as the likeliest focus for the nation's postwar expansion. Through its twenty-six train lines, six train stations, bus hubs, and the world's busiest airport, the city had welcomed millions of servicemen en route to somewhere else, and until 1959 the few transcontinental prop flights were long, expensive, and uncomfortable. Whether they liked it or not, Americans who traveled coast-to-coast had to smell the Stockyards. Chicago's seamy reputation as the capital of gambling, strippers, and good times enticed hundreds of conventions every year and turned the city into a circus most election cycles: between 1932 and 1960, nine out of sixteen political conventions were held in Chicago.

But the billions of postwar dollars poured into its industries only heightened the city's lingering problems, in particular its chronic housing shortage. Bauhaus founder Walter Gropius, now connected to the city through Moholy-Nagy and Mies, adopted the Near South Side as a test case for new postwar systems and structures, joining up Michael Reese Hospital with Mies's employer and other area institutions to create an enormous urban planning program; it would establish the legislative and business template for the redevelopment of other American cities. In Chicago, though, despite ostensibly utopian motivations, it would lead to the nation's most oppressive public housing system.

From 1945 to 1949, an explosion of creativity and destruction and a flood of new faces energized Chicago: migrants and émigrés; planners, architects, and designers; groundbreaking musicians and actors; innovators in technology and communications; leading minds in education, religion, and philosophy; European intellectuals and dirt-poor southern blacks—all came to the Third Coast to explore the postwar future. Because Chicago wasn't the big time of New York or Hollywood, it welcomed experiments and failures. In every art form, the process was as important as the product. Mies van der Rohe and the brilliant young veterans whom he trained turned the Illinois Institute of Technology into the laboratory of modern architecture. In music, the death of the big band and various technical and business revolutions opened the industry to independent labels such as Chess, home of Muddy Waters and the urban blues. Pianist Herman Blount, aka Sun Ra, up from Birmingham, studied space and Egyptian magic and attracted followers musical and otherwise to his "Afrofuturism" and avant-garde jazz, while Mahalia Jackson rose from the churches of the South Side to push gospel toward the mainstream. On television, WBKB became a workshop for a new kind of programming that put puppeteer Burr Tillstrom, DJ Dave Garroway, and actor Studs Terkel at the center of their own imaginary worlds. Curator Katharine Kuh and the Art Institute of Chicago helped explain abstract art to America; artists Leon Golub and the reclusive Henry Darger moved toward figurative styles distinctly unfashionable in the face of New York's Abstract Expressionism. The successor to Moholy's New Bauhaus, the Institute of Design, let Harry Callahan and Aaron Siskind teach photography both as a social tool and as an art form to a generation of educators and designers. Meanwhile Nelson Algren, novelist of Chicago's underbelly, penned his greatest work as he carried on a torrid love affair with Parisian intellectual Simone de Beauvoir.

All of this looked and felt different from what was coming out of New York, home of the academies, and it tells a different cultural history than the standard New York–centric narrative. Movements with catchy names didn't take hold in Chicago, the wine and cheese circuit was thin, and the city as a whole remained, as Sullivan had called it, the "City of Indifference." In contrast to New York's broad intellectual society, here the model was a family. Circles formed around the ideas and personalities of one or two visionaries like Mies and Moholy and Richard Wright. The Chicago School of Television centered on station executives Jules Herbuveaux and Ted Mills, and then on to the separate families of Garroway, Tillstrom, and Terkel. Without the nurturing and protection of a tight unit, the cold winds of the city's general disinterest might have blown most of them away.

Save for Mies's buildings, Chicago's artistic and intellectual creation during these years tended to share an aesthetic that blended turn-of-the-century Progressivism, the 1930s Popular Front, WPA regionalism, University of Chicago academics, Frank Lloyd Wright's industrial craft tradition, and an optimistic take on the possibilities implicit in being "regular." Chicago art in the postwar era was never art for art's sake; it was a tool. Like Sullivan, the cultural figures of the Third Coast mediated between the individual and the changing world; formally, that meant they worked with intimacy, figurative imagery, and a connection to social justice—qualities that midcentury "cool," from bebop to Abstract Expressionism to the New Criticism, avoided.

Like most everything else in postwar Chicago, the Machine was in transition too, trying to hold on to its power, and the business-friendly "reform" mayor Martin Kennelly lacked the backbone to drive an agenda, control his party, or lead 3.6 million Chicagoans. The end of restrictive covenants, the easing of the housing shortage, migration from the South, and the dislocation caused by big developments all together threw Chicago into racial chaos. The movement to the suburbs by whites became at least as much about race as it was about prosperity. When Senator Joseph McCarthy pushed onto the scene in 1950, the uniform consumer culture—urged by the government, and spread by faster, more extensive transportation and mass communications—cast the experiments and social consciousness of the late 1940s in a suspicious light. Whites who stayed wanted something more than new garbage cans in return for their votes—they wanted security. The brief era that Algren had called "a fresh time" came largely to an end in the early 1950s.

Chicago continued to build toward something, though. Home of mail order, soap operas, and conventions, the city redirected its creativity toward its knack for knowing what people wanted and how to sell it to them. That radical impulse to give the common man a voice now taught him how to express himself through what he bought; pride in his company and his job became brand loyalty. Hugh Hefner made sex clean, quick, and risk free. Selling out became the goal for most, a moral quandary for only a few. Even Robert Maynard Hutchins happily packaged Western civilization into fifty-four volumes and sold it on the installment plan as the Great Books, while Nelson Algren and Studs Terkel cried in what had suddenly become wilderness.

Nineteen fifty-five was a manic, climactic year. That winter, running as the consummate churchgoing, bungalow-owning father of seven, Richard J. Daley became mayor on the strength of black votes. Daley had a vision for the city. Plans and projects rose from their foundations. Suddenly Chicago felt on the move again, in a year everywhere turbocharged with sex and youth and music and theater. Chess launched rock and roll with Chuck Berry and Bo Diddley; Hef's Girl Next Door Playmates and McDonald's golden arches appeared, while Mike Nichols, Elaine May, and the Compass devised a new kind of improvisational theater to skewer it all. Meanwhile, the outlines of Daley's feudal empire took shape. When Woodlawn's Emmett Till was lynched in Mississippi, the new mayor mourned, then turned around and all but incarcerated the next generation of Black Chicago by announcing the construction of a breathtaking expanse of public housing on the South Side. Chicagoans had handed their city over to a man who could keep the jobs coming, the perverts out of their neighborhoods, and the races as far apart as possible.

With the Machine completely under his control, Daley consolidated City Hall, the business community, the Mob, and labor to produce an enormous building boom that delivered on the new city that had been promised since Mies van der Rohe arrived in 1938. At great cost to its soul, Chicago turned itself into the capital of modern architecture. Mies's spare, corporate style—as co-opted by Skidmore, Owings & Merrill—replaced

Sullivan's mediation as the look of Imperial Chicago. An artistic exodus began—Sun Ra, Leon Golub, Nichols and May, and Harry Callahan, just to start, all made for more receptive climes; Nelson Algren gave up fiction; and even though Lorraine Hansberry's *A Raisin in the Sun* was arguably the final great work of social realism to come out of Chicago, she wrote it in New York. Money and fame met in Hugh Hefner's mansion and the first Playboy Club; the city that gave the world May Day now offered it Bunnies. In 1959 the first transcontinental jets zoomed past overhead, rendering obsolete Chicago's role as the nation's meeting place. Skyscrapers would keep rising, but something had gone hollow in the great American city. The radical Chicago of Studs, Saul Alinsky, and Nelson Algren now lived mostly in the corners, seeds of what would become in the next decade the Counterculture. It seems inevitable that the iconic battle of America's culture wars, the 1968 Democratic National Convention, would be fought on the Third Coast.

Understanding America requires understanding Chicago. "Subtract what Chicago has given to it," claimed the pilot issue of *Chicago* magazine in 1953, "and you wouldn't recognize America." Whether or not you'd like what you'd see is another question. An America without McDonald's, naked centerfolds, and cold skyscrapers would also be an America without rock and roll, Frank Lloyd Wright, regional theater, and a labor movement. All these things are uniquely American precisely because they came out of the city that most genuinely expresses America as a whole. Restoring Chicago to its central place in American history is a crucial step toward reassembling a nation that has lost its shared sense of identity and experience.

PART ONE

PRE-1945

"Chicago has no tradition but modern."

Reyner Banham

CHICAGO SURVIVED the Depression—barely. But despite its slums and corruption, its aging buildings and dying core, the city's potential was immense. Over its hundred-year history, Chicago had cycled between tragedy and exuberant growth, and as it reemerged from its own rubble once again, opportunities presented themselves. From the late 1930s on through World War II, Chicagoans would examine new ways of building, thinking, making art, and encountering race. When publisher Henry Luce announced the "American Century" in 1941 and a year later Vice President Henry Wallace called for the "Century of the Common Man," no place better exemplified how those two very different visions of the same country were possible and in fact desirable when played against each other. After all, the tensions between the greater good of the community and the rights of the individual were what kept the structure of the nation standing. Chicago, in the center of the continent, was the keystone where they met.

CHAPTER 1

THE BRICK IS
ANOTHER TEACHER

CERES, ROMAN GODDESS of abundance, looked down this warm October night in 1938 from the top of the Board of Trade, a sheaf of wheat in one hand, a sack of corn in the other. Thirty feet high and made of aluminum, she marked Chicago's highest point, the way William Penn did for Philadelphia and King Kong for New York.

That, apparently, was all she was good for, because there wasn't much abundance to be seen through the murky smog below. The Loop was a dark place even in the best of times, always dusk under the El tracks, where flickering bar signs provided the light, and now resignation skulked among the money men on LaSalle Street, dogged the aisles of empty department stores on State. Chicago's economy had imploded in the Depression, along with its ballsy, built-overnight spirit, and while the New Deal had kept the city alive, the frantic drumming of Gene Krupa, playing everywhere as the Dow slid back down, sounded like the footsteps of a guy running away from another beating. Just this afternoon in the Pit, the value of wheat and corn had fallen to four-year lows, and up at Wrigley Field, Stan Hack, Gabby Hartnett, and the rest of the Cubs licked their wounds after Gehrig's Yankees swept them in four. *Hand it all back to the Indians*, the pessimists said. *Let them figure it out.* This muggy night of October 18, four hundred of the city's builders and power brokers assembled in the Palmer House to meet a new arrival from Germany who some hoped might make a difference.

The Red Lacquer Room where they sat embodied everything the best-known, if not most welcome, guest among them had fought the last fifty years. Frank Lloyd Wright, white hair billowing back over his velvet collar, hated the rococo chandeliers, the crimson walls, and electrified candelabra. But worst of all, he hated the rich mediocrities filling the room. Chicago, he'd once written, was the "greatest of machines," and he hadn't meant it as a compliment. The feeling was mutual; though Wright was world famous, his Prairie Style architecture beloved, no one was asking *him* to save the city. Cigar haze clung to the gilded chandeliers. The Master looked longingly off to the bar as Henry Heald, young president of the Armour Institute's engineering school, only thirty-three but with the fleshy lips and dark bags under the eyes of a much older man, extolled the portly German émigré hunkered before them on the dais like a rock formation.

The speeches went on—"superficial blah or labored lip service," thought Wright—until Heald at last called him up to the podium. "Ladies and gentlemen," Wright said, throwing his arm around the forbidding German, "I give you Mies Van der Rohe! But for me there would have been no Mies—certainly none here tonight. I admire him as an architect and respect and love him as a man. Armour Institute, *I* give you my Mies Van der Rohe. You treat him well and love him as I do. God knows you need him!"

At which point Wright dashed out of the room, leaving the new Director of Architecture of the Armour Institute alone at the podium. Unfortunately Mies van der Rohe couldn't speak English.

THREE MILES SOUTH and one block west of this grand introduction in the Loop, a young black woman finished her day's work wreathed in the sweet smell of incense. Gwendolyn Brooks didn't tell anyone what she did for E. N. French, "spiritual advisor," but it was all the state employment agency had had to offer. So for eight dollars a week she walked through this U-shaped apartment building called the Mecca at State and 34th streets, peddling "Holy Thunderbolts," dream guides and other sorts of quackery to desperate people who didn't know any better and a lot more who really should have. The incense helped create a heavenly atmosphere, and it also blocked the stench. As she stepped out the door, a complex mixture of smells told the stories of the thousand or so people who lived in the Mecca's 176 apartments: unattended children pissing through the railings; the shit and ammonia stink of boiling chitlins; simmering garbage; the cigarettes of those whiling away yet another day. Gwendolyn didn't belong here for many reasons, but mainly because she felt tainted by the lies of E. N. French; the work of a poet was truth of the most eternal kind, and Gwendolyn Brooks at twenty-one was above all things a poet.

She made her way quickly toward the stairs. The Mecca was a hard place for dreamers like her. It had two sections, each half a block long and four stories high with an atrium in the center lit by banks of uncleaned skylights that produced a watery gloom even on the sunniest days. Apartment life had still been a new concept in the 1890s when the Mecca advertised itself as Chicago's biggest and finest blend of residence and hotel, its design open and balconies wide to encourage tasteful sociability. Once the World's Fair closed, though, it slid straight down to blue-collar renters, and now tired black workmen tipped their caps as they slumped by. She was considering writing a poem about the Mecca. "To touch every note in the life of this block-long blockwide building," her notes say, "would be to capsulize the gist of black humanity in general."

In the days of the "Old Settlers"—anyone who'd arrived before 1910—Chicago had been integrated. The city's small number of blacks had risen from 6,000 in 1880 to a widely distributed 44,000 in that cut-off year—the census shows that blacks were living in nearly three-quarters of the 431 tracts counted, and none were all-black; Italians were more segregated. After 1910, however, new black arrivals gravitated toward two areas on the South and West sides. Panicking whites formalized the trend through the use of restrictive covenants that kept blacks within a three-block-wide strip starting at 26th Street, swelling east at 31st, and ending at 55th. Wealthy Chicagoans abandoned their mansions south of the Loop for areas north of the Chicago River and farther south along the lakefront, partly out of fashion—the crème de la crème Potter Palmers had moved to a castle on Lake Shore Drive—but mostly because of new factories and the growth of the city's notorious red-light district, the Levee. By World War I the Levee was gone; the police pushed its drug trade and prostitution south, over great objection, into the Black Belt, which was bursting now with some 65,000 more African Americans.

"Chicago," wrote John Johnson, founder of *Ebony*, "was to the southern Blacks of my generation what Mecca was to the Moslems and what Jerusalem was to the Jews: a place of magic and mirrors and dreams." Trains from all over the South met here, overwhelming the neighborhood with migrants who pushed established blacks out in search of better homes on white turf. Whites responded with violence and fire bombings. Racial and labor tensions at the Stockyards and the stoning of a black boy swimming at a "whites only" section of the lake at 29th Street culminated in the bloody Race Riot of 1919 that killed thirty-eight—five in front of the Mecca, when the residents of an all-white boardinghouse on 35th and Wabash clashed with black neighbors.

Soon after the riot ended, with the Mecca now all black, South Side musicians began playing a midtempo number called "Mecca Flat Blues," improvising new verses every night about "the trials, tribulations, and tragedies of the Mecca's inmates and visitors." Though home now to thousands of migrants, this ghetto was also "a creation of white hostility" enforced by vigilante violence, banks, and the law; by the 1940s Chicago would have more restrictive covenants in place than anywhere else in the nation. As better-off blacks pushed south into large, handsome buildings as far as 63rd, and as the opening of the Savoy Ballroom and the Regal Theater made 47th Street the main drag, the weary blocks around the Mecca rapidly collapsed into a slum. White landlords, many tied to the Mob, knew blacks couldn't live safely anywhere else in the city, so they gouged them on rent. With demand so high, they had no incentive to maintain their properties. Black apathy sped the fall; recent migrants often saw their white-owned buildings as a northern version of the farms they'd just been sharecropping. "We do not care if the barns rot down" wrote Richard Wright, "they do not belong to us, anyway." More and more people lived in less space. The original section of the Black Belt fell deeper into disrepair, and the intricate art nouveau grilles along the railings of the Mecca kept wandering toddlers from falling to their death.

The word commonly used to describe the spreading degeneration of neighborhoods, the surface rot of broken windows, collapsing buildings, and rats that defined a slum, was *blight*, a vague, prescientific term on a level with *humours*. It allowed politicians, journalists, and civic do-gooders to rail against the visible effects of poverty without having to address its uncomfortable causes. Most of urban America faced blight to some degree or another in 1938: waves of immigration and migration, topped off by the Depression, had left millions of the poor living in thousands of square miles of decrepit buildings, and Chicago's slums, acres of rotting wood-frame buildings thrown up during the postfire boom, were generally conceded to be the worst in the nation. When the Depression hit, "it was as if somebody had pulled a switch and everything had stopped running," wrote one. Property owners walked away from buildings or simply tore them down for parking lots. The housing shortage intensified. Landlords chopped six-room apartments into six separate "kitchenettes"; buildings meant for sixty families suddenly housed three hundred, in a warren of cardboard cubicles without running water, lit by kerosene lamps—fires were common and deadly. Rats abounded. Tuberculosis ran at twice the rate of the rest of Chicago. "The kitchenette," wrote Wright, "is the funnel through which our pulverized lives flow to ruin and death."

In the late 1930s the city had three primary blighted areas: north of the Loop, directly behind the high-rises along Lake Shore Drive; west of the Loop, around Maxwell Street, where Jane Addams had opened Hull House; and here around the Mecca, along darkened State Street. Wooden shanties leaned drunkenly against their brick neighbors while children lit small fires among the piles of boards left by those that had collapsed. Garbage drifted and lives sagged. Wild dogs and rats had the run of vacant lots. This wasn't the tight, ingrown ghetto of New York's Lower East Side; the rich had once lived here, so the streets were wide, and there was sky. On the facades of Baptist churches, Hebrew letters stood out, the lost language of those who had fled. More than a dozen Sullivan buildings, mostly homes, remained; the Falkenau row houses were just a block from the Mecca.

This third stretch of blight had brought Mies to Chicago, to this podium at the Palmer House, where he now shuffled his papers and conferred with his interpreter, Mr. Walterdorf, head of the local chapter of the American Institute of Architects. Historically, Chicago's government had lacked interest in much of anything beyond the next envelope of cash, so the business community had acted perforce as the city's planning arm. In 1934 a prominent realtor named Ferd Kramer had created the Metropolitan Housing and Planning Council (MHPC) to investigate ways private enterprise could work with Chicago's government—such as it was—to redevelop slums. Eliminating blight would save the money spent on social costs, but more important—since few things had ever been accomplished in Chicago for purely altruistic reasons—it would restore the land's value and, therefore, enhance its tax revenues. The land underneath the South Side blight had once been very valuable, and it could be once again. Serious study, some genuine sense of civic duty, and the promise of lucrative real estate deals let Kramer assemble a board of some of the city's most influential bankers, builders, and businessmen, along with progressives such as Saul Alinsky; Earl Dickerson, president of the nation's largest black insurance company; academics like sociologist Louis Wirth; and directors of other reform groups who spoke up, occasionally, on behalf of those who actually lived in the slums that the reformers were wishing away.

Henry Heald, tonight's host, was a prominent MHPC board member and president of the Armour Institute of Technology, an engineering school built by the meatpacking Armour family just east of the Stockyards. Located at State and 33rd streets, on the western edge of that South Side slum, the institute had since 1910 or so felt increasingly under siege and threatened to move to the suburbs. Kramer's efforts had persuaded Heald to line up with the MHPC. Not only would Armour stay, but it would buy up parcels of land as they became available, so that its current seven-acre campus could grow into a 110-acre rival to the likes of MIT and Caltech. Hiring Mies as the new director of the Architecture Department, and secretly as the architect of the new campus, was a dramatic step into the future.

Or so it seemed. Heald still had his doubts, even as he settled back into his seat on the dais. The newspapers this week were following the case of teenage "jungle Negro" Robert Nixon, a "sex moron" arrested in May for raping a string of white women on the South Side and then smashing in their heads with bricks. The *Tribune* had featured a map of his crimes that dotted the area around the school. If Armour were to stay, that sort of thing *had* to stop.

In architecture, a building whose parts are in perfect relation to each other is said to have "repose." So it was with Mies tonight, at ease at the podium, his German crisp, his voice deep and rich. Through his interpreter, he expressed his debt to Wright, whose Wasmuth Portfolio of Oak Park residential work had, back in 1911, directed European architects toward the clean lines of Modernism. Then, again via Walterdorf, Mies added a gentle remonstration: "Mr. Van der Rohe says he is sorry Mr. Wright left so soon." The message was clear: Ludwig Mies van der Rohe was not *that* sort of architect; he was not a showman or a scold. He was a burgher like them, eager to do a good job for good pay. He was "regular." Mies continued, outlining the importance of education and extolling the qualities of wood, stone, and brick, the promise of concrete and steel. At Armour he would "show that technology not only promises power and greatness, but also involves dangers; that good and evil apply to it also, and that man must make the right decision. . . . The long path from material through purpose to creative work has only a single goal: to create order out of the godforsaken confusion of our time."

On his way out, Heald found Wright at the bar, nursing a drink; even America's greatest architect had stayed to listen. It would be up to Mies now to create order out of Chicago's confusion. It would be up to him to make the right decisions.

Gwendolyn Brooks, meanwhile, reached the train safe and sound, eager to get back to her writing desk. She didn't know that a week before Mies's grand entrance, the Mecca had been sold to one Mr. Alfred L. Eustice, secretary of the board of trustees of the Armour Institute.

A YEAR LATER Mies van der Rohe stared out from a window on the fifth floor of the Railway Exchange Building. To his left, across Michigan Avenue, twin lions flanked the steps of the Art Institute of Chicago, where Armour's architecture department had its classrooms on the upper floors. Beyond, Lake Michigan stretched across the horizon: shades of white and cream filled the winter skies; in summer, Prussian blue until a great midwestern thunderstorm would come through all black and green and slash it with lightning. To the south, the shore curved east, plumes of steel-mill smoke smudged the lower corner of the canvas. Behind lay the rest of Chicago, a city Mies claimed never to think overly much about.

Daniel Burnham had built the Railway Exchange Building in 1904, and from its windows he'd watched Chicago fill, pave, and plant its way toward fulfilling his master plan for the City Beautiful, his ideal of an orderly urban habitat befitting the Edwardian gentleman. The plan's stunning Jules Guerin drawings, their colonnades iced with Beaux-Arts frippery, recall Haussmann's Paris or the Ringstrasse of fin-de-siècle Vienna. Great minds in the Loop had projected with pride and fear that by 1950 Chicago would have 13 million inhabitants, overtaking New York, Paris, and London as the world's biggest city. Burnham's plan had addressed the unpleasant fact that an overwhelming proportion of them would be lower-class—all the leafy parks and grand boulevards were designed as a way to control the coming disorder. Thirty-two years later that disorder had certainly come, but Chicago's place at the table among the major cities of the world had not.

Now in 1939, it was Mies's turn to do something about it. Burly, with a solid jaw and sleepy eyelids, he still looked like a stonemason's son. His office was small and surprisingly dusty for a man so meticulous. A few Paul Klees leaned casually against the wall. Two young architects, George Danforth and John Rodgers, stood poring over a drawing of the Armour Institute campus; between them, a turtlelike man Mies's age, balding, in round black glasses, toyed with his pipe. This was architect and urban planner Ludwig Hilberseimer, Mies's former Bauhaus colleague and his loudest advocate back in Germany; Mies had brought him to the States. John Rodgers had studied at the Bauhaus, as had one other Chicagoan with his own practice now, Bertrand Goldberg. During Mies's first visit, when he'd been considering the Armour offer, Rodgers and Goldberg had squired him around the city to see the Sullivan buildings and trekked with him to Wisconsin for an audience with Frank Lloyd Wright, a one-hour visit that became four days, during which Mies's one shirt turned gray and Wright sold him on Chicago. "The people have more initiative," one former student advised. "They get more naturally and directly to the point." In the end, Mies had chosen Chicago for practical reasons—Illinois had liberal laws for professional certification, while if he'd wanted to run either Columbia or Harvard, he'd have had to graduate from one of them first. Chicago it was.

A few purposeful steps brought Mies over to the circle. "It was more as if God were over there on the other side of the table," said a student once. He picked up his pencil with thick builder's hands, stuck out his bottom lip in a contemplative way, and gestured to Danforth to go ahead.

MARIA LUDWIG MICHAEL MIES (he took the name "Ludwig Mies van der Rohe" later, for effect) learned his lifelong devotion to materials in the family stone yard. Born in Aachen in 1886 to middle-class Catholic burghers, he moved to Berlin after his apprenticeship, to work in the office of architect Bruno Paul, the biggest name in German art nouveau, or *Jugendstil*. Mies, a quick study, polished off the rough edges of his provincial upbringing and joined the thousands of ambitious young men in frock coats and satin hats in a city bent dangerously on making the world pay attention to it. Mark Twain called Berlin "the Chicago of Germany," and the two cities shared an uncanny hunger for attention. "To see their city become a *Weltstadt* before their eyes," wrote Elaine Hochman, "was a source of almost unbearable pleasure to Berliners." At twenty, Mies scored his first commission, a vacation home for a wealthy professor that caught the eye of Germany's most important architect, Peter Behrens, then working on a complete factory-to-letterhead redesign for the German electric company AEG. Behrens hired Mies, who briefly shared an office with another Behrens protégé, the future Bauhaus founder Walter Gropius. To the manner born, brilliant and well connected, Gropius looked down on Mies's calloused background, while Mies considered him posh and pretentious, and yet there was mutual respect. Gropius would soon leave the firm, but their complex relationship would twine throughout the next fifty years, on two continents, particularly in Chicago.

Mies agreed with his boss Behrens that good architecture expressed the Zeitgeist, the spirit of the time. But the neoclassicism of Karl Friedrich Schinkel and the massive brick structures of the Belgian H. P. Berlage, both based on principles of order and clarity, resonated even more with him, as did the work of Wright, which Mies dubbed "genuine organic architecture." In 1912, when he left Behrens to open his own practice, Mies blamed the departure on philosophical differences (though it probably had more to do with the fact that he'd nabbed a commission from under his boss's nose). Creeping toward thirty, cushioned by the fortune of his new wife, Ada, by the time he was drafted in late 1915, Mies had done little more than build country homes, and when he returned from his remote Romanian posting in the spring of 1919, he expected to do more of the same. Instead he found Berlin devastated and the market for country house architects gone. So he gave himself over to the free-for-all of the "modern" flowing through the city and joined the Novembergruppe circle of artists who vented the explosive, bitter energy of Expressionism and Dada and explored their more rational cousin, Constructivism. Along the way he made friends with the likes of El Lissitzky, Naum Gabo, and Theo van Doesburg, while at the same time pulling away from Ada.

But the stonecutter's son was never entirely comfortable with the revolutionary impulse behind the chaos; instead, the greatest modern architect of the twentieth century built his intellectual foundation out of the stones of medieval Catholicism. Mies read voraciously, particularly Aquinas, who like Plato charged the artist with expressing the spiritual realm by finding the perfect order for each of his creations. Another more contemporary Thomist influence was Father Romano Guardini, chair of the philosophy of religion department at the University of Berlin. Ironic as it may seem, the Church then was trying to make sense of Modernism by reexamining Aquinas and his rational, universal solutions. Guardini's struggles with the question of how Man can maintain eternal truth in an age of chaos had led him to the answer that he must affirm life by searching for new forms in the changing world, but not in a way that glorifies the individual. Guardini's thought presaged the Second Vatican Council and allowed Mies to align Aquinas with Behrens and Berlage in a philosophy that embraced the whole of his personality: an intellectual Catholic, a man true to his time who glorified eternal truths by seeking order in all things.

During the next ten years, Mies pushed to the cutting edge of architecture. The Friedrichstrasse Office Building and the Glass Skyscraper never rose higher than their models, but they were seen as the first serious leap forward for the construction of tall buildings since the postfire Chicago builders led by Louis Sullivan. Le Corbusier (who also happened to work for a time with Behrens) had his own ideas for the modern building, but they largely remained just that—ideas—whereas Mies, even when brainstorming, imagined buildings one wanted to experience. The 1922 Glass Skyscraper, for example, with its thirty-story sheer glass walls bent in sensuous curves, suggested for the first time that glass could be used as an exterior surface. Mies's vision for what he called "skin and bones construction" took form in a series of masterpieces: the 1926 Rosa Luxemburg Monument, with its huge brick wall; the Weissenhof project, which brought together the world's greatest architects to propose urban housing solutions; and the German Pavilion at the 1929 Barcelona World's Fair, a simple study of space and planes of polished granite, steel, and glass executed so precisely that it seems there could be no other way.

Amid the hyperinflation and street battles of the Weimar period, then, Mies pledged allegiance only to the truth of whatever structure he was building. When Gropius in 1930 asked him to take over the Bauhaus, then flailing under Communist director Hannes Meyer, Mies accepted and immediately shuttered the political clubs to refocus the students on their classes. Sensible as that sounds, it also divorced the Bauhaus from the socialist values Gropius had built it on. Modernism strove for a new world structured on the needs and desires of the millions who'd never had a voice, so by taking socialism out of the Bauhaus, Mies also removed socialism from Modernism. To him, the spiritual value of expressing the modern world transcended both practical function and political aim.

Given the decade of turmoil prior to 1933, many reasonable Germans believed the Nazis would cycle in and out of office in the span of a few months just as all the other parties had; the apolitical Mies was very much one of them, willing to deal with the new regime on a "Give unto Caesar what is Caesar's" basis. Yet even as something curdled in Germany, the racial purity edicts mounted, the Bauhaus was closed, and the exodus began, Mies pursued as much business as he could with the Nazis and turned down opportunities to leave: the Armour Institute, for one, tendered him its first offer in 1934, and he was a candidate for director of Harvard's architecture school. (He pulled out when he found out they were also considering Gropius.) As the Nazis passed the Nuremberg Laws, occupied the Rhineland, and burned pyres of books, Mies sent word to the new Führer that he was interested in the monumental job of redesigning Berlin for the Reich. Unfortunately Hitler wasn't a fan—even if Mies wanted a future in Nazi Germany, the Führer didn't want *him*, so in August 1938, after sweating through a day of Gestapo questioning, Mies left for Rotterdam and then on to this new life in Chicago.

As MIES LIT his cigar, George Danforth produced a paper grid. The young draftsman had learned about the German's arrival while he was traveling in Europe. His friend Bill Priestley had sent a telegram: "Mies is here. Benny held over." Good news on both counts, since Danforth had missed Benny Goodman's last big gig at the Chicago Theater. Now he laid the grid over the map of the proposed Armour Institute campus.

Heald hadn't given Mies any specs for the project, only the broadest intentions of how the buildings would be used, so for the best part of the past year, Mies had puzzled away in a vacuum, every plan melting into speculation until finally he decided to ignore all the unknown realities in favor of a theoretical, one-size-fits-all solution. A twenty-four-foot-square room, he decided, would accommodate any of the uses Armour could possibly have in mind—classroom, lab, or workshop. Instead of creating big spaces and then dividing them up into different sorts of rooms, Mies could add or subtract modules according to a given need, all within a meaningful order. The design's impersonal, mass-produced aspect was exactly what made it strong.

Danforth's grid began the imposition of Miesian order on the South Side of Chicago, an interpretation of Chicago's existing street grid, which itself was derived from the grid that the Land Ordinance of 1785 had thrown over the entire nation west of Ohio. Because of it, the streets of Chicago align "with far-off country roads, soybean fields, and courthouse squares." Mies translated that idea not only through his design for the campus layout but in the buildings themselves, superimposing a Catholic sense of order on a predominantly Catholic city (though as later planners would discover, the city's Catholics understood the land in a very particular way).

According to Heald, Mies did not speak English regularly until Pearl

Harbor in December 1941, which meant that for the first three years he either spoke through associates such as Rodgers or relied on the most basic English phrases. Students helped by taking him to lunch at the Berghoff, the German *Brauhaus* on Adams where he "learned menu English and how to order beer." His apartment at 200 E. Pearson, two blocks from the lake, near the Water Tower, had the feel of an elegant bachelor pad, with dark hardwood floors, unexpected moldings, and his small but exquisite collection of Klees on the crème walls. Friendly, always willing to have a drink (or four), he was intimate with few. Socialite Inez Cunningham Stark threw a party for him, and he befriended gallery owner (and later Art Institute curator) Katharine Kuh when he admired a series of Klees that Thomas Mann pronounced *"schrecklich."* No one knew that he had left behind a wife—from whom he'd separated but never divorced—three grown daughters, and a grandson, Dirk, who would someday study under him. A cook and butler cared for his needs as he took in the American frenzy and the steel mills, gestating; between 1938 and 1945, he would build only one building, but he would develop three ideas that would bring him to his creative heights in the years ahead.

Mies's first plan for the Armour Institute showed how much he was still adjusting to Chicago. More Hilberseimer than Mies, it symmetrically situated immense buildings on a superblock that would require the closing of Federal Street. Symmetry and superblocks were two specialties of Hilberseimer, who'd gained notoriety in the early 1920s with his plan for *Hochhausstadt*, "Highrise City," its black monolith after black monolith receding into the distance like gigantic dominoes or the perspective drawing of a disturbed child. (In later years even Hilbs, as everyone called him, would admit that *Hochhausstadt* was "more necropolis than metropolis.") When the city refused to close Federal Street, Mies took to sliding wooden blocks around on the grid, testing sizes and arrangements, until he found the right flow of motion through the solids, as he had for Barcelona, but now with Armour's buildings instead of pavilion walls.

The politics remained. In January 1941, Henry Heald and the school, by now renamed the Illinois Institute of Technology (IIT), announced their grand building program at another Red Lacquer Room gala. To Mies's dismay, Heald proudly unveiled a timid plan that the recently deceased trustee Alfred Alschuler had been working on at the same time. Mies agreed to continue on the condition that Heald would present *his* plan when the IIT board was better prepared to encounter the Modern (a moment that would never really arrive). Acquiring the surrounding lots piecemeal was also proving to be wildly expensive for the school. That June, through the efforts of State Senator Richard J. Daley, the Illinois legislature had passed the Neighborhood Redevelopment Corporation Act, allowing private developers like IIT to condemn holdouts as soon as they bought 60 percent of the land within a proposed development area. The law was immediately challenged. (Two years later New York adopted this legislative strategy to acquire the land for Stuyvesant Town.)

As the courts deliberated, Mies prepared drawings for his first American structure, IIT's Minerals and Metals Building. Finished in 1943, its three stories of black steel and tan brick look like something extruded from a giant machine. The north wall carries the form of the interior—five squares and three rectangles that echo the offices and workspace inside. By exposing the power of steel—the product of those enormous mills to the south soon to drive the city's postwar economy—Mies captured his time and place. But whatever Heald told his board, they still weren't prepared. Heald recalled meeting later "with a committee of the faculty, who said in effect, 'Are you sure you shouldn't have your head examined for being a party to this construction?'"

One by one IIT bought the buildings around the school and demolished them, except for Gwendolyn Brooks's Mecca, which it could not take down. Alfred Eustice had since deeded it to IIT, making the school the "reluctant landlord" of some one thousand tenants. Its opinion of them is evident in a 1940 map showing the status of acquisitions—the corner where the Mecca stands is listed as "vacant." Funded by conservative businessmen (one of whom at the height of World War II slapped anti-Communist stickers on all his letters; another favored racist jokes), IIT had a reputation as a glorified technical school that produced competent draftsmen out of local, primarily ethnic students whose attitudes, racial and otherwise, surely jibed with the administration's. "IIT was in a slum, an absolute slum," said one student. Another called the area around IIT "one vast slum that was gradually cleaned out, people living in the utmost depravity." But IIT now did what it could to make conditions in the Mecca worse, on purpose. After it took the building over, for example, fire inspectors sent notice that a sprinkler system needed to be installed, but the school did nothing. "Because it has been planned to wreck the building, maintenance expenses had been kept to a minimum," stated one board report. The housing shortage may have kept IIT from evicting residents, but it operated the building with the minimum of services in hopes they'd leave on their own.

During the war, battleships and bombers used up all available steel, so the campus plan was halted, and the school became essentially a naval research base. Mies had little to do but teach. Most American architecture schools then still employed the Beaux-Arts system, an annual national design competition that required students to use a set of formulas and a uniform style of rendering, a process that produced some magnificent drawings but kept American architecture mired in what Frank Lloyd Wright called "Frenchite pastry." Worse yet, IIT "did pretty poorly compared to other schools" nationally. So Mies introduced a new three-stage curriculum: "Step I is an investigation into the nature of materials and their truthful expression. Step II teaches the nature of functions and their truthful fulfillment. Step III on the basis of these technical and utilitarian studies begins the actual creative work in architecture." The point, as Mies put it, was "the harmonious unfolding of one's own powers."

In practice, this "harmonious unfolding" was a grueling process. First-year students in empty, concrete rooms at the Art Institute drew nothing but brick walls for an entire semester. Then, after their year of learning how to render, Mies took handfuls of toy bricks out of a cigar box and demonstrated how to lay all the various bonds—English, German, Polish. Here was the essence of his system: a builder needs to understand, even love, his materials and know how to use them. "The brick is another teacher," he'd said that first night in the Red Lacquer Room. Materials were Mies's path to the truth. Stacking blocks became a way to answer real-world questions of how to turn corners and where to put windows. Wood and stone were next. Students saw nothing like a building until their third year, when they learned the functions of rooms in a house and then combined them into their own creations. Professional training came in the fourth year, along with urban planning. In this way, the practical ascended "through the different tiers of value into the realm of pure art."

Mies the instructor came off as a Zen master to some, a cipher to others. He could stare at a model for twenty minutes without a word, then say, "Try again." His rudimentary English certainly had something to do with it—Rodgers was known to translate long and clearly complex sentences of Mies's German as "no" or "start over"—but even when his language skills improved, Mies chose to say little; his performances at the weekly undergraduate class could be virtually gnomic. "He stood up front and very calmly looked out the window while the students sat there spellbound," reported Werner Buch. "One sat for several minutes and thought, 'Well, what's next? When does it start?' And he continued to stand there, unshakeable and calm, and said nothing. . . . Then he said one sentence, which, of course, was a platitude. But when he said it, the wheels began to turn." Or maybe the issue was English itself. Many German intellectual émigrés refrained from speaking English in America, deeming it too complicated next to good old straightforward German.

Hilberseimer was considered the emotional heart of the architecture school, which gives pause since he called his own most famous work a "necropolis." Pipe-smoking, avuncular Hilbs was the sidekick whom Mies needed to be an effective educator, accessible and chatty when Mies was silent, willing to wrestle through minor points that Mies grunted at enigmatically as he walked away. Rather than concentrate on how people used buildings, Hilbs's classes on "Urban Planning and the House" focused on outside factors, particularly the sun; every room, he taught, had to have at least four hours of sun per day. His fixation on sunlight became so notorious that in 1940 his students threw a party for him on December 21, the darkest day of the year, and celebrated "Hilbs's Day" annually until he died in 1967.

Most who came to study with Mies accepted his methods, but young Americans accustomed to choice and questioning could be put off. "Students were not allowed to express themselves or develop their own approaches," wrote one. "The school sought to develop in them a method by which they could study a problem in a deliberate and rational manner through which they could arrive at an appropriate solution." And what made a solution appropriate was that it was the one the instructor was looking for. The problems weren't open-ended—they were koans. Individual creativity was circumscribed, even suspect. (After meeting jazz cornetist Jimmy McPartland, Mies reportedly said, "Ja, but you must be careful with improvisation.") With its program of contemplative repetition under a silent abbot, Mies's IIT was becoming a kind of architectural monastery, producing a brotherhood trained to spread his word. Sigfried Giedion's *Space, Time and Architecture* in 1941 buttressed the sense that Chicago was holy ground by packaging the city's innovative nineteenth-century commercial architects such as John Wellborn Root, William Le Baron Jenney, and Louis Sullivan as the "Chicago School of Architecture."

The best way to get to know Mies was to see him after hours at a party or dinner, where liquor would open him up. Estranged from his wife, Ada, he took up with Lora Marx, the ex-wife of architect Samuel Marx, and became a sought-after guest in Chicago's top social circles—Mies was most decidedly not a bohemian. When he wasn't teaching, or drinking, he made plans. His office produced some 450 drawings for the Metallurgy Building, 870 for the proposed Library and Administration Building, and through them Mies had his third breakthrough of the period: a mastery of the horizontal, through open-plan rooms that could embrace the wide ranges of America.

By 1943 Mies could say that he had held up his end of the bargain. He'd transformed IIT's architecture department, created a critically admired campus plan, built the one building he'd been allowed to build, and completed drawings for two more. Aesthetically, he was making sense of

America's open skies and Chicago's grid, expressing the spiritual essence of the age with big steel. The *Tribune* even rolled him out to fight Hitler, claiming that "he came here simply because he no longer could confine his art and his work to the strait jacket of Nazi ideology."

But he hadn't made the blight go away.

Unlike most of the IIT board, Mies had seen slums before. He'd lived in Weimar Berlin, with its plagues of incest, prostitution, venereal disease, and drugs; Bertolt Brecht's *Threepenny Opera* was no exaggeration. Back then Mies had reacted to chaos and suffering by detaching himself from the day-to-day welfare of others in favor of the spiritual aesthetics of Aquinas and Guardini. "Questions of a general nature are of central interest," he wrote in 1924. "The individual becomes less and less important; his fate no longer interests us." His indifference to the South Side reflected less his attitudes about race—there's no evidence Mies was in any way racist—than his removal from the human condition. Mies's plan for the IIT campus made no attempt to integrate the school with its surroundings in even the most generic sense; among the materials announcing it was a telling illustration that superimposed the new campus onto a photo of the neighborhood, but with the entire school on a plinth, as if to keep IIT from having to touch anything around it. Mies seemed to have no particular animus to the troubled black neighborhood around the school; it just didn't live in his mind. His goal was to realize truth among the exigencies and traumas of mortal life, not to solve them.

And yet the IIT board couldn't stop thinking about blight. For all of Heald's support and the critical praise, Mies was an afterthought to an IIT administration that had no interest in creating a showcase for the architect; they'd hired him to accomplish *their* goal of remaking a neighborhood. Instead, Mies had ignored ideas such as Heald's appalling suggestion to build a wall around the entire campus using bricks from the demolished buildings. Matters came to a head in the hot summer of 1943. In May the school served all tenants of the Mecca with eviction notices, but courts blocked the wrecking permit. Racial tensions across America were running high; a Mississippi lynch mob was acquitted; riots flared in Texas and Alabama, then in June, Detroit, and in August, Harlem. When Chicago cops fatally shot a sixteen-year-old boy, the city looked next to go. So when the Army announced that it was selling the Stevens Hotel, with 2,750 rooms the largest in the world, Heald jumped at this chance to move the school downtown. Bids were due September 4, 1943.

What would happen to Mies was not discussed, but if IIT had won the Stevens, his entire campus plan would have been scrapped, and it's hard to imagine what reason there'd have been for him to stay on. He would have decamped to Boston or New York or London, none of which would have offered him much room to play with. Yet on the big day, the Kirkeby Hotel chain won by $581,000, paving the way for the Stevens Hotel to become the Conrad Hilton. IIT had no way forward now save with Mies and the Near South Side campus. By the summer of 1944, a model was on view at the Art Institute, and as the Allies pressed the Germans eastward, the school went to war against blight. Over the next fifteen years, Mies's IIT campus would become the nursery of modern corporate architecture.

In 1928 Mies wrote: "What does mankind need, or how can I earn the most? . . . The idea of earnings had to lead to isolation. The idea of service leads to community." Mies's concept of service was the monastic sort, a spiritual offering of the self to God rather than to God as revealed in man. His removal of socialism from Modernism didn't mean he was no longer a utopian thinker; it just meant that his vision of utopia discounted the value of collective social action. By throwing in with IIT, Mies had decided, as he'd said in his speech at the Red Lacquer Room, to create order. But *order* would soon carry meanings beyond rational clarity, and while Mies may have disavowed money as a motivation, his employers certainly didn't. IIT let the Mecca rot.

CHAPTER 2

WE WERE PART
OF THEM

E. N. FRENCH fired Gwendolyn Brooks after she turned down a promotion to "assistant minister," but her four months at the Mecca had shown her more than despair. "In the Mecca," she would write, "were murder, loves, lonelinesses, hates, jealousies. Hope occurred, and charity, sainthood, glory, shame, despair, fear, altruism. Theft, material and moral." Nor were broken windows and statistics the full reality of Black Chicago. If Chicago was the crossroads of America, Black Chicago was the crossroads of Black America, the natural home for the National Negro Congress in 1936, the Nation of Islam, the American Negro Exposition of 1940, the National Baptist Convention, and despite their name, the Harlem Globetrotters. Most major black press outlets—the *Associated Negro Press, Negro Digest, Negro World, Ebony,* and *Jet*—would be born here. "Chicago is the city from which the most incisive and radical Negro thought has come," wrote Richard Wright; "there is an open and raw beauty about that city that seems either to kill or endow one with the spirit of life." This oldest section of the Black Belt around the Mecca had a name bestowed by reporter James Gentry: Bronzeville.

Segregated as it was, Bronzeville shared White Chicago's gargantuan energy for making money, and had used its segregation to consolidate capital and power. Real estate mogul and banker Jesse Binga had started the Binga State Bank in 1921 across the street from the Mecca and built a protomall of shops and offices called the Binga Arcade in 1929. Anthony Overton's empire combined cosmetics and newspapers, and Supreme Life Insurance was the country's largest black-owned insurance company. Civil rights pioneer Ida B. Wells lived here, as did heavyweight champ Joe Louis and Dr. Daniel Hale Williams, who performed the first open-heart surgery. Though the name Bronzeville referred originally to the neighborhood around the Mecca, it came to embrace all the Black South Side, including places like Woodlawn and South Parkway, where successful professionals owned mansions. Middle-class black families pitied the poor whites and Chinese on the other side of the Rock Island tracks in Bridgeport, Back of the Yards, and Chinatown: "We had no idea that we couldn't live there because we never wanted to," said one resident. But restrictive covenants held working-class "Respectables" and the underclass close enough to the "Strivers" to keep a constant tension rippling.

More than money, though, what divided Black Chicago was New and Old, the tastes and values of the southern migrants versus the settled lives of those raised in the North, such as Gwendolyn's father, David Brooks, who'd come from Kansas in 1908. A true "Old Settler," his job as a janitor provided his family with propriety and an enviable security, both of which the *Defender* had tried to encourage during the beginning of the Migration: its "Wise Old Owl" columns offered strict advice about dress and behavior, as had the Urban League, with flyers listing do's and don'ts for newcomers: "Do not loaf. Get a job at once. . . . Do not carry on loud conversations in street cars and public places." Old Settlers weren't necessarily wealthy, but they'd enjoyed certain privileges back when black Chicagoans had flown under the radar, and they resented losing them now because of the new arrivals. The migrants, on the other hand, pushed back against northern mores and traditions that to eyes fresh up from Mississippi looked pretentious.

As a girl, Gwendolyn had seen herself as very much a part of that Old Settler world, puzzled at school by the country behaviors of the new kids in class. When she was seven, her mother, Keziah, read some snippets of her verse and at that moment created her daughter's rarified destiny: Gwendolyn, she declared, would become "the lady Paul Laurence Dunbar." Thereafter Keziah, a former teacher, tended and watered her gifted bloom. While Gwendolyn read the Harvard Classics, dreamed of living in the country, and produced at least one poem a day, her parents gave her an orderly, comfortable childhood in their house on South Champlain, summers in the backyard sandbox, and Christmases bright and busy with cozy rituals. Gwendolyn was assigned fewer chores than her brother Raymond so she could write, mooning "freely, often on the top step of the back porch—morning, noon, sunset, deep twilight."

Well into high school, shy Gwendolyn remained dreamy, blaming her lack of popularity on stupid boys who preferred lighter skin. Mostly, though, it was the insularity of her childhood that held her back socially. "I had not brass or sass," she would say; "I was timid to the point of terror, silent, primly dressed. AND DARK." So she bounced from school to school unhappy until Englewood High, where at last she found friends and wrote much, regularly placing poems in the school newspaper as well as the *Defender*. Unfortunately Gwendolyn had selected a poorly paid craft. When she graduated in 1935, the fortunes of the Brooks family were sagging, leaving her no choice but to enroll for a two-year degree at Wilson Junior College. An interview with Robert Abbott, founder of the *Defender*, came to naught. Domestic service next, but it was a poor match for someone who'd been given a pass on chores so she could compose; she walked out of each job after a day or two. E. N. French was the end of the road for Brooks; Old Settler pride, it seemed, didn't put bread on the table. Both the Mecca and Gwendolyn hit bottom, left to the mercies of the bigger white world.

Hoping to draw out the young poet, a friend convinced Brooks to join the NAACP Youth Council, where she marched for the Scottsboro Boys alongside energetic John Johnson, just out of his teens but already on his way up as a young editor and entrepreneur. Another marcher was her old classmate from Englewood High, artist Margaret Taylor, a self-described "young radical," petite, unstoppable, and constantly creative, equal parts

Nina Simone and Frida Kahlo, with enough brass and sass for both of them. It was Taylor who introduced Brooks, still dark, no longer so awkward but possessed of a blazing smile, to writer Henry Blakely, a man whose talents, quiet certitude, and lack of a big break mirrored her father, David. When he caught Gwendolyn's eye at a Youth Council event, Taylor shouted over, "Hey, boy, this girl wants to meet you." They married in 1939, and their son Henry Jr. was born a year later as they scraped by in a kitchenette on Champlain.

And it was Taylor who pulled Brooks into the center of the post–Richard Wright Chicago Black Renaissance. The Communist Party had publicly expelled Wright in 1937, literally pushing him out of the May Day parade, so he'd moved to New York, where Margaret Walker wrote him long letters full of gossip and hinting at her affections. Wright hadn't bitten on that score, but he'd asked her to send as many clippings as she could find about the Robert Nixon "sex moron" case—he was fascinated by a young black man driven to such violent extremes with so little visible remorse. The groups Wright had belonged to in Chicago carried on in his absence: the Mid-West Writers Group, for one, a North Side group that Algren attended, hosted by Lawrence Lipton, who'd later hook up with the Beats in San Francisco; and the Hyde Park salon of Ed and Joyce Gourfain—all integrated and politically oriented.

At the Youth Council, Taylor and Brooks started their own group, the Cre-Lit Club, which attracted young black intellectuals as well as the protective interest of South Side Writers' Group veterans Edward Bland, Margaret Walker, and Langston Hughes, then writing a series of columns for the *Defender.* With their help, Brooks began to make sense of being an Old Settler in the Mecca.

MORE THAN LITERATURE, though, popular music signified the social divisions in Black Chicago. Jazz was the establishment music. It had come up from New Orleans to the South Side, where Freddie Keppard, King Oliver, and Louis Armstrong evolved the improvised solo and the floor show; Armstrong's first Chicago gig had been at the Grand Terrace, a few blocks from the Mecca. The strip of clubs and theaters up and down that length of State Street (particularly the stretch between 31st and 35th that the Armour Institute now had its eye on) became "The Stroll," where the Pekin Inn and the Dreamland Ballroom offered the biggest names in jazz. Though the leading creative edge shifted to Kansas City and New York, Chicago remained the capital of live jazz, with the Regal and the Savoy, high-end white clubs like the DeLisa and the Rhumboogie, and countless neighborhood joints on the South and West sides. The hotels and nightclubs downtown featured white jazz, either the sweet stuff or the hyperactive Austin High brand.

If you weren't dancing to jazz on a Saturday night, you were in a joint like Smitty's Corner on 35th Street, grinding to the blues of Big Maceo, Big Bill Broonzy, Sunnyland Slim, or Tampa Red. The roots of the blues had simmered away in the South until W. C. Handy adapted them and sold them north in the 1920s. Despite all the visions of old bluesmen plucking away on guitars in cotton fields, the blues evolved as a call-and-response between North and South, especially between the Delta and Chicago, which became the center of blues recording. As the industry all but died during the Depression and migration slowed, the blues in the North turned toward the "Bluebird" sound, a jazzier style featuring barrelhouse piano and horns and favored by Lester Melrose, the A&R man for Columbia, Okeh, Bluebird, and Vocalion. Good times in 1930s Bronzeville called for the Bluebird sound, the hip-hop of the era, complete with thudding beats about booze and getting laid, while down south Charley Patton, Son House, and Robert Johnson kept developing the country blues, their anxious loneliness very much a product of the modern age. In either form, Old Settlers considered the blues distinctly low-class music.

Sunday mornings, churches like Greater Salem Baptist, Pilgrim Baptist (once Kehilath Anshe Ma'ariv Synagogue, designed by Louis Sullivan with three finished sides and a plain brick back facing onto the alley so that it looks as if it should be plugged into a wall), and Ebenezer Baptist echoed with gospel music, a form born and raised in Chicago largely by two giants, Thomas A. Dorsey and Mahalia Jackson. Back in the 1920s when he had been Ma Rainey's sideman, Dorsey had flipped between the sacred and the profane—"If You See My Savior" in 1926; "It's Tight Like That" with Tampa Red a couple years later—but ultimately God got the upper hand. In 1932 he established a gospel chorus at Ebenezer Baptist with Theodore R. Frye and when he returned from a trip later that year to find both his wife and infant son dead, the shattered Dorsey wrote the classic "Take My Hand, Precious Lord." Not long after, he moved the chorus to Pilgrim Baptist. As W. C. Handy was to the blues, Dorsey now became gospel's great popularizer and another Chicago mediator; as established black churches in the North struggled to come to terms with the thousands now arriving from the rural South, he set old-time communal suffering and hope to an urban beat.

Nobody lived that North-meets-South gospel life more than Mahalia Jackson, who'd arrived in Chicago from New Orleans on a freezing day back in December 1927, a sixteen-year-old girl only recently baptized in the waters of the Mississippi. Raised—and methodically abused—by her aunt Duke, she'd come north to her aunt Hannah's to start a new life, but the city was just too big and too cold for her, and she missed familiar faces. Lonely to her bones, she stayed in bed for a week in the apartment at 30th and Prairie Avenue until Hannah, who'd heard her incredible voice, coaxed her out to audition for the choir at Greater Salem Baptist. Mahalia's stomping, swaying version of "Hand Me Down a Silver Trumpet, Gabriel" shocked the church, but she very quickly established herself in the growing gospel community with her style—tall, thin, and dark, she growled and shouted in a voice crackling with an ecstasy that expressed a bit too much of the pleasures of this world for the comfort of conservative parishioners of the AME churches. (The temptation was more than abstract; according to one fan, she was notorious "for her hollering and getting happy and lifting her dress.") After days of cleaning hotel rooms or diapering white folks' babies, she'd sneak out and listen to Fatha Hines and Louis Armstrong for a taste of the Louisiana she missed. Her first recording in 1937, "God's Gonna Separate the Wheat from the Tares," didn't take off in

Chicago, but it hit big in New Orleans. Mahalia made no attempt to hide her dislike of "society negroes," who looked down on her for bringing the raw style of the Holiness denomination north. When a pastor once publicly accused her of blasphemy, she shot back: "This is the way we sing down South!"—a call, long before the Black Arts Movement, to keep it real.

Though Louis Armstrong begged her to join his band, instead she married Ike Hockenhull, a Fisk-trained chemist whose sad eyes expressed how he felt about working at the post office; his days at the track kept his mind off failure, while Mahalia found herself no less lonely despite the ring on her hand. Convinced his wife was wasting her talent, Ike begged Mahalia to audition for the lead in *Swing Mikado*, a jazzy adaptation of Gilbert and Sullivan set in the South Pacific, to be produced in 1938 by the Negro Unit of Chicago's Federal Theatre Project, run by dancer Katherine Dunham. Herself the product of an Old Settler family, Dunham had studied anthropology at the University of Chicago with some of the greatest names in the field, including Melville J. Herskovits, whose *The Myth of the Negro Past* established that African Americans had carried over, preserved, and adapted African cultural forms in the New World. Founder of the first black ballet company, Ballet Negre, Dunham's choreography "established for the modern dancer a new vocabulary of movement for the lower body"; African American dance began with her.

Against everything in her heart, Mahalia crept shyly into the Great Northern Theatre. Out of work, still tall but no longer thin, and way over her head among all the lithe, light-skinned girls, she walked onstage as if on her way to the guillotine. When she handed over her copy of *Gospel Pearls*, the pianist gave her a sour look, so Mahalia dashed out to Lyon & Healy on Wabash and spent a much-needed fifty cents on the sheet music for "Sometimes I Feel Like a Motherless Child." Last up, she stepped forward to face the dark theater, frightened and alone. The pianist changed the arrangement the first time around, so that Mahalia didn't know where to come in. On the next try, "I had it in my mind and I sang. And honeyyy, I forever more sang it, 'cause I *felt* it." While her final notes faded in the balcony, Mahalia dashed out, positive that she'd blown the audition, but when she arrived home, Ike was grinning ear to ear the way he did when he hit a long shot at Sportsman's—she'd gotten the part. Sixty dollars a week. Sick at heart from bringing her talents to bear in the secular world, she'd also hated not being in control. Mahalia turned down the role and never considered secular music again.

Swing Mikado turned out to be the biggest hit of the 1938 season and the inspiration for a subsequent rash of blacked-up versions of Gilbert and Sullivan, like *Hot Mikado* and *Tropical Pinafore*. George Balanchine brought in Dunham when he couldn't figure out what he wanted from his black dancers in 1940's *Cabin in the Sky* (though that didn't stop him from taking billing as the choreographer). Today it's regarded as the first Broadway show to use modern dance, before Jerome Robbins, Bob Fosse, or Agnes de Mille. Mahalia, meanwhile, went her own way, teaming up with Thomas Dorsey, who taught her "how to . . . shake at the right time; shout at the right time." The two went on the road together almost every weekend until 1942, when Mahalia was named director of the choir of St. Luke Baptist Church. Ike and Mahalia split up.

ONE WEEK AFTER Mies's Red Lacquer Room debut, October 25, 1938, white gallery owner Peter Pollack and officials from the Art Institute put some young artists—led by, of course, Margaret Taylor—around a table with black elites that included attorney Earl Dickerson. Their task was to explore the idea of a WPA arts center in Bronzeville. Interest in the visual arts had bloomed there alongside literature; the School of the Art Institute, especially instructor Kathleen Blackshear, had recruited painters such as Eldzier Cortor, Charles White, and Elizabeth Catlett on scholarship. Cortor specialized in long, smoldering paintings of black women reminiscent of Modigliani, while Catlett's best-known works were politically charged woodcuts of the poor. Charles White did similar subjects but in rich charcoals; he and Catlett would later marry, and White would study the murals of Diego Rivera in Mexico for the WPA.

The same interracial cooperation found in the writers' groups of the day fueled the artists. Around the corner from Nelson Algren and Rat Alley on Cottage Grove stood a "huge Louis Sullivan house [probably the Stearns House], run as a cooperative, . . . home to a collective of actors, painters, literati, mavericks and radicals, many of whom worked for the WPA," among them Simon Gordon, who taught art in the black community with WPA funding. Gordon introduced his students—including the young Margaret Taylor—to black history in the days before Black History Month and mentored Chicago's finest black artist of the period, sculptor Marion Perkins. Pensive, handsome, and natty, jailed at least once for distributing radical literature, when Perkins wasn't making change at his newsstand at 37th and Indiana, he carved sturdy, Brancusi-like figurative forms out of wood and stone recovered from the dilapidated buildings around his home. So as Margaret Taylor was getting the Cre-Lit Club off the ground, she was also there for the birth of the final hub of the Chicago Black Renaissance, the South Side Community Art Center (SSCAC) at 3821 S. Michigan.

"Margaret," wrote her friend Gwendolyn, *"lived up from the root."* Her opinions could be blunt: "Art itself should be used as a weapon . . . every artist or every writer, whatever they say should be a statement for the total, complete liberation of our people." Not everyone in the community was quite so strident. As soon as the doors of the Savoy Ballroom opened in October 1939 for the first Artists' and Models' Ball, held to match the WPA subsidy, the annual party became the prime social occasion of the city's black elites; debutantes sashayed in fabulous costumes with themes such as "Pan-Americana" and "Below the Border" while top-tier musicians played. Meanwhile Taylor, Gordon, and the starving artists stood on street corners with tin cans, begging dimes from passersby. Eventually the SSCAC collected enough to buy the mansion of Charles Comiskey, late owner of the White Sox, for $8,000, but clearly the socialites would be running things. The 1940 American Negro Exposition at the Coliseum, celebrating the seventy-fifth anniversary of the Emancipation

Proclamation with a show of black writing, music, and art, further stoked enthusiasm for black arts in general, so even as signs pointed to the end of federal funding for the WPA, renovations moved forward.

In the middle of all this, in March 1940, Harper & Brothers published Richard Wright's *Native Son*, and Margaret Walker suddenly understood why he'd wanted all those clippings about the Robert Nixon case. *Native Son* tells the story of Bigger Thomas, young, poor, black, and violent, much like Nixon, who accidentally murders the daughter of the Prairie Avenue white family he drives for. More than 200,000 copies were sold within three weeks, and the Book-of-the-Month Club named it a main selection; establishment tastemakers such as Clifton Fadiman and Malcolm Cowley lavished praise. Suddenly Wright was the most successful African American author ever and Black Chicago's main topic, but the fact that "we" had a best-selling book that Orson Welles was taking to Broadway tended to obscure the social issues Wright raised. Many resented his portrayal of black youth in the form of a violent rapist, and while he brought the work of the Chicago School of Sociology to life, Bigger's profound moral flaws blurred the book's call for justice. By lining up near sociologist E. Franklin Frazier, who argued that white America had all but destroyed black society and left it with no culture of its own, Wright seemed, to some, to present blacks as helpless, lending unintended credence to the paternalism with which the MHPC often coated its efforts. To Langston Hughes and W. E. B. Du Bois, Bigger Thomas was more stereotype than sociology; to White Chicago, he just inspired fear. The deepest impact of Wright's success, though, was that he'd achieved it without the Rosenwald Fund, the NAACP, or any of the other institutional sources that usually supported black artists. It made him into a wild card, but James Baldwin, Ralph Ellison, and the next generation of independent black thought followed in his steps.

On May 7, 1941, the top ladies of black society in their Sunday hats filled the main room of the completed SSCAC, along with precise little Alain Locke in his derby and cape, singers Ethel Waters and Bessie Smith, Daniel Catton Rich from the Art Institute, and First Lady Eleanor

Roosevelt, who cut the ribbon before being whisked off to a banquet. On behalf of the artists, Margaret Taylor-Goss (she'd married Bernard Goss by then) read some notes, in part: "As young black artists, we looked around and recorded in our various media what we saw. It was not from our imagination that we painted slums and ghettos, or sad, hollow-eyed black men, women and children. They were the people around us. We were part of them. They were us."

More than fifty thousand people visited the SSCAC that first year for its shows and classes, following from the idea that everyone could benefit from the arts. Young photographer Gordon Parks set up a darkroom in the basement, while upstairs the SSCAC hosted writers' groups. Inez Cunningham Stark—Mies's friend, who as president of the Renaissance Society had brought Prokofiev, Léger, and Le Corbusier to America—led a poetry workshop attended by Gwendolyn Brooks. Impressed by Stark's courage in venturing to the Black Belt, Brooks imagined the socialite's Gold Coast friends peppering her with insults: "You'll be raped." "You'll be killed." "They are savages." And yet every Wednesday at six, Stark came "tripping in, slender, erect, and frosted with a fabulous John Fredericks hat, which was as likely to sport vegetables as fruits, flowers or feathers. Her arms would be loaded with books."

Poverty, though, battered Gwendolyn and Henry. Unable to find a regular paycheck, they moved from bad apartments to dreary kitchenette, down to one with so many mice that Henry, then in the National Guard, marched them out "in droves." Seeing *The Wizard of Oz* one night reduced Gwendolyn to tears; those childhood days swinging in the hammock on Champlain seemed far away, but torn out of her middle-class upbringing, that foreign stench of the Mecca becoming her own, Brooks also met her muse. Under Stark's rigorous attention and with the encouragement of librarian Vivian Harsh at the George Cleveland Hall Branch Library, the back-porch dreamer took a harder, technical look at her work, focusing more on the city around her. "If you wanted a poem," she wrote, "you had only to look out of a window." The influence of Langston Hughes ("Mightily did he use the street") as well as Taylor-Goss and her concern with "the people around us" are evident in works such as "kitchenette building" and "obituary for a living lady." Stark urged everyone in the workshop to enter contests, but it was Brooks who won the Midwestern Writers' Conference award in 1943.

An editor from Knopf contacted her. And there were more parties; the best, according to Brooks, hosted by Evelyn Ganns (at 42nd and Drexel Boulevard) and by Taylor-Goss, who "served cheap red wine, tea and coffee, with black breads and cheese. Infrequently there would be a Creole or a spaghetti dish. . . . The talk was fantastic—and it might survive not only the dawning, but the next day's breakfast and lunch." Gwendolyn and Henry, despite their empty cupboards and radiators full of mice, were also famous hosts, including a memorable party they threw for Hughes, with a hundred people jammed into their two rooms, blues on the record player, and enough ham hocks, greens, and sweet potatoes on the table for all comers.

In 1942 FDR traded in the New Deal for "Win the War," and the gears of industrial Chicago lurched into action, creating jobs that put more money in black pockets, expanding the black middle class, and bringing a second wave of migrants north that deepened and complicated the divisions within the Black Belt. The lines between old and new, rich and poor, increasingly blurred: when Mahalia put together enough cash to buy an apartment building, she now had "tenants to move in, move out, make toe the line on the garbage and the trash. 'Don't you people want something nice?'" she would ask, sounding very much like an Old Settler herself. WPA projects wound down. Many leftist artists slipped away from Chicago, while those who stayed, like Brooks, Algren, Terkel, and Perkins, missed not just the funding but the community and the public respect the WPA had established for their work in a city with limited tastes. Margaret Taylor-Goss became an elementary school teacher. In November 1944 the SSCAC and the Abraham Lincoln Centre, a leftist community center housed in a striking red-brick Frank Lloyd Wright building on Oakwood Boulevard, held the Interracial South Side Cultural Conference, with a keynote by the literary editor of the *Chicago Sun,* A. C. Spectorsky. The event served as a coda for the years of "Black and White, Unite and Fight."

Profound as its intellectual and artistic interactions had been, the Chicago Black Renaissance never dented the city's consciousness the way the Harlem Renaissance created a mythic Black New York. Harlem had been all about style and fashion and drinking in tuxedoes—fun, white-friendly qualities that piqued curiosity more than fear. Chicago's Renaissance went unknown to most whites, and later, during the war and the McCarthy era, its connections with Communism and the WPA would make it easier, even necessary, to forget. There were no drawings in *Vanity Fair,* no embrace—Inez Cunningham Stark aside—from Chicago's wealthy white elites. So even as black Chicagoans factored on a national and international level, the city never found a place for them in its identity, never called Bronzeville by its name.

Whatever presence Bronzeville had on the city's grid, it meant competition for the only valuable resource to be found in the swampy patch of onions that was Chicago: land. Southern blacks coming north to work had nowhere to live, and black Chicagoans figured out that *they* were, in fact, what the city's businessmen and officials meant when they spoke of "blight." IIT, in the guise of battling blight, was making a land grab, bulldozing homes and looking for ways to take down the Mecca, even as Black Chicago grew more desperate for room. Increasingly, judges were refusing to enforce restrictive covenants, so the black middle class began to push out into white neighborhoods. Mayor Ed Kelly wished away the rising tensions with comments such as "There is no race trouble in Chicago." The 1942 election of William Dawson as the Black Belt's first black congressman seemed a positive sign, but a spate of firebombings in 1944 led the mayor to create the city's Committee on Race Relations and host a conference with all the usual sociologists and race spokesmen. Robert Taylor summed things up from a black perspective: "The race relations problem of Chicago resolves itself around the question of living for Negro citizens." But perpetually divided Black Chicago, which valued pragmatism over ideals, couldn't assemble a coherent leadership to confront the situation, while the conference moderator, columnist Herb Gaffis, expressed the typical white sentiment: "It would be a lovely thing for this community if the people could be sent on boat excursions and the South Side of Chicago could be very abundantly bombed. Then we could start with a rebuilding program that would have some sense to it."

SOME OF THE only places where blacks and whites lived together in relative peace were the city's few housing projects, where Chicagoans of both races lined up for units whenever they became available. Two strains of thought had evolved in the 1930s, as the Depression put people out of their homes and sped the decay of the nation's post–Civil War building stock. On one side, the old progressives simply wanted the New Deal to provide housing for the poor; on the other, reformers saw an opportunity to change America's housing system through the creation of nonprofit, working-class communities similar to those in England and Europe. A Modernist approach to design would keep costs low and might also defetishize housing from proof of one's station to a setting for an active, democratic life. The federal Housing Act of 1937 straddled the fence, and the seeds of its failure can be found right there. To appease the real estate industry, worried that everyone would suddenly abandon the private market for low-cost public housing, the law charged cities with the absurd task of building buildings that no one should want to live in. Cheap, stripped-down designs constructed with the lowest-grade materials let the government appear to throw a bone to the Modernists; the general public considered the structures ugly, while the imposed income limits guaranteed they'd become dumping grounds, federally mandated to inflict a stigma on their residents. No one had any incentive to maintain them.

It's doubtful that Mayor Ed Kelly had developed a sincere concern over the plight of Black Chicago (he still used the word "Hottentots" around City Hall), but his decision to keep the Chicago Housing Authority (CHA) clean, despite all the corruption in the rest of his administration, made political sense—the Machine needed black votes. He supported the election of African American Robert Taylor as its chairman and worked well with executive secretary Elizabeth Wood. Born in Japan to missionary parents, the schoolmarmish Wood had taught poetry at Vassar, served as a social worker in Depression-era Chicago, then was named executive director of the MHPC. Unashamedly liberal and integrationist, she agreed with the wholesale clearance approach favored by people like Henry Heald and fought attempts by Illinois state senator Richard J. Daley to create a nonprofit housing corporation to buy, renovate, and resell viable buildings in blighted areas. Like most involved in the creation of public housing, Wood saw rehabilitation plans like these as a half-measure and a sop to crooked landlords; she wanted slums leveled, period.

Even with all the built-in pitfalls of housing policy, what Elizabeth Wood and the CHA created in the 1930s and 1940s succeeded. For those, white and black, coming out of kitchenettes, these first projects were a godsend, clean and safe, with playgrounds for the kids and health clinics on-site. "We felt it was just paradise," said one resident. Wood and her staff of social workers established each project as "an engine for upward mobility and an incubator of the middle-class." Tenants were carefully screened, and inspectors made annual visits to enforce a list of rules and fines. "If the grass needed cutting and you didn't cut it, they cut it and they charged you," recalled residents of Altgeld Gardens. At the same time, positive behavior was reinforced. "If I'd see a man out shining his windowsills," recalled a manager, ". . . I'd send out a letter to the whole project congratulating him." The CHA gave out free seeds and lawnmowers, held yearly contests for prettiest lawn and prettiest flowers, and encouraged participation in sports teams, clubs, picnics, parades, and dances. " 'Project people' was a term of pride," Wood later said. ". . . Our problem was preventing the tenants from becoming snobbish." Wood wasn't afraid of social engineering. All public housing was supposed to follow the existing "neighborhood composition," and through custom and rule, the first projects maintained segregation; but during the war she began mixing people no matter their race, language, or religion. The projects urbanized black migrants from the Deep South even as their communal, primarily religious, values helped bind divisions. The Cabrini Homes on the North Side even picked up some of the bohemian vibe from Towertown a few blocks east, becoming "the center of a kind·of left-wing cultural and intellectual activity. . . . At the community center, people like Win Stracke, the Pete Seeger of Chicago, would be there regularly." Though racial tensions did erupt within the projects from time to time, Wood and the CHA saw integration as the only long-term solution.

The war squeezed construction standards down, and the federal government imposed an income limit that forced upwardly mobile tenants to either lie or be thrust back out into the private market, where they'd soon find themselves homeless again. Since the federal law required slum clearance along with new building, the CHA actually destroyed more units than it created during the war, and in a regrettable misstep, it gave no preference to those already living in the project neighborhood. The housing shortage only grew more desperate for both whites and blacks. By 1945, when the city most needed the CHA, Chicago was growing increasingly wary of it.

GWENDOLYN BROOKS STAYED in Chicago. Knopf rejected her poems, so she sent her next batch to Harper & Brothers, which bought the collection in 1944 that would become *A Street in Bronzeville*. Originally she'd planned to explore "a personality, event, or idea representing each of thirty houses on a street," and while the final book swerves from that plan, it stays true to the intention. In poems like "the mother" and "The Sundays of Satin-Legs Smith," Brooks no longer shouted her own feelings—she lent her voice to those with no words for their pain, their loneliness, their befuddlement, and their anger at a world so casually vicious. She'd become a witness to Bronzeville. "Abortions will not let you forget" opens "the mother," as a woman who has aborted any number of her own wonders at what's been lost; in "Queen of the Blues" a singer has a lonely onstage realization as to the real value of her fame; "Gay Chaps at the Bar" confronts the bitterness of the black war experience and is dedicated to Edward Bland, killed in action during the Battle of the Bulge. A book about common people, to be read by common people, *A Street in Bronzeville* is a first draft of that dream to "touch every note in the life of this block-long blockwide building."

As Brooks waited for copies of her book, Richard Wright published his autobiographical *Black Boy*, a huge hit that would sell upward of 600,000 copies in its first six months, and Harcourt, Brace brought out *Black Metropolis*, a many-layered, exhaustive, and brutally honest study of mid-century Black Chicago, conceived by Horace Cayton, built out of research he'd led for a WPA project in the late 1930s. The grandson of Reconstruction senator Hiram Revels, Cayton had studied sociology at the University of Chicago after knocking around as a reform school inmate, a ship's mate, and a policeman in Washington State; it was Cayton who had pointed Wright toward the Chicago sociologists and away from Communism. A tortured soul, Cayton was trapped between the white academic world, where he felt most comfortable, and his allegiance to the black community, where he ran the Parkway Community House. He would eventually flame out to alcoholism and depression, but for its scholarship and its examination of black society without reference or deference to white norms, *Black Metropolis* remains a landmark.

A week into August, Gwendolyn Brooks read her first review, a rave that launched her career:

> My husband and I, returning from yet another Saturday night movie, bought the early *Tribune* and ripped it open to the book pages. "For heaven's sake!" My Reputation! Henry and I read the entire review on the midnight street, then waited in ecstasy (forgive me, students whom I've

cautioned against the use of that weak word) for the bus. My husband looked at me meticulously. "Gwendolyn, tell me EXACTLY how you feel at this moment."

Exquisite and circumspect, she kept her words their secret. But *A Street in Bronzeville* announced shy, simple Gwendolyn as a challenger to Langston Hughes as the nation's premier black poet. Her mother had been right after all.

CHAPTER 3

WASHED UP ON
A FAVORABLE SHORE

LÁSZLÓ MOHOLY-NAGY LOVED light. He loved to see it move, dreamed of it painted onto passing clouds. A year before Mies arrived, August of 1937, this spry Hungarian in his early forties, a patch of white in his black hair, peered through his rimless glasses into the gloam outside the Art Institute. To the north, on the last building on Michigan Avenue, a beam of light swooped in circles, guiding fliers safely home to Municipal Airport, off in the brownlands to the west. It took fifteen or so hours now to fly across America. Moholy latched onto the beacon coming from a building near his hotel, up in the neighborhood called Towertown, and started briskly toward it.

He hadn't rested well since he'd arrived. Fire trucks. Police sirens. Hoppy jazz from every radio. Cars racing up and down Michigan Avenue with often tragic results; you didn't need a license to drive in Illinois, so the same number of people died in car wrecks in Chicago as in New York but with only half the drivers. He'd never have come here if not for this job. Miss Norma K. Stahle and the Association for Art and Industry had invited Gropius to open a new design school "along lines Bauhaus." Gropius had declined, then pointed them toward Moholy, in London at the time making educational films and designing window displays—increasingly, distressingly underemployed for the man who'd been Gropius's right hand at the Bauhaus. Since then Moholy had been meeting red-faced rich men who insisted on knowing his first name, pumping his hand, showing him around their big houses full of French antiques. In Europe only a lover addressed a man by his first name; why would they want to call him "Laci"?

Moholy crossed the new bridge connecting the Loop to the other side of the Chicago River and its unconsidered mix of warehouses, storefronts, vacant lots, wooden shacks, nickel bars, and burlesque houses, all under a string of atrocious skyscrapers: the Tribune Tower, with its flying buttresses and bits of other, better buildings stuck to its skin; the Medinah Athletic Club, sporting a Moorish dome; and a few blocks north the Allerton Hotel, a thirty-seven-story faux Italian Renaissance palazzo. Gropius loved Chicago; he called it a *toller Brodelkessel,* a "mad, bubbling cauldron." Literally so, in some places; the few hundred yards of Bubbly Creek boiled with gases from the shit and blood poured into it by the Stockyards.

The beacon spun again on the Palmolive Building. Everything in Chicago, even the names of buildings, seemed to involve selling, and yet the Palmolive was the best new building Moholy had seen here, lean and strong. Everything here wanted to be something great, even if it didn't know what, or how, or why. Chicago had achieved nothing yet, but it had built the set for all that it wanted to become, and it was selling tickets. More than anything, Chicago *yearned.*

A few weeks before he'd written his wife back in London:

DEAREST SIBYL,

If I didn't have to uphold my reputation as a valiant male before you I'd say that my heart sometimes sinks below the gray pavement of this strange town. I've never felt so alone. It all looks familiar but when you investigate it, it is a different culture—it is no culture yet, just a million beginnings.

Like, for example, the empty car barn he passed across from the Water Tower, where dozens of students and artists lived together, Bauhaus-style.

Towertown, the Greenwich Village of Chicago, harbored mad geniuses, bomb throwers, and advocates of free love—the kinds of people Moholy liked. In the evening, thousands sat in front of the bandshell in Grant Park. The fascist rebels were continuing their assault on Madrid, the Japanese were laying siege to Peiping, and in Munich, Hitler had opened his House of German Art. Here in Chicago (pronounced "schikago," he explained to Sibyl), children worried about nothing, and Moholy had two daughters. Gropius and Marcel Breuer were already at Harvard. All he had to do was say yes.

At the Palmolive Building, he walked on to the beach and the lake, dotted with the lights of a few boats content to float along the horizon. He'd written Sibyl about Lake Michigan: "But what a lake, oh Darling, what a lake! Its color changes constantly, and it remains calm and moving at the same time. No limitation. An endless aspect to a very limited civilization."

He turned. The white lights of the cars poured at him on the left; a stream of red dots rolled away on his right. Moholy was hypnotized.

> There's something incomplete about this city and its
> people that fascinates me. It seems to urge one on to com-
> pletion. Everything seems still possible. The paralyzing
> finality of the European disaster is far away. I love the air
> of newness, of expectation around me. Yes, I want to stay.

In mid-August Moholy signed a five-year contract and announced, with no teachers on staff, no curriculum on paper, that in two months the New Bauhaus would be ready for students.

IN ALMOST ALL WAYS, László Moholy-Nagy was the opposite of Mies, who could not stand him. Where Mies stood thick and stolid, lithe Moholy bounded with energy; when together, they reminded one "of a sturdy elephant brushing off a high-spirited puppy." If Mies was, as his biographer

Franz Schulze once said, "a black hole," sucking those around him into his gravity, then Moholy sent everyone off on their own chosen orbits, a man blasted apart, forever following his fragments. Born in rural Hungary in 1895, László Weisz had been only two when his parents separated. Mrs. Weisz gave her three sons to their uncle in Mohol, whose name László took. Like his uncle, he studied law until he enlisted into the Austro-Hungarian army in 1915. While Mies drank much beer and sat behind a desk, the Great War shattered László; a blaze of his black hair soon turned white. Stationed in Galicia, he survived the Brusilov Offensive in 1916, which all but decimated the Austro-Hungarian army—at one point, László saw his entire battery killed around him—but he was wounded the next July during the Kerensky Offensive. His drawings from then appear at first to be just masses of frantic lines until a dying soldier emerges, or a field of barbed wire.

Demobbed, László moved to Budapest, where he supported the Communist government until it fell, then wandered as a refugee from Szeged to Vienna and finally Berlin, his law career over. In Berlin he joined the same artistic circles as Mies; they had friends in common; and like Mies, he worked through the movements passing across the city like storms. He made Dada collages, created a cameraless form of photography called photograms, and performed arguably the first example of conceptual art, when he called in a description of a painting to an enamel factory that then produced the finished work. He did his best easel painting during these years, precise, geometric abstracts influenced by El Lissitzky and Kazimir Malevich. But where Mies ultimately chose to *express* the times, Moholy aligned himself with the Soviet Constructivists who believed art should *change* the times by using technology to unite art and everyday life. Long before Margaret Taylor-Goss, Moholy thought of art as a weapon, an offer of a clean new life. Constructivism let him explode within a confined space, paint lines and planes shooting off into endless dimensions, and yet still feel grounded to the collective effort of creating a better world.

In 1923 Mies's old office mate Walter Gropius hired Moholy to come to the Bauhaus, which he'd opened four years earlier as a reaction against mindless industry. The school's first years in Weimar had been a rage against the machine, full of bright colors and a strong Expressionistic, nearly mystical bent with Klee and Kandinsky on the faculty, and Johannes Itten in monk's robes, compelling students to practice an obscure cleansing discipline (created, incidentally, in Chicago) called Mazdaznan that involved breathing exercises and eating only raw vegetables. But Gropius soon realized there was no fighting technology, so he shifted from Expressionism to Constructivism and charged the Bauhaus with bringing industry to heel by creating well-designed objects for mass production. The key to that shift was Moholy. At twenty-eight the school's youngest professor, he took over Itten's mandatory Foundation Course (*Vorkurs*) and directed it toward the limited palette and straight Constructivist lines that would form the lasting image of the Bauhaus. By the time the Bauhaus moved to Dessau in 1925, Gropius, savvy administrator and politician, ran the show, as Moholy in his workman's overalls beat the drums. An enthusiastic and inspiring teacher, he rejected the title "Master" called for by the rigid German school system.

In 1929 his artistic theories gelled in his book *The New Vision*. Like Mies, Moholy was aiming at things of the spirit, and *The New Vision* links him to Rudolph Carnap, Ludwig Wittgenstein, and the Vienna Circle philosophers who tried to reduce all aspects of human experience to their most essential terms in order to find their ultimate unity. Moholy tried something similar in *The New Vision*, breaking down the arts to their most essential materials and forms, but not for the sake of art. "Not the product," he announced, "but man, is the end in view." Art isn't an expression of the divine or something to hang on museum walls; it's just one of the biological necessities of human life. "Everyone is talented," he said later, a phrase that would become central to his thought. Everyone needed to encourage and develop their creative energies to realize their *Gesamt-werk*, their "total design." It was a revolutionary idea that transcended the socialist rhetoric it had grown out of, and it breathed life into the nihilistic, intellectual forms European art had taken in the chaos since the war. Art was all about the making, and in Moholy's eyes it was now progressing past the easel, toward light, space, and motion. Beneath his dreams of light shows projected onto clouds are the beginnings of modern media theory. Walter Benjamin famously quoted him in "A Short History of Photography": "The illiterate of the future will be the man who doesn't understand photography."

Moholy left the Bauhaus with Gropius in 1928, spending the next few years doing graphic design, creating theater sets for the experimental director Erwin Piscator, and playing with short films. On one of these films he met Sibyl Pietzsch, a minor actress turned movie dramaturge. Moholy once boasted that he'd slept with a thousand women. In Sibyl, though, he met his match. Fiery, stubborn, if not brilliant then fully convinced that she was, horsey Sibyl was not especially attractive, but as in so many other areas in her life, she seemed to make herself so out of sheer force of will. Ravished by Moholy's constant energies in the arts and otherwise, she became his muse and then, against his wishes, the mother of his child. Theirs would be a tempestuous marriage.

When Hitler took control in 1933, Moholy settled in England near Gropius where he was accepted with a wan handshake into the Hampstead circle, concentrating mostly on photography and film, with some window design for Simpsons Department Store to pay bills. The English were bemused by all that amateur's energy but found Moholy ever so slightly, you know—*flimsy*. Plus, some unpleasant accusations had floated over the Channel. Josef Albers, later of Black Mountain College, who considered himself the top "Moholy hater," accused him of taking credit for aspects of the *Vorkurs;* Naum Gabo thought he'd stolen ideas, too. Man Ray challenged his claim to inventing the photogram, and it must be said that Moholy's sets for Alexander Korda's 1936 film of H. G. Wells's *The Shape of Things to Come* did bear an uncomfortable similarity to Mies's model for the Glass Skyscraper. Even among artists, the English class system demanded that everyone know exactly what you are and that, for Moholy, was nearly impossible to say. A quick trip back to Berlin to film the 1936

Olympics brought him face to face with former students now in SS uniforms. The telegram from Miss Norma K. Stahle came in spring 1937.

A N D   S O   B A C K to Chicago, with its soot and slums and meat on the hoof. As early as 1934, *American Magazine of Art* published an article, "Wanted: An American Bauhaus," and Chicago seemed the right place for one, despite being, as Moholy wrote, a very limited civilization. In the late nineteenth century, Chicago had embraced the Arts and Crafts Movement, even boasting its own William Morris showroom, and had then taken the next step with the Prairie School of Frank Lloyd Wright, whose 1901 speech at Hull House, "The Art and Craft of the Machine," announced the Machine Age twenty-five years before the Bauhaus. Given the impact both Wright's Wasmuth Portfolio and the Chicago School had on the Werkbund, Germany's craft association (whose members had included Behrens and Mies), continuing the Bauhaus in Chicago looked like a kind of homecoming. The city of very limited civilization also seemed prepared philosophically for the Bauhaus. Rudolph Carnap had come as an émigré to the University of Chicago, whose philosophy department focused on establishing the essential connection between all the sciences. At Gropius's urging—"Chicago seems to me the right place to be," he wrote—Moholy made his choice. The school would be called the New Bauhaus. The two discussed the name in their letters, and Moholy plainly stated in the first catalog, "Because of Dr. Gropius' confidence that Professor Moholy-Nagy and his faculty will continue and extend the best Bauhaus tradition he has granted permission that the School of Design be called The New Bauhaus."

Sibyl disagreed; as usual vehemently. With Hitler gearing up for war that summer, she felt a German name was a terrible idea. In fact, she was wary about the whole enterprise, especially this "Marshall Field" that Miss Stahle had cabled about, marching around the prairie—why would they have to be involved with the military? Unswayed, Moholy instructed his wife to sell everything and come to Chicago, where she saw that their benefactor was not a field marshal but millionaire Marshall Field III, who'd donated his three-story, twenty-five-room family mansion at 1905 S. Prairie Avenue to be the school's home, as part of his left turn into philanthropy. Ironically, it had been designed by Richard Morris Hunt, the "frenchified Yankee" most responsible for the spread of the Beaux-Arts in America and architect of the grotesque Vanderbilt mansion at 660 Fifth Avenue in New York that Louis Sullivan had mocked in *Kindergarten Chats* as a "Château de Blois."

Undaunted, Moholy furiously cobbled together his school. Working day and night, he sketched out a curriculum that basically replicated the entire Bauhaus system; when Gropius told him it was overly ambitious, he smiled and admitted that the catalogs had already been printed. The Field mansion was gutted, brocade torn off the walls, woodwork replaced with flat white paint, and Moholy added his own light fixtures, big spheres of glass hanging down on chrome rods. Staffing was a particular challenge. He asked Frank Lloyd Wright to join but had to be satisfied with Hin Bredendieck and György Kepes, the only Bauhaus alumni, who despaired at the "absolutely corroded sight of the South Side of Chicago, . . . the colored area. Dante's Inferno was really happening in comparison." James Johnson Sweeney pulled out at the last minute; Herbert Bayer couldn't get a visa in time. Photographer Henry Holmes Smith and sculptor Alexander Archipenko came aboard ten days before the school opened. Carnap introduced Moholy to University of Chicago philosopher Charles Morris, who, seeing the link to his Unity of Science movement, convinced the school to allow him and two other professors to teach at the New Bauhaus uncompensated.

Moholy now spread the Bauhaus idea through the city at large with long and occasionally incoherent speeches that fell on rocky soil. "We were among Philistines then," wrote Katharine Kuh, owner of what was then the city's only gallery of modern art. The Armory Show of 1913 had drawn mocking crowds to the Art Institute, where it had been the students and faculty who'd hung Matisse in effigy, and little had changed since. The *Tribune*'s art critic, Colonel McCormick's great-niece Eleanor

Jewett, a former agriculture major who'd quit school to avoid having to witness the wickedness of breeding animals, lent her support to a vigilante group run by Art Institute trustee Mrs. Frank Logan called "Sanity in Art"; its righteous blue-haired members harassed visitors to Kuh's gallery. The Renaissance Society at the University of Chicago and the Arts Club had the courage to present modern artists, but their small shows were geared toward cognoscenti, while Daniel Catton Rich and the Art Institute spun in the breeze, pushed in one direction by his good taste and intentions, and the other by the whims of its board. Chicago's most important art critic, the lively, inquisitive, and morbidly obese C. J. Bulliet, balanced out the lunacy. Before he began writing for the *Chicago Daily News*, he'd built up a large following as editor of the *Chicago Evening Post*'s weekly art section, generally welcoming new trends in art.

At last, on October 18, 1937, Moholy opened the doors to his first class. By the time Gropius arrived a month later, for a grand opening tea and dedication banquet, the school was already falling apart. Moholy's Bauhaus lacked the Germanic *Ordnung* that in Dessau had provided a stage for his free-form pedagogy. Here *everything* was free-form: board members walked the halls, giving their two cents; classes and schedules were in constant flux. Lectures by the likes of Bulliet and Sigfried Giedion made first-rate minds available to students but didn't add up to an accredited academic path. "The school," Kepes later admitted, "was not really clearly defined in its targets." Factions quickly formed. Those who believed in Moholy, such as Nathan Lerner, found themselves

> totally immersed in a program of sculpture, graphics, poetry, sciences, photography, industrial design and even music made on instruments of student construction, performed by our own orchestra. We were given strange exercises: picking up objects, feeling them, then drawing them; cutting and folding paper; shaping blocks of wood until we liked how they felt. This was all very mysterious and confusing until we realized objects and images we made were

not to be judged by faculty but were meant to reveal what
was happening to us, what we were absorbing, how we
were growing.

On the other side, a fringe of more experienced, fine-arts-oriented
students were angry that they had to go through the basic material explo-
rations of the *Vorkurs*, unhappy, according to Lerner, with Moholy's philosophy that "art was stuff and something to do with the world and people
and matter."

Miss Norma K. Stahle was unhappy too. Described by those who knew
her as an unlikely Lady Macbeth, cold and uncommunicative, Stahle
began plotting Moholy's demise within weeks of the school's opening,
enlisting Hin Bredendieck, teacher of the Preliminary Course. Gropius
squelched the coup, but then the board notified Moholy that the double-
dip had forced them to unload their holdings at a deep discount, costing
the school its entire $100,000 endowment. When news of Mies's pending
arrival spread to Prairie Avenue, Moholy approached the Armour Institute about a merger, an idea Heald immediately rejected. Moholy remained
resolute. Buoyed by excellent reviews of the June student show, he barn-
stormed across America to raise money. While he was gone, the Association of Arts and Industry closed the New Bauhaus. Lawsuits ensued.
Moholy won but got only the mortgage on the Field mansion instead of
back pay and had to endure embarrassing headlines such as "Bauhaus
Head Branded Flop," just as he and Sibyl toasted Mies at the Red Lacquer
Room. The Association of Arts and Industry faded away, and Miss Norma
K. Stahle—"a first rate gangster," according to Moholy—ended up deco-
rating windows at Marshall Field's, but his reputation had been dented.
Vindication came, as usual, from Gropius, who included a selection of
works by Moholy's students in the big Bauhaus show at the Museum of
Modern Art (MoMA) in fall 1938, officially extending its lineage to Chi-
cago. W. W. Norton published a new edition of *The New Vision* with Moholy
trumpeted on the cover, bittersweet, as the director of "The New Bauhaus
American School of Design."

Stranded in America, one of the key names in modern art now settled for a consulting job with the Spiegel mail-order catalog. This much was certain: he didn't want to leave Chicago, even if he'd just been cooked in the *toller Brodelkessel*. "Chicago is not only an unfinished canvas," he wrote Sibyl. "It is a smeared-over sketch which I have to clean up and set straight." He declined further help from Gropius. "I have to manage my life without bothering my friends," he wrote. "America was always a country of pioneers." Charles Morris provided Moholy with a letter of introduction to John Dewey, America's most influential philosopher, who'd fueled turn-of-the-century progressivism with a midwestern common sense and his driving impulse to experience, experiment, and connect. Dewey was especially popular in Chicago, where he'd founded the University of Chicago philosophy department, worked closely with Jane Addams, and started the Lab School to advance his theories on education. Moholy's brief meeting with him that November opened his mind to the potential of America, not just for its money and material but for its native philosophy. The *new* New Bauhaus—the School of Design—would be an American institution, not a European transplant, merging the Dewey-style pragmatism Chicago exemplified with Moholy's belief that artistic talent is innate.

Like Mies, Moholy removed socialism from Modernism, but he attached his understanding of it to populist strains of American thought. Embracing individualism and tolerating capitalism, the School of Design would create "universal designers," young men and women prepared to use aesthetics in service to the world, able, in Dewey's words, to "put the maximum of consciousness in whatever is done." With Sibyl happy to see light in her husband's eyes, Moholy convinced seven of his former faculty to teach for free and lined up a board of advisers that included Dewey, Gropius, Joseph Hudnut of Harvard, publisher W. W. Norton, and Alfred H. Barr, director of MoMA. The next issue was space. As Moholy and his crew wandered in search of a new home, Robert J. Wolff spied a series of dark windows on the second floor of an industrial building on the Near North Side. Taking a chance, he walked upstairs into a huge empty loft space that had once belonged to a now-bankrupt bakery chain. The next day, washing, painting, and hammering began at 247 E. Ontario. Walk-in refrigerators became darkrooms; massive bakery ovens would store plywood and heat plastics. All they needed now was money.

For that, Moholy turned to Walter Paepcke, owner of the Container Corporation of America (CCA). Paepcke's father had made a fortune providing crates to Chicago's great mail-order firms and department stores such as Montgomery Ward and Sears, and though not an émigré himself, prow-nosed Walter, product of a buttoned-down German family, had much of the Old World about him. His wife, the striking blonde Elizabeth Nitze, nicknamed "Pussy," thought him something of a philistine; her father was chairman of Romance languages at the University of Chicago, so Pussy had grown up surrounded by the world's intellectual high society. Prodded by his wife, Walter in 1936 pulled a minor version of what AEG did with Peter Behrens, using famous designers to sell CCA as a corporate good neighbor amid the Depression. As top Chicago socialites and patrons to some of the world's leading artists, the Paepckes had supported the New Bauhaus, but they'd shrugged off Moholy's touch. Now the Hungarian talked his way into dinner at the Paepckes' apartment at 999 Lake Shore Drive. "I have to be the advertisement," Moholy told Sibyl, and that night he spun a web, laying out his vision for the School of Design and all the other great Bauhauslers, such as Walter Gropius, who'd surely love to know a genial, German-speaking millionaire willing to put his money behind their art. Paepcke "did not want the world's most famous school of modern design to breathe its last breath in Chicago," but with business as bad as it was, he only had $8,000 socked away. "Valter," Pussy reported Moholy saying, "kann you help uss?" For the first of many times to come, Paepcke opened his wallet for Moholy.

The School of Design opened to eighteen students on Washington's Birthday 1939, the whole scene even more chaotic than the New Bauhaus. Wolff hadn't noticed that the space he'd found was below the practice floor of the Chez Paree nightclub—if the penniless students weren't distracted by chorus girls tap-dancing overhead, the smells coming from the club's kitchen did the job. The Preliminary Course remained, but no grades, no tests. In 1940 the talented and unpaid faculty included a young composer deeply influenced by *The New Vision* named John Cage who conducted "Sound Experiments." Moholy's followers were as fanatical as Mies's; one referred to him as "my Christ." "He . . . had a million ideas a minute," recalled Katharine Kuh, "but his students got a great deal from him. He revolutionized their thinking." "At the bottom of the infinite faith we had in Moholy," wrote painter and sculptor Richard Filipowski, "was the fact that he never criticized the work of a student in terms of good or bad." The result was "an electric atmosphere which is almost overwhelming," said the *Chicago Sun*. His daughter Hattula remembered him going to work every day in a lab coat over his suit, a black metal lunchbox in hand.

With housing tight, most of Moholy's students lived hand to mouth in that dodgy area just west of North Michigan Avenue, the center of North Side bohemia known as Towertown. "Chicago at that time had a seminal environment," said architect Bertrand Goldberg, who lived in what he referred to as a "commune" in the Stables, the coachhouse of the Farwell mansion on Michigan and Pearson, a block away from Mies, owned by muralist Edward Millman, art director of *The Chicagoan* magazine, and home to *Life* photographer Wallace Kirkland. Painters such as Richard Florsheim, who lived in the Tree Studios on Wabash, would chip in fifteen cents toward a communal stew, though Mary Lynch, owner of the restaurant behind the Stables, fed artists for free. The Allens, at 645 N. Michigan, owners of one of the last mansions on the street, rented rooms to students from both the School of Design and the School of the Art Institute of Chicago and held regular "evenings." Towertown, home to an estimated 1,500 dice girls, 1,000 priests and nuns, 3,000 art students, and 500 strippers, had the city's highest concentration of bars, strip joints, and hotels, and the fewest cops on patrol.

Chicago's North Side bohemia had political roots that reached back to the 1860s, when a friend of Karl Marx had tried to organize the city's German laborers. Throughout the second half of the nineteenth century, Chicago collected anarchists, socialists, and freethinkers who promoted the cause of labor as a radical impulse native to the soil. Pre-Bolshevik Reds, they drew as much inspiration from Walt Whitman as from Marx. Radicals like to talk, so they gravitated to the half-acre park in front of the Newberry Library at Walton and Dearborn officially named Washington Square but better known as Bughouse Square. Here miners and hoboes, free-love advocates and out-and-out nuts all gave speeches to crowds that sometimes numbered in the thousands. They battled hecklers, analyzed Kierkegaard, rabble-roused, and most of all entertained, because this was free theater, full of passion, improvisation, and humor, and everyone understood the game. Smaller speakers' clubs opened throughout the area, already a seedy part of town "lined with cheap hotels, the winter quarters of carnival and cheap circus people, burlesque queens and comics, stars of the Chautauqua circuit and pitch artists and grifters," to let the conversation continue into the night and through the bitter winters.

Of all these clubs, the most famous appeared at Michigan and Pearson. The first description of the Dil Pickle Club, in 1914, calls it a tearoom "on the dry end of Pearson Street," but it came to fame when its founder, a former union saboteur with mangled hands named Jack Jones, moved the show west a few blocks to a hole in the wall at 18 Tooker Alley, where they went on a search "to find Chicago's great soul." Through its door, painted with the motto "Step Down. Stoop Low. Leave Your Dignity Outside," visitors crouched along a passage (it really *was* a hole in the wall) into Chicago's version of Cabaret Voltaire, a place Jones called "the world's greatest university, where all isms, theories, phantasies and other stuff can have their hearing." Coffee, tea, and snacks were on the menu, but no alcohol; the talk provided all the excitement. Along with crackpots, Wobblies, and anarchists, the visitors and speakers into the 1920s included Carl Sandburg and the Andersons, both Sherwood and Margaret, William Carlos Williams, Djuna Barnes, Ben Hecht and Charles MacArthur, Clarence Darrow, Ring Lardner, Dorothy Day, Katherine Dunham, and the young Kenneth Rexroth; professors from Northwestern and the University of Chicago; and anyone changing trains with an expertise in human sexuality, the topic that drew the best crowds. The speaker would give their speech, and then the assembled Picklers would have at them with comments and arguments and insults that went through the night. It was Chicago Dada, an intellectual free-for-all, part cabaret, part poetry slam, part performance art. "We of the Dil Pickle believe in everything," began its manifesto. "We are radicals, pickpockets, second story men and thinkers. Some of us practice free love, and some, medicine. Most of us have gone through religion and have tired of it. Some of us have tired of our wives."

Then Al Capone muscled in. By forcing liquor into the place, he turned the coffeehouse into a bar, and by the late 1920s it had devolved into radical chic, a stop on the tour of decadent Chicago. Tourists jammed out the old Wobblies, and the Dil Pickle died of popularity. Jones shut it down for good in 1933 to concentrate on his invention, a metal toy duck called the Du-Dil Duck.

Though gentrification had already begun to boost prices on the area's grungy sprawl of cheap lofts and storefronts, Towertown maintained that spirit of a separate place just across the river from the Loop, in no small part from the Dil Pickle imitators throughout the Near North Side, like Rexroth's favorite, Green Mask at Grand and State, various "at home" salons, and bars such as the College of Complexes and Riccardo's, Chicago's version of Café de Flore. In the 1940s veterans would move to Towertown, "a haven," wrote one, "for the broken soul as well as the earnest and rebellious. The drug addict, the petty thief, the sex deviant and the alcoholic are generously mixed in among the sincere and aspiring. . . . There are call girls and crowds of visiting firemen, second hand clothing stores and smart shops, pawn brokers and art supply stores," all drawn by an indefinable pickle-tinged scent of homegrown intellectual freedom. As housing activist Catherine Bauer once said, any sensible city planner doing a new town would always include a good slum. Towertown was a very good slum.

Moholy, then, had landed in the perfect spot for a chaotic school of design based on leftist principles, Dewey-esque philosophy, and faith in the abilities of the common man. "Art is a community matter," he declared at every opportunity, and "Everyone is talented"—a philosophical balancing act suited to his adopted hometown, at once fiercely individual, community-oriented, and identical to that of the SSCAC. Instead of pulling up the drawbridge, as Mies did at IIT, Moholy saw the way Chicago's bohemia worked, or at least wanted to see itself—as a function of the community. "He intended to create communities of artists in Chicago that would be as cohesive as the one he had experienced in Dessau," said John Walley, director of the WPA Design Workshop, who once brought the Hungarian in for a speech to the nearby Artists Union that turned into an all-night debate at a bar. Walley and Moholy collaborated on an industrial arts manual for the Chicago public schools that would have offered Bauhaus-style training to every child in the system. Through Walley's offices, the School of Design did the SSCAC renovation Margaret Taylor-Goss had collected dimes for in 1940.

Then the WPA shut down and the war began. Moholy scrambled to keep the school open. Lectures by Fernand Léger, Richard Neutra, Charles Eames, and others couldn't hide Moholy's inability to pull in any great Bauhaus names for faculty. "Things would get terribly gloomy," said one student, "and everyone would know there wasn't any money in the bank, and then Moholy would go out and persuade someone to buy one of his paintings." He gave speeches and sat with the ubiquitous Inez Stark on whatever committees he could; Mayor Kelly put him in charge of camouflage for the city, as he stood next to Bears coach George Halas and Archbishop Samuel Stritch in the line of famous older men signing up for the draft. In doing all this, his sincere enthusiasm took on a craven edge—he assumed the role of what Sibyl called the "prooofessor" around prospective donors, most of whom were skeptical of the whole "design for life" concept. "He wears rimless glasses," reported the *Tribune*, "and talks with such an accent that he is difficult sometimes to understand." The *New York Herald Tribune* said terms such as "painting with light" and "kinetic sculpture" had a "cultist ring." "I think he was friendly and fond of me in a way," said Kuh, "but mainly he saw me as a conduit. I think he saw everyone more or less that way." Paepcke aside, Moholy valued Chicago's businessmen by how much they gave. When meeting new people, he was "known to pull Paepcke aside and inquire all too audibly: 'Tell me Valter, how much ar' zey vert?'" Worse, he continued to take credit for the work of others, though maybe Moholy was simply ahead of his time in believing that content was free. According to Sibyl, all that mattered to him was spreading ideas; the details of ownership were secondary. Then as now, that reasoning sounds thin.

Over countless games of chess, Walter Paepcke and Moholy became close friends. Paepcke lent him a run-down farm in the village of Somonauk, two hours outside Chicago, where the school held summer classes while his two daughters, Hattula and Claudia, got some sun. "I know what little interest you have in expressions of thanks," Moholy wrote in 1942, "but allow me to say that our life here in America would have been sometimes very dark without your and Pussy's friendship." Walter's voluminous correspondence badgering friends for contributions and fairly blackmailing CEOs into sending men to night classes at the school attest to a profound commitment, yet even he found things disorganized. As the first class graduated in May 1942, Paepcke again tried to convince Henry Heald at IIT to take in the School of Design. Heald was intrigued, but there did "seem to be some difficulty in connection with the personalities involved." Which meant, Mies said no.

No one hated Moholy-Nagy and the School of Design more than Mies van der Rohe. According to Katharine Kuh, Mies "thoroughly disliked Moholy's methods, didn't admire at all the way he operated and found him too aggressive. But those weren't the real reasons." Though Moholy and Mies had come out of the same Modernist trunk, they'd grown in opposite directions; Mies applied the Bauhaus method to one field of study, while Moholy applied it to every aspect of life. When it came to power and money, Mies had arrived already connected to institutions, whereas Moholy was a permanent supplicant, Paepcke's pet cause; his unsightly begging surely repelled Mies, who considered him more a charlatan than a threat. That Moholy was a teetotaler and Mies a functional alcoholic didn't help, but the real reason for Mies's animosity was that Moholy had, according to Mies, stolen the word *Bauhaus,* which he considered his own property, through Bauhaus bylaws after the school's closing in 1933. In this case, though, Moholy's sticky intellectual fingers hadn't come into play; Gropius himself had insisted he use it, and if anyone had claim to the word *Bauhaus,* it was its founder. In 1967 Mies actually "gave" the word back to Gropius, an acknowledgment that it wasn't his in the first place.

Moholy wasn't always popular at home, either. Tight money had forced him to move his family from a large apartment on exclusive Astor Street to something cheaper on Lakeview Avenue. He worked six days a week, gone before his daughters woke and back home after they'd crawled into bed. A difficult, demanding husband, he was dismissive of Sibyl's writing career, and the little they had belonged to the Paepckes, from whom she couldn't escape "the definite feeling that in [Pussy's]—oh so pretty—blue eyes we are just Schnorrers." Yet as much as Sibyl feared and resented Moholy, she loved him, "a total man" with "a voracious appetite for strong sex and strong food, and there was absolutely nothing he permitted as obstacle in his reach for fulfillment."

By 1944, the school was on the verge of collapse, and so was Moholy, doing everything and none of it well. Paepcke issued an ultimatum: the School of Design had to change from a one-man show into a structured institution that worked with industry: the Institute of Design (ID). He'd serve as chairman of the board for this new ID, and he'd enlist power hitters such as William Patterson, the president of United Airlines, and E. P. Brooks of Sears to sit on the board. For his part, Moholy would have to create a more coherent curriculum. "So, let me repeat once more," Paepcke wrote him in April 1, "that everybody expects you to be a leader, educator, and creative artist and not an individual doer of a thousand and one miscellaneous relatively unimportant mechanical duties."

The story of the three iterations of Moholy's school is as simple as the typefaces on their letterheads. The name "new bauhaus" had always been set in all-lowercase sans serif, a direct link to the Weimar original. "School of Design" had been written in elegant script, artsy and fanciful, maybe a little too dreamy and delicate for its own good. "INSTITUTE OF DESIGN," though, was written in block letters, all caps. The ID, like all of postwar Chicago, would mean business. Still, Moholy's humanist ethos would weave itself into the city's most important creative currents and constitute one of its greatest artistic legacies.

CHAPTER 4

THE IDEAL WORLD OF MR. HUTCHINS

SOUTH OF BRONZEVILLE and Mies's industrial IIT, far, far away from the patched-together genius of the Institute of Design, lay a resort village on the lake. Though swallowed by the city in 1889 to accommodate both the World's Fair and John D. Rockefeller's plan to create the world's greatest university, Hyde Park would always remain a place apart from the city at large, and Rockefeller's school, the University of Chicago, would be regarded with as much suspicion as pride, when anyone paid attention. With only an occasional tip of the mortarboard to Northwestern, its faculty and administration considered themselves the city's intellectual elite, stationed in a frontier outpost of the mind. The gothic spires and gray limestone, the quadrangles, and leaded glass windows all called to mind Oxford; the lawns and wide, satisfied homes, especially the one built by Frank Lloyd Wright for Frederick Robie, lounging along Woodlawn Avenue like a lazy summer day, exuded an East Coast sort of security—financial, social, and intellectual—rarely found in the rest of the city. By the 1930s, two generations of academics had lived in Hyde Park, raised children, intermarried. "Living here is like living in a very delightful 'village,'" wrote one new arrival. Jackson Park and Promontory Point, jutting into the lake, provided places to walk and fish and row; the busy, if run-down, strip along 55th Street offered shopping, and the southern boundary of 63rd and Cottage Grove had movie theaters and clubs for the adventurous.

As the city devolved into its 1920s daze of Capone, Chicago's upper crust shipped their sons off to Yale and Princeton, leaving the college a "social escalator" for bright Chicagoans who lacked old school ties. Contrary to its current bookish image, it was a party school then, frat happy and in thrall to coach Amos Alonzo Stagg's Maroons, the "Monsters of the Midway." Stagg had introduced the idea of using big-time football to make a school's name, a plan that worked then, as now; watching local boys in Maroons jerseys, rooting for Jay Berwanger, winner of the first Heisman Trophy and first player picked in the first NFL draft, Chicago's clock punchers and freight haulers found a way to embrace the university without worrying they'd come away smelling like rosewater.

All this changed in 1929 when Robert Maynard Hutchins became president of the University of Chicago and the de facto mayor of this academic company town. There was no getting around his looks: he was a taller, more refined version of the young Tim Robbins. Unfortunately this man who wanted to be profound was best known for his surface, which was probably to his benefit, because Chicago's most famous intellectual was not particularly well read. Hutchins's family had moved from Brooklyn to Oberlin College when he was a boy, so his minister father could take a job teaching homiletics, the study of giving homilies. After a childhood of virtuous simplicity, Hutchins enlisted in the army and in August 1918 served briefly in Italy. Like Moholy, his view of human nature got creased, but unlike the Hungarian, he developed a taste for liquor that would later place him in Mies's league as a drinker. He finished his undergraduate degree at Yale. A gifted orator, sharp-tongued and handsome, Hutchins was voted Most Likely to Succeed in the Class of '21; from there, he taught boys at the ivy-covered Lake Placid Florida School, where arguably he should have stayed and as a tweedy headmaster lit fires in generations of young hearts. But it was assumed that life had bigger and better plans for Robert Maynard Hutchins. He scaled the next rungs quickly: hired by President James Angell to be secretary of Yale, then on to Yale Law, where he graduated magna cum laude in 1925 and became a lecturer there the next day; two years later a full professor; after three months, just weeks short of his twenty-ninth birthday, he was named dean of Yale Law. Finally in November 1929, the board of the University of Chicago elected him president, in the throes of what Hutchins himself later called "that spirit of wild emotional adventurism that characterized the boom." He was thirty.

Along the way Hutchins had married socialite Maude Phelps McVeigh, who was remarkable in two ways. First, for her beauty, at least the equal of her husband's. Exquisite, tall as Hutchins, with bobbed dark hair and Audrey Hepburn's long neck, Maude presumed herself a sculptress, playing the wilting, sensual artiste to great effect. Second, those who knew her fail to offer even a backhanded compliment on her behalf. Hutchins's casual, clubby arrogance became in her hands a knife; her wit "often transgressed the boundaries of polite discourse to become downright rude." No one liked Maude, but more to the point, Maude didn't like anyone else. As soon as she and Robert arrived in Hyde Park, she decided never to see anyone socially, insisting that he be home straight away from the office so the martinis and brilliant banter could begin. The result was that Hutchins, the public face of the university, had little to do with its tight-knit community huddled together on the lakefront. He was alone and his rise was already attracting negative attention. His curt notes, ostensibly full of wit, in fact bruised feelings and had an air of his being above the messy details. Hutchins needed help. Along came Mortimer Adler.

A Brooklyn native, schlumpy Adler had climbed the ivory tower from the outside, a very Jewish Jew at a time when Gentlemen's Agreements were still in force. His memoir, *Philosopher at Large*, reveals a man utterly puzzled by the subtleties of human interaction, aware that he was unable to engage with others but confused as to why. After night school classes at Columbia, Adler had received a scholarship, taking a special honors class with John Erskine that featured a close reading of certain classic texts.

Then in his senior year, he'd taken a class with John Dewey, who had since left Hyde Park for Morningside Heights. Adler took to sending Dewey long recapitulations of his lectures accompanied by batteries of questions that he followed up with yet *more* questions, all in a manner less curious than aggressive. Says Adler, "I was an objectionable student, in some respects perhaps repulsive." He stayed at Columbia for graduate work, but in psychology instead of his first love, philosophy. He made his rift with Dewey final by delivering attacking lectures that caused Dewey to "explode with rage." Considering that the philosopher was famous for his plain manner, one can only imagine.

While at Yale, Hutchins had contacted Adler after reading proofs of an upcoming book. Adler, in black suit and briefcase, waited outside the office expecting to meet some bearded old man, when the door opened and there he was—Hutchins, in tennis shoes, duck pants, and a white T-shirt. They became great friends, each able to do and be what the other could not. But they had another bond. Adler at that time was also in an unhappy marriage to a sculptress, and when he met Maude that first night, surprisingly—shockingly—she liked him. For his part, Adler found that the smell of her sculpting compound stirred "embarrassed excitement in me, even to the point of my blushing." Though he had turned down Hutchins's offer of a job at Yale, Adler happily moved to Chicago, where Hutchins was looking for a platform and a friend. "Bob confessed to me that, in his career so far, he had never given much thought to the subject of education. He found this somewhat embarrassing now that he was president of a major university." "Mert," as Adler was known, told him about Erskine's General Honors class, which inspired Hutchins to challenge the university's emphasis on departmental specialization. Mert and Hutchins were a devastating pair, but largely to their own cause. Hutchins's unrelenting moralism—he was a prig about smoking, for instance—and his tendency to be personally cutting while being himself unable to actually argue a point were already widely discussed. Adler, for his part, in a matter of months became the most universally disliked figure in American intellectual history—"unfunny, ungraceful and unquiet," "a one-man infestation of the ivory tower, a bulldozer in the academic grove."

The war Hutchins waged is still debated: Which matters more—ideas or facts? Should you go to college to learn a shared set of fundamental knowledge that you'll build your adult life on, or should you go in knowing what you want to do and specialize at a school with a vocational direction, like IIT? To Hutchins and Adler, the university needed to be saved from Dewey and pragmatism: truths were knowable and constant, therefore everyone should get the same education built on those knowable truths—but only as they were explained by the metaphysics of Aquinas and the neo-Platonists. On an intellectual level, it was as if the new head of the astronomy department believed the earth was flat. Even the Catholic Church had a more up-to-date approach; while Cardinal Mundelein "studiously ignored" the university's turn to the antique, Adler in a public debate argued the higher value of angelic knowledge. Beneath the academic battle was the question of control: Would two men, one thirty and the other twenty-seven, be allowed to disrupt a way of life and a community that they both looked down on? Adler once compared Hyde Park to an army base. With the machinery of the university against him, Hutchins backed down.

The two things Hutchins is best remembered for—the Great Books program and the experimental "Hutchins College"—both sprang from his devotion, via Adler, to the study of a prescribed list of classic texts. Reforms to the college were already on the boards when Hutchins came and were approved as part of a general restructuring of the university in 1930; one two-year general college would now feed students into the five professional schools. Class attendance was optional; all students had to do was pass a final exam. In no small part because of the dashing young president, the press made much of the change, and student quality shot up. Hutchins, though, saw all this as only a half-measure. What he really wanted was a four-year college covering the junior and senior years of high school and what were traditionally the first two years of college, with all students following a single curriculum (though not the Great Books, as often assumed) before selecting a specific field for graduate studies. Bit by bit Hutchins fought on, bringing the University High School under the college and lowering the entrance age to sixteen. Outside the classroom, the sorry last years of the Monsters of the Midway, including a punishing string of four losses in 1939 that saw them outscored 255-0, finally gave Hutchins the excuse to kill the football program. (George Halas then appropriated the Maroons "C" logo and combined it with the blue and orange of the University of Illinois for the Bears' new helmets.) Not everyone was thrilled. "This will be a seminary in about seven years," student Richard Salzmann told the *Tribune*.

At any moment, Hutchins would have happily packed his bags for Washington, D.C., if President Roosevelt had offered him the right job. "The greatness of the University of Chicago," said Hutchins, "has always rested on the fact that Chicago is so boring that our professors have nothing to do except work." He all but campaigned for the Supreme Court opening FDR eventually gave to William O. Douglas. As a consolation prize, the president offered him the chairmanship of the newly created Securities and Exchange Commission, a post Hutchins declined in a huff. He cajoled Harold Ickes to pass a note to FDR about the vice presidency in 1940, but Roosevelt did not respond, so the next year Hutchins committed political suicide with a national radio speech explaining why the United States needed to stay out of the war. Overnight Hutchins found himself persona non grata in Washington, adrift in the America First movement with Henry Ford, Colonel McCormick, and Charles Lindbergh. His marriage to Maude had dissolved into a series of gin-streaked arguments and pained apologies to those she offended—one year their Christmas card was a nude drawing she'd done of their daughter Franja.

Mies made an appearance in Hyde Park, as part of an effort to save the Robie House, Frank Lloyd Wright's masterwork. An IIT student inadvertently found in March 1941 that the Chicago Theological Seminary, owner of the Robie House, planned to demolish it as part of an expansion. Wright rallied Buckminster Fuller, Carl Sandburg, and Lewis Mumford to his cause, while Mies, Hilbs, and Daniel Catton Rich formed a Committee for the Preservation of Frank Lloyd Wright's Robie House. Much exalting of Wright ensued, but it was the war, not the protests, that stopped the seminary. This was probably the first serious landmarking coalition in Chicago.

After Pearl Harbor, Hutchins did an about-face on the war. Though months earlier he'd believed that "the American people [were] about to commit suicide," now he declared the University of Chicago to be "an instrumentality of total war"; by 1944, two-thirds of its budget came from the government, in support of the science departments that Hutchins had previously slighted for being too specialized. Men in uniform swarmed the campus, and the atmosphere thickened with an anxious knowledge of something enormous, very secret, and not at all metaphysical being created in Hyde Park, where photographs were no longer allowed in front of certain buildings. Its code name on campus was "the metallurgical project," but it would be better known as the Manhattan Project. In a squash court under the stands of dormant Stagg Field, Enrico Fermi, Harold C. Urey, and Leó Szilárd built a radioactive pile that, on December 2, 1942, yielded the first nuclear chain reaction. The Atomic Age began under the nose of a man devoted to medieval Scholasticism. "I didn't think they could do it," Hutchins would later say by way of explanation, and apology. Until 1943, when J. Robert Oppenheimer took the Manhattan Project to Los Alamos, the university controlled the multimillion-dollar budgets of the Hanford plant in Washington State, the Argonne National Laboratory, and Oak Ridge, Tennessee, the new community that the Chicago architectural firm Skidmore, Owings & Merrill (SOM) designed and built for the secret production of plutonium.

Hutchins now made a new push for humanism, a psychic counterweight to the destructive seeds he'd planted on his own campus. Late in 1942 the university board agreed to form one four-year college with a single required curriculum, open to qualified high school juniors. After thirteen years, the Hutchins College was finally born, its worship of pure knowledge suddenly heroic as Hitler went about extinguishing Goethe's light across Europe, its students envied not for their class or affluence but for their intellectual performance. As the start of educational meritocracy, it introduced competition to the study of dead white men. Classes were interdisciplinary investigations of the humanities and sciences, all capped with "Observation, Interpretation, and Integration," a culminating philosophy course. Smart, motivated, "offbeat" students worked to excel within a culture of constant debate and exploration; the rich kids who'd been going east to Princeton and Cambridge for social reasons now went there because they couldn't cut it in Chicago. Hutchins welcomed new students with a convocation at Rockefeller Chapel. "You are now members of a community of scholars," Robert Silvers recalls him saying. "You are not in kindergarten. You are not in a club. You are not an agency of propaganda. You are scholars where each person has the responsibility and the opportunity to learn." Students took his message to heart and worshipped him. "If he ever gave a talk, the place would be jammed."

The bad news was that even as student quality rose, enrollment dipped. On top of the military draft, a general education seemed a luxury after a devastating depression; specialized degrees appeared more sensible, and those who left Chicago were dismayed to learn that their credits from this experimental school weren't always transferrable to mainstream institutions. Some prospective students (and their parents) worried about living on the South Side as blacks moved south along Cottage Grove west of Hyde Park and into Kenwood. For all the humanist philosophy spouted in Hyde Park, the neighborhood had always been deeply and violently segregated; fiery homeowner meetings there had helped spark the 1919 Race Riot. While Bronzeville limited IIT's future, blacks threatened Hyde Park's cherished, genteel lifestyle. The school bought up as much surrounding land as it could and honored restrictive covenants, even when the black buyers were faculty members. The few black students at the University of Chicago faced racism on personal and institutional levels; they couldn't buy or rent a place to live on campus; black fraternities were shut down; the barbers in Reynolds Hall refused to cut black hair. The school's own hospital would not treat black students. Hutchins claimed to be appalled and distressed by the situation, and once when a black assistant professor wasn't admitted to the exclusive Quadrangle Club, he offered his resignation, but he did little to defuse racial tensions, let alone improve relations. Though he found restrictive covenants "morally offensive," he never contested the board and in fact supported the university when it funded the legal battle against black businessman Carl Hansberry, who had bought a house just south of Washington Park from a white landowner intentionally breaking a covenant. Hansberry's family, including his eight-year-old daughter Lorraine, were regularly surrounded by "howling mobs." The case went all the way to the Supreme Court. When two black graduates of the law school requested that Hutchins stop funding it, he refused and added, "Why don't you people stay where you belong?" Real estate and academics were two separate issues for Hutchins—"But don't ask me why," he told the *Defender.*

SELLING HUMANISM CAME more easily to Hutchins than practicing it. The Great Books program started back in 1930, when Hutchins and Adler held a special year-long seminar on Adler's list of "great books" for a select group of freshmen. The class was a curiosity; the press focused as usual on the dapper university president nodding sagely at the head of the table rather than on Adler bullying students on the finer points of Saint Anselm. The seminar became a calling card for the school: Gertrude Stein attended a class and fought with Adler; everyone from Orson Welles to Lillian Gish stopped by while switching trains. Hutchins then introduced the classes into the adult education division. By now Adler had given up on academia to court the world at large. The great books, he decided, were wasted on the young, but if the adults who ran the corporations and waged the wars learned the wisdom of Plato and Aquinas, the world could still be saved. In 1940 he wrote (with Charles Van Doren) *How to Read a Book* and promoted it all the way up the best-seller list. Two years later, Hutchins at his side, Adler began a reading series for a group of thirty Chicago businessmen and their wives (including Walter and Pussy Paepcke)—the grandees and upper executives whom Heald and Moholy were chasing for checks—that came to be known as the Fat Man's Class.

Hutchins and Adler bit the apple, unlike Moholy, who just constantly nibbled at it. The start of the Great Books should be seen in the context of books being burned in Germany; content aside, the idea of cultivating serious intellectual discussion among mainstream American adults was about as hopeful and utopian as the Bauhaus plan to save the world through better furniture and light fixtures. Though it might have made a Dil Pickler squint warily, advocating that Everyman could and should understand Spinoza and Rousseau displayed remarkable faith in the American public and presaged the coming postwar liberalism, at least on the part of Hutchins, who'd become something of a lost soul. More than a worldly man probably would have, he put stock in the ideals of the Great Books, in a much more innocent way than publicity-hound Adler.

Enter William Benton, a college classmate of Hutchins, whose résumé ranges from the depths of American greed to the heights of American aspiration; he's the Colonel Kurtz of the American Century. As an ad man, he invented "laugh" and "applause" signs, the live radio audience, and the entire field of market research. During World War II he was head of the Commission for Economic Development that laid the foundation for America's postwar economic expansion; then he became assistant secretary of state, started UNESCO, and founded the Voice of America. As a senator in the 1950s, he was the first man to call for Joe McCarthy's censure. Hutchins introduced Benton to others as "a man who invented things that he now apologized for."

Benton had come to Chicago in 1936 as a consultant to help sell the school's image. A man without much downtime, he expected his demands to be met; once when he missed a flight, he ran onto the taxiway and chased after the departing airplane until it stopped and took him aboard. On December 9, 1941, he had lunch with General Robert E. Wood, chairman of Sears, Roebuck. One of the company's more unusual holdings was the *Encyclopaedia Britannica*, which, Wood moaned over their shrimp cocktails, was bleeding money. The solution was obvious to Benton; Wood should give the entire thing to the University of Chicago. After lunch, Wood called Benton and offered it to him. The deal took over a year to consummate; the university's reluctant board of trustees seemed puzzled by the windfall, though the return would be immense.

Around this time Benton took the Fat Man's Class and had trouble finding copies of the books. The solution was again obvious, to him at least: *Encyclopaedia Britannica* and the University of Chicago would publish a big, hardcover, and very deluxe edition of the Great Books, a white elephant that would serve as a tax write-off against the massive profits Benton was taking in on the *Encyclopaedia* and his recently purchased *Merriam-Webster Dictionary*. At first Hutchins was reluctant, thinking with justification that the point of the Great Books was to discuss them, not own them, but Benton soon convinced him to become a figurehead editor-in-chief. The real lifting would be done by Adler, who'd also concocted a companion index to all human thought (or all dead white male thought), to be called the Syntopicon. The term *Great Books* was copyrighted, and Hutchins selected an advisory board, starting a process that would soon fall into a rabbit hole.

CHICAGO SAW THE terrors of World War II secondhand, but it took special pride in its job of hosting the thousands of passing GIs, who regarded the city as the most hospitable in the nation. Rationing was onerous and shortages acute—good luck finding shoes, sewing machines, fabric, vacuum cleaners, washing machines, fans, irons, beds, cutlery, toasters, waffle irons, baby carriages, lamps, refrigerators, or even a bottle of Coca-Cola. Chicagoland industries led the nation in producing war matériel, flushing money through the city; $1.3 billion went into building new factories, and unemployment, once at 40 percent, dropped to under 2. Many feared another Depression would hit as soon as all this spending stopped, but in fact the United States was about to launch into the height of its industrial power, and this reawakened Chicago—rail hub, air hub, manufacturing giant—would be the engine. During the next fifteen years, as America's industrial might exploded, Chicagoland would build more factories, produce more steel, handle more freight, employ more construction workers, and bank more money than any other part of the nation.

But Chicago itself was not transformed. As the saying goes, having money doesn't change you—it just makes you more of who you are. Though Chicagoans, for the first time since the 1920s, had cash in their pockets—a lot, since rationing had left little to buy—Ceres continued to stare down on the same soot-choked Loop, the same failing schools and corrupt cops, the same irresponsible government, the same slums swelling with new arrivals looking for work. The war effort had frozen local construction, which meant the city's building stock continued to degrade. The housing shortage became a housing crisis. Homes and land took on a totemic value; the black population continued expanding and becoming more middle class, yet its political leadership was chained to the Machine. Meanwhile, the war had invigorated homeland connections among ethnics, hardening neighborhood borders. As Chicago got rich, its problems got worse.

Over the next fifteen years Chicago would use the ideas of Mies, Moholy, and Hutchins to decide whether Henry Luce's American Century could coexist with the Century of the Common Man. One side of the debate imagined a single national mass market, driven by uniform ideals spread by Big Business (with much government help); the other called back to the populist ethos of the WPA and the New Deal coalition. The rift cut straight through the city, in all kinds of circles. An Information Age would soon transform the culture, spreading art and information faster and more completely: would that democratize art and knowledge or cheapen it? As Hutchins, Adler, and Benton kicked off the Great Books, the networks were feverishly developing television; James Petrillo, head of the musicians' union headquartered in Chicago, was enforcing a recording ban, to preserve live music and hopefully cut radio and jukeboxes back down to size. Would people follow Moholy's optimistic path of making art within their communities? Or, *à la* the Great Books, would the Establishment and the

Fat Men decide what the truth was and disseminate it at a price? Government and Big Business considered the future of thousands of buildings
around the city, but how much would individual Chicagoans, black and
white, have to say about where they would live? Would the Cook County
Democrats, the country's last big political machine, be able to hold on to
power, or would independent voters take over as the city spread north,
west, and south?

The answers to all these questions depended on what *regular* would
mean in postwar Chicago.

PART TWO

1945-1949

"YOU'RE IN CHICAGO NOW!
IS EVERYBODY HAPPY?"

Willard Motley,
Knock on Any Door

A T THE end of World War II, the U.S. government had
unprecedented control of American life. The New Deal
had reined in corporations, and the war had subjected individuals not just to the draft but to rules on what they could buy, sell,
charge, say, and do. Americans had gotten used to both. But the
net result of saving the world for democracy had been to give
Institutional America back its strength; after a decade of global
slaughter, rational planning struck most as only good sense. The
assumption (made particularly by those in power) was that great
minds would sit down and make wise decisions about how things
would work in the Atomic Age, while everyday Americans
would drive the economy with the money they'd earned during
the war. Big Business would tell them how to spend it, where to
live, and when to punch the time card, while the world opened
itself to the American Way.

Though Americans wanted to enjoy their new prosperity and stability, they hadn't forgotten the Depression or the trauma and shared sacrifice of the war. Those years had fused a national identity out of populism and communal values as much as any singular drive to win battles. As the city's most powerful institutions banded together to resume redevelopment along business-friendly lines, the old New Deal spirit made its voice heard again in Chicago. The word *regular* could still carry a Whitman-esque air. In the arts, Chicagoans' particular attitude in many ways ran counter to East Coast trends; they met the possibilities of peacetime with experiments and improvisation. New sounds would emerge from the street corners and the storefront churches; social justice still mattered, as did the human form. Between the end of the war and 1950, radical new ideas swirled in Chicago that would lay the groundwork for much of postwar American life.

It was, according to Nelson Algren, "a fresh time."

CHAPTER 5

THE CHAOS OF OUR CONCEPTIONS

KNOCKING THE SLUSH off their shoes, blowing on their hands, twelve hundred Chicagoans in double-breasted suits filed into the Red Lacquer Room for lunch, buzzing about the Marines on an island called Iwo Jima. Midday February 23, 1945. The war was entering its endgame. Everywhere the world's best minds were looking at large maps and making big plans. Allied leaders at, Yalta, Bretton Woods, and Dumbarton Oaks framed out a postwar order dominated by two new superpowers, the United States and the Soviet Union. Only oddballs like Friedrich Hayek, whose *The Road to Serfdom* was a surprise best seller for the University of Chicago Press, proposed *less* planning.

They were looking at maps in Chicago too. The city's contribution to the war effort indicated that it would likely become the center of postwar industry, so the power brokers were preparing for opportunities to come. The crisis at hand was the housing shortage that had Chicagoans crawling on top of each other. "All over town basements and attics are being adapted for living quarters," wrote the *Tribune*. Kitchenettes now existed outside the Black Belt. Families were putting out boarders, so their children-turned-veterans could have their rooms back. The state even had to cancel the annual high school basketball tournament because the boys had nowhere to stay. The obvious solution—build more buildings—was blocked by sky-high labor costs and the lack of basic supplies like lumber and nails. Even if a developer managed to cost out a project, rent controls meant he wouldn't see a profit for decades. Ostensibly, the war's end would restart outward growth in the third residential ring, but no one knew how long it would take. If the city proper wanted to stay the focus of Chicago-land's coming expansion, it would have to act before the middle class followed the rich, leapfrogging out to the suburbs. In 1944 the toothless Chicago Plan Commission (CPC) had tweaked Burnham's plan, adapting, for example, the broad boulevard meant to extend out west from Congress and Michigan into an expressway—but the CPC's report was at best a statement of intent. As usual, the disorganized, diffuse, and generally corrupt city government was waiting for the businessmen.

Long-faced Walter Gropius had come today from Harvard to make some suggestions in his speech, "Rebuilding our Communities after the War." Gropius was well thought of in Chicago. The product of an affluent Berlin family, he'd spent a year as a hussar before studying architecture and working at the Behrens office, until he made his name with the Fagus-werk shoe factory in 1911. As an officer in the Great War, he cuckolded the revered composer Gustav Mahler with his much-younger wife, Alma, who married Gropius as soon as the composer died; she then promptly began an affair with the novelist Franz Werfel, bearing *his* child while Gropius recuperated from shell shock. In 1919 Gropius combined the Saxon Academy of Fine Art and the Saxon School of Arts and Crafts into the Staatliches Bauhaus, which for its dramas must have still seemed calm by comparison. His boxy and then-revolutionary entry for the 1922 international Tribune Tower design competition finished out of the running but gave him profile in Chicago. He appreciated the city's lack of East Coast refinement; on his first visit to the States, he found "Chicagoans totally . . . unrepressed, unembarrassed." After a year under Hitler, he emigrated to England in 1934 and then in 1937 took over the Harvard Graduate School of Design, where he also shifted his school's curriculum out of the Beaux-Arts and worked on prefab housing schemes and the sort of urban plans he'd be sharing today at the Palmer House. His stake in the Institute of

Design and his friendship with Moholy had drawn him closer to Chicago, in particular to Walter Paepcke, who enjoyed the fact that he didn't ask for money or require explaining at the Tavern Club. Behind Moholy's back, Gropius and Paepcke, the two courtly Germans, plotted how to make best use of his genius while minimizing his diva propensities.

Moholy flitted about, introducing his very good friend "Pius." This was his show, sponsored by the business-oriented ID, along with the Chicago Plan Commission and the Chicago Association of Commerce and Industry. Given it was a Friday and damned cold (and the new curfew shuttered all bars and clubs at midnight), whiskey was surely enjoyed at the head table by the likes of Mies, Mayor Ed Kelly (at sixty-nine still with lush, wavy hair and the face of a chummy principal with a dark side), Bishop Sheil, Robert Hutchins, and of course Paepcke. The luncheon was lily-white. (Earl Dickerson had sued the Palmer House in 1942 for refusing to seat him; the hotel had lost, but never paid him on principle.) Gropius's real audience was the businessmen. Blustery as Chicago's weather could be, its nickname "The Windy City" actually referred to the regular cycles of boosterism and Babbittry produced by its business community; but now the Great Books had endowed art collector Leigh Block of Inland Steel, Weyerhaeuser Timber heir Laird Bell, and kilt-wearing, curling fanatic Hughston McBain, chairman of Marshall Field's, with the sense that they were philosopher-kings. Along with Material Service's Henry Crown, who $30 million or $40 million ago had been a delivery boy on the West Side, and of course Marshall Field III and Paepcke, they were preparing to step forward together to remake the city. "The business people are really identified with the city, much more than ever in New York," said one executive; they "were all fellows who knew one another." And if all that enlightened noblesse oblige just happened to produce billions of dollars in profits for them, would that not be their due?

Lunch finished and cigars now lit, Gropius, with his glum basset hound face, gripped the podium. After bemoaning "our present chaotic cities," he described a vision of new ones made of "self-contained neighborhood units" of five or six thousand residents that scaled up to a precinct of 30,000 to 50,000 people. "All points of activity and interest in the neighborhood unit . . . should be within 10 to 15 minutes walking distance at most. This would confine its size to an area with a radius of about one half mile or less." Rather than massive developments like Stuyvesant Town in New York, which he deemed "a potential slum area," Gropius envisioned a rural idyll, with all homes at a "proper size," filled with "wife-saving devices" and "hobby rooms," the buildings largely prefab or at least made of materials that would render them obsolete in twenty years. Swaths of green space would run between buildings.

If you'd been living in a kitchenette with eight other people, this all sounded fabulous—it was called the suburbs. No one sipping on his after-lunch Benedictine (except maybe Hilbs) had any interest in turning the city into what Gropius described. But what they heard loud and clear from the director of the Harvard School of Design was permission to do what the MHPC, IIT, and others had been saying all along—tear it all down and start over. "We have to go the whole hog," Gropius said. ". . . It is obvious that piecemeal plans, partial reforms, and appeasing concessions are but retarding factors on the way to a tightly-coordinated, over-all pattern of planning which would promote a healthy 20th century community life."

Two months later the ground shifted. FDR died on April 12, 1945, and Harry Truman, no one's choice for the White House, couldn't restrain the military, the anti-Communists, or Big Business the way Roosevelt had. His order to drop the bomb on Hiroshima and Nagasaki in August changed the calculus between the United States and the Soviets; America no longer required cooperation or consensus to exercise its will. The American Century began with a surge of swaggering optimism and a frightening, liberating sense that the bomb had suddenly blown the ceiling off of man's limitations. In Chicago, back in 1942, Mies's human-free, hyper-orderly IIT campus on a plinth had looked unnerving, but with two "chaotic" Japanese cities wiped entirely off the map and many of Europe's great cities just piles of brick, Herb Gaffis's dream of bombing the South Side suddenly didn't sound so strange or even unpleasant—at least *he* wanted to put everybody on a boat. Theoretical solutions like Gropius's seemed possible, and "slum clearance" took on the deceptively benign sound that "Free Soil" had had before the Civil War.

The cannon fired on a land rush in Chicago. Marshall Field III sold the four-million-square-foot Merchandise Mart to a new player on the scene, former ambassador Joseph Kennedy, who with one pen stroke became the city's biggest landlord; that same week, an experimental jet plane traveled 544 miles in 62 minutes, persuading Mayor Kelly that the Douglas C-54 aircraft factory northwest of the city was the perfect site for a new airport, Orchard Place. South of the Loop, about a mile and a half northeast of IIT, an even larger development scheme moved forward. Faced with the same choice as IIT as to whether to stay in its deteriorating neighborhood, Chicago's largest private hospital, Michael Reese (MRH), had in spring of 1945 brought in urban planner Walter Blucher, who advised the hospital to join ranks with IIT and reclaim the area. Taking baby steps, the MRH board named Gropius's former student Reginald Isaacs as director of an exploratory Planning Staff charged with essentially the same task as Mies, though on a bigger scale. Gropius signed on as a senior adviser.

Planners across the city got to work. What needed to be fixed now, according to Hilberseimer, was "the chaos of our conceptions." Gropius's emphasis on the "human" presupposed that there was one preferable way to be human. As blinkered as Hutchins and Adler, his hyperrational, sanitary vision of inevitable Western progress applauded the arrival of "complete meals which have been pre-cooked, quick-frozen and packed in plastic containers ready to put in the oven!" Everyone made suppositions based on his own preferences, like Hilbs with his formulas that quantified exactly how much space a bed required, where a table should be placed. One student described the approach as "You start with a kitchen and you end with the world." "The idea that those in authority know best," wrote historian Tony Judt, "was not born in 1945, but it flourished in the decades that followed."

Isaacs explicitly declared war on Chicago's neighborhoods with a three-stage plan that covered a twelve-square-mile radius around the hospital campus. The MRH Planning Staff, he wrote, was "forcing a re-examination of the neighborhood concept . . . urban dwellers generally become members of groups larger than neighborhoods, and the complex needs of modern urban life are not answered by the facile formula of the neighborhood theory." Gropius, Hilberseimer, and many other city planners made no secret of the absurd contradiction ticking inside their work, namely, that they didn't like cities. Not only did they consider cities outmoded, but in the Atomic Age urban density waved a big "Bomb Me" sign. Superblocks were meant to minimize fatalities; expressways to speed evacuation. To Hilbs, it wasn't just slum dwellers who suffered; *everyone* was a captive of the city. When planners like Isaacs rolled their big maps of Chicago out across the table, they didn't read the city the way most Chicagoans did. They saw money; some of them saw race; but mostly they saw their own preconceptions and theories. Despite their claims to intellectual superiority, they really didn't know black or white Chicago or any of its social structures. The planners' goal was to improve the city out of existence.

Although there were attempts such as the *Herald-American*'s "Better Chicago" contest to interest everyday citizens in the planning process, Chicagoans remade the map in their own violent way. Between 1944 and 1946, there were forty-six racial incidents in the city, nearly all connected to housing. On July 1, 1946, at 7200 S. Eberhart, within sight of the green copper steeple of St. Columbanus Church on 71st Street, a group of boys threw rocks at Dr. Eugene Cooper and his wife, Osia, as they moved into their new two-flat. Until now a zone of light industry had separated the Black Belt from this neighborhood—Park Manor—but the Coopers had breached the levee. The rocks turned to firecrackers. The boys didn't leave, and as the day turned to evening and men came home from work, the crowd grew. By the time the police showed up, nearly two thousand people had surrounded the house, about as many as fit into St. Columbanus for

Sunday Mass. Rocks pinged off the windows. Three days later the Coopers sold, but more blacks would follow.

ANCHORED TO HIS old swivel chair, Congressman William Dawson hung up the phone and propelled himself across the floor with his one real leg. Thick set and glowering like a linebacker on fourth and one, he rolled past the wooden leg, placed the good one, with its two-toned shoe, atop a box, and then waved for the first visitor to enter. Every weekend when he came back from Washington, Dawson, only one of two African Americans in Congress, held court here in his office above the Grand Terrace Ballroom on 35th Street. Today's audience was no different than usual—old winos, whores, and storefront preachers, folks fresh up from the Delta clutching their caps, still trying to figure out life in the city. Could he fix a ticket? Call off the fire inspector? Move them up the list for Dearborn Homes? The answer was usually yes, for the price of their vote. Southern blacks were proud of their vote after generations of having it stolen, and they were proud of being able to do whatever they wanted with it, including make a trade. Bill Dawson exchanged small, immediate favors for all those individual votes, bundled them together, and built a career with them.

He was no country boy himself; he read poetry and collected jazz records. After graduating from Fisk, he'd made first lieutenant in World War I before he was gassed. Following his recovery, he moved to Chicago for law school and passed the bar in 1920. Eight years later he ran for Second Ward alderman on the revolutionary platform that he was more fit to represent the black ward than the white incumbent; though he lost, he'd put himself in the game. After losing another aldermanic race in 1939 to Earl Dickerson, Dawson announced his switch to the Democrats, for which he received the post of committeeman, top party rep in the ward. That effectively gelded Dickerson, since Dawson now controlled the patronage. He was Kelly's man; the mayor not only let Dawson oversee the policy business in the Black Belt but backed his run for Congress in 1942 against Dickerson. Dawson had one other important fan whose support would have national implications—Mahalia Jackson, who took to him from the start, beginning her cozy relationship with the Machine. "Not only for the big meetings," she said, "for all the precinct-captain meetings too," she would riff on one of Dorsey's hymns: "'Dawson has brought us all the way, and he carries our burdens. Oh, he's such a wonderful leader, we always got to vote and keep him . . . Dawson has brought us a long way.' And baby, all the politicians would go crazy!"

Dawson's down-home appeal and street-level pragmatism posed a problem for the Old Settlers and black upper classes, who couldn't help feeling some pride at his place within the Machine's inner circle and especially that seat in Congress. "Big Bill Dawson lived a few blocks from us," wrote Ronne Hartfield, "in a looming red-brick mansion secluded by an imposing black iron fence. We children used to stand outside the house hoping for a glance of this man who everybody said could fix anything." And the small favors he doled out were crucial for survival in a place Nicholas von Hoffman described as "a honeycomb of conspiracies to confine black people to 'their' part of the city," where even the fire and police department sometimes refused to respond to calls. "Politics back then was not just electing someone," said one small business owner. "It was an essential part of accomplishing the day to day things that you needed to get done." But Dawson's power had little to do with Old Settlers and everything to do with Southern migrants like Mahalia.

As a staunch admirer of Booker T. Washington, Dawson wasn't concerned about civil rights, a point he'd made clear back in '39 when he'd ambushed Dickerson after a rousing speech on black independence. "I make the decisions with the mayor," warned Dawson, "and I don't want to hear that kind of speech again." Powerful as he was reputed to be, though, he was toothless on major issues, especially housing. None of his constituents wanted to live in slums, but slum clearance encroached on what turf they had and threatened their hold on the balance of power. They didn't dislike living in the Black Belt; as St. Clair Drake reported, "they resent being *forced* to live there." Reducing blacks' *Lebensraum* without safely opening any other areas to them would cause more situations like that of the Coopers in Park Manor. Dawson the politician had to walk a tight path here, since segregation was in his interest—open housing would make it harder for him to get elected. Hence his efforts on behalf of the Mecca's tenants, an entire precinct in one building. "Those people were all Democrats," he said later, "and I was a Democrat and I was playing politics." He had to tiptoe around redevelopment too, given that City Hall was pushing it. "Dawson used the word 'power' more often than anyone else I ever knew," Dickerson wrote, ". . . but he was subject to the dictates of Kelly and other white people."

Chicago's black community saw itself as more independent than that. In November 1945, in an office behind Horace Cayton's Parkway Community House, John Johnson had published the first issue of a glossy magazine based on an idea of a white South African Jew named Ben Burns. Burns hadn't been able to afford the start-up costs, so Johnson provided the cash, changed the name to *Ebony*, and hired Burns to edit it. "In a world of negative Black images," wrote Johnson, "we wanted to provide positive Black images. In a world that said Blacks could do few things, we wanted to say they could do everything." The magazine was an immediate hit. The nation's worst ghetto had inspired not only the most caustic vision of black life, in *Native Son*, but also the sunniest, in *Ebony*'s light-skinned models and invitation to consumer culture. Burns and Johnson had met on Earl Dickerson's failed congressional campaign, and *Ebony* captured much of the spirit of Dickerson, who managed to promote black wealth and success even as he fought for economic and social justice.

The most memorable photos in those early years of *Ebony* were taken by Wayne F. Miller, and they form the definitive portrait of Black Metropolis. Raised in Uptown, a graduate of the University of Illinois, Miller had apprenticed under Edward Steichen in his naval photography unit. Assigned to cover the enlisted men, he learned to see the war through their eyes and discovered the vision that would guide his career—showing the emotions of his subjects mattered more than expressing himself. At the war's end, angered by the years of devastation, he turned down an offer from *Life* and instead won a Guggenheim to document the Black South Side. One of the first people he met was Horace Cayton, who quickly introduced him to Ben Burns. Whether on assignment for *Ebony* or shooting for his own project, Miller captured everyday life in Black Chicago— the women sweeping bad spirits off their stairs, high school football games, pool halls, factory workers, church ladies, junk collectors, and Lena Horne—the entire range of the postwar black experience. He passed on doing a book with Nelson Algren because he didn't want his work politicized. Nor did he think of himself as an artist. "I was a storyteller with a camera," says Miller.

But Miller was the exception: few wanted to talk about what was happening in the streets of Chicago. In any American city today, the story of a racist mob threatening a house would lead the news, but the *Tribune* buried twenty lines about the Coopers and Park Manor on page thirty-two. Chicago's press, the *Defender* included, would soon agree with City Hall to gloss over racial conflict. As the violence rose, this absence of mainstream press coverage and the silence of city officials served as a wink to the Regular Guys and made Black Chicago believe that the white power structure was lined up against them. Leaning back in his swivel chair above the Grand Terrace Ballroom, Bill Dawson tapped his five real toes as he counted his votes one by one.

MEANWHILE, IN PARK Manor and Englewood, the regular whites believed essentially the same thing, but in reverse—faceless government power and meddling institutions were cooperating to help blacks get *their* land. And they were also right. Chicago Housing Authority plans to build forty thousand integrated units rang alarm bells. Though veterans would have priority, the agency was seen as working for blacks and promoting integration—which it indeed was, but only because decades of racism required it. By 1946 Elizabeth Wood directed the CHA to ignore neighborhood composition rules, believing that they only exacerbated the problem.

Whether on purpose or out of ignorance, the planners also ignored an enormous organizational structure that ran parallel to the wards and neighborhoods. The Archdiocese of Chicago was the largest in the nation. Its nearly two million Catholics saw the city as a collection of 262 parishes, each with its own borders ideally covering a square mile (about the size that Jane Jacobs would later identify as ideal for a neighborhood). Parishioners weren't born in Chicago as much as they were born in St. Ambrose or Visitation or St. Kevin. The church building—the core of the parish—was usually surrounded by a school, a rectory, a convent, and often a gym or community center; some were so large they had their own high school, and in the case of St. Leo its own hospital. All together, the parish provided much of the structure and service that Gropius dreamed of in his speech, but with a clan mentality. Many were "national" churches that offered mass in Polish or Italian and did all they could to reproduce life in the old country, down to excluding outsiders.

The main difference between Gropius's concept and the parish was home ownership, which the German was leery of. When Chicago's large parishes were built in the late nineteenth century, the archdiocese had promoted home ownership to immigrants as a way to guarantee a future flock, future income, and future power. Tethering people to parish turf would buoy the value of the approximately $2 billion worth of real estate owned by the archdiocese. Home ownership in Chicago was, therefore, less the American Dream than the Vatican's. Protestants and Jews had a much lower percentage of ownership and were traditionally more mobile. In the face of racial change, they were more likely to simply pick up and run to the suburbs with their congregations. Gropius and the planners never saw, or admitted, that they were essentially trying to secularize the city by reconstituting the Catholic parish along rational principles. When they criticized neighborhoods, they were criticizing the very things white Catholics held nearest to their hearts; not just real estate values and stability but deep cultural and religious values.

Housing exposed serious disagreements within the postwar archdiocese. Without question an enormous, conservative institution, "the city's largest property owner, largest hospital operator and largest private social services provider," under Cardinals Mundelein, Stritch, and later Meyer, it was also the nation's most progressive archdiocese on family life, labor, and social justice. A generation of young activist priests trained by the intense, heady Monsignor Reynold Hillenbrand went into the city streets carrying a gospel of social justice as the archdiocese, spurred by the same consolidating impulse driving the nation's corporations and government, tried to melt the neighborhood fiefdoms of ethnic-national churches into one modern and universal Church. Ending racial discrimination was part of this effort, practically and theologically. Throughout the war Bishop Sheil had spoken out against racism and anti-Semitism, and in May 1946, in a speech to the Chicago Council Against Racial and Religious Discrimination, he blasted restrictive covenants. Cardinal Stritch had ended institutional segregation of Catholic schools in 1945. Though all this came on orders from Rome, Chicago's ethnic Catholics increasingly saw the Church hierarchy as just another institution working against them. When struck by the blunt realities of race, the foundation of the Church's power cracked. Racist priests and parishioners desacralized their parishes by rejecting the "infallible" Vatican and shifting the loyalty that bound their communities from their faith to their race. "Cafeteria Catholicism" began over racism, not birth control.

White resistance did contain some legitimate concerns. First, open housing, the right to live where you wanted, wasn't interchangeable with integration, which had no standard definition. Most black Chicagoans didn't want to integrate any more than whites did, but they did want the higher quality of housing and services found in white neighborhoods, and most of all they wanted the freedom to live wherever they wanted, be it castle or slum. Public equality and private segregation more honestly describe their goal. The other issue was proportion. While whites generally believed a 15 to 20 percent black presence constituted "integration," blacks saw the threshold at 50 percent, in a city where they were closer to 30 percent of the total populace. In fact, once the balance tipped over that point, blacks encouraged whites to leave. Many neighborhoods in Chicago had both blacks and whites, but they were almost always seen as in flux, changing toward one direction or the other, rather than as stable neighborhoods with a mixed racial makeup. Clearly whatever tortured discourse the city would have over integration over the next decades would be a discourse over very different goals. Whites' economic concerns were also grounded in brute realities. FHA policies disallowed mortgage insurance in integrated and changing areas on the grounds that they were unstable, so whites were actually encouraged by the federal government to be the first on their block to abandon their neighborhood for a lily-white "stable" suburb. Predatory agents would then immediately step in to buy the rest of the block from panicking whites at fire-sale prices and sell them within days at a premium to blacks, sometimes on "contract," binding the buyers to usurious, unethical, often bankrupting deals.

By 1946 only upper-middle-class, educated whites and blacks had any interest in living together. With the smoke and excitement of the war still hanging in the air, Chicagoans of both races grafted its martial vocabulary onto their conflicts for land. What blacks called a "bastion . . . breached," whites described as an "invasion" or "incursion." Hunkered down and prepared for, according to Wood, "a most violent though invisible state of war," Chicagoans now read the city map the way they'd recently read the European Theater. Parishes in Park Manor and South Deering hosted neighborhood "improvement" organizations that plotted violent attacks; a Ku Klux Klan offshoot called the White Circle League sprouted up. Even where the "guerrilla warfare" was only heard as distant fire over the hill, whites fought in subtle ways, turning civic pride into a weapon; priests instructed them to keep their lawn mowed, their hedges trimmed, and their windows clean as a sign of resistance to "blight," which meant blacks. Monsignor William Gorman, pastor of St. Columbanus, was reassigned later that year because of his segregationist attitudes. But everything else remained the same.

. . .

IN ORDER TO invoke eminent domain and tear down everything within a certain area, a developer had to buy 60 percent of the land in it. Michael Reese Hospital quickly learned, as IIT had, that buying up that much land piecemeal was too expensive for a private developer alone. Two leaders of the Metropolitan Housing and Planning Council—Milton Mumford, an executive at Marshall Field's, and Holman Pettibone, CEO of Chicago Title and Trust—went at the problem. First, they convinced Mumford's boss, Hughston McBain, to fund a study that would eventually show that the most profitable sort of real estate development possible in Chicago would be a middle-income apartment complex for blacks on the South Side. (Racial uplift was not the motivation—Chicago Title and Trust continued issuing titles to housing sales within restrictive covenants long after the Hansberry case, and Marshall Field's still sent black shoppers to the basement.) Mumford and Pettibone identified a section of Bronzeville as the future home of what they christened Lake Meadows. Then the two crafted a new bill for the state legislature, the Redevelopment Act, which would allow the city to invoke eminent domain on a parcel of land, clear it, and sell it to developers at a deep discount. Now considered a basic tool in urban redevelopment, it all began with this MHPC legislation. In spring 1946, with the Loop business community on board, Mumford and Pettibone pitched Lake Meadows to Mayor Ed Kelly, who promptly handed it off to the CHA, which in turn ignored it because it wasn't public housing.

That spring the Chicago Plan Commission offered a preliminary revised city plan. So along with this new CPC plan, three massive redevelopment projects—Mies's campus at IIT, Gropius's project at Michael Reese, and Lake Meadows—all located in the same twelve square miles of the city, were staged to begin at the same time. On top of all that, the CHA was looking at the same twelve square miles for its own housing projects, and the archdiocese hoped to keep Mercy Hospital and Loyola Medical School where they were, just north of MRH. The goals overlapped. The boards overlapped. The architects overlapped. The obstacles overlapped. Working separately, they might get what they wanted, but together they'd be invincible.

So in May 1946 they announced the establishment of the South Side Planning Board (SSPB), with Henry Heald head of the executive council. The SSPB would coordinate all their separate efforts into one general plan; then, as each group pursued its own goals individually, the SSPB would lobby, connect, influence, and generally try to ram through whatever needed to happen, politically or otherwise, in order for each piece of the puzzle to fall into place. "The Board was not organized by an individual or group," it stated. "Its origin was in the spontaneous expression of individuals and organizations on the Central South Side." In fact, no one who actually lived in Bronzeville had a say. In October 1946, Heald presented the MHPC's four-point plan for South Side redevelopment centered on Mumford and Pettibone's eminent domain legislation. The report was titled "Stand and Fight."

CHAIRMAN JACK ARVEY took a whiff of the chrysanthemums and coughed; for all the smoke, there might as well have been a locomotive in Room 441 of the Morrison Hotel. A photographer had taken a shot of the flowers going in, a not-so-prescient gift from the Allied Florists Association of Illinois in honor of a historic Democratic victory this Election Night 1946, so they'd had to keep them. No need to lose the florist vote too; they'd lost everybody else.

Al Horan, an old insider hiding out here with Arvey and the mayor, cracked the door open an inch, took the latest slip of results from a runner, and without peeking handed it over to Ed Kelly. The mayor shook his head. Every Democrat in America was getting his ass handed to him tonight.

Five foot four, bald and professorial, with a prominent jaw and a hint of a lisp, Arvey, as tonight, was often the smartest man in these smoke-filled rooms. Born in a West Side Jewish tenement, as a boy he'd delivered milk around Maxwell Street with his devout father and later passed the bar by answering, ironically, a question about the then-obscure concept of eminent domain. The Party ran him for alderman in 1922, then made him committeeman in 1934. Two years later he delivered the Twenty-fourth Ward in dramatic if not suspicious fashion—29,000 for FDR versus a paltry 700 for Alf Landon, leading Roosevelt to call the Twenty-fourth "the greatest Democratic ward in the country." He did it (ostensibly) by providing excellent service.

Arvey understood the Machine's transactions as the way it earned its keep: drop off a bag of coal, a Thanksgiving turkey, or some matzoh to folks out of luck, find people jobs, pay respects at their wakes, make sure benefit checks came, offer free legal advice. During World War II a conservative faction of the Party, led by John Duffy from the Irish Southwest Side, had begun chipping at Ed Kelly's base. Instead of getting caught in the middle of a power play, Arvey resigned his county and city jobs, faked his eye examination, and took a commission in the U.S. Army. Four years later he'd returned a lieutenant colonel, and though he still sat next to Kelly at the big tables, he was now a bulletproof veteran with clean hands. During the summer the Duffy faction had let the mayor give the chair of the county party to Arvey, but only because they'd seen this night of reckoning coming and figured he'd go down with the ship.

A knock. Any comment? Too early to see any trends in the voting, croaked Kelly. He looked old. Arvey stuck his face in the crack and gave the reporter a big smile. "It's too early to accept victory!"

Long into the night, the three of them sat together in the room, little slips of paper piling up on the floor like an early snowfall. Losing the national races was one thing, but getting hammered in the state and city was unforgivable. Arvey eyed the old man. Rank and file were getting tired of garbage piling on their streets while Kelly flew off to Palm Springs to "rest." Not only was the old man not out in front of the South Side redevelopment, but all those years of giving the CHA run of the show had just bit them in the ass. The Machine couldn't afford to be faceless; it kept power by putting a face on power, by sending a precinct captain out to say

"Jak sie masz" to Jerzy and "Top o' the mornin' " to Jimmy O'Shea. You convinced people to vote for candidates because they were *your* candidates. The mayor hadn't run for anything tonight, but he'd lost.

Dick Daley had lost the race for sheriff, too. Arvey was sad to see *that* slip of paper. Daley was just about the only state senator who came home from Springfield every weekend instead of whoring it up; he was smart and patient, and he'd been making noises for more, so Arvey had offered him the county sheriff's job. It would have kept him out of the way and probably ended in the usual indictment—at least that had been the plan. Now he'd have to keep an eye on Richard J. Daley.

THE EXPLOSION CAME December 5, 1946, as the Christmas windows twinkled along State Street, the day President Truman announced the formation of the Committee on Civil Rights. Temperatures had risen overnight, so John Fort and Letholian Waddell had to mind a few inches of slush as they unloaded furniture in front of their new units in the Airport Homes veterans project at 60th and Karlov. A survivor of the Battle of the Bulge, Fort owned four battle stars, and Waddell had fought in the Pacific. They were watched by some two hundred housewives in cloth coats and babushkas, rubbers over their shoes, shuffling in the snow like a flock of pigeons until they began shouting; then the rocks. The windshield of the truck shattered. With a cry of "There they are!" the crowd came at Fort and Waddell. Cops tried to stave it off as the men dashed into the project office. White rioters turned over cars and trashed the truck, finally dispersing around midnight.

The next day 350 policemen fought another mob that lobbed bricks and tried to flip a squad car. Kelly promised the black community that the rioters would be prosecuted. Meanwhile the black families lived for two weeks under guard until they moved out. At first Kelly called Airport Homes a federal matter, but then he released a statement standing behind the CHA's need-based policy, declaring that "all law-abiding citizens may be assured of their right to live peaceably anywhere in Chicago."

White ethnics steamed. Arvey ordered a secret phone poll. The caller went through a fake survey about Hollywood stars and then at the end, when things were all friendly-like, they'd toss out something along the lines of, "Hey, that's some mayor ya got there in Chicago. Whaddya think of him?" Over and over whites slammed Big Ed for siding with "the coloreds." Arvey confronted the mayor with the survey and the consensus that he'd lose in a primary. Kelly accepted his fate and suggested the moving-van magnate and Red Cross fund-raiser Martin Kennelly as his successor. Arvey could run Kennelly, an officious old bachelor, as a business-friendly reformer. After Arvey swore not to interfere at City Hall, the gullible Kennelly accepted the nomination and with promises to clean house won the general election going away in April 1947.

The MHPC now had a staunch ally in the mayor's office. On his first day Kennelly spent an hour with Henry Heald. The Redevelopment Act passed the state legislature in June, allowing the city to declare eminent domain, with a bill attached that required a percentage of land be devoted to housing the displaced; the newly created Chicago Land Clearance Commission would buy, clear, and resell the land instead of the CHA, now persona non grata with Kelly gone. The act set the terms for urban renewal: profits and the private sector would drive development, with affordable housing a distant secondary concern.

Within days of its passage, the SSPB presented the master plan it had been working on in anticipation of this moment: titled "An Opportunity," its sixty-two pages consolidated the plans of IIT, Michael Reese Hospital, and Lake Meadows, along with CHA proposals for public housing, into one Sears Christmas catalog of what Gropius and the planners thought a city should look like, all the buildings in high Miesian style (though not designed by Mies or Gropius; neither got the job from the Jewish, conservative board of Michael Reese). A month later Pettibone and Mumford met with New York Life Insurance to underwrite Lake Meadows.

Still committed to integration, Elizabeth Wood gave a speech in May to a community group leery of the new Fernwood Park Homes on Halsted and 104th, only a few blocks from St. Helena of the Cross. "We are the government," she told the crowd, "and we do what we do," which was exactly what white ethnics feared. The CHA tried to prepare the neighborhood with an advance wave of educators and church leaders who created a "Community Goodwill Council," but on August 13, 1947, five thousand whites rioted against the first eight black families in Fernwood Park, smashing windows, attacking cars, and pulling blacks off streetcars. Thirty-five African Americans were injured; more than one thousand police officers were called in to make hundreds of arrests. Violence continued well into autumn. In October, a rash of deadly arsons swept through integrated buildings on the West Side; parents threw their children out windows. "It was like it was raining babies," said one bystander.

Reginald Isaacs once said that the neighborhood folk of Chicago didn't "know themselves what is good for them much less for the city as a whole." On November 4, 1947, they voted through bond proposals that would let the city move ahead with the land acquisition and clearance the SSPB wanted. Isaacs may well have been right.

CHAPTER 6

BELIEVERS IN THE CITY

WHEN EXACTLY DR. Edith Farnsworth fell in love with Mies van der Rohe, no one knows. They met sometime in 1945, while Mies was sifting through letters from IIT full of deadlines and niggling complaints, and famous as he is for his apocryphal saying "God is in the details," Mies tended to lose interest in the divine when it hid in places like plumbing specs and roof flashing. Storklike, tall and awkward, staring out of photos with goggle-eyed intensity, Dr. Farnsworth was a renowned kidney doctor, violinist, and spinster of means from Chicago who wanted to build on ten acres of land alongside a slow-moving skid of water called the Fox River some fifty miles west of the city. That spring she offered Mies a commission for a small country house entirely of his devising, a jewel where every detail would matter, crafted for someone willing to put herself utterly in his hands. Her hopes that this would happen in a literal sense seem to be at the heart of their later court battle, though without question Mies gave all of himself to the house, the genesis of much of his later work.

The first sketches for it appear in April 1945, but in fact he'd been playing with the idea since at least 1937. The plan was for a house that would transcend even the refinement of the Barcelona Pavilion, a structure of ultimate simplicity and transparency that would state the essence of shelter as materials and space: two flat white planes for roof and floor, raised five feet off the ground in case of flooding; eight white steel columns; walls made of glass. Adjacent to the building a smaller, slightly lower plane with steps up to the house. That's it; *"beinahe nichts,"* as Mies often said was the goal for his work—"next to nothing." Inside, all the functional aspects of the home stood open to the world. Mies once said, "We should attempt to bring nature, houses, and human beings together in a higher unity." The Farnsworth House would force those inside into a complicated intimacy with the natural world: anyone floating by on the Fox River would see you tossing your salad or reading Faulkner, going about your business like any other wildlife on the banks, while the interior framed the world outside for your viewing pleasure. The drama of autumn leaves tugged free of their branches, snow tossed in broad brushstrokes— that was the art on your walls. Where the Barcelona Pavilion was introspective, the Farnsworth House is exhibitionistic, shameless in a most American way. Ironically, a 1945 watercolor rendering by Mies—two long white horizontals connected by four white verticals, the blue and yellow chairs reduced to squares of color—looks just like one of Moholy's Constructivist abstractions.

While this was Mies's most crystalline composition to date, crisp and clear as one of his beloved martinis, spiritual in its simplicity, Dr. Farnsworth could be excused for taking the whole thing in a more personal vein. Mies had, in his way, captured her in the design—elegant, cerebral, made of sharp angles, without shame or deception. She knew who she was, what she looked like, and she did not hide, and Mies had found the beauty of that. Mies had found *her.* And she gave herself to him, budgetwise to the tune of $40,000 (around $470,000 today). Once he assured himself she could afford it, Mies planned only the finest materials, travertine marble he would select himself, handcrafted wood—she agreed to everything. They were collaborators, after all. He was creating a work of art; she was its patron and model. His office crafted an intricate maquette.

The question now was siting. After a fast start, the process crawled to a languorous pace. Mies and Dr. Farnsworth enjoyed long drives and picnics out to the site in Plano, where they considered the big black sugar maple, how its branches would cut across the planes of glass like a Japanese painting; which trees had the most color at the peak of fall and where the first buds appeared. Surely there was wine and discussions of deep and meaningful things; she even read Guardini for him. There seemed to be no hurry and no limits as the two dreamed what would turn out to be very separate dreams.

ALL THIS WAS a charming distraction from events at his new office at 37 S. Wabash, smaller than before and already dusty, where Mies opened letter after complaining letter from IIT. His architecture department had survived the war years with a skeleton staff and a student body consisting not of the best and the brightest but mostly rejects from the draft. Like Gropius, he'd had time to experiment; for example, he revived his flirtation with the skyscraper, asking his class to design a steel high-rise. (He especially liked one by Earl Bluestein and had Joseph Fujikawa, a student and later employee, do a version clad in concrete. Both went up on the shelf.) As a client, though, IIT was the most difficult Mies had ever had, its staff of engineers and scientists a running chorus of requirements and opinions. In mid-March the school's treasurer dressed Mies down for his "lack of progress," cost overruns, disorganization, and poor communication. With few clients to bill aside from Edith Farnsworth, Mies had no choice but to knuckle down. Action restarted with the Engineering Research Building, a forgettable brick and concrete bunker, and in January 1946 IIT approved construction on three more: the Navy Building, the Metallurgy Building, and the Chemistry Building. On an architectural level, they show Mies arriving at a nuanced relationship between structure and exterior. While much of his fame comes from showing the structure, in fact fire codes wouldn't allow the beams to be exposed, so he created a brick and steel skin that expresses what's going on behind, most visibly at the corners of the Navy Building (later renamed Alumni Memorial Hall), which display the steel work arrangement inside without actually bearing weight.

For all of Mies's talk of spiritual truths, his buildings came freighted with some very earthly meanings. As American money and power swept across the globe, and Europe tried simply to feed itself, the United States asserted its role as the new center of Western culture. The Museum of Modern Art made plans for a Mies retrospective in 1947, its largest architecture show ever, intended by curator Philip Johnson to launch the idea of American ascendancy in the field. With Mies now identified as the vanguard, IIT became a magnet for so many talented and ambitious students that classes were forced out of the Art Institute and into a floor of Louis Sullivan's Gage Building across the street. "Practically all the student body had been GIs and they had a great sense of camaraderie," said Reginald Malcolmson, a student then. "Many of them were quite angry at the government having used up so much of their lives in the war and they were determined to graduate as quickly as possible. . . . It created a very exciting kind of atmosphere." Never had so many Americans been abroad at once, shattering for a moment the nation's traditional isolationism. These young men, attending class in their fatigues, wanted to make sense of their exposure to Rome and Paris and Kyoto and build in a way that balanced the long legacy of human culture against the technologies and terrors of the Atomic Age. "We were going to rebuild the world," said one of Mies's students. "We were building, and would talk about it. . . . There was a whole new era about what could be done." No longer a school for bohunk draftsmen, IIT began to emerge as the world's most influential school of architecture, with Mies as the object of what even Hilbs described as "a cult."

In order to handle all the new students, Mies added faculty, most notably a voluble landscape architect named Alfred Caldwell, who would become Mies's living connection to the Prairie tradition and a pillar of IIT's architecture department. Impetuous, romantic, a self-taught philosopher, Caldwell grew up poor on the North Side, reading stories of King Arthur and Atlantis and sneaking into Wrigley Field. After quitting the University of Illinois to start his own landscaping business, Caldwell worked with Bunyan-esque ecologist Jens Jensen, a towering man with a bushy white moustache who landscaped the city's grand estates when not delivering emotional speeches on the importance of conservation. With Jensen, Caldwell developed a distinctive style that echoed Frank Lloyd Wright's, piling slabs of horizontal stone in a primordial way, perfect for climbing and sitting. Sporting long hair and an ascot, Caldwell was a hot-head and an official Dil Pickler in good standing who spouted leftist, agrarian views. Instead of taking up any of Wright's invitations to stay at Taliesin, he ended up at the Chicago Park District, where he landscaped Riis Park on the Far Northwest Side, Promontory Point in Hyde Park, and his masterpiece, the Lily Pool just north of the Lincoln Park Zoo, a long, sheltered pond surrounded by his signature layered stone that Mies and Hilbs both admired. After taking some classes at Armour, Caldwell was asked to join the faculty under Mies who, beyond their mutual admiration for Wright, shared his sense of nature's importance to architecture. For all his industrial austerity, Mies saw that his steel and glass buildings were incomplete without grass and sky; he drew in the trees of the IIT schematics himself, to say nothing of the Farnsworth House. Caldwell became IIT's mad prophet, an American original among the foreign imports, inspiring students with his demanding take on architectural history. A master draftsman, he illustrated Hilbs's urban planning books, and lent his voice to Mies—that speech in 1938 was one of Mies's last; fiery Caldwell went forth now in his stead. His devotion knew no bounds. "Mies cast an aura over everything," he once said. ". . . He was absolutely infallible."

Outside of IIT and the glacial progress of the Farnsworth House, Mies had little professionally to do in 1946. As Winston Churchill declared that an "Iron Curtain" was falling across Europe, a restaurant owner named Joseph Cantor hired Mies to design a drive-in for a long stretch of highway in Indiana. Mies was hardly consumed by the commission; long months would pass with no action until a letter from Cantor would send the office into a spasm of show-progress work. He played with a trussed, clear span design, a spare structure that would have been a striking alternative to the golden arches to come, but his interest in producing a functioning fast-food restaurant was minimal. "Function is sweeping dirt!" he once said. But there was urgency in the office. Key members of his staff, Joe Fujikawa and John Weese, left for other jobs just so that Mies could stay afloat. "He was living, basically," said Fujikawa, "hand to mouth." If Mies was to transcend the role of cult figure and keep his doors open, he would need a patron.

Herbert Greenwald arrived on Wabash Street just in time. Slim, witty, and effusive, only twenty-nine, "Squiff" Greenwald had traded his rabbinical studies for philosophy at the University of Chicago and the spell of Hutchins. Left a sizable inheritance at the death of his mother in 1946, he went into real estate with car dealer Samuel Katzin, starting with a complex of coops in Evanston. Now he was a consultant to the South Side Planning Board, a self-proclaimed "believer in the city." What he had in mind was a spec co-op high-rise on a lakefront site in Hyde Park, across from Alfred Caldwell's Promontory Point; it would be cheap to build but full of apartments worth owning as an investment. Mies pulled Earl Bluestein's high-rise project from 1943 off the shelf; it could be built at a lower price per square foot than the city's public housing. Greenwald and Mies were in business.

The next day Fujikawa came back to his old desk, and the practice leaped to life. The Promontory was announced in May 1947. ("It will have no outside ornamentation," wrote the *Tribune*. "However, it will have an unusual amount of window space.") When ground was broken two months later, Greenwald already had Mies working on three other commercial developments. Architecturally, the Promontory wasn't a breakthrough; though the original plans called for a single-slab, all-steel building, costs and code requirements pushed them toward the final twenty-one-story, concrete version, along with two additional wings on the west face, and all-masonry sides to the north and south. Mies considered it "primitive" because of the concrete.

Throughout the summer of 1947, Mies kept his office on a constant boil, shipping materials out to Philip Johnson for the MoMA retrospective. One afternoon Frank Lloyd Wright dropped by Johnson's office. MoMA had just closed a small show on Taliesin, and now as he saw the spreads for the monograph accompanying Mies's show jealousy bubbled up. As Johnson recalled in a letter to Mies, Wright became "quite high-hat" and insisted that he refer to the German as "merely a renegade pupil of his 1910 work." The crack between the two architects split wider when the show opened September 16, 1947, to great acclaim. Chicago's Mies van der Rohe was the first name in international architecture. Wright visited MoMA, entourage in tow, to sniff at the photographs and the maquettes (including the beautiful one of the Farnsworth House for which Edith had volunteered to make little sponge trees). It was, said Wright, "Much ado about next to nothing."

Word got back to Mies, who was not amused. Wright tried to explain himself in a letter—the "next to nothing" line was a reference to Mies's desire to do *"beinahe nichts"* with his work. "You are the best of them all as an artist and a man," he wrote, inviting him out to Taliesin for a long visit. Mies gave a cordial but terse response. The power between them had shifted; he had no need to kowtow. *His* style and the graduates coming out of *his* school were being touted as the force promising to transform Chicago and the entire postwar world, just as Sullivan's Auditorium Building came perilously close to demolition until Roosevelt College bought it for its new campus. Through Mies, Modernism no longer belonged to socialist bohemians. Modernism belonged to big business, big government, and big institutions. Corporatism had been born, and its cradle was being designed and built in Chicago.

CHAPTER 7

A DISCOVERED BEAUTY

SIBYL BEGAN DINNER as Moholy took Claudia and Hattula in their matching blond braids and flowered headbands hand in hand across Lakeview Avenue. Often they'd go to the Lily Pool a block south, but this cloudy, cool Sunday in October called for the North Lagoon, with its snapping turtles, owls, and herons. As he began this week's installment of the adventures of a certain green-checkered pig, scouring the ground for a pod of milkweed or a smooth, speckled rock, noticing the trees thrashing in the breeze, a wave of fatigue slammed Moholy. To the south the beacon on the Palmolive Building still swooped in its circle. After a life of constant motion, László Moholy-Nagy was suddenly very tired.

The last two years had been touch and go. Materials they needed at the Institute of Design—wood, plastics, metals—were exactly what the war effort used; food rationing had forced them to shut down Somonauk. Even so, they'd kept going: the occupational therapy classes for veterans; new departments in dress design and advertising; they'd approached Balaban and Katz about developing programs for their new television station, WBKB. The girls ran ahead a bit, flapping their arms. Moholy had found an unexpected peace in turning fifty. Every night he painted; then, during the day, he carried the canvas back and forth to work just to have it nearby. Few Chicagoans collected him, but that wasn't why he painted. His client, Parker Pen, was happy. He had money in the bank. And among the hundreds of students crawling over the school, there were still gems like BJ, puckish Robert Brownjohn from New Jersey, rejected by the army, a misfit like so many of the others, given sanctuary in the studios of the ID.

But the weariness dragged on Moholy. Enrollment was up 500 percent—the classrooms packed with young men, anxious in foxholes a few months ago, now anxious to land a job, anxious to start a family, anxious to find a home. The board was unhappy; staring across the chessboard, Paepcke would purse his lips, holding back words. It had only taken a year for the businessmen to lose interest, pick apart his methods, or wonder where the famous Bauhaus teachers were. He and Sibyl kept bitter track—Kepes, Breuer, and Bayer were in New York and Boston, Albers ran Black Mountain College in North Carolina, while Moholy got this boiling cauldron on the lake. Paepcke and Heald had a luncheon set to discuss IIT finally taking it over.

The wind kicked up, bringing the smell of burning leaves. Hattula tilted her chin to regard a passing goose. Moholy smiled, at the school, the leaves, his daughters, the geese. When they'd gotten notice on the Ontario building, they'd walked the streets until they'd found a new place, at the triangle of State, Rush, and Oak, two blocks from Bughouse Square. When Paepcke used Herbert Bayer instead of him to design the big Art Institute show of CCA posters, Moholy had applauded in the face of the insult, resigned to the fact that Walter was a rich man above all, resigned about Chicago. "Creative people don't seem to thrive in the Chicago atmosphere," he'd written Sibyl from the road that fall. ". . . The enthusiastic support given to new projects, new ideas, dies too quickly. There's no stamina, because there are no convictions."

In a couple months the pond would freeze and the girls would skate back and forth in front of the warming hut. He could already feel the cold.

A MONTH LATER Moholy collapsed in the apartment. It was leukemia. Sibyl canceled a Christmas visit to Paepcke's new hobby, a town in the

Rockies called Aspen. The merger with IIT went on hold, and board members made for the exits. Hughston McBain pulled his support; memos circulated calling Moholy a charlatan; the lease on the space at Rush and Oak was canceled, forcing another real estate hunt—no convictions indeed. Still, enrollment remained at an all-time high, and the students and faculty rallied around Moholy's courage. In the face of death he lived with the same drive, and while he was dying, he created the ID department that would have the deepest legacy.

Chicago's concentration of retailers, ad agencies, mail-order catalogs, magazines, and printers fed a surging market for commercial photography. Early in 1945 the ID had offered an orientation course on photography for veterans, taught by the high-strung Arthur Siegel, whom Moholy then asked to expand the class into a full department. Swamped by the response, Siegel soon needed more faculty, so he called a friend from Detroit trying to break into art photography. To a school desperate for marquee instructors, the name Harry Callahan meant nothing; he was an unknown thirty-three-year-old college dropout working at GM who'd picked up photography as a hobby. But in 1941 that hobby had become a vocation for Callahan when he'd met Siegel and Ansel Adams, who pointed him toward the work of Alfred Stieglitz. Callahan progressed quickly. "The camera was a machine," he realized, "and it could make machine-like pictures which were very beautiful." Rather than a way to magically capture a moment, photography was a form of technology that a regular guy from Detroit like him could use to make art—a very Moholy-like thought. "Weeds in Snow" (1943), for example, an almost abstract image of black lines rising out of a low covering of snow, is a product of a development process that saturated the white to heighten the contrast as much as it is the product of his discovery and precise framing. Callahan quit GM in October 1945 and dragged his wife, Eleanor, to New York to take his shot. Though he met the likes of Helen Levitt and Paul Strand, six months later he was back in Detroit, a washout. That's when Siegel called.

Intimidated by the prospect of teaching college-level classes, Callahan had to be convinced to come down to Somonauk, where Moholy was trying to build up strength in the spring of 1946. Callahan wasn't a people person; in no way abrasive or mean, but a cipher. Private, serious, and prematurely bald, as devoted to his solid, dimpled Eleanor as she was to him, he gave few of his thoughts away to those he didn't know. With money tight, Moholy had told Siegel that the ID wasn't taking on anyone new, but he'd meet his friend as a favor. Callahan handed over his photographs with few words. Jumpy, doing five things at once even with leukemia, Moholy slowed down as he examined Callahan's work—a single leaf atop a crust of late snow; a series of three photos of the same fire escape; Eleanor against a building in New York. Each photo as silent and deceptively simple as its maker. The dust hung in the air. Callahan seethed, positive Moholy hated his work. The Hungarian finally shook his head and whispered, "Only once in my life have I been moved like this." One shot in particular fascinated him; he asked Callahan why he'd taken it. The photographer mustered an embarrassed shrug, and Moholy, sensing how ill at ease he was, butchered the language in a most touching way: "Oh, I only asked. I don't think it matters if it's only for a wish." Moholy hired him on the spot.

The Callahans arrived in the summer. Eleanor found work as a secretary and Harry, when not teaching three days a week, began walking the streets, methodically, patiently, photographing the faces and forms of his new home. In July the ID hosted an eight-week seminar that brought Berenice Abbott, Erwin Blumenfeld, Beaumont Newhall, Paul Strand, and Weegee to Chicago and that stamped a high-art imprimatur on the photography department. Moholy's prediction—that the illiterate of the future would be the man who couldn't read a photograph—was coming true because he was helping to make it so.

But Moholy was fading. At the seminar Siegel had had to follow him onstage with a chair in case he exhausted himself. Paepcke roused what remained of the board to buy the former Chicago Historical Society Building on Dearborn and Ontario, while Moholy spent as much time as he could in his borrowed country house painting until, after a final rush in

September, he cleaned his brushes for the last time and carefully stowed them away. When not sleeping on the couch, he twisted wire into forms and even stuck one favorite outside to sway in the wind. As they were packing to move back into the city, Sibyl went to bring it in, but Moholy said he wanted to see what would happen to it when they came back next year. "Our eyes met," Sibyl recounted, "and I realized that he knew his fate. . . . It was the only time that he broke down and cried."

The new ID building was a mess, but Moholy pitched in to help paint and plaster. For Sibyl's birthday, October 29, he presented her with a lavish fox jacket—the first birthday present he'd ever given her. At the beginning of November, barely able to walk, Moholy flew to New York for a conference on industrial design at MoMA. These days were to be Moholy's final work of art. "He knew he was dying," wrote Robert J. Wolff to a mutual friend, "and I have never seen a human performance like the one he put on. He made a point of seeing all his friends, and made a joke of his illness and seemed to generate more bright and optimistic energy than ever before." As the two took a final walk alone together, Wolff asked if he was satisfied with his body of work. "I don't know about my paintings," Moholy said, "but I'm proud of my life."

László Moholy-Nagy died at Michael Reese Hospital on November 24, 1946.

The funeral was held the next Wednesday afternoon at the Institute of Design, with Mies and Hilbs among the thousand in attendance. Gropius's eulogy managed to praise and patronize at the same time, comparing the man who'd spent the last nine years in a frenzy of work to "an unprejudiced happy child at play." Gropius might have envied Moholy's innocence, but he also made clear that Moholy hadn't moved big shafts of steel or bought and sold companies the way the Fat Men did. A vocalist from the University of Chicago performed some songs by Béla Bartók. Sibyl, now a forty-three-year-old widow with two young daughters, set about fiercely maintaining her husband's legacy, out of love but also because her future depended on the quality of his reputation. Panicked, lonely, and eager to start her own career among Old World men who found her pushy, unqualified, and worst of all, female, she needed to keep his spirit alive.

But what, exactly, *was* Moholy's legacy? He left no signature designs behind, no Eames chair or Aalto table to make his name a household word; his easel painting and sculpture have a significant place in early Modernism, but instead of showing how he connected the Bauhaus and Constructivism, histories often let him fall in the crack between. The art he made was secondary to the methods he used to make it and to the ways he helped others find methods of their own. As an artist of process and performance, as a teacher of awareness and of life lived as an organic, aesthetic whole, he stands next to Marcel Duchamp, but without a defining masterpiece like *The Large Glass* to make the point tangible. Unlike the Alberses at Black Mountain, Moholy at the ID produced more educators than artists; they brought his methods of approaching art, and life, onto campuses across America; students learned them, even if they didn't put up posters of Moholy in their dorms. The swift diffusion of his ideas—for every one that he filched from Bredendieck or Man Ray, he gave away a dozen—made the cult of Moholy a difficult flame for Sibyl to tend. His philosophy that everyone was talented, that humans had an essential need to make art, and that satisfying this need could change society for the better sounded fatuous when bruited by those who didn't live with his commitment and melted quickly around cynics.

And then there was Mies, whose shadow Moholy couldn't escape even in death. In the fall of 1947 the Art Institute mounted a retrospective on Moholy, something it had never considered while he was alive; but the exhibition opened the same week as the grand Mies van der Rohe show at MoMA. Though Katharine Kuh wrote aptly and fulsomely about Moholy in the museum bulletin—"Singleness of purpose coupled with heroic faith can work wonders"—the sense was that Moholy's account was now closed, just as Mies's fame was becoming general. Two men from the same time and place, who shared friends and quoted the same paragraph regarding the perfect structural design of the seal from D'Arcy Thompson's *On Growth and Form* in their own writings should have had some relationship. Both men devoted their careers to space; Moholy investigated motion in space and simultaneity, while Mies once told a reporter, "I manufacture space." But if taste kept Mies from Moholy, it's likely that Moholy was repelled by Mies's past. Before the Nazis shuttered the Bauhaus, Mies had negotiated down the official cause so that his ongoing career wouldn't be tainted by charges of "degeneracy"; worse, in August 1934 he had signed a proclamation in support of Hitler. According to Sibyl, "of the leading group of Bauhaus people, Mies was the only one who signed. This was a terrible stab in the back for us." While Moholy and Sibyl were hiding émigrés in exile and Jewish Bauhauslers were being arrested, Mies was currying Hitler's favor, even after the Degenerate Art Exhibition of 1937. Mies's claim to higher spiritual values might have had a hollow ring to Moholy.

Their differences, personal and philosophical, endured beyond the grave. In *Vision in Motion*, his final testament, published posthumously by Paul Theobald, Moholy revealed what he thought of the schools of Mies and his ally in metaphysics, Hutchins: "the classics of the liberal arts— without the brake of social thought—may condition the student to petrified forms of class-determined thinking." If IIT and the Farnsworth House show Mies celebrating and guiding the industrial might of postwar America, in *Vision in Motion* Moholy looked beyond the smokestacks into a post-industrial age where media had the power to alter man psychologically and physically. No other artist had Moholy's comprehensive understanding of the issues that would inform art in the late twentieth century and well into the Digital Age. Art, he saw, was no longer about mysteries and inspiration; it was about tools and perception. The artist of the future wouldn't be a genius, he'd be a witness, and his media would be the products of light—photography, television, and film. The ID didn't produce great works of art; it produced the methods to create and replicate them, and a structure for teaching others. Moholy had identified reproduction as an opportunity forty years before Warhol, discussed the rise of amateurism thirty years before Marshall McLuhan. Control of the image was paramount. Documentary photography interested Moholy less than "discovering an interesting picture when he developed the print."

His death in 1946 came just as many were dismissing art as a social force. Art hadn't stopped the war and it couldn't stop the bomb, so taking Trotsky's advice, New York School painters such as Jackson Pollock and Mark Rothko positioned themselves as a third force, alienated from society and, like Mies, avowedly apolitical. But Moholy was already a few generations past questioning whether *Guernica* should make you start a revolution or feed starving children or vote a certain way. To him, works of art themselves were next to pointless, discussions of styles absurd; arguing the merits of Pollock versus Utrillo merely helped set prices in the marketplace. The point of art to Moholy was the *act* of making art, the serious play of experimentation. Art was by its nature political to Moholy, because art making acted as the corrective to greed and power. Spreading the faith that everyone is talented, and teaching others to do the same, would not only reconnect man to his community, bridging the gap between Reinhold Niebuhr's moral man and immoral society; it could transform human consciousness. Moholy, who carried a painting along with his lunchbox, lived his ideas. Art was his work, and he liked to work, as did most of the people around him in the city of smokestacks, slaughterhouses, and union jobs, whereas Hilbs and Mies maintained an aristocratic view of work as a necessary evil. Even his sense of urban planning showed a better understanding of Chicago. "It is no longer possible to praise the classics and let the people live in slums," he'd written in 1945. Raised on a farm, Moholy had no illusions about the rural life Gropius pined for; he loved the city's randomness, the constant opportunities to see light and color and motion.

EARLY IN 1946 a controversial new book energized the idea of the regular with populist meaning. *Reveille for Radicals* (published by the University of Chicago Press) called for the rebirth of the Tom Paine radical and full participation by the common man in the American system. Its author, Saul Alinsky, was to politics what Moholy was to art. Alinsky had made his name as a sociology grad student at the University of Chicago, when he'd infiltrated Capone's mob and an Italian youth gang. In 1939, funded by Marshall Field III and Bishop Sheil, he'd brought the various Catholic parishes and the social and labor groups around the Stockyards into the Back of the Yards Neighborhood Council (BYNC), the first grassroots community organization. As anti–New Deal as he was anti–big business, Alinsky placed self-determination and the neighborhood's preferences above everything else, even when good sense argued otherwise. Settlements, for example, that offered birth control were blasted for challenging the Catholic beliefs of the residents. *Reveille for Radicals* hit the *New York Times* best-seller list, and commentators left and right battered Alinsky for his bombast and his less-than-accurate reporting of what the BYNC had actually accomplished, even as he gained a legion of devoted friends and everyday Americans grateful for how he'd returned a sense of agency to their lives. Though demonized now, his definition of a radical has more to do with Whitman than it does with Red Square:

> The radical is that unique person who actually believes what he says. He . . . wants a world in which the worth of the individual is recognized. He wants the creation of a kind of society where all of man's potentialities could be realized; a world where man could live in dignity, security, happiness, and peace—a world based on a morality of mankind.

The defining elements of so much of the next fifteen years of creativity in Chicago—improvisation, vernacular, experimentation and a sense of play, intimacy, social purpose, figurative imagery—all fit within Alinsky's definition of radicalism, itself the extension of a tradition that reached back to Dreiser and Sandburg, up through Margaret Taylor-Goss to Moholy-Nagy, the spine of the city's cultural history. In Chicago, the regular had always had a touch of the radical. But would it survive America's success? Could Chicago—and America—learn to connect the best impulses of Mies *and* Moholy? Could the United States enjoy the peace and still bestride the world?

CHAPTER 8

UNTIL MY CHANGE COMES

MAHALIA STARTED HER catfish stew with some bacon, a welcome sign of better times. She crumbled it into the pot with fingers she'd kept delicate through the years of scrubbing hotel floors and spreading lye. "My hands," she once said, "demonstrate what I feel inside." She poured off some of the grease, then tossed the scallions in to sizzle. Next a big can of tomatoes, some ketchup and water, thyme and cayenne, salt and pepper. Then she left it to steam up.

The house was full, which seemed to happen whenever she set the big pots on the stove. Every gospel singer in Chicago seemed to know when she was putting up pig's feet or gumbo, and this was the golden age of Chicago gospel. Roberta Martin, classically trained, challenged Mahalia for the top, while Sallie Martin (no relation) built her following with the sincerity of her singing, not her voice (her former pianist Ruth Jones was now known as Dinah Washington); the Soul Stirrers had moved up from Texas (though the quartets considered themselves a more manly breed apart from gospel, where women held power); the young James Cleveland was the mascot of Thomas Dorsey's choir at Pilgrim. Mahalia had broken off with him—no ill will; it had just been time. You're going to be a star someday, Dorsey said. She'd told him to shut up. The Detroit singers called her place home when they were in town, the Reverend C. L. Franklin and his four-year-old daughter Aretha, already singing. Dellareese Taliaferro—who'd trimmed her name down to Della Reese—had lived with Mahalia for two years like a daughter.

So how could she be lonely with such a house full of people?

She stirred the pot, scraped up some brown from the bottom the way Aunt Duke always did, then fell into herself a little, the way thinking about Aunt Duke made her do. Not quite time for the potatoes. All these people were her family now. At least that's what she told herself, though sometimes she couldn't help wondering how many of them were just here to eat. Sooner or later everyone wanted something from her. She'd come up with nothing, the only child in the world to never have a doll, but *she* didn't ask for favors; she just sang for the Lord. The pot boiled. Mahalia threw in the potatoes, watched them bob in the stew the way Rosetta Tharpe—*Sister* Rosetta Tharpe—bounced across a nightclub stage. *She* was making money, *white* money, because *she* was willing to sing gospel in any white honky-tonk that'd pay her. A man claimed he could get Mahalia $10,000 if she'd sing in nightclubs. $10,000 a *week*.

The thought of all that money opened something inside her, a hunger and a fear. There could never be enough; every night she rocked in bed between the fear of losing what she had and the need to have more. She'd told the man he could book her, but no theaters and no contract. The hollow wind howling off the lake shook her windows while she dropped the catfish into the stew. She never heard back. She'd cut four sides with Apollo Records, same label as Dinah Washington, but they weren't selling; she and the owner, Bess Berman, went at each other like cats in a bag. The fish turned white. All those people in the dining room would have something to eat now.

But what was there for Mahalia?

THE GOSPEL COMMUNITY on the South Side was one of the city's many cultural circles, islands in a vast sea. Some travelers navigated between them all, the most prominent being Irv Kupcinet, known to generations of his readers as "Kup." A Russian Jew from 16th and Kedzie, Kup had played football at the University of North Dakota, then briefly for the Philadelphia Eagles, before writing sports at the *Chicago Times*. In 1943 he was given the gossip column, which he turned into a civic institution, a chronicle of the world as it passed by his roost in Booth One at the Pump Room. A midwestern Walter Winchell connected to major figures in Hollywood, Washington, and the Mob, Kup made nightly rounds of the city's clubs with his wife, Essee, on his arm, then wrote it all up the next morning into a surprisingly intelligent column blending flack tips, paid quips, and starlet sightings with actual reports on politics and entertainment. Parsing his ethics was impossible—he had brains and good taste, was ahead of the curve in matters of race, but he loved trading favors and cherished his access to the rich, famous, and beautiful. The city had no greater chauvinist than Kup.

If anyone held together the scattered worlds of Chicago culture, though, it was Louis Terkel. Like so many great Chicagoans, Terkel was born somewhere else; in his case New York, as the son of a sickly tailor named Sam, whose brother staked him to a boardinghouse on Chicago's West Side. Nine-year-old Louis immediately took to Chicago—his first whiff of the south wind coming up from the Stockyards in August 1921 cured his asthma (or at least that's what he would claim). The boardinghouse and then their next property, the Wells-Grand Hotel in Towertown, taught Louis the secrets of a good host—discretion, the ability to listen, and an acceptance of the infinite wonders and horrors of humanity. Every sort of person bounced in and out of the Wells-Grand during the 1920s; retired Wobblies, grifters on the lam, faded actors—Louis treated them all the same. A half-mile walk north, he befriended the raconteurs and revolutionaries in Bughouse Square and learned to leave his dignity at the door of the Dil Pickle Club. Law school at the University of Chicago cured him of wanting to follow in the steps of his hero Clarence Darrow, but all those long trolley rides down to Hyde Park took him through Bronzeville, where he fed his catholic tastes in music with 78s by Big Bill Broonzy and Memphis Slim. Blackballed from an FBI post by a former professor, he was left with only the WPA for a job. Terkel's raspy voice and his theatrical way of spinning a story made him a natural for the stage: director Charles DeSheim convinced him to join the Chicago Repertory Group (CRG) for a 1935 production of *Waiting for Lefty*.

Underwritten by Ruth Page, Harriet Monroe, and Darrow, the CRG was a small but significant moment in Chicago's theatrical history. At the turn of the century, with spectacles like *Ben-Hur* on mainstream stages, Chicago's theater types considered New York productions overstuffed and overhyped. Hull House mounted restrained versions of Shaw and Chekhov, and Maurice Browne opened the Little Theatre in the Loop in 1912 with both professionals and amateurs, inspiring the Little Theatre movement that spread across America as community theater and then finally regional repertory. The Dil Pickle and a number of other Towertown cafés and bookstores absorbed the Little Theatre ideal, throwing locals on with the occasional professional in rough, inventive sets and keeping alive what Bernard Sahlins calls "theater without heroes"—vernacular traditions such as commedia dell'arte that trade the fourth wall and set text for improvisation, experimentation, topicality, and audience participation. When the Depression hit, the Chicago Workers Theater, soon renamed the Chicago Repertory Group, was the next to carry the flame.

Joining the CRG set the path of Terkel's life. Now a member of a "farm club of the Group Theater," he read Stanislavski and prepared for roles using the Method, but the plays they did—by Langston Hughes, John Dos Passos, and Kurt Weill—and where they did them were right out of Brecht. "Its audience," Terkel later wrote, "was made up of teachers and social workers and cabdrivers.... We'd perform street theater at picket lines and soup kitchens; we regularly appeared before unions, performing *Waiting for Lefty* as various strikes were being organized." One night during the taxi drivers' strike, the audience beat up the actor playing the fink. The day after the 1937 Republic Steel Massacre, the CRG staged the play at the steelworkers' favorite bar. Terkel took bad guy roles in Chicago radio shows to pay the bills. Through the WPA, he wrote radio scripts for the Art Institute and worked on the *Living Newspaper*, a prophetic brand of "multimedia theater: It might be a piece of newsreel, a narrator, a dramatic scene, a bit of music. It always involved the social issues of the day"—unsubtle, earnest fare like *Spirochete*, which tackled venereal disease, or *Power*, a tribute to the Tennessee Valley Authority. (One of the carpenters at the CRG, Ed Spolin, was married to a young drama teacher for the WPA named Viola Spolin who, under the tutelage of social worker Neva Boyd, was developing a series of improvised theater games for inner-city children, including in 1939 the first performance based on audience suggestions. The Chicago press praised her work, and Terkel aired one of her children's shows on the radio.) Terkel, brought by Ed Gourfain into the city's bohemian circles, popped up at every party and salon, black and white, that would have him, signed every petition that came his way, and raised money for antifascist causes. During all this, James T. Farrell's *Studs Lonigan* came out, and Terkel's style, seemingly pulled from its pages, earned him a new nickname: Studs. Thus did these years in all ways create Studs Terkel.

His two perforated eardrums brought a discharge from the Air Force in 1943, so he returned to radio, and when the war ended, WENR offered him his own show, with carte blanche. *The Wax Museum* was entirely new, a radio version of the low cement flower beds, decorated with shards of china and broken glass, that fringed many homes out in that third ring of bungalows. The first show started with "Villa-Lobos's 'Bachianas Brasileiras #5,' sung by a Brazilian soprano, and Burl Ives singing 'Down in the Valley'; Louis Armstrong's 'West End Blues'; a Lotte Lehmann *Lied;* and then a piece from an opera," after which Studs told the story of the opera in Runyon-esque slang out of *Guys and Dolls*. Its racially integrated playlist also broke ground, and *The Wax Museum* soon developed a cult following.

One cold day in early 1947, Studs stopped by the record department at Concord Radio-Camera, where he bought many of the records for his show from George Hoefer, a jazz columnist for *Downbeat* magazine and salesman touted by the store in its ads: "Come in to Concord's Madison Street Store and meet George . . . tell the man with the widest knowledge of records in America what you want." That morning Hoefer played Studs a new gospel side from Apollo Records. The needle went down on "I'm Going to Tell God," the first few slow notes on the piano, and then the voice, starting low on "I'm" and "gonna," but by "tell" it was a wave already swelling, and by "God" the hair was up on Studs's neck, the voice expanding, booming forth but under total control. This wasn't raw emotion, this was an artist; the catch in her voice, its husky, sensual edge even as she sang about God, the strong low notes. Studs had him play it again. She lives on the South Side, said Hoefer, sings in churches there.

Studs bought a copy, and the next edition of *The Wax Museum* began this way: "There's a woman on the South Side with a golden voice. If she were singing the blues, she'd be another Bessie Smith. What she sings is called gospel. Listen." And he put the needle down. Over the next months, Studs wore out his copy of "I'm Going to Tell God" and its flip side, "I Want to Rest." In the meantime, he sought out his discovery, though all he had to do was ask a few ministers—they knew exactly where to find her. Studs and Mahalia made quite a contrast, the tall, bountiful black woman and the schlubby Jew with eyes always excited by something new. She was gratified by his offer to sing live on his show, by all the praise from a white man who seemed awed by her talent and spoke to her so honestly. "So many white people talk at colored people," she'd say once in an interview, "but not *to* them." Studs meanwhile, a veteran of "Black and White, Unite and Fight," loved introducing a black singer to white radio as the smoke of the Airport Homes riots hung in the air.

One Sunday morning Studs went down to Greater Salem Baptist and sat down, the only white face among hundreds of "parishioners, bone-weary after a weak of unsung work, for a wage not worth singing about." They gazed up at Mahalia, hands waving, calling back to her, begging her to take them higher, to take them to heaven the way the intricate stained glass windows of gothic cathedrals once took poor laboring peasants up to see God, for just a few minutes.

Studs realized that he hadn't discovered Mahalia Jackson.

They had.

CHAPTER 9

A LOCAL YOUTH
IN LOVE

FROM HIS STOVE, Nelson Algren saw a dark shape stumble out of the bar across Wabansia Avenue. It teetered once, then slumped under the Nectar Beer sign, sizzling neon in the bitter February cold. Eight degrees, an army fatigue jacket, and too many shots of Old Taylor; he'd be face-down dead in a snowbank before the end of the night. Algren felt a pang. Did the guy's cat die? Was his wife fucking the precinct captain? It was only a pork chop frying in the pan, but he had an urge to drag the rummy up here and give it to him with a cup of coffee. There were only the two rooms—kitchen and bedroom, plus a shared head for ten bucks a month— but they were warm, full of books, and Algren had another pork chop . . .

The phone rang.

A woman with a foreign accent shouted on the other end—shrill, like he'd just bought the last plum pierogi; nothing new when you lived in the middle of half a million Polacks. Algren shouted "Wrong number!" and got back to his dinner, but twice again the phone rang with the same gib-berish, until finally the fourth time a voice said, "Would you mind hold-ing the phone for a minute? Don't hang up. There's a party here would like to speak to you."

Then the same foreign accent, a woman's. French, he could tell, now that she'd slowed down a bit, though he still couldn't make sense of her name. Their mutual friend Mary Guggenheim had given her his number, she said. Algren looked over at the unmade double bed, the iron frame, with some fond memories of Mary, remembered that she'd sent a note warning him this broad might be stopping by on her way across America. Cold as it was outside, he offered to meet her; she suggested the "leetle café" at the Palmer House, her hotel. The good news was that he'd been at the Y today working the heavy bag, so he'd had a shower. Across dark Wabansia, another drunk stumbled out the door. Algren poured some milk into a bowl for the cat, grabbed his own army fatigue jacket, and switched off the light. There'd always be another drunk, stumbling out of some door, somewhere. That was the problem.

EVERY YEAR NEW YORK had a new crop of literary stars, but being Chicago's Famous Writer was like winning the heavyweight title—there was only one at a time, and you kept the belt for as long as you could beat all comers. In 1947, with Carl Sandburg retired, James T. Farrell out of fashion, Richard Wright gone for good, and Gwendolyn Brooks not allowed in the ring, the title remained vacant. Nelson Algren was about to get his shot.

He'd been born in Detroit, out of a family notable for its weak, wandering men. His grandfather Nels Ahlgren converted to Judaism in the 1850s, changed his name to Isaac Ben Abraham, and emigrated from Sweden to America, where he bounced west to San Francisco and then, wife and children in tow, went to Palestine, where he seems to have made no attempt to earn a living, forcing his wife to beg money from the U.S. consulate for boat tickets back home. As they pulled out of the harbor, Abraham threw what was left over the railing, and once back in the States gave his family the gift of abandoning them for a career as a paid prophet for esoteric religions. Rather than follow his father's erratic trail, Abraham's son Gerson hunkered down to a lifetime of abuse from his wife, Goldie, described by those who knew her as "cold, domineering and cruel," and did nothing to protect or inspire his three children, especially the youngest, Nelson Algren Abraham, born in Detroit in 1909.

The family moved to Chicago in 1913, and after a barren youth at 71st
and Cottage Grove, a few blocks east of St. Columbanus, the reedy, intro-
verted Nelson escaped to the University of Illinois in 1927, where he buried himself in books, leftist writings, and the breasts of his landlady—even
then, he was never far from a fuck. Journalism jobs weren't to be had
when he graduated in 1931, so he dropped the weighty name *Abraham* and
joined the millions of other American wanderers shivering in culverts and
dodging train yard dogs. He picked grapefruits and oranges, worked as a
carny, played—and was played by—cons, and concluded, bruised and
angry, that real life supported the Marx he'd read in college. A confirmed
Communist, he crawled back to his parents' house in 1933 and joined the
John Reed Club, where his new friends Jack Conroy and Richard Wright
encouraged his graphic realism. His break came when Vanguard Press
commissioned a novel off a piece he'd written in *Story* magazine. A
hundred-dollar advance in hand, he retraced his travels through the
South, holing up for a few months at Sul Ross State Teachers College in
Alpine, Texas, where he lectured in return for use of a rare Royal typewriter. He was caught trying to steal it when he left in January 1934. The
experience of sitting in the county jail for a month awaiting trial burned
itself into Algren's mind the way World War I had traumatized Moholy—
the swelling boredom, punctured only by the random, almost playful violence of the inmates and the callous jailers. Virtually the same jail scene
appears in every one of his major works of fiction, reworked and refined,
as if he could never fully make sense of its horror. Finding him guilty, the
State of Texas sent him back to Chicago on his own recognizance.

Vanguard published *Somebody in Boots* (originally called *Native Son*)
in March 1935, a desperate travelogue of Depression America that follows
Cass McKay through the scoured plains of West Texas to the docks of New
Orleans where he, as Nelson had, lives off rotting bananas for weeks at a
time. Boxcar gang rapes, jail time in a Texas backwater, lovers and sisters
turned into whores, are all told in a deeply, sometimes overly, poetic style.
Cass can't help but to be as brutal and ignorant as his upbringing, yet as
he tries to find a way to live as a man in a nation that punishes its people

for the crime of poverty, he has an innocence, an animal desire to be of some kind of value. When he finds love with Norah Egan in Chicago during the Century of Progress, redemption seems possible. Of course, it's not. Later Algren called it "an uneven novel written by an uneven man in the most uneven of American times," all of which is true.

The book's commercial and critical failure crushed Algren, whose independence and biting wit hid an extremely sensitive core. After a suicide attempt, a breakdown at Yaddo, and a brief commitment under the care of Karen Horney, he found stability in the South Side bohemia of the 1930s, living with his then-wife, Amanda, on the white side of Cottage Grove Avenue in one of a string of abandoned storefronts known as the Arcade or Rat Alley. Going deeply into Communist writing circles with Wright and Conroy, he became secretary of the Chicago chapter of the League of American Writers, where he met Langston Hughes, Malcolm Cowley, and Upton Sinclair. Wright found him a new job as an editor and writer at the Illinois Writers' Project in September 1936. Permanently rumpled, tall and sardonic, Algren cast a long shadow at the WPA office, equal parts lothario and encouraging mentor to younger writers like Margaret Walker. He liked to go bowling at lunch with Studs Terkel. His belief that the WPA "served to humanize people who had been partially dehumanized" and that it "provided a place where they began to communicate with people again" sounds like a description of its effect on him as much as the nation as a whole. Though he sided with Stalin's realism over Trotskyist abstraction and alienation, a stray cat like Algren wasn't meant for party discipline. In 1939 he left the Communist Party to schmooze editors, apply for grants, and start the agitprop magazine *The New Anvil* with his old friend Conroy; they raised money through raucous theatricals featuring Algren vamping onstage in a wig that Studs borrowed from the CRG.

In the spring of 1940, as Wright hit it big with *Native Son* (a title officially bequeathed to him), Algren, now divorced, moved to Milwaukee Avenue and Division Street in the heart of old Polish Chicago near St. Stanislaus Kostka, at the time the largest parish in the United States, nicknamed *Stanislawowo*. Dubbed by Wright "the Proust of the proletariat," Algren immersed himself in the guts of a city he saw getting "bigger and greyer and sootier and more clamourous every day." He bought *kolaczki* at Polish bakeries, hung around syphilis clinics and courtrooms, listened to the old lushes on the last stool, the pool hustlers, and ladies in babushkas. At the turn of the century, this had been the city's densest slum, and things were only slightly better now. Unlike "blighted" Bronzeville, there'd been no renaissance in these parts; humanity here fell below the reach of Communism and salvation. "God has forgotten us all," says one of his characters. "He has even forgotten our names."

Harper & Brothers published *Never Come Morning* in early 1942, to strong reviews. Malcolm Cowley in *The New Republic* called Algren "a poet of the Chicago slums." Its story is simple, maybe too simple for its own good. Bruno "Lefty" Bicek dreams of being a boxer, but for all his muscles, he's gutless inside, and when the boys in his gang want to share his girl Steffi, Lefty doesn't have the courage to keep them off—the need to be regular matters more than the need for love. As men line up, the furious, frustrated Lefty breaks the neck of a Greek waiting his turn. While Steffi goes to work as a whore for the local fixer, Lefty pulls some petty crimes and ends up doing time. When he comes out, he works as a bouncer at Steffi's brothel; admitting everything to her, he begs forgiveness. They have no one but each other, so together they cook up a plan to buy her out. Lefty will get a rigged bout through the fixer and then double-cross him. Lefty wins the fight, but the fixer turns him in for the murder of the Greek.

There's barely enough for a novel there, which Richard Wright and Algren's editor at Harper & Brothers continually told him. But both *Somebody in Boots* and *Never Come Morning* reveal in rich detail the lives and souls of thugs, hookers, and dirty cops. Algren dodges the trap of most lumpen naturalist fiction by never mistaking his sympathy for an excuse. Yet it's his prose style that elevates these books, with its echoes of Ben Hecht at his most poetic, ornate and so beautiful that it threatens to overwhelm its subjects, like Louis Sullivan's late banks. Hemingway called

Never Come Morning "the best book to come out of Chicago," and Algren believed a life as the city's Baudelaire was possible for him now. He wanted to write "honestly, for honest men; for the milkman, for the janitor, for the street-car conductor." Though he sounds like Gropius when he writes, "The chief thing should be to share, as fully as one is able, in the common experiences of common humanity," he could not be farther away.

But rather than put Algren on a pedestal, Chicago kicked him in the shins. Despite local reviews comparing the book to *Native Son*, the *Polish Daily Zgoda* accused him of comforting the Nazis with anti-Polish propaganda, so Mayor Ed Kelly, well aware that Nelson Algren had one vote versus the thirty thousand or so vulnerable Polish ones in the Twenty-sixth Ward, had the book pulled from the shelves of the Chicago Public Library. Meanwhile the FBI stirred up an old investigation of Algren's Communist past. The message was clear: it was okay to depict black depravity; it was not okay to depict the depravity of being regular. Sales ground to a stop, and by the summer of 1942, Algren was a syphilis inspector for the Department of Health. Drafted the next year, he made an abysmal soldier; his short service was most notable for the illegitimate daughter he fathered in Germany and his three-month stint of nonstop gambling as he waited to be demobbed in Marseilles.

Algren arrived back in Chicago in December 1945, lucky to find the dumpy one-bedroom without a bath where he could inflict his dark moods on no one but the cat. He often dropped by a tiny Rush Street bookstore with a creaky floor, a barrel of apples, and a thoughtful stock selected by its stout, mercurial owner, Stuart Brent. Over the next five decades the Seven Stairs would become the city's prime literary outlet and Brent his biggest booster. Doubleday bought a collection of short stories from Algren, *The Neon Wilderness*, and it had just hit the stores when he fielded the unusual phone call on February 21, 1947.

THE PALMER HOUSE had no "leetle café," but it did have Le Petit Café. Algren was stung that she took him for a rube. He cased the room, its women *très chic* in their mink stoles. One gal in a thin coat with tricky cat eyes kept walking in and out. He suspected it was her; well, he *knew* it was her: the copy of *Partisan Review* tucked under her arm was a dead give-away, but it also kept him at bay. None of the scenarios he'd imagined on the streetcar coming down here had involved *Partisan Review*. But no other woman in the room had such regard for herself, and no other woman had eyes quite like hers, slanted downward at the corners with such natural elegance.

At last he stepped forward, lean and straight if disheveled. Her name—Simone de Beauvoir—rang a bell. He bought her a drink, and they talked haltingly, each mangling the other's language while they took stock. She was French, so Algren explained his contribution to the war effort—lucky for him she didn't understand much. He watched her full lips circle the edge of her glass, her eyes glazing a little. Good looking and tightly wound, she didn't pretend to be interested, and Algren found that intriguing.

He had no clue what to do with this Simone de Beauvoir. She was here until tomorrow evening, then off on the Super Chief to L.A. Would she like to go hear some jazz? Simone sniffed—there was no good jazz anymore. She nodded up at the Bing Crosby playing. Americans had killed it with their "sweet jazz," she said. Jazz ended with Armstrong. Maybe a nightclub? Tony Martin at the Chez Paree? He was relieved when she rolled her eyes. Burlesque? Algren regretted the word as it came out of his mouth—snare drums and conventioneers eager to see a little titty. She made a small moue. This De Beauvoir was a tough room to play; no girly "whatever you want to do" business from her—she was the heavy bag. Algren dragged a hand through his hair, already a mess but now standing up straight on his head, wondered what Frenchy here'd make of the joint across Wabansia. Well, said Algren, I could show you the city that none of the tourists see. You know, the rough side.

She tilted an eyebrow. Now *she* was intrigued.

So they left the flashing signs of the Loop, the honking cabs and tall buildings, to head west on Madison, past the opera house and over the river to where the streetlamps were few and far between, the sidewalks cold and empty; the only proof that spring would happen was the "Vote Kennelly" signs in loyal windows; Election Day was in early April.

You could hear the thumping rhythm outside the door of their first stop; heat and sour stink hit them as they walked in, the blare of the small band. Heads turned, then turned back to their beer—Algren was a regular. Simone registered the details: toothless bums bobbing their heads while a cripple leaped into the center and began a hop-frog dance amid other clutching dancers; bright, cracking makeup on the wrinkled face of a drunk old woman; vaguely melodious shouting and occasional pitched screams. It was a voluntary madhouse, a museum of expired vices, a final cry of joy for ruined lives.

He may as well have shown her a Van Gogh.

"It is beautiful," said De Beauvoir, breathless.

Right then he knew. Any other woman in Le Petit Café would've run out of this dump in tears, but she saw it with the same wonder and affection as he did. Their eyes caught. He pulled her away and on to the next bar, where she met more characters. It turned out Richard Wright was a friend of Simone's in Paris. Another whiskey, and then back to Wabansia and Bosworth. The sex was phenomenal. Algren had never made love to a woman on anything like even terms, but Simone examined his body and his bookshelves with equal curiosity and energy. The cat made himself absent. The next morning Simone got back to the Palmer House in time to answer a call from the French consulate—there was to be a tour of the Art Institute and the Loop, a lunch with the Baroness de La Paumellière who was also in town, along with members of the Alliance Française. After lunch in the Arts Club, they whisked her into a black sedan for a tour of the city's wonders, the skyscrapers, floes of ice rolling on the lake, the statue of Ceres atop the Board of Trade, the opera house she'd passed last night. All very nice. She drummed her fingers. Dinner was at six. There was still time. She directed the driver to Wabansia and Bosworth; Algren bounded out of the door without a coat. He nodded at the sedan. "My neighbors are going to start asking me for money."

Upstairs they reunited as if they hadn't seen each other in years. Then they got dressed, and she insisted he take her for a walk around *Stanisla-wowo*, a piece of America fermented in Polish backroom vodka. They downed shots, ate sickly sweet sour cream cakes, and strolled through the cold as Algren told her his story, talked about his writing. Already he was her "crocodile" and she was his "frog." There needed to be more. She would be coming back east in April. There would be more time then . . .

Back at the Palmer House, lobster and martinis for dinner, spent in a fog. Simone made a last call to Algren; the phone had to be taken from her so she wouldn't miss the late train west. Since the 1920s she'd been with Jean-Paul Sartre as his helpmeet, his partner, his servant, once and even now occasionally his lover. But the experience with Algren, her "local youth," had been illuminating, to say the least—the American, for example, did not feel it necessary to argue philosophical points while inside her. That alone had changed her world. Heading toward L.A., she read *The Neon Wilderness*, recalled his "hovel, without a bathroom or a refrigerator, alongside an alley full of steaming trash cans and flapping newspapers." Mostly she recalled how much it hurt to say goodbye. Meanwhile, at Wabansia and Bosworth, she'd left behind a copy of that week's *New Yorker*. At a certain point it dawned on Algren that the Simone referred to in "Talk of the Town" as "the prettiest Existentialist" was indeed his Frog Wife.

SIMONE DE BEAUVOIR was thirty-nine, a year older than Algren, born of a formal, old French family that could trace its lineage back to the twelfth century. Brilliant, methodical to a fault, she'd been nicknamed Castor, the Beaver, for her unrelenting, humorless nature. In 1929 she'd come in second to Sartre in the French national examinations, and they'd stay that way through their lives, bound but in a definite order. Before the war and through the occupation, she and Sartre had been the center of a circle of French artists and intellectuals, known as the Family, who developed existentialism. Its influence was spreading as her relationship with

Sartre became more complicated. The romance had ended back in 1930, leaving her "so dissatisfied sexually that . . . whenever a man brushed against her on the Metro or the bus, the mere touch suffused her with violent physical urges." Now she honed and edited and refined Sartre's writings, for which she received little if any credit; nor did she for her work as a procuress for his particular fetishes. Yet she was utterly committed to their work revitalizing thought and action in a devastated world. Following in the footsteps of Sartre's 1945 visit to the United States, she'd come to assess America as it swelled with postwar vigor. She drank orange juice and scotch, ate club sandwiches, and made broad pronouncements; Diana Trilling later called her visit "a four months psychological contest whose terms had been established well before [she] set foot on our shores." She knew more about jazz than any American, for example, pronouncing it dead the year Dizzy Gillespie introduced Chano Pozo and Charlie Parker formed his quintet with Max Roach and Miles Davis; meanwhile, she marveled at jackalope postcards.

Back in Towertown, Stuart Brent pumped *The Neon Wilderness.* "To keep the book alive, we held periodic parties," wrote Brent. "One month we would call it Nelson's birthday, another month the birthday of the publication of the book, still another the birthday of the book itself." When he wasn't signing at the Seven Stairs, Algren pecked at *High Yellow and the Dealer.* From the road, Simone sent her first letters, tentative not just because her English was stiff and young but out of a reluctance to see the magic of those thirty-six hours erode. "Good bye," she closed a letter in March. "I am happy to have met you and I am sure we'll met again, this year or next year." In late April, she convinced her local youth to meet in New York. Algren had never been on an airplane, and their first hours together were awkward; slumming the Bowery in an attempt to recapture their night on Madison Street, he was snappish and irritable. Only back in their bed at the Brevoort Hotel did they find each other again, so that's where they spent most of the next two weeks, during which Simone reported later that she had her first orgasm. When it came to sex, Algren was in charge, while she fussed over him "just like all the American women I had ridiculed for the way they catered to men's needs. I was surprised by how much I enjoyed it."

The more time she spent with Algren, the more his peculiarities came out, his sensitivity and stormy moods, a rudeness she saw as his defense against those with tougher hides. As their visit neared its end, he grew more unstable, at times even hostile, and she fell deeply in love, knowing all the while what he wanted and could never have—a life with her in Chicago. Simone could never leave Paris: her career as a writer grew out of that place as surely as Algren's did from the alleys of Chicago; she'd told him that many times, but he was unable or unwilling to hear her. And yet if she ever succeeded in convincing him that their future was hopeless, she'd lose him. If Simone surrendered herself to Nelson in the bedroom, she controlled his heart. Before she left for Paris on May 17, Algren produced a wide silver ring that he slipped onto her finger. They were married now, in their own way. "In the sad streets of Chicago," she wrote as soon as she landed, "under the Elevated, in the lonely room, I'll be with you, my beloved one, as a loving wife with her beloved husband."

Through a summer hot in both Chicago and Paris, they suffered apart. She endeavored to get his books published in France, while he begged her to come back, still not comprehending the magnitude of her commitment to Sartre. Simone sank into a depression, crying and drinking, putting aside an essay about the state of women to help Sartre, even though women were first given the vote in France that summer of 1947. Before the emergence of modern feminism, their intellectual partnership could be understood only as a product of a complicated romance. If she'd been able to present her relationship with Sartre as a job that she could not, did not want to, leave, rather than in terms of affection, all parties might have been spared some torture. She and Algren continued to pledge their love and dissect their relationship in increasingly turgid letters. "Nelson, I love you," she wrote. "But do I deserve your love if I do not give you my life? I tried to explain to you I cannot give my life to you. Do you understand it? Are you not resentful about it? Will you never be? Will you always believe yet it is really love I am giving you?"

For her visit in September 1947, Algren took her on the grand tour, from Stockyards to slums to Seurat's *La Grande Jatte*. They saw the electric chair, went to midnight missions, and visited Maxwell Street, where she bought wide shoes at Big Jack's. At Poole's Healing Services on Lake Street, he gave her a bottle of "Compelling Oil." Precise and perceptive, De Beauvoir proved to be one of the most astute observers Chicago has ever entertained:

> In the evenings especially, a provincial poetry floats through the streets. At the corner of a dead-end street, children smoke and whisper about their plans. Sitting on their porches, women watch the city lights on the horizon. The groaning of the El shakes the silence; the foliage of a tree rustles; a cat rummages in a trash can: the slightest sound lingers. You feel far, far away from human ventures and follies, in the heart of a calmly ordered life that repeats itself day after day. Yet tomorrow morning you'll read in the paper that they found a corpse cut into pieces in one of these alleys, that two men slit each other's throats in a nearby bar, that a barkeeper was shot down with a revolver two steps away. The sweetness of Chicago nights is deceptive.

These weeks together were probably their most relaxed and happiest. In hopes of making sense of her personal life, Simone had begun work on a sanitized version of her diary, to be called *America Day by Day*. They listened to "Lili Marleen" on his record player, heard Studs on the radio, drank Southern Comfort, read and wrote and made love. He encouraged her to expand her idea for an essay on women into a book—it would eventually become *The Second Sex. Poetry* published his "Epitaph: The Man with the Golden Arm," a poetic coda he'd already written for *High Yellow and the Dealer*. Each was privately convinced they were the superior writer: Of her work, Algren once told a friend, "It's like eating cardboard.

If she didn't think I was so great in the sack and had such a great mind, I'd send her back to Jean-Paul Sartre." Still, by any reckoning, they were equal partners, the crocodile and the frog. "Quite simply, he thought she was 'wonderful,' and unlike Sartre, he didn't hesitate to show it with a quick hug and spin around his kitchen, by staring at her with open delight on his face." Yet the more they shared a normal life, the harder it was to explain why Sartre's needs would always come before Algren's, and as the weeks came to a close, he again began to curdle, flying into rages and paranoid rants that didn't improve with whiskey.

They said goodbye September 24, with plans for a long trip together in the spring down the Mississippi. While she waited at Midway Airport, a messenger handed her a white corsage from her "gentle wild man." Sartre's confrontation with De Gaulle loomed; in tears, Nelson's "loving little frog" headed back to Paris and her work.

CHAPTER 10

LET ME DO ONE
BY MYSELF

I N POLAND THEY'D been shtetl Jews called Czyz, but when shoemaker Yasef joined his brother-in-law Morris Pulik on Maxwell Street in 1922, he became Joseph Chess, and six years later when he sent for his family, eleven-year-old Lejzor and seven-year-old Fiszel became Leonard and Phil. Joseph's carpentry business dried up in the Depression, so the brothers-in-law started Wabash Junk Shop at 2971 S. State, across the street from a church, where the two boys sorted scrap to the music of an upright piano and tambourines. In 1942 Leonard went out on his own to run Cut-Rate Liquor on South State, and when he married, instead of heading west to the suburbs like most of his Lawndale neighbors, he moved east with his new wife, Revetta, to an apartment on Drexel Boulevard, in the old Jewish neighborhood bordering Bronzeville along Cottage Grove Avenue, near Si Gordon's commune and the Abraham Lincoln Centre. Leonard, though, was no Marxist agitator. He saw money in Black Chicago, and the fact that some people didn't want to touch it only made his life easier. The Cut-Rate, with its small bar and jukebox, did fine, but when Leonard saw a vacant storefront just a few blocks away from the Regal and the Savoy on 47th, he leaped. A bigger and better version of Cut-Rate, the 708 Liquor Store lasted until he cashed out in 1946.

He had big plans for his next place, a hole-in-the-wall diner at 3905 S. Cottage Grove called the Congress Buffet, across the street from the Ida B. Wells Homes, just south of Gropius's reach. The urban planners eliminated nodal intersections like this one at 39th and Cottage Grove, known as Drexel Square, a crossroads within a city of crossroads where blacks and whites mingled. Mixed crowds attended the nearby Abraham Lincoln Centre and Elder Lucy Smith's All Nations Pentecostal Church, but most came for its nightclubs and its nationally known concentration of prostitutes. Blacks from out of town stayed at the DuSable Hotel on Oakwood Boulevard, Chicago's equivalent to Harlem's Hotel Theresa. Leonard opened the Macomba Lounge in February 1946—in time for Phil to come on board after the Navy—and the locals made the Macomba their place to party, and they *did* party: dealers taped bags of heroin and cocaine under their stools, and hookers worked openly as marquee players dropped by to listen to Tom Archia's house band.

Tom Archia wasn't a breakthrough saxophonist. Well regarded, he'd led backup bands for name singers, but the music he played at the Macomba is best described as transitional. Jazz was in chaos. By December 1946, eight of the big bands, including Benny Goodman's, Harry James's, and Tommy Dorsey's, had all broken up, as Dizzy Gillespie, Charlie Parker, and Thelonious Monk pushed bop into the mainstream along with the goatee-sporting, beret-wearing, heroin-shooting style that came with it. Bop was great music, but Monk and Diz played for you to listen, not dance, and its coterie of white followers liked talking about art more than having a good time. Old white record collectors, "the moldy figs," listened to Dixieland and Chicago jazz (Studs's pal George Hoefer was one of those); sweet jazz, the pop crap of Bing Crosby, still clogged the airwaves. Louis Jordan, Nat King Cole, Dinah Washington, and Billy Eckstein (the last three all from Chicago) had staked a space between white pop and the more overtly sexual, dance-oriented material called race music before the war but now reclassified in the trades as rhythm and blues. Yet Chicago in the late 1940s remained "the best city in America for jazz musicians," with by one count some seventy-five jazz clubs just on the South Side. *Downbeat,* the influential if stuffy jazz magazine, was headquartered here, as was *Esquire,* whose annual jazz awards were a public battleground. You could hear bop in Chicago—Tom Archia played it some—but what really went down at the Macomba and elsewhere on the Third Coast were big, wallowing saxophones and boogie piano. "Chicagoans' attitude toward nightlife," wrote *Holiday* magazine in May 1947, ". . . is basically barrelhouse and the conditioning factor, more often than not, is the desire for a large evening."

But the evolution in taste was formed at least as much by changes in business and technology. After a hiatus during the war, the government licensed new radio stations again, filling the airwaves with small outfits that played a wide range of music and drew listeners away from the big New York networks. Chicago disc jockeys began to make a name for themselves as mass communicators. Phonograph and record sales shot up, as Petrillo's recording ban and the shellac shortage ended, and small companies, encouraged by the surprise hit "I Wonder" by Cecil Gant, flooded the market with records by unknowns that gave all those upstart stations something to play. One such hobby label in Chicago was Aristocrat, founded in April 1947 by two married couples, Fred and Mildred Brount and Charles and Evelyn Aron. Their first record, "Chi-Baba, Chi-Baba" by Sherman Hayes, was a novelty bedtime song with an Italian flair later covered by Perry Como, Peggy Lee, and most recently the Wiggles.

Leonard, meanwhile, charged up on coffee, cigarettes, and a brazen love of money, saw the talent passing through the doors of the Macomba and lined up his first recording: seventeen-year-old vocalist Andrew Tibbs, a high-pitched tenor with clear, uptown diction. At the time dozens of labels and distributors were operating in Chicago, but Aristocrat was the obvious choice since Tom Archia had cut some sides with them and Leonard knew the Arons socially. Leonard packed his car full of Tibbs's rough efforts, "Union Man Blues" and "Bilbo Is Dead," and drove them around the northeast while Phil held down the fort at the Macomba. By October 1947 Leonard was on the company masthead as a salesman, and Aristocrat moved further into "race" music.

.   .   .

AFTER THIRTY YEARS of picking Mississippi cotton, Muddy Waters had packed his Sears Silvertone guitar, two fragile records he'd made for the Library of Congress, and everything he'd learned from Son House and Charley Patton to come north. He'd landed at 36th and Calumet on a Saturday in 1943; by Monday he had a job making more in a week than he'd make in a year down on Stovall Plantation. But that acoustic guitar killed Muddy at the clubs. "You'd go in and tell [the club owners] you played blues," he'd said later, "and a lot of them, they'd shake their head and say, Sorry, can't use you."

The old 1930s bluesmen still hung together in Bronzeville—men like Sunnyland Slim and Memphis Slim and Tampa Red, with his beer-drinking dog; Big Maceo thumped away at his piano. Big Bill Broonzy was the biggest name of them all, but Muddy's first real friend in town was Jimmy Rogers, another guitarist from the Delta who lived on the West Side, where most migrants now settled, Muddy included. Rogers bought him a pickup and an amplifier, and soon they were playing parties with a small band that had more country to it than Big Maceo and Broonzy, who still had that Bluebird sound. Muddy and Rogers played for the folks in the Ida B. Wells Homes, men in do-rags setting out on the wooden porch back of their flat wondering what the fuck they were doing in a place where it *snowed*. As Charles Keil wrote, "The bluesman is in a sense every man," and Muddy meant to play an everyman kind of music.

The leap came when Muddy finally bought his first electric guitar. "It was a very different sound," he'd say later, "not just louder." It was a sound that captured the moment. As he learned his way around the sensitive strings, Muddy re-created modern, industrial life with ears still startled by screeching El trains, police sirens, and factory whistles. He used the slide less and picked more, lost those long, acoustic slurs that felt like slow evenings in Mississippi. A familiar name on the Chicago blues scene now, Muddy did odd jobs in the daytime and played parties at night. In September 1946 he sat in on a Columbia session under Lester Melrose himself. Hidden behind the heavy piano, Muddy only hinted at what he could do.

The final piece fell into place one Sunday when Jimmy Rogers heard a harmonica playing out his window on Maxwell Street, the city's running outdoor junk shop, flea market, and bluesfest. That morning Rogers heard the fastest, wildest blowing ever coming from a "little squirrel-faced boy," whom he recognized from back home, named Walter Jacobs, soon to be known as Little Walter. Flashy and fly, he'd picked up the harp at the age of eight and played on the streets of New Orleans before he'd found his way up to Chicago on VE Day 1945, all of fifteen years old. Rogers brought him to Muddy. "He had more nerve than brains," said Rogers later, who'd compare his improvisations to Charlie Parker's. Unfortunately, he'd also copy Parker's self-destructive ways.

Everything clicked. Muddy and Rogers had their own play going, and now here was Little Walter to skip like a spark on their two rails. Around this time, a few blocks from Muddy's apartment at Ashland and 13th Street, Club Zanzibar opened. The three moved in as the house band in the fall of 1946 and spent the winter working on their new pared-down sound, Muddy with his hooded eyes and placid Buddha face. The break came during that hot summer of 1947—four days over one hundred degrees, the beaches full, most rationing and price controls ending. Jackie Robinson had made his Chicago debut to a packed and extremely hostile Wrigley Field. Sunnyland Slim was going into a recording session at Aristocrat, and talent scout Sammy Goldberg, who'd heard Muddy play, wanted him on backup. No one knows anymore what exactly happened next: one version has Muddy making a delivery for Westerngrade Venetian Blind Company when someone hunts him down and tells him that his mother or aunt or cousin is either sick, dying, or dead, so he can leave early; more likely he knew beforehand and cooked the story up on his own. However it fell out, Muddy took the afternoon off to drive up to Universal Recording Studios.

Three blocks from Moholy's old School of Design at 111 E. Ontario, Universal was on its way to becoming the world's most advanced recording studio. Its owner, Bill Putnam, was a lifetime electricity geek from

Danville who'd gone to high school with Dick Van Dyke and Bobby Short. In 1946 he'd opened Universal and a year later scored a huge hit with a version of the Irish standard "Peg o' My Heart" by the Harmonicats. Its haunting, reverberating harmonicas had marked Putnam as a creative genius, and starting this summer most Chicago labels, as well as a growing number of national acts, did their important recording there.

All the technology in the world, though, couldn't give Sunnyland Slim a new sound. On "Johnson Machine Gun" and "Fly Right, Little Girl," he shouts the blues over a tinkling, whorehouse piano, Muddy deep in the background, adding twang and attack when there's an opening. Imitation Bluebird, but Sammy Goldberg knew there was something more there. He let Muddy cut two numbers of his own once Slim finished. "Gypsy Woman" and "Little Anna Mae" both took a full stride away from what they'd just cut. Now it was Muddy up front, with his unique combination of heavy Delta accent and crisp diction springing certain words the way he sprang notes on the strings. The guitar set a deliberate pace that felt less like a slow piano blues and more like foreplay. Muddy didn't talk dirty like the old hokum music; his stuff *sounded* dirty, the guitar squirming around like a girl with her hips hard up against you.

Leonard Chess and the Arons weren't ready for all that quite yet. They shelved the two sides, while Muddy went back to his delivery van.

HOT AS IT was in Chicago that summer, it was hotter just south in Calumet City, "the Barbary Coast of the booming Midwest," flush up against Indiana, where the Capital Bar and the Ozark Club and Sid's Oasis offered watered drinks, laff-riot emcees like Tiny Roy, and "The Man with the Glass Head" but mostly strippers pulled right off the farm and stuffed into garters and pasties.

At the Peacock Club, a sweet-faced pianist named Herman "Sonny" Blount, soft-spoken to the edge of ethereal, reminded himself that he was not of this world. He began another verse of "Buttons and Bows" with Lonnie Fox the trumpeter and Buggs Hunter on drums. A tatty velvet curtain strung on a pipe hung between them and the sloppy, sweaty flesh of the white women dancing on the other side, the drooling white men; a scrap of petty racism that Sonny was actually grateful for. An entire room full of people thinking about nothing but sex made it clear that he was supposed to care, but Sonny Blount wasn't like everyone else. He wasn't of this world. Buggs snapped him back—ba-dum-*dump*. Strippers needed a steady beat, so in Calumet City bands, the drummer led. They didn't care what they stripped to—Sonny had played everything from "Rhapsody in Blue" to "The Woody Woodpecker Song"—all they needed was that steady beat.

He was not of this world. Ba-dum-*dump*. And Herman Blount was not his real name. He had no name or age or mother or father. He was not black or white or even human. He'd had a vision once, in college. Spacemen had taken him to Saturn, where they put him in robes and said that there'd be trouble on Earth. Someday he would have to explain the universe to the people of Earth. He would know when the spaceships were going to land.

Ba-dum-*dump*.

Herman Blount was born in Birmingham, Alabama, in 1914, a year after Muddy Waters, but the two couldn't have been any more different. Abandoned by his mother, Herman was raised by his grandmother and his aunt. A withdrawn child, constantly reading, he didn't like sports and was discovered to have an undescended testicle, a condition that added to his sense of separation. "I've never been part of the planet," he'd say later. ". . . Right in the midst of everything and not being a part of it." Herman's passion was Fletcher Henderson, the sophisticated bandleader of the Harlem Renaissance, so on his eleventh birthday his great-aunt gave him a piano; within a year, he was composing music. As soon as he graduated from high school in January 1932, Herman formed a small band and began to arrange charts. After a few years on the road, Blount and most of the band entered Alabama A&M. By now Herman had become "Sonny Blount," and in his short stint in college he studied Bach, Haydn, and

Mozart all the way up to Schoenberg and Shostakovich, while back in his dorm room he lost himself in close readings of biblical commentaries. It was here in Huntsville that he'd had his vision of Saturn and space travel, what some consider a story of alien abduction. If it were true, Sonny Blount would turn out to be the most eloquent and successful spokesman the aliens have ever found.

It must have been ninety degrees in the Peacock Club. Sonny wanted water or grapefruit juice—he didn't touch liquor. Another song, and the set would be over. He could read a chapter then dash over for the next set across the street, and then back to the Peacock and that's how it was, five nights a week from eight at night to five in the morning.

After his astral vision, Sonny had returned to Birmingham and moved back in with his great-aunt, where he read, wandered, and listened to music, wrestled with angels and received visitors in his room, called by one "a pool hall for the metaphysically minded." He also got up a new band to rehearse his compositions. Drafted in 1942, he convinced a judge that he deserved conscientious objector status, no small feat for a black man in Birmingham, but he took it even farther. Demanding placement in a Civilian Public Service camp rather than prison, Blount revealed his soul in desperate letters to the National Service Board. "I have never been able to think of sex as a part of my life though I have tried to but just wasn't interested," he wrote in one. "Music to me is the only worthwhile thing in the world. . . . Unfortunately, I have learned not to trust people. I am a little afraid of normal people." The surprising candor seemed to work—he was directed to a CPS camp, but now he refused that as well, threatening self-mutilation to his remaining testicle. Clearly more was going on here than philosophical objections to combat, so the government finally deemed him 4-F. Sonny returned to Birmingham an angry, driven, sexually confused man.

When his aunt died in 1946, he headed north to Chicago and right away got jobs with Wynonie Harris and the quirky Sir Oliver Bibb, who dressed his band in Revolutionary-era costumes complete with epaulets and tricorns. Sonny's real quarry in Chicago, though, was his boyhood idol Fletcher Henderson, then playing out his career as the big bands crashed like the last dinosaurs. Henderson had a standing gig at the city's hottest jazz club, Club DeLisa on 55th Street, and Sonny—by now Sonne or Sonny Bhlount, depending on his mood or whatever other currents dictated his actions—lobbied him until he was allowed to sit in one night for a missing pianist. Sonny stayed on after Henderson left in May 1947, and he was still playing there two days a week with Red Saunders while he put together a new band and pulled these Calumet City shifts.

By the wall, the tape recorder rolled on, as it did through every session Sonny played. Back in his small apartment, a cocoon of books, he'd listen to it as he played and as he read, searching for what it was he should be searching for in the universe, and himself. He spent hours in the Egyptian collection at the Field Museum, his reading now focused on the days when black men built the great cities and erected pyramids. He talked about all this to his new band—Sonny's quiet, penetrating character, his unquestionable talents, gave him a solidity and depth that always drew players to him no matter his eccentricities. Day by day he crawled deeper into his head, into the stars.

Glass broke over by the bar; someone screamed.

Sonny Blount had seen Saturn. It was nothing like Calumet City.

IN THE LATE summer of 1947, as Leonard Chess drove through Pennsylvania with his trunk filled with Andrew Tibbs records, and Nelson and Simone had their two weeks of sex and sightseeing, Mahalia Jackson went into the studio for a final run at blowing down the walls of Jericho. Her dismal sales had Apollo on the brink of pulling the plug, so for this last chance she'd picked a song by the Reverend W. Herbert Brewster called "Move On Up a Little Higher." After weeks of practice, finally, at the most silent hour of the night on September 12, 1947, Mahalia did three takes at St. Luke accompanied by piano and organ that turned the song into a stately six minutes built to a triumphant exclamation of pride and will that some thirty years later Chicagoan Curtis Mayfield would echo in his own "Move On Up." Bess Berman wasn't thrilled with giving over both the A and B sides to one song, but at this point it didn't matter. Or as Mahalia would say, it was in the Lord's hands now.

In fact, it was in Berman's hands. Apollo sat on the record all through the fall of 1947, an agonizing wait, but "Move On Up a Little Higher" finally hit the racks that December. Studs immediately played it on *The Wax Museum*, but he didn't need to—disc jockey Al Benson on WGES was the man who put her over. A former storefront minister, WPA interviewer, and Dawson precinct captain, Benson dominated radio in Black Chicago, the nation's center of black radio, with his chronic stutter and a slurry West Indian accent that combined "northern being and southern memory." His street pose deepened the cultural split between Chicago's old blacks and the new ones who kept coming to fill the factories. "I talk the way the common people of my race do," he told the *Tribune*. "They understand me." By now he was the nation's most influential black disc jockey, "the cultural padrone in post-Depression Black Chicago," and when he began to play Mahalia in regular rotation, she took off. Over time, two million copies of "Move On Up a Little Higher" would be sold. Mahalia's agent couldn't keep up with the bookings, and Berman got her back into the studio for a session that would produce two more million-copy sellers, "Even Me" and "Dig a Little Deeper." Mahalia had arrived, but she wasn't satisfied. Not yet.

DESPITE LEONARD CHESS'S best efforts for Andrew Tibbs, "Move On Up a Little Higher" blew him away that December, at all the hairdressers and candy stores where people bought records then. Still, Tibbs did well enough, establishing early on the Chess strategy of doing "well enough" with a lot of titles. Two months later Aristocrat released the two sides Muddy had cut in that first Sunnyland Slim session, and they did "well enough" too, so with the Macomba in Phil's hands, Leonard took the leap. With $10,000 from his father, he bought out the Brounts and Charles Aron, who divorced Evelyn in the spring of 1948. Leonard was now her sole partner.

Just then James Petrillo, head of the American Federation of Musicians headquartered in Chicago, tried once again to stop the rising flood of recorded music that threatened the livelihoods of working musicians. With the big bands gone, DJs taking over the airwaves, and jukeboxes everywhere, Petrillo called for another recording ban in 1948 with an argument that wasn't all that different from those heard today regarding intellectual property: the artists deserved a cut of the money created by the new technology replacing them. The major labels froze, while indies like Aristocrat kept bringing eager nonunion artists into the studio. In April 1948, Muddy went back into Universal, with Sunnyland Slim to play piano and Big Crawford on bass. The results of this session are the musical equivalent of watching a prehistoric fish climb out of the primordial ooze, sprout legs, and run. His first two cuts, "Good Lookin' Woman" and "Mean Disposition," could have been made by any bluesman in the previous twenty years, the thudding tempo, twinkling piano keys, sax blurring the background, all at Leonard's insistence. Sunnyland Slim recorded two more forgettable sides, and then Muddy spoke up: "Let me do one by myself."

He chose the same two songs he'd recorded seven years earlier, when Alan Lomax had come through Stovall Plantation, but Muddy had been to the city now. The first guitar sting of "I Can't Be Satisfied"—three simple, descending notes plucked on the electric guitar—get under your skin, an earworm if there ever was one. In the insistent beat, the stab and retreat of the guitar, Muddy's up-in-your-grill tone, the lyrics all sex and violence and a desire to go back south, away from the false promise of life in the North, the urban blues were born.

Behind the glass, Leonard was livid. "What's he singing?" he shouted, biting back the *motherfuckers* in deference to Evelyn, who absolutely felt the very *very* basic thing Muddy was expressing when he plucked those strings. Still dubious, Leonard waited to distribute "I Can't Be Satisfied" until a Friday night in June, a few weeks after the *Shelley v. Kraemer*

Supreme Court decision outlawed restrictive covenants. By the next morning almost all copies were sold. Muddy found a few at Maxwell Street Record Company, but the owner had jacked up the price, and Muddy could only convince him to sell one. Like Mahalia, Muddy Waters had arrived, and neither one could be satisfied.

Coming as they did and where they did, in a city tearing itself up over race, there was more than partying going on with the success of Muddy's new sound, and more than redemption with Mahalia's. Muddy Waters and Mahalia Jackson each said in their own way that the people of Black Chicago, and Bronzeville in particular, still existed—something you'd never know from looking at Gropius's SSPB Opportunity Plan.

Rather than rebuild the neighborhood around IIT, the plan would turn the city into a campus: a mix of high-rise and low-rise modernist residences and one central shopping area that looked like a student union. The cultural, historic, and political heart of Black Chicago was gone, along with any sign of black life, like Mies's montage for IIT. Gone were the offices of the *Defender*, Supreme Life, Pilgrim Baptist, and other Louis Sullivan buildings; instead of storefront churches of every denomination, there was one. Bars line every street in Chicago, but the Opportunity Plan had exactly zero, just Miesian buildings and wide planes of grass more suited for Ultimate Frisbee than the web of complex interactions involved in daily urban life or winter in Chicago. Clearly the "opportunity" to live here was not going to be extended to many of those who lived there now.

The reaction in Black Chicago to the first section of the plan, Lake Meadows, was mixed. Upper- and middle-class blacks leaned toward it—after all, they were the intended residents—but the land being claimed belonged to a functional middle-class neighborhood that wasn't blighted. Dawson kept his voice low, the Urban League and the NAACP offered little resistance, and most of the cultural voices of Black Chicago went quiet. Richard Wright was in Paris for good; most of the painters had gone to New York or Mexico; Frank Davis was in Hawaii. Margaret Burroughs (she'd dropped the Taylor-Goss for her second husband) was finishing her master's, teaching art at DuSable High and doing what she could to keep the SSCAC open. Gwendolyn Brooks, Guggenheim in hand and marriage on the rocks, was working on a new book of poems after Harper & Brothers rejected ten chapters of the novel they'd asked her to write. *Ebony*'s considerable editorial talent, such as Era Bell Thompson (whose memoir of growing up black in North Dakota, *American Daughter,* is a forgotten jewel), urged more pragmatism than protest. WPA veterans Frank Yerby and Willard Motley both published best-selling novels, but their characters were all white. Elijah Muhammad's voice was still a low whisper on the other end of the spectrum but was growing louder.

So it was up to black musicians to announce black presence, impatience, and pride. As Ronald L. Fair described this Second Migration, the people "were ill-informed and they were loud and they were sometimes vulgar, and sometimes they didn't have much respect for the law because the law had no respect at all for them, but they were vibrant with a will to belong and they were not afraid to fight for what they knew to be their right to remake Chicago."

Country blues weren't dangerous; for all their talk about selling their souls to the devil, Son House and Robert Johnson sounded like Job talking to God. Muddy, on the other hand, flaunted the hyperbolic sexuality that fed white paranoia. His urban blues belonged exclusively to black America, at a moment when white listeners and white players were tapping into bop and its interior world of heroin and slang. Though young, mostly poor blacks produced the music and took the heroin that gave the whole bop scene its "cool," middle-class blacks watched and consumed it as an affect and an art form; everyone else was looking for something to dance to.

Muddy and Mahalia—far away from each other in every way—both catered to people who wore aprons all day, who did for others, whose hands cracked, who drank beer and worked in factories, the people Wayne F. Miller photographed for the pages of *Ebony.* Muddy spoke straight about the supposed promised land of the North; he'd seen war heroes stoned by white women who couldn't speak English. Blues was music of individual identity, the music of Me, while gospel was a vehicle for shared values and hopes that only the best of whites could understand and maybe relate to, but never claim—the music of We. "They'd tell me, 'Girl, you could be a blues singer,'" Mahalia said once. "I'd answer, 'What Negro couldn't be a blues singer?' I knew that wasn't the life for me. . . . Blues are the songs of despair. Gospel songs are the songs of hope." And they were all being sung in Chicago.

CHAPTER 11

A FRESH TIME

AFTER CONSIDERING CANDIDATES such as Buckminster Fuller, Ansel Adams, and Robert Motherwell, the board of the Institute of Design finally selected for its new director Serge Chermayeff, the man Moholy had wanted as his successor. He'd been born in the Caucasus to an oil-rich family and raised in England, where he'd developed, according to Sibyl, a "200 per cent English personality." A borzoi of a man, dangerously thin with protruding ribs and White Russian elegance, he'd done his best architecture, namely the De La Warr Pavilion at Bexhill-on-Sea, as Erich Mendelssohn's partner. Brusque Chermayeff was nobody's holy fool—he had no time for things like the jar filled with soap bubbles that had once entranced Moholy for the better part of a day—and that suited Gropius and Paepcke, who gave him the mandate to cultivate professional designers. The Russian cleaned up the curriculum and separated the wheat from the chaff. An in crowd of talented students formed, led by Moholy's old favorite Robert Brownjohn, "so gifted," said Chermayeff, "that it was inescapable that he was the best man around the place." Blond and snarky, the precocious BJ and his circle interacted with the faculty on a level beyond the less-talented sorts who paid the bills. Sibyl, meanwhile, bit her tongue as she helped the Chermayeffs find an apartment and carried on an affair with the school librarian. The ID's new energy bubbled up from a very combustible mix.

The same could be said of the nation as a whole during these expansive, exuberant, belligerent years just before cars and televisions changed everything. Inflation spiked as corporations jacked prices to celebrate the end of federal controls. Truman's handling of housing rights, civil rights, and Soviet relations satisfied no one. In December 1947 in Chicago, Henry Wallace declared himself the Progressive Party candidate for the White House. As FDR's secretary of agriculture, he'd authored the policies that stabilized and reinvigorated America's rural economy, and as vice president, he had watched over the remains of the New Deal while Roosevelt concentrated on the war. His ideas on world peace and civil rights, suffused with a mystical worship of the land that appealed to midwestern agrarians, countered the postwar Liberals, who blasted him for allegedly harboring Soviets in his campaign. The black intelligentsia joined the Wallace camp, along with just about every Depression-era socialist and ex-WPA employee, including Terkel and Algren, who actively campaigned for him; Terkel even emceed Paul Robeson's fiftieth birthday party.

But Wallace's promise was undermined by his considerable weaknesses. As large plates moved across the world in the summer of 1948— the Marshall Plan began, and the Soviets blockaded Berlin—Wallace's candidacy foundered amid revelations of embarrassing dealings he'd had with Russian mystic Nicholas Roerich during the Roosevelt administration; most damaging, his letters referring to Roerich as his "guru" and FDR as "the Flaming One." Claims that he was a Soviet shill gained weight as he spoke in outright support of the Soviets, while Truman laid down a hard line. Dwight Macdonald said he was "fuzzy-minded," lacking integrity and courage. The leftist challenge to postwar liberalism was being made by a fool.

Still, Wallace's message of peaceful optimism was popular with left-wing intellectuals, certainly around the Institute of Design. With Moholy gone, the school reconceived itself as a place inspired by its founder's spirit and Bauhaus roots but no longer restricted to them. While IIT remained largely insulated from its surrounding community, students and faculty here spread out into the life of the avant-garde around them. Moholy's process-oriented philosophy and the ID circle, which some deemed too "fashionable" for their taste, met the growing desire for self-expression and the optimism of the moment, and though the school still produced mostly arts educators, it began to influence popular culture. At one of the regular Sunday salons of James Prestini, a popular instructor who specialized in delicately turned wood, architect Harry Weese and his wife, Kitty Baldwin, met Jody Kingrey. As they griped about how hard it was to get an apartment, Weese pitched the idea of selling affordable, well-designed furniture to returning veterans. Later that year the three opened Baldwin Kingrey at 105 E. Ohio, the first store to sell modern furniture to the American mass market. Its first employee, Don Dimmitt, was an ID student, and Serge and Barbara Chermayeff themselves stayed up one night to help assemble the first shipment of Aalto stools. Its impact extended throughout the Chicago arts community. Celebrities between trains now had someplace other than Marshall Field's to visit, a store "ahead of its time in immersing American consumers in an environment of good design." By presenting in one place the work of Charles and Ray Eames, the Finnish designers Eero Saarinen and Alvar Aalto, and the ID/Bauhaus lineage, Baldwin Kingrey began the marketing of postwar design under one coherent banner. "We were, in a sense," said Dimmitt, "the precursor of Crate and Barrel." The store was a first green shoot of a new kind of urbanism that stressed accessible quality design; Modernism as consumerism. The question was, could there be such a thing as an enlightened consumer? "The people that rushed into Baldwin Kingrey weren't from Lake Forest," said Kitty Baldwin. "They were mostly from the city, and they didn't have very much money. Instead, they had some sort of a new outlook—a vision." Baldwin Kingrey's landlord, Arthur Rubloff, was hoping to cash in on that vision too; he was developing the stretch of Michigan Avenue just east of the store into a high-end shopping strip he dubbed "the Magnificent Mile."

Meanwhile the tension between Chermayeff and Sibyl grew into a rift, then a full rupture. "There is a morbid coldness in him that frightens students and stymies the faculty," wrote Sibyl, while he described her in biting, brutally psychiatric terms, to Gropius and anyone else who'd listen. At last she resigned from the faculty and left Chicago, "an old flowerpot" that she'd "become unreasonably attached to." In her subsequent career as an architectural historian, educator, and critic, she took aim against the old world men of the Bauhaus, dubbing Gropius's Pan Am Building "Hitler's Revenge" and missing no opportunity to call out Mies for what she considered his crimes, both architectural and political.

But new instructors energized the school. The Swiss-born painter and sculptor Hugo Weber took over the Foundation Class. Hired by Moholy just before his death, Weber had an impressive European pedigree and an open, engaging manner that made friends of Brancusi, Arp, Giacometti, and Duchamp in Paris, and Mies and Harry Callahan here in Chicago. Though Jack Kerouac described him as looking like "a submarine commander for Karl Doenitz," Weber was loose and creative—"a sort of blue-green Mephistophelian flame," wrote one student—and unbound by any allegiance to the Bauhaus. Also on the faculty were the painter Emerson Woelffer and photographer Wayne F. Miller, who taught a class in 1948. Miller too became close friends with Callahan: his journalistic approach balanced Callahan's meditative formalism while his method of selecting and mounting his student show was the model for the *Family of Man* show he'd later curate with Edward Steichen, the most-widely seen photography exhibit ever mounted. Chermayeff also brought in Paul Strand, Herbert Bayer, Richard Neutra, and Alvar Aalto for lectures, and to replace Moholy in the role of mad guru and Wizard of Oz, he signed up Buckminster Fuller.

A self-described "comprehensive anticipatory design scientist," Fuller traveled on Spaceship Earth, but in many important ways he'd been launched from Chicago. A descendant of the commander of Fort Dearborn, his mother had watched the Great Fire of 1871. One night back in the 1920s Fuller had had his *satori* moment on the shore of Lake Michigan. His young daughter had just died from polio, and his business was a failure, but as he stood on the rocks considering suicide, he heard this thought in his head: "You do not have the right to eliminate yourself; you do not belong to you. You belong to the universe. Your significance will remain forever obscure to you, but you may assume that you are fulfilling your role if you apply yourself to converting your experience to the highest advantage of others." Fuller stepped back from the edge, then went on to devote himself almost madly to the human race, as a mathematician, architect, and philosopher, with a dash of huckster thrown in; his famous term *dymaxion* in fact was produced by Marshall Field's marketing department.

Chermayeff had hired him at a crucial moment. Earlier in the summer Fuller had tried—and failed—to build a geodesic dome at Josef Albers's Black Mountain College, as a form of self-expression. At the ID, he operated within a new program that examined the concept of "shelter" for the masses. Fuller saw the future of structure in mathematics and computers. Possessed by ideas, his letters ran on for dozens of long-winded, semi-alchemical pages, typed single-spaced, all caps. Sleeping only in small fits, he turned the basement of the ID into "a Merlin's cave" of Ping-Pong balls and geometric models. Like Moholy, he enjoyed hearing his own voice, once to a Homeric extreme, as reported by Ivan Chermayeff, Serge's son, then attending the ID—a full twenty-four hours, pausing only for the occasional bathroom break. An intrigued Mies was known to sit attentively through these marathons.

Jazz, particularly bebop, became the ID's informing spirit. "As a strong component of modern painting," wrote Katharine Kuh, "the phenomenon of jazz should never be minimized." Hugo Weber's paintings combined the whimsy of Klee with Pollock's action, but he described his "Chicago Style" as "jazzy, bumping, grinding and shaking while stripping." To get started at the easel, he'd access his unconscious by giving himself over to a rhythm of swirling sketches. Callahan also claimed jazz as an influence, as did Fuller, who could riff for hours on his ideas, engaged in complex wordplay, and referred to himself as "your bebop representative." "Bucky loved jazz," said Serge. "He could do his little beats and stuff." And so "Bucky and a few chosen students went to night clubs." Bebop had its own secret language, a hermetic knowledge of cool that the white artists and teachers tapped into with little sense of racial connotation.

Bebop had a dark side, though: its connection to the cheap,

high-quality heroin then coursing through Chicago, being used with little knowledge of its dangers and relatively unpoliced. The resulting heroin epidemic resembled the Haight-Ashbury scene in San Francisco two decades later: "In both cases a hip, rather innocent and open drug-using subculture was suddenly converted, into a dangerous, criminally-oriented community." Along with thousands of young black men, heroin claimed Robert Brownjohn, who'd told a fellow student that he had "started getting in trouble, by which [the student thought] he meant heroin abuse, because he was mixing with these gods at the Institute of Design, people like Buckminster Fuller. I remember his saying that he felt very insecure and nervous, out of his depth." Chermayeff brought in the police to help clean up the ID, while Brownjohn, now regularly going into the Black Belt to score, lived in his house; "a wonderful tenant," according to Barbara Chermayeff, who didn't recognize people like Billie Holiday and Charlie Parker when they dropped by. "They would all come over and they were so quiet, and then I realized they were all on drugs!" Serge sent Brownjohn to rehab.

He returned in 1949 to freelance at *Esquire* and *Coronet*, teach briefly at the ID, and through Chermayeff, design the *Chicago Plans* exhibition with the Chicago Plan Commission. Brownjohn then moved to New York, where he extended his drug and jazz friendships to Miles Davis, John Coltrane, and Stan Getz. In the late 1950s he went into business with Ivan Chermayeff and Tom Geismar to form the graphic design agency that would create the logos for Chase, NBC, Mobil, PBS, and MoMA. But Brownjohn never got clean. He moved to Swinging London and burned himself out on King's Road, even as he designed album covers for the Rolling Stones and the credits for James Bond movies; the ones for *To Russia with Love*, projected onto the body of a dancer, are a tribute to Moholy. He died of a heart attack in 1970.

ON MICHIGAN AVENUE, Daniel Catton Rich, director of the Art Institute (AIC), tacked the museum through stormy waters. The Chicago

Symphony Orchestra could stay up to date simply by recording the same musical canon on whatever new technology Bill Putnam, over at Universal, might invent. Rich, on the other hand, had to explain, collect, and promote modern art in a city whose attitudes toward easel painting were conservative to the point of being unhinged. Vandalism at the Art Institute actually rose after World War II—the eyes of a major portrait were gouged out, a Léger was cut, and another painting was spat on, forcing the museum to protect its most important works behind glass. The AIC had tiptoed through the 1930s and 1940s, supporting black painters and buying as much modern art as it could without stirring up the bees in the antiquated bonnets of Mrs. Logan and Sanity in Art. It couldn't afford to shock or, like MoMA, present modern art as a fait accompli; it had to be more subtle. Al Benson, Baldwin Kingrey, and Hutchins and Adler had all proved that selling taste worked better than issuing style diktats, so rather than shame Chicagoans into accepting modern art, Rich brought in Katharine Kuh to sell them on it. Together they'd become the Tracy and Hepburn of modern American art, down to the long-running, secret affair; Rich the taciturn, warmhearted establishment man and Kuh his spirited career-girl protégée.

Kuh's life was shaped by her polio. The daughter of a wealthy Chicago silk merchant, nine-year-old Katharine was diagnosed while traveling in Switzerland. Though she spent her next ten years in a full body cast, her mother, a buck-up, morning-cold-shower type, didn't allow Katharine to brood: at fifteen she went back to high school, then attended Vassar where a class taught by the young Alfred Barr fired her love for art. The cast finally came off while she was studying for her master's at the University of Chicago. She married the much older George Kuh, but instead of settling down, Katharine, on her own two feet at last, soon left him to open Chicago's first modern art gallery, an immediate lightning rod for Sanity in Art. Plugged into both the North and South Side bohemian scenes, possessed of a taste for married men, Kuh befriended Katherine Dunham, unsuccessfully pursued Horace Cayton, and rebuffed a clumsy proposition from Nelson Algren, until she fell into a long-running affair with Guatemalan painter Carlos Mérida. She became fast friends with both Mies and Moholy when they arrived (though it was Mies on whom she had the unrequited crush).

In 1943 Kuh accepted Rich's challenge to remake the AIC's Gallery of Art Interpretation. In return for her permission to smoke in the museum, Mies designed Kuh a small, elegant gallery where she would expand the role of the museum as an art educator and tastemaker. Her methods, though, were all Moholy, a "marvelous teacher," in her mind, even if she and Rich had shrugged at his paintings. Rather than discuss symbols and meanings and history, she followed Moholy's edict to simplify and demystify art in order to make it more accessible. So instead of relying on blocks of explanatory text, her exhibits—such as *From Nature to Art* and *How Real Is Realism?*—showed the play of light and shadow on a sculpture or the deceptions involved in realism. As much as possible, she wanted the viewer to *experience* things as visual realities rather than know them as abstract concepts. The shows were up front about appealing to a middlebrow market, affecting the same tone of corporate expertise found in those other intellectual class markers produced in Chicago: the *World Book Encyclopedia*, the *Encyclopaedia Britannica*, and the coming Great Books series.

Kuh's work not only set the standard for museum education, it heightened the value of the Art Institute's collection and laid the foundation for more challenging shows to come. In late 1947, alongside the Moholy retrospective, Kuh ran *Explaining Abstract Art* as a lead-up to the museum's groundbreaking *Abstract and Surrealist American Art* show. Painter William Baziotes won the $1,000 first prize for *Cyclops*, a work that bridges a divergence: some call it Abstract Expressionist (and the prize the first major award won by an Abstract Expressionist), while Peter Selz ties it to the mythic surrealism of the period's Chicago painters. Either way, President Truman called Kuh's show "the vaporings of half-baked, lazy people" and conservative congressmen accused Rich of Communism. The New

York School may have been producing the most important modern art, but Kuh (with Rich providing cover) was trying to bring it to the masses.

In June 1948 the collectors and art patrons Walter and Louise Arensberg accepted the AIC's offer for Kuh to catalog their unmatched collection of modern art, which included the core works of Marcel Duchamp. Kuh worked for months in Beverly Hills with the erratic Arensbergs and their adviser Duchamp, until she at last secured a coup: their consent for the first public showing of their collection, to be held in the fall of 1949 at the AIC—the first step toward making Chicago its permanent home.

Ironically, the city's young artists were just then feeling stifled by the museum. In 1947, at the AIC's annual exhibition by artists of Chicago and vicinity, students from the School of the Art Institute (SAIC) had won most of the prizes (and money), with modernist works far superior to the rest of the field sent in by local artists. Caving to pressure from trustees and the press, Rich banned the SAIC undergraduates from entering the 1948 show, a decision that united them with the ID students, who up till now had tended to operate in separate worlds. Where the ID students still saw themselves as Moholy's universal designers—theoretical, disciplined, and focused on social responsibility—the SAIC fed Chicago's commercial art community with graduates such as LeRoy Neiman, Robert Indiana, and Claes Oldenburg and just then a handful of passionate fine artists led by Leon Golub and Nancy Spero. Students at both schools, many of them war veterans and just as eager to move ahead in their careers as the architects at IIT, resented the ban and signed a protest written by the voluble Golub (once the arts and crafts teacher at Ner Tamid Hebrew School under Herb Greenwald).

Rich remained firm, though, and so the renegades created the Exhibition Momentum. Open to all, it would run annually for the next four years at various venues with judges that included Robert Motherwell, Pollock, and Alfred Barr, as well as Josef Albers and Clement Greenberg. Some Chicago artists caught a patronizing whiff off the visitors, but if anything the feeling was mutual—before the Internet and television, the visual arts spread slowly; according to Golub, no one in Chicago had ever seen a painting by Jackson Pollock before 1947, and when they did, they weren't impressed. Left cold by the alienation that informed Abstract Expressionism, Chicago's painters favored a figurative, cerebral surrealism influenced by the Freudian psychologist Franz Alexander, hours spent at the Field Museum and the Art Institute looking at works by James Ensor, Bosch, Munch, and Goya, and a belief that art still had a purpose.

"Chicago art is not naive," wrote Franz Schulze, "but it is fiercely, resolutely hermetic." While he was referring to its art scene as a whole, no single artist was more hermetic than a middle-aged dishwasher living on the second floor of 851 W. Webster, known for digging magazines out of trash cans on his way back from work at Alexian Brothers Hospital. It's unknown where exactly Henry Darger was at this point in the progress of his masterwork, *In the Realm of the Unreal* or *The Story of the Vivian Girls in What Is Known as the Realms of the Unreal, of the Glandeco-Angelinian War Storm, Caused by the Child-Slave Rebellion*. Its fifteen-thousand-page manuscript and hundreds of massive illustrations combine to tell the story of a planet dominated by Glandelinia, an empire of adults that keeps children as slaves. While the narrative is remarkable if nothing else for its length, the illustrations, measuring two feet high and as wide as ten feet, are overwhelming, unsettling, and absurdly beautiful pastiches. Darger culled thousands of images from newspapers and magazines, then arranged and painted them with watercolors in tableaux of medieval complexity to depict scenes from the war—battles, massacres, celebrations, heroic escapes and rescues, concentration camps, and flower gardens; Moholy's photocollage and manipulation of media taken to an extreme. The subjects in most cases are little girls, often naked, some hermaphrodites, in moments of high peril, down to scenes of butchery such as mass hangings from trees. Once the viewer absorbs the shock and registers that Darger's interest isn't prurient, the beauty of his work bursts forth in all its glorious color and intricacy.

Henry Darger was not a healthy man. When he was a young boy, his mother died and his infant sister was given up for adoption, a double loss he never recovered from. When he was twelve, his father was put into an old-age home, forcing Henry, bright enough to have skipped two grades in school, into a Dickensian orphanage where something slipped inside; intermittently violent, he was sent to an asylum for the "feeble-minded" in downstate Illinois to suffer through fresh horrors until he ran away at seventeen to Chicago where he worked for the next sixty or so years at menial jobs, attending mass three or four times a day, then at night holing up in his apartment in Lincoln Park to compulsively create his art. He saw it all as illustrations for his epic fiction, *à la* W. W. Denslow's illustrations for the Oz series he loved so much; but the images took on a life of their own, addressing his emotional issues at the same time as he consciously explored his abilities and limitations as an artist. *In the Realm of the Unreal* combines his many interests, all intricate worlds unto themselves—the Oz books (written not far from Darger's apartment), the Civil War, and Charles Dickens—along with his sense of loss and memories of abuse. Rather than inflicting his pain or anger on others, he named his demons in this alternate universe and enlisted female innocence to help fight them.

In keeping with the mood in Chicago, Darger improvised and invented. Since he couldn't render, he collected cartoon and advertising images in folders and traced them as needed into his tableaux, long before Lichtenstein or any Pop artists. During the war he began having images resized by a photo developer, which let him suddenly create perspective and depth. Nature in Darger's world is lush, bizarre, and fantastic, thrumming with his tensions, the currents of subsumed sexuality, and a child's visceral experience of the world's terrors. Without knowing it, he was producing work that fit right into the mainstream of Chicago art.

Today Henry Darger is considered arguably the greatest "outsider" artist. His fame and influence outstrip that of all his trained Chicago contemporaries, save for possibly Golub. Most of his work is held in New York's American Folk Art Museum, the subject of much scholarship but also public curiosity, far ahead of its time for its gender ambiguity and feminist air.

. . .

ROBERT MAYNARD HUTCHINS, meanwhile, chose alienation. One spring evening in 1947, he ended his captivity to Maude by simply packing a bag and walking out the door of the chancellor's mansion, never to speak to her again. That this would have a thunderous impact on his children was never considered, and in the end not surprising for a man who, according to a friend, "felt that he had to have time for every student who wanted to see him—with three exceptions: his daughters." The settlement added up to some $30,000 a year, putting Hutchins forever at the mercy of his old friend William Benton for creative ways to meet an annual nut that allowed Maude to at last pursue her career as a sculptor and writer of literary erotica.

Hutchins had transitioned into the honorary position of chancellor to devote more time to the cause of one world government and nuclear activism, but now he took a year's leave of absence to concentrate on his new job as chairman of the board of the Great Books Foundation. Though the board had chosen the 443 books and 74 authors back in 1944, work on the series had ground to a crawl and the $60,000 originally budgeted for the project was now well on its way to its final tally of nearly $1 million, in large part because of Mortimer Adler's Syntopicon. Hutchins had given over an entire three-story building, known as Index House, to the massive task of cross-referencing everything the 443 books had to say about 102 topics. Since the value of the Great Books was their ability to make you look smart just by owning them, the Syntopicon—called "superficially awesome" by one later critic—had sounded ideal to Benton, but the planned two volumes were sucking everyone's time and Benton's money into their swirl, as fifty readers (including the young Saul Bellow) and a staff of seventy-five created millions of index cards.

The Syntopicon (really a Web site waiting for the Internet) was bankrupting *Encyclopaedia Britannica,* whose receipts were plummeting as inflation-strapped consumers paid other bills. Salesmen hawked it so hard that the Federal Trade Commission reprimanded the company. When

Benton warned Hutchins that he was about to pull the plug on Adler, one of Hutchins's Fat Men found enough money somewhere between the sofa cushions to keep things going. Meanwhile the Great Books Foundation, with Walter Paepcke as vice president and Pussy on the board, continued its somewhat more altruistic work of training volunteers. Hutchins predicted there'd be 15 million Great Bookies by the early 1950s; a television show was in the works; and in September 1948, Mayor Kennelly gave the city over for a Great Books Week that climaxed with Hutchins and Adler leading a discussion from the stage of Orchestra Hall. And so at a moment when the Chicago public school system was deaccredited and so strapped for money that many children had classes only half a day in metal trailers, the Great Books movement rolled on. When it came to education, the Fat Men had their priorities.

With Moholy gone, Paepcke diverted more of his energies to Hutchins and brought him along in his schemes. For one, the Paepckes had been methodically buying up an old mining town in the Colorado Rockies called Aspen. The area had inspired development plans since the late 1930s, when skiing arrived in the States, but the war had scotched them until the Paepckes began encouraging friends to buy as well. Millions of Chicago dollars poured into Aspen, whether those living there liked it or not. Hutchins came up with an idea for a festival celebrating the two hundredth birthday of Goethe, a program of music and lectures that would bring together all the great minds of the age, promote Aspen, and reintroduce Germany to the community of nations. Paepcke and Hutchins (by now preparing to wed his fetching and most wonderfully named secretary Vesta Sutton Orlick) scheduled it for the summer of 1949 and immediately began selling Goethe to the world.

Hyde Park, though, suffered from the inattention of its chancellor. Crime soared, robbery and rape became so common that students and faculty traveled in packs, though Hutchins liked to point out that teenagers in the Middle Ages went on pilgrimages alone across Europe. Admissions fell. Wright's Robie House sank into disrepair. Like Hutchins, the university and in particular the college, beaming with intellectual energy, removed themselves from the surrounding city. The veterans like Kurt Vonnegut who'd enrolled immediately after the war had helped even out the "intellectual pride and emotional immaturity" of the sixteen- and seventeen-year-olds, but as they graduated, the college turned in on itself. Little about its course of study encouraged engagement with the world. Extracurriculars were left to the students; the school pulled entirely out of the Big Ten in 1946, and after his breakup with Maude, art in general repelled Hutchins. Intrepid sorts like Robert Silvers participated in the city, but those arriving in the postwar era tended to make their own fun within a closed, idiosyncratic, and extremely verbal culture, a never-never land for maladjusted teenage geniuses. While this sparring forged many great and nimble minds, others developed the ability to, for lack of a better word, bullshit. In a place where defending and attacking ideas was honored more than analyzing them, those who could talk the longest and the loudest succeeded.

Hyde Park's bohemianism became more pronounced; interracial, coed cooperative apartment buildings formed. Wrote anthropologist Sally Binford, "My father would visit and say 'How can you stand to live surrounded by communists, faggots, and niggers?' I would say, 'But I like communists, faggots, and niggers.' " The neighborhood hosted the city's most extreme salon, run by painter Gertrude Abercrombie, an ungainly friend of James Purdy, collected by Dizzy Gillespie, who claimed her as *the* bop visual artist. Though that hints at colorful canvases slashed Pollock-style with jagged lines, the reality is dreamy and figurative, closer to the mood of heroin, only one of the vices available at her crash pad on Dorchester Avenue. Trumpeter Clifford Brown named the song "Gertrude's Bounce" for her, and the entire Modern Jazz Quartet lived there for a year. Towertown may have been Greenwich Village, but Gertrude Abercrombie's house was the Lower East Side.

CHAPTER 12

THE BALANCE
OF POWER

SMOKE AND SOOT swirled through the platform of LaSalle Street Station. A redcap whistling "Move On Up a Little Higher," just out that week of December 1947, pushed a luggage cart through mohair coats and the scent of Arpège. The bell rang. The Twilight Limited had left for Detroit ten minutes ago, and now, down at the end, just visible in the dusk, the brand-new diesel engine of the 20th Century Limited faced out into the cold, ready for another sixteen-hour run to New York. The through cars from Los Angeles had been linked in, packages from the layover afternoon spent at Marshall Field's loaded aboard. A few coast-to-coast runs had started in 1946, over Chicago's objections, but most travelers still preferred their quick visit to the Loop. The train's manicurists and barbers, not busy until the morning, hung to the sides while chefs and waiters prepped dinner. Though its famous Deco steam engine had been retired, the 20th Century remained the train of Chicago power, timed to allow starlets a PR appearance at the Pump Room and a morning arrival that let businessmen walk straight into a boardroom just as trading began.

The train pulled out. Nestled into the club car, Jake Arvey placed his order for a Century Steak dinner with Tommy the steward, then flipped through the *Daily News* as they rolled south. He liked riding the 20th Century; he liked sitting in the biggest chair in the smoke-filled rooms.

But the world had changed, and the 1948 slate would have to show it; for one, like a lot of Democrats, he wanted Truman out and Eisenhower at the top of the ticket. Eisenhower wasn't just a veteran—he was *the* veteran, at a time when veterans could do no wrong. Plus, Arvey had a Senate seat and the governor's mansion to fill.

As Indiana flashed by, a familiar face plunked down beside him. "I'd like to talk to you about Adlai Stevenson," said Dutch Smith, a big insurance man who joined the long line of people talking up this Stevenson: Secretary of State Jimmy Byrnes, Ferd Kramer, and Nat Owings, whose firm Skidmore, Owings & Merrill was landing huge government contracts. Smith made his case—Adlai was a New Deal Democrat with Republican-style money, experience in foreign affairs, and a good name from his war work. Arvey stopped him. "A fellow was telling me the other day," he said, "I'd better lay off Stevenson, that he went to Oxford." Smith assured him that wasn't true, but promised to verify it with the man himself, and the two made a date for dinner on their return ride on Thursday. "Never went to Oxford not even to Eton," Stevenson wired to Smith, who relayed the news as they headed back.

Arvey agreed to visit Stevenson that Sunday in Lake Forest. The 20th Century pulled into Chicago the next morning on time as always, at eight-thirty. A new chapter in Democratic liberalism had begun.

ADLAI EWING STEVENSON grew up in the town of Bloomington, some 125 miles southwest of Jacob Arvey's boyhood tenement. On the surface he was as rich and regular as the corn that covers most of Illinois outside Chicago, numbing empty miles of even growth and horizons that never come closer. Amid this land of Ambersons and *American Gothic*, the Stevensons were WASP royalty, land rich and political on both sides—Whigs-turned-Republicans on his mother's and Democrats on his father's, to the extent that Grandfather Adlai had been Grover Cleveland's second vice president. His father, Lewis, was a dabbler out of a comic novel, full of schemes for health cereals *à la* C.W. Post, franchised opera houses, and Zeppelin publicity, yet he managed to end up Illinois secretary of state. Raised to have few cares, young Adlai saved his serious attention for matters such as The Hunt. The family traveled a good deal, often for no particular reason, haunting exclusive enclaves in Michigan, dude ranches out West, where Adlai had met Pussy Nitze and the rest of Chicago society. When it came time for college, he would go to Princeton, of course, but not before failing the entrance exam three times, thus forcing a few remedial semesters at Choate. Clubbable, sporting but not *too*, possessed of a crafty tennis game, soft eyes, a ready wit, and great taste for the ladies, "Rabbit" did only enough to graduate; the Ivy League version of Algren's "regular."

Many aspects of Adlai Stevenson were unexpected, though, in some cases even shocking; for example the fact that he had shot his cousin Ruth Merwin dead with a rifle when he was twelve. By all accounts it was a horrible accident, but some blamed it for the Hamlet-like indecision that he would display throughout his political life, usually to his own detriment. His politics were also unusual. Once ensconced in a white-shoe law firm, Stevenson charmed his way into the Gold Coast and Lake Forest scenes, where he married Ellen Borden, a shrill sort of girl, almost beautiful, from the core of Society. Instead of following his friends like the Paepckes into quiet conservative exile during the Depression, though, Adlai threw in with Roosevelt, a heresy so inexplicable in his circles that they indulged him with an affectionate pity, as if he'd been born with a sad deformity. Post-law-school travels as a reporter had given him a global perspective rare in the isolationist Midwest, which brought him to the Council on Foreign Relations. He worked in the Roosevelt administration and tried without success to break into the Cook County Regular Democrats. In 1944 he tested party leaders about running for governor but ended up at the State Department instead, where he was involved in the formation of the United Nations. As early as January 1947, he'd looked into the Illinois Senate race. So this meeting with Arvey was the culmination of a long road toward electoral politics.

And yet Adlai wasn't home when Arvey came to call. He was out playing tennis, according to Ellen, so the boss spent a while chatting with his brittle and extremely unhappy wife, who, like Maude Hutchins, failed to understand how her husband could be bothered with such trifling concerns as running the state of Illinois when she needed his full attention. Whether as a matter of gamesmanship or a patrician belief that "people like us" didn't chase after jobs, Stevenson at last walked into his living room in his tennis whites late for a meeting he'd been desperately chasing for months. Arvey was impressed despite the insult. He offered him the state on the same terms he'd given Chicago to Kennelly: cabinet and staff would be his, but the party would expect a say-so when it came to patronage. Stevenson flopped back and forth until the morning of the slating meeting, December 30, 1947, when he finally accepted. That night Ellen descended the stairs in a ballgown, greeted Adlai and two friends with a poem she'd just written, and never mentioned once that her husband was running for governor.

Ellen Stevenson wasn't the only person with reservations. The boys at the Morrison Hotel weren't sold on Adlai's Gold Coast digs, the horse farm in Libertyville, his friendships with Republican swells like Jinx Falkenburg. Machine bosses like Paddy Bauler and Vito Marzullo had come up the dirty way and now here was Stevenson in his velvet knickers asking to join the toughest gang in the schoolyard. Arvey, as the brains of the operation, had to continually vouch for the new guy, along with Dick Daley, one of the first members of Adlai's committee; he was just then assembling his own base in the Eleventh Ward. On the stump, party handlers helped Stevenson capitalize on his warm sense of humor and very attractive willingness to make fun of himself; that his bedside reading wasn't Plato but the Social Register (and he sometimes moved his lips while he read it) let him connect to everyday voters in a Reagan-esque way, and his platitudes played well against the fear-mongering of the red-baiters and Dixiecrats. He refused to join the Americans for Democratic Action, the liberal anti-Communist group of Eleanor Roosevelt, Reinhold Niebuhr, and Hubert Humphrey, even though he agreed with their platform; that lack of precision and commitment let him slip around critics. Adlai was doing his part at a bad time. Henry Wallace's collapsing campaign could still draw away enough votes to hurt Truman, as could Strom Thurmond and the Dixie-crats, sending Jake Arvey back to his first solution: Draft Ike. He approached the general about running as a Democrat, and hopes rose briefly when the Republicans nominated New York governor Thomas E. Dewey, but on July 5, Ike officially announced he wasn't a Democrat. Arvey and the entire Chicago Machine now had to kiss and make up with Truman.

Through the summer and fall of 1948, as Buckminster Fuller puzzled over his geodesic dome, Preston Tucker made cars in his massive factory on Cicero Avenue, Algren bore down on his masterpiece, and "I Can't Be Satisfied" played on the streets of the West Side, Arvey and the Machine pulled out all the stops for the president, capped with a gala dinner at the Blackstone Hotel, fireworks, then a parade down Madison Street, lined with 250,000 Chicagoans (their signs included the less-than-inspiring BETTER SAFE THAN SORRY), leading to a monster rally at Chicago Stadium, where Truman delivered a fiery speech condemning "the crackpot forces of the extreme right wing." Whether or not they loved him, the Machine had delivered, though Kennelly, typically misguided, was convinced Truman would lose; Arvey had to cajole him into introducing the president.

The tide had begun to turn at another huge rally in Chicago back in June that had featured Bill Dawson and his friend Mahalia Jackson who, breaking big just then with her records, signed on to campaign for Truman in Ohio, Missouri, and Indiana, plus a constant push in Chicago. While most black intellectuals lined up behind Henry Wallace, Truman had let himself be prodded into forming the Committee on Civil Rights, and a month before the rally, the *Shelley v. Kraemer* decision against restrictive covenants had come down. By throwing in for Truman just before the convention, Walter White and the NAACP essentially unhitched the van of African American civil rights from the cause of anticolonialism and Pan-Africanism; the price of domestic change was surrendering global idealism. In return, Hubert Humphrey battled for the first inclusion of a civil rights plank in the Democratic platform.

"If we've got Illinois," said Truman on election night, "we've got the election." Early in the evening, Arvey called campaign director Howard

McGrath. "I think it'll go our way," said Arvey. "If the edge is that close, the margin can come from the city wards here in Cook County." Though Stevenson demolished his Republican gubernatorial opponent Dwight Green by some 500,000 votes, Truman won Illinois by only 33,612: a difference likely from Bill Dawson's Second and Third Wards, which delivered a plurality of more than 50,000. For better and for worse, the path of modern African American activism had been determined, and the New Deal Left would have to gather under Truman if it wanted to stay out of the rain.

The victories by Stevenson and Arvey's Senate candidate, Paul Douglas, along with Truman's come-from-behind hold made Arvey look like a genius. One of the governor's first appointments in January 1949 was Richard J. Daley as state director of revenue.

MARTIN KENNELLY HAD risen up from earning two dollars a week working at Marshall Field's to owning a moving-van company that ironically profited from all the whites heading out to the suburbs; that and the fact that he wasn't a lifelong politician summed up his qualifications to be mayor of Chicago. Promising to work hard and bring his business acumen to City Hall, the city's new bachelor uncle had a pleasant enough honeymoon with Chicagoans tired from fourteen years of Ed Kelly's corrupt inertia. With the SSPB writing his script, Kennelly rammed through the laws and bond acts necessary to set the Opportunity Plan into motion. The main opposition to development at this point didn't come from the black community but from the aldermen who were in bed with the corrupt, absentee, and often Mob-connected property owners in the slums slated for clearance.

To push the cause, Kennelly hired architect Nate Owings from Skidmore, Owings & Merrill (SOM) to run the Chicago Plan Commission. So began an intimate relation between the city and SOM; over the next ten years, it would become the nation's biggest architectural firm. Owings went forth to sell a new Chicago Plan and a view of the city that balanced commerce, industry, and housing. For all his sincerity and passion, however, the only real motivation for change would be what it always is: money. There'd be more than enough of it for everyone if both the Opportunity Plan and the CPC's new Chicago Plan with all its expressways went through, a wave of money both public and private, plus side deals involved in eminent domain, demolition, materials, and labor contracts.

Such a massive undertaking, involving dozens of city, county, state, and federal agencies, not to mention the private stakeholders and the residents of the affected areas, called for leadership. Unfortunately, Martin Kennelly was no leader of men. A police captain once told the City Council that "the trouble with Mayor Kennelly is that the only thing he learned in the moving business is never to lift the heavy end." Rather than accept the responsibility of exercising his power, Kennelly washed his hands of anything not explicitly named as one of his duties. Instead of cracking heads in the City Council to advance a program, he allowed the aldermen, soon known as the "Gray Wolves," to take over the chamber and slice up the budget for themselves. Corruption expanded to historic proportions. The one place he found his guts was Black Chicago, where he let schools and other city services slide further downhill. On open housing, he made his interests very clear. As the City Council debated Lake Meadows in March 1948, Alderman Archibald Carey introduced a bill that would "require non-discrimination in all housing built with city funds or on land obtained . . . by the exercise of the city's power of eminent domain." Given that Lake Meadows had been planned as integrated and New York Life had signed a nondiscrimination clause in its deal, this was all largely symbolic, but Mayor Kennelly spoke out publicly against the Carey Ordinance. Meanwhile Cardinal Stritch, worried that Lake Meadows and a new Catholic Mercy Hospital nearby wouldn't get off the ground because of it, worked back channels to be sure the ordinance failed.

The issue of relocation helped the violent sparks around the city merge into a single opposition. Here Kennelly's weakness and racism did lasting damage. By 1948 all the entities of the SSPB were ready to charge ahead: Michael Reese Hospital had already built two of the buildings in its twenty-year plan and was clearing land for more; Lake Meadows was approved and looking for an architect; IIT had more Mies on the drawing board. But the residents of the condemned buildings had nowhere to go, and the Opportunity Plan lacked any comprehensive relocation scheme, even as critics inside and out stressed how important it was to have one. Instead of creating a separate agency to handle relocation from the South Side redevelopment, Kennelly handed the problem to Elizabeth Wood and the CHA, who then had to deal with the various organizations demanding the CHA deal with *their* dispossessed first so they could begin demolition. The CHA didn't have enough units, and the furor over where any new units would go triggered more white resistance and flight—between 1945 and 1949, just over 137,000 private housing units were built in Chicagoland, and 77 percent of those were in the suburbs. The redevelopment program intended to ease the housing shortage actually made it worse.

Although Kennelly had closed his door to the CHA, Elizabeth Wood continued looking for creative solutions to public housing. Some had unintended effects. SOM, for instance, copied the look of Mies's Promontory Apartments for their Ogden Courts project. Given that Promontory was a middle-income apartment building with a lower per-square-foot cost than any public housing in Chicago, it made sense to look at what Mies was doing there; but over time CHA architects would so overuse the concrete frame and dark brick infill of Promontory's back side that it became the signature look of the city's hopeless public housing projects. Young architect Harry Weese at first won praise for the innovative buildingwide balconies he built at Loomis Courts; later critics would identify them as one of public housing's greatest flaws. The CHA and Wood, now hated in the white community, became even more committed to integration and recommended mixed-race low-income housing scattered throughout the city—the city's Commission on Human Relations agreed. But a fully open housing market would require a strategy to keep Chicago from exploding and no one wanted to go near that. The MHPC and the Public Housing Association, run by Saul Alinsky, with sponsorship from the B'nai B'rith, the CYO, and Marshall Field III, could do little but appeal to the better natures of Chicagoans.

So Kennelly fiddled as many of Chicago's neighborhoods burned. In July 1949 Congress passed the Federal Housing Act, a law based on Chicago's, that provided funding for public housing. Immediately thereafter the CHA submitted a plan to the City Council for 40,000 new units, the closest thing to an overall plan for integration that Chicago would ever have. Days later at 71st and St. Lawrence, a few blocks from St. Columbanus, whites threw Molotov cocktails and railroad flares into the home of Roscoe and Ethel Johnson; 350 policemen were needed to keep the peace. A parish priest was escorted through the mob to visit Mrs. Johnson, who'd attended mass there once under guard. Unlike Kelly, who had at least bothered to appear the mayor of all Chicagoans, Kennelly said nothing.

In October the CHA submitted to Mayor Kennelly the sites for the first 10,000 units, with priority given to those displaced by Lake Meadows. The selected sites were superblocks, some in vacant spots on the city's fringes (where whites had already moved once to escape blacks), the rest in built-up black areas. The CHA hoped Mayor Kennelly would act as a go-between with the City Council, but for three weeks it heard nothing. When finally pressed, the mayor claimed he'd lost the plan on his desk, and anyhow it wasn't his place to take a position. By now the sites had leaked to the press, causing hell to break loose in white neighborhoods. Cutting any pragmatic, backroom deal was now out of the question—the aldermen felt the CHA had sandbagged them. They'd now have to play this out as theater for their white constituents, while the CHA couldn't afford to publicly back down. The plan was officially given to the council in November, and public hearings scheduled for February 1950. The mayor, meanwhile, professed to be powerless on an issue that would scar Chicago forever.

As all this was happening in City Hall, rumors spread on the South Side that blacks were moving in within two blocks of another major parish, Visitation, in Englewood. Thousands of whites took to the streets in gangs around 56th and Peoria, tipping cars and asking strangers what parish they were from before deciding whether to beat them. On the eighth, another mob threatened a six-flat just sold to a Mr. Edward Blanks.

White Catholics threw bricks and firebombs into black homes, sneaked their children under police barricades to break windows. That same night a small interracial group in Hyde Park, mostly Jews and Quakers, formed the Hyde Park–Kenwood Community Conference, to address the changing racial balance in their neighborhood with something other than Molotov cocktails or flight. If there was a way for blacks and whites to live together in Chicago, Hyde Park seemed to be the place to figure it out.

CHAPTER 13

THIS PROGRAM CAME
TO YOU FROM CHICAGO

AT EIGHT P.M. on January 12, 1949, a small clown puppet popped his head, only slightly larger than a tennis ball, over the edge of a stage on the nineteenth floor of the Merchandise Mart. More quickly than the Internet fifty years later, television was about to utterly transform American society. Already ads for fifty-two-square-inch GE Daylight televisions (its screen slightly smaller than an iPad) at $325 and Philco consoles at $599 muscled aside news of Truman's budget, loaded with new taxes to pay for a national health insurance plan. Already almost 81 percent of Americans with TVs went to the movies less often and 59 percent read fewer books. Two days earlier Adlai Stevenson, a lookalike for this puppet with his bald pate and tonsure, had announced the cultural shift in his inaugural address. "The world," said the new governor in a Springfield drizzle, was settling down "to a long trial of strength between individualism and collectivism." The night before, the coaxial cable between the East Coast and the midwestern television networks had been connected, plugging millions of individuals between the Atlantic and the Mississippi into a uniform national culture. In this puppet Kukla, his dragon friend Ollie, and their "big sister and girl friend" Fran Allison, America met one of the paths that culture could take, a style of television unique to Chicago that defined the technical grammar of the medium and explored its possibilities in ways done nowhere else. "Chicago . . . was an extraordinary, vital, exciting time for television," Mike Wallace said. "This was the birth of television."

Radio had really been just a dry run, an opportunity to test production, sales, and distribution models while engineers hammered out television's scientific details. As the networks had grown, Chicago's location made it the natural center of production. The soap opera was invented here and the cavernous NBC studios, in the top floors of the Merchandise Mart, sent *Amos 'n' Andy, Ma Perkins,* and *Fibber McGee and Molly* across America, while WLS popularized country music—WSM's *Grand Ole Opry* copied WLS's *Barn Dance.*

In 1939, with maybe a dozen television sets in all of Chicagoland, former submarine captain Bill Eddy took over W9XBK, an experimental television station owned by the Balaban and Katz movie theater chain. Six foot seven, Captain Eddy was a natural inventor, credited with developing television lighting and the basic rules of filming baseball. Entirely deaf, he'd sometimes switch off his hearing aids during meetings and rely on a pipe he'd made that transmitted sound waves through his teeth. There were no rules or schedules—TV owners would call the station and ask them to turn on the transmitter for the daily hour or so of free-form content that passed for programming. All this changed after the war. Like the early days of Silicon Valley, techies with an entrepreneurial spirit now came to television, along with actors, writers, and theater students who saw its potential. Northwestern doctoral candidate Bob Banner, for instance, interned at WBKB, as Eddy's station was renamed when it became the city's first commercial station in 1945. Radio announcers such as Hugh Downs moonlighted; Mike Wallace was positive that his acne scars would keep him off camera. Small, low-rent dramas, amateur musicians, and stiff instructional shows made up the content.

The only serious draw was sports—in early 1947 WBKB admitted to *Time* that two-thirds of its viewership came from the 250 Chicago bars that had bought TVs for hockey, baseball, and Notre Dame football. Bar business wasn't good enough, though, for the businessmen behind television, like GE's General David Sarnoff, who'd done their projections based on selling sets. Millions of dollars had been plunged into the experiment with little return so far. In Chicago, an executive from RCA Victor went to Bill Eddy with the problem: they needed programming that would convince individuals to buy televisions. Eddy called a young puppeteer named Burr Tillstrom.

Tillstrom had staged his first puppet show at the age of five, a scene with two teddy bears performed out a window for the kids in surrounding Rogers Park. Encouraged by his parents, Burr played with dolls, read the Oz books, and made puppets all through grammar school, finally going "professional" at fourteen with a sell-out run of two shows, ten cents a ticket, held down the street in Mrs. Polak's garden. He studied drama at Senn High School and earned a scholarship to the University of Chicago, but the summer he graduated, he joined a WPA unit, putting on marionette shows throughout the city at beaches, hospitals, and nursing homes. Not only did he cut his teeth as a performer, he saw the positive impact that puppetry had on his often beaten-down audiences. After one semester of college, he and his puppets rejoined the WPA.

That year, 1936, a friend asked Burr to design him a puppet. What he came up with—a clown with a red felt body, round head, bulb nose and eyebrows arched in some mixture of consternation and surprise—turned out to be more personal than he'd planned; Burr kept it and pulled it out at random moments with friends, letting this snarky but good-natured clown with a falsetto voice say what he couldn't. When the Ballet Russe came to town, Burr sneaked backstage to hover near his then-idol Tamara Toumanova. Too shy to speak, he produced the puppet—"Ah, Kukla!" said the dancer, *kukla* being Russian for "doll." Thus was the cornerstone of Burr's creative universe set. By 1939 his troupe consisted of Kukla; Madame Ooglepuss, a Margaret Dumont character; Ollie, a blustering one-toothed graduate of Dragon Prep; a difficult little girl puppet named Mercedes; and Bill, who only spoke gibberish. RCA Victor broadcast the Kuklapolitans, as they were now known, throughout Marshall Field's via closed-circuit TV, beginning a long relationship with RCA that would include demonstrating television at the 1939 New York World's Fair. During the war Burr brought the Kuklapolitans to USOs and hospitals, crafting his show to appeal to injured GIs as much as children. Captain Eddy put him on W9XBK a few times, and it was those shows that the lanky station manager remembered when RCA Victor asked for help.

Eddy was giving Burr an hour a day, a great yawning gap of time. To help him fill it, he'd need an interlocutor figure between the real world and the fantasy of the Kuklapolitans, "the Alice who wanders through Wonderland," he once said, "the Dorothy who goes to Oz." Fran Allison, a broad-shouldered ex-teacher from Iowa who did a daily gossipy comedy bit on *The Breakfast Club* radio show. was curious for a look at television, so she came aboard. True to his WPA roots, Burr always improvised, and "the kids," as he called the Kuklapolitans, seemed comfortable with Fran, who was sharp and well read, motherly to children, nonthreatening to mothers, and if not exactly a knockout, then at least easy on the dads' eyes. Their rapport developed quickly as they ad-libbed their way through that first week of *Junior Jamboree,* though Burr still suspected that Fran hadn't accepted the puppets quite yet as people, so one afternoon, with no one else around but her, Kukla and Ollie began a long, provocative discussion about women that she listened to until she dove into the conversation full bore, losing sight of who she was arguing with. The ground rules were established: The world of the Kuklapolitans was entirely true; the kids existed as living beings, and anyone who voided that compact was off the show.

The response was immediate. "In less than a week," the *Tribune* reported, Ollie had "become a fast friend of many Chicago youngsters." A year later Mrs. George Levison told the *Tribune* that the television was "just about the best investment we've ever made," especially when it came to her three-year-old daughter Carole. "When *Junior Jamboree* is on," said Mrs. Levison, "I can just forget about her for an hour for she sits perfectly quiet, absorbed in Kukla, Fran and Ollie." The accompanying photo of Carole's blank face, eyes glued to the screen, makes a reader today slump; she may as well have a Camel going in the ashtray, too. But Mrs. Levison can be forgiven because all through 1948, Burr and Fran constructed a wise and innocent world, bristling with the energy of the unexpected, and that ached a little, too: Ollie's childhood in Dragon's Retreat, Vermont, and the whistling act he once did at Chautauqua; Fletcher Rabbit's suffragette mother; and Madame Ooglepuss's Olympic medal in the decathlon.

Wherever Burr and Fran went the night before provided the starting point for a half-hour that rarely stumbled, sometimes rambled, but most often glowed with an elegiac warmth. Composer and pianist Jack Fascinato added songs—usually brief, wistful numbers—interspersed with short movies and, yes, the occasional animal visitor, including a most memorable one from Dr. Marlin Perkins, then head of the Lincoln Park Zoo. Though his guest, a skittish baby skunk named Sweet William, had seen Kukla in rehearsal, Ollie's appearance a few seconds into the segment sent him into a panic, and he bit Perkins. As Fran dashed offstage for a bandage, Sweet William bit Perkins again, then began shooting feces and musk across the room, while Perkins continued to bleed heavily. The camera shook with laughter and finally went blank. When the show came back on, there was Kukla with a little mop. He turned to the camera and said, "It happens in the best of families."

Though *Junior Jamboree* aired only in Chicago, NBC noticed that WBKB sent the monthly *Kuklapolitan Courier* out to 22,000 homes. With the coaxial cable ready to connect all viewers east of the Mississippi, NBC lured Burr with a five-year, $1 million contract, and on January 12, 1949, *Kukla, Fran and Ollie* made its debut to the East Coast. Much of the staff at WNBQ was embarrassed to have what they considered a high-end Punch and Judy show in their lineup, especially Bob Banner. Made the show's stage manager against his will, he walked into his first meeting shocked to find that three hours before they went on air, Burr and Fran had no plot, no lines, no story. Burr asked Banner what he'd done in the last couple days; Banner said he'd seen *La Bohème.*

"Great," said Burr. "Let's do a parody of *La Bohème!*"

Doing his best to be patronizing, Banner offered to run down to the music library for the score, but no one was paying attention to him. Jack had already launched into the overture while Fran suggested she sing

Mimi's aria from the second act. Three hours later the show aired live; subtle, funny, and geared to a wide audience. Banner was suddenly proud to be putting on a puppet show.

Within two weeks, *Kukla, Fran and Ollie* was a phenomenon, an oasis on the dial between Milton Berle lumbering across stage and *Howdy Doody,* a show for "moron kids," according to one of *Kukla's* cameramen. Even though *Time* found *Kukla, Fran and Ollie* "mildly irritating," it had to fess to its "odd, narcotic pull" and "ephemeral sadness." Subscriptions to the *Courier* rose to more than 200,000, and everyone from Orson Welles and John Steinbeck to James Thurber (who credited Burr with "helping to save the sanity of the nation and improve, if not even to invent, the quality of television") publicly expressed their love for the show. Like *Pee-wee's Playhouse* and *The Muppet Show* in years to come, *Kukla, Fran and Ollie* didn't just appeal to the whole family; it appealed to its best self. By March there were an estimated 1.2 million televisions in American homes. They weren't all bought to watch Kukla and Ollie—*Howdy Doody* got better ratings, and so did *Lucky Pup*—but the show went a long way toward legitimizing the medium.

Burr enforced strict rules in order to maintain the show's reality. Though big stars on their layovers filled the seats of Studio A, no one was ever allowed backstage, where Burr, in a T-shirt, watched the show on a monitor as he switched back and forth between characters. Fran avoided ever seeing the kids hanging on their hooks, and only three people could ever touch them: director Lewis "Gommie" Gomavitz, Burr, and his assistant, costume designer and interior decorator Joe Lockwood (or "Monsieur Josef" as Burr called him). A new announcer who referred to Ollie as "an alligator" was fired on the spot. But it wasn't the fantasy that made Burr's world so influential and beloved; it was that on screen and off he created a particular sort of community, one way ahead of its time. By all accounts generous and genuine, Burr had built a protected place; for Fran, whose face was the product of reconstructive surgery after a terrible car crash and a miscarriage; and for his own homosexuality. (Marriage, Burr told an interviewer, would come as "a very noisy surprise.") The production team was as close as the Kuklapolitans; they lived near each other, vacationed and celebrated holidays together. But what neither the staff nor the kids were was a nuclear family. With the 1950s suburban idyll about to swamp America, along with a new medium that was going to not only keep families like the Levisons in their homes but reinforce a certain idea of how those families should look, here were a clown, a dragon, a witch, a dowager, a gardening rabbit, and more, all learning to live with each other on the most accepting terms, wrapped in an atmosphere of "ephemeral sadness." Watched today, *Kukla, Fran and Ollie* is a model of the gay, urban experience.

IT WAS ALSO the first example of the Chicago School of Television, nurtured and spread largely by two men, WNBQ station manager Jules Herbuveaux and producer Ted Mills. Suave and well connected, Herbuveaux hired Ted Mills away from the *Tribune*'s new station, WGN, admitting that he liked golf and that he'd be happy to play a lot of it while Mills ran things. NBC had brought them both on board in 1948 to develop new programming in Chicago with only one requirement—it had to be cheap. Costs had skyrocketed for New York programs, essentially filmed vaudeville and Broadway, and L.A. shows with their Hollywood production values. An episode of *Milton Berle* cost something like $25,000 every week, and *Your Show of Shows* came in at $85,000. As had happened during the advent of radio, New York executives looked to Chicago for a solution.

Kukla, Fran and Ollie exemplified two fundamental aspects of Chicago television—improvisation and intimacy. "The main thing about the 'Chicago school' of TV," said *Look*, "is this: The viewer doesn't always know what's going to happen next and next and *next*." Nor did the performers, because in some of the most influential and popular Chicago shows that followed, their scripts were rarely more than loose outlines. Improvisation cut out the cost of a writing staff, but it was a high-risk venture that demanded considerable skill and it didn't always work; even Fran and Burr sometimes stepped on each other's lines, and their loose banter could drift off into the ether. When it worked, though—when Ollie offered a thought that Fran batted back with a little spin, and then Kukla jumped in—the energy came through the screen. Mills, who'd made propaganda films with Frank Capra during the war, credited this breezy, unpredictable approach in some degree to the fifteenth-century commedia dell'arte tradition, connecting Chicago television to the same "theater without heroes" populist tradition as the Dil Pickle, the CRG, and Viola Spolin, more than any progression from film.

THE NEXT BIG SHOW out of Chicago interacted with the viewers in ways that exposed the power—both good and bad—of the medium. Mills brought in disc jockey Dave Garroway to host a variety show. Every frat boy at Northwestern and probably a goodly share of Hutchins's college had tuned their radios to *The 11:60 Club* religiously at midnight for Garroway's low, late-night tones, somewhere between chilled and totally stoned. "Hello, Tiger," he'd start, almost seductively, and go on for an hour of jazz as if he were talking to them and just them, a clean-cut version of a bebop junkie. The initial plan was to do the show live in a Loop theater, but Garroway, six foot two and owl-eyed in his big glasses, was the same person offstage as he was on air; laid-back, thoughtful, friendly, if a bit reserved—and a world away from the bucktoothed vaudeville of Berle. Adman Charlie Andrews, who joined WNBQ to create the show, saw that Garroway's style matched the intimacy of television, where a handful of people huddled together around each set like a campfire. And then there was the money, or lack of it. NBC budgeted only $750 a week for the Garroway show, plus the cost of the orchestra, so Mills and Andrews took a gamble. Staffed with a crew that knew barely more than the viewers did about television production, they let the format of the show express their collective curiosity, enthusiasm, and imagination.

To start, *Garroway at Large* tore down the fourth wall. From their debut on April 16, 1949, Dave and his guests directly addressed the viewer in the manner of "respectful and charming visitors," offering them a window back into the world of television. Though every line of the show (save for the ads) was improvised, Garroway maintained a graceful, relaxing tone. Second, that peek into the world of television meant experimentation, both in style and in production. Early viewers wanted to know how television worked, so when Dave moved around the studio, the camera followed him, showing the boom, the musicians, the other cameramen, all of whom he addressed, joked with, and otherwise used as part of the action. (When David Letterman talks to his crew during the show, he's simply repeating a trope created in 1949.) Approaching television not as a mutated version of theater or the movies but on its own terms, *Garroway at Large* explored the medium to such a degree that even *Popular Mechanics* covered its innovative stagecraft: glass building bricks that created multiple images; forced perspective sets; green-screen tricks that made Les Paul's hands play the guitar on Dave's body; and split screens that let ten people jump out from behind a tree five inches wide. "The stars of the show and the idea-people behind it," wrote *Popular Mechanics,* "are young, daring and unafraid of new ideas. So many trick effects are used in the show that among some wits in the business it's known as 'Gimmicks at Large, with Garroway.' " Just as quickly, though, as one of the "gimmicks" would appear, Dave would show how it had been done. When dancers seemed to jump into the ocean, he brought the camera over to the mattresses they'd fallen onto; or he'd pop his nose through the tiny doors at the end of a long, forced-perspective hallway. Where Ernie Kovacs played with television, Garroway pulled back the curtain, showing it for the genial fakery that it was, dispelling the mystery and magic from a thing that was already growing out of control but also bolstering the show's tone of living-room intimacy by showing that it had nothing to hide.

If Andrews, Mills, and Garroway were connected to Chicago's tradition of popular theater, Wee Risser and Buddy Doremus, in the show's workshop, had a deep link to Moholy, who had died before he could play with television as a light-based medium. The ID curriculum remained focused on film even as *Garroway at Large* engaged television in a seat-of-the-pants way that epitomized Moholy's sense of artistic wonder; TV was his kind of living, breathing art form, and in a way that Moholy would also have approved, Garroway used the show as a vehicle for constructive communication with his audience, encouraging them to listen and look at new things.

The show's gentle, quirky sense of humor had deep midwestern roots and mocked New York's preconceptions. Charlie Andrews's mentor had been Paul Rhymer, creator of the radio show *Vic and Sade,* a kind of great-uncle to Garrison Keillor's *Prairie Home Companion,* with offbeat, small-town tales of people such as "the most beautiful girl to ever drown in Miller's Pond" and the man who builds a locomotive in his backyard. On *Garroway,* visual puns became a trademark; for instance, Dave brings a glass of milk over to a singer after she finishes "Black Coffee Blues," or sight gags such as finishing the show by whacking the coaxial cable in half with an ax as the screen goes black. A few seconds later the show popped on with Dave holding up the garden hose he'd cut, but the suits in New York were not amused. Forced to sign off with the line, "This show came to you live from Chicago," because NBC considered it a "remote" production, Garroway came up with variations, such as saying "This program came to you from Chicago, the friendly city," with a knife sticking out of his back. Amid his growing fame, Garroway remained calm on the surface; he tinkered with telescopes and collected old cars. Director Bob Banner called him "a very private person, rather aloof, quiet," and that translated to the set, which stayed low-key even as Garroway fought off bouts of depression. His trademark closing—"Peace"—seemed to come from a more personal place than the Merchandise Mart.

WNBQ's other shows in spring of 1949 included *Walt's Workshop, Quiz Kids,* and *R.F.D. America,* described by the *Tribune* as "the farm show for city folk"; not strange in a city that had hundreds of thousands of cattle in it at any given time and put country music on the radio. *Saturday Night Square* was an hour-long show built around a set of a town square, with a cop on patrol who'd drop by an apartment house, a shop, and a nightclub for fifteen- or twenty-minute segments. The most successful one turned out to be the nightclub, featuring Carolyn Gilbert at the piano and Studs

Terkel as the crusty bartender. Charlie Andrews spun it off into its own show, now set in a basement beanery named Studs' Place, with Studs out in front as the man-of-the-people owner. Gilbert didn't last long as second fiddle, so a retooled and recast version appeared in April 1950.

Studs' Place didn't hide its connection to old Lefty Chicago and its egalitarian understanding of "regular." Not only was the show improvised, its cast barely qualified as actors: Chet Roble, a lounge lizard pianist, played Chet, a lounge lizard pianist; Win Stracke, Studs's activist friend from Depression days who'd sung at the Cabrini Homes, played a big potato-headed folk singer much like himself; and Studs could never really manage to be anyone other than Studs. Only Beverly Younger as the waitress Grace, who always wore a union button, had any significant acting experience. *Studs' Place* was essentially the precursor to *Cheers,* "a neighborhood restaurant," explained Studs, "an arena in which dreams and realities of 'ordinary people' were acted out." On Mondays, Charlie Andrews or Studs would bring an outline to the balcony of the Civic Opera House. Studs, Beverly, Win, and Chet and any guest actors would then construct the dialogue out of their own lives and experiences. Charlie, a big jazz fan, would work the beats and the pacing to capture the flow. The action always took place in the evening, just before the joint opened for business. "People were never put down," said Studs. "The stories were about little aspects of their lives. It was built on character." For example, two shabby old con men spin an elaborate story in hopes of selling Studs a penknife. Grace and Win want to throw them out, but instead Studs stands the two to dinner, buys the knife, and slips them both some cash to boot—he's been on to them the whole time. "It was acting, good acting," Studs tells Grace. "Isn't that worth a meal?" Other times Studs made himself the foil, holding out on giving a young married couple a bottle of cognac as a gift until the gang shames him into it, or being embarrassed of his friends when a famous opera singer comes by. Like *Kukla, Fran and Ollie,* the stories were about individuals within a community that accepted all different kinds of individuals. *Studs' Place* was the first television program to show a pregnant woman; another episode ended with a deaf couple dancing to music they felt by touching Win's guitar as he played. Visitors to Chicago looked for the real Studs' Place, but unlike the original Bull and Finch Pub in Boston, it was too good to be true. Even Studs knew that: "It was, of course, El Dorado." As a work of populist, multicharacter realism, *Studs' Place* belongs next to Algren's novels and Gwendolyn Brooks's poems. "We never underestimated the audience," wrote Studs, and when he delivered the network-mandated "This program came to you from Chicago" after the credits, he looked straight into the camera and growled it with pride.

By early 1950, with the start of the fourth groundbreaking WNBQ show—*Hawkins Falls,* an early television soap opera—the Chicago School of Television was the darling of critics. Fred Allen, one of the great stars of radio, whose wry style wasn't translating well to the screen, said, "Radio City should be torn down here in New York and rebuilt in Chicago, where it might be rechristened Television Town." Television was becoming the new ritual for America, and the Chicago School of Television provided rituals with intelligence, integrity, and calm. "After half an hour of being beat over the head by New York," said Herbuveaux, "people enjoy a half-hour of leaning back with Chicago."

And yet that calm was being produced in a city that was, in places like Park Manor and Airport Homes, a virtual war zone. At first glance *Kukla, Fran and Ollie, Garroway at Large,* and *Studs' Place* may seem airily oblivious to what was going on around them, but Studs brought Big Bill Broonzy and Odetta to parties and put Mahalia on his show; meanwhile Garroway emceed the annual American Negro Music Festival at Comiskey Park and not only made Sarah Vaughan a star but once very publicly confronted one of her racist hecklers. It's more likely that all three shared not just a general philosophy but also a hope that Chicagoans could somehow find a way to live together in peace. The brief life of the Chicago School of Television had shown how television could be something other than a vast wasteland.

CHAPTER 14

A CITY OF SLIGHTBROWS

THE FEBRUARY 1949 issue of *Harper's* featured an article by cultural critic Russell Lynes, entitled "Highbrow, Lowbrow, Middlebrow." Lynes saw American society reorganizing itself into a new class system based not on money or breeding but on taste, and in semisociological and somewhat ironic fashion, he defined the groups. The highbrows were grungy intellectuals who eschewed Early American furniture, iceberg lettuce, and French wine; the lowbrows liked westerns, went to lodge meetings, and couldn't care less about art while the real villains were the middlebrows, whose upper end packaged and sold taste to its lower end, the dreary Book-of-the-Month Club members and lecture attendees. There were no heroes; Lynes skewered everyone equally and had the grace to out himself as an "upper middlebrow," since he wrote for magazines and liked Roquefort on his salad (not to mention that the article itself was a lower-middlebrow reinterpretation of Clement Greenberg's 1939 "Avant-Garde and Kitsch" essay).

Money and choice had overwhelmed American culture. By 1949, even in a mild recession, the issue for most Americans wasn't so much whether they had money but what they would spend it on and to that degree Lynes was right: people now defined—or redefined—themselves by what they bought and owned, and not so much by the objects themselves as by their brands. A deepening flood of media, led by television, helped advertising saturate the culture, increasing the importance of brand specificity not just out in the new suburban developments but also in the higher aeries of taste. Baldwin Kingrey didn't just sell chairs and tables; it sold Eames chairs and Aalto tables. Americans were embracing consumerism, so an Episcopalian, insurance broker, and father was now also a Lucky smoker, a Buick driver, and a Canadian Club drinker. And when it came to culture in these last minutes before the Red Scare, they were displaying a surprising curiosity, even if it was all done for appearances.

Chicago in 1949 was still the belt buckle holding America together. Names like Schwinn, Brach, Weber, and Ford meant the factory where you worked, not just what you bought; Chicago—and America—still made things. Flying was expensive, often uncomfortable, and just a bit too unnerving for most. Car ownership was shooting up, but train travel still ruled, and in Chicago the train yards bundled tracks like muscle fibers; any crosstown drive risked a long wait for freight cars crawling past at grade. That summer more than a million visitors celebrated Chicago's connection to trains at the Railroad Fair where they wandered happily in a barren patch of lakefront just south of Soldier Field among the Pioneer Zephyr, the DeWitt Clinton from the 1830s, and the largest steam locomotive in the world, Union Pacific's Big Boy. Train tracks weren't just Chicago's muscles, they crisscrossed its imagination; model railroads took over countless basements. Though Midway was proudly the nation's busiest airport, few Chicagoans, including Mayor Kennelly, made note of a prediction by the civil aeronautics board that within ten years, all travel over one thousand miles would be by air. Consultants warned the city that it would need an airport able to handle 12 million passengers a year, yet Kennelly made no allocation for the new airport at Orchard Place to accommodate the coming jet engine planes.

On the verge of its peak population of 3.6 million, Chicago had to be reckoned with as a tastemaker. What highbrows the city had huddled together in Hyde Park scanning Middle English poetry; if you placed a "regular" Chicagoan on Lynes's chart, he'd most likely land somewhere on the upper end of lowbrow, where the beer drinkers and comic book readers lived; but every impulse of Chicago's cultural circles was about the middlebrow. While Lynes believed that art's purpose in postwar America was to divide society, everything here was now going toward the creation of a common culture, from both sides of "regular." From the populist Alinsky radical side came Algren, Studs, and the Chicago School of Television, as well as the vernacular music of Mahalia and the blues and the Moholy spirit still clinging to life at the Institute of Design. On the other side came the drive to mass-market high culture, and that came in a number of forms. One was Mies; his work was becoming the face of institutional Chicago. Another was the Hutchins-Adler-Paepcke-Benton swirl of Great Books, *Encyclopaedia Britannica*, and Aspen, all aimed at putting high culture in the hands of the middlebrow masses; still another was Katharine Kuh and her educational efforts at the Art Institute. The corporate mechanism geared toward creating a uniform culture needed Chicago as a clearinghouse, and in 1949 the common culture that Chicago pointed toward was resolutely middlebrow—but most definitely not lowest common denominator. Chicago's "great soul" lived in that tension, that mediation between extremes, and America was fascinated by it. *Look* magazine asked Kup for a piece about the city of contrasts and dispatched twenty-one-year-old staff photographer Stanley Kubrick to shoot it. Even then the future director had a cinematic eye, spotting the swooping depth and geometry of State Street, a platform at Union Station and a line of hanging beef carcasses, as well as the intimate dramas of models at an underwear wholesaler and traders at the Board of Trade.

Kukla, Fran and Ollie had at Lynes directly in a May episode, when Kukla pores over a tongue-in-cheek *Life* magazine chart that let you place yourself amid the high-, low-, and middlebrows and eventually decides Ollie is a "slightbrow." *Studs' Place* tackled the same issue with a bit more drama. Transported by a night at the opera, Studs walks into the restaurant the next day and tells Grace, Chet, and Win the story of *Tannhäuser* in his streetcorner style, turning Wagner into a soap opera. When an opera singer he met drops by, Studs waves his ostensibly lowbrow friends away, even as they start up conversations with the Englishman about cricket, French cooking, and the town of Bath. Mr. Seaton-Seaton isn't interested, says Studs, who then tries to impress his new friend with lame details memorized from Milton Cross's *Complete Stories of the Great Operas*. Annoyed, Win picks up his guitar and sings an Irish folk song, then Chet plays a slow piano blues. Studs cringes as bumbling Win, with his campfire singalong voice, launches into an aria from *Tannhäuser*, but Win nails it, reducing Studs to the brink of tears. I never knew you could sing that kind of music, he says to Win, who replies, "You never asked me." In that instant, everything is connected: Grace's fish stew becomes bouillabaisse, and operas draw from folk music. Culture belongs to everyone and no one at once, a product of the people, not institutions. Engagement and connection still matter at *Studs' Place*. Chet doesn't make fun of cricket; he asks with genuine curiosity who the game's "big hitter" is, eliciting probably the only mention of Sir Donald Bradman in American television history. The preconceptions of culture—from music to sports to food—that Studs puts up as barriers are revealed to be the means to connect. It's the perfect statement of the Chicago aesthetic and of Moholy's ethos.

The blues were as lowbrow as anything could be. (Since Lynes called jazz the product of lowbrows, it must be assumed that he considered *all* African American culture lowbrow.) At Aristocrat, Leonard Chess had hired as a performer and songwriter a huge man named Willie Dixon, whose wide, pegged-tooth grin made his head look like a black jack-o'-lantern. Dixon brought a feeling for the blues that Leonard was still groping for; he helped him to sign top talent and get the most out of recording sessions. As an operator, he was a man after Leonard's motherfucking heart, his eyes, ears, and right hand in a community he wasn't really a part of. Dixon could get hold of just about every bluesman and his women at any given time.

But the key to Aristocrat in 1949 was Muddy Waters. Leonard well knew that nothing else had sold like "I Can't Be Satisfied" that past summer, and thus began one of the more unlikely friendships in music history.

Muddy had no illusions that this chain-smoking Jew always offering him a sandwich really wanted to be his pal, but as John Johnson pointed out, "It was important in that era for a Black family to have a kind of 'protective custody' relationship with a strong and important White family. If you worked for such a family, the head of the family would protect you from other Whites. He didn't always protect you from himself or members of his family, but he protected you from others." A wobbly sort of friendship often resulted, wherein each side took advantage of the other and played out uncomfortable roles, yet still managed to share genuine affection. The decades of loose accounting that followed; the cash advances and Cadillacs instead of royalties; Muddy's lack of any responsibility toward his own finances or behavior—all played out against a sincere bond between the two men. For all their obvious differences, Leonard and Muddy were both immigrants who wanted to make as much money as soon as possible, a couple of lowbrows who spoke the same language of ambition. They never signed a contract. Said Muddy, "It was just 'I belongs to the Chess family.' "

As Muddy drove around the West Side now, he still heard "I Can't Be Satisfied" coming out of windows. His band got nonstop work, playing from the Zanzibar on the West Side to places like Silvio's and the 708 Club in Bronzeville, and now Muddy wanted to get back in the studio, with a new sound. Leonard liked it, but stubbornness and superstition were at the core of his strategy. "He could be an absolutely charming man," said producer Malcolm Chisholm, "and a master politician. He often was bone-headed and arrogant when running a session, but it wasn't that he was nasty or personally difficult. He was just absolutely sure about what he wanted." Last summer's formula—Muddy on guitar and Big Crawford on bass—had worked once, so Leonard was sure it would work again. As good as "Little Geneva," "Burying Ground," and "Train Fare Home" are, they don't capture where Muddy was live at that point.

Up in the office where the checks were signed, Evelyn Aron understood the appeal of the blues and their sales, but she hadn't started Aristocrat to have a blues label, and Leonard's charms, such as they were, had long ago worn away to expose his superstition and mulishness, his foul mouth and driven personality, not to mention the chain smoking. In December 1949 she sold out to Leonard, who immediately brought in his brother Phil and made Willie Dixon talent scout, producer, and writer. Aristocrat now belonged to the Chess brothers.

AS THE SUN rose over the lake, Harry Callahan scooped up his camera bags and tripod from where he left them packed every night. Careful not to wake Eleanor, he closed the door behind him and began his daily exploration of Chicago's streets, what he called his way "to regulate a pleasant form of living." Weber considered him "the hunting type, chasing his own shadows." Alone with his cameras, Callahan captured the bare, formal qualities of storefronts and trees, made the low hiss of snow skittering across ice and the sound of reeds shaking in a breeze almost audible. More than any artist who's ever worked in Chicago, he understood the value of snow; silent, blank, endured by most but used by him as a canvas and a source of light. His attachment to Mies leaps out in photos such as "Chicago," where a thatch of trees in snowy Lincoln Park echoes a grove of black steel columns. A vision was evolving on these expeditions—intimate and human, yet at the same time cool and often abstracted; a refined expression of Moholy's hopeful engagement with the modern. Callahan was gaining notice, and his eventual recognition as one of the greatest photographers of the twentieth century would be based largely on work taken during these walks through sleepy Chicago.

In summer of 1949 he captured one of his most famous images—Eleanor as a naiad in Lake Michigan, eyes closed, the ends of her long black hair dipped in the water and floating away to her left like Botticelli's Venus. While the self-possessed Eleanor loved Harry, Harry *needed* Eleanor, who offered herself as a model at all times, stripping on his command, assuming whatever pose he requested, indoors or out. His photos of her are a remarkable statement of their marriage, of how she met his constant need by freely giving herself to him without restraint or exploitation; if there's any sense of power being exercised, it's Eleanor's. Not long after the naiad shot was taken, she became convinced she had cancer. Happily, she turned out to be pregnant; their daughter Barbara would be born in February 1950, setting him off in another burst of creativity, notably the "Eleanor Snapshots," which feature his wife standing amid broad urban landscapes, swallowed by the scale but very much the focal point; Barbara soon became another constant model.

The three of them moved to a vast second-floor ballroom in an old mansion two blocks from Moholy's last apartment on Lakeview Avenue, hushed and filled with light, furnished with only some Eames chairs and a platform bed. For art, Hugo Weber drew sketches on the walls. For a dark-room, Callahan used a small alcove off the kitchen with an ironing board for a table; instead of studiously cataloging prints, he kept them loose in boxes without dates or titles. Only the act of making them mattered.

Despite his quiet, more and more Callahan became central to the Institute of Design. The Art Institute had opened its new photography gallery with his first one-man show. Arthur Siegel had finally snapped under Serge Chermayeff's pressure, so Callahan took over the photography department; his friendships outside the ID and his growing reputation helped buoy the school, and his admiration for and debt to Moholy kept the founding principles in mind as the ID began a difficult transition. All through 1948 Serge Chermayeff had been trying to unload the school, and in November 1949 he finally signed the deal for IIT to take it over; a victory, it would seem, for Mies, though he'd been dead set against it. In March the German had written Henry Heald in a lather: "The school is not good, and the man is not good. . . . The school was not good under Moholy-Nagy, and in the last two and a half years has steadily deteriorated. . . . Our school is based on discipline, and the Institute of Design exists on extravagances. The two are not compatible." Despite his interest in Buckminster Fuller, Mies regarded the ID's Shelter program as a conflict with his architecture department, and he only got testier when Fuller was replaced with Konrad Wachsmann. (Fuller, meanwhile, proved to share Moholy's less-than-admirable tendency to appropriate ideas. He created the first geodesic dome in 1949 out of his research at the ID, but it also derived to a large degree from the work of a Black Mountain and ID student named Kenneth Snelson, who soon found his conception of a continuous tension structure repackaged as Fuller's "tensegrity.")

Gropius, Paepcke, and Chermayeff all expressed reservations about what Mies and his cult at IIT would do to the ID. But the ID had no choice, really. After more than a decade, Paepcke was "getting old, tired, and worn out" when it came to the New Bauhaus ideal and the petty fractiousness that seemed attached to it; and Chermayeff had wound the school into a state of constant febrile tension. In fact, Mies wanted nothing at all to do with the ID, but Henry Heald had a vision, and the continuing demolition of the Near South Side showed just how overwhelming his visions could be. He planned to convert the ID into the vocational school that Moholy had always resisted; Chermayeff, meanwhile, considered Heald "not very bright" and "fundamentally a money collector."

As the signal from the Bauhaus grew dimmer, Walter Paepcke set his eyes on another, older light. He and Hutchins launched a round of intellectual hoopla for that summer's Goethe festival. Paepcke built an enormous Eero Saarinen tent at Aspen to house the Minneapolis Symphony Orchestra; and old friends such as Thornton Wilder and Martin Buber signed on for an all-expense-paid visit to the Rockies. But the big fish was the modern Goethe, Albert Schweitzer, musician, thinker, and doctor who'd given his life to the people of Gabon, "The Greatest Man in the World," according to *Life*. Paepcke's ability to lure him out of the bush thrust the festival into the spotlight and put Aspen on the map as the most exclusive suburb of Chicago. Though Goethe-mania was short-lived, the festival would morph into the Aspen Institute think tank, still thriving on the flowery sides of the Silver Queen more than sixty years later.

Across Wabansia the rummies still stumbled, the Nectar Beer sign still flickered, and not only did the whole business stink to Nelson Algren, but nobody else seemed to care. Truman had leveled Hiroshima, and now

America was blowing itself apart, every man his own plush island—and if you didn't own an island, you'd better like to swim. He'd tried to sound the alarm. In the months after Simone's return to Paris, he'd thrown himself into the new book and politics. Though he complained that no one was listening, *The Neon Wilderness* got strong reviews, and he'd won fellowships from the Newberry Library and the American Academy of Arts and Letters. When someone tried to resurrect the old anti-Polish debate, the *Tribune* shot them down with the news that Algren "has for years crusaded against the conditions of life which have distorted the personalities of young people in that area." Even after he staked out a very visible position in the fall of 1948 as head of the Chicago Committee for the Hollywood Ten and campaigned for Henry Wallace, he spoke regularly at writers' groups and ladies' clubs. If he wasn't selling, he *was* respected.

With only Simone's letters to keep him warm, Algren had locked himself inside the tiny apartment on Wabansia and cranked out the pages of his next novel. The joint across the street, with its windows of bleary glass brick, became one of the book's main settings—the Tug & Maul, a corner bar well stocked with those left behind—while Algren took up with some heroin addicts, not so hard to find those days. Living alone amid a culture drifting farther away from his values, he felt that these junkies, unconcerned with upward mobility or the Red Menace, were "real." When he described the heroin world to his agent, she recommended he use it to help beef up the plot, so he turned Frankie's crippled wife, Sophie, into an addict.

What he didn't like about heroin were the "campus fellows, authentic paperfish authorities, . . . certain prebeatnik cats . . . searching Chicago's South Side for ways and means of passing for black." Whether he was talking about Robert Brownjohn and the ID crowd isn't clear, but writing later about the time, he wasn't as sanguine as Studs about prospects for racial amity: "Wright had made us aware that the Christianity of the white American middle class had lost its nerve: now we saw it to be a coast-to-coast fraud. And the fraud lay in this: that property was more valuable than people." By 1948, he wrote, "the image of America reflected in editorials in *Life*, on TV, in movies and on the stage, was a painted image that had nothing to do with the real life of these States." Still a Stalinist in that aesthetic way (he signed an open letter to him that May), Algren thought this new book would "reach" white, middle-class America and give it the good slap it needed.

On the other end of all this work was the four-month vacation with Simone they'd been planning through the winter of 1947. They were still Frog and Crocodile, but De Gaulle's election, *Les Temps Modernes*, and a divided Berlin consumed her attention, along with work on what would become *The Second Sex;* her letters set scenes of domestic bliss to soothe his touchy hide. Simone had realized that their situation suited her quite well, actually: forty now, she could produce pages in St.-Germain, the world's cultural center, and then once in a while play house with a brilliant, sensitive man who loved to fuck. Her letters turned more on points of the mind now than of the heart; when Algren's letters wandered to the mawkish, she pulled him back with warnings that her life would always be in Paris.

At last in early May 1948, Simone arrived in Chicago, not mentioning to her Crocodile that she planned to cut their four months together down to two so that she could get back to Sartre. After a few rainy days of provisioning and reunion sex, the trip began with a train ride to Cincinnati. Few great journeys begin this way. De Beauvoir's biographer paints the next six weeks in lyrical terms—puttering down the moonlit Mississippi on a paddleboat; hot nights in Mexico, naked in front of the fire—while Algren's biographer reads the joint diary they kept as the chronicle of a running battle; Simone marching them off on daily adventures like a pair of Victorian explorers, Algren swamped by sour moods. The itinerary was as follows: a week or so on the boat, with stops in Louisville, Natchez, and Memphis, ending up in New Orleans, a disappointment to Algren, who found the city nothing like he remembered. On they flew to Guatemala, then to Mérida in the Yucatán, where the poverty of Mexico pulled them down to the point where even the ruins at Chichen Itza represented oppression to Algren. Simone kept them going at quick march through markets and churches while Algren begged for coffee breaks. In the diary, Simone describes him as "very bad" one night, then he calls her "very bad" the next. It's likely they were both correct. On June 12 they hit Mexico City, and it was on a drive between there and Morelia that Simone dropped the bomb about cutting the trip short.

"Oh all right," said Algren.

That was it for Mexico. Algren insisted they return to New York, where he sulked, pouted, and snapped for the better part of two weeks. His tricky sense of humor, self-deprecating and mocking at once, became a public embarrassment. "One evening, we ate at an open air tavern in the middle of Central Park," Simone wrote, "and then went downtown to listen to some jazz at Café Society. He behaved incredibly badly. 'I can leave tomorrow,' I said to him. We had words, then, suddenly, he said to me, fervently 'I'm ready to marry you on the spot.' I understood then," she continued, "that I could never again hold anything against him; any missteps were mine." She flew back to Paris on July 14, with no plans for a reunion. After a harrowing transatlantic flight, Simone found that Sartre didn't need her after all, so she immediately wired Algren that she was coming back, to which he snipped, "No. Too much work." Not a native speaker, or maybe just a hopeful one, Simone read that as "Not too much work" and cabled her plans so he could meet her. He wired in no uncertain terms that he did not want her back. Period.

Algren threw himself into the manuscript, working through changes from his editor Ken McCormick at Doubleday. The book, they decided, would be called *The Man with the Golden Arm*. After handing it in that October, Algren celebrated by sleeping with a divorcée he worked with on the Wallace campaign, news he shared with Simone. The divorcée had represented marriage, home, family—everything that Simone refused to offer—but he knew he'd tire very quickly of any woman who gave all that to him. As much as he wanted a conventional life with Simone, he was stuck in Chicago, "as far away from everything as Uxmal," he wrote, ". . . because my job is to write about this city, and I can only do it here." Simone suddenly became intrigued again—she was not above jealousy.

The Union Stockyards

Ludwig Mies van der Rohe and
Ludwig Karl Hilberseimer, Illinois
Institute of Technology, c. 1940s

IIT Dormitory

*Mildred Mead, University of Chicago Photographic Archive, Special
Collections Research Center, University of Chicago Library*

860–880 N. Lake Shore Drive, 1948–1949

*Pace Associates; Holsman, Holsman, Klekamp and Taylor,
architects. Richard Nickel Archive, Ryerson and Burnham Archives,
The Art Institute of Chicago. © The Art Institute of Chicago*

Alfred Caldwell's Lily Pool

© Bill Guerriero

The Farnsworth House

Jon Miller © Hedrich Blessing

Mies van der Rohe and Crown Hall

Arthur Siegel/TIME & LIFE Pictures/Getty Images

The Mecca

Inez Cunningham Stark and her poetry class
at the SSCAC

Gwendolyn Brooks

Wayne F. Miller/Magnum Photo.

Courtesy of Stephen Daiter Gallery

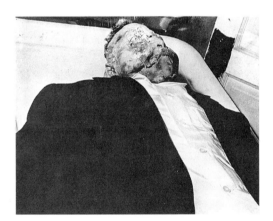

Emmett Till's Body

Courtesy of the Chicago Defender

Robert Taylor Homes

Mildred Mead,

University of Chicago Photographic Archive,

Special Collections Research Center,

University of Chicago Library

Moholy-Nagy sitting
beneath one of his
Atomic paintings

Vories Fisher, courtesy of
the Moholy-Nagy Foundation and ARS

Walter and Elizabeth Paepcke,
Aspen, 1949

© *Ferenc Berko. Courtesy berkophoto.com*

Wire Sculpture, 1946, László Moholy-Nagy

László Moholy-Nagy, courtesy of the Moholy-Nagy Foundation and ARS

Chicago, c. 1950 by Harry Callahan

Robert Maynard Hutchins

Myron Davis/TIME & LIFE Pictures/Getty Images

Mortimer J. Adler

George Skadding/TIME & LIFE Pictures/Getty Images

Mike Nichols and Elaine May

Alfred Eisenstaedt/TIME & LIFE Pictures/Getty Images

When Algren announced that he was coming over to Paris for a look around, she agreed.

In May 1949 he flew to New York to check in with Doubleday, continued on by boat to Le Havre, and then took a train to Paris, where he arrived weighed down with gifts of food, clothes, and liquor. Simone installed him in her fifth-floor apartment on the Left Bank at 11 rue de la Bucherie, down the street and through Viviani Square from Shakespeare and Company, a view of Notre-Dame out the window. No other man would ever sleep here, she promised. Algren loved Paris. Much to his surprise, he actually got along with Sartre, though he thought the philosopher looked like a shoe salesman, and even Simone poked fun now—Sartre, she said, would fall in love with any woman who'd stick her tongue up his ass. Evenings in Café de Flore, Algren drank with Albert Camus, Raymond Queneau, and Boris Vian, author of the potboiler *I Spit on Your Graves,* inspiration for the 1959 crime film (though Vian allegedly had a fatal heart attack at its screening; his last words—"My ass!"). Juliette Greco in a black leotard wriggled in his lap while he regaled the Family with hyped-up tales of back-alley Chicago. A reunion with Richard Wright did not go well, though. Algren saw his old friend now as less of an expatriate than a deserter, while Wright expected Algren to stay.

Social pleasantries, and unpleasantries, aside, the big news was Simone, whose Algren-inspired book *The Second Sex* had just been published in France. The primary text of modern feminism, it upset nearly every aspect of French society and made her the target of violent threats. Through the summer Simone leaned mostly on Algren for support, amusing Sartre and their circle. In June the couple left for a trip that took them through Italy, then Tunisia and Algiers, then back up to Paris via Marseilles and Monte Carlo. In September they parted. "I never loved you so much," Simone wrote him. ". . . We shall stay together even across the ocean, now I know it for sure." Nelson seemed to finally accept the difficult terms of their relationship; what she brought him beyond the sex had been made clear.

In Newfoundland, as his return flight refueled, Algren read *Time*'s review of his new book *The Man with the Golden Arm*. "A true novelist's triumph," it said. And it *is* Algren's masterpiece. Frankie Machine comes back from the war with a habit he wants to kick. A card dealer now, he dreams of being the next Gene Krupa, but it's hard to know whether it's the morphine keeping him down or his wife, Sophie, confined to a wheelchair after Frankie crashed their car. Zosh claims she can't walk, but it's really her way to torture Frankie with her anger and neediness. Frankie's true love is Molly, a prostitute who lives a couple floors below, but even she can't keep the monkey off his back. (That's where the phrase comes from.) Afraid of sliding back onto the needle for good, he kills his dealer, but instead of taking a rap for murder, he gets caught stealing irons with his mangy sidekick, Sparrow. In prison, Frankie cleans up and plans to save Molly, but once he's out, the cops force Sparrow to snitch on Frankie, who hangs himself. Poetic, gripping, heartbreaking, raw: no better novel has ever come out of Chicago.

Algren landed home a hero, every review from the *Sun-Times* to *The New Yorker* a rave, comparing him to Gorky, Dickens, and Dostoyevsky. "This is a man writing," Ernest Hemingway wrote, "and you should not read it if you cannot take a punch. . . . Mr. Algren can hit with both hands and move around and he will kill you if you are not awfully careful." Chicago suddenly adored him; the *Sun* even reprinted a photo of the paper Hemingway had written his quote on, scribbles and all, like a proud mother showing off a good report card. Stuart Brent went into overdrive hosting book parties, John Garfield, star of *Body and Soul*, optioned the movie rights, and then the kicker: Eleanor Roosevelt would be presenting him with the first National Book Award next March.

Just then *Life* sent to Chicago a talented young writer, photographer, and former bomber pilot from the Bronx named Art Shay. At that time a profile in *Life* was like a segment on *60 Minutes;* in April, Jackson Pollock had exploded into the national consciousness after one, and now Shay proposed the same thing for Algren: a big feature following him through Chicago's alleys and dive bars that wouldn't just cement him as heavyweight champion of Chicago, but put him in the ring with Hemingway for the national title. And he would finally *reach* people. The two hit it off from the start. Fearless, wisecracking, and literate, Shay was up for every adventure Algren had in mind, be it in a courtroom, a Madison Street flophouse, or the upper deck at Comiskey. Shay captured the spirit of Chicago as it swaggered and stumbled into a new decade, an off-key polka band to Callahan's single flute. Empathetic, poetic, ballsy, and humorous, Shay's work was the visual complement to Algren's writing. Not only was Algren famous; now he even had a sidekick.

THOUGH ALGREN WAS certain he was the only serious writer in Chicago, Gwendolyn Brooks was still on 63rd Street looking over the El tracks, still with Henry and Henry Jr., still writing and now reviewing books for Chicago papers. Algren was right in that there weren't many active writers in the city, but it had a community of critics big enough for the *Sun* to bring out the first stand-alone book review in America outside New York. On the night of June 1, 1949, Gwendolyn drank champagne with John Johnson at the new offices of *Ebony* at 1820 S. Michigan. In 1947 the magazine had topped 300,000 in monthly circulation, the largest of any African American–interest publication, but Johnson had had to wait a year until the likes of Pepsi, Colgate, Beech-Nut, and Seagram's finally decided to advertise. That recognition of the black presence in the marketplace was overdue, but it also brought the not-necessarily-positive focus of American advertising, its emphasis on consumption, and white, middle-class mores that weren't always "regular" on the South Side. Either way, the money rolled in after that. Johnson had had to hide behind a white agent to buy the building, but he was a millionaire on his thirty-first birthday, and *Ebony* was here to stay, its pros and cons twisting around each other like a Möbius strip.

Gwendolyn, however, was by no means a millionaire. After Harper's rejected *American Family Brown*, she'd returned to poetry, publishing *Annie Allen* in August 1949. Its cornerstone is "The Annead," a technical tour de force about a young black girl. Dense and florid, *Annie Allen* feels less like an expression than a self-consciously important work written with a white audience in mind. Which is not to say that it's bad, but it lives on the bridge in Brooks's creative life (and of Black American writing) between Richard Wright and Ralph Ellison. Writing poetry was no more lucrative than it had been in the 1930s; nor had Henry, solid and smart as he was, found a way to share in the postwar prosperity, and book party wine and cheese didn't feed the babies. Though her life was dramatized on the radio show *Destination Freedom*, though *Poetry* magazine awarded her its Tietjens Prize in 1949 and gave her major coverage for *Annie Allen*, she was still sitting in the dark with her children, wondering how they'd scrape together the money to get the electricity turned back on—when the phone rang. A reporter notified her that she'd just won the 1950 Pulitzer Prize for *Annie Allen*, making her the first African American to win a Pulitzer. She'd beaten out Robert Frost's *Collected Poems* and William Carlos Williams's *Patterson III*. If she'd been trying to impress the white literary powers, she'd succeeded. But the room stayed dark.

A RECORD 1,338,761 people visited the Art Institute in 1948, and Daniel Catton Rich and Katharine Kuh had even higher hopes for 1949, when it would host the first public showing of the Arensberg Collection that fall. On the morning of October 19, the Commodore pulled in from New York bearing Marcel Duchamp, the Arensbergs' emissary: he checked in at the Palmer House and then recorded an interview with local critics. Like Gropius, Duchamp had pleasant connections to Chicago, in particular the Arts Club, which had mounted an exhibition of his Brancusi collection in 1927; plus Brookes Hubachek, brother of his longtime on-and-off lover Mary Reynolds, served on the board of trustees of the Art Institute. Duchamp and Kuh had developed a mutual respect and friendship while they'd worked together for the flighty Arensbergs. Director Rich hosted a small dinner for him at the Tavern Club, and then came the gala opening at eight p.m., a landmark event in American art—for the reason that it was entirely uneventful. Though the collection included works that had been shown in the original Armory Show, this time no one was burned in effigy—in fact, Chicagoans *liked* it. Kuh's educational efforts had helped Chicago find some peace with modern art, paving the way for mainstream America's acceptance. Three days later, on his way back to New York, Duchamp notified the Arensbergs that the show had been mounted beautifully, and though he didn't tell them, the most influential artist of the twentieth century left hoping that the permanent home for his work, and the world's most important collection of modern art, would be here, in a city whose artists had rejected Abstract Expressionism.

AMERICA HAD SPENT four years alone at the top of the world, bomb in hand, flush with cash, spinning in an equilibrium of paranoid anti-Communism and consumer optimism. At the center were Chicagoans, wrestling with new styles of television, blues, jazz, and gospel, winning awards for the year's best novel and best book of poems—all accessible, all intimately scaled, and all aimed at humans, not markets. On Lake Shore Drive, construction workers were digging the foundation for an apartment building that would change modern architecture and urban living forever, about a mile from a museum that was on the brink of becoming the only serious challenger to MoMA. The Midwest Stock Exchange opened, and the city's unemployment rate was below the rest of America's. Without the density or ballyhooed cultural impact of the East Coast, Chicago could feel at times an industrial Florence to New York's Imperial Rome, a place where man and modernity might co-exist. The stink of the Stockyards, the smoke of the factories enforced a reality that no longer existed on Park Avenue or Sunset Strip. "The gap," wrote De Beauvoir, "that separates the world of profit from the world of work is more obvious here than elsewhere because the smell that infests the dungeon is so close at hand."

Toward the end of 1949, America teetered to the right. In late August, the Soviets tested their first atomic bomb, and six weeks later Mao proclaimed the People's Republic of China. Suddenly the insidious subversives who had once existed mainly in the imaginations of the House Un-American Activities Committee and the prosecutors in the trial of Alger Hiss became 800 million atheists ready to drop nuclear weapons on your home. On February 9, 1950, just weeks after authorities arrested scientist Klaus Fuchs for passing atomic secrets to the Soviets, Senator Joseph McCarthy stood up at a ladies' club meeting in Wheeling, West Virginia, and waved a piece of paper that listed, or so he claimed, 205 known Communists in the State Department. The Red threat was now very real in the minds of Americans.

The trains still stopped in Chicago. But a very deep kind of winter was about to set in.

PART THREE

1950-1954

"There are two kinds of people in this country.
There are the ones who love Chicago and the
ones who think it is unmitigated hell."

Louella O. Parsons

THE RED scare silenced the dialogue about what "regular" meant. Chicago's ethnic, mostly Catholic homeowners, led locally by priests and nationally by anti-Communist Catholics like McCarthy, rolled all their fears of the Red menace, blacks, and the bomb into a potent, often violent force. The game had always been rigged against them, but instead of continuing the New Deal spirit, they'd redefined "regular" as a belligerent conformity that turned at times into guerrilla race war. While that conservative force emerged throughout the North, nowhere did it spread so viciously or completely as it did in Chicago. To maintain power, the city's Democrats would have to make a drastic adjustment.

The market meaning of "regular" moved into the foreground, too. Algren's "fresh time" of experimentation ended, as television and speedier transportation spread a uniform vision of America. While the Red scare drove many Chicago artists into the corners, others happily cashed in. Redevelopment rolled on; Sullivan's old hopeful city began to fall under the wrecking ball, and *Playboy* hit the stands. The nation's culture wars began in the streets of Chicago.

CHAPTER 15

STAND UP AND
BE COUNTED

By the end of February 1950, all Chicago was in the dark. Coal strikes and a deep freeze forced off store lights and neon signs; schools went onto a four-day schedule, and radio stations cut broadcasts down to six hours a day. People lined up for whatever coal could be had. Just weeks into McCarthy's anti-Communist hysteria, it was a frigid, frightening reminder of the Depression.

With the city in this Siberian state of mind, Alderman William Lancaster called to order the first of four days of hearings on the CHA's public housing sites. Usually the Gray Wolves wiled away their hours in the City Council chambers napping, chatting, and studying the odds at Sportsman's, but today, February 23, 1950, more than five hundred protesters, the same sort of working-class housewives who'd touched off the Airport Homes riots, packed the gallery to jeer any witness who spoke in favor of the CHA or its plan. Public housing, said one speaker to a stomping ovation, put the city "on the road to communism." Four days later the council approved only two of the seven sites, and a serious issue sank to farce when some of the Gray Wolves loaded up a bus full of reporters and drove around the city to scout out new locations in the wards of the few aldermen who'd dared support the CHA. The city looked out of control, but neither Kennelly nor Arvey reined things in. The CHA offered a revised proposal, which the council ignored in favor of its own "compromise" plan that placed all the housing in black neighborhoods; an exasperated federal government advised the CHA to accept. The deal was done that summer, forever poisoning open housing and integration in Chicago.

Any hope for a national thaw in the anti-Communist hysteria disappeared in June, when North Korean troops crossed the thirty-eighth parallel, and three days later a Red-baiting organization published *Red Channels*, a list of 151 media figures and their alleged associations with alleged Communist subversives. The enemy, claimed McCarthy and his ilk, hid everywhere among us—at home, in the office, at school, in the movie theaters, and especially on television, a medium that had quickly proven its unique powers to persuade. But for all its dramatic impact, network television didn't invite innovation in social matters or politics; big corporations and the military had created it, and as the FBI arrested Julius Rosenberg in July, television fell into line. Along with loyalty oaths for everyone in the industry, the networks established certain rules regarding content: in mystery or crime shows, for example, businessmen and bankers, heroes of the free market, could never be suspects. The white suburban nuclear family pushed aside ethnics like *The Goldbergs;* Chicago-style intimacy and community were suddenly suspect, and as part of the general move toward consolidation, the networks pulled most production back to New York.

Dave Garroway was the first to leave Chicago. In the fall of 1951, NBC announced a new show to debut on January 14, 1952, at the unheard-of hour of seven a.m. *Today,* shot in a glassed-in studio at Rockefeller Center, did well enough in its first week that the network announced a spin-off, *Tonight!* The talk show, a format that acknowledged the intimate nature of the medium and people's willingness to watch people converse, was essentially a product of Chicago-style television. Initially the show ventured wary little gimmicks amid the news and features to remind viewers of what *Garroway at Large* had been like without scaring off the incurious. A chimp named J. Fred Muggs came aboard as a cohost to draw in younger viewers and their moms. NBC made full use of Garroway; after waking up at three a.m. for *Today,* he did two other television shows and a radio show. The grinding schedule sent him down into the depression he'd fought off in Chicago. Just before the on-air light went on, he'd hit a small bottle of liquid codeine he called "the Doctor" to get through the show. The long-term effects were devastating; he became convinced that his phones were tapped, that a Communist invasion was imminent, that machines were conspiring against him. He stole props and occasionally hit J. Fred Muggs. (In fairness, the chimp turned abusive, to the point that he once knocked down a little girl in crutches live on air. Marlin Perkins came to get him after that.) Burned out, Garroway left the show in 1961 for a patchwork career stitched across TV and radio, unable to shake the darkness. He committed suicide in 1982.

Ten days before the premiere of *Today,* though, the Chicago School of Television had already been pronounced dead by none other than Ted Mills, who'd gone to New York himself. Writing in the Roosevelt College alumni magazine, Mills declared Chicago's future in television "hopeless." The talent drain could not be stopped. Chicago, one ad executive told *Billboard,* was being "clubbed and beaten insensible by . . . New York production giants." Hugh Downs and Mike Wallace left Chicago and went east, as did Charlie Andrews, Dan Petrie, Bob Banner, and Bill Hobin, all of whom filled New York's corner offices and production studios with Chicago attitude. Some shows, mostly educational ones, survived the exodus and wove their way into national consciousness. *Zoo Parade,* hosted by the self-styled great white hunter Dr. Marlin Perkins and his sidekick Jim Hurlbut, would later become *Mutual of Omaha's Wild Kingdom,* and *Mr. Wizard* with Don Herbert ran for fourteen years. Fred Rogers and Jim Henson both adopted the slow, direct delivery and cosseting tone of *Ding Dong School,* hosted by the motherly Frances Horwich, who went to New York in 1954 to run NBC's children's programming. *Super Circus,* Mike Wallace's show, though out of Chicago, was hardly an example of the Chicago School. Remembered by most boys and their fathers for its bandleader Mary Hartline, a stacked peroxide blonde in a sparkly majorette uniform that *just* covered her rear end, its animal acts included a smoking chimpanzee. One episode involved elephants relieving themselves with such volume and abandon that the boy who was being paid to eat a sandwich made with the sponsor's peanut butter instead wept on camera.

The bigger, faster, louder world of the Cold War affected *Kukla, Fran and Ollie* too. From an hour, it shrank down to half an hour, and then the same week Garroway left for New York, NBC announced it was going to fifteen minutes, five nights a week, spurring a fruitless letter-writing campaign. Now shot in huge Studio 8H at the Merchandise Mart, the show drew visiting celebs from Arturo Toscanini to Tallulah Bankhead, who became what could only be called a groupie; General Sarnoff gave her a special telephone so she could call the studio from wherever she was and talk to that night's guest, argue with Madame Ooglepuss, and kibitz with Ollie. If she was in town, she came to the studio. One night she forgot about the time and simply threw her fur coat over what she had on— which was nothing. Sitting down in the studio under the hot lights, Kukla repeatedly asked her if she wanted to take off her mink, until finally she stood up and opened her coat in his direction.

Tillstrom meanwhile made himself a familiar face on the north end of Oak Street Beach, where gay Chicago congregated. He brought the Kids to schools and hospitals and resisted every offer to sell out to toymakers, as rich as it would have made him. The worst anyone could say about him was that he was a lousy tipper, though he did begin to unnerve some. Once Hugh Downs saw him do a late-night show where he and somehow Ollie had both been drinking, while Kukla managed to stay "cold sober. With clear disapproval and without any slurring of words, he said, 'don't come to me with your big head tomorrow complaining about a headache.'" As the show became more famous, it seemed to fall in love with itself; according to stage manager Lynwood King, it "got inbred." Since Burr liked to base the show on the events of that day, episodes were now based on precious subjects like that morning's chat with Tallulah. Young viewers were not impressed. Ratings slid. *Kukla, Fran and Ollie* hung on to half an hour on Sundays.

Studs couldn't even do that. His show had opened its doors right as the

McCarthy storm hit in spring of 1950, a refuge of trust and brotherhood in the middle of the witch hunts. The first calls from the network came about Win Stracke, but the head of NBC soon called about Studs. Though he hadn't been named in *Red Channels* (Studs attributed his omission to "New York parochialism"), he'd signed every antifascist, Soviet-amity, civil rights petition that had passed his way for twenty years. NBC didn't want to pull the plug—*Studs' Place* had a devoted following and critics loved it—so they sent Studs a loyalty oath. He refused to sign. *Studs' Place* without Studs was impossible. The pressure built until it came down to the oath or the show.

An executive flew in. "Say you were duped," he suggested.

"Suppose the Communists come out against cancer," asked Studs. "Should I come out *for* cancer?"

The suit didn't wince. "It's time to stand up and be counted."

At that, Studs jumped out of his chair and stood up.

The man from New York didn't laugh. When he pulled another loyalty oath out of his briefcase, Studs told him to "fuck off," ending not only the meeting but *Studs' Place* on the NBC schedule. A local sponsor picked it up until June 1952. In the last episode, Studs loses his lease. Chet shuts the piano, Win hangs up his guitar, and Grace blows out the candle stuck in a Chianti bottle. After taking a final look around, Studs turns off the lights on the show—and on a way of creating television as what Jules Herbuveaux called "a small-scale, intimate kind of thing that had the quality of fresh baked goods in the kitchen."

Now "graylisted" if not officially on the blacklist, Studs tried to make a living from lectures and local radio. While Ida Terkel paid most of the bills as a social worker, Studs and Win toured college campuses with *I Come for to Sing*, a musical review that told the story of American vernacular music, primarily folk and blues. In October 1952 one Owen Vinson testified to HUAC in Los Angeles that Studs had invited him to join the Communist Party in 1943 "with the idea of improving radio booking conditions." Now that Studs was implicated, the FBI regularly searched his home, while Studs read them excerpts from Thoreau and Tom Paine.

He continued with *The Wax Museum,* and his jazz column in the *Sun-Times* lasted until the paper notified him that it needed the space. A few weeks later a new jazz column appeared—a longer one, written by a conservative.

One of the stations Studs approached for work was WFMT, the first all-classical FM station, just started by Bernard and Rita Jacobs. Its unusually stringent rules about programming and advertising flew in the face of every commercial impulse: no piece of music could be played more than once every three months, for instance, and all ads had to be vetted and read live. Studs fit right in with the other announcers—Norm Pellegrini and an actor living in Hyde Park named Mike Nichols—and though it paid, of course, no money, he had freedom. Encouraged by his experience with another radio show called *Sounds of the City* and by Algren's advice, Studs opened up his microphone to average people and just let them talk about what they knew. The result was *The Studs Terkel Program,* an hour of conversation punctuated by Studs's cackle, guided by his occasionally windy questions, and imbued with intelligence and that faith in the value of every man fired long ago in the lobby of the Wells-Grand Hotel. While the gossip columnists fucked passing starlets, Studs interviewed the great minds and punch-drunk ex-champs, the firemen, and the artists. *Red Channels* and McCarthyism might have kept Studs Terkel from cashing in as a big television star, but they also made it possible for him to help establish the voice of the people in the creation of history. In that way, the blacklist failed miserably.

CBS liked Fred Allen's idea of building a Television City so much that it did so in 1952—only they built it in Hollywood. Corporate America on both coasts had swallowed—and in some ways suppressed—the ideas and approaches of the Chicago School. Moholy had seen this coming in the 1920s:

> "The danger of the photographic medium—including the motion picture—is not esthetic but social. It is the enormous power of mass-produced visual information that can

enhance or debase human values. Brutal emotionalism, cheap sentimentality, and sensational distortion can, if they spread unchecked, trample to death man's newly won ability to see gradation and differentiation in the light-pattern of his world."

The Honeymooners debuted in 1953.

CHAPTER 16

LIVING SEPARATE LIVES

T CAME DOWN to the curtains. Mies insisted on beige shantung silk; Edith Farnsworth wanted either yellow or brown, but to be honest, she didn't want silk at all.

Site finally determined, Mies had broken ground on the Farnsworth House in the fall of 1949, over budget before construction even began. Steel went up early in the spring, long spans that demanded meticulous leveling before they were sandblasted smooth and painted white. The marble arrived. Mies in shirtsleeves directed construction of the wooden interior core by a German craftsman and there'd been some talk about the furnishings, something more casual than Barcelona chairs; maybe leather cushions strewn across the floor.

But at no point had Mies and Dr. Farnsworth discussed his fee, and this unspoken yet increasingly uncomfortable issue swelled just a little more with each contractor bill. Dr. Farnsworth might have been able to deal with all this, if not for the now obvious fact that it was the house Mies van der Rohe loved, not her. Once he asked her to "walk up to the terrace level, so that I can have a look at you." She did, in as winsome a way as the nephrologist could, to which Mies said, "Good. I just wanted to check scale." She'd been thinking about a painting, an important one, for his payment, but as he ignored her questions, and worse, her feelings, she grew angry; no longer his collaborator or his muse, all those lingering picnics bitterly recalled, she was simply the banker now. Their relationship soured. She stopped paying bills in August 1950, and on her first stay at the house over New Year's, she discovered she'd spent some $74,000 on a building that didn't work: the windows steamed up, the fireplace didn't draw, and there was barely room for a change of clothes. When the sun was out, the house became an oven. Curtains would at least create shade, but even now Mies wouldn't yield—they had to be beige shantung silk. In February they stopped speaking. "If I would have known that she would be so difficult," Mies said, "I would never have touched the house."

Nonetheless it was finished in March 1951, two years after Philip Johnson completed his own derivative Glass House. (Johnson often dropped by Mies's office with a notebook and quizzed the staff about their projects.) Upset as Mies was by his friend's shameless crib, the Farnsworth House transcends it; the white planes float amid the trees, imposing yet light, with two sets of low steps up to the patio; its steel beams a restatement of Grecian columns for the modern age, the seeds of all that Mies would achieve in the coming years. But its perfection had a price: he was out of pocket for some $4,000, as well as almost six thousand man-hours and his own design fee, so on July 13 he sued Edith Farnsworth for $28,173; she countersued three months later for $35,000, charging "fraud and deceit," "negligence," and financial misdeeds.

Homes were the main topic everywhere in Chicago now, whether you were a young married couple living with your in-laws, a black family looking to get out of the slums, a white ethnic homeowner afraid for your investment, or a spinster nephrologist. The shortage was over, and a home-buying mania swept Chicagoland such that in the summer of 1950 the city even traded in the popular Railroad Fair for a low-end Century of Progress–cum–State Fair called "the Chicago Fair of 1950." Its main attraction was the "Avenue of the American Home": a street of eight model homes constructed Three Little Pigs style by different architects using different materials. (The "television home" featured walls arranged so that the set could be seen from every room.) This was housing for the people, off the rack and ready to go up, at an average of $9,000. But certain values attached to home-owning often work at cross purposes with others and in Chicago this friction—stability, community, long-term thinking, and investment pressed against insularity, greed, and class—underpinned much of the city's postwar culture, good and bad. Whether he liked it or not—whether he *knew* it or not—Mies would be in the middle of this struggle to define the importance of "home."

BAD NEWS CAME for the Art Institute in spring 1950: the Arensbergs had double-crossed it by deciding to send their collection to Philadelphia, thereby ending the delicious possibility that Marcel Duchamp and his *Large Glass* would become fixtures of Chicago's cultural landscape. Instead it was Mies, monosyllabic, Teutonic, who was officially becoming the face of the city's cultural life, as the Arts Club of Chicago reopened that June at 109 E. Ontario with a lobby, staircase, and second floor that he had designed. Since 1916 the consistently progressive Arts Club had kept Chicago's artistic Ner Tamid alive through wars and depressions but most of all in a local cultural market that continued to buy the bulk of what hung on its walls from the painting department at Marshall Field's. Having lost its lease in the Wrigley Building in 1947, it now reemerged, holding up Mies's work as the image of Chicago's movers and shakers at midcentury: luxurious, monumental, institutional, and built of steel. The new Arts Club's first major show, a Jean Dubuffet retrospective in December, would have a profound impact on the city's art scene. His lecture on "Anticultural Positions" connected easel painting to deeper, "primitive" cultural traditions that held meanings language couldn't transmit; artists, he said, had "a much more worthy job than creating assemblages of shapes and colors pleasing for the eyes." The Chicago painters loved the jab at the New York School and built on it: Leon Golub and Nancy Spero, newly married and living just off Clark Street, considered that lecture the foundation of their subsequent careers.

Down at IIT, Mies's full campus was emerging sleek and sharp amid the battered old buildings of the Near South Side. Ten structures were now either completed or were under construction, including his Mechanics Research, the Institute of Gas Technology, and the Chapel of St. Savior, the latter easily mistaken for a shed or a power plant until its doors were opened and its ascetic power revealed. But what had the trustees excited was a demolition: given the expanding housing market, it was time for the Mecca to go. Over the last twelve years, IIT had let it fall apart physically and socially, dropping rents to attract low-income residents who then drove out stable, middle-class families whose flight IIT then brandished as proof that the Mecca had turned into a slum. Eviction proceedings began May 22, 1950, with demolition scheduled for the end of 1951. As a building a week came down around the tenants, the CHA, pushed on all sides, could do little to help, while IIT kept the pressure on the Mecca's residents; the school ignored squatters while *Harper's* and *Life* both ran features that presented the building as evidence that degraded African American life—"blight"—was devastating urban America. A final flurry of action got everyone out just under Heald's deadline; only a fraction of the former Mecca residents went into public housing. No one bothered to track the rest. "Arrangements," said a board report, "[were] made for a small ceremony to mark the beginning of the end of the Mecca" at eleven on the morning of December 31, 1951; in January, the massive ball of the Speedway Wrecking Company crashed through Gwendolyn Brooks's microcosm of Black Chicago.

MIES'S GRADUATES HAD spread throughout the city's architectural firms. Some (like Joe Fujikawa, Gene Summers, Reginald Malcolmson, and for many years George Danforth) stayed at his side, but a large number (notably James Ferris, Skip Genther, Myron Goldsmith, Gertrude Kerbis, and Ambrose Richardson) had landed, or soon would, at Skidmore, Owings & Merrill, where business was booming. Rather than feature star architects, Louis Skidmore and Nat Owings had created a company uniquely suited to take advantage of corporatism; using the model of an old-fashioned builder's guild, SOM practiced "group design," mirroring the institutions it served and relieving them of any possible *Farnsworth v. Mies* dramatics. Corporate America and the U.S. government pushed huge, complex projects their way: entire towns and military installations in Africa and the South Pacific; Bellevue Hospital in New York; Ford office blocks in Michigan. To keep their big talents, such as Gordon Bunshaft, then beginning work on New York's Lever House, the firm started to vote in new partners in 1949, but only under the SOM name. The Chicago office (led by Owings, William Hartmann, and designer Bruce Graham) was muscling its way into the city's inner circle, with commissions for a new Greyhound Bus Terminal, public housing, a dormitory at IIT that did not please Mies, and the most visible of all, Lake Meadows, known officially as "Redevelopment Project Number One." Nat Owings was the public face now, with his post at the helm of the Chicago Plan Commission nearly an adjunct to City Hall, where he took seriously his mandate to publicize the value and meaning of planning. Skidmore, for instance, wrote pro bono a needed update of the building code, and in 1951, the CPC used the ID and Robert Brownjohn to produce *Chicago Plans,* a show explaining the social concerns supposedly motivating Chicago's planning effort, issues the City Council and the city at large didn't always care to hear about. But having New York Life, the developers of Lake Meadows, as a client was a bomb waiting to go off.

As the city cleared the land, SOM came up with something astonishing for the Lake Meadows design: two long buildings pointing like knives toward the lake, each twenty-three stories high, 832 feet long, and only one forty-foot apartment wide, separated by a twelve-hundred-foot grass field. Their thin profiles would allow the surrounding neighborhood to see the lake while residents would have their own vistas. New York Life loved the plan; the City Council did not. The buildings were enormous, out of scale, sailing amid the barren expanse of the superblock; even Hilbs, of *Hochhausstadt* fame, disliked them. Fronting each was to be a nine-foot wide-open "gallery in the sky"; SOM referred to the building cozily as stacked row houses, but the idea of a January morning, wind off the lake, twenty-three stories up in the "gallery in the sky," makes the heart pound.

And there was another problem: New York Life wanted to close Cottage Grove Avenue within the Lake Meadows superblock. Nat Owings, with his connections at City Hall, clouted through the request despite loud opposition. Hearings resulted, and suddenly SOM was defending itself on all sides: against whites who were using the road closure as an excuse to try to kill an integrated project; against traditionalists who were scared by the design; and against blacks who saw the destruction of a viable neighborhood. The developers themselves admitted that blight wasn't the target. "It wasn't necessarily a slum area," admitted Ambrose Richardson, designer of Lake Meadows. ". . . There were well-kept neighborhood homes and communities. . . . We were displacing these poorer people who had been really maintaining a good neighborhood. . . . In some cases, the people wouldn't get out of their places, and the city turned off their water and their utilities and everything." The design ultimately changed, but the development didn't. Though Lake Meadows began with some good intentions, the fact was, as one architect would later say, "We were living separate lives." At a lunch held two years later to celebrate progress on Lake Meadows, everyone in attendance save Mayor Kennelly lived in the suburbs. Owings soon resigned from the CPC, blaming the City Council for colluding with slumlords to retard urban progress, which it surely was, but he couldn't recognize that Lake Meadows was the architectural version of cutting off a weak but viable limb to attach a nifty new prosthesis. His reputation dented, Owings relocated to the San Francisco office.

To keep momentum going on the whole Opportunity Plan, Reginald Isaacs brought Gropius at Harvard, Mies at IIT, and sociologist Louis Wirth and city planner Martin Meyerson of the University of Chicago together with a host of other agencies for another study of the South Side. Isaacs's dream of leveling entire neighborhoods was proving harder than it had looked. The SSPB was showing cracks—for one thing, various local architects had produced designs not to the liking of Michael Reese Hospital, which now wanted Gropius to fix them. In Hyde Park, as the Hyde Park–Kenwood Community Conference was organizing block by block to stop white flight and prevent illegal conversions, the university administration was undermining their efforts with businessmen and real estate owners. The study, completed over a year of intense work, produced little of tangible use: Harvard offered an over-the-top drafting exercise, while Hilbs and his team ventured an out-of-touch plan to replace Chicago's grid with an angled, suburban "fishbone" street approach. His new traffic patterns replaced a large number of quiet streets with fewer—but much busier—ones. Bland, undefined open spaces would replace the backyards that Chicagoans saw as their own personal kingdoms. Even his supporters found it "much too drastic."

AS BUS DRIVER Harvey Clark, a twenty-nine-year-old Fisk graduate and former Tuskegee Airman, arrived at his new apartment at 1639 W. 19th Street in Cicero on June 8, 1951, it should have been clear to him that the fifty or so policemen at the door were not there to help him lift furniture. Just over the western city line from Chicago, the same grid held the same brick bungalows and two-flats you'd find in Park Manor and Lawndale, but Cicero was wound a few turns more tightly, the way certain Austrian villages are more German than Germany. No one stumbled into living in Cicero; they came for its fearsome insularity. Once home to Al Capone's crime empire, it now harbored white families who'd left changing neighborhoods to live among an immigrant population that pledged allegiance first and foremost to their own real estate. "They have acquired homes," said one Catholic priest of Cicero's Czechs, Slovaks, and Lithuanians, "but they made them the golden calf to be worshipped and possessed at all costs." In his subsequent lawsuit, Clark claimed the officers kicked and beat him, his wife, Johnetta, and two children. Despite Clark's claim for $200,000 in damages, Judge John Barnes insisted that the Cicero police had a responsibility to treat the family "just like white people." "See to it they are not molested," he said.

What followed surprised few in Chicago. Clark, a man willing to sue the Cicero Police Department, obviously wanted to make a statement, and the newspapers were covering the story, so on July 10, five hundred whites gathered as he made his second attempt to move in. Sheriff John Babb and eight cops managed to calm the crowd, but the next night it was larger and the sheriff's resolve was weaker; 3,500 whites surrounded the building with bricks; vandals trashed the Clarks' apartment as the mob burned their belongings in the street. The next day Clark announced that his family wouldn't be moving in, but Governor Stevenson still sent in the National Guard, and that night, for the first time, the world watched a race riot live on television. The unsatisfied mob overturned police cars and broke through police lines. Five hundred National Guardsmen countered with bayonets pointed and guns drawn. By two that morning, fifty-four rioters had been arrested.

Photos of young white Americans in violent rebellion against black civil rights spread as far away as Pakistan, Singapore, and Ghana. Walter White, executive secretary of the NAACP, rushed to the scene and said he'd never faced as much "implacable hatred as I found in Cicero," whose residents he dubbed "plodding, stodgy, intellectually limited human beings who desperately seek the security which they never had in Europe." Earl Dickerson led a "rally for justice" at the Chicago Coliseum. The grand jury indicted the landlord, Clark's lawyer, and three other blacks—but none of the rioters. Under pressure, Chief of Police Erwin Konovsky and three policemen were convicted on civil rights violations, but the charges were quietly overturned in 1954; the landlord, on the other hand, was judged insane. Though Adlai had scored politically, the real winners were the whites who'd defeated the blacks and the government. Encouraged white neighborhoods would continue to fight integration and open housing until the cards would fall and they'd run to the suburbs, now as much racial sanctuaries as proof of postwar prosperity. Moving Up as a goal was replaced by Moving Away. Through July 1951 the building remained wrapped in barbed wire, lit by floodlamps, under a state of siege; like the Mecca, another apartment building turned from home into symbol.

As Cicero burned, builders topped Mies and Herb Greenwald's next project, a pair of all-glass-and-steel co-op apartment buildings at 860–880 Lake Shore Drive. Exacting and harmonious, they were simply two twenty-six-story black steel frames with glass windows—essentially the skeleton of the Promontory Apartments, freed from its concrete. No decoration, save for the single I-beam running up the mullions. Each open plan unit had floor-to-ceiling glass windows, with a service core in the center similar to the Farnsworth House; a breezeway connected the two buildings across an expanse of marble. For months, ads had run aimed at older buyers who, it was assumed, were the only people who'd want to live in high-rises. "Worried by the insecurity of your present housing situation," they asked, "the threatened breakdown of rent controls?" But by November, as the first families moved in, it was clear Mies had achieved something greater than a safe investment for seniors. As the first tall buildings to go up in the city since the 1930s, 860–880 were instantly iconic; like the Arts Club, they represented everything that Chicago's—and America's—power class wanted to believe about itself and the country. "America, Americans, and most of all, the image makers of Madison Avenue," writes Stanley Tigerman, "were thoroughly ready to embrace Mies van der Rohe and his monuments as symbols of the 'spirit of the age.'"

Life inside 860–880 was anything but mass-produced; it was more a constant work of performance art that spoke to man's relationship to nature as much as the Farnsworth House did. So close to the shore, rooms fronting east seem to float over the lake. One visitor said sleeping there on a starry night made her feel she "was between heaven and earth," while John Cage, overwhelmed by a storm exploding around him, the building swaying in the wind, said, "Wasn't it splendid of Mies to invent the lightning?" What Moholy had dreamed of, Mies had accomplished; he'd turned every moment into art, made lightning his medium.

Mies often said, "You can't tell anybody how to live," but his faith in the beauty of industry, just when the city was producing more steel than all of Great Britain, sent a message. By tilting the city grid upward, Mies showed Chicago how to express its enormous postwar industrial and tech-nological power in a way that was intellectually rigorous, aesthetically vigorous, and attached to the long traditions of Western Civilization. "Technology is our fate," Mies told the *Tribune* in June 1951. "His mis-sion," wrote Peter Blake, "has been to *direct* the industrial process." And though some members of the Tavern Club might not have wanted to hear it, the new world didn't have to belong only to the wealthy; in terms of cost, 860–880 came in at only slightly more than Promontory per square foot. While Greenwald had planned them for an older, more established market, those airy, open apartments on the lake became the goal of young strivers shopping at Baldwin Kingrey (and who hadn't visited the Avenue of American Homes). Where Gropius and Hilbs denied the virtues of city life, Greenwald sold them, planting the seeds for a market-driven urban revival. 860–880 proclaimed a future of urban life based on density and an educated, prosperous upper middle class, very much the opposite of Cicero (and the opposite of what Mies himself professed to believe about the coming end of urban life); a vision of the city that threatened more people than just angry whites in their bungalows.

In late May 1952, *Mies v. Farnsworth* began in the Kendall County Courthouse. Both sides had agreed to arbitration before a special master, but it did little to speed the case. Through six weeks of attacks from Farns-worth's lawyer, Mies, hobbled by arthritis in his hip, displayed that same grand repose that had attracted his cult at IIT, meticulously and confi-dently answering questions, providing evidence that proved Farnsworth knew all along what was being built, down to a budget memo for $65,000 that she'd written. A photo taken of her in Mies's office as she points at a blueprint, pencil in hand, particularly damaged her claim to be a helpless spinster fleeced by a sly, sweet-talking artist from Europe. Oral arguments would come in January 1953, then the master would issue a final report. The evidence, in legal terms, was loaded in Mies's favor.

Except now the case went to the court of public opinion. Resolutely middlebrow *House Beautiful* decided to try Modernism as a whole and Mies in particular with the April 1953 issue, themed "The Next American Home" and featuring a splenetic rant from editor Elizabeth Gordon entitled "The Threat to the Next America." The buildings of Mies, Le Corbusier, and other "bad" modernists, she wrote, were "bad in more ways than in their lack of beauty alone." Gordon had broken the code. "They are all trying to sell the idea that 'less is more,' " she snapped, "both as a criterion for design, and as a basis for judgment of the good life." Her major gripes followed in bold type: **"They are promoting unlivability, stripped-down emptiness, lack of storage space, and therefore lack of possessions."** And for a magazine that opened with one hundred pages of advertisements, possessions were everything. **"For if the mind of man can be manipulated,"** she went on later, again in bold, **"in one great phase of life to be made willing to accept less, it would be possible to go on and get him to accept less in all phases of life."** Anything less than gleeful participation in consumer culture signaled a Red, and Mies was a fifth columnist. Gordon went so far as to provide a handy sidebar to help readers identify "The International Style" as if it were enemy aircraft.

There are reasons to not like Mies and the International Style, and Gordon made valid points about comfort and functionality, but tying them to a Marxist conspiracy was ludicrous; Mies and Edith Farnsworth had split over beige shantung silk, rarely found in a gulag. The truth was, Mies didn't really care how anyone lived. Controlling the look of a house in Plano intended as a work of art mattered to him; he couldn't care less about controlling a spec apartment building. His only requirement for 860–880 was uniform curtains, but he'd learned his lesson; the owner could use any material facing inward, as long as they were backed with his. Sales brochures made a point to feature rooms decorated in various styles including (gasp!) Early American. Even as Greenwald plotted to build more like them across the country, Mies got bored and handed it all off to Joe Fujikawa. He never lived in the two units of 860–880 that he'd received as part of his deal, claiming that he didn't want other residents nagging him in the elevator with their complaints. His other reason was more telling: there was "no place to put the furniture." "I can dream and imagine this new world," he told Bruce Graham, "but I can't live in it." Content to sleep under his chenille bedspread on Pearson, furniture against the wall, he watched boxing on the largest television available, puffing on one of his two dozen daily cigars while his youngest daughter Waltraut, who had come from Germany in 1948, aired out her room down the hall.

The controversy brought Gordon a telegram. "Didn't think you had it in you," wrote Frank Lloyd Wright, turning against his old friend Mies. "Am at your service from here on." She continued the campaign in her June issue with an article about the Farnsworth House, quoting the doctor herself. "In this house with its four walls of glass," Farnsworth said, "I feel like a prowling animal, always on the alert." Her complaints about her garbage can and lack of hanger space were all evidence of Mies's shrugging attitude toward the messy details of human life; he did once say, "The reason the Gothic church is such a great building is because it doesn't have plumbing." Certain aspects of 860–880 worked no better than the Farnsworth House; the apartments heat up to an alarming degree (though it was Greenwald who'd nixed air conditioning), and without double-paned glass, the windows ice over on the inside. The porous marble cracked. But confronted with the gulf between his supposedly functional architecture and its faulty reality, Mies said he wasn't exploring how materials function *now;* he was studying their potential. It was the job of the next generation to make it all work. If he agreed with Le Corbusier that a home was a machine for living, then he was an inventor, not a mass-marketer. And Dr. Farnsworth had hired him because of that.

The era of the "glass box" began at 860–880. A year after it topped, as Mies sweated in the Kendall County Courthouse, Gordon Bunshaft of SOM completed Lever House on Park Avenue in New York, and the race to build more Miesian (and Corbusian) skyscrapers was on, fueled to a large degree by Mies's former students and employees. While many of them, like most modern architects then, counted Le Corbusier as an influence, Mies exercised a more personal and practical sway in the direction postwar America took. His buildings weren't theoretical exercises; given their lower per-square-foot cost, they offered companies with swelling coffers a new place to put their money and make their presence known. In the coming decades, urban centers across America would be demolished and rebuilt with countless structures inspired by Mies. America demanded transparency now. His buildings didn't hide their problems; nor do they, as Gordon rightly suspected, allow *you* to hide behind your possessions. Yet as much as they expressed the potential of American power, they also unconsciously expressed how appearance now mattered more than the reality of things. Don't worry, Mies seemed to say, someone else will figure out how to fix the problems we create.

In 1952 Carl Condit's *The Rise of the Skyscraper* further spread the gospel of Mies. The *ur* text of the history—or legend—of Chicago's architecture, it expanded on Giedion's argument that the nineteenth-century Chicago School of Architecture was a movement consciously motivated by aesthetics rather than simply commercial imperatives to build tall buildings. By hitching Mies to Jenney, Sullivan, and Root, Condit now cast the German's unique perfectionism as a continuation of a longer historical movement, a technical advance anyone could replicate, which was definitely not true. Mies did nothing to dissuade this notion, and if he could ever be mistaken for a Marxist, it came from his teaching his personal style as an inevitable product of progress. Each building for Mies was a spiritual journey, yet he was loath to admit that his buildings caused enormous change, that his antimaterialist style became a cheap and brutal way for American institutions to state their power. If his style countered suburban conformity, it also helped effect devastating control on the South Side. Ultimately, Miesian architecture was all about class. The cultural gap between elite postwar liberals, intellectuals, and businessmen in Brooks Brothers suits, and the masses looking up at their towers was widening. To working-class Americans, Miesian austerity represented power and money that they weren't a part of.

THE MASTER'S REPORT came back in May 1953 in Mies's favor. The two sides settled in 1955 with the doctor coming off, in the end, as a much sillier person than she ever was. One of her quotes in the *House Beautiful* article spoke volumes: "Indeed, there was no thought of me at any time." Brilliant like Sibyl Moholy-Nagy, but bitterly shortchanged by the Bauhaus, she let the house run down until finally selling it in 1968 to someone more sympathetic to its beauty and unattached to the pain it represented.

That same month, May 1953, Walter Gropius turned seventy. Joseph Hudnut, dean of architecture at Harvard, couldn't get rid of him fast enough and set his official retirement date as June 30. Gropius came to Chicago for the dedication of a plaque in his honor on the grounds of Michael Reese Hospital and a gala birthday dinner for three hundred that night at the Blackstone Hotel, where his old comrade and rival Mies van der Rohe gave an affectionate speech. At one point Katharine Kuh overheard Gropius lean over to Mies and say, "All that work and what have we got to show for it—the picture window?"

CHAPTER 17

NOBODY KNOWS MY NAME

Revetta Chess filled the Thermos upstairs, while Leonard squeezed a few more records into the trunk of the Chrysler; its sideboards barely cleared the ground. Ten hours and twenty cups of coffee from now he'd be in Memphis breaking bread with their distributor, Buster Williams. Then he'd light out for hamlets and small southern towns to get Aristocrat sides into every jukebox he could find, stopping under the antennae of five-hundred-watt stations to leave new records and a fifty for the deejay; he'd restock stores, get drunk with producers who might have a line on some talented kid, make handshake deals with a cigarette always dangling from his lip, sprung on coffee and booze—just the way every other *farkoyfer* built a business. The thing was, Leonard knew about as much about smoked fish as he did about the blues. He'd come a long way from that first session with Muddy and no less than Langston Hughes had singled out the Macomba in a *Defender* column titled "Things I Like About Chicago I Like, And What I Don't, I Don't." The poet had praised "Hindu drumming like mad at the Macomba with a good little group who raise a boppish fog." But at the start of 1950, the Chess brothers had only enough confidence to react. Instead of taking a risk on Muddy's electric blues, Leonard hopped in the car and headed down the same old roads.

In his absence, stumpy Phil Chess in his fedora kept one eye on the Macomba and the other on Aristocrat—"Phil made a wonderful vice president of everything," said one producer—while Revetta held down the fort at their apartment on Drexel Boulevard. Leonard's new friend Muddy wasn't as patient. He wanted a hit record, so when the Leaner brothers, nephews of Al Benson, asked Baby Face Leroy to lay down some sides for their new Parkway label, Muddy got on board. In a cash business run on handshakes, everybody looked out for their own interests; Leonard's spiral notebooks surely didn't capture every dollar he took out of juke joints and hairdressers, and now Muddy took advantage of the fact that he had no signed contract with Aristocrat.

Recorded in a warehouse in January 1950, the Parkway session consists of eight energetic, playful cuts that, as Gwendolyn Brooks might say, came up from the root. Baby Face (a double for the basketball player Kevin Durant) was known to hop on one leg for an entire city block when he'd had enough to drink, and the mood on these songs is tight like that, his sinuous voice sliding around words and running phrases together. The highlight is "Rollin' & Tumblin' Parts 1 & 2," a five-and-a-half-minute hybrid of Delta and the West Side. As Baby Face hammers the drums, he snakes around the melody until halfway through, when he gives over to a fever of moaning and vocalizing that Little Walter and Muddy both sting at with their harp and guitar. It's a hypnotizing few minutes, right out of a circle dance as genuine as any Alan Lomax field recording. When Leonard heard about "Rollin' and Tumblin'," he promptly brought Muddy back in to record a studio version that wasn't as good as the original, but it still killed on the racks. Muddy had made his point to Leonard, though—from then on, he recorded with *his* band.

Muddy wasn't the only person who shoved Leonard toward success. Down in Memphis, Buster Williams suggested that the brothers trade the name "Aristocrat" for the catchier "Chess." A month later Leonard and Phil released the first two Chess singles: #1425 (after their first home, 1425 S. Karlov), a big weeping-in-your-Tom-Collins tenor sax version of "My Foolish Heart" by Gene Ammons, and #1426, "Walkin' Blues" by

Muddy Waters, whose flip side would inspire five young Englishmen to name their band after it: "Rollin' Stone." That fall a fire destroyed the Macomba Lounge. Cleared of arson, Leonard and Phil cashed the insurance check and went all in with the record business. The first Chess list shows a company making bets across the board; jazz and R&B crossovers like Ammons, Tom Archia, Andrew Tibbs, and Al Hibbler outnumbered Muddy, Jimmy Rogers, and Baby Face. Al Benson played Muddy and the rest of the Chess list in heavy rotation on WGES, while Leonard kept loading up the Chrysler and working his network of distributors, accounts, producers, and deejays, particularly one in Cleveland named Alan Freed, who'd debuted an R&B show aimed at white kids in July 1951. In Memphis, Buster Williams introduced Leonard to Sam Phillips, a minor producer who later sent up a number by Jackie Brenston and the Delta Cats called "Rocket 88." Released by Chess in June 1951, it shot to number one. Some consider it the first rock and roll recording.

If Black Chicago had tipped the balance of power in America, the cultural balance of power within Black Chicago was tipping toward its migrants from the South, and the blues were on the rise. Muddy's "Louisiana Blues," released that fall, captured what Mike Rowe calls "the very springtime of Chicago blues." A run of solid hits paid for Chess to move to an office in a nondescript building on the corner of 49th and Cottage Grove Avenue, next to an auto supply store. On July 11, 1951, Leonard and Phil brought Muddy and the band to Universal for a session. Leonard rigged up something with a sewer pipe for an echo, while Walter, just to try it out, plugged his harmonica directly into the amp. The result was a hard steel and glass sound as modern as Mies's breakthrough on Lake Shore Drive or Callahan's epiphany about the technology of photography; it matched Muddy's guitar and could be manipulated on the soundboard. The last defining element of the Chicago Sound was now in place. Another grueling night in the studio followed, and another slog of pissed-off retakes, especially on "She Moves Me," a slow grind that drummer Elgin Evans just couldn't get the hang of. Willie Dixon's tutoring was helping Leonard's gut sense of the blues, if slowly. "I would argue," said Malcolm

Chisholm, "that Leonard didn't know shit about blues, but he knew an awful lot about feeling." Unable to stand it anymore, Leonard ran out of the control room. "Get the fuck out of the way!" he shouted, shoving Elgin off his stool and grabbing the sticks. "I'll do that." The tape rolled. If you listen to the song today, that heavy, thumping beat—it has to race like a little brother here and there to catch up—belongs to Leonard Chess.

Over the long haul, B.B. King and his melodic, big-band approach to the blues, with its horn sections and delicate guitar work, would appeal more to mainstream America than Muddy; the Clean Blues versus the Dirty Blues. But only one man challenged Muddy Waters when it came to those Dirty Blues. If Biggie had Tupac, Paul had John, and Mozart had Salieri, then Muddy had Chester Arthur Burnett, better known as Howlin' Wolf. No one in Chicago had seen him yet; all they'd heard were two songs sent up from Memphis by Sam Phillips—"Moanin' at Midnight" and "How Many More Years," both number-one hits for Chess in the fall of 1951—but they were all you needed to know there was another genius in the room. Tonsillitis as a boy had made Wolf's throat a natural Auto-Tune, twisting his deep, rough voice with a lonely intensity that went all the way down to something universal, to the place, as Phillips called it, "where the soul of man never dies." "Moanin' at Midnight," for instance, starts with a contemplative hum that could belong to a man standing in a field at dusk, but a flash of guitar turns it into a howl—someone's after him, knocking on his door, calling him on the phone. Cutting harp runs, lightning stabs of guitar, and thundering distortion build the sense of pursuit as Wolf bellows in fear and ultimately resistance. There's no story beyond a man being hunted—the blues equivalent of Camus—but it conveys the reality of centuries of black life, and as the statement of a soul, it belongs next to Blind Willie Johnson's "Dark Was the Night." The B side, "How Many More Years," lives in Muddy's world of sex—Wolf's walking out on a no-good woman—but without Muddy's player attitude, it sounds like a man with factory dust on his boots sick of a trifling wife. Wolf had worked Delta juke joints until he moved to West Memphis in 1948. His unusual voice landed him a radio show on KWEM, where he howled and woofed and created the shtick that Wolfman Jack later lifted. A family man in his late thirties, he was content to stay in West Memphis for now, leaving Chicago to Muddy, while Leonard worked out a deal with Phillips and the Modern label in L.A. that made Wolf an exclusive Chess recording artist for the musical equivalent of a few draft picks.

In May 1952 Chess produced another homegrown star. Twenty-two-year-old Little Walter, Muddy's mascot, was bouncy and restless, qualities that made his harp playing sparkle, but he was impatient too, and he'd long ago given up Pepsi-Cola for whiskey and pot. To keep him happy, Leonard and Muddy let him cut a solo number, with the band laying down a dance beat—Leonard insisted on a dance beat for everything—then shelved the result. A few months later, windows open to catch the warm breeze, someone pulled the demo off the shelf. Outside, an old woman loaded with bags waited for the bus. A few seconds after the needle went down, her feet began to move, and soon she was flat-out dancing on the corner—Chess market research, circa 1952. Leonard released "Juke" in August, just as the Democratic National Convention came to town.

The springtime of the blues went into full flower. Leonard Chess had the good sense now to let Muddy do what he wanted. He replaced Little Walter, off on his own now with Junior Wells, and brought in pianist Otis Spann, who skittered around like Walter's harp but with an added sophistication (unless he was drunk, which was too often). With his new band, Muddy recorded "Mad Love," famous for introducing the stop-time beat (Ba-dum, ba-*dum*. One two. Ba-dum, ba-*dum*. One two), and he defended his title as the King of Blues with a string of now-classic Willie Dixon songs. Though in his autobiography he portrayed the Chess brothers as conniving and greedy, Dixon himself was a prime operator, "in cahoots" with Leonard and known to put his name on riffs, mash-ups, and often outright copies of existing material. "I'm Ready," for example, came from waiting for Muddy to get out of the shower one evening before a show. "I'm ready," Muddy announced when he was done. "Ready as ready can be." And there was Dixon's song. "He was a fabulous song writer and song stealer," says Marshall Chess. His ability to whip up a hit out of scraps of a playground chant or a street-corner toast evidenced a resourceful brand of genius, and his talents as a bluesman often paid off for everyone. One night between sets at the Zanzibar, he accosted Muddy in the men's room and handed him a new song that used the stop-time rhythm. The two squeezed into a stall, where three-hundred-pound Willie schooled him through the chords and what lyrics there were. Muddy opened the next set with the debut of "I'm Your Hoochie Coochie Man," a monster hit in 1954 and one of the defining songs of his career.

Leonard and Phil still ran the business like a family; from the South Side to their later tonier suburban abodes, they kept their doors open to Muddy and their whole roster of performers, lent money, hired lawyers, and treated them at all times as social equals, even as their way of doing business crept toward the plantation. Muddy started to live larger. On Leonard's advice, he bought a house on the South Side for his wife, Geneva; during gigs he sat at a side table working through a bottle of champagne while his band played onstage.

Such coasting ended when Howlin' Wolf drove his DeSoto up from Memphis in 1954. Wolf landed hard, living with his sister in Gary and working at a steel mill until Leonard asked Muddy to put him up. As usual, Muddy did what Leonard asked, though not for free; Wolf paid for his room and Geneva's cooking. Muddy enjoyed the freedom that his bargain with Leonard allowed—for one, Leonard's lawyer knew how to get him out of paternity suits. Wolf, on the other hand, played his first gig at the Zanzibar as if he were auditioning for the rest of his life. Six foot six, three hundred or so pounds, he bellowed and shook and threw everything he had into it; he crawled on the stage and danced on the bar. The rivalry was on. Wolf and Muddy pushed each other musically, both live and in the studio, while Willie Dixon played them off each other. "Rockin' Daddy," "Baby How Long," and "Evil (Is Going On)" were all big hits for Wolf.

By now Leonard had bank enough to move from Drexel down to South Shore. He had new hits from Willie Mabon and Little Walter, and his deepening friendship with Alan Freed was paying dividends not just in airtime but in material: Freed sent Harvey Fuqua and the Moonglows and their doo-wop anthem "Sincerely" to Leonard. But the cash didn't all come from records. Leonard and Phil had made a deal with Benny Goodman's brothers to form ARC Music. At this point, the music business was still about the song, not the singer; songwriters and publishers encouraged as many covers as possible so three or four could be on the charts at any one time. (Complaints decades later about white artists covering black music in this era tend to ignore the fact that white artists were just as busy trying to screw other white artists.) ARC Music took the Chess brothers out of that innocent place where handshakes were a bond and back-of-a-napkin accounting balanced an artist's record sales against what Leonard laid out for legal bills, doctors, cars, and out-of-pocket "I gotta have a hundred bucks" cash advances. Chess regularly shifted royalties among artists to keep everyone afloat, the way Magnum paid all its photographers off the work of the successful few. But as Chess's new revenue stream grew, who wrote what began to matter, and names were added to copyrights as promotional incentives or as payment in kind. Radio and TV increased performers' power to drive sales, but their participation in the profit stream remained the same pennies per record. The greed of the old Chess Records was no longer communal.

OVER ON 35TH STREET, at Second Ward headquarters, Bill Dawson wobbled in his old wooden throne. The Mob, blessed by City Hall, had violently taken control of "black policy" (aka "the numbers"), and policy was Dawson's sole program for black empowerment. "If anybody is to profit out of gambling in the Negro community it should be the Negro," he said. "It is purely an economic question. I want the money my people earn to stay in the community." On top of the prizes, a single wheel could pay out $200,000 in salaries that everyone up the ladder spent in Black Chicago, all the way to the Jones and McKusick brothers, policy kings who'd poured their profits into legitimate businesses and even the SSCAC. Under the mafia, though, policy sucked money out of the black community, and Dawson had to keep quiet about it.

In early 1950, just months after Joe McCarthy began his Red hearings, Tennessee senator and presidential hopeful Estes Kefauver went after the Mob; he subpoenaed mobsters and held hearings, in a dramatic build to an autumn climax in Chicago, the city he called "perhaps the one most important center of criminal activities" in the nation. According to Kefauver, the Mob had spread into some ninety-two legitimate businesses; no surprise to Chicagoans. The Korshak brothers, attorney Sidney and politician Marshall, for instance, who'd represented the Mob since the days of Capone, had fingers in every aspect of the city—labor, entertainment, business, government. Sidney had gone to L.A. in the late 1940s to burrow into the movies and California politics, while Marshall stayed in Chicago with the Machine. As Kefauver's witness list dribbled out, mobsters like Sam Giancana and Tony Accardo disappeared, joints like the Macomba went up in flames. Even Big Ed Kelly had a well-timed fatal heart attack that October. Hapless Mayor Kennelly, who'd once said he didn't believe organized crime existed, decided to clean up the city—but only Bill Dawson's wards, where cops clamped down on gambling and jitneys. Furious, Dawson stormed to the mayor's office, but an offended Kennelly threw him out—a stupid move considering that Dawson controlled five wards and Kennelly was up for reelection in a year. A regretful Arvey later called Kennelly "the most inept man I ever met." The Gray Wolves still wanted a weak mayor in City Hall, though, so a secret peace conference was arranged, one unprecedented for America in 1951: the white mayor of the nation's second-largest city was forced to silently subject himself to a dressing-down from a black politician. "Who do you think you are," Dawson shouted, perched on his peg-leg, pointing at Kennelly. "I bring in the votes. I elect *you*. *You* are not needed, but the votes are needed. I deliver the votes to you, but you won't talk to *me?*"

With no one else in the wings, Kennelly got his next term, and Dawson looked like the most powerful black politician in America. Unfortunately, he seemed to believe it. "These people aren't going to get things [Dickerson's] talking about for a long time," he told John Johnson. "And while they're waiting, they need me to look after their needs." He slated his own candidates for alderman in the Third and Twentieth Wards, a move promptly squashed by rising Democratic star Dick Daley. Meanwhile, policy went underground until it reappeared as the daily numbers in Your State Lottery. The Mob pulled big-time gambling out of Chicago, "the fountainhead of the crime situation," according to one senator, and relocated it in Las Vegas. The strippers kept stripping, and you could always find a poker game, but as much as Dave Garroway moving to New York, or the jet engine, it signaled the beginning of the end for Chicago as the nation's center. The city sprouting up in the Nevada desert was a miniature of Ed Kelly's convention-friendly, Mob-friendly, vice-friendly Chicago—but without factories, Louis Sullivan, or snow.

THE FINAL ITEM in Langston Hughes's column of Chicago favorites was Mahalia Jackson, who could, the poet said, "out-sing an angel when it comes to gospel songs." By January 1950, Mahalia was as famous as a black woman could be in America, traveling cross-country to sold-out arenas. In Chicago she added Mahalia's House of Flowers at 47th and Michigan to her expanding business interests; now anyone who asked her to sing at a church event had to buy their flowers from her. She appeared on *Studs' Place,* and the French ate her up—"I Can Put My Trust in Jesus" won the Grand Prix du Disque. *Ebony* ran a feature on her, and Detroit even had a Mahalia Jackson Day. But she wasn't satisfied. Being as famous as a black woman could be in America in 1950 was still nowhere near being as famous as a white woman could be.

In spring of 1950, black radio pioneer Joe Bostic called her bluff: he offered her the headline for a gospel show that October at Carnegie Hall, where Paul Robeson and Marian Anderson had sung, where Sister Rosetta Tharpe had strummed her guitar in John Hammond's *From Spirituals to Swing* concert. But as the day came closer, and Mahalia was being driven east to New York, the legend loomed larger. A friend in the car reminded her over and over of all the famous opera singers who'd stood on the stage of Carnegie Hall. What it would mean for her. "She had me vomiting from Chicago to New York," said Mahalia later. They pulled into town so sick with nerves that their first stop was the emergency room at Bellevue. That night she shared the bill with the Famous Ward Singers, starring one of her biggest rivals in the world of gospel, Clara Ward, the black Judy Garland. Despite her homely, mannish looks and mental health shredded by her tortuous relationship with her domineering mother, Ward's febrile energy and warbling alto drew lovers that included the Reverend C. L. Franklin.

When it came her turn, Mahalia edged out into the spotlight as if she were back at the Great Northern Theatre, hands held up at her chest for the first few songs like a proper Negro trying out for *Swing Mikado*. On "It Pays to Serve Jesus," she finally closed her eyes and did what she did at small churches—she imagined herself as a big shimmering peacock, glorifying the Lord. Her hands began to move. Her knees bent, and she launched into the heights of the song, a swelling musical rose window that let all the light of God into Carnegie Hall. The next songs were faster—"bounce" songs, she called them—and the finale, "Amazing Grace," wrecked the place. Clara Ward was an afterthought in the reviews.

The dam had cracked but it didn't break, partly because Mahalia didn't want it to—she turned down the role of Berenice in the Broadway production of *The Member of the Wedding;* Ethel Waters then took it and parlayed it into the television show *Beulah.* TV ideas came and went as Mahalia seemed to wrestle with the price of success. She collected an entourage that she'd bully one day and mother the next; she'd stash tens of thousands of dollars in cash in her bra and underwear, and what she couldn't carry, she invested in real estate on the South Side. Yet she still didn't feel secure.

On August 26, 1951, she swallowed hard and walked into a roomful of very serious-looking white folks sitting in a converted barn in Stockbridge, Massachusetts, not far from Tanglewood. Encouraged and assisted by critic and Hunter College professor Marshall Stearns, Philip and Stephanie Barber were renovating Music Inn, amid the low mountains of the Berkshires, to be a casual, integrated forum for the academic study of jazz. As much as Mahalia hungered for white acceptance—she'd felt flattered by Stearns's invitation—she still had her guard up here, especially when she'd learned she was expected to answer questions *and* sing for free. Dr. Willis James of Spelman College started with a lecture building on anthropologist Melville Herskovitz's ideas about the roots of African American music, then shifted into a technical discussion of scales and rhythm that flummoxed Mahalia—field cries and African drums had nothing to do with singing for the Lord. Music, for her, was not an intellectual pursuit; she couldn't even read notation. She stepped forward and began to sing. But something felt wrong. It was strange enough to see only white faces, but in every church, hall, or tent that she'd played, the heads had moved, hands waved and clapped. These white folks, though—the likes of Leonard Bernstein, Aaron Copland, and even famed A&R man John Hammond—couldn't even clap in time.

Finally she stopped. "No-no, you got to clap on the *off*-beat like this, see?"

After a brief master class on keeping time to African American music, Mahalia picked up a house-breaking version of "Didn't It Rain." The clapping didn't improve much, but the earnest faces in seersucker suits tried, and afterward, Mahalia gave a short history of gospel, all the academics "picking at my music like birds at a box of corn." No one but Studs had ever taken her this seriously. She stayed for a week, opening gospel to the white musical establishment. Word spread. Walter Winchell touted her second appearance at Carnegie Hall and the resulting sell-out crowd, mostly white, went wild. In March she went on *The Ed Sullivan Show,* many years and many pounds away from the young woman who'd scandalized the Old Settler churches of Bronzeville, but she displayed the same public ecstasy, blasting out a passion in these pre–rock and roll days that most whites hadn't seen, an almost frightening energy that kids were beginning to circle around. John Hammond whispered in her ear that it was time to leave Bess Berman and Apollo for Columbia Records.

Mahalia let things stew as she prepared for her first tour of Europe in 1952; it was the white people's turn to wait. She let them wait the better part of two years before meeting with the head of talent at Columbia Records in New York. The Mephistopheles of midcentury American music, Mitch Miller in his plaid jackets and goatee wrote large checks that damned great artists to years of overproduced, cheesy records. After lunch at his plush Central Park West apartment, he offered her four years at $50,000 each, four sessions a year. She said she'd think about it, then went to her hotel. "When I stepped in there," she later said of her room, "it was like a castle. I mean the walls, the rugs, the furniture, the paintings. . . . I said, 'No wonder these people strive so hard.' Honey, I didn't want to go back. . . . I was ready to move on up. . . . Once I saw what was to be had, there was no turning back."

Everyone gave her advice. Studs didn't like Bess Berman at Apollo either, but he liked the recordings; Hammond warned that Columbia wouldn't support her if she didn't break out, and she'd have no creative control. But all she could picture was that posh hotel room. Just before Easter 1954, Mahalia shook the devil's hand and signed, figuring she'd be able to outsmart him. Miller immediately called William Paley, head of CBS (and another Chicago native), and by the end of the week, she had her own radio show, scheduled to debut in September. Her one condition: Studs had to be the writer. "If he hadn't of kept plugging me," she said, "you all might not have known me past 12th Street."

So Studs started work on the show, thrilled to be out of the cold, until one day during rehearsals at the Wrigley Building, when a network suit sidled up to him with a familiar-looking piece of paper and a pen. Studs shook his head. He'd sacrificed his beloved TV show for McCarthy, and now he was about to lose Mahalia's radio show.

Just then, Mahalia walked by, knowing full well what was happening. "He want you to sign that, baby?"

"Uh huh," said Studs.

"You goin' to?"

"Uh uh."

"Okay. Let's rehearse."

Now the factotum shook his head. "Oh, but he *must* sign it, Miss Jackson."

She stopped. "If Studs don't write the show, Mahalia Jackson don't sing."

And that was that. A deal was quickly struck whereby Studs could continue on as a writer and as a voice, but without credit. This strange balance ran throughout their relationship. Mahalia, his patron and caretaker, not only made sure he had a job but gave him a camel-hair coat for Christmas, taught him how to eat gumbo, protected him from a world that had gotten meaner since the heyday of the WPA. Studs's role was to be the expert, to be the bestower of white approval when he in fact was powerless. But after rehearsal he could go to the Wrigley Building restaurant, which would most certainly throw Mahalia out, and treat himself to dinner with money she'd paid him. That they negotiated their complicated friendship with candor, respect, and affection, in a city bristling with racial violence, speaks well of them both.

Before the red light went on at nine-thirty p.m. September 26, 1954, Mahalia ran through her by-now standard pep talk for the whites in the audience. "You all got to learn how to clap, babies; you got to help Mahalia." Then she reminded the blacks that they were under no circumstances to "fall out." The director pointed at her, and *The Mahalia Jackson Show* went live. Twenty-five minutes later, she was the host of a hit radio show. The national press lined up for interviews. She began seeing the very handsome, and wealthy, the Reverend Russell Roberts of Atlantic City. Kup worked her into columns in the *Sun-Times,* and after headlining the annual Harvest Moon Festival in November, she dashed straight off the stage for a flight to New York and her first session with Columbia. The result, "A Rusty Old Halo," was an irredeemable two minutes of corn unearthed by Miller himself. It was also a big hit. Going forward, there'd be reasonable and even excellent recordings of Mahalia on Columbia, but for each of those there were two or three head-shakers with chirpy white background singers, bizarre arrangements, or ponderous timing. The Mahalia who danced and wrestled with God was back on Apollo.

IN NOVEMBER 1951, as the first families moved into 860–880 Lake Shore Drive, a single mother and her ten-year-old boy hauled boxes into the second floor of a two-flat on the 6400 block of St. Lawrence Avenue, owned by her mother, Alma Spearman. Mamie Till Bradley was short and pert, a black Betty Boop with round face and big eyes. Her first husband, Louis, had been a bad sort, court-martialed and executed during World War II, but their boy Emmett was the center of Mamie's life, especially after a bout with polio left him with a slight speech defect and a stammer. Bobo, she called him, ten years old, collected Little Lulu and Superman comics and seemed to come down with everything going around, mumps, measles, you name it. He'd begun school at McCosh Elementary on South Champlain Avenue, and though a game of football in nearby Washington Park would have been fun, he stayed home to help his mother.

The rest of Black Chicago seemed to be out in Washington Park, and on a sunny afternoon like this one, all the speakers came out to the South Side version of Bughouse Square. Amid the Communists and nutjobs, three men in black suits, white shirts, and bow ties—Fruit of Islam—circled a fourth in a leopard cape and black beret. *The white man is a spook,* said one of the three. *God is not a spook. There is no Holy Spirit. God cannot be. . . .*

Sonny Blount waved a mimeographed sheet of paper that looked like one of Buckminster Fuller's letters, covered in single-spaced type, all caps. *You are the spook,* he said. *The Negro is the spook, and Jesus is not our god.*

The men in suits nodded. Blount rearranged his beret and continued his explanation of why the Earth was an evil place, why Negroes should be happy to be uncorrupted children, and the spacemen. . . .

All three Black Muslims smiled. So you believe in the spaceship?

A young man stepped forward and pulled Sonny away. Twenty-four-year-old Alton Abraham, when not training at Provident Hospital to be an

X-ray technician, spent his time with Blount and a few other men studying Egyptian history, the secret languages hidden within words, and primarily what Blount's thought meant for the American Negro. Left to
himself, Sonny would have been happy to just read and practice music, so
Abraham had formed a company, Thmei Research, to spread his mentor's
message through performances and recordings of his music, but without
all the white record producers buzzing around Mahalia.

Blount left some of his mimeographed sheets behind. They set forth a
philosophy directed only at the black man, abandoned by all the other
races who had followed their own gods. Jesus didn't care about blacks—if
he did, their lot wouldn't be so hard. No, the cosmos wanted the black man
to educate himself, to look toward science and space for his salvation, and
then save the rest of the Earth's people, collapsed in failure and evil. "THE
NEGRO RESURRECTED FROM HIS STATE OF IGNORANCE," he wrote in a broadside, "IS THE ONLY MEANS OF SALVATION LEFT FOR AMERICA." If these words
had come out of Martin Luther King, Jr.'s mouth, they'd be carved on
walls. In shades of Gertrude Stein, with a pinch of Duchamp, Sonny
Blount's broadsides made points through wordplay, etymology, and exege-
sis, skipping across thousands of years of language and culture in obses-
sive, intricate, almost musical ways, modulating rhythms and repeating
phrases the way you'd riff on a theme, improvising and developing until it
exploded into meaning, even if the meaning was silly.

By 1951 Blount had boiled down his twelve-piece orchestra to a quintet
that he trained not just musically but philosophically and ethically, in his
secret knowledge of music as "a bridge to another dimension." The music
was melodic, even romantic, but just slightly off center, built on Duke
Ellington, Fletcher Henderson, and Fats Waller, whom he considered "the
creators" as much for their social importance as for their music. "A band,"
Blount once said, "can demonstrate unity among men more than anything else in the world." He saw an agenda behind the death of the bands:
by breaking them down into small groups, "you destroy initiative and
cause total chaos and confusion of the people in the black communities."

The Nation of Islam (NOI) was curious about Sonny. Since getting out of prison in 1946 for resisting the World War II draft, Elijah Muhammad had slowly built up Chicago's Temple No. 2 in wealth, if not yet in numbers. Even as it advocated separation, reparations, and a total repudiation of white America—the NOI had no interest in moving into Park Manor or attending mass at St. Columbanus—it still took advantage of the capitalist system. Its clean-cut men were highly employable, and its restaurant, farm, and real estate holdings were soon to kick off meaningful revenues. The weekend before Labor Day 1952, as "Juke" streamed out of windows all over the South Side, an ex-convict named Malcolm Little arrived in Chicago along with a group from Detroit's Temple No. 1. As Little found his seat, Elijah Muhammad came out, tan-skinned and trim in a golden fez, to deliver a long speech on the history of the black man in America and how knowledge would restore him to his primacy. Then he called out to Malcolm Little. Would the new convert be able to stay clean and live within the ways of Allah? "We will see how he does," said Muhammad. "I believe that he is going to remain faithful." A few weeks later, back in Detroit, Malcolm Little received his new Nation of Islam name: Malcolm X.

It's very possible that Malcolm and Blount debated in Washington Park; under all the talk of space, Egypt, and mangled Islam, Blount and Elijah Muhammad held similar philosophies centered on black achievement and self-definition. Both stressed practical action, from eating healthy to doing business in an ethical and black-oriented manner. Both men advocated education (albeit alternative), taught temperance and personal responsibility; no smoking, cursing, or extramarital sex. Blount's vision, though, didn't demand separation from whites or believe they were devils, and it had something the NOI never had, which may be the key to understanding his work. "People have to have a sense of humor," he said later. ". . . That's where the real conscious comes in." How much of all this Sonny really believed and how much might have been a gimmick we'll never know, though page after page of obscurant writing, all the hermetic puzzling and wordplay scribbled in the margins, seem to indicate that he was in the main serious.

Just as Malcolm X believed that "Malcolm Little" was not his true name, so did Blount not recognize himself in his signature. His true name was Ra, same as the Egyptian sun god, but he offered his earth identity to Thmei Research. On October 20, 1952, the office of Richard J. Daley, county clerk, affirmed that Herman "Sonny" Blount was now Le Sony'r Ra, the name Thmei Research would use to promote him and the idea of black self-activation through science and space—"Afrofuturism." His friends took to calling him "Sun Ra." And as Sun Ra, he would lead jazz beyond bop to the limits of the avant-garde.

CHAPTER 18

THE LONELY CROWD

JOHN GARFIELD WANTED to finish their *Man with the Golden Arm* deal, so despite Simone warning him not to go to Los Angeles without "a good contract," Algren pointed himself west, reviews still warm in his hand, planning to show those movie types what a genuine writer looked like. The bard of derelicts and his junkie friend, Ken Acker, clambered aboard the Super Chief. Algren's source in the world of heroin and the loose inspiration for Frankie Machine, Acker was coming along as a "technical advisor," hoping to clean up half a continent away from the dozen addicts who were waving goodbye from the platform of the LaSalle Street Station. McCarthy's Wheeling speech and the beginning of the Red scare were a few days away.

The trip did not go well. Deposited in a seedy-chic apartment at the Garden of Allah, where Robert Benchley and F. Scott Fitzgerald had tippled away their own Hollywood exiles, Algren schemed for a better deal. A few years earlier Garfield had screwed boxer Barney Ross by making *Body and Soul* without buying his life rights, so the wary Algren reopened negotiations, and things turned ugly; in particular, him. As much as the crowd on the Left Bank spoke a different language, they'd shared his understanding of the world, and Simone had kept his skittish psyche on a leash, cheering him up when his mood tugged toward dark alleys. But here he was in over his head and trying to hide it with a pose that was part tough guy, part clown. Shouting and subpoenas ensued. Garfield stopped paying for the Garden of Allah, so Algren moved into Acker's efficiency until Bob Roberts, the producer, finally caved to the minor point he insisted on. The cost to Algren, though, would be profound.

Elsewhere, things were pleasant and promising for him. He'd accepted his National Book Award from Eleanor Roosevelt, then given it to Shay, who was scrambling around the West Side getting releases from every bum and hooker he'd photographed for the coming *Life* piece. Algren insisted that one shot be recaptioned—"Just because a woman wants to party in the afternoon and needs three bucks don't make her a whore." Doubleday had bought an expanded version of the *Life* article to cash in on the novel, but Algren's proposal for *Nobody's Old Chicago* sounded like true love: "New York is the place where they bind books and write blurbs and arrange the publicity and print the galleys. . . . But Chicago is the place where the book is lived out before it is bound and the song is sung before it is recorded."

He worked on the screenplay, taught a fiction class at the University of Chicago, and turned up at every party that passed for literary, often bumping into *New Yorker* writer A. J. Liebling, temporarily relocated here for 1950. Out in L.A., Algren had reconnected with his ex-wife, Amanda, no longer the docile young Polish girl she'd been, but still willing to follow in a way that Simone wasn't; there were signs it could turn serious. Simone, meanwhile, sent along letters begging him to have her for a few months that summer—Sartre insisted they take their vacations at exactly the same time. Her promises of food, sex, and housekeeping finally earned an invitation to the tiny white cottage he'd just bought in the dunes of Miller, Indiana, where Chicago's skyline flecked the western horizon. Then he handed in the screenplay and waited for his destiny to arrive.

Shay went to the printer to watch their issue of *Life* come off the press. Instead of West Side drunks and hookers, though, it featured prisoners in a Mexican jail. *Life* had spiked the article—and with it, Algren's overnight fame. Doubleday canceled *Nobody's Old Chicago*. In L.A., the screenplay had sunk soundlessly into the depths of movie development and though *The Man with the Golden Arm* sold well, Algren's advances over the years meant he wouldn't see much in royalties; what he got, he was gambling away. To top it off, hosting Simone was a mistake. Her presence plunged Algren into a funk, and at first he even refused to touch her, though when he saved her from drowning in the cold water of the lake, they began to make love again. In fact, *he* was the one drowning. He'd written a great book. A masterpiece. But it was dawning on Algren that he hadn't reached anyone. He'd shouted his best shout, the bar had gone quiet for a second, and now everyone had turned back to their drinks. Evenings, he drove back into the city to lose at poker, everything he'd ever wanted slipping through his fingers quietly, softly. That fall he and Simone departed friends once again, her heart, she said, a "kind of dirty, soft custard inside." Everything had become a little too messy to enjoy.

Art Shay stayed at his side, snapping pictures as Algren offered famous visitors his tour of the city's wild side. What had once been a quest to touch the depths of his fellow man was hardening into a star turn for his bummy image. In May, Shay landed him a long feature for the decidedly middlebrow *Holiday* magazine, a prose poem about his hometown that Doubleday, still in his corner, bought to publish in fall 1951. Far from celebrating the go-go spirit of Mies's new buildings, however, Algren let fly that October with a Valentine wrapped around a brick. Loving Chicago, he said, was like "loving a woman with a broken nose, you may well find lovelier lovelies. But never a lovely so real." Squeamish *Holiday* defanged the piece, but Doubleday published it uncut, with a title Shay had come up with: *Chicago: City on the Make.* "An ugly, highly scented object," ruled the *Tribune,* though most other reviewers saw it for the sad testament that it was: a goodbye to all the shabby addicts on the platform waving so long to an America pulling out of the station to sunnier climes.

Chicago: City on the Make may be the most beautiful, heartfelt thing Algren ever wrote, but the boosters and Fat Men who'd once dutifully lined up for their third signed copy of *The Man with the Golden Arm* now penned huffy letters to the editor. Already hurting, Algren seemed stunned. His love affair with Chicago had turned into the same kind of long, bitter strangle as his love for Simone. He wanted them both to love him unreservedly, to do what he said, to thank their stars that he loved them, but they'd both changed. Only spoilsports mentioned the poor and oppressed now, in the city that had once been labor's hope. Chicago still gave America characters it loved, but they were out of inkwells at Leo Burnett's ad agency: Tony the Tiger and the Jolly Green Giant. "Our myths are so many," Algren wrote, "our vision so dim, our self-deception so deep and our smugness so gross that scarcely any way now remains of supporting the American Century except from behind the billboards." Doubleday claimed to be happy, but sales stunk.

Just as the furor hit and Algren was deciding whether to remarry Amanda, Simone came for a visit. They slept in separate beds for two weeks until the last day, when according to her, "his face crumpled, he fell to his knees beside the bed, he told me he loved me." They made love, of course, and once again they staged the same freshman drama. "What I've tried to do since is to take my life back from you," Algren pleaded. "My life means a lot to me, I don't like its belonging to someone so far off, someone I see only a few weeks every year." Simone's response was a few decades ahead of the times: she would always love him, she wanted him in her life, but she could never commit to a life at his side, so could they be Friends with Benefits? Algren refused. Simone was obviously the stronger of the two and she'd used him even after that had become apparent—she would carry the guilt for that forever. She promised her very private Crocodile Husband that she would never write about their affair. He let go of the apartment on Wabansia.

The two things that Nelson Algren ever truly loved had made it clear that they did not love him the way he wanted them to. He would never recover.

A LONG A. J. LIEBLING piece ran in the January 12, 1952, *New Yorker.* "Second City," part one of a three-part series, took down Chicago with greater efficiency than either the wrecking ball tearing apart the Mecca or the shovels breaking ground on Lake Meadows. Over the next three weeks, Liebling continued to employ his dyspeptic style to dismember the city. The upper middle class and wealthy, he rightly said, had disentangled themselves from the source of their wealth: most businessmen lived out in the suburbs, and even the intellectuals chatting away in Hyde Park were increasingly insular. He called Hutchins out by name, nailed the buffoonery of the city's tribal politics, its fascination with crime, and the marks it left when it pressed its nose against the glass to watch New York; its casual and constant racism.

But on another level, Liebling's series was a deeply incurious, if not dishonest, bit of work, packed with as much pettiness as insight. If there was a reason to live in Chicago, Liebling couldn't find it—just at the moment when its population hit 3.6 million people, the seventh largest city in the world. Nothing—not Caldwell's Lily Pool, not the Auditorium Building, not even Bushman the Gorilla—merited the great connoisseur's interest. The restaurants were awful, the women dressed poorly and shopped foolishly, his apartment was small with neighbors either too friendly or not friendly enough, depending on his mood. The newspapers defied reading, the ball teams defied rooting, and the tap water wasn't quite to his taste. Lake Michigan was too cold. If he'd ever visited the Art Institute or IIT, he didn't let on. Algren he described with a pat on the head hovering over the buffet tables at cocktail parties in a turtleneck. There was no mention of the Chicago School of Television, nor of anything musical that wasn't opera or classical: no Mahalia, no blues or jazz. In fact, no African Americans except as proof that the city had something higher than the lowest rung of ethnic whites; otherwise, their presence and contribution went unnoticed.

Out in Hegewisch and Jefferson Park, on the banks of Bubbly Creek, response was muted, as no one there had ever heard of either A. J. Liebling or *The New Yorker.* But those who lived in Astor Street mansions and Mies's apartments, swaying in storms, felt as if they'd walked in wearing a cardigan when the invitation said BLACK TIE. The name stuck. "The Second City," like "The Windy City," another dismissive moniker issued from Manhattan.

LIEBLING HAD RESERVED a special dose of venom for Robert Maynard Hutchins and his experimental college, "whose inmates" the writer "viewed with sympathy, like the Little Princes in the Tower, or Hansel and Gretel in the cage." In mid-December 1950, Hutchins had resigned to become vice president of the Ford Foundation and also guide the publication, at long last, of the Great Books. Liebling took aim at the trivializing effect that Hutchins and Adler were having on the city's collective culture, with the ubiquitous Great Books groups and "determined ladies who want to discuss Lionel Trilling." Again, Liebling got many things right, and Hutchins's departure was overdue; his lack of interest in running the university hadn't been apparent to undergrads inspired by his rhetoric. Winning the "Chicagoan of the Year" award as he packed his bags, he and his second wife, Vesta, happily decamped for Pasadena, where he wrote checks for his friends' think tanks and seeded probably his most lasting legacy: public television. Ironically, at his farewell address in Chicago, Hutchins had attacked his new enemy: "The horrid prospect that television opens before us, with nobody speaking and nobody reading, suggests that a bleak and torpid epoch may lie ahead." Between the atomic bomb and TV, Hutchins seems to have made his greatest contributions to the things he hated most.

That fall Lawrence Kimpton took over as chancellor and almost immediately began to undo aspects of the Hutchins college. More important, he focused the university's full attention on the condition of Hyde Park. In February 1952 a spate of physical assaults, including one on the wife of a faculty member, roused a special meeting of the Hyde Park–Kenwood Community Conference. The university had been waiting for this opportunity. Kimpton made a speech in essence commending the HPKCC for doing such nice work and for being such good neighbors, but now it was time for the grown-ups to take over. The result was the South East Chicago Commission (SECC), charged with working with City Hall and the business community, while the HPKCC kept making nice with the neighbors. The reality was that the SECC, dominated by the University of Chicago, would now direct Hyde Park's renewal.

Maybe the most famous product of the University of Chicago then was a book that implicitly criticized Hutchins's Great Books and their commodification of culture. *The Lonely Crowd*, written by sociology professor David Riesman, claimed that societies go through three phases: High Growth Potential, Transitional, and Decline. In the first, most people conform to traditions; in the second, they "acquire early in life an internalized set of goals" that makes them "inner-directed." In the third phase, which he saw postwar America slipping into, individuals care only about "the expectations and preferences of others." These people are "other-directed" and only found themselves through the approval of others—by driving the right car, living in the right suburb, dreaming the right dream. In the United States of the 1950s, society, media, and business were now structured to provide Americans with needs and the way to satisfy them; cradle-to-grave consumers, they were losing any personal motivation beyond their own comfort. Chicagoans were no different, and maybe a bit worse. The growing race and class conflicts that were redefining "regular" reinforced the "other directed" in unhealthy ways; community was becoming conformity, your mowed lawn, washed car, and face at church on Sunday proved to your neighbors that you were in line and not just in some vague, sociological way.

Crossroads Chicago would play a major role in determining what "other" would direct everyone, from Tony the Tiger to *Great Books of the Western World*, finally unveiled on April 15, 1952, in the Grand Ballroom of the Waldorf-Astoria. After eight years of toil in the intellectual mines, Hutchins and Adler now stood in tuxedoes before all fifty-four volumes, flanked by Nelson Rockefeller, Conrad Hilton, Henry Grunwald, and Jacques Barzun. As recently as a year ago, William Benton had again threatened to board up the money pit, whereupon Adler devised a plan to pre-sell a "patron's subscription" for twice the price; luckily Paul Mellon had fallen for it. Printed on Bible paper, in minuscule type, the books expressed their solemn mission to be "the means of continuing and revitalizing Western civilization for the sake of the West and for the sake of all mankind."

In the first volume, titled *The Great Conversation*, the only sort of introduction or explanation in the entire series, Hutchins made his case for the Great Books, and it wasn't strong. "Democracy," we are told, "requires liberal education for all," but it had always been the province of the elite. Now, since everyone who wanted a liberal education could get one, those "not capable of acquiring this education . . . should be deprived of political power and probably of leisure. Their uneducated political power is dangerous, and their uneducated leisure is degrading and will be dangerous." Hutchins followed this breathtaking statement with the caveat that this did not "require the immediate adoption in any given country of universal liberal education." Proposing a kind of intellectual vagrancy law, the book says in effect: *If you don't have an education or can't handle it, you should be locked up, but there's no requirement that anyone offer it to you, so . . . you'll have to be locked up.*

Just under two thousand sets were sold in 1952; the next year, only 138. Hutchins and the *Encyclopaedia Britannica* brought in adman Leo Burnett, whose new promotional pieces made the "other directed" point clear: "If you have gained a measure of success in this Great America—these are the books that can help you to even greater attainment." Door-to-door salesmen spread out, and by 1977, one million sets of the Great Books had been sold. Medieval Scholasticism, once the province of monks, now belonged to the masses, at a low monthly price.

CHAPTER 19

CONVENTION SUMMER

S TATELY, PLUMP DICK Daley grabbed hold of the brass rail and lifted the casket up and out through the doors of St. Nicholas of Tolentine Church. Death was clearing his path again. Fourteen years ago he'd won his first election when State Representative David Shanahan died just before voting day, leaving an open ballot line for him to jump onto. Now, on January 6, 1950, as he slid the body of Cook County Clerk Michael J. Flynn into a hearse, Daley could consider the vacant office his. The funeral cortege began its long drive through a light flurry of snow to the cemetery in Evanston.

Though sixteen years younger than Mies, Daley was carved of the same stone: thinning hair combed back, fleshy ears and jowls, paunch buttoned into an expensive Duro suit. Neither one had command of the English language; Daley bumbled and botched words, dropped *dem* and *dose* like rocks onto flowerbeds. But like the architect, he too understood the value of bricks. He had no plans to ever move to the lakefront, as Kelly and Kennelly had; instead he'd built a brick bungalow like all the others in Bridgeport (his was just a little larger). Neither Mies nor Daley was driven by money; what they craved was the power to move large things, to build structures meant to last forever. For them, time moved in slow cycles. Mies often said, "You do not invent a new architecture every week," and for Richard J. Daley, politics was just as slow and simple, an expression of unbending will. Monuments are made with that attitude. So are dictators.

Daley was a mama's boy at heart. Lillian pampered and powdered her son to kill the Stockyards stink, dressed him in little suits that made his family's lace-curtain aspirations very clear, but Dick had no illusions. Diligent, unremarkable, he plowed through the business curriculum of De La Salle Institute at 35th and Wabash, a block from the Mecca. Unlike Studs, his daily visits to the Black Belt bred contempt; he belonged to the Hamburg Social and Athletic Club, one of the gangs that instigated the 1919 Race Riot, which helped get him a spot under the wing of Eleventh Ward alderman Big Joe McDonough. In the wild world of Chicago politics, young Daley stood out for not standing out, working his precinct for ten years as he plodded toward his law degree at DePaul. Being the apple of his mother's eye had taught him the most crucial lesson about succeeding in an organization: Please your boss. So Daley made himself necessary to McDonough. He didn't make waves, didn't take risks, didn't display great personal initiative. He just showed up every day and did his job, and when McDonough became county treasurer in 1930, he brought Daley along as his deputy to learn the ropes and the secrets. Only twenty-eight when Big Joe drank himself to death, Daley was passed over to run the Eleventh, but he cozied right up to the new man, Babe Connelly, and when David Shanahan died in 1936, the party owed him the state representative seat.

So Mr. Daley went to Springfield, a town that had slipped down a few moral pegs since Lincoln called it home. Again Daley kept his head down. He voted for what he was told to vote for, and he came back up to Bridgeport every weekend for mass at Nativity of Our Lord with his wife, Eleanor, and the kids. In the statehouse, he developed a reputation as a "progressive force" who knew his way around a budget and advocated tax reform, school lunches, and urban renewal. Two years later Bridgeport's state senator died, and not only was Daley the obvious choice, but three years later the Democrats elected him minority leader—at thirty-eight, the state's youngest ever. Jake Arvey rated his potential high enough that he sidetracked him into that ill-fated sheriff run in 1946. Without a job, Daley pushed aside the aging Babe Connelly as Eleventh Ward committeeman and got in on the ground floor of the Stevenson campaign. His appointment as state revenue director had the look of spoils, but in fact he was probably the most qualified man for the job.

As the hearse bore County Clerk Flynn's body away, the battle lines were being drawn: on one side the forward-thinking (if still ethically challenged) reformers like Arvey, Daley, and Stevenson, and on the other the old school bosses led by John Duffy who were orchestrating the public housing circus. As soon as the dirt was tamped on Flynn's grave, Daley resigned his state job and accepted an appointment as interim county clerk. By the time Senator Kefauver arrived in Chicago for his threatened hearings on organized crime in the fall of 1950, he'd realized that he'd need Machine support (and Mob silence on his philandering) to reach the White House, so he sent signals that he'd pull punches. But Arvey's ill-advised choice for county sheriff, the lazy and corrupt county prosecutor Daniel "Tubbo" Gilbert, still volunteered to meet behind closed doors with the Kefauver panel. Asked how he'd put away close to $400,000 on his salary, Tubbo replied, "Gambling," apparently unaware that it was illegal. When the story broke, the entire Democratic slate of 1950 went down—except for Richard J. Daley, who kept his county clerk seat in a landslide. Arvey resigned as party chairman and took a "promotion" to national committeeman, Mayor Kennelly got his second term, and Daley waited to have it out with Duffy for control of the party. With civil war on the horizon, the city welcomed Convention Summer.

CHICAGO DIDN'T LIFT its pinky the way Liebling liked, but for a little while longer, it was still the national playground; in the summer of 1952, it hosted both the GOP and Democratic conventions. Buckingham Fountain shot high into the blue July sky as the Republican delegates poured into the Conrad Hilton. A few blocks up Michigan Avenue at the Congress Hotel, more than four thousand paying visitors peeked in the room where

248 | THE THIRD COAST

the front-runner, Senator Robert Taft, planned to lay his conservative head. Chicago loved political conventions—the original "smoke-filled room" was a suite at the Blackstone Hotel where the Harding nomination had been hashed out. But mostly it just loved being on display; the city's favorite museum, the Museum of Science and Industry, was essentially an industrial trade show, and two of the four stars on the Chicago flag represented exhibitions. "Nobody in Chicago is inclined to be standoffish," warned *Life*. Restaurants like the Mob-run St. Hubert's Old English Grill, Fritzel's, the Cape Cod Room at the Drake, Henrici's, and Don the Beachcomber served the power brokers, at prices hiked accordingly, while curious delegates could try the deep-dish pizza, invented during the war, at Pizzeria Uno. "Hippy Shyanne St. Clair" performed "anatomical tricks" at the Silver Frolics. No ballgames because of the All-Star break, but with highs in the nineties, beaches would be full. Cabbies wore white shirts, under orders from City Hall. At Lake Meadows, the first steel of a more restrained design had gone up. The Shedd Aquarium had sharks, the Art Institute had French paintings, and Marshall Field's had everything else.

The Republicans convened July 7 at the International Amphitheatre at 43rd and Halsted, a pedestrian but well-located arena that served as the city's meeting place for dog shows, flower shows, boat shows, cat shows, midget racing, circuses, religious revivals, and most of all, conventions. This one was wide open. Neither Taft nor Eisenhower had enough delegates to claim the nomination, so their forces fought it out in conference rooms and on the convention floor. General Douglas MacArthur's surprisingly dull keynote on Monday left the spotlight to Chicago alderman Archibald Carey, whose speech ended, in part: "This is exactly what we mean, from every mountain side, let freedom ring. Not only from the Green Mountains and the White Mountains of Vermont and New Hampshire, not only from the Catskills of New York, but from the Ozarks in Arkansas, from Stone Mountain in Georgia, from the Great Smokies of Tennessee and from the Blue Ridge Mountains of Virginia . . . let freedom ring." (Whether you think Dr. Martin Luther King, Jr., plagiarized it for his "I Have a Dream" speech depends on how strict your standards for plagiarism are.)

Beyond politics, what made the convention truly "open" was that it was the first to be fully televised. Seventy-seven strategically placed cameras brought all the mayhem, boredom, and theatrics of a national convention into some 18 million homes that had never seen the absurd floor demonstrations or the men in hats waving signs. The brand-new zoom lens focused on napping congressmen; the "teleprompter" allowed candidates to deliver their speeches more naturally. Dave Garroway came back to Chicago to cover the show; Betty Furness hawked refrigerators. Don Hewitt, later of *60 Minutes* fame, invented the term *anchorman* this week as well as the use of superimposed letters on the screen. It was, according to *Life*, the "most widely viewed event in history." ABC's coverage won awards, largely because Red Quinlan, station manager of WBKB, fixed it so the Amphitheatre guards kept out reporters from other networks.

Ike took the nomination with upstart Richard Nixon at his side on the ticket. He promised to get out of Korea and hinted that he'd muzzle Joe McCarthy. As the Republicans stormed out of Chicago ready to fight, at the Conrad Hilton, hundreds of maids changed thousands of sheets, janitors swept up the Amphitheatre, and hammered in brand-new bunting. Two weeks later the Democrats rolled in like a fog, confused and drifting. Kefauver held the most delegates, even though no one really liked him. *Life* said he came off as "a splendidly successful undertaker." His best asset was his wife, Nancy. New York governor Averell Harriman was your father's Studebaker, a well-polished East Coast New Dealer, while Richard Russell of Georgia, number two in delegates, was only slightly more rational than his fellow Dixiecrat Strom Thurmond. The man the Democrats really wanted just sighed and paced and told everyone within earshot the same thing he'd been saying for going on three years now—that he just didn't know whether he wanted to be president.

As soon as Adlai Stevenson had moved into the governor's mansion in 1949, his name had bobbed to the top of possible presidential candidates and stayed there. Though his term as governor had been lackluster, his wit and his mailing address earned him comparisons with Lincoln. The limits of his thought were summed up in his official portrait: on the shelves behind him sat the Great Books series. (He was on the board.) Stevenson was to politics what the Great Books were to knowledge, something that looked a lot like what people were told it was supposed to look like. "He complained that he never had time to read a book," said Newton Minow, "but the fact is that he did not want to read a book. But he knew it was important to read books."

As early as 1949, Truman had called him in to hand over the baton, thus beginning three years of dithering. Stevenson's initial qualms were reasonable—he and Ellen had finally divorced, and Adlai was convinced America would never accept a divorcé in the White House. Arvey talked him out of that, but there was always another reason. He met with Truman twice and left him hanging and insulted both times. The party leadership flailed through the primaries as everyone hoping for a Stevenson run held back from picking new horses, thus gumming up the entire process to the brink of the convention, when *Life* published a long, fawning profile of Stevenson, exactly the sort of coy, disingenuous move that drove his allies crazy. If he wasn't considering a run, why had he cooperated? Instead, he dangled himself out there, his mouth saying no no no, while the photos of him under a sturdy oak, looking pensively into America's future, said yes yes yes.

A copy of the article awaited every delegate, courtesy of Jake Arvey, as they arrived for the opening session on July 21. After a prayer led by Cardinal Stritch and a mealymouthed welcome from Mayor Kennelly, Governor Adlai Stevenson took the podium. As the cameras rolled, he delivered the speech of his life. "Here on the prairies of Illinois and the Middle West," he began, "we can see a long way in all directions. We look to East, to West, to North and South. Our commerce, our ideas, come and go in all directions. Here there are no barriers, no defenses, to ideas and aspirations. We want none; we want no shackles on the mind or the spirit, no rigid patterns of thought, no iron conformity."

He went on with all the good humor and eloquence that would make him famous, midwestern common sense bundled with eastern intelligence and gentility. "What America needs and the world wants," he said, "is not bombast, abuse and double talk, but a sober message of firm faith and confidence."

The convention went up for grabs. A draft movement swept through the floor, and a platform battle between conservatives and liberals increased the chaos. "Such strains and such spurting of ambitions operate constantly in every American national convention," wrote Theodore White, "only, at Chicago, more so." Finally Stevenson asked Truman if he'd be embarrassed if he accepted the nomination, to which the president angrily replied, "I have been trying since January to get you to say that. Why would it embarrass me?" The night of the vote, Kefauver led through the first two ballots, but when Harriman threw in with Stevenson, it was all over for the senator from Tennessee. Stevenson met the press outside the house where he was staying on Astor Street, then rode in a motorcade back to the Amphitheatre, where at two a.m. he gave his acceptance speech, a strangely biblical address in which he compared himself to Christ accepting his fate in the Garden of Gethsemane. But its most memorable line—"Let's talk sense to the American people"—became his motto.

With no organization or staff, and the election a little more than three months ahead, Stevenson launched into a campaign that put all his considerable strengths and flaws on plain view. His first mistake was to distance himself from Truman, undercutting his support within the party; second and more damaging was that even though his televised speech had won him the nomination, no one in his campaign, including the candidate himself, understood that this was the first televised presidential race. Like his friend Hutchins, Stevenson disdained the new medium, while the Republicans made the most of it. If the cheesy "I Like Ike" commercials were on par with Howdy Doody, Adlai was the political version of the one TV show he liked: *Kukla, Fran and Ollie*—thoughtful, civilized, and dropping in popularity the longer it was around. Given that Adlai represented

Burr Tillstrom and Lewis Gomavitz was his television consultant, this was no coincidence. Unlike Kukla, though, Candidate Stevenson came off badly on-screen; he never rehearsed, he froze, he rambled over people's heads and often past his allotted time, forcing directors to cut him off midspeech. Stewart Alsop called him an "egghead," further driving a wedge between the American public and the intellectual "elite." Stevenson's dislike of ethnic Catholics cost him in cities, particularly Chicago, where he ignored Daley's stated interest in succeeding him as governor.

And yet Adlai Stevenson was beloved as few presidential candidates have ever been. His campaign, created on the fly, had "a gaiety, a spontaneity, a freshness, an insouciance about it that was extraordinarily appealing to countless people weary of pompous politicians." Intellectuals ran to his side—even the appearance of thought was better than no thought at all—and he was a cheerful tilter at windmills, summed up by William M. Gallagher's photo of Stevenson displaying a hole in his shoe, soon his trademark image. "Politically speaking, it was the Christmas morning of our lives," said journalist Mary McGrory. Volunteers flocked to him; the system of retired ladies and college kids canvassing for candidates began. Tallulah Bankhead loved him almost as much as she loved *Kukla, Fran and Ollie*. When asked once whether his fame was affecting him, he said it was all right so long as he didn't inhale. Stevenson reminded Americans of many of their best qualities, and like a later presidential candidate from Illinois, he offered them hope.

But he couldn't convince them to vote for him. Polls showed that he at best pulled voters into the undecided column; even the *Sun-Times*, a liberal paper owned by his friend Marshall Field III, endorsed Ike. "The sad part," said his campaign manager later, was that "the fellow had actually convinced himself that he could win." On Election Day, Stevenson won only nine states, and Illinois wasn't one of them. His image—the disengaged, effete egghead—replaced the rolled-up sleeves of the New Deal as what a Democrat was, creating a false sense that this brand of intellectualism was the only way to fight ignorance and greed. Lured by the charms of Adlai and his campaign, the party would imitate it for decades to come, with candidates like Hubert Humphrey, Michael Dukakis, and John Kerry, all to similar ends. Stevenson went back to the farm in Libertyville, and the Eisenhower Era began.

DEATH HAD ONE more gift for Richard J. Daley. In the summer of 1953, Joe Gill announced that he was stepping down as Cook County Democratic chairman. Daley, his forces in line, walked into the July 8 meeting at the Morrison positive that he'd be strolling out as his successor, but John Duffy and his crony, alderman Clarence Wagner, finagled a two-week delay to give their own candidate time to mount a run against Daley. Bill Dawson, still bitter over Mayor Kennelly's insult, leaned toward Duffy's side, even though they were even worse on race. Daley stumbled out of the room on the verge of tears, then crawled back to the Eleventh Ward while a pleased Wagner headed to Canada for a fishing trip; at International Falls, Minnesota, he died in a car crash. Daley's path was clear. On July 21, 1953, taking a very public vow never to run for mayor—surely too much power for one man, he said—Richard J. Daley became chairman of the Cook County Democratic Committee.

CHAPTER 20

PLAYWRIGHTS
AND PLAYBOYS

FOUR HUNDRED MILES to Indianapolis. Eight more hours of chasing taillights in the dark. A sandwich, a piss, then pick up a bed of prefab houses and head right back. A gust off Lake Erie rocked the cab. The driver blinked. The tires hummed, his eyes were dry. . . .

Suddenly, outside Erie, he saw a figure waving on the shoulder ahead, duffel bag at his feet. He stopped and pulled down his window. "Where you headed?"

"West," said the lanky hitchhiker in horn-rimmed glasses. David Shepherd hopped aboard. "Tell me when we get to Cleveland," he said, then the shivering twenty-six-year-old proceeded to pay his way with non-stop conversation. He'd been teaching in India not long ago when he realized that he wanted to start a cabaret theater. His late stepmother had just left him the ten thousand dollars he needed. Should he do it in Cleveland, Detroit, or Chicago? The driver didn't really have an opinion.

Shepherd had been born in Manhattan at 86th and Madison, a Vanderbilt, his love of theater fired by seeing Walter Huston sing "September Song" in *Knickerbocker Holiday*. Diplomas from Exeter, Harvard, and Columbia, a few years in the army during the war, travels through Europe, and classes at the Sorbonne had produced a socialist eager to put his passion to work for the masses. He described the London music halls; La Rose

Rouge in Paris, where he'd listened to Juliette Greco; Bertolt Brecht's "Smokers' Theater"; that's what America needed, he said, a theater where the workingman could see himself and his own problems addressed on-stage. He would call it The Compass. Shepherd went on like this until the lights of Cleveland appeared to the right. Three hundred more miles to go, the night only more inviting. "Hey, Chicago is on your list, right?" asked the driver. "Well, why don't you go to Chicago first? Then you can tell me stories and keep me awake so I won't crash the truck."

Jack Kerouac was about to start writing *On the Road* that January 1951, another young American hungry for speed, sex, and meaning. Shepherd rode as far as Gary. No takers there for his workingman's theater, so he went on to Chicago where he crashed in a West Side fleabag and took a factory job in Cicero, another town not well-known for its artistic sensibilities. In the fall, an old roommate pointed him toward Hyde Park, where Hutchins's presence still clung to the gothic walls. The scene was "very mixed and very flowing," Shepherd would later say. "There were hardhats and intellectuals, steelworkers and students and professors and homosexuals." Outlaw speech and action were encouraged.

In 1950 the Loop saw only a quarter of the theatrical productions it had hosted twenty-five years before; the biggest thing to happen there in recent memory was Tennessee Williams's pre-Broadway tryout of *The Glass Menagerie* in 1944. The Goodman Theatre and Northwestern produced talented performers but didn't draw audiences; the Chicago Repertory Group had closed during the war. Most everything that wasn't a road company, dinner theater, or a Marshall Migatz summer stock production now came out of the University of Chicago, even though—and many would say *because*—it had no drama department. Faculty members had their tradition of play-reading clubs, monthly living-room gatherings of professors in straight-backed chairs. The University Theater staged serious drama on its own terms, so unhappy students started Tonight at 8:30 to produce one-acts by Shaw, Williams, Yeats, Lorca, and Brecht, with casts that combined trained and amateur actors. In Hyde Park, everyone was talented or at least was convinced they were.

Ed Asner, a self-professed "good old boy" from an Orthodox Jewish family in Kansas City, had dropped out of the University of Chicago in 1947, after his first year, but later returned to Hyde Park to reconnect with a girlfriend. While working at the Ford Assembly Plant at 126th and Torrence, he fell in with the University Theater but got his "ass booted" after a performance of *Antigone,* during which he shared the stage briefly with Susan Sontag as Ismene. He then took his gruff menschiness to Tonight at 8:30 where he stayed until he left for the army.

Another Tonight at 8:30 standout seemed to go out of his way to annoy people. "You had to endure him," a fellow student said of Mike Nichols. "He was a pain in the ass." Nichols was indeed not a happy young man. His accomplished Jewish family had fled Berlin because of the Nazis, landing on the Upper West Side of Manhattan in 1939. Ten-year-old Nichols went off to boarding school in 1942, but when his father died of leukemia two years later, the family's fortunes sank, and his mother scraped to put him through prep school. New York University was not to his liking— he left after one day—so he tried Chicago. Fellow freshman Sontag "considered him her closest friend," though Asner found him "effete" and took great pleasure in once sleeping with a girl he was thought to be pursuing. Nichols made it through a year and a half before dropping out, but he stayed in Hyde Park, gaining a name for himself with his bitter wit, desperate poverty, and low-end jobs that smacked of self-punishment even as he took out his anger on everyone else. A busboy at the diner where Nichols snatched uneaten food had brought him in to Tonight at 8:30.

In October 1952, David Shepherd walked into a Tonight at 8:30 rehearsal of Shaw's *Arms and the Man.* An odd duck for those parts, a kind of patrician scarecrow, he landed a minor role in the next production, which he pulled off with some flair. That earned him an invitation from the young director, Paul Sills, who'd been the busboy at the diner and who also happened to be a central figure in the Hyde Park theater scene. The two met at the Steinway's Drugstore on 55th, Hyde Park's Russian Tea Room. A year younger than Shepherd, with dark curly hair and a workman's body, he was "intense, charismatic, and had the gift of getting people to follow," says a contemporary. His devotion to dramatic theory came from his mother, Viola Spolin, WPA veteran and Studs's friend who'd been teaching drama in California since leaving Chicago in 1943. Unlike Stanislavsky's Method, which required actors to embroider entire lives for their characters, Spolin's actors created characters out of themselves by focusing on the tension within a scene. Simple, emotionally based, and easy for untrained actors to use, when it worked, Spolin's approach led to clear, effective performances and lean productions. "We're making games out of what you call actors' exercises," Sills would later explain, ". . . in which the people, instead of concentrating on the scene they are to produce, or the effect they are to have, concentrate on playing the game. . . . It comes close to an athlete playing a sport." Paul directed productions both at Tonight at 8:30 and at the University Theater, tramped cross country for a while, and now, in the fall of 1952, was back from exile.

Shepherd joined Sills's circle, with Nichols, Eugene Troobnick, and Joyce and Byrne Piven (parents of actor Jeremy Piven), juggling classes and jobs around his workshops. After rave reviews for Sills's January 1953 production of Jean Cocteau's *The Typewriter,* the University Theater let the young director mount Brecht's *Caucasian Chalk Circle,* the play's second international production. Sills was now ready to move beyond 55th Street. As Shepherd toyed with starting his cabaret in the Stockyards, Sills pitched the idea of a repertory theater. It was close enough; Shepherd wrote a check for $7,000, and Playwrights Theatre Club (PTC) was born. Sills recruited Ed Asner, back from two years in the army, Zohra Lampert, the Pivens, and a dozen or so more actors. Shepherd, Troobnick, and Sills produced, Sills usually directed, and everyone was onstage at some point. An announcer now at WFMT, Mike Nichols couldn't commit full time.

On Tuesday night, June 23, 1953, in a stuffy room over a Chinese restaurant at 1560 N. LaSalle Street, on the fringe of Towertown, PTC opened with a restaging of *The Caucasian Chalk Circle.* The stage imitated an Elizabethan theater, jutting forward into the 150 director's chairs set up for the audience. The *Tribune*'s intimidating drama critic Claudia Cassidy, often accused of strangling good things in their cribs, called them "lustily intrepid amateurs playing happily and violently over their heads." Over the next two years, PTC mounted a remarkable twenty-five productions, from *Wozzek* and *The Dybbuk* to *Peer Gynt* and *Murder in the Cathedral*—in short, a kind of refresher course on the theatrical canon for drama-starved Chicago.

The University of Chicago background shared by most of the troupe forged them into a commune of sorts, that and the poverty. "We slept in the theater when we started because we had so little money," claimed Troobnick. "Since it had been a restaurant, it had little alcoves and each person took an alcove as a sort of room of his own." Mike Nichols dipped in and out of a few productions, then left for the Actors Studio in New York. Shortly thereafter, a delicate seventeen-year-old girl walked in the door—one cast member compared it to the appearance of an angel. Senn High School grad Barbara Harris was immediately accepted as an intern, silently sweeping, in time making small appearances as graceful and delicate as her features. The death of her brother in the war had devastated the Harris family—her father, Oscar, once a Dil Pickler, had gone from writing for the *Tribune* to driving a cab; so the constant chaos and discovery of Playwrights became a secure place where she could construct and reconstruct some sort of self under the attention, theatrical and otherwise, of Paul Sills.

The other woman who came aboard in 1954, busty, smoldering, and brilliant Elaine May, attracted and frightened men in equal measures. Her persona exploded everything an early 1950s woman was supposed to be: she wore dirty, torn clothes and had a less-than-fastidious approach to personal hygiene; she consumed cigarettes and apple cores; but most of all she was, according to one, "a ballbreaker. You didn't tangle with Elaine and come out intact." Possessed of a devastating wit, May had grown up on the road, the daughter of two Yiddish theatre veterans. At fourteen she'd quit high school; at sixteen she'd gotten married and had a child, whom she left with her mother after the inevitable divorce in order to pursue a career as an actor and writer. May first came to Chicago to pitch a film to *Encyclopaedia Britannica,* then stayed to audit classes, where she fell in with Sills and his friends and now joined PTC. The volume and energy of her creative genius compensated for how unpolished it could be at times. "Everyone was trying to make her," says Asner, "except me."

Playwrights had two thousand subscribers after the first year. Troobnick was gently ushered out as a producer in favor of the slightly older Bernard Sahlins, a Garfield Park native and University of Chicago math major who now made a good living as vice president of a tape recording company. The company moved to a new location at Dearborn and Division ("Queerboy and Perversion," as it was known), where the tensions between art and commerce went on display: on opening night, David Shepherd could be seen scrubbing a piece of railing with a toothbrush, oblivious to the backstage chaos. Asner said he had an "Eastern mysticism about him that I never quite fathomed."

Everyone burned out the second year. Paul Sills married Barbara Harris and applied for a Fulbright to study theater in England; for Shepherd, Playwrights now represented everything that he'd jumped into that truck outside Erie hoping to destroy. "In a year and a half," he wrote in his journal, "I have helped build a miserable self-centered arts club which talks over the heads of its bourgeois members at the same time it licks their feet for patronage." The Red scare rhetoric in the air made the atmosphere tense; leftists like Asner were "scared shitless of the Blacklist." "I would hear people talking on the subway or the streetcar," said one performer, "very convinced about the Rosenbergs' guilt and taking pleasure in their execution." Playwrights had earned its reputation from what Sahlins calls "the liberal-progressive theatrical tradition," and Shepherd had opened the stage to Studs for *I Come For to Sing,* hired a blacklisted director, and pushed to screen the Communist film *Salt of the Earth.* All this (plus some occasional raciness) finally hardened City Hall's heart. In February 1955 fire inspectors shut PTC down for minor violations. More relieved than angry, Shepherd had something new in mind, and Chicago was still the perfect place for it.

. . .

FOXLIKE, HUGH HEFNER stood on the Michigan Avenue Bridge on a cold December night in 1952, sniffing up at what he imagined himself missing behind the lights in the windows: women in mink stoles and silk stockings curled around men in tuxedoes; jazz combos and martinis. He was twenty-six and running out of time. To the south lay his tedious job in the Loop, the apartment in Hyde Park where his wife sat wondering where he was right now, their month-old baby crying in her lap. And to the north the whole Toddlin' Town that he'd wanted to belong to since high school: the bars along Rush Street, jazz at Chez Paree, the Black Orchid, and Jazz Ltd, strip joints, *Esquire* magazine on Oak Street, and the Mies van der Rohe towers on Lake Shore Drive. The nurse he was screwing. Middle-class, middlebrow, and middle American, Hefner wanted them all. Below, the Chicago River rolled on.

Hefner's dreams were the products of a solitary childhood spent on the Northwest Side back when the edges of the city were still prairie. His block on New England Avenue had only three or four houses; tall grasses covered the rest, with birds and crickets and snakes, yet if he wandered the patch of woods around Caldwell's lagoon at nearby Riis Park and stood on the hill, he could see the tips of the skyscrapers downtown. Like Burr Tillstrom and Sun Ra, he dreamed away his early years, rarely touched by his straitlaced Methodist parents, allowed to drift into a world of movies and his own cartoons, soon so detached, stuttering and inattentive in class, that his mother had him tested. The doctors informed her that her boy was incredibly immature, emotionally stunted, and had an IQ of 152; they suggested she be more demonstrative with him. Hugh finally joined the world at Steinmetz High, where he reinvented himself as "Hef," a rebellious Big Man on Campus who chronicled his life in a cartoon diary, wrote a jazz column for the school paper, and was voted "Third Most Likely to Succeed." Mrs. Hefner even allowed him to pin up *Esquire* girls. He and his best buddy, Jim Brophy, made movies down in the basement starring Hef as the mad scientist and Jim the Frankenstein monster; they imagined sophisticated lives surrounded by babes. The skyscrapers seemed close enough to touch.

And then he was drafted. Too young for combat and a good typist, Hefner spent his brief turn in the service behind a desk, dreaming his way through what was left of the war, but this time it was the same dream millions of other GIs had: a job, a house, and a wife. Demobbed, he made the most of the GI Bill: at the University of Illinois he learned to fly, started a humor magazine called *Shaft*, got good grades, and listened to Dave Garroway's *11:60 Club* every night. He and Millie Williams became a couple. The problem was sex. At the age of twenty-two, Hefner was still a virgin. Maybe if he'd been living in Omaha, it wouldn't have been such an issue, but living in the capital of stripping with a girlfriend almost as conservative as his mother, poor Hef suffered the tortures of sexual continence until finally, in the spring of 1948, he and Millie made love in a Danville hotel room. Convinced they now *had* to wed, he finished school while Millie had a brief affair to which she tearfully confessed after viewing *The Accused,* starring that icon of Catholic purity, Loretta Young. They should have parted for everyone's good, but on June 15, 1949, they married at St. John Bosco, back in the old neighborhood. With no apartments to be had, the newlyweds moved into his bedroom on New England Avenue, the holes from his pin-ups still visible in the walls.

Hefner was no closer to the lights downtown. He went for his master's in sociology at Northwestern but dropped out, bounced through Carson Pirie Scott (where he met LeRoy Neiman) and *Esquire*, his dream job until someone handed him a time card. When Arnold Gingrich moved the magazine to New York, Hef stayed in Chicago. However he'd eventually make it, Hefner wanted to make it here in this swanky new town. His idea for a monthly city magazine called *Pulse* went nowhere, but Kup gave his self-published cartoon guide *That Toddlin' Town* a nice write-up in 1950. Hefner had tasted just enough fame to know what he was missing.

He also knew what he was missing in the bedroom. Millie simply didn't like sex all that much, while Hefner craved it; he didn't bother hiding his growing porn collection or the dirty cartoons he drew. His next job was all sex; seedy Publisher's Development Corporation put out a string of men's magazines that included *Sunbathing for Health* and *Art Photography.* Though he disliked owner George von Rosen, Hef made connections and learned how magazine distribution worked. And then he had a new idea. "If Von Rosen could make a living with what I thought was really second rate junk, I saw the possibilities of doing a variation of what *Esquire* had given up."

At which point Millie got pregnant. Apartments opened up in a changing section of Hyde Park, so Hef immediately rented one on South Harper, eager to get away from his parents but also relishing the rebellion that living in an integrated neighborhood implied in Chicago. They decorated the place in high Baldwin Kingrey style down to the Saarinen Womb Chair, earning a write-up in the *Daily News* style pages. The months passed, his daughter Christine was born, and he was trapped even deeper, the only guy in free-love Hyde Park not getting laid. Then he and Jim Brophy reunited to put on the alumni show. "It brought back to me the memories of what had previously been the high point of my life," says Hefner. That December night on the Michigan Avenue Bridge, he replayed the show in his mind. "It just reminded me of the dreams put away." As it went, Hefner turned south, back to life as it was, but "it was in the days and weeks that followed that I began to make the plans."

So began the most famous media start-up of the American Century. Hef unfolded a card table in the living room and pushed all his chips to the middle. Though fueled by his obsession with sex, *Stag Party* was a business proposition first and foremost, a product created to fill a need in the market and the means to bring it there. Men's magazines then "were all rural, outdoor books devoted to hunting and fishing and chasing the abominable snowman over mountain tops," he told *Chicago. Stag Party* would be "an entertainment magazine for the city-bred guy—breezy, sophisticated." For the first issue, he pasted together forty-two pages of public domain nuggets by Sir Arthur Conan Doyle and Ambrose Bierce, with party jokes and articles about football and office furniture by writers willing to take stock for payment. The real draw—the eight or so nude photos—came from the John Baumgarth Calendar Company at North and Harlem, whose owner, "a shirt sleeve kind of guy," saw himself in the young publisher and cut him a great deal: $500 for the Tom Kelley Marilyn Monroe session, plus six months of topless women throwing beach balls and reclining on divans; Hefner decided to call them "playmates." Designer Art Paul, who'd attended both the SAIC and the ID, brought a Moholy-esque sensibility to the layouts: lots of white space, images silhouetted and arranged to create new images.

When Hefner wasn't writing, cutting, pasting, phoning, or selling, he was raising the $8,000 he needed to print the first issue. His confidence, and the sizable advance orders, convinced a few friends to pony up, and some even took jobs in the new HMH Publishing Company in exchange for stock. Hefner's brother Keith kicked in, as did his mother, who gave him $1,000 even though she disapproved. For the last $600, Hefner borrowed against his new furniture. On the inside front cover, Paul had designed a buck with antlers smoking a pipe; a legal threat from *Stag* magazine forced him to turn the antlers into a pair of bent rabbit ears. The name would have to change too, but the first issue of *Playboy* did finally come off the presses in November 1953. "I felt I had succeeded beyond my wildest dreams just having that in my hands," says Hefner. "It was important enough so that I actually sat down in the Womb Chair and Millie took a picture of me holding it. Dreams don't get better than that."

The struggle ended there. *Playboy* was a hit from the start, selling 80 percent of its initial 70,000 run. The numbers were even higher for the second issue. Hefner made no pretense to profundity. "Affairs of state will be out of our province," read page one, issue one. "We don't expect to solve any world problems or prove any great moral truths. If we are able to give the American male a few extra laughs and a little diversion from the anxieties of the Atomic Age, we'll feel we've justified our existence." Not only had Hefner given American men a magazine that didn't make them feel bad for liking sex, but he'd cast a lifeline toward all the "other directed" young men desperate for someone to tell them what to wear, what to buy, what to listen to, how to *be* amid midcentury consumer culture.

Hefner was suddenly rich. "I'm my own boss and I'm doing a job I love and believe in," he said. But in true Chicago style, he'd made it a point of pride to stay regular—"I haven't stepped on anyone on my way up." Instead of taking the magazine to New York, he kept *Playboy* in the convention city with a five a.m. curfew, a town that laughed just a little too loud after everyone else had gone to bed. In January 1954 the scrawny dreamer with way-too-intense eyes, sunken cheeks, and a very present WASP-y chin folded up the card table and moved into new offices on the third floor of 11 E. Superior, across the street from Holy Name Cathedral, and over the course of the year took over the entire building. At any given hour, he could now be seen shuffling about in his pajamas, tearing up layouts with Art Paul, editing text, or enticing some tasty secretary up to his private lair. If he had pants on, he was bar-hopping down Rush Street. Along with the party spirit of the place, Hefner recognized Chicago's pool of cheap talent, and the fact that he was now a very tall tree on the prairie, sure to be always in the news. With stripping on the wane, he continued the proud Chicago tradition of packaging sex for a new generation.

That he'd all but abandoned his family may well have come as a relief to Millie. Juices flowing, Hefner had been pushing the sexual limits of his marriage, for one, trying to convince his wife to swap partners. One doesn't have to be a prude to feel put off by that idea, but Hefner took her reluctance as further evidence that she was sexually uptight; it appeared that he hadn't really emerged from the narcissism of his childhood. It was still all just a game to him, a break from real life. "*Playboy* isn't very serious," he told *Chicago*. ". . . In a sense it's a kind of spoof on the kind of life part of the reader would like to live. It offers him an imaginary escape into the world of wine, women and song. Then the other part of him says he has to go back to his family responsibilities and his work." He and Millie stayed married, Christine still had a dad, and once in a while he even dropped by their new apartment downtown.

CHAPTER 21

CHICAGSKY TEMP

CERES GLANCED NORTH toward the skeleton rising at Michigan and Randolph. The Prudential Building, planned for fall of 1955, would be the city's first skyscraper since 1934. Chicago's industrial output had quadrupled in the years since Mies's arrival in 1938; the money was pouring in, the rich were getting richer, and the middle class was doing pretty well too. That rumble of excitement Hefner felt through his loafers was more than hormones. According to *Newsweek*, Chicagoland was "the world's largest steel and rail center, the country's biggest breadbasket and livestock market, and the nation's largest industrial area." It produced a quarter of all the nation's electronics; every day its stations handled 35,000 freight cars and 1,770 passenger trains; 15,000 trucks rolled over its streets carrying 300,000 tons of goods, more than anywhere else in the country. It was the center of mail order. "How many," asked *Newsweek*, ". . . really know that Chicago is a powerhouse of the American people?" The Soviets apparently did—the term *Chicagsky Temp* there meant "an exciting tempo of growth."

Chicagoans weren't so bullish. As McCarthyite paranoia gave way to the more abstract anxieties of nuclear annihilation, they noticed they were dusting the same soot off the shoulders of their Brooks Brothers suits as they once had off their fatigue jackets. Chicago still hadn't solved many of its prewar problems. Below Ceres, the dingy Loop was only dingier; the high-end nightlife crept north to Hef's haunts along Rush, leaving cheap b-girls to roam dimmer, emptier, after-work streets. Legit theater was all but dead, and suburban shopping centers like the new Old Orchard had sliced the veins of State Street. On the South Side, rats had recently eaten a nine-month-old girl alive. For all its postwar Opportunity Plans and Redevelopment Acts, Chicago had little to show: a scattering of buildings at Michael Reese Hospital and Lake Meadows peeking through the rubble of Bronzeville; Mies's IIT campus and the Glass Houses. The other construction projects were still holes: a seven-mile gorge through the West Side that would be an expressway, and that pit across from the Prudential, someday a garage. Extending Lake Shore Drive north had cut the Edgewater Beach Hotel off from the beach, killing the grand old resort; refrigerated trucks on the new interstate system were making stockyards obsolete. Fine buildings left to decay over the decades—many built by Sullivan himself—faced demolition.

On the other side were more enormous plans. Developer Arthur Rubloff, still pushing his "Magnificent Mile," hooked up with Skidmore, Owings & Merrill for "Fort Dearborn," a proposal to transform 151 acres of delirious Towertown into government buildings, a new campus for the University of Illinois, five thousand luxury apartment units, and six thousand parking spots. Hughston McBain was on board, but Loop interests were fighting it; said John Taylor Pirie, Jr., of Carson Pirie Scott, "We just can't let the Loop rot away." A new water filtration plant was needed, and digging was under way on the St. Lawrence Seaway; soon ships would be able to travel straight from the Atlantic to the Great Lakes and the new Port of Chicago in Calumet. The SSPB had Mies working on a new convention center just north of Michael Reese, and in Hyde Park two redevelopment plans had been approved, with the major SECC proposal on the way. Waves of federal money and bond issues were pending.

The problem was, for all that was happening, and was about to happen, and *could* happen, no one knew what it all added up to, and that included the mayor, whose "clean" City Hall had all the energy of a principal's office. Kennelly couldn't explain what Chicago was becoming and why it mattered, not to the world and not to itself. The wonderful absurdity of being home to atomic scientists and strippers, architects, chitlin joints, a Baha'i temple, race wars, and *Playboy*, *Ebony*, and *Poetry* magazines all at once felt simply confusing rather than proof that the Third Coast was still America's crossroads. No one was in charge.

Of course, the *real* problem went largely unspoken. Flight to the suburbs, said University of Chicago president Kimpton, was "dictated by a refusal to face an issue." But what was the issue? It was no secret that Chicago's whites didn't want to live with blacks, and blacks were fine with that. The city's population had peaked in 1950, and now the numbers would begin to fall as blacks kept coming north and whites kept heading out to the suburbs. So was Kimpton's "issue" racism, or the presence of undesirable blacks? In years to come, Kimpton would show what he'd meant. Without question, the city had a future. The next mayor would have to make sure whites hung around long enough to be a part of it.

MIES EXPANDED HIS office to thirty people in a new space at 230 E. Ohio. He designed a new neighbor for 860–880: the Esplanade, at 900 Lake Shore Drive, a more refined version of its older and bolder siblings, with air conditioning and dark glass windows that give it a mysterious aura. But Mies preferred to concentrate on his new convention center, intended for a stretch of brownlands just north of Michael Reese Hospital. With no residents to worry about, he experimented with pure form; the plans called for a 500,000-square-foot clear span building, almost twice the size of the Louisiana Superdome. Enormous X-shaped trusses would bear the roof over a space seating 50,000, plus theaters, restaurants, and parking for 10,000 cars. Sponsored by the SSPB, the plan had the support of Chicago's business community, but things that didn't involve City Hall from the get-go had little chance of happening, and the convention center was no exception; Cardinal Stritch got the land for his new Mercy

Hospital. Aspects of the convention center would live on—the X-trusses would reappear later in SOM's John Hancock Center, and the clear span would figure in one of Mies's next works, Crown Hall at IIT.

Crown Hall was intended to house Mies's architecture department, while room would be found for the Institute of Design down in its basement; that says it all about the merger. Mies resented having even the spirit of Moholy nearby; in Gropius's mind, Mies was "too much the tyrant teacher." Instructors now had to administer tests and give grades, while under the pretense of IIT's federal contracts, the FBI investigated ID students, mostly black ones with ties to the South Side Community Art Center. In August 1951, after letting his temper chase away much of the senior faculty, Serge Chermayeff resigned from the ID's helm with "gall and bitterness" for a position at Harvard; his assistant director, Crombie Taylor, was named temporary head. Though generally considered a seat warmer, Taylor had attended the ID and had played a vital role in preserving Sullivan's Auditorium Building in 1945.

Harry Callahan continued his restless meditational photographing of Chicago, but he now punctured the quiet around him by hiring someone his complete opposite. Aaron Siskind had come through Chicago briefly in 1948, and the two had met again in the summer of 1951 at Black Mountain. Outgoing, almost ten years older than Callahan, a natural in the classroom after decades teaching public school in New York, Siskind was farther along in his career. In Chicago, he bridged worlds—he hosted the likes of Willem de Kooning, Roberto Matta, and Robert Motherwell, who then spread the word about Callahan and Hugo Weber back in New York. Like Callahan, he looked for abstracted forms in his work, and like David Shepherd, he provided a booster shot of leftist idealism from his days with New York's Photo League in the 1930s. The 1953 pilot issue of *Chicago* magazine featured Siskind on the masthead and a photo essay by an ID student about a family moving into the Cabrini Homes (along with articles by Studs and Saul Alinsky and artwork by Claes Oldenburg). Wearing baggy pants, his hair uncombed, Siskind was a schlub compared to the buttoned-up Callahan, yet together on the third floor of the building on Dearborn, they became known as "harryandaaron" and expanded Chicago's reputation beyond commercial photography.

In 1952, troubled that so many Sullivan buildings were threatened with demolition, Crombie Taylor suggested Siskind teach a seminar that would record them. Eight students under Siskind's guidance began applying the techniques of fine art photography to the broad arches of the Walker Warehouse, the treelike mullions of the Gage Building, and the jungle of ivy that overwhelms the entrance to Carson Pirie Scott, the simple dignity of the Barbe, Rothschild, and Adler homes, victims of years of disuse, abuse, and now, as Chicago lurched forward, indiscriminate destruction. A Korean War veteran named Richard Nickel quickly became the heart of the project. A round-faced Polack from *Stanislawowo* whose father had delivered the *Polish Daily Zagoda* for thirty-five years, he was about as regular as you could get. After IIT rejected him in 1946, he joined the army for a two-year hitch, then studied photography at the ID in 1948. In June 1950, after a whirlwind courtship, he married seventeen-year-old Adrienne Dembo, but before they'd barely gotten to know each other, he was drafted. Though he saw no combat during his year in Korea, somehow he was wounded; when he got home, he began having nightmares, turned distant and cold with Adrienne. The couple divorced in 1953, but he told no one until his mother dropped by and found him sitting alone and penniless on the floor of his apartment. Mrs. Nickel promptly scooped up her son and installed him in her basement where he built a darkroom and burrowed deeply into Sullivan's life as a way back from the gray, empty place he'd wandered into. Sullivan's Whitman-esque philosophy recharged Nickel, who returned the favor by bringing Sullivan back to life with photos that convey the spirit behind the stones and the melancholy of time passing; if the work of his teacher Harry Callahan ached with something existential, Nickel's spoke, like Algren's, to how Chicago was losing something vital. The project culminated in a March 1954 show that began to reclaim the nearly forgotten architect, just as John Szarkowski's book *The*

Idea of Louis Sullivan was published. Nickel and Siskind signed a contract with Horizon Press for a *catalogue raisonné*, an artistic quest that would in time change the face of American cities—and cost Richard Nickel his life.

That year Katharine Kuh, now curator of modern painting and sculpture at the Art Institute, mounted the first major museum show for Mark Rothko. Leon Golub sold his first painting in 1954 while a loose agglomeration of artists gathered around him: Cosmo Campoli, maker of delicate, unnerving, Boschian bronze sculptures; Seymour Rosofsky, with his dense, Kafka-esque scenes; H. C. Westermann, who built Duchamp-like constructions; and George Cohen, assembling doll part collages. Former ID instructor Peter Selz called them a new Chicago school, though they followed no intellectual or aesthetic program; instead, according to Franz Schulze, they held that "one's immediate and actual surroundings are an altogether abundant source of magic and marvelousness." Humor abounded, as did a pre-Pop interest in found objects. Schulze dubbed them "The Monster Roster."

NELSON ALGREN HANDLED rejection from his city and his lover by going back for more: he led the Chicago committee to keep the Rosenbergs out of the electric chair and resumed his correspondence with De Beauvoir. Simone had been quite taken with *Kukla, Fran and Ollie* and had described it to Sartre, who liked the sound of it so much that he immediately bought a television. The problem was, there was no *Kukla, Fran and Ollie* in France, just bad French programs, and Sartre's mother was especially put out. His secretary tried to fix the set, but nothing he did could deliver Kukla. John Garfield refused to name names before the HUAC; instead his own went into *Red Channels* and in May 1952 he died of a heart attack. There'd be no movie of *The Man with the Golden Arm*.

Algren distracted himself with women, mostly a heroin-addicted stray named Margo, but there were many more. Adlai Stevenson's politics weren't left enough for him, but the two bachelors did share an interest in getting laid. Once they passed each other in the doorway of a well-to-do mutual acquaintance. "I was first," said Adlai, to which Algren responded, "So why did she send for me?" At least that's how Algren told it, and she probably wasn't the only one. Adlai's ex, Ellen Borden, turned her family mansion at 1020 Lake Shore Drive into a not-for-profit Art Center that housed *Poetry*, Artists Equity, and for a while the WFMT studios; in the basement Algren hosted a running high-stakes poker game. Given that, according to Shay, "Algren's dick always got in the way," Ellen was likely another of his conquests. "Women liked him, despite his caddishness and boorishness," wrote Studs Terkel, and now Algren pulled a supremely caddish move with his ex-wife, Amanda. With Simone in Paris, in the arms of Claude Lanzmann (later famous for his Holocaust documentary *Shoah*), Algren decided to remarry Amanda and then fly her over to Paris to be rubbed in Simone's nose. But in March 1953, the Rosenbergs waiting in their cells for the electric chair, Algren was denied a visa and became, as he now signed his letters, "the American Prisoner." The comment had a bitter double edge since he regretted remarrying Amanda the moment he said "I do" and loathed their domestic life in Miller, Indiana. He pleaded his case to Simone. "I cannot help you," she wrote him in April, distracted by her new lover, her fame, her work on a *roman à clef* about their affair; "nobody can. It is a sad story."

Algren's next novel, *Entrapment*, followed a grifter junkie couple on the lam; Little Daddy thinks he's running the show, but in fact it's Beth-Mary who's pulling the strings, and she eventually leaves him to run off with another guy—a plot line that may sound familiar. Writing in the first person from both viewpoints, Algren stops observing the depths and joins them, alienated not just from power but from society as a whole. He'd told Shay once that if you could get down on paper the life of one street in your lifetime, you'd be doing a good job, but now he increasingly saw those lives as complicit in the system. For all its crisp dialogue and pacing, *Entrapment* lacks the human tragedy of his earlier work, and here addiction, unlike in *The Man with the Golden Arm*, is a badge of honor. Concern for the victimized becomes outlaw chic. *Entrapment* marks the end of social realism for Algren. In 1953 social realism meant suburban angst and boardroom struggles, the stuff of television writers. Nothing interested him less.

When Doubleday offered him money to rewrite his first novel, *Somebody in Boots*, Algren stuffed *Entrapment* in a drawer. He needed the cash, but he also felt the sting of losing his heavyweight belt. Former WPA writer and Syntopicon researcher Saul Bellow had left Chicago during the war to serve in the merchant marine, went on to teach at the University of Minnesota, then traveled to Paris to write his third novel, *The Adventures of Augie March*, set in his old neighborhood of Humboldt Park. Bellow landed a punch with the first line: "I'm American, Chicago born—Chicago, that somber city—and go at things as I have taught myself, freestyle, and will make the record in my own way." By the end of Augie's picaresque search for success, he'd taken the heavyweight belt from Algren, even if his ambivalence about Chicago had him holding it at arm's length. Complex and cerebral, the novel won the 1953 National Book Award and made Bellow a literary star, while Algren's poetic cries on behalf of the Forgotten Man began to feel *de trop* with so much bounty now bulging off the nation's shelves. He spent the summer of 1954 looking for new things to say about Cass McKay that would make him fit competition for Augie March. It was hard work and not going well when word came that Simone had won the Prix de Goncourt for her *roman à clef*, called *Les Mandarins*. Algren didn't know what it was about, but he was happy for her.

NINE DAYS AFTER Richard Daley's assumption to the Cook County throne in late July 1953, the Howard family moved into an apartment in the Trumbull Park Homes at 105th and Bensley, a low, grim 462-unit project way down in South Deering, three blocks from St. Kevin. Betty Howard was extremely fair-skinned, so when she'd applied for housing at the CHA office, no one had noticed that she was black. But her new neighbors certainly did. On Monday, August 5, teenagers attacked their home with rocks and bricks, swelling to a mob of thousands by the end of the week. Now that former police chief Erwin Konovsky's conviction in the Clark case had been reversed, local whites knew there was nothing to stop a second Cicero. The saga of Trumbull Park answered any remaining questions about how White Chicago wanted to deal with race.

Into the fall, the Howards and their two children stuck it out behind the plywood that replaced their shattered windows. At night, their neighbors shot fireworks at their apartment. "Not one, not two, but bomb after bomb after bomb," wrote Frank London Brown in his compelling novel *Trumbull Park*, based on his own experience there. ". . . the explosions splitting deep down in the hollow of your ears—not once or twice, but three, four, and a hundred times more than that—one after the other for minutes and minutes." Mobs prowled the streets of South Deering, breaking windows and attacking vehicles carrying blacks. The police required the Howards to have an escort whenever they left their apartment. The CHA rushed three more black families into the project to shore up the black presence while the protesters, organized and paid for by the South Deering Improvement Association (SDIA), a local intimidation squad, reinforced the siege. Every night up to 250 policemen stood watch. And the bombs continued. "We tell them it's fireworks," one mother said of her anxious children. The archdiocese urged the pastor of St. Kevin, Father Michael Commins, to intercede, as many of the blacks were Catholic, but Commins was unmoved by the not particularly Christ-like spectacle of Betty Howard requiring policemen at her side in order to receive the Eucharist. The tension spread through the rest of the city; at one stretch that fall, a third of all Chicago cops were assigned to some racial conflict. Even as the world tuned in once again to observe Chicago's race war, Mayor Kennelly did not consider it his job to act. Eric Sevareid featured Trumbull Park on *American View*, and *Life* sent Art Shay to photograph. In the spring, South African novelist Alan Paton visited for *Collier's:* "It's an unreal world," he wrote, ". . . the sun shining and the trees coming out in leaf, and the bombs." A white resident explained, "We mean to get the jigs out, that's all." The Howards finally did move out in May 1954, just before *Brown v. Board of Education.* By then fifteen black families lived in Trumbull Park.

The situation came to a head on the afternoon of July 10. A group of blacks led by Willoughby Abner, head of the local NAACP branch, took bats and balls onto a contested baseball diamond on 105th Street. Some 400 policemen and a crowd of whites massed along the left-field line, and at the first foul ball, the melee exploded. By the time it was over, fifteen whites had been arrested. The next Sunday thirty whites ambushed three black women after eight o'clock mass at St. Kevin. At City Hall the person responsible for all the turmoil was obvious: Elizabeth Wood. Quickly and quietly, the city brokered a quota deal with the SDIA and reorganized the CHA. When Daley appointed his wildly unqualified nephew as a CHA attorney, Wood went on the record against the appointment. Now not only were her integrationist policies unacceptable, but she'd made herself a personal enemy of Chairman Daley. Wood was fired and the Machine pulled the CHA under its control.

LATE IN 1954, Congressman Bill Dawson brought Mahalia Jackson into a room with a fleshy middle-aged Irishman wearing an expensive suit. She'd met presidents, senators, and governors, cut off Bill Paley when he ventured an opinion about her music, and this Richard J. Daley seemed like he could run with the best of them. He looked her in the eye, spoke to her with respect, and even if she couldn't make out half of what he mumbled, he said it with conviction. "That man's engine's turning over," she told Dawson afterward. "He's going go." Mahalia committed to campaigning for him in the coming mayoral primary.

Dawson may not have liked Daley, but he absolutely hated Martin Kennelly, a common feeling in the Cook County Democratic Party now that the mayor had decided to go after the patronage system. The public liked the idea, but turning twelve thousand patronage jobs into civil service ones killed him with the party. In the spring of 1954, Daley reslated himself for Cook County clerk, a campaign all observers saw as a test run for the mayor's office. Young Massachusetts senator John Kennedy, son of Merchandise Mart owner Joe Kennedy, spoke at a fund-raiser for him; the candidate took speech lessons to help his accent, and he went on television as much as possible to stump for a job that was actually his for the taking. He was awful in a televised debate, stumbling over his words. When a reporter asked if he was running for mayor in 1955, he snapped that he was "not and never was a candidate for mayor." Daley well understood what the next mayor would inherit.

And because Kennelly really was as foolish as he appeared to be, he believed Daley. On December 1, a reporter asked the county clerk if he'd be dropping by the mayor's office to lend his support for a third term. "I promised to take my kids to Santa Claus," replied Daley. Two weeks later Kennelly presented himself to the party's slating committee at the Morrison Hotel. "He was sure," said one of his staffers, "that when he went into the committee and talked to them, he'd con them and charm them, and that they wouldn't have the guts to dump him." The mayor read his statement, then waited for questions. There were none. Instead, they thanked him and showed him the door—in and out within four minutes. "They gave me a fast deal," he said. Then Dick Daley sat down with the committee for two hours. The vote came in unanimous: Draft Daley. Richard J. Daley, fifty-two years old, was the Cook County Regular Democrats' candidate for mayor. "I never dreamed it could happen to me," he said afterward.

AS WORK BEGAN on Mies's Crown Hall, most Chicagoans had already forgotten what once stood on its site. People had once sung songs about the Mecca, had seen it as the epitome of life in Bronzeville, but the plans to redevelop the neighborhood from beneath its residents plowed that memory under. Henry Heald had left IIT in 1952 to become president of NYU, but Gwendolyn Brooks remembered the Mecca. Pregnant with her daughter Nora, her marriage cracking under the weight of her husband Henry's disappointments, her success, and their general lack of funds, she'd briefly left him in early 1951 with Henry Jr. in tow. A few months later she came back, but the family couldn't find an apartment to live in together. She'd returned to work on *American Family Brown* too, and under the attention of her editor Elizabeth Lawrence, it became *Maud Martha,* a short auto-biographical novel about a bright young black woman, dark and plain, with literary dreams, who's dragged down to earth by the South Side. Critics have largely overlooked it, but as Maud Martha loves dandelions because it was "comforting to find that what was common could also be a flower," so this novel is a bouquet of exquisite simplicity. Algren got her an assignment to write a piece on Bronzeville for *Holiday,* and she was invited to judge the National Book Awards, but one of America's greatest living poets still existed on the edge. Even as she raised two kids, struggled to make ends meet, and keep her marriage afloat, Gwendolyn was known to put on an Erroll Garner record and dance through her housework. That deep and painful engagement with the realities of American family life, and her ability to celebrate it in all its delicious mundane details, seeps through her work. Brooks wasn't just the poet of Black Chicago; her appreciation of the common and domestic made her by now, with Sandburg in his last years, the greatest poet of Chicago. Along with James Baldwin and Ralph Ellison, she examined what exactly black literature was in these years of limbo before Rosa Parks and Dr. King. In 1953 she and Henry were finally able to buy a small house. The next year she began a young adult novel about a little girl abducted somewhere in the long galleries of the Mecca.

KUKLA, FRAN AND OLLIE moved to WBKB in 1954. Emmett Till didn't go for them, though; he was an Abbott and Costello, Martin and Lewis kind of guy. He'd grown into a gentle giant on St. Lawrence Avenue, still Bo to his mother, Mamie, laughing and playing basketball, but his stammer kept him quiet around grown-ups, and though Mamie'd been a straight-A student, he hadn't exactly burned up McCosh Elementary. Every Sunday morning he'd take the 63rd Street bus west for an hour to go to church out in Argo, where he and Mamie had lived before they moved to the South Side. If he had to pick right then, Bo would say he wanted to be a motorcycle cop. As December went by, he got more and more excited. Mamie put up a big spruce tree, and on Christmas morning, he woke up to a mountain of presents, including a whole new outfit: suit, shirt, shoes, tie, hat, and coat, plus a hundred dollars cash to do whatever he wanted with. Emmett had bought her a scarf.

Buying all those gifts had put Mamie in the red; it was crazy, she knew, but she couldn't stop smiling all day. Her own mother, Alma, had always had to keep an eye on her as much as Bo, as if they were brother and sister not mother and son, and Mamie felt that way too, sometimes. A confidential secretary for the air force now making $3,900 a year (almost four times the average for a woman in 1954), she'd married Gene Mobley, who got along great with Bo, though the boy still wore his father's big silver signet ring, wrapped in tape so it would stay on. Christmas was so wonderful that Mamie asked a friend to photograph her and Emmett in his new suit so she could always remember her one baby boy all dressed up. Bo leaned against the television, left leg crossed casually across the right, striped tie ending a couple inches short of his buckle. He looks proud in the photos; thirteen, and about "going go" himself. The pictures "captured something more than just a moment in time," Mamie would later write. "They caught that perfect light that you see sometimes just before darkness falls."

PART FOUR

1955

"They ain't found it out yet, but Daley's the dog
with the big nuts."

Alderman Paddy Bauler

WITH MCCARTHY gone from the scene, Eisenhower's
looser attitude unleashed profound change: rock and
roll, car culture, fast food, and skyscrapers; centerfolds and improv theater. Richard J. Daley ran for mayor of Chicago not as an
expert but as the most "regular" guy in a city full of them. His
election signaled a choice by whites to embrace the Machine in
exchange for leadership and security in a world changing way
too fast for them. As Chicago began its program to contain its
black population, a teenage boy from the South Side was murdered in Mississippi. His mother's brave choice to show the world
her son's battered body catalyzed the modern civil rights movement.

CHAPTER 22

A FAMILY MAN
FOR A FAMILY CITY

THE CAMPAIGN SEASON was short and intense, with the primary on February 22 and the election on April 5. The Machine still had firm control over the Automatic Eleven and the black wards, but that wouldn't be enough to put Daley over. Kennelly had caught the scent that voters weren't happy the party had taken away their right to decide whether they still wanted him, so after eight years of fronting as a reformer, this time he ran as a real one. Electing Daley, he warned, would mean a return to the worst days of Cermak and Kelly-era corruption. Polls had him ahead, especially in non-Irish, ethnic neighborhoods.

The Cook County Organization hoped Kennelly was right, that Daley would let the Gray Wolves continue divvying up the city budget, so the Machine was motivated. Checks arrived from labor, the Mob, and the mobsters-turned-businessmen. As one precinct captain in the 42nd Ward said, "It is the duty of every American to help and nominate Richard J. Daley." Brandishing Stevenson's endorsement, Daley slammed the mayor's lack of leadership and his cozy relations with Republican business interests, plus he had one of his usual strokes of good fortune. Poles, the single largest ethnic group in the city, had been loyal Democrats for years but had never gotten their fair share of money and jobs from the Irish bosses; so to make the point, Ben Adamowski ran as an independent. In wards where Daley didn't have a shot, the Machine put money and bodies toward boosting Adamowski at Kennelly's expense. Plus, Daley had the black vote. Blacks may have been divided about Bill Dawson, but they all hated Kennelly. Down to the wire, the mayor kept his lead, but on the day of the primary, Adamowski drew off 112,000 votes, and the black wards delivered huge pluralities for Daley that overcame his poor showing on the North Side. Kennelly conceded at nine p.m. Alderman and saloon owner Paddy Bauler, of the bulb nose and top hat, told a reporter, "Chicago ain't ready for a reform mayor," a line then massaged into the legendary quote "Chicago ain't ready for reform."

Either way, Bauler's buffoonery was a gift for Robert Merriam, the do-gooder Hyde Park alderman who'd left the Democrats to run on the Republican ticket. Intelligent, honest, and well spoken, his good looks shone next to mumbling Dick Daley, the epitome of an Irish politico, but Merriam was too liberal for the *Tribune* to fully support. "Chicago is unique," Liebling had quoted him saying. "It is the only completely corrupt city in America." Picking up Kennelly's failed campaign themes, Merriam turned off blacks by attacking Dawson, whose "ruthless use of power and a low appeal to prejudice maintained and expanded his grip on a series of south side wards."

Daley went a different way. Postwar prosperity was pulling Chicagoans up into the middle class without Machine help. If the Machine wanted to survive, it would need middle-class votes, and to get them, it would have to look and act middle class. Arvey and Stevenson had tried in their own egghead ways to improve appearances. But Daley understood that for most of those new members of the middle class, all that had really changed was the size of their wallets; the tribalism remained. So he went for the gut; he packaged himself to appeal directly to those white ethnics drifting away from the party. "Let's talk sense to the people of Chicago," said one campaign ad, dusting off Adlai's old motto above a photo of the Daley clan lined up in front of the brick bungalow at 3536 S. Lowe. "A Family Man for a Family City" touted another, with head shots of all the Daleys—including Patricia, a novitiate with the Sisters of Mercy in Des Plaines—all in a circle, with Papa Daley at the top. The issue of *McCall's* that hit the stands the week of the election explored the "New Togetherness." Americans were living in a new "way characterized by more family homogeneity and solidarity," read the copy, with a "feeling of fun, of inspiration, of completeness in being a participating member of a family." That was the Daleys in a nutshell: the adorable kids, the wife with her lace-curtain dignity, and the daughter in the convent. For all of Merriam's accusations, the Daleys looked more like most Chicagoans than did some bloodless Lakefront liberal, and dodgy as Daley's associates certainly were, the candidate didn't have a black mark on him—he'd passed legislation to give schoolkids milk, called for more women in politics, and suggested, way ahead of his time, that schools be used as community centers. Dick Daley had been a Man in a Gray Flannel Suit his whole life.

The message coded within that image was that he was regular, and by 1955 that included a certain attitude toward blacks. Despite Dawson and Mahalia's dogged efforts on his behalf and the *Defender's* endorsement, white Chicagoans heard his real message when he dodged questions about public housing and talked about cleaning up the city. A *Sun-Times* poll taken the week before Election Day outside various churches showed Republican Merriam with numbers north of 80 percent at Lutheran and Baptist churches on the North and Northwest sides, while Daley had similar numbers at Baptist churches in the Black Belt, as well as a two-to-one advantage across the board at Catholic churches, up to 84 percent at St. Columbanus. In other words, the two segments of the city literally at war with each other were both backing the same candidate.

Daley left no prints on any of the countless dirty tricks—his proxies handled them. Instead, to all appearances, the nation's most corrupt Machine found God. Daley attended mass visibly and often, and took to ending speeches with a prayer from Saint Francis. He slated Morris Sachs, longtime host of a radio amateur hour and Kennelly's former running mate, for city treasurer, to siphon off what he could of the Jewish vote. He made fast friends with Mahalia, not because he loved gospel but because she spent her days with preachers, who then spread the word in their congregations. Daley's religious offensive even pulled in his opponent; Merriam's staffers insisted that their candidate had to have a quote to match Daley's Saint Francis prayer, so they appropriated some lines from the patron saint of Hyde Park, Saint Thomas Aquinas.

Election Day was windy and damp. Two days before, Colonel Robert McCormick, millionaire owner of the *Tribune* and the New York *Daily News*, died at seventy-five. The Rupert Murdoch of his day, McCormick had given voice to America's right-wing paranoia for decades; his passing ended an era, just as this Election Day would begin one. Moments before Merriam walked into the funeral at Fourth Presbyterian Church, he heard turnout estimates around 1.5 million, enough to wash out the Machine wards. Sitting through the eulogies, he mulled his cabinet. A few hours later he was writing his concession speech—actual turnout had stayed below 1.3 million. "I got 600,000, approximately," said Merriam later, "and Daley got 700,000. I carried the white vote of Chicago, and what carried Daley was the black vote." Merriam wasn't far off. Daley's 55 percent tracked closely with his primary performance; the pluralities in the Automatic Eleven and Black Belt had overwhelmed the wards he lost, especially on the North Side. The party bosses raised their glasses for happier days to come.

It hadn't escaped Paddy Bauler's notice that Daley was now mayor *and* county Democratic chairman. "They ain't found it out yet," he said, "but Daley's the dog with the big nuts." The mayor-elect sent his first message that night. The old warhorses like Joe Gill, Al Horan, and even Daley's rabbi, Jake Arvey, got their thank-you calls, but no invitations to the Morrison to celebrate and no pledges to share the wealth. The papers welcomed the mayor-elect with wary editorials, though not everyone was so polite. As hard as Daley pleaded to throw the first pitch at Wrigley Field on Opening Day, the Cubs insisted that they'd promised the honor to one Jacob Walter, a maintenance man from Zenith Radio who'd been to an average of twenty-five games a season since 1902. Mayor-elect Daley, a very public White Sox fan, could try again next year.

The evening of April 20, wearing a blue suit, with Sis and the four boys at his side (Patricia watched on TV—she'd gotten special permission from the mother superior), Richard J. Daley took the oath of office, lost in the sea of onlookers crowded into the hot City Council chamber. The only way to pick out Daley, five foot nine standing straight, was by the battery of lights trained on him. There was tension, and rightly so, because Daley in his inaugural speech essentially announced a minor coup, claiming vast new powers for his office. The state's home rule committee was taking the city's budget out of the Gray Wolves' hands and putting it in his; all spending above $2,500, whether legitimate or corrupt—the driveway permits, the padded labor bills, the insurance deals—would have to go through him. With control of both the city budget and the Cook County Democratic Party, Daley could now personally direct all negotiations with the governor and how Chicago Dems would vote in the statehouse. (Home rule in Illinois wasn't established until 1970, when the state adopted a new constitution.)

Daley's shakeup continued through the weeks after his inauguration. He laid down rules for behavior in the City Council chamber; assumed responsibility for investigating "wrongdoing on the part of city employees"; removed the long-standing police tap on the mayor's phones. He filled job openings with cronies, starting with William Lee, formerly of the Chicago Federation of Labor, now his head of civil service; all the jobs Kennelly had converted Lee now turned into mayoral patronage. The mayor's assistant, the fire commissioner, the sewer commissioner, the general counsel of the CTA and more—all came from Bridgeport. Tom Keane, Daley's closest ally, became floor leader of the City Council; the aldermen found out where they stood when he bulled through a thirty-four-page agenda in seven and a half minutes, warning one who asked a question "not to be so inquisitive."

Daley now positioned himself to ride the wave of concrete bearing down on Chicago. The day after his swearing-in, he flipped the first shovelful of dirt on a thirty-five-acre extension of the Cabrini Homes public housing project just west of Towertown. He explained the need for more expressways and announced another round of public housing—3,500 units to be built in twenty-one sites, all in black neighborhoods. In his first month in office, he pushed through a sales tax and cut a deal with airlines to open O'Hare International Airport in October—with them footing most of the bill. The statehouse took up the Fort Dearborn plan and the bond issue for a new convention center (not Mies's), then killed a bill that would have taken Chicago's judges out of Machine control. Ever meticulous, he doubled the number of street sweepers. To win over those parts of the city that still didn't trust him enough to throw out the first ball, the mayor charged into a frantic personal campaign. One observer called him "a man of inexhaustible energy": wakes, weddings, and Little League games, a meeting with the mayor of Taipei—Mayor Daley did them all. In black neighborhoods and white, for dinner and lunch, more and more people wanted to see him until his secretary finally had to put a stop to any request that wasn't official city business. The family stayed in the picture; on May 16, the mayor's fifty-third birthday, there were photos of the kids handing Daddy his presents. The cult of personality had begun.

By May 21, Armed Forces Day, an almost giddy feeling was in the air. Some of it may have been the polio vaccine announced the day after the election; for the first time in decades, parents could send their kids to camp or the park pool without worrying that they'd wake up the next morning crippled for life. But Daley's surprising first month had energized the city. Sixty-five thousand Rotarians were arriving for their annual convention, military might bristling in open view as if the city were threatening war on Wisconsin. At the Museum of Science and Industry, citizens could inspect Nike missiles, "the matadors of the Air Force" said the *Daily News*, along with a "model of the atomic cannon," a navy plane, and twenty-six other military exhibits. At O'Hare, F-86D Sabre Jets would mock-scramble at 600 mph while citizens on the ground examined hundred-ton transport planes and fighter jets.

Sun shining, Mayor Daley bounded off the 20th Century Limited at Englewood Station, 63rd and State, pushing Sis ahead in her polka-dot dress, back from the U.S. Conference of Mayors in New York. Though the big banks hadn't given him much encouragement on raising Chicago's bond rating, everything else had been a win, starting with the ride out, when they'd sat with Joan Crawford and her new husband, Al Steele, the president of Pepsi. Eleanor Guilfoyle, aka "Sis" Daley, was five and a half feet of stout Irish housewife whose impeccable manners, drilled into her by the nuns, had let her glow comfortably on the fringes while Dick scored on his first national stage. In eight years Kennelly had never made anyone on either coast turn their heads the way Daley had in just three days, arguing the merits of sixteen-inch softball versus twelve-inch with Robert Wagner, passing judgment on New York traffic and parking, tooting his horn everywhere about how Chicago was now the place to be.

Though he'd bestowed the lead spot in today's parade to Lieutenant Colonel Joseph McCarthy, a fire department captain and Medal of Honor winner, Daley changed plans: Sis went back home to see the kids while a motorcade whisked the mayor north toward the Loop. At State and Wacker, McCarthy and the Fifth Army Band were just about to begin the procession, when suddenly cops and crowds parted to let a convertible pull up. His Honor the Mayor, Richard J. Daley, gestured for the colonel to climb aboard. With a blare of trumpets, the parade moved south, Daley waving left and right at the 125,000 Chicagoans lining State Street, drums battering the windows of department stores, nut shops, and Wimpy's burger joints all hanging on for dear life against the suburbs. The Cadillac crept past the Chicago Theatre with Ernest Borgnine, cut from the same burlap as Daley, starring in the role of his life in *Marty*. The crowd went wild. When they looked at Daley, they saw a middle-aged guy with a gut who could still park a softball into the outfield, who went to mass, took care of his house, and got red in the face when someone pissed him off. If that wasn't them exactly, it was someone they knew—their father or their uncle or the guy next door. Three navy jets ripped by just above the rim of State Street's canyon. Kennelly hadn't led Chicago, and not only did Chicago need to be led—it needed to *see* that it was being led. And no one loved leading a parade like Richard J. Daley.

The next week both *Fortune* and *U.S. News & World Report* landed with long features about Chicago, packed with lines that would make any chamber of commerce drool. "Right now," said *Fortune,* "the most exciting city in the United States is Chicago, Ill. . . . What is happening in Chicago amounts, in many ways, to a rebuilding of the city. Chicago has needed the rebuilding in the worst way; it is getting it in a big way. . . . All over the city there is a fury of blasting and leveling."

"Do you feel," the *U.S. News* reporter had asked Daley, "that the Negroes will be a real asset to Chicago?" To which the mayor answered, "I think they're an asset in any community." The real message was in the rest of the sentence, though: ". . . as far as they are like any other citizens and contribute what they can to the betterment and development of their community and city." And then came *the* question, the absurd question that Chicagoans had given up on in the 1930s. *U.S. News* asked him if he could see Chicago overtaking New York. Daley didn't miss a beat "Yes," said the mayor, "I can." In the following week, all the major papers ran chuffed editorials. "New Breeze Is Blowing Through Windy City," claimed the *Sun-Times;* "Chicago on the Move," said the *Daily News.* "Chicago the Greatest?" asked the *American,* having taken the bait. When Seagram's announced that Mies van der Rohe would be designing its new headquarters on Park Avenue in New York, the *Tribune* headline read "Chicagoan Designs 38 Story, $20 Million New York Building." Henry Crown, head of Material Service, a guy from *Stanislawowo,* personally bought the Empire State Building. Even Soviet Minister V. M. Molotov, making a surprise visit en route to the UN, had to admit he was impressed—*Chicagsky Temp* indeed!

All eyes now were on Mayor Daley, though in the Tavern Club and the Commercial Club, those eyes remained doubtful. For all his new friends, Daley couldn't get the time of day from the big businessmen, literally— one afternoon Jules Herbuveaux noticed the mayor sitting quietly in a corner at the Tavern Club and had to encourage other members to talk to him. For all his faults, Kennelly had spoken the businessmen's language, whereas candidate Daley had called them the city's problem. Yet as the weeks passed, the tommy guns didn't reappear. During the summer, the

Tribune raved, "the pile driver has replaced the machine gun as the symbol of Chicago's reputation." Lillian Daley's only son Richard, altar boy, Hamburg tough, was no longer "Dick" or "Richard," even to his old friends from the neighborhood. He made it known that he was to be called only "Mr. Mayor," or in Chicago parlance, "Hizzoner Da Mare."

CHAPTER 23

THE BLUES
HAVE A BABY

CHESS RELEASED A new song the week of the election, a twangy number with a throbbing "bump dee bump dee *bump*—bump *bump*" rhythm that echoed back to the Delta, a guitar that shimmered like asphalt in July, and of all things, maracas. It wasn't exactly blues or R&B; it didn't make you want to dance, really, but it forced you to rock your head. Stocky twenty-seven-year-old Ellas McDaniel had learned to play classical violin at Ebenezer Baptist Church before he'd picked up a guitar at twelve and worked his way up to clubs like the 708. Within days of hearing the catchy, almost physically irresistible beat, Leonard and Phil hustled McDaniel into Universal Recording Studios and wasted no time in getting out "Bo Diddley," backed with "I'm a Man," a straight-ahead, boasting blues in stop time. Alan Freed pounced. As Marshall Chess celebrated his bar mitzvah with an integrated party at the Morrison Hotel and Mayor Daley made his rounds of Chicago, "Bo Diddley" climbed the charts, and Ellas McDaniel took the song's title as his new stage name.

Surely Chuck Berry listened to it on the radio a few times during his long drive up from St. Louis on May 9. Berry played guitar himself, but he was twenty-nine years old with a wife and two daughters, and it was the carpentry work he picked up at his father's contracting business that paid the bills right now, that and some hairdressing. He'd taken Friday off to drive up to Chicago with his friend Ralph to hear as much music as they could in one night, hopping bar to bar in the chilly damp: Howlin' Wolf, Elmore James, and then in the wee wee hours, at the Palladium, Berry's idol, Muddy Waters. They paid their cover just in time to hear his last song of the night, but Ralph shoved up front for an autograph before Muddy could get to the wings. Berry later compared it to an audience with the pope. He asked Muddy who to see about making a record.

"Yeah, see Leonard Chess," he said. "Yeah, Chess Records over on Forty-seventh and Cottage."

If Muddy had known what was about to happen, he might have sent Chuck Berry back to St. Louis. Too excited to go back home, Berry stayed in Chicago over the weekend so he could lie in wait outside the Chess offices until first thing Monday morning when he saw a man walk in who looked like the boss. Berry followed and asked to see Leonard Chess—Muddy Waters had sent him. City born and bred, with a professional attitude, Berry made a good impression, and that week he drove home to St. Louis to cut four demo songs. He spent most weekends tweaking and testing his music at the Cosmo Club in East St. Louis, less interested in getting a sound that he liked than in getting a reaction out of the white kids. Making music for the black kids was no way to make a living, and Chuck Berry couldn't stand to hammer another nail or relax another curl.

When the brothers sat down to listen with Willie Dixon, one number got everyone nodding: "Ida Red" layered Louis Jordan's jump blues, Bob Wills, and a little R&B, threw in a pinch of gospel and topped it off with Berry's hepped-up vocal, a rush of hyperclear Nat King Cole diction so that the white kids would understand all the words about cars and girls and driving cars with girls in them. It had that same push that "Bo Diddley" had, and "Bo Diddley" was a hit. Leonard, Phil and Willie agreed it was rough but worth recording; a date was set for May 21.

As Mayor Daley was hijacking the Armed Forces Day parade a few blocks south in the Loop, Berry, his drummer Ebby Hardy, and pianist Johnnie Johnson, a big soft man with a wary look, unloaded instruments from his red Ford station wagon in front of Universal Recording Studios. Once all the equipment was upstairs, Phil, the good cop with his hat perched on his head, situated everyone around the smaller of the two studios, Studio B, and generally made nice while Leonard swore vividly and often in the control room. One look around told the men from St. Louis that they were in deep. The room was so acoustically pure that they might have missed out on the atomic bomb if it had been dropped in the neighborhood. An empty mascara bottle shook on the piano as Johnnie sat down, probably left behind by a secretary.

Leonard called the proceedings to order. They'd start with that "Ida Red." First, a few run-throughs. Ebby counted the beat, and the three others jumped in. After a couple lines, Leonard waved them off with a *motherfucker*. They tried again, but Berry kept pulling back and forth from the mike the way he did at the club, to manipulate the sound. Another *motherfucker*, plus a *goddammit*. Phil explained to Berry that he just had to sing up at the mike, and they'd do the effects later on Bill Putnam's console. A few more, and Leonard signaled it was time to start.

Berry swallowed hard, the artificial silence in the studio deeper and lonelier than any silence outside could ever be. He held the dice in his hand, and everybody was waiting for him to throw. . . .

He peeled off the opening notes, Ebby Hardy joined in, and the four of them played a clean version of the song. They looked at each other, then at the booth. Leonard sneered and shook his head.

No, motherfuckers! Do it again!

And so they did, scared and sweating more each time as Leonard gritted his lantern jaw and leveled his eyes at them through the glass. More than once Berry was sure they'd nailed it, but there was always something wrong—Ebby wasn't sharp enough, Berry's voice just wasn't . . . *something*. Phil and Leonard couldn't put their finger on it, mostly because they were in over their heads with this new sound. They pulled some tricks out of Putnam's playbook. Leonard tried a take himself, using Ebby's sticks on a phonebook. That didn't work. They sent Berry to the bathroom, hoping to imitate the Harmonicats, but no luck.

Leonard called for a break. As everyone tried to let some life seep back into this grueling session, he brought up the name. "Ida Red" sounded like something for that Polack cowboy Pee Wee King and his accordion. Thoughts simmered. It had to have three syllables. Leonard pointed to the box of mascara that Johnson hadn't bothered to move. Maybelline. *Eye*-duh red. *May*-buh leen.

Berry sang it a few times low. *May buh leen. May buh leen, why can't you . . .*

He smiled and sang it again, this time plucking the notes on the guitar. *Oh May buh leen.* It was all about the long vowels; he could stretch and twist them. They picked up their instruments, and a couple takes later, somewhere around number thirty-five, Leonard nodded. They'd have to change the spelling, but "Maybellene" it was. Fifteen minutes later they'd cut "Wee Wee Hours" and everyone broke for lunch. By eight-thirty that evening, they'd recorded two more songs, "Thirty Days" and "You Can't Catch Me," then ate a round of hamburgers. Berry, Johnson, and Hardy packed up the red Ford and followed the brothers down to the Chess offices on Cottage Grove.

There was no ceremony. Leonard smiled and slid a pile of papers across the desk for Berry to read through. He skimmed over much that he didn't understand because no matter how much he wanted to appear like he was looking out for his own interests, Chuck Berry needed this record to happen. The first contract he signed covered the recording, the second the publishing rights. All he could do now was trust the Chess brothers. Handshakes, and then Berry went back out to the car. Rock and roll had just been born, not in some great outpouring of teenage lust and angst, or even in some gritty late-night gutbucket session. Leonard and Phil had cut a record in the world's most advanced studio, with an ambitious man whose musical style was the product of his own rough market research. Business and technology were under every spark of inspiration; "Maybellene" and the music that followed was a product created for teens by a group of middle-aged men looking to make money. Three days after they recorded "Maybellene," the Chess brothers went back in the studio with Muddy

Waters to record a riff on Bo Diddley's "I'm a Man," called "Mannish Boy." Using the same stop time rhythm as "I'm a Man," the rhythm that *he'd* made popular, the old man schooled the young one, swaggering and swatting away his claims, listing his titles—a rolling stone, a hoochie coochie man—over a relentless chest-beating drum. Leonard held on to both sessions, hoping to first ride Bo Diddley as far as he could.

MARSHALL'S BAR MITZVAH that spring had been quite an affair—350 people in the Cotillion Room of the Morrison Hotel, with a special number by the Flamingos—it was maybe the height of Chess Records' days as a family. Marshall began to hang around the office more often to fetch coffees and sandwiches from Deutsch's and run deposits to the bank while his father stomped around, cursing and playing casino deep into the night, until he'd come home and wake up his son for some predawn perch fishing. Big Gene the former bouncer offered the thirteen-year-old tips about numbing his dick with cocaine. It was a good time for Marshall.

Too many other teens were left to their own devices. The night after Berry cut his first record, cops broke up a gang fight at 2900 S. Halsted, arresting a hundred kids and confiscating knives, hoses, bats, clubs, a pipe, and a croquet mallet. When the Memorial Day weekend was over, 346 drivers had been killed in accidents. General Motors announced a three-for-one stock split. The whole summer was mad like that. Police in suburban Bedford Park discovered a marijuana field four miles long and four hundred yards wide. July brought nineteen days in the nineties. The body of eight-year-old Mary Manzo was found under the 46th Street railroad viaduct, defiled, coal dust in her hair; police launched a manhunt but never solved the crime. The Shriners arrived, ninety thousand of them, be-fezzed and many in blackface, for their annual seven-hour parade down Michigan Avenue. In the next three days, a seven-year-old girl was pulled into a vacant building and raped by a teenager, Disneyland opened, and a Braniff plane crashed at Midway, killing twenty-two. The President's Council of Economic Advisers reported that so far in 1955 Americans had "spent more money, produced more goods, and held more jobs than ever before." The mercury broke 100.4; hydrants ran dry. Mayor Daley banned watering lawns. Someone tried to steal a baby in broad daylight.

Into the middle of it all, Leonard released "Maybellene," a song as frantic and buoyant as the world felt just then. The label on the sheet music named Alan Freed and Russ Fratto, Chess's landlord and fellow casino player, as songwriters with Berry, who later claimed it had been done without his knowledge, but he'd likely accepted it as the cost of doing business. In return, Freed plugged the song hard, and Leonard sent a touring contract to Berry, who packed away his carpenter's tools for good; he went on the road nonstop for the rest of the year. By the beginning of August, all hands were on deck at Chess to handle the demand. Sam Phillips had brought out ten sides by his discovery Elvis Presley, whom he'd kept from Leonard because of hard feelings over the Howlin' Wolf deal. Elvis remained a local phenom, while Chuck Berry roared across the country. On September 3, after a big Apollo date, "Maybellene" was the most-played, most-bought R&B record on *Billboard*'s charts. Chess Records had its first monster hit.

Muddy meanwhile spent a lot of time with Geneva at home, in a scene not unlike Mahalia's place—a big pot of something or other always simmering on the stove, Geneva puttering with the flower garden outside while Muddy sprawled across the sofa in a wife-beater, Sox game on the TV; James Cotton, Jimmy Rogers, and Otis Spann drifting through, playing with ideas. He toured the South that summer, and Wolf played the Apollo, where he tried with no luck whatsoever to get Etta James into bed. Muddy's "Mannish Boy" had come out along with "Maybellene." The first ads even promoted the songs together, but while it was Muddy's biggest hit of the year, it earned peanuts compared to Berry and Bo Diddley. Rock and roll felt like a sports car full of wiseass kids zipping by in the passing lane.

CHAPTER 24

AMERICAN HUNGERS

RAY KROC SQUATTED down on his arthritic knees to grab another pickle. People who didn't like pickles peeled them off their hamburgers and tossed them on the ground, leaving the lot covered in bright green dots, and for a man who came in on weekends to scrub the yellow parking lines, scrape up gum, and once in a while clean out the mop wringer with a toothbrush, this was unacceptable. He stuffed them into the bag full of the discarded cups and wrappers he'd scooped up when he'd arrived, as he did every afternoon, after a day at the office of Prince Castle Sales on LaSalle. Since he'd opened the store a few weeks before, on April 15, he'd driven in every morning to pick up the pickles in the lot; then he'd take the train to the Loop to sell Multimixers. At four p.m. he was headed back west here to Des Plaines for a few hours around this sleek, white-and-red-tiled drive-in, whose roof seemed held up by a pair of giant golden arches. This was Ray Kroc's last shot at something big. "If I lost out on McDonald's," he later said, "I'd have no place to go." He'd scrub as many mop wringers and harvest as many pickle slices as he needed to for it to work.

Grinning, elfin Ray went around back to dump the bag, then went inside. The Greek boy, youngest man on the crew, looked up from cutting a block of American cheese. McDonald's had no female employees, and especially no carhops giving hand jobs in the parking lot, a practice more common than anyone liked to admit. All the countermen wore white pants, white short-sleeved shirts, and white paper hats as spotless as the stainless-steel surfaces of the kitchen, every inch visible through the glass windows at the front, where customers came up to be served. McDonald's had nothing to hide: no hearts ground into the meat or holes in the patties, no rancid oil and filthy floors like so many of the other drive-ins popping up like roadside weeds. Planned in minute detail, McDonald's No. 1 would be the template for a new way of eating in America. A fresh batch of French fries sat under a heat lamp, draining into a metal pan; Ray bit into one and stopped grinning. Not a true fan of the French fry—he considered the best of them just a transition between hamburger and milkshake—even he knew these were below par. Out they went.

Ray Kroc was fifty-two, the same age as Richard J. Daley, but he was betting *against* Chicago; he'd put his last penny on cars and suburbs, on speed and mobility—car registrations in Chicago were already up 15 percent in just the first three months of 1955. A product of the suburbs himself, Kroc was born west of the city in Hemingway's broad-lawned hometown of Oak Park, and though he never ran with the bulls in Pamplona, he took risks that Daley, dug badgerlike into Bridgeport, never dreamed of. At fifteen he'd dropped out of high school and lied about his age to enlist in the army ambulance corps, where he became friends with another young Chicagoan named Walt Disney. (That Disneyland was opening that summer of 1955 and every little head he saw through the glass wore a Davy Crockett coonskin hat hadn't escaped Ray.) The war had ended before he shipped out, so while Daley worked his precinct through the 1920s, Kroc, of lighter heart and nimbler fingers, played piano in clubs and the occasional whorehouse, got married much too young, and became a paper cup salesman. Daley ground away at his law degree; Kroc moved Mrs. Kroc and their daughter down to Florida, so he could take a flyer on selling boggy plots in the Everglades, until that bubble burst and he was behind the keyboard again, passing the tip snifter.

Soon it was back to Lily Cup for Ray, where he expected everyone to welcome his innovative ideas, but instead, like Hefner, he found the corporate world frustrating. All his hard work paid for a nice house in Arlington

Heights and a poolside chair inside the midlevel country club set of the western suburbs, but never the big win he was looking for and never the support of his wife, Ethel, who might have been happier with boring security than a husband who repeatedly butted heads with his superiors. In time he jumped to his own firm Prince Castle to sell Multimixers, a tidy dollar immediately after the war but unsatisfying, because in the end Kroc wasn't motivated by money. He wanted to build something, and time was running out. When he went out to visit an account in San Bernardino that owned eight of his Multimixers, stirring up forty milkshakes at any given moment, he saw his last best chance for a future.

The brothers McDonald, Dick and Mac, weren't motivated by money either. Or so they said. They, not Kroc, had created virtually everything about McDonald's down to the pair of giant golden arches and Speedee, the cartoon hamburger running across the sign. Drive-ins were everywhere nowadays, but despite familiar signs like Howard Johnson's, Kentucky Fried Chicken, and Dairy Queen, you could never be quite sure what you'd find when you pulled in. The McDonalds had perfected an easily replicated drive-in system, laying out their burger joint in precise detail to maximize efficiency and transparency, commissioning the golden arches which unconsciously echoed the trusses of Mies's Cantor Drive-In, reducing the menu to a minimum of items (including those peerless French fries) that let them turn over customers fast. But in true California fashion, they'd done it with something of a Zen attitude and never licensed the plans. Instead, they gave them away to anyone who asked; a national chain was too much of a bother.

This, to Ray, was incomprehensible. To have lines around the building; to have invested so much and not want a maximum return bordered on insanity, so on the spot he pitched them a deal wherein he'd do all the franchising and pay them a royalty. Kroc wouldn't see a dollar for years, but he quickly developed a passion for the Speedee Service System that bordered on the religious and left him vulnerable to the brothers, who weren't quite the laid-back Californians they posed as, toying with Ray and his frantic energy in a not-so-good-natured way. Just weeks before

McDonald's No. 1 opened, for example, he discovered that even though the brothers had given him rights to the entire nation, the one spot they'd held back and licensed themselves was Cook County, Illinois. Kroc had to put himself deeper in the hole to buy out his home territory. McDonald's would be a kind of machine for food, each store "a small factory" delivering a fast, consistent, quality product in a clean setting, at a reasonable price. Now the target of documentarians and nutritionists, Kroc's 1955 McDonald's represented the cutting edge of responsible business. Kids liked the independence of going to the window and ordering for themselves; dads liked having a fun place to go when they were trying out some of that New Togetherness; and it was a destination at a time when the suburbs offered little in the way of entertainment.

If McDonald's didn't single-handedly change how America ate, it sped the change in how Americans thought about eating. In this way, McDonald's completed a process that Chicago had begun back in the nineteenth century, as the headquarters of western expansion, when farmers had sent their wheat and corn to huge grain elevators on the Chicago River. The invention of the commodity future hypercharged agriculture by changing grain transactions from the sale of a particular bushel of corn to the purchase of the *promise* of a bushel of an agreed-upon standard of corn; a liberating business idea, but one that took "food" a step away from its physical reality. The Stockyards served essentially the same purpose for meat, concentrating and performing the rituals of slaughter not just out of sight but out of consciousness, muffling what Upton Sinclair had called "the hog squeal of the universe." By 1955, Americans loved those time-saving, frozen foods that Walter Gropius had praised back in the Red Lacquer Room, and now McDonald's all but severed the connection between what went into their mouths and where it came from. A visit there conveyed no information about the food served other than its taste and cost; cows and potatoes had nothing to do with hamburgers and French fries, though the miasmic stink of blood and shit and fear that hung over the Stockyards, the vile ooze of Bubbly Creek, were only a short drive away.

Kroc's other goals for McDonald's were also progressions of what agricultural Chicago had started: ever speedier production from ever cheaper labor had always been the primary goal of Chicago's packing-houses and an underlying cause of the endless labor strife there. Kroc's expanding web of suppliers, whose product would be altered by McDon-ald's volume, was a new version of Chicago's nineteenth-century agricul-tural network. The first McDonald's, in San Bernardino, was indeed the invention of the brothers, but McDonald's the Corporation, McDonald's the Social Phenomenon, would be all Ray Kroc, the pinpoint of food ser-vice efficiency that Chicago had been working toward for more than a century.

The other American hunger Kroc wanted to feed involved food only tangentially. A McDonald's franchise offered guys like him an alternative way of doing business—smart, ambitious entrepreneurs eager to work hard and succeed but misfits in their own way, unwilling or unable to function effectively within the corporate world. But until Ray Kroc, the norm in franchising had been for the parent company to bleed what it could out of the little guy frying the burgers until he took down his Burger Chef sign and went independent. Ray, instead, advertised a mutually ben-eficial relationship. He resolved to do ethical business, to sell each fran-chise one at a time, to accept no kickbacks from suppliers, and to charge almost ridiculously small royalties to franchisees. The company that today for many epitomizes mindless conformity was conceived as a profoundly American innovation—a mammoth corporation built out of every man's hunger to be his own man. That business model eventually would let Kroc parlay this store in Des Plaines into a global behemoth that represents to much of the world all that's bad about America, and all that they want.

What Ray Kroc really needed to figure out right now though, in May 1955, was how to fix his damn French fries. The brothers didn't just slice potatoes and throw them in oil; they peeled them, cut them into slices, then soaked them in cold water to draw out the starch. Then they hosed them off and put them in fresh oil used only for fries. But it wasn't work-ing. The fries were good but not great. It would be another late night at the store, it seemed. By this point, Ethel didn't seem to care when he came home.

EARLY IN JUNE a scientific paper reported the discovery of unusual changes in the lungs of cigarette smokers. "Some authorities consider this thickening pre-cancerous," said the *Tribune*. The news didn't stop the Leo Burnett Company from unveiling its ad campaign for the new Philip Morris cigarette, called Marlboros, featuring a weathered cowboy known as the Marlboro Man. Philip Morris had hired Burnett for a "west of the Hudson" take on its product. Michigan-born, Leo hadn't come to Chicago until he was forty but had always considered it "a kind of Rome to which all roads led, with a side-order of Babylon. . . . When we rubes came flocking in from all quarters of the cornbelt we recognized each other and knew we were home." And that gave Chicago advertising a unique power: "our sod-busting delivery, our loose-limbed stand and our wide-eyed perspective make it easier for us to create ads that talk turkey to the majority of Americans. . . . The language of our ads has been ventilated in the fresh Chicago breezes and rinsed in the clear waters of Lake Michigan." Burnett had opened his shop in 1935 with three clients, and now, in 1955, he was billing $70 million a year by providing comfortable, indulgent ways for America to see itself, from the responsibility embodied in the Good Hands of Allstate to the unconditional love offered by the Pillsbury Doughboy's crescent rolls. No long blocks of text or testimony from scientists; Burnett's ads took the thinking out of buying things and replaced it with feeling good. In Burnett's hands, consumerism became shorthand for living. By the end of 1955, Marlboro sales were up 3,000 percent.

THOUGH MAYOR DALEY took communion every day and brought milk-shakes home for the kiddies, these times weren't quite as puritanical as they're now billed. "Key clubs" were the city's nightlife fad, led by the

Gaslight Club, where flirtatious—but untouchable—former models in fishnet stockings and velvet corsets served drinks. Sex simmered in provocative underwear and stocking ads; as the Senate heard testimony about a massive pornography ring featuring UCLA coeds, Marilyn Monroe thrust out her chest to promote *The Seven Year Itch*. *Playboy*'s circulation hit 175,000 in December 1954, evolving from its wide-eyed freshman year into a more credible tone, with regular pieces by writers like Ray Bradbury and Erskine Caldwell. The May 1955 issue, for example, featured an Irwin Shaw story next to a profile of Steve Allen, a long introduction to cheese ("Roquefort and Ricotta are not the food of virgins"), and a pictorial of Bunny Yeager, famed for her photos of Bettie Page. There was also the requisite public domain filler by Boccaccio and rules for some "adult party games." Miss May, a redhead in black pantyhose, had no top and no name.

The scene at 11 E. Superior was its own constant adult party game, played by the small core of employees. One new addition to the subscription department that spring was Charlaine Karalus, a busty twenty-year-old blonde with a big, wide-open Chicago face. Hefner made his move, and they were a regular item by June, which arrived with a problem: they'd run out of stock nudies. What would they do for July? Hefner's idea: Charlaine. As beautiful as Kim Novak, under the name "Janet Pilgrim" (his way of answering the pieties of Kefauver), *she'd* be Miss July. Charlaine's mother was not pleased, at least until Hefner gave her a job.

A million people hit the beaches for the Fourth of July and 400,000 picnicked in the forest preserves. Millie Hefner sweated through the heat, pregnant with their second child, David, to be born later that year. Twelve-year-old Peter Gorham disappeared from his Scout camp, yet another gang fight left a De La Salle senior dead, and the July *Playboy* hit the stands with the first Girl Next Door Playmate looking out from the centerfold, topless, her arms pressed together to hide her nipples; demure stuff even then. The caption for a shot of "Janet" reviewing paperwork with a pencil-necked Hefner (a ringer for Dick York in *Bewitched*) read, "Actually, potential Playmates are all around you: the new secretary at your office, the doe-eyed beauty who sat opposite you at lunch yesterday, the girl who sells you shirts and ties at your favorite store."

The result, Hefner would later say, was "an absolute sensation" but also an unsolvable question as to whether a great leap forward in American sexuality had taken place, or a great leap back; whether sloe-eyed Janet called for the enjoyment of life as a sexual being, or set in motion the mass-market exploitation of women and sexualization of American culture. On the face of it, there was something liberating and mature about the Girl Next Door. Hefner, untouched as a child, wanted sex to be admitted and discussed as one facet of a healthy human life, a process already under way thanks to Dr. Alfred Kinsey's 1948 and 1953 reports on sexuality. Kinsey's findings had shaken attitudes even in the Catholic Church and particularly in the Archdiocese of Chicago, where the Reverend Jack Egan began leading classes for married couples that discussed sex as a positive and divinely approved aspect of marriage. (Called Cana Conferences, they're still required before you can be married in the Church.) In fact, the American puritanism that Hefner railed against was usually more of a public pose than a private reality. At the turn of the century, Chicago's sudden growth had thrown thousands of young singles together, and they made the most of it; the progressives who shut down the Levee were also hoping to tamp down free love, a sell-out topic at the Dil Pickle Club and a fact of life in the Roaring Twenties. The migrations, chance passings, and death of the Great Depression and World War II had made sex something turgid and tinged with desperation that the postwar years channeled toward the altar—Chicago issued 66,000 marriage licenses in 1946, compared to 44,000 in 1945—and a more uniform national consciousness made this era of transition appear an eternal truth.

Hypocrisy and confusion were Hefner's real targets. The media titillated even as it reinforced sexual repression. Women, removed from their wartime positions in the workplace and academia, were now sent off to suburbia to be goddesses of the ranch house. Ironically, married couples were having less sex because they were talking *more;* husbands weren't forcing sex as much, but they still wanted it, and while conformity pressed down on them too, they had trouble enlisting women as their partners in the bedroom because women wanted sex to be *better*. Hefner understood just how scary women, and in particular their sexuality, were to most men. Sexually available women were dangerous, unnerving fetish objects in porn rags, and then there was VD. More effort was being expended on landing on the moon than on exploring the mysteries of feminine desire. So Hef's solution was sexual liberation—for men.

The Girl Next Door domesticated female sexuality. For all the hype, "Janet Pilgrim" was hardly "the first nice girl to take off her clothes for the camera"—Eleanor Callahan could testify to that. Janet's choice appears daring, but one can't tell from her eyes just how much of a choice it was for a twenty-year-old girl who was sleeping with her boss and encouraged by her mother. Eleanor Callahan, on the other hand, was the real girl next door—physically imperfect, confident, and strong, her sexuality not to be consumed but given as a gift. Harry and Eleanor Callahan shared power and intimacy. Sex in *Playboy*, on the other hand, was a transaction performed for mink coats and Lobster Newburg; the word *love* rarely if ever appears in its pages—in 1955 the archdiocese was more explicitly concerned about a woman's sexual pleasure than was Hugh Hefner. "Janet Pilgrim" was not so much a woman as an ideal of consumer sexuality offered every month among all the other products on display, in a city that had amassed much of its wealth through the mail-order business. In these preimplant years, the women ranged in types and cup sizes, but increasingly Hefner's personal taste was presented as every man's, and as *Playboy* went forward, it treated sex the way McDonald's treated food: hygienically packaged, well-priced, pumped-up, quality-controlled—and born in Chicago under the same sign as the Fast Food Nation and Rock and Roll.

In order to please all those who'd written in praise of Janet Pilgrim, Charlaine posed again for the Christmas issue, this time wrapped only in jewels and a white mink stole. Chicago's great love story was no longer the yeasty coupling of Algren and De Beauvoir, but a ménage between a shy man with intense eyes, his fantasies, and the half-million or so monthly readers of *Playboy*.

CHAPTER 25

THEATER
WITHOUT HEROES

Homeless since the fire department had shut them down in February, Playwrights Theatre Club performed Sean O'Casey's *Juno and the Paycock* in college auditoriums and rented spaces. No one minded when the production closed on May 28—the reviews had been terrible. Ed Asner had made a credible Captain Boyle, but as for Viola Spolin, "a legitimate theater director," says Asner, "she was not." The *Tribune* critic Claudia Cassidy expressed some hope that PTC would return in the fall. At the *Daily News*, Tony Weitzel suggested that Playwrights might "come up with a startling summer drama dream." Something remarkable would indeed happen that summer in Chicago theater, but it would have nothing to do with Playwrights. Out of a Hyde Park dive bar scheduled to be torn down, a new kind of theater would emerge that would eventually transform American comedy from shtick into a form of commentary and opposition that would rival music as an expression of the nation's soul.

As David Shepherd spun PTC off under different management, he circulated a pamphlet laying out the vision he'd had ever since that truck ride from Erie: a new theater aimed at "the newspaper vendor, the waitress and the machinist," who'd be expected "not to sit still or leave, but to comment, applaud, hiss and stay." The Compass would offer "plays with a juggler, a hypnotist, an argument, a song, fight, game, impersonation—anything you can watch or listen to for itself." All that mattered was economy, intensity, and "a form that can be recognized by the man-in-the-street." Once a week the actors would ask the audience for ideas about what they should act out. The other staple would be improvised "scenarios": a step past the germ of an idea that Charlie Andrews would bring to the cast of *Studs' Place* every Monday morning, Shepherd planned to give his actors characterizations and the beats for a dramatic arc that they'd then figure out how to get through with improvised dialogue and action.

While he searched for a home for the Compass, Shepherd produced the first "scenario" on May 14 at the Reynolds Club at the University of Chicago. *Enterprise* was a roughed-up version of Arthur Schnitzler's play *La Ronde,* about four teenage boys who trade a jalopy up into a successful jewelry business and eventually a new car. Lively and amusing, it persuaded Elaine May and Roger Bowen to sign on, but the man Shepherd really wanted on board was Paul Sills.

Back at the Steinway's Drugstore, they'd bonded over Brecht and his idea of a "Smokers' Theater," meant "for the sort of people who just come for fun and don't hesitate to keep their hats on in the theatre." To pitch his neighborhood cabarets, Shepherd played a tape of *Enterprise*—the laughter proved to Sills and Barbara Harris that he knew what he was doing. The couple agreed to join until August, when Sills would have to leave for England and his Fulbright. As producer and director now searched for players, Viola Spolin ran a series of her theater game workshops to help sort through their largely amateur catch. Bar owner Fred Wranovics rented them the side room of his Hi-Hat Lounge on 55th Street, one of the twenty-three taverns slated for demolition in the redevelopment of Hyde Park. In all ways, impermanence was central to the venture.

Shepherd's dream was becoming real, but if the Compass was to be like a stadium, as Brecht suggested, they now had to decide what kind of ball they were going to play with. For that they turned to Spolin, whose dramatic theory held that what animated a scene was its "point of concentration," its anxiety. Acting was for her serious, philosophical play that heightened your awareness and reinvigorated your ability to experience, allowing you to break away from the Lonely Crowd—Spolin made that connection clear by requiring everyone to read Riesman's book along with the newspaper. Though later some Compass alums would claim that the importance of Spolin's games was overhyped—the experienced actors may not have needed them, and improvisation was around long before Spolin—the spirit of the games informed the venture. "You forget yourself as the process takes hold," said Harris. "You sort of become part of the form itself."

By late June, the cast was in place. Ed Asner moved on because it was "not meet that one made a living improvising"; nor were his strong but conventional acting skills what Shepherd and Sills were after. Andrew Duncan shared Asner's working-class-hero appeal—he was finishing his master's in English at the same time as he was renovating the Hi-Hat—but he could also play a straight man. Plus, he tended bar. Bowen, May, Shepherd, Harris, and Duncan would form the core, along with six or seven amateurs. After Shepherd had greased all extended palms and opening night approached, the ward's alderman wanted them to ante up for a cabaret license they couldn't afford. In true Chicago fashion, People Who Knew People were called, until their plight was submitted to the mayor along with a gushing *Time* article about Playwrights. "These guys are culture," Hizzoner reportedly said. "Lay off." And so it was with the mayor's personal blessing that on the evening of July 5, the Compass Theater debuted in the middle of a deadly heat wave. The show began with *The Living Newspaper,* a cousin to the original WPA version, then came the scenario; that night it was *The Game of Hurt,* featuring Shepherd as a salesman who sells his wife, played by Elaine May, to a laborer. As much as he regrets it the next day, he can't convince his wife to come back because she actually prefers her new husband. Like most scenarios, it ran close to an hour, then ideas were solicited from the crowd for a final improvised piece—Bowen claimed they did it to keep the audience in their seats for another round.

It was a long night, but no one had seen anything like it since the Dil Pickle closed. Fresh, young, smart, and topical, the Compass offered something real the same week Hugh Hefner gave America an airbrushed Venus and Ray Kroc perfected mass-produced fries. There was no censorship, so imaginary joints were smoked, curse words uttered, rapes simulated; bracing stuff, even in that part of the city.

Word spread, and the next night the Hi-Hat was packed, the small round tables covered in beer bottles, as they'd be all through the summer. At one end of the long, smoky room was the stage, not much more than ten feet wide, with a series of movable panels to stand in for scenery, the actors in shorts sometimes when it was too hot; at the other end a window where anyone walking along 55th Street could stop and look in. People wandered in and out. Some nights the scenario lumbered along, and the improvisations could be incoherent and rambling. "People would sit out there for two or three hours trying to figure out what was happening onstage," said Shepherd. But the energy bursting off the stage expressed truths about American life that no one wanted to say, dramatized the anxieties and confusion the audiences voiced in their suggestions. "We were articulate, we were as educated as they were," said Duncan, "and we were as perceptive about what was going on politically and socially. . . . We were their representatives, in a sense."

For the actors, it was exhilarating. "Nobody knew what was going to happen," said Harris, "but it was happening." If a set went badly, they'd dash the mile or so east and jump into the lake to cool off, or play a game of chess. It was a brutal grind: eight shows a week while preparing next week's during the day, and on top of that, only a few of the actors were paid, so they had jobs to go to in what little time remained. The scenarios quickly proved to be extremely difficult. Though they didn't have the high-wire excitement of the improvs, Shepherd saw them as the basis of a new kind of direct, confrontational theater; there were laughs, but not jokes. *Georgina's First Date,* for instance, told the story of a fat girl preparing for the prom, with her proud parents May and Shepherd guiding her through the social rituals. Unknown to them all, her date is only taking her on a dare; he rapes her after the dance, and all Georgina can do when she comes home is say she had a wonderful time. *The Drifters* followed the gristly, greedy escapades of two con men; in *The Minister's Daughter* a clergyman reveals to his children that they'd been adopted out of the low-class neighborhood around them that they've looked down on their whole lives. All the cant of the McCarthy and Eisenhower years was fair game. "I'd like to see neighborhoods all over the city form groups like this," Sills said, in terms Moholy would have approved of. "It's a search for a community."

In those two months, David Shepherd truly did realize his dream of a Smokers' Theater. But the fall changes Hyde Park more than the rest of Chicago; thousands of new faces arrive for the semester, others leave, and that autumn the entire neighborhood was in the throes of rancorous community meetings as the university and the SECC pursued their own agenda for transforming the neighborhood. The departure of Paul Sills and Barbara Harris in September hurt most. The Compass was now in David Shepherd's hands, and he wasn't prepared. "I didn't expect it to happen so fast," he told Janet Coleman. "I've tried to do things I couldn't do, compose symphonies when I couldn't play an instrument." His philosophical convictions couldn't make up for the loss of an experienced director who understood actors; Shepherd didn't really even like actors that much as a group, suspecting that they considered themselves "vastly superior to the audience." To reach out to the community, he made Tuesday nights an open improv night and invited random viewers to try something that was hit or miss even in the hands of the professionals. Sills had dialed down the politics, but Shepherd's overtly socialist scenarios bombed with audiences out for a night of fun. Wranovics complained about plummeting beer sales; Elaine talked about leaving.

Shepherd scouted talent in New York. The first recruit, Severn Darden, was extreme in all ways, from his oversize bearing to a near-encyclopedic knowledge that let him take improvisations into the strange, cerebral, and funny places Hyde Parkers wanted to go, such as his character Professor Walther von der Vogelweide, who delivered hour-long mock lectures in academic gibberish. While a student at the University of Chicago, Darden had built a reputation as a cape-wearing eccentric; now, pushed out onto the stage his first night with no training in improvisation, Darden dove into a *Living Newspaper* bit based on a *National Geographic* article about a village in the Amazon, and immediately became one of the troupe's driving forces.

The second new face was an old one. Mike Nichols's flirtation with Method acting had left him penniless in New York, so he returned to Hyde Park. But he had a hard time fitting into the Compass: though he was a famous wit, his emotion-driven Method training often left him yelling and crying onstage. Ultimately he found his way in through Elaine May. Years earlier they'd circled each other on campus, two spiny creatures unsure whether they were natural-born enemies or belonged to the same species. One night while both were taking the Illinois Central train up to the Loop, Nichols approached her and asked in a German accent if he could sit down, to which she said, "If you weesh." They played spies the rest of the ride, and after a brief affair just to get All Of That out of the way, they flowered together onstage. Nichols usually set the scene with characters much like himself—smart, cutting, snobby, and a bit put upon by the world—while May, who had the range to play Yiddishe mamas, society matrons, and moony girls with equal finesse, lived in the details. In scenes such as *Teenagers* (a less fraught redo of *Georgina's First Date*) and *Pirandello* (which punctured layers of reality until other actors finally rushed onstage to separate them as if they'd really begun to fight) their exchange could be as fast and intricate as Barcelona's passing or a pas de deux, challenging each other while supporting their shared reality. "You would literally be possessed and speak languages you didn't speak," said Nichols. ". . . You'd be drained and amazed afterward, and you'd have a sense of your possibilities."

As people began coming to see the two of them work, the Compass evolved. "You had the right to fail," said Bobbi Gordon, along with her husband the other two Shepherd recruits of that fall. ". . . You couldn't do that in New York because . . . you knew you were being judged. But in Chicago, you could experiment." Improvisation, experimentation, watching something being made: all were basic to artistic expression in Chicago, part of its mediating function as the belt buckle of America; what Ralph Ellison called "antagonistic cooperation." The epitaph on Nelson Algren's tombstone is, along with Mies's "Less is more" dictum, the ultimate statement of a Chicago aesthetic: "The end is nothing. The road is all." "Chicago was the best audience we played for," Severn Darden would say later. "Chicago liked watching things being built. New York audiences like to watch things that are already completed and polished." Chicagoans today still watch the Cubs for the same reason they watched the Compass—to follow the anxiety, to see what will happen next; Chicago has always understood play, maybe more than it's understood how to win.

On November 1 the Compass relocated to the Dock, a restaurant at 53rd and Lake Park Avenue. But something was changing in the company that cut right to the core of Chicago's own ambiguous heart; the Compass's quasi-socialist mission was being executed by professionals who'd found something they could sell. While Shepherd still saw himself as the head of a worldwide movement, this new cadre of pros had no clue about Spolin's games aside from the fact that improvisation provided a great vehicle for their talents; the Compass was a job to them, not community service, and their job was to entertain. As the outspoken liberals in the neighborhood around them got very quiet about their convictions now that "renewal" was coming to Hyde Park, the idea of theater for the "community" sounded hollow. Brecht had gone from inspiration to punch line.

CHAPTER 26

WHAT KIND OF WORLD DO WE LIVE IN?

THROUGH SWELTERING AUGUST, the lines ran long at Riverview Park, charged with that dark energy carnivals have. One big draw was the "African Dip," a black man in a dunking booth. It did enormous business. Ten-foot storm waves slammed into the lakefront, and children kept disappearing. Susan and Sandra Pasternak, both eight, went missing in an unsettled area southwest of the city; the decayed body of Peter Gorham was finally found in a dump five miles from his Scout camp, molested, with a bullet in his head. Yet it's still been written, "if ever there were 'good old days' in Chicago, it was in 1955." In white neighborhoods "kids didn't worry about the future or the world," said an Albany Park native. ". . . We didn't have a fear of people, or pretty much anything during those years." The musical *Grease,* the primary text of 1950s nostalgia, was written by two alumni of Taft High School in nearby Norwood Park.

Feelings weren't quite the same in Black Chicago. "I felt great anger," said Warner Saunders, ". . . but I didn't even recognize it as anger because I was so wrapped in fear." When Mamie Till's uncle Moses Wright came up for a funeral that month, parts of the city were definitely off-limits to him. "Everybody enjoyed their civil liberties," wrote Nicholas von Hoffman, "yet the place was almost like pre-Nelson Mandela South Africa." Bo and Mamie could take him to the Museum of Science and Industry, the Shedd Aquarium, or the Field Museum, all known to allow blacks, but the 57th Street Beach was off-limits, as was the North Side. It wasn't illegal to go, but it would *not* be safe.

For Uncle Mose, an occasional minister from a dot on the Mississippi map called Money, about thirty miles from where Charley Patton sang the blues, 63rd and Cottage Grove was more than enough. During the war, migrants had poured into Englewood Station, then walked east on 63rd with their bags. Now the area boasted one of the city's best-educated, most comfortable black populations, at a time when the median income for blacks in Chicago was almost twice the national number. The intersection popped with nightclubs like the Pershing Lounge and Birdland, the Kitty Kat, Basin Street, the Trianon, and the Crown Propeller Lounge; the Pelican had a woman swimming in a mermaid costume behind the bar. Barber Leon Cooper and his partner, George Johnson, were turning his new hair-straightening process into Johnson Products, eventually the first black-owned business listed on the New York Stock Exchange.

When it was time for Uncle Mose to head back south, Bo announced that he wanted to go too; he wanted to fish in slow streams and count the stars. He wanted to see where they came from. Mississippi still crackled from *Brown v. Board of Education,* and Belzoni, where the Reverend George Lee had been lynched in May, was only about fifty miles from Uncle Mose's house; *Jet* had published pictures of Lee's body lying in the casket. Mamie had bought a red Plymouth back in February, planning to join the 50 million other Americans taking road trips that summer, but she understood the calling Bo heard; though the idea chilled her to the bone, she agreed. Now fourteen-year-old Bo had to go to a school very different from McCosh Elementary. There were rules in Mississippi he had to learn before he got on any train: Never look at a white woman. Never speak to a white man unless spoken to. Get off the sidewalk to let a white person pass. Say "Yes sir," and "No, sir." These weren't points of etiquette; they were rules of survival. Bo had no wallet, so they bought one with a picture of Hedy Lamarr, and on the morning of August 20, he and Mamie rushed to Englewood Station to catch the 8:01 City of New Orleans.

A shoebox packed with fried chicken under his arm, he clambered onto the train to meet Uncle Mose inside.

"Bo," shouted Mamie. "You didn't kiss me good-bye. How do I know I'll ever see you again?" He ducked down to kiss his mother, then ran back in. That night Mahalia Jackson headlined the twenty-sixth annual Chicagoland Music Festival at Soldier Field. Just about the time Emmett's train was rolling into Winona, Mississippi, she was singing "Move On Up a Little Higher."

When Mamie got home from the station, she took to her bed and stayed there all week. She missed Bo, but there was more to it than that; her heart felt like it'd been taken out of her. That week Senator James Eastland made a speech to the White Citizens' Council of Mississippi demanding violent resistance to the Supreme Court's desegregation order. On Friday she called Bo, who told her he was having fun fishing, but he could use some money because he'd been treating everybody to candy at the grocery in Money, and would she please get his motorbike fixed before he came home? Aunt Lizzie, Mose's wife, reported that Bo was as good a boy as could be; letters came on Saturday that pretty much repeated all of that, down to the bike. Mamie felt better, and since she was on vacation too, she decided to take a train down to Mississippi on Monday; in the meantime she met her ladies' club, Les Petites Femmes, for cards. At one point she stopped, and out of the blue, like she wasn't even the one talking, said, "If Bo Till could get his feet on Chicago soil he would be one happy kid." For a second everyone held their cards until the spell broke.

The phone woke her at nine-thirty Sunday morning, her cousin Willie Mae on the other end. Apparently Bo had whistled at a white woman at the grocery store in Money. Some white men had come during the night and taken him away.

Alma's husband, Henry, called his nephew, Rayfield Mooty, an official in the Steelworkers Union, and Monday Mamie met with the NAACP and a lawyer who together with Mooty activated every connection they had; by the end of the day, Mayor Daley, Governor Stratton, and Senator Douglas were making calls, the FBI was involved, the president of Inland Steel had offered help, and the *Tribune* had run a page-one story. On one hand, it didn't help that he was from Chicago, a city with a reputation down south as the capital of uppity negritude. The poet William Alexander Percy had written in 1941, "Every black buck in the South today has gone or will go to Chicago, where it is not only possible but inexpensive to sleep with a white whore." But on the other hand, if Bo hadn't been from Chicago, no one would have said a word. Roy Bryant, the owner of the grocery store, and his half-brother J. W. Milam, were being held for questioning. Bryant admitted to kidnapping Emmett but claimed they'd let him go.

Tuesday, *Jet* reporter Simeon Booker came by the house and convinced Mamie to give him the photos from Christmas with Bo in his new outfit. Uncle Mose had finally come out of hiding and explained how four white men had come in the night waving guns. He'd promised them he'd punish Bo, but they woke the child up and told him to come with them. Bo'd either been the coolest customer in the world or he had no clue as to what all this meant, because he didn't say "sir" and insisted on putting on socks before they left. When they threatened to "blow his head off," he might have started to understand. A few hours later Mose had gone to the store looking for Bo, but Bryant said they'd let him go. Rumors and hoaxes filled Wednesday, and then, as Mamie packed in Chicago, her friend Ollie Williams called. They'd found Bo. Dead. Floating in the Tallahatchie River, shot once in the head, a 150-pound cotton gin fan tied to him with barbed wire. Chicago TV stations broke into *I Love Lucy* (though many complained). The state of Mississippi insisted that he be buried immediately, but Bill Dawson worked a deal with the governor to release the body to the family in a sealed crate, to be buried unopened.

But no one told Mamie Till. The box arrived, brown and massive as an Egyptian sarcophagus, at Central Station, where a huge crowd waited, Mamie in a wheelchair. A. A. Rayner, Chicago's leading black undertaker, tried to explain the situation, the seals and signatures, but she wouldn't hear it; she needed to *see* her boy. With the sudden good sense to decide he was on her side, Rayner had the box loaded onto a truck, Mamie screaming, "Oh, God! Oh, God! My only boy!" Simeon Booker and photographer

David Jackson came to the funeral home. Everyone begged Mamie not to view the body—its smell was infesting the entire area around 41st and Cottage Grove. "I will never forget that smell," she'd write. The officials in Mississippi had packed it with quicklime, hoping to hide what Rayner now reluctantly revealed. Mamie crumbled; Simeon Booker had to hold her up and try to keep himself standing too. What lay before them was "something from outer space," she'd say later; drooping flesh, bulging tongue, sockets gouged with the eyes hanging out on their stalks, a body not just beaten but mangled until it was no longer human. Bryant and Milam hadn't just beaten and killed Emmett Till—they'd tried to reduce him to a *thing*. Only the signet ring on his finger identified him as Bo.

Rayner promised to do his best, but Mamie stopped him. She'd been an immature sort of parent, loving and concerned but often a bit too young herself. Seeing, touching Bo's body had changed that in an instant. Her next choice would spark the modern civil rights movement. "Let the world see what I've seen," she said. Mamie demanded an open casket. After great efforts to reassemble Bo into a human form, his body went on view for four days. Tens of thousands passed by shocked and weeping, often fainting, the Christmas photos tucked into the edges of the casket to remind you that this wasn't just another helpless victim; it was a boy named Emmett who loved his mother and climbing trees and Abbott and Costello; a boy in whom all African Americans could see themselves; a city kid with country roots raised by a hardworking mother whose success hadn't taken her away from her community; a boy reclaimed from the four centuries of dead black flesh piled in America's backyard. On September 10 thousands packed the Roberts Temple of the Church of God in Christ at 40th and State for the funeral; the street outside blocked with thousands more listening on loudspeakers. State Senator Marshall Korshak, on behalf of the mayor, called the boy "a martyr and inspiration to God fearing people." Emmett Till was then laid to rest in Burr Oak Cemetery.

Five days later *Jet* ran David Jackson's photos of the body in the casket. White lynchers, just like the Nazis and the Pol Pot regime, commonly documented their work; sometimes they even sold the photographs of the mob and the strange fruit as souvenir postcards. But these photos showed the world what happened when the mob left and the family came to cut the charred body down. "There were people on the staff who were squeamish about the photographs," wrote John Johnson later. "I had reservations too, but I decided finally that if it happened it was our responsibility to print it and let the world experience man's inhumanity to man."

The impact was immediate and profound. After decades of running on separate tracks of geography, culture, and philosophy—Old Settler v. new arrival; the Talented Tenth and those who set their buckets down; assimilationists and communists; black, ebony, tan, and lighter than the paper bag—Black America reunited to witness Emmett Till's body. The *Defender* ran the photos next, and then the Pittsburgh *Courier*, The *Crisis,* and a four-page spread in *Life.* Michigan congressman Charles Diggs called Jackson's photos "the greatest media product in the last forty or fifty years." African Americans from Muhammad Ali (who "felt a deep kinship" to Emmett, born only months apart) to Eldridge Cleaver, Shelby Steele, and many of those who in the years to come would fill the ranks of the Southern Christian Leadership Conference, the Student Nonviolent Coordinating Committee, and other civil rights organizations have written that seeing the photos was a catalyzing moment. No matter what club you belonged to, how many commissions were named or promises made, you could win awards, die for your country, and pray all you wanted, but *that,* that monstrous face, told you where you and your children stood in the mind of White America in 1955.

The international press came to Sumner September 19 for the murder trial of Roy Bryant and J. W. Milam—"A Good Place to Raise a Boy" said a sign in town. Few expected justice; the community had collected $10,000 for the defense fund, five local lawyers had volunteered their services, and despite the ring on Bo's swollen finger, Mississippi officials expressed doubts that the body was actually Emmett's, claiming that the NAACP had set it all up. Bill Dawson was conspicuously quiet, though Congressman Diggs attended the trial. President Eisenhower remained silent too, while J. Edgar Hoover hinted that Daley's agitation for a federal investigation evidenced Communist leanings. When Moses Wright was called to the stand and asked to identify the men who'd taken Bo, he stood and did the unthinkable by pointing at Bryant and Milam. Still, the all-white, all-male jury returned a verdict of not guilty after only an hour of deliberation. "If we hadn't stopped to drink pop, it wouldn't have taken that long," admitted one juror. A year later, Bryant and Milam would admit in *Look* that they had in fact murdered Emmett Till.

David Halberstam called the trial "the first great media event of the civil rights movement." But it wasn't as if the white mass media underwent some great awakening—the editors of the *Sun-Times* went out of their way to remind its man in Sumner that the paper cared about the rape and murder of "white girls by negro assailants" as much as justice for Till. It was John Johnson who'd slapped the press awake by publishing the photos in *Jet.* The photos caught in some nightmare place in the mind and demanded justice. The photos did not let you forget. "A generation of black people would remember the horror of that photo," said Diggs, "and it steeled the determination of some of them to reduce their own vulnerability." Black Chicago, for now at least, came together at Metropolitan Community Church, where ten thousand attended a rally to hear speeches by Mamie, Abner, and Booker; a thousand members of the United Packinghouse Workers held a mass meeting. Said historian Adam Green, "All of Black Chicago seemed intent on recovering and exercising their collective powers of memory."

A little more than two months later, a tired Rosa Parks sat down on a Montgomery, Alabama, bus. "Rosa Parks," Mamie wrote later, "would tell me how she felt about Emmett, how she had thought about him on that fateful day when she took that historic stand by keeping her seat."

TWO PHOTOGRAPHS TAKEN in Chicago that summer had changed the world, one of a beautiful woman and the other of a mangled teenaged boy. The images vindicated Moholy's belief that the future was in photog-

Muddy Waters and
his wife, Geneva

Howlin' Wolf

Leonard and Revetta Chess

Sun Ra

© Adam Abraham/Saturn Records. Courtesy of Corbett vs. Dempsey

Mahalia Jackson

Paul Schutzer/TIME & LIFE Pictures/Getty Images

Studs Terkel in the studio

Stephen Deutch/Chicago History Museum/
Getty Images

Nelson Algren and
Simone de Beauvoir

© Art Shay. Courtesy of
Berlanga Fine Arts

Burr Tillstrom with Kukla, Fran, and Ollie

NBC/NBC Universal/Getty Images

Dave Garroway

Hank Walker/TIME & LIFE Pictures/Getty Images

WNBQ Performers. The cast of *Kukla, Fran and Ollie* are at the left; *Studs' Place* in the foreground; and Dave Garroway stretches out on the couch. Jules Herbuveaux stands in the center of it all

Adlai Stevenson

Richard J. Daley and Jacob Arvey

Francis Miller/TIME & LIFE Pictures/Getty Images

Mayor Daley presents his vision for
Chicago, 1958

Francis Miller/TIME & LIFE Pictures/Getty Images

Hugh Hefner

© Art Shay. Courtesy of Berlanga Fine Arts

Ray Kroc

Self Portrait, Circular Mirror,
1951-55, Vivian Maier

Henry Darger's table with paintings, 1974

Richard Nickel

Richard Nickel, photographer. Richard Nickel
Archive, Ryerson and Burnham Archives,
The Art Institute of Chicago.
© The Art Institute of Chicago.

Schiller Building,
1890–1892

Adler and Sullivan, architects. Richard Nickel
Archive, Ryerson and Burnham Archives,
The Art Institute of Chicago.
© The Art Institute of Chicago.

raphy and we must learn how to read it with the same care and depth we apply to words. In the fall, a snippet of film would speak to how the great soul of the city had changed.

Mayor Daley had been vocal in pursuing justice for Emmett Till, maybe even sincere. He could like a particular African American such as Mahalia, especially one who'd done so much to get him elected; marching alongside her in the Bud Billiken Day Parade in August, he'd said: "Anything I can do for you, Mahalia, you just let me know." His anger over Bo was possibly real. Negroes as a group, as an idea—*that* he wasn't so crazy about. Two days after he'd paraded down South Parkway with Mahalia, Daley announced a $500 million "urban renewal" program to clear slums and build what would become the State Street Corridor of public housing. Since few whites wanted to live in public housing, white preference was no longer necessary. All Elizabeth Wood–era restrictions were removed; no more intake screenings, no more income requirements. The CHA now existed solely to warehouse blacks. The second ghetto, as Arnold Hirsch calls it, was born. In July a delegation of black leaders petitioned the mayor for help in Trumbull Park, which was boiling again. Daley made promising statements and named a blue ribbon committee of well-credentialed, largely unknown, and heretofore silent members of the black community to study the problem. Much studying ensued, but no action, so in October, just weeks after the Till trial, Willoughby Abner led the local NAACP branch in a protest at City Hall. Daley responded with what could be called white signifying: a speech at Trumbull Park that managed to avoid mentioning race, an omission made more remarkable by the fact that just hours before, a black woman had been assaulted at St. Kevin.

White Chicagoans continued running north and south and west, away from blacks. Their neighborhoods, full of grimy packs of kids scampering through hydrants and chasing the Good Humor man, were little different from any other urban neighborhoods in America during Ike's 1950s. But the constant threat of black invasion lent them the poignancy of something believed to be eternal suddenly threatened with extinction, an antebellum quality that crystallized white Childhood in Chicago and sprinkled it with a false innocence no matter how many Pasternak twins went missing or Peter Gorhams were found raped and killed.

On the afternoon of Sunday, October 16, way out in Jefferson Park—on the Far Northwest Side of the city, one of the "safe" neighborhoods white ethnics had filled after the war—thirteen-year-old Bobby Peterson set off in his White Sox jacket for an adventure with fourteen-year-old John Schuessler and his brother Tony, age twelve. It was a school night, so their parents Eleanor and Anton Schuessler insisted they be back by seven. No one knows exactly what the boys had planned, nor what really happened that day; the trail patched together later offers at best a guess. After a bus ride to Logan Square, the three bowled a few games at Monte Cristo Bowl, then took the El to see Disney's *The African Lion* at the Loop Theater; though they'd told their parents they were going to the movies, they hadn't mentioned the part about Downtown. Bobby stopped briefly at the Garland Building at 111 S. Wabash for reasons unknown—To use a bathroom? To meet someone? His loopy signature is in the security log. Then they headed back to the Northwest Side, where they hitched rides from bowling alley to bowling alley in search of an open lane. It began to rain. By now it was nine o'clock. Angry at first, now the parents contacted each other. The last sighting, around ten-thirty, had the trio in the vicinity of Lawrence and Milwaukee, either huddling under an awning, the biggest one thumbing a ride, or all climbing into a battered white pickup truck with a man they were overheard calling "Ed." The panicked parents went to the police and continued their fruitless scouring the next morning.

Tuesday afternoon, the WGN-TV newsroom intercepted a police radio call—something had been found in the Robinson Woods at Lawrence and River Road. Cameraman Richard Ritt got there first and filmed a scene as sickening as what David Jackson had shot at Rayner's Funeral Home: the dead, naked bodies of the three boys, bound, beaten, strangled, and dumped together in a low depression. Police from both the county and city arrived along with the rest of the press, and before anyone could positively identify the corpses, Chicago's television stations ran special reports showing the film, the papers splashed a ghastly photo across their front pages. Today the film is pixelated to hide the bodies, but in October 1955 the entire city saw the pale skin, the genitals, the open eyes; a slaughter of innocents straight out of Henry Darger. The families were devastated. Anton Schuessler, a Yugoslavian tailor, fell to the ground when he heard. "Mother," he cried to his wife, "what kind of land do we live in?"

Hysteria gripped those parts of Chicago that had complained when *I Love Lucy* had been interrupted for the news that Till's body had been found. Cops searched house by house and interrogated students in their classrooms. Police suspected Mr. Schuessler, a groundless suspicion that drove him insane; he would die before the year ended during a shock treatment. What trail there was went cold. Mamie Till sent a message of condolence to all the parents, while rumors spread on the Northwest Side that blacks had done it in revenge for Bo's murder, or Jews had done it for the blood. Parents locked doors, enforced curfews. White Chicagoans were proud to say that they'd moved to neighborhoods like Jefferson Park to get away from blacks—they cushioned it in terms of values. But they refused to admit that the fate of those three dead boys proved that Algren was right: out where the lawns were mowed as tight as a crew cut, being regular had curdled into something more than just an insistence on conformity. With the murders unsolved, the answer to tragic Anton Schuessler's question was: a land they no longer could control. Their kids were listening to crazy music, the niggers were coming, homosexuals were murdering little boys; all the challenges to white ethnics that would explode in the Sixties—sex and drugs, rock and roll, black and white—were peeking up just past the blades of their hedge cutters.

When they saw Mayor Daley marching at the head of a parade, they saw a man who understood the need for control.

SUN RA SAT down at the piano at the Parkway Ballroom. It was time to go. He'd distilled his group from a quintet to a trio, with two students of DuSable High School's fabled music teacher Captain Walter Dyett, who'd taught Nat King Cole and Dinah Washington. Robert Barry played drums and Pat Patrick (soon to be the father of future Massachusetts governor Deval Patrick) played sax; when Patrick left for college, John Gilmore came in. Sun Ra had told the Space Trio, when they'd first started together last year, that they might rehearse for ten years before they ever played a gig, if they ever played a gig at all. Assembled to study and learn the secrets, they rehearsed long into every night, then woke up the next morning and started again, sometimes at his book-lined kitchenette on South Prairie, other times at Pat Patrick's mom's. Unlike New York sax players, who worked tight to notes, in Chicago they played around them, which lent itself to Sun Ra's experiments. Eventually they'd surrendered to him—how long they played, what they played, and what they ate. They practiced until he could take away the sheet music and they'd keep going, practicing until the names of the songs didn't matter, until there were no notes and they all simply played.

Sun Ra looked out at the audience. Since the days of the slaves, there'd always been a place to run to if you followed the drinking gourd. Sometimes it was Diddy Wah Diddy, a magical valley in the mountains where runaways, Indians, and whites lived together like the Seminoles. Sometimes it was just Canada. But he was not of this earth. And it was time to leave a planet where boys were killed for simply whistling. If there was any hope left, it lived in music.

He played a few low notes on the keyboard, then added an off-kilter chord higher up that the drums joined in their own stiff way, like a clock striking or a countdown. Tonight they'd jump in place, march through the audience, chanting, playing songs that touched the essence of all things. Whoever wanted to come was welcome to grab hold of his robe and fly along. If the aliens weren't coming back, then it was up to Sun Ra to deliver his people.

CHAPTER 27

WE LIKE IT THIS WAY

WHENEVER," ALGREN ONCE asked, "is someone going to come along who'll say right out, 'We like it this way?'" For ten years, Chicago had been trying to make sense of itself in the postwar world, when Richard J. Daley offered White Chicago the dream of getting back both the control it felt it had lost and its identity, either stolen or ignored by those who'd really cashed in. White Catholics had turned away from the Vatican on matters of race and handed over their vote in return for segregation. And so did most blacks. The city of Al Capone and Tubbo Gilbert had never been pure, but a midwestern hope always fueled its myth of the phoenix rising from the ashes, the renaissances, the perseverance of men like Kroc, Hefner, and Shepherd, and all the "Chicago Schools" with their better ways of doing things. But the deaths of those four boys, and the unwillingness of blacks and whites to mourn together, marked the end of what passed for innocence in Chicago.

The compromises between commerce and art weren't really compromises anymore. To replace Crombie Taylor as head of the Institute of Design, IIT hired a designer from Raymond Loewy's slick New York practice named Jay Doblin. Not only did Doblin consider Moholy's philosophies and the ID the product of dilettantes, he felt that contact with fine art actually hurt designers. Doblin was a corporate servant, and that's what IIT wanted to produce. The faculty and students joined to protest, but Doblin didn't step down and the exodus began—Hugo Weber, Taylor, Peter Selz, and many others resigned; some like Konrad Wachsmann were let go, and Doblin had Callahan and Siskind's photography department very much in his sights. Concerned alumni, friends, and faculty met at Ellen Borden's Art Center to create Friends of the Institute of Design, an advisory group whose advice the ID had no intention of listening to. Approached for support, Serge Chermayeff just sounds tired as he writes: "Are not the good intentions of the Friends of the Institute of Design likely to succeed better if the school is left in peace to work?" The rebellion was quashed in a whimper. In September the ID relocated to the IIT campus as it waited for its new home in the basement of Mies's Crown Hall. Once an integral part of Chicago's cultural scene, a messy, navel-staring generator of ideas, it was now essentially a trade school. One of the few people to benefit was Richard Nickel, who took Alfred Caldwell's classes on architectural history and made pictures around the city—at Riverview, in the Loop—that echo Callahan's street work. He also made two trips to find more lost Sullivan buildings.

NELSON ALGREN NEEDED money. Badly. What his agents came up with was surprising: a new screenplay for *The Man with the Golden Arm*. Without Algren's knowledge, John Garfield's producer had sold the rights to Otto Preminger, who planned to take a run at the Motion Picture Production Code with Frank Sinatra as Frankie Machine and blousy Kim Novak as Molly. Though he was working on an Off-Broadway adaptation, Algren couldn't resist $1,000 a week, but he had more in mind than just a writing gig—he had a score to settle with Hollywood. Otto's brother Ingo Preminger had picked up the rights from Garfield's estate for what may have been as much as $100,000, which would have entitled Algren to around $40,000; but producer Bob Roberts showed no profit on his books, thereby cutting him out.

Algren had a case, but unfortunately he was no savvier now than he'd been five years earlier. As soon as he landed in L.A., Preminger lowered his rate to $500 a week, settling finally on $750. Meanwhile his high-end digs made him so tense, he checked out and, according to Preminger, moved "downtown where nobody lives, because he said he has to be in a rundown hotel with a bar." Requested to be on the curb the next morning for pickup, so as not to delay Mr. Preminger, Algren instead had to be summoned down to the director's red Cadillac. What meeting of minds they had was short. Otto, the son of a well-to-do Viennese lawyer, asked, "How come you know such terrible people you write about?" (Since Algren recounted all this in various ways in various places, it took place either in the car while Preminger displayed his power windows or at the studio as he had his makeup done; a major director but a minor actor, he'd play Mr. Freeze in the original *Batman* TV series.)

"They live around where I live," Algren says he responded.

"Why you live around such people? . . . You *like* underdogs?"

The next few days proceeded along these same bumpy roads, and Algren seems to have handed in a short, undercooked treatment after seeing "no chance of having a relationship with this guy at all." While Algren swans it up in his retellings, he seems to have made valid attempts to add the kind of realism that would come into favor only decades later, asking that there be Polish songs in the jukebox and such. "While he's a wonderful writer," Preminger said of Algren, ". . . he cannot write dialogue. He cannot write scenes at all. So after a few weeks I had to reluctantly let him go," adding, "Thank you for letting me meet such an *interesting* person." Tossed aside and left out of pocket for a trip he couldn't afford to make, Algren returned to Chicago broke. Hollywood had "made a horse's ass out of him," said his friend Dave Peltz. "Totally and completely. I think that was shocking for him, a rude awakening in terms of his own abilities and strength." Instead of consulting a lawyer, he dashed off a pissy letter that effectively waived any claim. "He not only made it impossible to do our jobs," said his agent, "he frustrated all our attempts to get any more money back by writing that letter." Nor did he hurt Preminger's feelings. When a writer sells his property, Otto would say, "I have no obligation, nor do I try, to be 'faithful' to the book."

The Man with the Golden Arm, advertised as "a film by Otto Preminger," was not a good movie at all. For all the credit he receives for confronting drugs, homosexuality, and race in his films, Preminger was an above-average talent who exploited topics to sell tickets, and the lack of empathy he expressed with Algren makes *Man* a hollow, lifeless enterprise; only the theme song by Elmer Bernstein is memorable. The sets bear no resemblance to Chicago, and the actors have Brooklyn accents except for Novak, who had to have many of her lines dubbed afterward. Sinatra's Frankie jumps around and sweats and threatens his way to another Oscar nomination, instead of crawling into a corner and falling asleep into sorry dreams of drumming the way a junkie really would have. Algren found it "sort of comical. It had nothing to do with drug addiction. I thought it was cheap."

Worst of all, it was a hit, and he wouldn't see a penny.

Divorcing Amanda a second time, he went out on the road, taught for a short stint in Montana, and holed up in upstate New York in order to meet *A Walk on the Wild Side*'s fall deadline. After reading it, Algren's editor at Doubleday took him out for lunch and enough martinis until he had the guts to say that they were rejecting the book because it was too raunchy. Farrar, Straus and Cudahy snapped it up, but he was falling deeper in debt, and Amanda was countersuing him. At Christmas, his faith in himself and other people nearly snuffed, Algren washed up in Cuba, where he knocked on Hemingway's door. Papa took him in with pleasure. Under the stuffed heads of various wild animals, Algren acted out the last movie he'd seen, Disney's *The African Lion,* drank whiskey, and ate Christmas dinner with people who admired him and his work. For a day or two, he was the Dostoyevsky of Chicago again. Then the holiday ended. Beaten by Hollywood, left to remember the good times, Algren returned home, the canary in the mine shaft for Chicago.

BILL PALEY HAD little patience for the slow progress of racial enlightenment. Despite strong ratings and reviews for her radio show, Mahalia's inability to penetrate the South meant that February 6, 1955, would be her last broadcast. The local CBS television affiliate tried her as a guest on a late-night show called *In Town Tonight* (ever the crossroads mentality). The station owner called in with the order to "Get that big black gorilla off the air!" but otherwise the response was positive, and two sponsors quickly stepped up. Mahalia let it be known that there wouldn't be a television show without Studs Terkel, so a deal was cut: at the taping of the first show in the Garrick Theater early in March, and for every show thereafter, Studs's disembodied voice drew out as much of her big personality and warmth as possible for the camera, without ever showing his face. In this way, Communism would be defeated.

A tape went out to Paley in hopes of a network pickup, while Mahalia launched into a busy spring and summer that pushed her further into the challenging position of racial pioneer with a nonthreatening persona. Whereas the big, black, God-fearing women on TV had always worn a maid's uniform, Mahalia answered to no one but God, so even as Mitch Miller sanded down her music, she maintained an independence and a musical integrity. Her first Columbia album, despite its cloying production, was a popular and critical hit. She made guest appearances on network TV shows like Arthur Godfrey's; topped a monster concert in Detroit over Ella Fitzgerald, Count Basie, and Dinah Washington; sold out Carnegie Hall on Mother's Day; and just as Bobo Till rode the train south, she headlined the huge Chicagoland Music Festival with the Justin Bieber of his day, Eddie Fisher. But there were limits to just how much Mahalia white America wanted. Bill Paley never responded to her demo tape, and discussions with NBC floated away; as Bryant and Milam prepared for their sham trial in Mississippi, word came that the South wouldn't take Mahalia's show, and so no national sponsors wanted to sign on. Her local sponsors dropped out.

On October 28 she was given a gala forty-fourth-birthday dinner at the Morrison Hotel to raise money for a girls' shelter, to be built at 90th and South Park Avenue. Mayor Daley sat next to her, told her again that he'd give her anything she wanted, walked up with her to the birthday cake. After he handed Mahalia a bronze plaque, nine-year-old Rachel

Washington, on behalf of "all the little girls in the world," presented her with the thing she'd never had: a doll. It had black braids, a yellow dress. And a white face.

AS THE YEAR ended, Richard J. Daley's Chicago began to emerge from the scaffolding. In December two segments of the Congress Expressway opened on the West Side, with many more miles to come. Flights landed at O'Hare Airport, already slated for expansion. (In June, Douglas Aircraft had announced its plans for the DC-8, a jet airplane that could travel from Los Angeles to New York in four and a half hours, ready for use in 1959.) On the Near South Side, Michael Reese Hospital dedicated the Kaplan Pavilion, and forty more acres were being prepared to become Michael Reese's residential development, Prairie Shores. Just south, at Lake Meadows, the twelve-story buildings and the shopping center were completed, and work had begun on the twenty-two-story towers. Most of the "opportunity" left in the Opportunity Plan at this point involved demolishing Bronzeville buildings. Soon after the Congress Expressway opened, the Prudential was finished, a block of gray that owed more to Rockefeller Center than anything around it; Chicagoans flocked to Stouffer's Top of the Rock restaurant for long views down the lakefront. At Dearborn and Monroe, work had begun on the Inland Steel Building, designed by Bruce Graham and Walter Netsch of SOM, just then finishing the Manufacturers Hanover Trust Building at 43rd and Fifth in New York and working on the new Air Force Academy in Colorado. Ceres was soon to be eclipsed.

On December 23, Richard J. Daley extended his holiday wishes to his fellow Chicagoans. "As mayor of Chicago, it is my hope and prayer that you, your families, and your loved ones will be blessed with health, prosperity, happiness, and peace in the years to come." He would extend similar wishes for the next nineteen Christmases. The city was now his, and it would survive by remaking itself in his image—industrious, racist, and provincial.

PART FIVE

1956–1960

"Well, we're all born equal. Anyone in Chicago can now
become an expatriate without leaving town."

Nelson Algren

DALEY'S ARRIVAL in the mayor's chair launched a building boom in Chicago that brought together City Hall, big
business, the Mob, and labor. The only people left out were the
citizens of Chicago, who paid higher taxes and saw their needs
pushed aside when it served the administration and its friends.
Their racism had been turned against them even as it was pla-
cated. The creative climate grew chilly. While the skyscrapers
rose and Daley played kingmaker for JFK, the city turned
inward. But the loss wasn't just Chicago's. Jets replaced railroads, and the nation lost touch with its center—physically at
first, but soon in every way.

CHAPTER 28

CHICAGO DYNAMIC

RICHARD J. DALEY, family man, woke up at six every morning to beat everyone else to the bathroom then, showered and dressed, with all six children sitting up very straight at the table, he ate his poached egg and toast and drank his coffee. The mayor's detail, no one taller than him, waited outside until he emerged with William, John, Michael, and Richard M. in tow, and everyone trouped two blocks to Nativity of Our Lord for eight o'clock mass, the Cadillac limo idling at the curb. Half an hour later, recessional hymn sung, the boys went off to school, and the mayor of Chicago bore east on 33rd Street, right through the IIT campus. At Michigan they took a left and headed north to Congress. Daley walked the rest of the way to City Hall. "The mayor," wrote a *Tribune* reporter, "is like a high powered sports car in a dapper gray suit."

Once in his office, he got to work, desk clear except for a pen set and a small box stacked with slips of paper. Meetings were to the point, no schmoozing or chatting; over the course of a day, he rarely ran more than five minutes late. If he agreed to do something or look into a matter, he made a note on one of the slips and put it in the upper-right-hand drawer of his desk, to be collected later by his assistants. If he grew impatient, he rubbed the flesh between his thumb and forefinger, sometimes so much so that it got raw. Whatever his personal feelings were, he never indulged in public slurs as Ed Kelly had; he kept his thoughts to himself, save for a defensive little sign in a corner: "When I'm right, no one remembers. When I'm wrong, no one forgets." To any meeting held outside the office, he always arrived first, looking "like he just came out of the shower— neat, fresh, eager to go, always well groomed and immaculate." On nice afternoons in the spring and summer, he held court in his box at Comiskey Park.

Daley's whole first year was matter-of-fact and businesslike this way, setting a tone. The city now worked. Streets were clean and better lit. The budget made sense. Behind all the ribbon cuttings of the first year, Daley had been extending a hand to the Republican business community he'd run against in '55, in particular the Chicago Central Area Committee, whose membership included the big names of the SSPB and other development groups. After all, many of his goals were the same as theirs: clean up the Loop, pull Chicagoans back from suburban shopping centers, and keep out blacks. To help jump-start things after Kennelly's glacial pace, Daley packed the Chicago Plan Commission with marginally qualified "experts," while Nate Owings's successor, John Cordwell, steered a new Central Area Plan to address the needs of the city—as identified by the business community. "Chicago business has made up its mind it will hold onto the Loop," Owings told the press at SOM's annual partners meeting. "Having decided that, now it will have to modernize the Loop." In the Kennelly years, Owings had loaded the CPC with SOM employees as a way to keep the Chicago office afloat; now, with business booming, the firm acted as a virtually independent entity within the CPC, in charge of designing half of the Central Area Plan, while city employees worked on the rest. City Hall wasn't so much helping big builders and developers as it was merging with them. The days of Gropius and Mies ordering the urban grid were over. Now Richard J. Daley would dictate how, where, when, and who played. As for the Mob, he'd conveniently shut down the police division assigned to pursuing it. You can't stop them, he shrugged. You just have to keep them in line.

With the mayor now clearly directing traffic, the building frenzy took off. The Inland Steel Building went up on Monroe; work on the Borg-Warner Building at Michigan and Adams began. On the Near South Side, ground was broken on the final towers of Lake Meadows, and the first two neared completion. Just north, the city had acquired almost 70 percent of the land Michael Reese Hospital wanted for its next expansion; by the fall nineteen acres would be sold to Ferd Kramer's company, and in the spring of 1957, construction would begin on the five twenty-story buildings of Prairie Shores. Fort Dearborn moved forward. Public housing projects like the Cabrini Homes extension and Stateway Gardens poured money directly into the Machine. In May the City Council approved the Robert Taylor Homes, along with the South (later Dan Ryan) Expressway and Calumet Skyway, a fourteen-lane river of cars to safely divide the projects from the white neighborhoods—namely Bridgeport—to the west. On the North Side, the Northwest Expressway would connect the Loop with O'Hare.

Biographers Adam Cohen and Elizabeth Taylor aptly call Daley the "American Pharoah," but construction's central role in the rise of his Chicago wasn't just a matter of personal obsession. Hundreds of millions of dollars flowed into Chicago's economy in various ways legitimate, illegal, and usually some combination of both. Insiders sold information about what sites were being scoped out, or bought the plots themselves at a bargain price to sell back to the city; the inner circle of plugged-in contractors kept up the appearance of competitive bidding but somehow managed always to make just about the same amount of money by the end of each year; Material Service, the city's main provider of building materials, made a billionaire of its owner Henry Crown. Henry's older brother Sol had founded the company in 1919 and never lost a dime up to his death, when Henry took over. Crown now owned a mansion in Evanston, a string of polo ponies, and of course the Empire State Building. (In 1959 Material Service would join the military-industrial complex, merging with General Dynamics, maker of tanks, submarines, and fighter jets.) Daley's version of the New Deal made labor happy too; he repaid its support for his

1955 campaign by providing plentiful jobs loaded with overtime, all billed at exorbitant rates paid by Washington, the state, and the rising local tax bills of everyday Chicagoans.

But those for whom rebuilding had symbolic value saw only their rising city when they looked out from the top of the Prudential, allowing Daley to define *progress* going forward solely in terms of building. Through it he orchestrated a major change to the Machine and to life in Chicago. "Good government is good politics," he liked to say; public servants who did a good job providing services for their constituents got re-elected. In Chicago, where the average alderman answered to fewer than a quarter of the residents his counterpart in New York did, politics had always been service-oriented: patch my alley, help me get a liquor license; retail, as opposed to the wholesale sort concerned with policy and ideas. (Dawson stood out only because his constituents required more of that loftier sort.) But the word *retail* implies one has a choice, and Daley was eliminating choices for the people of Chicago. Under him, the Machine no longer made any pretense of helping "regular guys" work the system; the Machine *was* the system, and its purpose was to rake in money, create jobs, and keep blacks in their place yet still voting Democratic. Big business, labor, the Mob, and the Machine had always been connected through people like the Korshak brothers, but now they met openly at construction sites.

Not only were the schools still terrible, but *Life* said the Chicago Police Department was "probably the worst . . . of any sizable city." Corruption saturated the system. A small businessman, for example, would get a call insisting that he buy supplies from a certain vendor or insurance from a specific outfit; if he didn't, city inspectors would be at his door. White Chicagoans whose homes, businesses, churches, and schools had been plowed under left for the suburbs; the blacks went into the projects or were pushed into white neighborhoods, accelerating the flight. The day-to-day functioning of city government became what *Daily News* columnist Mike Royko would call "service for favors." Where the Machine once provided something extra as an incentive, now the question was what you could do for the Machine, be it a sign in your window come election time, some tickets to the ward golf outing, or maybe—if it was something really important to you—some cash in an envelope. In black neighborhoods, it was a threat: vote Democratic, or you might lose your benefits or apartment. Mayor Daley's famous temper—he'd turn red in the face and bellow—served to back up the warning, as did the cops, in Chicago an ambiguous moral force at best. Those who brought a complaint to City Hall got a dose of Daley's technocrat charm. "He had a very clever knack," said one politico, "of listening and letting everybody think he was for them." That quality allowed him to construct what former alderman Richard Friedman has described as "a very intelligent political program to co-opt . . . the business community, the academic community, and the ethnic groups" with those powerless blue ribbon panels whose existence hid the fact that the mayor intended to do nothing. Daley's retail politics was to democratic government what McDonald's was to food and *Playboy* to sex: a processed and mass-marketed simulation.

Meanwhile his inner circle enjoyed raises and sweetheart deals. To get around Kennelly's patronage reforms, he stopped hiring civil servants and added approximately forty thousand "temporary" employees who served at his pleasure, each of them personally approved down to the guy sweeping up the slips after the day's races at Sportsman's, recorded on a card, and managed by aide Matt Danaher. Bridgeport received most of the spoils. "I think patronage is just doing favors for friends," Daley once said at a party meeting. "It would be a lousy world if you couldn't do a favor for a friend."

Most Chicagoans didn't mind, as long as the buildings went up, union jobs kept paying, and their block stayed one color. A regular guy could do nothing except figure out how to get his and stay out of trouble, so Chicagoans could now absolve themselves of any responsibility. "Daley is undeniably a politician," wrote *Chicago*, "and a thoroughly professional one. But in the long pull is that necessarily bad? Would the knowledgeable citizen of Chicago call in a physician to repair the house plumbing?" Boosters went even further. "What's wrong with Chicago?" asked the

Tribune in August 1956, just over a year since it had drawn a desperate portrait of what the city would look like under then-candidate Daley. "The answer is nothing. Nothing can possibly be wrong with Chicago which is not also wrong with the 20th century, with the American way of life, with the achievements and spirits of an age of mechanization." That statement contained more truth than its author likely intended. The American way of life in the postwar world was a product of Chicago, from the steel in its new Miesian skyscrapers to its sacks of golden crispy McDonald's French fries. The city was navigating the transformation of the cultural ideal of the common man into a national mass-marketing strategy.

THE REASON FOR the article, modestly titled "Chicago Rises to Mighty Gem in the Prairies: World Leader, That's Chicago in Two Words," was the 1956 Democratic National Convention, once again being held at the Amphitheatre that August. Despite Daley's rise on the Prairie, it was shaping up to be a bad year for Democrats. Most Americans could see no reason to force Eisenhower out of the White House, and only his heart attack in September 1955 had stirred the Democrat field into action, on the off chance they'd get to run against the unpopular Richard Nixon. Estes Kefauver hadn't taken the hint that America wasn't interested in what he was selling, and Averell Harriman had Truman's backing, but the obvious choice was Adlai Stevenson, who'd played the role of party leader over the past four years when he wasn't sleeping around or performing damage control with his increasingly disturbed ex-wife. Not only had Ellen shown up to the wedding of their son Adlai III wearing all black and packing a pistol; she'd also recently published a cringe-worthy poem in *Chicago*, a conversation between Plato, Aquinas, Bacon, Voltaire, Freud, and the "Modern Woman," who delivers the following: "Doctor, I feel so strange! / My libido is hard to restrain; / My psyche gives me a pain. / I want an ideal / With sex appeal, / I want some brawn with a brain!"

An air of futility hung over the convention, frustrating to the mayor, since he'd wanted to make a grand display. The highlight of the first day was Mahalia singing "I See God," though an Alabama delegate started a fistfight with some catcalls. A few nights later, Stevenson waited through the roll call at the Stock Yards Inn restaurant next door to the Amphitheatre. When his nomination was official, Daley turned to Jake Arvey, the man probably more responsible than anyone else for his rise to the top, and snapped, "Go get him." The national committeeman meekly obeyed.

Stevenson gave over the selection of his running mate to the floor, leading Mayor Daley to nominate the junior senator from Massachusetts, John F. Kennedy, much to the horror of his father, Joseph Kennedy, who through business, politics, and crime was drawing his clan closer to Daley's Machine. In the end, JFK and Peter Lawford would console themselves at Chez Paree while Kefauver, the man in the coonskin hat, won the chance to stand beside Adlai for a second, if possible even more eggheaded, campaign than the first. More interested in being right than winning, it seemed, Stevenson delivered deeply considered speeches that paralyzed listeners. Centrist to a fault last time around, he now split himself in two: on one hand advocating the abolishment of the draft, limiting nuclear testing, and attacking Nixon's character (history would vindicate him there), but then going limp on civil rights. Not only would he refuse to use federal troops to enforce *Brown v. Board of Education,* at one point he even suggested to a black audience that January 1, 1963, the one-hundredth anniversary of the Emancipation Proclamation, should be the goal for school desegregation in America. The Soviet invasion of Hungary and the Suez Crisis, just weeks before the election, destroyed what little chance he might have had. Daley led the traditional torchlight parade to the Stadium, but this time there'd be no Truman-esque magic; Ike finished with forty-three states. Adlai once again lost Illinois. Jake Arvey would later call him "a patsy," a soft man who considered himself above it all. "This is my politician," Stevenson said once, pointing at Arvey. "I don't have to be one, I've got Jake Arvey." The Machine's best chance to install a direct line to the White House was now through the Kennedys. County party insiders weren't thrilled with Daley's performance—two crowns were too many for one man, they thought. But no one had the power to take one away.

THE BUILDING MANIA continued. Nineteen fifty-six was on its way to being the busiest year of building ever in Chicago history, bigger than the years after the Fire. New construction would top a billion dollars. "It would be an error to say everybody was putting up a building in the Chicago area," said one builder. "A few were not. They were still working on the plans." That included Frank Lloyd Wright. With Sullivan's hundredth birthday noted—barely—that September with a small exhibition at the Art Institute, Wright weighed in with plans for a mile-high skyscraper, The Illinois. Mayor Daley, a lover of big plans, proclaimed October 17 "Frank Lloyd Wright Day" and at a benefit dinner in his honor at the Hotel Sherman, Wright unveiled a twenty-foot-high rendering of the 5,680-foot, 528-story tower topping out amid passing clouds, angular, inspiring, and gradually more ominous the higher up you went. The Illinois, Wright said, would be "a finger in the right direction of humanity," though which finger he was showing humanity no one could tell, since he'd done nothing but slam Mies and every modern skyscraper for years. "I detest seeing the boys fooling around and making their buildings look like boxes," he told reporters. Calling Daley "the only Chicago mayor since 1893 who has boldly enlisted himself on the side of culture," Wright went on to lambast the sorry state of education, architecture, and car making until it sank in that The Illinois was little more than a publicity stunt.

Mies had designed the Barcelona chair for a visit from King Alfonso XIII of Spain to the German Pavilion at the 1929 International Exposition, so it was appropriate that its creator, stiff with arthritis and nearing three hundred pounds, sat back in one for this gala November evening at Crown Hall. At the dedication in April, Eero Saarinen had declared Chicago "the center of the universe in modern architecture." Of Mies, he had said, "The moral fiber of this man can be a measuring rod and inspiration that we can carry through our lives." This night, the IIT student government's annual I-Ball, felt like a celebration not only of what Mies had accomplished with Crown Hall but of his position as the spiritual father of this current building explosion.

Bucking trends during this Year of Elvis, the students had blown their budget on the by-now-somewhat-retro Duke Ellington, whose band played atop a series of white platforms in the center of the hall. Aaron Siskind and Cosmo Campoli had arranged the lights outside so they bathed the structure in blue and green; on either side of Mies sat Hilbs and IIT instructor Walter Peterhans in their own Barcelona chairs, watching the students dance as reflections of the Duke Ellington band wavered in the thin glass behind. At sixty-nine, Mies more than ever resembled a medieval abbot with his creased brow and deep, stern silence, trying to think his way into heaven. These days he usually had lunch and a martini at the Arts Club, then worked in the afternoon, keeping to himself until evening, when a few more drinks would let a shy kindness seep out in his smile. He could be too cross with Waltraut, still living with him on Pearson, though Lora Marx had come back after a breakup to dry out. Peterhans tapped a toe. Mies did not. Rhythm for him was an ordered thing, a matter of materials, the different bonds of brick and the staggered columns of this room as close as he came to the polyrhythmic.

Crown Hall was, as Saarinen had described it, a "serene temple of the present," a clear span, a comfortable medium between the Farnsworth House and the yawning Convention Center never built. It stretched just to the limits of one's sight, a single long box of steel and glass 18 feet high, 220 feet long, and 120 feet wide. Four trusses bore the weight of the roof, as he'd planned for the Cantor Drive-In. The plate girders and the columns supporting them seem to lift the space out of the ground and create one vast bright room. "A girder," Mies told *Time*, "is nothing to be ashamed of." As usual, the IIT administration had hated it. Too expensive, they'd said, and too big, but he'd eventually prevailed. He had little time for them anymore.

The truth was, as soon as he'd stepped onto the frayed red carpet of the

20th Century Limited, bound for New York to work on the Seagram Building, Mies had begun to detach from IIT; discussions were being had as to who'd replace him as head of the architecture department. His new right-hand man, Gene Summers, had done most of the work on the Commons Building, put up in 1954. Of course, IIT had only complaints about that, too, and claimed it had no money to build the Library or the Student Union, so Mies now peered down a miniature Park Avenue for hours at a time, mulling the perfect placement for Seagram's. In the end, though, for all his battles with its penny-pinching, conservative administration, IIT was his home in the States. He had forged his American style here, instilled its precepts in his students; without him, it would have remained a trade school. In his mind and in the mind of the world, Mies van der Rohe still *was* IIT and the coolly brilliant, impersonal building he produced, the face of this new Chicago promised by his arrival eighteen years earlier at the Palmer House, and the expression of the corporate American empire.

But Mies never really loved the city, just as he'd never loved Edith Farnsworth. Richard Daley, on the other hand, loved it with all his heart. Cynical and power hungry as he was, the mayor believed every dollar skimmed and neighborhood demolished was for the greater glory of Chicago. And part of what his city deserved was culture, the way Sis deserved the biggest Fannie May sampler on Mother's Day. Raised wearing clean collars in a neighborhood of slaughterhouses, Daley knew culture was important, though it bounced right off him. He'd see a musical downtown to make Sis happy, but honestly he'd rather go smelt fishing or watch the Sox. Big, approved names were the limit of what he could handle, nothing bohemian, and so his new friends in the business elite came to his aid. An inner circle formed, including William Hartmann, to steer the mayor toward the big-ticket arts organizations they supported: the Art Institute, the Chicago Symphony Orchestra, and the Lyric Opera. Many honorary days were proclaimed. "Poetry Day," for example, initiated by *Poetry* editor Henry Rago, brought Robert Frost and Wallace Stevens to town.

Frank Lloyd Wright was one of those brand names Daley liked; not only had he publicly praised the mayor, but his bombastic proposal for The Illinois was full of the same speculative hot air then filling the city's sails. In January 1957, Daley let Alderman Leon Despres, usually his enemy, enter a motion to create a Landmarks Commission. Ironically or cynically, one of those who spoke in favor of it was architect John Root of Holabird & Root, just then designing a dormitory that the Chicago Theological Seminary (CTS) intended to build on the site of Wright's long, tawny masterpiece, the Robie House. The March 1 announcement of their plan sent Wright and architects around the world into a panic. The original 1941 committee to save the building was quickly revived, with Wright himself making the case for the Robie House's seminal place in American culture. At the age of ninety and about to start work on the Guggenheim Museum, he'd seen his greatest early works—the Midway Gardens and Tokyo's Imperial Hotel—both fall, so to him saving the Robie House was a matter of preserving his legacy. That it was located in Chicago fired him even more. Not only would this be his last battle against the Mobocracy, but it would also give him a platform from which he could shoot spitballs at Mies. Leading a press tour of the old house, Wright swung his cane around and pronounced it "sound as a nut." Given that Wright's friend Richard Daley was the leader of the Mobocracy, though, just how much progress would the mayor halt to save a masterpiece? In April the city's landmarks committee, led by Daniel Catton Rich and including William Hartmann, designated the Robie House a landmark, which pressured the CTS to negotiate a purchase price with Wright's foundation.

In the middle of this, with the Inland Steel Building nearly complete and a deal for the Robie House looking possible, US Steel hosted a weeklong "Chicago Dynamic" festival in October 1957. Ostensibly a commemoration of the city's building heritage, it was more a display of sleight-of-hand. Five days of seminars, speeches, and forums were scheduled around two guests of honor: Wright and the hallowed Carl Sandburg, brought up out of retirement from his home in North Carolina. Both *éminences grises* happily let themselves be carted around the city whose identity they'd helped create. "We live in the time of the colossal upright oblong," opened

Sandburg's poem for the gala banquet; burdened with lines such as "Millions of outdoor privies banished in behalf of indoor/plumbing and flush toilets," it was not his most inspired work. The old poet, hair still parted down the middle and pasted back like a nineteenth-century schoolboy, only hinted at deeper concerns about America's "fat-dripping prosperity." Wright, on the other hand, didn't pull his punches. "In another fifteen years," he said, "this city will be on the way out."

But by then "Chicago Dynamic" had achieved what its sponsors wanted. Just as backing Wright had made Daley and City Hall look enlightened, so Sandburg and Wright lent their credibility to the idea that Daley's Chicago was another history-making epoch. Showering praise on Sullivan, Jenney, Root, and Burnham diverted Chicagoans from noticing the bags of cash changing hands, the racial divides being carved and erected like so many Berlin Walls, and the painful irony that among the hundreds of structures being leveled during the building boom, a shocking number had been designed and erected by the very architects Chicago Dynamic purported to honor. On December 21, a few weeks after Mies resigned as director of the department of architecture at IIT, William Hartmann announced that the Robie House had been bought by New York developer William Zeckendorf, who then in August 1958 made a gift of the house to Wright's foundation.

More public works bulled ahead. Over loud protests from the MHPC and nearly every public advocacy group, the city moved on plans for a new convention center, a vast white concrete tomb, 340 feet by 1,050, designed with a graceless hand by old boys Shaw, Metz, & Dolio, embellished with the blocky reliefs of Constantine Nivola, an instructor at the Harvard School of Design. Worse was its lakefront location, on parkland used for the Railroad Fair back in '48 and '49, since left in disrepair by the Park District and nowhere near any public transportation. Only the cabbies were satisfied. But as this vast white elephant was to be named after its late great publisher, Colonel McCormick, the *Tribune* flexed its muscles. The Illinois Supreme Court ruled in its favor, and work began on McCormick Place.

There were other, better, new buildings: SOM's Inland Steel turned out to be a snappy addition to the Loop made of two parts, a main office section with a Miesian glass face, seemingly buttressed along Dearborn Street by beams the height of the building that projected out like exaggerated versions of 860–880's mullions; and a second, taller wing that holds the elevators, wiring, and ductwork. Only nineteen stories high, it operates on a human scale, with a welcoming street entrance and a handsome interplay between steel and green glass windows that's more mature than Bunshaft's shiny Lever House.

Blessed with the greatest concentration of architectural talent in American history, if not entirely grown by Mies then raised under his shadow, Chicago would remake its skyline over the next twenty years. Daley-era Chicago had found the one art form that it truly understood. "Chicago could not create, or at any rate could not suffer very long, an Henri Matisse or an Andy Warhol," wrote critic Franz Schulze in the summer of 1968, at the apex of Daley's power and notoriety. "Perhaps it will never be much of a town for painters, or actors or the classical ballet. But it understands commerce and technology as it reveres them, and it happily raises temples to these contemporary deities, attaining its most admirable creative momentum in the process. Architecture is thus the one art Chicago's spirit can serve, at least—and probably only—as long as architecture returns the favor." A source of pride and identity, the city now has the greatest collection of modern architecture in the world. The price it paid—the buildings lost, the lives displaced and destroyed—can never be calculated.

CHAPTER 29

BETA PEOPLE
FOR A BETA WORLD

T HIRTY-YEAR-OLD SHELLEY BERMAN nervously worked his rubbery face, waiting for the right moment to enter a Rumpelstiltskin bit. Though the oldest member of the Compass, he'd never heard of Kierkegaard; no one had explained to him David Shepherd's philosophy of theater. He'd gone from cantorial studies on the West Side of Chicago to Greenwich Village, written jokes, and scraped together parts in TV dramas, the sum of which hadn't added up to a career, and though his wife hadn't said as much, this gig had the feeling of a last chance. Berman needed it to work.

He stepped into the footlights.

"Suddenly the whole scenario was about The King," remembered Bobbi Gordon. "... It was a running comedy monologue.... Everybody turned to everybody else and said, 'Uh, oh.'"

Walter Benjamin once wrote, "There is no better trigger for thinking than laughter." But David Shepherd didn't buy it. PTA groups, atomic scientists, and famous radio personalities were filling the Dock, to laugh at themselves through the mirror of Elaine May's acid portraits of Jewish mothers and airheaded starlets, Mike Nichols's status-craving snobs. Laughter had never been his goal though, no matter how much Brecht stressed that a Smokers' Theater should be fun. Surrounded now by even more laughter, Shepherd fell into a depression. "I lost control," he says.

Back in the summer, the humor had evolved out of situations, but Shelley Berman didn't have time to wait for anything to evolve; he went straight for the laugh, and he stole lines that got *other* people laughs. Shameless about wanting "to be most loved by the audience, to be chief of the night," his huge emotions overwhelmed the group's cool intellectualism. The laughs proved corrosive, a quick high that sent everyone off in search of their next fix. "People began to harbor resentments," said Mark Gordon. ". . . It became a contest of who could be funnier. That's when things really began to fall apart." Shepherd and Nichols, never close, split further; Berman began picking up an imaginary phone in the middle of scenes, conducting very funny one-sided conversations that were the dramatic equivalent of grabbing the steering wheel from the passenger side. On May 17, 1956, the Compass moved to the Argo Off-Beat Room at Broadway and Devon, a bigger venue with better pay, and with a new kind of audience: the North Shore money crowd that worked in all the new buildings downtown. Here, said Mark Gordon, the Compass "went from being a potential theater to a nightclub act."

Between sets there was jazz, including for one stretch a quintet featuring a pianist named Sun Ra. The Chicago tradition of improvisation was that rare instance of white culture encountering black culture without co-opting it. Though theatrical improv comes out of that "theater without heroes" tradition, it shares many of the same values and methods of black music, particularly jazz. Both are means of communication and reinvigoration; both assert identity and opposition to the establishment. In Chicago, jazz and improv often worked the same room, literally and figuratively. Jules Herbuveaux and Charlie Andrews at WNBQ were both former jazzmen, and white Chicagoans as far back as Bughouse Square and the Dil Pickle Club had used improv as a way to speak against political and social institutions. Stylistically, they were the same, too; good performers didn't deliver lines as much as swing them, and improv at the Compass was about individual genius within a group dynamic as much as Pat Patrick taking his solo with the Arkestra. Nor did using humor mean selling out, the way Shepherd supposed. "In laughter as in blues," wrote Lawrence Levine, "the line between the commercial and the folk is not easily delineated because of the close interaction and the bonds of identity between professional entertainers and their audiences." Laughter and improv didn't teach communities; they *created* them.

Except, it seemed, *within* the Compass, floating adrift in the tonier seas of the Argo. The show lost coherence, and the audiences got smaller. *Playboy* said it was "a little like the *commedia dell'arte* of Renaissance Italy, Dr. Moreno's therapeutic psycho-drama, and the Acting Tech class of any drama school. . . . It's not exactly acting, and it certainly isn't drama, but it *is* theatre (in the broad sense that includes flea circuses)." A burned-out David Shepherd, still trying to decide whether he wanted to continue his mission or join in the "industrialization of gags," asked for help from Paul Sills, who boiled down the cast. "Baseball is commercially supportable," he wrote, sounding more like George Steinbrenner than Bertolt Brecht. "People turn out to watch the players play and if I have artists among these players, then I'm going to get the higher levels." He fired Andrew Duncan, then lost Mark Gordon and Barbara Harris, who found the Argo Compass too slick. Outside directors were brought in, but the situation was beyond hope. Good teams need utility players. On a very cold Sunday in January 1957, the Compass gave its final performance—the scenario that started it all, *Enterprise.*

Shelley Berman went off as a solo act. The rest fell back on their old friend Bernie Sahlins, who with Lewis Manilow leased the Studebaker Theater to mount ten productions a year that would let Chicago "initiate theatre of our own." "If we do the right thing artistically," said Sahlins, "we will do the right thing commercially." A strong start with Geraldine Page in André Gide's *The Immoralist* and a vigorous production of Arthur Miller's *A View from the Bridge* ran up against the reality that ticket sales alone couldn't pay the bills. Claudia Cassidy's acid reviews didn't help either. Its two final productions in the spring of 1957 were landmarks of a sort. First, a *Lysistrata* featuring Severn Darden in drag as leader of the women's chorus, and starring a C-list Hollywood actress continually upstaged by Harris, Duncan, Nichols, and particularly Elaine May, who played Myrrhine with a Yiddish accent. Cassidy called it "the Worst Lysistrata since the Athenian Premiere." The second, the show that closed the Studebaker, was *Waiting for Godot* starring Mike Nichols as Lucky and Harvey Korman of *Carol Burnett Show* fame as Vladimir.

Meanwhile Darden's friend Ted Flicker had, in partnership with Shepherd, mounted a tighter, faster, louder version of the Compass in St. Louis. Heavy on audience suggestions, it was a huge hit, so when the Studebaker died, Nichols, May, and Darden made their way there. One night they all sat down at a kitchen table along with Flicker and cast member Del Close to write the rules for improv that would once and for all end the confusion: Spolin's theater games were for private use; they had value for training and for amateurs, but audiences shouldn't have to pay to watch something a national magazine compared to a flea circus. Staged improv had three basic imperatives: (1) Never deny verbal reality. If some-one onstage says there's a penguin on the table, there's a penguin on the table. (2) Take the active choice. (3) Characters come out of an exaggerated version of yourself and always establish who, what, and where; buying, selling, and arguing are not viable "dramatic transactions." These remain the foundation of improv.

Audiences loved the results, the show turned a profit, and, according to Flicker, David Shepherd's first words after seeing it were, "You've ruined my dream." Then he reminded them that he owned the rights to everything.

Lawsuits, machinations, backstabbings, and tearful reunions ensued. Shepherd dissolved his partnership with Flicker, while Nichols and May alternately turned on each other, Berman, the rest of the St. Louis Com-pass, Flicker, and Shepherd. In 1957 the two sat down for lunch at New York's Russian Tea Room. Over blinis and borscht, they did their act for Harry Belafonte's manager, Jack Rollins, who signed them on the spot. Later that month they performed at the Village Vanguard, then quickly moved uptown to the Blue Angel in Midtown, where the good press convinced Hyde Park native Steve Allen to have them on *Tonight* on December 29. Alistair Cooke booked them on *Omnibus* that weekend, and on Monday morning, the first day of 1958, Nichols and May woke up as hot young stars a long way from the Compass.

David Shepherd, in Paris on a Fulbright, seethed.

IN JANUARY 1956, Alton Abraham and Thmei Research incorporated El Saturn Records, putting Sun Ra—unlike Mahalia, Muddy Waters, Chuck Berry, and virtually every other African American musician—in complete control of his own work. He'd moved back up to a bigger band, dressed them in bright, two-tone outfits instead of tuxedoes, and settled the 8 Rays of Jazz into a standing gig at Cadillac Bob's Budland ("Birdland" until the one in New York threatened to sue), downstairs from the Pershing Lounge, at 64th and Cottage Grove. Sometimes he pulled a quintet out for a smaller gig such as the Argo Off-Beat in May 1956. The real focus, though, was recording. El Saturn's first records are best described as space doo-wop; acts such as the Nu Sounds, the Cosmic Rays, and the Lintels produced strange, exuberant versions of standards, part Moonglows, part Mills Brothers, plus originals such as "Chicago USA," a cheerful ode to the capital of "Mid-west, Mid-USA." Sun Ra and his Myth Science Arkestra (the names of the band changed like the names of the songs) produced approximately fifty sides in 1956; Abraham and Ra tested the waters with three 45s and squirreled away the rest for later release. None of the three singles hit the charts, but El Saturn placed enough orders and paid promptly enough that in the fall RCA offered the company a line of credit. Sun Ra copyrighted everything in the names of the composers; Thmei Research did business straight up.

While Abraham ran the office, Sun Ra and Pat Patrick passed out tracts on corners and streetcars. "Sun Ra was another kind of being," said Pat Patrick. "... He was a black self-help organization run on a shoestring." One of the people who benefited most from his teachings didn't belong to his band: John Coltrane joined the Miles Davis Quintet in December 1955 and played with Miles that Christmas at Budland. Coltrane, stunted by his alcoholism and heroin addiction, was still nowhere near the "sheets of sound" style he'd make famous; he'd sunk to nodding off on the bandstand and, much to Davis's disgust, picking his nose. Over the next two years, the saxophonist met with Gilmore, Patrick, and Sun Ra himself, who steered him toward the esoteric philosophies that would gird his later work. "I had to play my things for him," said Sun Ra, "so Coltrane would have a broader understanding, to protect himself, because he unleashed some cosmic forces in his mind." Everything was music to Sun Ra. "In my intergalactic music every person is a key to something. . . . The people are the instrument. That's the intergalactic principle." In spring of 1957 Coltrane kicked his habit.

As much as Sun Ra wanted to control his own entry into the marketplace, another fledgling label called Transition—owned by young Fisk-and-Harvard-educated Tom Wilson, who'd go on to produce Bob Dylan, Simon and Garfunkel, and the Velvet Underground—recorded Sun Ra's first LP, *Jazz by Sun Ra: Vol. 1*, at Bill Putnam's new Universal Recording Studios on Walton Street in July 1956. As LPs grabbed a growing share of the market, El Saturn's first, *Super-Sonic Jazz*, came out in March 1957, all numbers from the 1956 sessions. For all the talk of space and Egypt, it's extremely accessible stuff, from "India," with its then-innovative electronic piano and clanging Eastern gongs, to John Gilmore's lush saxophone in "Blues at Midnight" and two more Chicago songs, "Springtime in Chicago" and "El Is a Sound of Joy." (The double meaning of *El* was surely intentional.) Sun Ra stated El Saturn's mission on the order form: "Beta Music for Beta People for a Beta World." A few weeks after the release of *Super-Sonic Jazz*, the Arkestra played Hines Veterans' Hospital. During the gig, a woman who hadn't "moved or spoken for years got up from the floor, walked directly to his piano, and cried out, 'Do you call that music?'" Sun Ra was very pleased by that, and when the Soviets launched Sputnik in October 1957, he suddenly didn't look so crazy after all. Space really *was* the place.

.   .   .

LEONARD AND PHIL picked at the mortar between the bricks of a non-descript two-story building on the west side of the 2100 block of South Michigan, three blocks south of the Johnson Publishing Building. Among independent labels, only Atlantic Records had had a better 1955 than Chess. Sam Phillips may have kept Elvis Presley to himself, but the singer's unprecedented popularity all through 1956 had burned rock and roll and teen culture into the American psyche. Chuck Berry had four hit singles that year—"No Money Down," "Roll Over Beethoven," "Too Much Monkey Business," and "Brown Eyed Handsome Man"—and appeared in two Alan Freed movies, *Rock Around the Clock* and *Rock Rock Rock*, along with Chess acts the Moonglows and the Flamingos. While Berry duck-walked across the country, sleeping in his car and cooking on a hot plate both to save money and avoid segregated restaurants, the Chess brothers spent the cash. Leonard moved Revetta and the kids to the plush northern suburb of Glencoe where Marshall suddenly had a new bike and a grand lifestyle that in the years to come he'd always thank Berry for.

The off-white terra-cotta fixer-upper the brothers were now inspecting would become the home of Chess Records, the newest addition to Chicago's Record Row along with Vee-Jay and a host of other distributors that Mayor Daley drove past every day on his way to work. In time, 2120 S. Michigan would become a legendary address, but the brothers weren't interested in erecting a temple to themselves. Aside from replacing the crumbling first floor façade with glass windows, they built a recording studio designed by the men who did Bill Putnam's new Universal; everything else from the offices to the one tiny bathroom stayed down and dirty, as befit a couple of chain-smoking immigrants who worked 15-hour days.

As black music pushed into the mainstream, the act of recording multiple covers took on a racial significance: one version would be for blacks, and the other desexualized, generally enervated, and usually lucrative versions would be for whites. Since the Chess brothers made money on their songs no matter who sang them, they now sometimes encouraged white covers even at the expense of versions recorded by their own black artists. Just as Daley had turned the Machine from the working man's friend into a means of controlling him, so Leonard and Phil betrayed many of their young rock and roll performers this way. Chuck Berry played it the best he could, not only writing his own songs but performing them in a style that made *his* version *the* version. In 1957 his "School Days" went head-to-head with Elvis's "All Shook Up," and his other two hits from that year, "Rock and Roll Music" and "Oh Baby Doll," could only inspire imitators, not rival covers. Yet canny as he managed to be, Berry still had to trade shares in his copyrights in exchange for promotion if he wanted to stay on top of the charts.

The money wasn't all coming from Chuck Berry and rock and roll: in the second half of the 1950s, Leonard and Phil Chess had success in every aspect of black music. Though the brothers never made it a secret that they followed the money, Chess had no intention of abandoning the steady revenue stream of the blues. Once the renovated 2120 S. Michigan opened in early 1957—Leonard was recovering from the heart attack that had just been a matter of time in coming—Chess did all its recording there in tight surroundings, amid what Marshall would later describe as the "funk" of all those big, hard-drinking men playing in one small, unventilated room.

Muddy seemed stunned by the turn of events. Just as he was about to go big, rock and roll had punctured the blues. Gigs had dried up, record sales plateaued, even as he and Howlin' Wolf and Little Walter produced some of their greatest records. James Cotton drove him around the streets of the South Side, Muddy nipping at a pint, hoping to hear their music billowing out of a corner tavern, until they'd pull up at Silvio's or Smitty's Corner at 35th and Indiana, a block from IIT. Plopping down at a side table with a bottle of champagne, he'd listen to his band play. Soon Muddy stopped touring altogether, claiming he wanted to spend more time with his family, and hunkered down for a standing gig at Smitty's. The king of the blues ruled a very small empire.

Howlin' Wolf, meanwhile, faced the challenge by climbing higher up the curtains and creeping lower under tables, shaking up Coke bottles to shove down his pants so at the right moment he could unzip his fly and pop the cap to no small effect. Women sat on his back while he crawled across the floor. For all the romping onstage, though, the man who cut "Smokestack Lightning" was no novelty act. Clean as a knife blade, a train roaring down the tracks, Wolf sounds desperate but in control as he ranges over a chugging bass and drum rhythm, echoing when he goes into his falsetto howls. Philip Larkin compared it to "an impression of Coleridge's demon love wailing for his woman." Producer Malcolm Chisholm called him "vaguely menacing" with "the paranoia of the very stupid"; in fact, he had a reputation as a fair, if tough, boss, and a firm union man who paid his bills on time. Though Muddy and Wolf never really hated each other the way the story has it, Wolf didn't let his band members hang out with Muddy's because they drank too hard for his taste. After Muddy briefly hired away guitarist Hubert Sumlin, things were never the same. Willie Dixon took leave of Chess for an outfit called Cobra, where he led Magic Sam, Buddy Guy, and Otis Rush to the last stop for the urban blues, the West Side Sound, with its virtuoso guitar playing and a stripped-down sound. Though the legend is that 2120 S. Michigan was the birthplace of the Chicago blues, it was actually their nursing home.

Jazz, the mainstay of the old Aristocrat catalog, reemerged now as the music of grown-ups. Chess's two new jazz stars both had refined styles far from the rugged Macomba. Raised in the Cabrini Homes, Ramsey Lewis and his trio had a steady gig at the Lake Meadows Lounge, where they played listener-friendly piano with concert hall dramatics—middle-class music for middle-class blacks. The other was Ahmad Jamal, a thin young pianist with a tight beard who had passed up Julliard to follow the woman he loved to Chicago in 1948. By his own description, Jamal was "very withdrawn, an introvert," a highly disciplined artist whose effortless, airy style sounded easy to critics accustomed to the oblique angles of Thelonious Monk and Art Tatum's fireworks, but only a master's sense of rhythm and harmony could do so much with such a delicate hand. As Mies had with architecture, Jamal reduced his playing to an essence. His 1958 album *Ahmad Jamal at the Pershing: But Not for Me* stayed on the *Bill-*

board LP chart for 107 weeks. In contrast to his back alley, motherfucker relationship with the bluesmen, Leonard deferred to his jazz players. "Leonard treated me with the optimal amount of respect and vice versa," says Jamal.

Gospel came to Chess through a single record store in Detroit owned by Joe Von Battle, who in 1953 convinced the Reverend C. L. Franklin of New Bethel Church to record his very popular sermons onto LPs that he turned around and licensed to Leonard in the spring of 1956. Franklin had already been touring based on the strong sales of Von Battle's records, and his connections to the gospel world through his friends Mahalia Jackson and Clara Ward, but Chess distribution made Reverend Franklin America's most famous black preacher. WLAC in Nashville offered him a Sunday-night radio show that became, according to the Reverend Jesse Jackson, "the common frame of reference for the black church prototype." Everyone listened, from Al Green, James Brown, and Bobby "Blue" Bland to the growing civil rights movement led by his friend the Reverend Martin Luther King, Jr. His style of sermonizing—an African American *Sprech-gesang,* swooping and growling in a trance-inducing rhythm full of pauses and held breaths and then rushes of power—influenced as many bandstands and stages as pulpits. In 1956, Chess put together a collection of gospel standards sung by the reverend's fourteen-year-old daughter Aretha with a sound all her own, sensuous, mighty, and hurt, like Mahalia, from being a motherless child.

Says Marshall Chess, "We had Mozart, Beethoven, and Bach all together."

A NEW CLUB opened in February 1956, down a flight of stairs at Dearborn and Chicago, a block and a half from the old Dil Pickle Club. The Gate of Horn was tiny: a six-seat bar right when you squeezed in, then a room to your left described as "chiseled out" of whatever was under the Rice Hotel. While early rock and roll was running its course, the folk revival sprouted in the background. Albert Grossman, a Lane Tech graduate, former CHA employee, and now a music manager opened the Gate of Horn as a showcase for his clients, who'd over the next decade include Bob Dylan, Odetta, Peter, Paul and Mary, Gordon Lightfoot, the Band, and Janis Joplin. Roger McGuinn of the Byrds began his career there; Howard Alk worked there, making it the unofficial clubhouse both for the swanky sorts and for Studs Terkel, a folkie since WPA days. Down in the brick-lined basement, "dark and hot and crowded and great," wrote Shel Silverstein (once known for his louche cartoons but now mostly for *The Giving Tree*), performers and audience interacted in boozy intimacy. If the Dil Pickle had a true successor, this was it; Katie Lee, the opening-night act, sang a madrigal based on something she'd read many years before written on the wall of its ladies' room.

The immediate success of the Gate of Horn inspired Studs's old friend, Win Stracke. During a three-week run at the Gate of Horn, he met Frank Hamilton, a young guitarist with an engaging personality and a communal method for teaching guitar perfect for novices. On December 1, 1957, they opened the Old Town School of Folk Music. "The interest in folk music by city people," said Win, "betrays their search for the basic realities which they don't find expressed in commercial popular music." The Gate of Horn lasted only five years, but it and the Old Town School of Folk Music, still going strong, reconnected Chicago to its rural, folk past in a communal way that Moholy would have loved. With the ID gone, the bohemia of Towertown now re-formed around folk music and a few galleries in what people were calling Old Town.

CHAPTER 30

GAINING A MOON
AND LOSING OURSELVES

NELSON ALGREN SHIFTED the bag of groceries to his other arm as he paused and stared at the ice. A gust of wind tossed snow over the surface. In the summer he either rowed across this lagoon separating his house on Forrest Street from Pignotti's Store on Lake, or else he walked the long way around, but it was in the thirties today. Taking the shortcut would save him ten minutes.

It was New Year's Eve 1956. Miller, Indiana. Algren was forty-seven years old, untethered and helpless. He tapped his toe on the ice. For a minute there it had looked as if things would work out. The Screen Writers Guild thought he had a case against Preminger for billing *The Man with the Golden Arm* as "by" himself, so he'd sued the director, United Artists, and Bob Roberts for $250,000. The publicity from the movie and the lawsuits had made his new publisher, Roger Straus, so optimistic about *A Walk on the Wild Side*, due out that May, that he'd turned down a hefty offer for paperback rights. All that money would have let him pay off Amanda along with the rest of his debts, then maybe take off for Paris.

The ice sounded hard.

Things hadn't worked out that way.

A Walk on the Wild Side wandered through the same bloodshot Depression-era America as *Somebody in Boots*, but instead of brutally crushing his protagonist Dove Linkhorn, as he had Cass Mackay, Algren left him performing in sex shows in a New Orleans brothel until, beaten within an inch of his life, he slinks back to Texas for a cynical, unsatisfying happy ending. Algren said in his *Paris Review* interview that he wanted *A Walk on the Wild Side* to be "a reader's book," with "one ear to the audience for yaks," which sounds like a writer who doesn't really know what anyone wanted anymore, since no one who'd praised *The Man with the Golden Arm* and *Never Come Morning* had ever asked for "yaks." Once again he asked, who are the real grotesques? Banged-up lushes and losers? Or the Lonely Crowd suburbanites fixated on their lawns; the racist old women who beat blacks with their umbrellas on the steps of St. Kevin; the admen on LaSalle Street paid to sell breakfast cereal to toddlers? "I certainly did not set out to make 'heroes' of these people," he said of Dove and Kitty Twist, but he did cop to finding a "certain overall satisfaction" in "scooping up a shovelful" of drug addicts and whores and "dumping them in somebody's parlor."

Though he considered *A Walk on the Wild Side* better than *The Man with the Golden Arm,* and the book did have a few defenders, most critics, especially the likes of Alfred Kazin, Norman Podhoretz, and Leslie Fiedler, pulverized it and Algren. *Time* deemed him a "museum piece." De Beauvoir's judgment was the most accurate. Praising the first half, she told Algren he'd never written in "more poetical and strong and moving language," and she was right; technically it's a tour de force, lean, lustrous prose from a man who still liked to spar at the gym. But then she laid it on the line: "The second part is too much of the same stuff as your other books, too much a remake." Indeed, after what plot there is crawls to a halt, he's content to rewrite scenes out of old novels and stories. The result is a bright and entertaining sparkler, not a torch. *A Walk on the Wild Side* was on the *New York Times* best-seller list for fifteen weeks; good, but not good enough to salvage a reprint sale or royalties or Algren's literary reputation. Many today regard *A Walk on the Wild Side* as a key inspiration for Joseph Heller and Ken Kesey, a tragicomic indictment of self-satisfied, hypocritical, postwar America.

Algren stepped forward. The question wasn't how thick the ice was, but how thick he actually wanted it to be. It crackled and held. "Everyone is guilty of everything," a character in *A Walk on the Wild Side* said.

It wasn't just his own book that had brought him to this edge. When the English translation of Simone's novel *The Mandarins* finally came out in May, he'd taken to forging her signature under the dedication to him with the note "on account of becuz he is mah ideel!" Then he'd sat down and read it. That the book is numbingly long, entirely without humor and backs up Algren's assertion that "she couldn't write a scene in a restaurant without telling you everything on the menu" were all beside the point. His Frog Wife had rendered her Crocodile Husband as Lewis Brogan, a soft man naïvely consumed with the good of mankind but unable to deal with intimacy, by turns petulant and macho. Simone related conversations verbatim, made passionate moments very public. "I think the lady invaded her own privacy," he told one reporter, but his wit couldn't conceal the hurt. She'd held him up for ridicule, and even if her portrait of him was spot on, he had a right to feel betrayed. He called her a few times but hung up when Claude Lanzmann answered the phone.

Algren's mind slipped into a rut of paranoia, regret, and anger that led to a nervous breakdown in the fall. Dave Peltz had stayed with him at the admissions desk of a mental hospital as he signed one letter at a time of his name, debating his choice letter by painful letter. No matter; he escaped within a few days. Writing fiction "used to be as easy as laying bricks," he told Art Shay, but he'd lost one of the essential qualities of fiction—hope.

He ventured another step, heard a deeper crack. The water would be cold. But it would all happen fast, and it would be over.

He'd proposed to his former junkie friend and like-soul Margo. She'd turned him down. He took another step. He owed his lawyer money, so she'd dropped the suits against Preminger, UA, and Roberts and put a lien on the movie rights to *A Walk on the Wild Side*. He owed the government. He owed Amanda, who had let him come back to the house on Forrest Avenue when he had no other place to live. She found another home in Gary. He'd wasted all his chances. "I have been trying to get a start in life since 1929," he once wrote, "and if it isn't one damned thing, then it's another. One decade it's a nationwide depression, so that if you make a living you're a fink; the next decade it's a war, if you don't go you're 4-F; and the next decade if you don't get your picture on the cover of *Time*, your relatives are ashamed of you especially your mother."

Cracks shot from under his feet, bolts of lightning trapped in the ice. Ten yards across, Algren plunged into the freezing water.

Three men working on a house nearby heard his screams. Treading, he warned them not to come any closer; instead, they threw him a rope he couldn't hold on to with his numb hands. He struggled to wrap it around his arm, and then they dragged him ashore. The next day the *Tribune* ran the story on page four. Algren survived, but he'd never write fiction again. He was "like a comet," says Art Shay. "He'd reached his apex and then flared out."

Having given up on the common man and himself, Algren now began thirty years of addictive gambling and a second career writing exclusively nonfiction of wildly varying quality. Without telling his agent, he sold the movie rights to *A Walk on the Wild Side* at a deep discount to someone who turned around and resold them for three times as much. No publisher would give him an advance, so he wrote for magazines like *Esquire* and *Playboy,* which published an excerpt from *Entrapment* in 1957. He played the role of a Cassandra now, "large-hearted, funny, angry, lonely," said Russell Banks; like Darrow, forever committed to the basic rights of the bottom turtle in the pile.

AT NOON OR thereabouts Hugh Hefner got up and opened himself the first of the two dozen Pepsis the day would bring. If someone had shared his bed, she'd dress and leave while he threw a maroon silk robe over his black pajamas and headed to the office downstairs. With its print run now bumping up around a million copies a month, *Playboy* had bought 232 E. Ohio, right around the corner from Moholy's old School of Design and next door to Mies's offices at 230. A major focus of the renovation had been this bedroom suite that let Hef live his life in one place—his business was his life, and his life was his business. Editing copy, reviewing layouts, and bedding a pair of Norwegian twins were all of a piece now, all part of being a playboy. Pipe in his teeth, he scuffed through busy halls. Hugh Hefner was a very happy man.

"What is a Playboy," wondered an ad for the magazine. He had to be aware and sensitive to pleasure, take joy in his work, and "see life not as a vale of tears, but as a happy time." Hugh Hefner was not the only happy man in those days of plenty; 70 percent of the magazine's readers were college educated, 88 percent had cars, and almost two-thirds were professionals or businessmen. This was the vanguard of Ayn Rand libertarianism—freedom for all, responsibility for none. The average *Playboy* reader might nod knowingly as Beth-Mary shot up in Algren's excerpt from *Entrapment*, but he didn't hear a call to action. "I'm very very selfish," said Hefner. "I'm very self-oriented and I think everybody should be. Intelligent self-interest is for the good of everyone. The person who spends all of their time thinking about others accomplishes nothing." Pro-integration and civil rights, pro-free speech, he had no desire to clamp down on anyone else, no sticky politics beyond a call for "freedom." And that was the nub of Hef's creepy, appealing avant-garde ambiguity: It was fine to tilt the balance toward the self and away from postwar conformity, but the pursuit of 200 million separate self-interests would mean some people would get screwed. An intelligent self-interest that considers the greater good isn't the same as Hefner's selfishness, but the *Playboy* life-style did all it could to blur the two.

Hefner rarely came home alone from a night on the prowl. Though he and Millie didn't officially separate until the middle of 1957, he had an extensive list of girlfriends and an even longer list of brief encounters in his little black book. Those who have gone on record describe a gentle, boyishly enthusiastic lover, an adolescent in white socks and loafers who's woken up to find himself in a world of wet dreams. Only Janet Pilgrim seemed disturbed, angry to see Millie at the office Christmas party, hurt when she caught him with other women. Totemic as she was to *Playboy*'s ethos of sexual freedom, Janet (no one called her Charlaine anymore) seemed to want the same old love and commitment that Hefner had run away from. Eventually she got married, had two kids, and moved to the suburbs.

With profiles in *Time* and *Newsweek* and a television interview on Mike Wallace's show, Hefner shifted the magazine into a higher gear. Hunting for someone "with Eastern establishment connections for advertising purposes and who'd bring some *New Yorker* sensibilities," in July 1956 he hired former *Chicago Sun* editor A. C. Spectorsky. As a literary figure, Spectorsky had never quite lived up to expectations, a fact he was painfully aware of, and if he forgot it, others reminded him. When he told Lionel Trilling he was worried that he'd be selling out if he took the *Playboy* job, the author of *The Liberal Imagination* said, "You have nothing to sell out." Spectorsky had spent a few early years at *The New Yorker,* came to the *Sun* for six years, then returned to New York, where in 1955 he published his one book of note, *The Exurbanites,* a stilted mix of journalism, cultural critique, and satire about the lifestyles of the media power elite in places like Bucks County and Chappaqua. Lincoln Steffens he was not, and that was fine because Hefner didn't want Lincoln Steffens breaking the mood of his sexy cocktail party of a magazine. "I don't want articles that preach, or are pompous, or are primarily concerned with international affairs, religion, or racial fracture," read one memo. Hef's checkbook and Spectorsky's Rolodex would deliver enough Kerouac, Steinbeck, and Bradbury to make saying you read *Playboy* for the articles plausible.

If Spectorsky represented the limits of Hefner's intellectual aspirations, his other hire, Victor Lownes III, set the rest of his imagination loose. Like Hef, Lownes had recently walked away from his family to embrace bachelorhood, yet he was in many ways everything Hefner aspired to. A University of Chicago graduate raised in Florida country clubs and mansions, Lownes rode, sailed, played tennis, and was at least as sexually insatiable as Hefner; his apartment featured a "playpen" made of four double beds nailed together. Introduced to Hef at a party for comedian Jonathan Winters, Lownes thought him "a highly intelligent, switched-on character with a mind-blowing belief in his personal destiny, and in his magazine," and the admiration was mutual. Hired as head of special projects, Lownes became much more. "Hefner listens to everyone," Spectorsky would say, "but when Lownes talks Hef sees it all in Technicolor." Charming, suave, and very smart, famously abusive around the office, Lownes would direct the company toward the brand extensions that would make the Rabbit Head an icon, but he would also give Hefner permission to let his inner satyr run free.

In June 1957, Hugh Hefner stepped from behind the curtain. A special editorial in that month's magazine presented "Hef," once the hero of his high school comics, as the epitome of the *Playboy* lifestyle. "He likes jazz, foreign films, Ivy League Clothes, gin and tonic, and pretty girls," read the piece introducing him to his acolytes, ". . . and his approach to life is as fresh, sophisticated, and yet admittedly sentimental as is the magazine's." Back in 1955 he'd said it was all partly a spoof; the reader knew he'd have to return to his normal life. But as Hugh Hefner, formerly of New England Avenue, opened another Pepsi and popped another Dexedrine, the spoof was over. *Playboy* was real.

THE LAST EPISODE of *Kukla, Fran and Ollie* came and went quietly the evening of August 30, 1957; the next week ABC canceled *Zoo Parade*, sending Marlin Perkins back to the cages of Lincoln Park. "There's no right place in TV for us any more," Tillstrom told *Time*. "If a man has anything in his heart, he has to break away." America had sped past the gentle intimacy epitomized by the Kuklapolitans, and though Burr talked about coming back, he was off the air after ten years because he couldn't find a sponsor. Just as Moholy had warned, the media had physically altered viewers' ability to take in the show's slow pace. The networks drove home the uniform culture that served the corporate/government combine. Game shows did Hutchins and Adler one better, polishing knowledge and ideas down into chits of trivia traded for prizes on programs like *Twenty One*, which was exposed, with bitter irony in August 1958, to be fixed, when Charles Van Doren, son of Columbia professor and Great Book selector Mark Van Doren, confessed to having been given the answers. Called on the carpet in Washington, network executives claimed that no one expected reality from television; it was all entertainment, including the things that were real. Burr packed the Kuklapolitans into their specially made Mark Cross cases and prepared for a show on Broadway.

"I suspect," wrote Algren in the fall of 1957, with America's first satellite soon to lift off, "we are well on our way toward gaining a moon and losing ourselves."

CHAPTER 31

WILL SOMEBODY PLEASE LISTEN TO ME TODAY!

The Cry of Jazz, a cult half-hour film made between 1956 and 1958 by composer Edward O. Bland, opens as a meeting of an interracial jazz appreciation club is breaking up. Friendly discussion quickly devolves into a not-so-friendly argument about what jazz is and whether whites can truly understand or play it. As the black president explains Bland's pre–LeRoi Jones Afrocentric views on jazz history and theory, the camera dissolves to black-and-white documentary scenes of the South Side ghetto—kids playing basketball and double dutch, 47th Street at night, pool halls, rows of women falling out at church, babies in a kitchen crawling with roaches—all overlaid with the music of Sun Ra, songs like "Blues at Midnight" and "Demon's Lullaby" from the 1956 sessions; brutal, tender interludes that include rare footage of Sun Ra, Pat Patrick, John Gilmore, and the Arkestra playing at Budland. A dark, desperate film, it's as if Wayne F. Miller's photography had come to life. MoMA film curator Willard Van Dyke would later call it "the most prophetic film ever made" for predicting the urban riots of the 1960s. Seen now, it's an angry cry at the collapse of Horace Cayton's Black Metropolis and its reconstruction under Daley.

On the Near South Side, Crown Hall, standing on the ghosts of the Mecca, declared a victory over what the city's institutional interests still called blight. By mid-1958, the Cabrini extension on the North Side was finished, but more dramatically, three-quarters of the State Street Corridor was in place, the four-mile procession of public housing projects starting at 26th Street—the Ickes Homes, the Dearborn Homes, and (after the interruption of IIT), the completed Stateway Gardens, ready to absorb more low-income African Americans. Low-grade materials, vandalism, and inflated maintenance contracts stole whatever savings had been realized from Stateway's high-rise design, so for the last piece of the Corridor—the Robert Taylor Homes—the initial plan called for four-story confidently modern buildings, family friendly, and in Jane Jacobs's word, defendable. They'd be expensive too, at least the way the CHA padded its budgets; $4,000 more per unit than the $17,000 limit that even New York managed with. Federal housing authorities rejected the plan. The city refused to relocate the projects to white neighborhoods, which would mean lower land costs. Instead, hiding behind its supposedly high motives, it demanded that the nation pay for its racism.

Much of the Black Belt had greeted Daley's election with optimism; after all, their votes had put him in office. Unlike Kennelly, who once greeted a visiting Louis Armstrong with no clue as to who he was (and to be fair, Armstrong afterward asked, "Is that the fella who fixes up divorces?"), Daley nodded with furrowed brow as black leaders spoke, and had been out front on Emmett Till when Bill Dawson had been noticeably quiet. So before any backlash could emerge over public housing, the mayor moved to cripple black opposition with a long game of his own.

Despite his fighter's rep, Congressman Dawson was really no more than an operator now; his local prominence built on the sand of small favors, his House record on civil rights thin. Fellow white congressmen appreciated how well he knew his place, how he sat at his own table in the congressional dining room and never made a scene. "His approach is of the silk-stocking texture," wrote one white analyst, with no "ill-advised racial tub-thumping." Local NAACP president Willoughby Abner, who had brought a much-needed confrontational bite to the Chicago branch, went after Dawson, publicly accusing him of cowardice on Till and

of fobbing off years of accommodation as smart politics and black empowerment. Dawson roared back at Abner, but the blow had been struck. Then
on July 28, 1957, a gang of white teens stoned a gathering of black families
in Calumet Park; the black men fought back with bats and bottles, and the
resulting battle left two dozen blacks injured and one white. Trumbull
Park erupted once again, and again Congressman Dawson did nothing.
With awareness of Martin Luther King, Jr.'s movement spreading, Black
Chicago's power brokers decided someone had to go—and that would be
Abner, whose growing political base threatened the old guard.

This is where Mayor Daley stepped in. Since all you needed to do to
vote in the Chicago NAACP branch was join and pay your dues, he told
Dawson to pack the December annual meeting with his flunkies and cast
their ballots for the other guy. Dawson did as instructed, and that was the
end of the local NAACP branch as a voice of challenge. Daley rewarded it
by proclaiming May 28, 1958, "NAACP Tag Day." Dawson had the thorn
pulled from his own paw, but that was only Daley's setup for the kill. A
few months later black alderman Claude Holman cosponsored an open
housing bill, which put *him* out front as Chicago's most outspoken black
politician and the city's leading voice on civil rights. Hizzoner let the bill
fail, but without publicly slapping down Holman, thus embarrassing
Dawson. City Hall Kremlinologists read the message: Dawson had lost his
clout. A year later the Machine brought Holman to heel.

City Hall held fast to its inflated numbers for the Robert Taylor Homes
until September 1959, when it finally caved and tossed out its family-
friendly plan. Instead of scattering the housing as recommended, the CHA
began work on the William Green extension to the Cabrini Homes, creating the infamous Cabrini-Green project, and on the South Side twenty-
eight sixteen-story buildings that would soon form the nation's largest
public housing project, Robert Taylor Homes—4,400 units holding 27,000
black Chicagoans, most of them children. It was the final piece in a stretch
of barrackslike architecture that consumed the Manhattan equivalent of
everything between Ninth and Tenth Avenues from 14th Street to 96th.
With Mies's campus amid slab after slab of life-denying buildings, the

South Side had become a bitter realization of German modernist dreams, of what Hilbs had rightly called his "necropolis."

IF POOR BLACKS on the South Side had the State Street Corridor to look forward to, *Ebony* called the finished Lake Meadows "a suburb within a city . . . the nation's biggest and most successful venture in high-grade interracial housing." Like *Ebony* itself, Lake Meadows inspired black pride, hope, and anger, all at once. The "envied residents of Lake Meadows" were mostly the sort Black Chicago would envy no matter what— "a high percentage of professional people, business executives, bankers and civil service employes [*sic*]." Photos showed the well-tailored Mrs. Lauraine Duncan working on her backhand, sitting at the playground with white mothers, and ordering dinner at the Lake Meadows Lounge (as Ramsey Lewis likely played in the background). Instead of a gym or a community center, "the Meadows" offered a two-story country club space for bridge and cocktail parties. German shepherds patrolled the lawns. Meanwhile outside, in what remained of Bronzeville, cultural activities starved. Vivian Harsh, the esteemed librarian at the George Cleveland Hall library, retired, and her lecture series, her book and history clubs that had been popular after the war, were replaced with remedial adult education classes. Margaret Burroughs, back from a sabbatical in Mexico and ever the optimist, worked with New York Life and Lake Meadows's management to create the Lake Meadows Art Fair in July 1957, an institution that lasted into the 1970s. Earl Dickerson, disappointed that public sentiment had kept black-owned Supreme Life Insurance from investing in Lake Meadows, settled on remodeling its offices across the street, where the State Department brought by visiting foreign dignitaries in hopes they'd file glowing reports on conditions in Black Chicago.

Despite *Ebony*'s staged photos and Ferd Kramer's heroic efforts to integrate Lake Meadows, whites occupied less than 5 percent of the first five hundred units, and many of those were ID students. Lower rents would later lure more whites, but ultimately it served as a middle-class version of the State Street Corridor, meant to absorb blacks who might otherwise consider moving into a white neighborhood. Prairie Shores Apartments, directly north, had a quota system tied to Michael Reese staff needs well into the 1980s. The Gropius-planned Michael Reese development, started in 1946, would expand to an eventual hodgepodge of twenty-nine buildings, some bearing signs of the master's own hand and landscaped by his colleague Hideo Sasaki, but most designed by a mix of local architects. The 1961 Harvard Design Conference, with MRH planner Reginald Isaacs and former CHA head Elizabeth Wood on the panel, deemed Prairie Shores "too brutal" and "a mass which is destructive both to the human scale of the area and to the scale of its sponsoring institution." Before they were even completed, the Near South Side projects—which had started the city toward its Daley-era regeneration, and whose strategies, laws, and designs had created the template for much of the nation's urban renewal—were quietly deemed not worth repeating. In the end, the planners had loved their theories more than they loved Chicago. Meanwhile, the rest of the South Side desperately needed hospitals.

THE FUTURE WAS now considered to be in "urban renewal." In March 1957 the City Council approved William Zeckendorf's first two projects in Hyde Park; one included plans for the Hi-Hat, birthplace of the Compass Theater, to be torn down and replaced by a firehouse. Zeckendorf's purchase of the Robie House in December 1957, brokered by Julian Levi and university president Kimpton, was a public relations coup as everyone up to the *New York Times* pointed to Hyde Park as the model of how to preserve a neighborhood. Surely the home of the University of Chicago, bastion of humanism that gave the world liberals like Robert Merriam, Alderman Leon Despres, and Senator Paul Douglas, would deal wisely with a nonwhite population that between 1950 and 1956 had risen from 6.1 percent to 36.7 percent. Two new buildings by Eero Saarinen gave a taste of the enlightened thinking at work. The Hyde Park–Kenwood Community Conference was still calling for interracial peace.

But Levi, head of the university-dominated Southeast Community Council, and President Kimpton made no secret that they didn't share the HPKCC's desire for an interracial community, and the truth was, not many whites in Hyde Park did. Most residents claimed they were liberal (save for those in the economics department, then fermenting into the Chicago School that would produce Milton Friedman and his followers), but Julian Levi called their bluff by working for what they were too embarrassed to admit they wanted—an upper-middle-class white neighborhood. The SECC defined *blight* mainly as black overcrowding, but most blacks living in Hyde Park didn't consider their conditions overcrowded, so the SECC can be credited for finally saying what everyone since Henry Heald had danced around: *blight* simply meant the presence of too many blacks for white comfort. On February 18, 1958, Levi presented the Final Plan, designed by Zeckendorf's Webb & Knapp (with the young I. M. Pei on staff): it would clear 106 acres and tear down 638 structures, forcing some four thousand families, 59 percent of which were nonwhite, to move. Instead of Mrs. Duncan relaxing on the lawns of Lake Meadows, gingerly approached by a couple of safe whites, here whites would lean back on the Midway Plaisance, visited now and then by carefully selected blacks who would fit in with what a university spokesman once called "our people." Both fantasies involved twenty-four-hour guard dog protection. Conspicuously absent were the five hundred units of public housing included in the original plan; Levi had decided they'd be too off-putting for investors. At a benefit appearance in Hyde Park, Mike Nichols joked that the attitude there now was "White and Black together, shoulder to shoulder, against the lower classes."

City Hall was all on board, leaving the last hurdle for Levi and Kimpton to be God Himself. Ironically, the one institution with doubts about Daley was the one he made the biggest show of supporting. According to Nicholas von Hoffman (then a community organizer with Saul Alinsky's Industrial Areas Foundation, or IAF), Cardinal Stritch was "so repulsed by . . . Mayor Daley's ways of doing business that he could not stand being in the same room as the man." With the cardinal's encouragement, Hoffman penned a series of editorials questioning the plan that were published in the archdiocese newspaper in April under the byline of Alinsky's ally Monsignor Jack Egan. Lashing out against "the unreasoning evil of bigotry," they said the goal of urban renewal had to be "human need." Described by Von Hoffman as a "smallish, invincibly likeable man . . . neither sanctimonious nor preachy," Egan had joined the Catholic Action movement after overhearing Alinsky tell a group of seminarians that on the day they were ordained, they should choose whether they wanted to be a bishop or a priest—everything would follow from that choice to either rise or serve. Once ordained, Egan aligned with a faction of parish priests engaged in labor activism and community organizing. French Catholic philosopher Jacques Maritain introduced him to Alinsky, and the two became the Hutchins and Adler of Chicago's underclass, Alinsky the fiery Jewish Tom Paine and Egan a simple Irish priest out of a Bernanos novel. The archdiocese funded independent IAF studies on Near South Side redevelopment and a pilot integration program on the Southwest Side, while Stritch made Egan the head of the archdiocese's Committee on Conservation. In Chicago, the Catholic Church was heard even when most Catholics didn't agree with what it was saying—*New World* counted 1,982,030 Catholics in the city—so to the dismay of Levi and Kimpton, public hearings on Hyde Park were delayed until September.

That August Mayor Daley held a press conference behind a vast model of a restructured and rebuilt downtown Chicago. This was *his* plan for *his* new city, the successor to Burnham's City Beautiful: a federal courthouse and a federal center; a civic center; more parking and more expressways; the development of Navy Pier; islands to be built into the lake; upscale housing on the Near North Side; more apartment buildings along the lakefront; and a massive new West Side campus for the University of Illinois. All the deliberation over Fort Dearborn ended up in just a few buildings on the river. The whole thing looked terrific—so terrific that it masked the fact that average Chicagoans were sending all their tax dollars downtown while their own neighborhoods were ignored. Chicagoans wanted to believe as much as they wanted to build—as long as it wasn't *their* house being demolished, of course, or *their* kid going to school in a trailer. (Most Catholic children attended parochial schools, which explains in part why the public schools remained bad; two-thirds of the population considered them vaguely immoral, on principle.) The Pan-American Games were coming in 1959, along with a visit from Queen Elizabeth and an International Trade Fair. Twenty years before, Moholy had been swept into the speed and light and raw possibilities of Oz, and now here was the same town on its way to becoming the Emerald City.

In September, Monsignor Egan faced the City Council at the hearing on Hyde Park. "The major moral problem of our generation," he testified, "the segregation of the bulk of the Negro population into nightmarish shanty towns, will continue to disgrace us unless we house all our population in a manner consistent with their dignity as human beings." But the archdiocese spoke too late; groundbreaking in Hyde Park was the next day. Skeptical Jewish and Protestant leaders, who for decades had watched the Church hierarchy say one thing as its parish priests orchestrated race riots, now accused Egan of speaking for Catholics who didn't want the Hyde Park blacks moving near them. Pressured by the mayor, Egan had no choice but to back down; in November the federal government and City Council approved the University of Chicago's Final Plan. Levi and Kimpton had saved Hyde Park, and the upper-middle-class residents could reassure themselves that since they were intellectuals and liberals, they could never be racists. "The people who will live in the rehabilitated neighborhood will be able to condemn the racial barbarities of Little Rock without a tongue-in-cheek, hypocritical feeling," said Rabbi Jacob Weinstein of KAM Temple, without a tongue-in-cheek, hypocritical feeling. Egan went on under Cardinal Stritch's successor, Albert Cardinal Meyer, to march at Selma with Dr. King, form a priests' union, and petition the Vatican for married clergy and the ordination of women.

A few weeks after the City Council approved the Final Plan for Hyde

Park, on the cold afternoon of December 1, 1958, only a few minutes before dismissal, fire ripped through the parish school at Our Lady of the Angels on the West Side. The heavy old wood furnishings and floors went up too fast for any orderly escape. Nuns tried to keep their classes calm: some led their children to exits only to find them chained shut; some helped them leap out windows into the arms of firemen and parents below, or death. The body of one nun was found at the head of her classroom, rows of small bodies sitting at their desks, hands folded in prayer. Ninety-two children and three nuns were killed, yet another Darger scene of devastated innocence. Firemen wept, staggering under the charred bodies in their arms. Fire Commissioner Robert Quinn said it was "the worst thing I have ever seen or ever will see." Jack Egan temporarily quit all his other duties to minister to the families, while the rest of the archdiocese withdrew into a defensive shell, since it had lobbied the city to keep from having to meet new fire codes in its older school buildings. Like the child sex abuse scandals decades later, the Church spent most of its postfire energies protecting itself; with City Hall's help, it quashed the questions and the pursuit of a young Catholic arson suspect. The West Side Italian neighborhood around the parish never recovered, not just from the trauma and the loss of its children, but from the abandonment it felt at the hands of City Hall and the archdiocese.

SINCE THE FIRST Leeds Triennial Music Festival in 1858, it had debuted works by Dvořák, Elgar, Vaughan Williams, Holst, and Walton. This October 1958 Festival boasted Otto Klemperer directing Beethoven's *Missa Solemnis,* Yehudi Menuhin playing Schumann's *Sonata in D Minor,* and Peter Pears singing Benjamin Britten's *Canticle No. 2,* accompanied by Britten himself on the pianoforte. For those with more adventurous tastes, Mr. Ravi Shankar would offer two sitar recitals while Duke Ellington from America would play jazz.

And then there was this man in a tight suit, high white collar, and processed hair, standing behind the curtain of the Odeon Theatre. The band backing him, the 'Jazz To-day Unit' led by trumpeter Kenny Baker, was about as good as British jazz got in 1958, for what that was worth. Otis Spann, who'd come along with Muddy, looked up from the piano and met his eyes. For a moment the question as to why they were here in dark, spitting Leeds hung heavily between them.

Muddy wriggled his fingers on the frets, working some oil back into the joints. America belonged to Chuck Berry right now. "Johnny B. Goode," "Sweet Little Sixteen," and "Reelin' and Rockin'" had all been huge hits that year, and now that hatchet-faced man who'd learned his licks from Muddy was traveling coast to coast with Jerry Lee Lewis like a running heavyweight fight, though the two were more likely to punch themselves out than actually hurt each other. Marrying his thirteen-year-old cousin had proved a bad career move for The Killer, while Berry had been arrested outside St. Charles, Missouri, changing a flat tire with two very dangerous things in his possession—a pistol and a white teenager named Joan Mathis. Still, the only turf left for Muddy Waters seemed to be England's green and pleasant land.

The curtain opened. The English audience expected tricked-up country blues, overalls, and aw-shucks deference; instead Muddy and Otis unleashed a set of pure, raw Chicago blues, circa 1958—loud, hard, fast, and sexy. "Screaming Guitar and Howling Piano," blared the Leeds newspaper. In Newcastle, they met Chris Barber, the leader of the jazz band that had set up the tour. Over the course of the ten-day tour, Barber's band would start with a set of what the Brits called "traditional jazz," a polite, holiday camp version of Dixieland, and then bring on Muddy and his swaggering, gritty sound that said more about life in the slums of Newcastle and Manchester than all the cheery skiffle bands on the BBC. Critics and folk fans went mad; kids like Eric Clapton, Eric Burden, and Mick Jagger went forth. Muddy had planted the seeds for the next stage of rock and roll and became the de facto international ambassador of the Chicago blues. During the Beatles' first visit to the United States in 1964,

Paul McCartney told reporters that the man he most wanted to meet was Muddy Waters.

MAHALIA JACKSON SLAPPED the pillows of her mustard Regency sofa. The gold swags on the windows needed dusting. No one had wanted her to buy this red brick ranch house at 8353 S. Indiana: not her agent, not her manager, not her friends, and certainly not her new neighbors in a white area called Chatham—"You'd have thought the atomic bomb was coming instead of me." But Mahalia did what she pleased, and it had pleased her in the spring of 1956 to take $40,000 out of her bra and hand it to the white doctor willing to break the now unspoken rules. Out back she grew greens, tomatoes, and string beans so she'd have fresh to cook with; the Reverend Russell Roberts had always loved her cooking.

She'd lived her life playing all sides: a hotel maid who'd pushed her way into palaces and opera houses; a woman known as a servant of God who fired her longtime pianist Mildred Falls when she asked for a small raise. On the road, she was an idealist. In December 1956, she'd gone down to Montgomery to sing for C. L. Franklin's young friend the Reverend Martin Luther King, whom she'd added to her list of people she cooked for. She'd stood behind him May 17, 1957, on the steps of the Lincoln Memorial, when he'd called out "Give us the ballot!" and in the years to come she'd use her status inside the National Baptist Convention to help push him forward. But in Chicago, she played by Chicago rules. When Dawson and Daley schemed to hijack the NAACP, she'd been on the phone with them constantly; but when Daley checkmated her old friend, she'd stuck with Daley (and didn't care that Studs hated them both). When neighbors shot her windows at 8353, robbed and harassed her, she called the mayor, who gave her a year's worth of round-the-clock police protection and spread word that the FBI was looking into it.

The floor-length shades rippled as Mahalia vacuumed under them. "I hadn't intended to start a one-man crusade," she said about the house. "All

I wanted was a quiet, pretty home to live in." A home to live in with Russell, the sharp and educated "café society minister" she'd edged aside Clara Ward and Dinah Washington to land. They'd planned to get married on the eve of her European tour, but then her agent called, and Mahalia always took calls that meant money. She put the marriage on hold. And the marriage kept holding as more and more offers came—movies, concerts, TV appearances—each just a bit more important at that moment than ending her loneliness. Bored by now, Mitch Miller handed her off to producer Irv Townsend, who hooked her up with Duke Ellington for the "Come Sunday" coda to his *Black, Brown and Beige* suite. An improvised version of the Twenty-third Psalm, the coda sank under its pretentions; Ralph Ellison called it "a most unfortunate marriage and an error of taste." Signed to the same label by the same agent, Duke and Mahalia were producing white-friendly imitations of their earlier work, and she, at least, knew it. "When I wasn't getting a dime for singing," she told an interviewer, "I had a more glorious feeling for singing than I have now." The devil was taking his due. "Those humble churches are my filling stations," she said. "If I didn't get in one every time I can, I would run empty." But even there she got cash up front.

That fall Sidney Poitier begged Mahalia to try the theater. He was going to star in a new play about a South Side black family moving into a white neighborhood, and there was a role for her. Lord knows, Chatham had taught her all she'd need to know about *that*. Edward R. Murrow had filmed her sitting in one of those red chairs and asked her why white Chicagoans had trouble with the presence of one of the world's most beloved performers. Mahalia had fed her famous red beans and rice to the crowd surrounding the house while children white and black waved at the camera. The next week the whites surrendered en masse; "for sale" signs sprouted up and down the block. She turned Poitier down and instead sang a number in *Imitation of Life*.

And then Russell was diagnosed with cancer of the spine.

On February 13, 1959, Mahalia sang for the first time at Orchestra Hall; Studs and the Old Town School of Folk Music had booked her and

Langston Hughes for *An Epic of Americana from Spirituals to Gospel Song.*
That morning in the middle of rehearsal, she learned that Russell had
passed. During lunch she bought a black dress for the funeral. The night
was long and heavy. Hughes read an essay on gospel, then handed her a
cold room that she couldn't light up, and frankly didn't care to. Claudia
Cassidy walked out.

Mahalia looked through the window of her big empty house. There
were mostly black faces in Chatham now; that wasn't a tragedy, or a
triumph—just some of both. Standing at King's side, she sang down walls,
and then she sang them back up again whenever she encouraged black
support for Daley. But Mahalia stood wherever she wanted to stand, and
for now that was 8353 S. Indiana. "The same birds are in the trees," she
said. "I guess it didn't occur to them to leave just because we moved in."

FOUR DAYS BEFORE Mahalia's concert, Claudia Cassidy had watched
the curtains at the Blackstone Theater open on a tired old room on the
South Side where "all pretenses but living itself have long since vanished."
A young boy slept on the couch. An alarm clock rang in a room offstage,
and through a door came his mother, Ruth, played by Ruby Dee, starting
a scene of aching reality in the Younger apartment, sweet and true in its
moments between Ruth and her boy Travis, painful and true when Sidney
Poitier as Ruth's frustrated husband, Walter, damned all the eggs that
ever were as Walter's mother—the role Mahalia turned down—waited
for the insurance check that would set the stage for his fall and rise. The
next day Cassidy wrote that *A Raisin in the Sun* "has the fresh impact of
something urgently on its way." That spring the play opened on Broadway,
and playwright Lorraine Hansberry became the first African American
to win the New York Drama Critics' Circle Award for Best Play.

A Raisin in the Sun was a return to social realism, with roots deep in
the same troubled Chicago soil that Dreiser, Wright, Algren, and Brooks
had drawn from. Decades before her life in Greenwich Village, Hansberry's father, Carl, had battled the University of Chicago and Robert

Hutchins all the way to the U.S. Supreme Court while she suffered at the hands of her new white neighbors at 6140 S. Rhodes, just south of Washington Park. But black kids beat her up too, for reasons that seemed to now drive her landmark play. Both active Republicans, her parents had created a foundation at the NAACP; Carl had run unsuccessfully for congressman in 1940, and Nannie was the Republican committeeman for the First Ward. Their home had been a minor cultural center, host to Robeson, Ellington, and Walter White; her uncle was a Howard University professor and while she described her father as "simply . . . a reasonably successful businessman of the middle class," Hansberry Enterprises had twenty-five employees and $300,000 worth of Depression-era real estate that it cut up into those same kitchenettes that Richard Wright had called "the funnel through which our pulverized lives flow to ruin and death." In her autobiography, she refers to herself ironically, even bitterly, as "a 'rich' girl," which she *was*—because her father was a slumlord. Shunned by whites and blacks, Carl eventually moved to Mexico, where he died in 1946; Lorraine graduated from Englewood High the next year, from there on to the University of Wisconsin, New York, Paul Robeson's *Freedom* magazine, and her marriage to poet Robert Nemiroff. The day back in the 1930s when young Lorraine was beaten up by other black kids for her fur coat was the day she became, she said, "a rebel," the only choice left when you're both victim and victimizer. With it comes the ability to tell the truth from all sides, and in her case the truth was a vision of being black in America that, like Ellison and James Baldwin, accepted no limitations. Worried less about making a case for blacks than about expressing their lives, on their terms, for them, Hansberry deftly and lovingly mined the hearts of the Youngers, embraced all of Black America's yearnings through the eyes of the sort of family that had paid for her fur coat, redeeming her father's tarnished name.

Algren hated the play, said it was "a soap opera so corny that it would scarcely have been tolerated on afternoon TV." Compared with *Native Son*, "*Raisin in the Sun*, enacted by Negro players, was not a play about Negro life at all. It came straight out of the turn of the century Yiddish theater." How exactly Algren knew this is a question Hansberry answered by calling him one of the New Paternalists, a romantic like Norman Mailer who had "mistaken the *oppression* of the Negro *for* 'the Negro.'" In fact, Wright and Hansberry were not so far apart; she'd simply changed Bigger from a monster to a man and inserted him into Gwendolyn Brooks's kitchenette.

Fine as the 1961 film version is, the real Younger apartment lives in those scenes of *The Cry of Jazz* that show the back porches Hansberry wrote of in her autobiography: "All travelers to my city should ride the elevated trains that race along the back ways of Chicago. The lives you can look into! I think you could find the tempo of my people on their back porches. The honesty of their living is there in the shabbiness." The anger behind *The Cry of Jazz* is the same that drives Walter to shout, "Will somebody please listen to me today!" As much as Baldwin and Hansberry disdained the blind rage of Bigger Thomas in *Native Son*, it was smoldering again in the generation of children being roughly shepherded into those four miles of public housing down State Street. It was no coincidence that two of the greatest literary works to come out of Chicago deal with housing (Chris Ware's 2012 master piece *Building Stories* is a recent third), yet neither Brooks nor Hansberry ever lost hope. Gwendolyn Brooks's original pitch for "The Mecca" well describes *Raisin in the Sun:* "I wish to present a large variety of personalities against a mosaic of daily affairs, recognizing that the grimmest of these is likely to have a streak or two streaks of sun."

CHAPTER 32

THE REALM OF
THE UNREAL

ANOTHER DAY FINISHED, the old man walked home through Lincoln Park from Alexian Brothers Hospital, where he rolled bandages, now that he was too weak to wash dishes. Protruding ears and a white walrus moustache, lips moving in a dialogue only he could hear. Sad, deep-set eyes that saw only enough not to stumble. At 851 W. Webster, a red-brick three-flat, he made his way slowly up the stairs, leaning hard on the banister. At the second floor, he took a breath and opened the door.

In an apartment cluttered and worn as he was, Henry Darger began to live again: paintbrushes and pictures of the Holy Family; Crayolas; magazines he'd snipped apart for the images of little girls or soldiers or masses of clouds. Papers and magazines stacked on the floors; bricks under his bed in case of attack—along with everything else, the old man was paranoid. As he worked, he replayed whatever the nuns at the hospital had been on about that day, acted out the scene he was depicting loudly enough that the other tenants thought the harmless crazy man who made pictures was entertaining guests.

When the sun set that evening, he went to the window and recorded the temperature on the first page of a new project, a weather chronicle. A tornado had dropped Dorothy into Oz, and Darger had witnessed one himself back in 1908, a sight that had scorched itself into his mind. Nothing in nature shows personal malice the way a tornado does, and like most Chicagoans fascinated by stockyards, slums, and gangland murders, Darger found beauty in what was terrible. He'd check the weather again in a few hours and note his measurement, as he would continue to do for the next ten years, a record that soon turned into a running comparison of what the weatherman predicted and what he saw out his window. The exact opposite of *In the Realm of the Unreal*, it was a constant check on reality versus what the newspapers and radios told him was real. This evening he celebrated New Year's alone, in another world far from the Third Coast.

"FOR BETTER OR worse, for more or less, Mayor Richard J. Daley is Mr. Chicago Culture," wrote the *Daily News*. ". . . Anything Big and Important in culture in Chicago generally succeeds if the Big and Important Daley clout is behind it." "The word 'culture,'" wrote Algren, "now means nothing more here than 'approved.' Thus the Chicago of the 1940's is forgotten and unrecorded and that of the fifties is gone for keeps." And those artists and writers who weren't approved had better look over their shoulders. Daley's Chicago would be a *clean* Chicago. The Sanity in Art crowd had been the province of blue-haired biddies, but now the beefy former Bridgeport altar boy, head of a crooked political machine, took a stand for all that he considered good and noble in America's former Good Times capital. His police department harassed booksellers who stocked undesirable titles, and staffed a movie censorship bureau with six doughty women and Sergeant Vincent Nolan, who felt that "children should be allowed to see any movie that plays in Chicago. If a picture is objectionable for a child, it is objectionable period." The women made their determinations largely on visible violence and whether they were at any point sexually aroused, which given how many films they deemed "for adults only" apparently occurred with minimal provocation. Despite rising taxes, the city cut funds for libraries and park drama programs and studiously ignored anything relating to African American arts or any other minority group.

Artists began seeping away. Daniel Catton Rich was among the first to go. Exhausted from years of dealing with a board that had once decided whether or not to buy a Mark Tobey painting by flipping a coin, he resigned in 1958 to become director of the Worcester Art Museum. His partner Katharine Kuh was next. Back in 1955 when she'd bought Jackson Pollock's *Greyed Rainbow*, the *Tribune* had run an article titled "Kuh-Kuh Must Go." She'd hung on long enough to organize the 1956 Venice Biennale, but finally left for New York in 1959. For years the art editor for the *Saturday Review*, she eventually returned to Chicago as art buyer for the First National Bank, where she orchestrated the installation of the Chagall mosaic. Kuh and Rich would remain lovers until his death in 1976. The city's most accomplished painter, Leon Golub, had (with Herb Greenwald's help) taken his wife, Nancy Spero, and the kids to the island of Ischia in 1956, then on to Florence, where the couple soaked in the Etruscans. Considering themselves a movement of two, they both worked in dark grays, blues, and ochres, Golub creating rudely Classical colossus figures while Spero used similar forms to explore her ideas on motherhood.

They returned to the States in 1958, and though a teaching spot at the University of Indiana stuck them in Bloomington, they still felt connected to Chicago, at least for now, where a new generation of students at the School of the Art Institute went deeper into dark, fantastic dream imagery under the tutelage of surrealist Roberto Matta. Some new galleries, like the Wells Street Gallery Old Town, had popped up. Peter Selz featured Chicago artists Golub, Campoli, and Westermann in the *New Images of Man* show he curated at MoMA in 1959, and for a moment it looked as if Chicago, with its "anti-mainstream, anti-idealistic penchant," might step out of New York's shadow. William Rubin sank that hope with a review that deemed Golub's work "phonily expressive" and "badly painted." Chicago's art reputation sank too, and Rubin's next job as

MoMA's director of painting and sculpture all but locked Golub and Chicago out of the upper reaches of contemporary art. Devastated, Golub and Spero moved to Paris. The Wells Street Gallery closed; painters June Leaf and Robert Barnes moved to New York; Westermann followed his wife to California. Chicago was once again a place to paint in isolation.

Talent also left the Institute of Design and IIT. James Prestini, salon host and wood-turner extraordinaire, left for Knoll Design and then Berkeley, where he taught with fellow ID faculty member Jesse Reichek. ID alums staffed faculties across the nation. What marked the end of the old institute, though, wasn't so much its relegation to the basement of Crown Hall as the departure of the last link to Moholy—Harry Callahan. Awarded a fellowship by the Graham Foundation, Callahan went to France for 1957 and 1958, leaving the photography department to Aaron Siskind, who had never really bought into the Bauhaus or Moholy. Within the next ten years, Andy Warhol and Marshall McLuhan (who created his landmark *The Medium Is the Massage* with Moholy's New Bauhaus student Quentin Fiore) would build their careers on ideas that Moholy had aired forty years earlier. In 1961 Callahan would leave the big white apartment on the lakefront, the storefronts and street corners he'd so memorably captured, for a position at the Rhode Island School of Design, where he'd teach until 1977. As a final tribute to what he'd accomplished in Chicago, *Aperture* published a special volume on five ID photographers, and the ID brought out Callahan's monograph, *The Multiple Image*. "I think," said Callahan later, "that going to the Institute of Design in Chicago saved my life." Much as Richard Nickel kept the memory of Sullivan alive in return for saving him, Callahan passed along Moholy to a decade of ID photographers that included Art Sinsabaugh, Charles Swedlund, and Ray K. Metzker. "I was learning photography as art," said one student, "but I was also learning how to be a person in the world: a man, a husband, a father, a teacher, all this stuff together." Callahan died in 1999.

The net effect of the exodus was an institutional marginalization of Chicago's people-oriented aesthetic. Nothing could be farther from

Moholy-Nagy and "Everyone is talented" than Richard J. Daley. Yet the ultimate irony of Chicago art in this period—and Moholy's vindication— is that the two Chicago artists most discussed today were completely unknown then, working between the cracks of the city's established culture. That Henry Darger vindicates Moholy is no hyperbole; his landlord since 1956 had been Nathan Lerner, Moholy's student and interim successor, one of his most faithful Universal Designers whose heightened sensibilities allowed for the possibility that an old recluse who talked to himself and collected scraps of paper could actually be an important artist. Everyone in the neighborhood knew about his pictures, but only when Darger moved into a nursing home in 1972 did Lerner and his wife, Kiyoko, discover the enormous tableaux, the novels, and the weather chronicle. Darger died the next year, and in 1977 selections from *In the Realm of the Unreal* were first shown at the Hyde Park Art Center, run by another ID alum, Don Baum. Darger himself was clear that he was an artist—he referred to himself as one in his writings, and when Lerner, having seen the work, visited him on his deathbed, Darger said, "Too late now." For all the Freudian obsessions, dreamscapes, and Dubuffet *art brut* of the postwar Chicago artists, only he had truly lived in that realm of the unreal they'd all aspired to.

The other was a nanny, a daughter of French immigrants, who moved to Highland Park in 1956 to take care of the three sons of Mr. and Mrs. Avron Gensburg. Whenever Vivian Maier wasn't leading her charges on a Mary Poppins adventure, she had a camera in her hand. A self-portrait taken in the reflection of a window shows a long-faced woman, not beautiful, but poised and dignified, with intelligent eyes drooping at the same angle of sadness as the ends of her mouth. Beloved as she was by the Gensburgs and most of the other families she would work for well into the 1990s, Maier led her life on her off days, when she would dress in men's shoes and floppy hats and roam the city taking photos on the streets, incidental portraits uncommon for their immediacy and formal strength, sometimes documenting events and parades. Though she may have once taken a class at the New School in New York, the power of her works, the striking contrast and structure, all point to an elegant eye and a wry creativity that could only come from a native talent. It's her individuality, her intense personhood, that presses forward most. Without the veil of being a student or an artist, without position, title, or settled home, resolutely single, Maier seemed to offer herself in the simplest way to the world, and in return its everyday working faces gave themselves back. Her families knew about her obsession, one even gave her space for a darkroom, but she never let anyone see her work, and it remained unseen until 2007, when a photo researcher and real estate agent bought several boxes of her negatives at auction for forty dollars. Maier died two years later, and since then a minor industry has grown to assess her work as it gradually comes to light. Whether or not the photography establishment affords Maier a place next to Helen Levitt and Garry Winogrand, her life, like Darger's, speaks to the ultimate truth of Moholy's supposedly naïve belief in the animating importance of art in the lives of individuals.

ON PEARSON STREET, another silent old man made his way slowly into a much nicer apartment, one with paintings by Paul Klee and Max Beckmann on the walls. Arthritis would soon put Mies in a wheelchair; these days he moved slowly, aiming toward the next place to sit, the pain driving him even more deeply into himself and the distilled purity of his work. Liquor kept him sociable, if not exactly convivial; he saw whom he wanted to see, worked on what he wanted to work on, avoided confrontations. The author of instant classics like the Seagram Building, he saw no need to explain himself any longer, so Joe Fujikawa dealt with IIT, though he considered the campus, like the Farnsworth House, irrevocably his.

The school, like Dr. Farnsworth, was not happy about being taken for granted, and the result was the same: that summer Fujikawa received a page-long list of grievances that he summed up as "Board's attitude was that they were not 'building a monument to Mies' on campus." If Mies made nice, he *might* be allowed to do the Library. In the meantime, IIT announced that the next building on its campus, the Student Union, would be designed by Skidmore, Owings & Merrill. It turned out to be a public relations disaster both for the school and for SOM. Accused from all quarters of stealing the masterwork of the man who'd made their rise possible, suddenly regretful Hartmann and Owings offered Mies a role as consultant. "No," sniffed Mies. "I'd rather accept doing nothing than half the torso."

SOM moved ahead, but instead of putting one of Mies's former students in charge, Owings gave the job to Walter Netsch, a Chicagoan who'd gone to MIT, not IIT. "We will not do Mies's working drawings," Netsch recalled Owings as saying. Things came to a head at a conciliatory birthday dinner SOM hosted for Mies at the Chicago Athletic Club. After a pleasant enough meal, all retired to a back room to continue drinking, including Hilbs, who should have stopped a few glasses of straight gin earlier. Mies's oldest friend and defender, the turtle-headed German pointed his pipe at the SOM contingent. "Why are you here, at Mies's birthday party? You are his enemy, you have taken his campus away." Embarrassed, Mies tried to restrain Hilbs, but, as Alfred Caldwell told the story later, Hilbs would not be stopped and egged on SOM's William Dunlap, who then challenged Caldwell to resign if he was so upset. Caldwell quit on the spot. "They were all yellow," he said later. "There wasn't a man in the bunch." The glory that was Mies's IIT architecture department was essentially over. Caldwell went off to teach at USC, while Hilbs, his rival Caldwell gone, ran the department until his death in 1967. In the meantime IIT, a school known to the world only because of Mies van der Rohe, decided that his designs were "too radical" even as he won the Royal Gold Medal, the AIA 1960 Gold Medal, and, in May 1959, the commission for his last great work in Chicago, the three-building Federal Center.

Meanwhile Netsch, an otherwise brilliant architect, struggled with his charge to create a Student Union "in the spirit of Mies" yet distinctly SOM, since no one could define precisely what was distinct about SOM. Reflective glass replaced Mies's wide, clear panes; lengths of steel crossing the roof seem to echo the ones at Crown Hall, until a closer look reveals they have no structural role. What makes the building less "radical" than what Mies had proposed is not clear, but it's clearly not as good. One architect told *Fortune* what he thought: "S.O.M. took Mies's stainless-steel standard, warmed it up, and sold it as a prestige package to the U.S. businessman. That's all to the good, but now *rigor mortis* is setting in. They're becoming a conservative force in U.S. architecture—they've stopped inventing." But as SOM became the world's largest architectural firm, it wasn't evident that inventing was ever the point.

JANUARY 25, 1959. At nine in the morning Pacific Standard Time, American Airlines flight 2, a Boeing 707 christened the *Flagship California*, took off from Los Angeles carrying 109 distinguished passengers. For the next four hours and nine minutes, a crew of five specially trained stewardesses, led by a dead ringer for the young Shirley MacLaine, doted on a planeload of CEOs, corporate presidents, and media honchos that included California governor Pat Brown, actress Jane Wyman, and the head of the William Morris Agency, Mr. Abe Lastfogel. The plane touched down at Idlewild at four in the afternoon, after a flying party of lobster, cocktails, and cigarettes, ushering in regularly scheduled nonstop jet service between New York and L.A. The newly minted "jet set" would never need to change trains in Chicago again. Terms like *bicoastal* and *flyover states* came into being. Balloons would no longer land in Oz. Instead, earlier that week, the first episode of *The Untouchables*, set in a fantasyland of Capone-era Chicago, had aired on ABC. Whatever else the city was responsible for would be lost in a hail of bullets from Robert Stack's tommy gun.

TWO WEEKS LATER Herb Greenwald fastened his seat belt in preparation for landing at LaGuardia. It was late—going on eleven—and the lights of the skyline were hard to see as American Airlines flight 320 cruised up the Hudson River, then banked right through a wintery mix of rain, sleet, and dense fog. His secretary, Elizabeth Ann Kalnicky, stowed her notebook away. The day before, Greenwald had announced that after spreading the gospel of Mies throughout America, he'd made a deal with SOM to build a big new hotel just south of the Conrad Hilton, at Michigan and 8th. He was coming in to New York to line up investors.

The four engine turboprop dropped through the clouds somewhere over Washington Heights and the South Bronx. The tugboat *H. Thomas Teti, Jr.* heard it explode as it crashed nearby into the shallow water just east of Rikers Island. Greenwald and Kalnicky were among the sixty-five killed. "Herb needed no hope to begin, and no success to persevere," said Mies at the funeral at Anshe Emet Synagogue (sadly only his first of the year; Waltraut would also pass in 1959). "Squiff was," said Leon Golub, "pre-eminently a great patron," and that he was; along with supporting two of the city's finest artists, Golub and Mies, Greenwald had also funded the three short years of Maurice English's *Chicago* magazine, a highly intelligent run at a local version of *The New Yorker.* His death cut deeply at the cultural heart of Chicago.

A few rows away from Greenwald and Kalnicky on flight 320 sat another Chicagoan heading east to sound out investors. Beulah Zachary, Burr Tillstrom's producer, defender, and the inspiration for Beulah the Witch, was en route to start up a new Kuklapolitan Workshop Theater in New York. Fran Allison may have been the tissue between the Kuklapolitans and the world, but Beulah had been the wall protecting Burr. After her passing, he wandered for three decades of one-man commedia dell'arte: a brief run on Broadway, guest spots on TV specials, hosting the Macy's Thanksgiving Day Parade, a few more tries at a regular show. As the years passed, even the youngest in the audience found the Kuklapolitans out of their time. In the late 1970s, they discovered a warmer home in the theater; back in 1948 the young Stephen Sondheim had submitted a song to Kukla, Fran, and Ollie that had been stupidly sent back without a listen, and now, on Broadway in *Side by Side by Sondheim,* Burr sat on the lip of the stage with Kukla and Ollie—revealed for the first time on his hands—singing "The Two of You." After Burr's death in 1985, his will donated the

Kuklapolitans to the Chicago Historical Society with one proviso: no other person shall ever be allowed to put their hands inside Kukla, Ollie, or any of the Kuklapolitans.

In April 1959, Frank Lloyd Wright died in Phoenix, Arizona, following abdominal surgery. He was buried in a circle of pines in Spring Green, Wisconsin.

FIVE HUNDRED YARDS off the coast of Chicago, the royal yacht HMS *Britannia* drew closer through shimmering July waves. Boat horns tooted, guns sounded, and on the specially made jetty at Congress Street, a very tanned Richard J. Daley adjusted his tie, ready to welcome Her Royal Highness Queen Elizabeth II and her husband, Prince Philip, here to celebrate the opening of the St. Lawrence Seaway. The State Department chief of protocol stood waiting; the red carpet rolled behind them toward the honor guard and bands; Buckingham Fountain poured upward.

Mayor Daley was doing all he could to make the summer of 1959 the greatest in Chicago history. That April he'd been reelected in a landslide over Republican Timothy Sheehan, an Edison Park soft drink distributor and importer of specialty Swedish foods. Chicago was now essentially a one-party city; the list of contributors to the Non-Partisan Committee to Re-Elect Mayor Daley had included just about every Republican businessman and powerhouse in Chicagoland. The queen's arrival all but served as Daley's coronation.

The royal barge skimmed over the lake.

Only four days before, in front of a three-story missile at Navy Pier, he'd opened the Chicago International Trade Fair, laying the wares of twenty-eight countries at the feet of Chicagoans, along with fashion shows and a floating stage in the lake where "Voodoo warriors from Haiti" would perform what the *Tribune* described as "their strange rites of black magic and dance their weird jungle dances." The fair's true horizons can be measured by the answer an IBM 305 Ramac computer gave to the mayor's son William when he asked it what was the most important event of 1948. Its reply: "The Chicago railroad fair opens."

The gracious young queen, almost fetching from certain angles in her sundress, pearls, and hat, stepped onto Chicago soil accompanied by the prime minister of Canada, with Jack Brickhouse, voice of the Cubs, and Lloyd Pettit, voice of the Blackhawks, calling the action. Cameras whirred. So began a whirlwind thirteen hours: a motorcade through downtown streets lined with royal-loving Chicagoans; twenty minutes at the trade fair; lunch at the Ambassador West; then down to the Museum of Science and Industry, where her most serene royal highness walked through a gigantic washing machine, saw, quite briefly, some baby chicks hatch, then shot up the Drive for a twenty-minute visit to the Art Institute. The queen particularly admired El Greco's *The Assumption of the Virgin*. After a spot of emergency dental work, Elizabeth R. in tiara and white satin was taken to the Hilton for the gala dinner—each course named after a lock of the Seaway. (She later received kudos for pronouncing *Chicago* correctly and "not using the Shi-cah-go pronunciation of eastern Americans.") The queen's seatmate, Da Mare, glowed in his white tuxedo, while Sis did very well with the prince. Whisked away after fond farewells, the royals were back on the *Britannia* just after twelve under a shower of fireworks. It was, according to the CEO of the Chicago Association of Commerce and Industry, probably "the greatest reception she has ever had outside of Great Britain itself."

Of course, the queen hadn't gone more than a mile from the lakefront. She didn't visit Milwaukee Avenue for pierogies or 47th Street for ribs. While it's true the visit lasted only thirteen hours, the Potemkin Chicago she saw was the city Mayor Daley had all of Chicago believing in, the one that Jack Reilly, the city's director of special events, said had, with this visit, "proved it can do anything that any other city in the world can do." The queen saw none of the crumbling neighborhoods torn by racial strife; she visited no bad schools, understaffed hospitals, or housing projects. None of the cops she met were involved in the burglary ring that had almost implicated Daley and forced him to bring in a new police commissioner,

Orlando Wilson. The trade fair closed two weeks later to great acclaim, and the U.S. Conference of Mayors elected Daley its president.

In late August 1959, with royal magic still twinkling over Glencoe and Barrington Hills, the Pan American Games opened, the largest international sporting event to be held up to that point in the United States. Seeing the lack of preparation the summer before, Avery Brundage of the U.S. Olympic Committee had warned, "We can't tolerate failure. . . . It would be a disgrace to the city." It turned out he'd been right to worry; the games were a fiasco from the torch relay, when a Boy Scout runner had the torch stolen from him in Oklahoma. The Peruvian rifle team had their rifles taken at the airport, while the Mexican pistol shooters, with nowhere to practice, began shooting squirrels in Lake Forest. Eisenhower, as promised, attended the opening ceremonies—Dr. Milton Eisenhower, the brother of the president, who was otherwise engaged. Sculls rowed through the fetid Cal-Sag Channel, an industrial waste canal; the Haitian soccer team went on strike; and a member of the Brazilian rowing team was shot dead in Naperville while trying to buy a gun. The *Los Angeles Times* called it "perhaps the worst-staged track and field event ever." The United States won an embarrassing 121 out of 164 events.

Chicagoans paid little attention. Attendance was dismal. What mattered, at least on the South Side, was that at ten-thirty on the night of September 22, at Cleveland's Municipal Stadium, bases loaded, bottom of the ninth, Vic Power ground the first pitch he saw into a double play, Aparicio to Kluszewski, giving the White Sox their first pennant in forty years. Mayor Daley, watching at home in his suspenders with sons John and William, ordered the air raid sirens sounded for five minutes. Thousands of panicking Chicagoans ran into the streets expecting imminent nuclear holocaust; parents led their screaming children down into the basement to await the end. The next day Daley explained that he'd ordered the sirens "in the hilarity and exuberance of the evening. I regret if anyone was inconvenienced, but after 40 years of waiting for a pennant in the American league I assume that everyone who was watching the telecast was happy about the White Sox victory." What he did not say was that he was sorry. If the summer of 1959 was not great for Chicago, it certainly was for Dick Daley. What he and his city lacked in subtlety, they offered twice over in enthusiasm, citizens be damned.

LATE THAT OCTOBER a white Mercedes convertible cruised north on Lake Shore Drive and pulled up in front of a modern apartment building. One by one the elevator buttons blinked until at the very top a bunny head flashed. The door opened onto a party, Cy Coleman playing "Playboy's Theme," the suave, on-the-town anthem Victor Lownes had commissioned. Mad Men and busty Playmates in satin sipped scotch and danced lazy mambos. Then a man tapping his foot at the piano turned, took the pipe from his mouth, and said in a halting voice, "Hello there. Glad you could join us this evening. I'm Hugh Hefner, editor and publisher of *Playboy* magazine."

It's hard to know what was real about the premiere episode of Hef's syndicated *Playboy's Penthouse* that October 29, 1959, and much of its charm lies therein; an avowed fan of Dave Garroway and *Studs' Place,* Hef wanted to "bring the magazine to life" with a "sophisticated weekly get together." Ad-libbed, no fourth wall, the show was a direct descendant of the Chicago School of Television. But instead of you inviting Garroway into your home, Hef invited you into his. Of course it wasn't *really* Hef's place, but it *was* a real party, with real booze and real people pretending to be at one. In this first episode, Lenny Bruce switches between hepcat rambling and filling uncomfortable silences, while the surprisingly hot young Rona Jaffe, who'd clearly worked bigger, tougher rooms, swats away envious questions from Spectorsky. The highlight was always the music, drawn from those in town working with Bill Putnam. Here Ella Fitzgerald does two live numbers, and Coleman debuts "The Best Is Yet to Come," just sold to Sinatra (referred to by all as simply "Frank" or "The Leader"). In later episodes Sarah Vaughan, Nina Simone, Tony Bennett, and Count Basie dropped by; Pete Seeger gave a fifteen-minute concert ending with a group sing of "Wimoweh." That Nat King Cole and Ella were guests at the "party" kept the show from clearing in the South. (*Playboy* gave much of the proceeds from its jazz festival that summer to the NAACP; Hef resolutely supported the civil rights movement.)

Like the early years of *Playboy*—and Hef himself—the show manages to be sophisticated, compelling, and cheesy all at once; swinging and striving. At one point Lenny Bruce says to Hef, "You're not interested in people without money." Which was not exactly true. Back in December 1952, Hef had imagined parties like this happening in all those bright windows, and now he was hosting one for all the other regular guys standing on the Michigan Avenue bridges of their own lives. In one show, Hef introduces a thick-set, crew-cutted rocket scientist, who happens to be his pal Jim Brophy, to explain the Van Allen belt. Then, as a special surprise, Hef shows a loooong clip from one of their New England Avenue monster movies. Another episode ends with pizza being passed around. Hef holds up a slice and says to the viewer with utter sincerity, "I kinda wish at this particular moment I could offer a slice of pizza to you too, but it's difficult to push it through the video screen." In New York, they built walls around the jet set; in Chicago, Hef from the Northwest Side wanted *you* at the party too. *That,* as much as any pair of bare breasts, was what created the *Playboy* empire.

If Mayor Daley was the city's father figure, Hugh Hefner was the black sheep brother who bought you beer. On the record as disapproving of the *Playboy* lifestyle, Daley barred the first Playboy Jazz Festival, scheduled for August 1959, from Soldier Field under pressure from the new archbishop, yet he needed Hef; all those lakefront towers in the mayor's big diorama required people to live in them, but the population was still flowing out to the suburbs—by now one-third of Chicagoland's families lived outside the city in that terra incognita of manicured lawns and bridge clubs. Like Herb Greenwald, Hef was a believer in the city, and the city he believed in most was Chicago; when Tony Bennett sings "Chicago" on the show, a delighted Hef literally bounces up and down on the sofa.

Masculine living, according to *Playboy*, meant living downtown in a bachelor pad. "Since ancient times," read one ad, "men have associated true sophistication with cities." In September and October 1956 the magazine ran a feature on the dream penthouse, with all its push-button hi-fis and timed dimmers a fantasy bridge to the urbane lifestyle that Mies and Greenwald had announced with 860–880. William McFetridge, one of Daley's key allies, used millions from his labor union to fund Bertrand Goldberg's Marina City complex, started in 1959 specifically for singles and young couples.

The parties kept going for Hef even after the cameras went off. After finally divorcing Millie, he tried to buy a building at 28 E. Bellevue, but local zoning wouldn't allow him to dig an indoor pool, so instead he purchased the Henry Isham mansion at 1340 N. State Parkway. Its eleven rooms and seven thousand square feet became a playhouse, complete with in-house movie theater, bowling lane, ring-a-ding-ding Dean Martin–style firepole, and most important, a zoning variance for that indoor pool and plaster grotto. The running party began. The Pump Room, a block away, used to snag stars in transit; now they made special visits for anything-goes fun in Hef's Mansion. Spectorsky presented him with a nudge-nudge sign for the doorbell that read *Si Non Oscillas, Noli Tintinnare*, "If You Don't Swing, Don't Ring"; a more creative use of Latin than either the Church or Mortimer Adler had made in a long while.

What had started as fantasy for Hef in 1952 was now his reality, and it had happened because he wanted it to happen for his readers as well. Going further would require more than the imagination; no more pizza through the television, it had to be something *real*. So they updated the Gay Nineties–meets–speakeasy atmosphere of the Gaslight Club, transformed the French-leg corsets and fishnets of the Gaslight Girls into the Bunnies, and on February 29, 1960, opened the first Playboy Club at 116 E. Walton. Visitors to Chicago with fifty bucks in hand could get a Bunny-head key and lifetime access to five floors of bars, top musicians, and a constant buffet. No one went searching for *Studs' Place* anymore; they wanted to find that "meeting place for the most important, most aware, most affluent men of the community." There'd be fifty thousand key holders by the end of the first year.

"Well, no use to call out the hook-and-ladders," wrote Nelson Algren, who overcame his dislike of Hefner's commercialized sexuality just enough to drop by the Mansion once in a while for cold cuts at the buffet. Art Shay and just about everybody who was anybody in Chicago went too, though Studs preferred evenings with Ida: "So long as Jerry Lewis Jr. is doing such a good job of handling children's diseases for us and Sammy Davis Jr. has integration in hand, I see no reason why our city should not be proud in giving America Hugh Hefner to handle sex." With no need now for the outside world, Hef boarded up the windows to eliminate night and day and turned back in on the perfect dream world he'd created. Daley had done the same thing. Chicago's isolation began. "The stockyards stink," wrote John Bartlow Martin, "the streets are filthy, restaurants are overcrowded, a hotel room is often impossible to obtain, and so is a place to park. Many people are afraid to go abroad on the streets at night. On Lake Shore Drive, life in Chicago is lovely—for the few. For the millions, life in Chicago is toil and ugliness, if it is not squalor and privation." That was the New Chicago of Dick Daley and Hugh Hefner, a city chasing out, even demolishing, what was best about itself.

NICHOLS AND MAY were off in New York by the spring of 1959, appearing at Town Hall in an evening of their old Compass scenes, while Shelley Berman had broken out as arguably the father of the "Don't you hate it when . . . ?" school of stand-up, with his hit album *Inside Shelley Berman*. Back in Chicago, the remnants of the Compass drifted toward the Gate of Horn, where Elaine May's boyfriend, Howard Alk, worked the lights and Paul Sills was now the house manager. Andrew Duncan, who'd gone into social work, dropped by for long talks with Sills about doing something new, something more finished than the Compass had been. The idea gained more traction over the summer: Sills and Harris had divorced by then, but she was still interested, as was Eugene Troobnick, now an editor at *Playboy,* and Bernie Sahlins, undaunted by the failure of the Studebaker. David Shepherd passed. Married now but sinking under the weight of another season of depression, his new traveling company of the Compass, including Jerry Stiller, Anne Meara, and Alan Arkin, bombed badly—in the lounge of a Cleveland honeymoon hotel, guests threw rolls and silverware at the stage. When Anne Meara asked for suggestions, the audience said, "Go home." Sahlins staked Alk and Sills each their $2,000 investment, and while in Greenwich Village they came up with a name: The Second City.

Sills and Alk fixed up a new space above a Chinese laundry at 1842 N. Wells and assembled the cast. From 55th Street to the Argo, from St. Louis to New York, many lessons had been learned and Sills applied them all. If the Compass had been a constant attempt to catch lightning in a bottle, everything here was planned to provide a sophisticated evening on the town. Second City's first show, *Excelsior and Other Outcries,* began with Barbara Harris singing a light little song called "Everybody's in the Know." The entire cast had grown up since that steamy night back in July 1955. Out of her shell and in charge of her dramatic powers, Harris commanded attention; Andrew Duncan added layers to his Everyman; Severn Darden reined in his excesses. With Alk, Troobnick, Roger Bowen, and newcomer Mina Kolb filling out the cast and Allaudin Mathieu on piano, the first act established character types through short sketches, and then the second act usually went for something longer and more substantial, like an opera parody. There'd be improv, but only in special sets five times a week after late shows. Viola Spolin's exercises were used only to sharpen what happened onstage.

The Second City was an immediate success, the result, according to Paul Sills, of how guilty Chicagoans felt for what they'd let go the first time. Though it sprang from the family structure that had always kept Chicago arts afloat, Second City now became an institution, the only level of success that guaranteed survival in Daley's Chicago. A few months in,

Alk and Bowen both left, to be replaced by Paul Sand and Alan Arkin. Into the 1960s, Second City would act as a meeting ground between the Gate of Horn/Old Town School of Folk Music circle and the swinging *Playboy* types, an anchor of Old Town and one of the few public outlets of discontent during the Daley era. The following performers would work at some point in one of David Shepherd's various Compass companies, Ted Flicker's the Premise, or the Chicago and Toronto companies of Second City: Alan Alda, Joan Rivers, Bill Murray, John Belushi, Gilda Radner, Robert Klein, David Steinberg, Fred Willard, Peter Boyle, Tina Fey, Steve Carell, Chris Farley, George Wendt, John Candy, Harold Ramis, Dan Aykroyd, Eugene Levy, Rick Moranis, Martin Short, Dan Castellaneta, Mike Myers, Adam McKay, Bob Odenkirk, Amy Sedaris, and Stephen Colbert (thus can *The Colbert Report* trace its lineage back to the malcontents and raconteurs of Bughouse Square and the Dil Pickle Club, via the Compass). In the early 1960s, even the young David Mamet could be found at Second City, waiting tables.

On October 8, 1960, *An Evening with Mike Nichols and Elaine May* opened at the Golden Theater on Broadway, and the two never looked back. Nichols would go on to become a director: *The Graduate, Who's Afraid of Virginia Woolf?*, and *Primary Colors* are just a few of his films, while his stage work ranges from *Barefoot in the Park* to *Monty Python's Spamalot*. Elaine May's own career as a screenwriter and director has been quirky and decidedly less glamorous; her disastrous film *Ishtar* was for a long time code for a Hollywood bomb. Though his original vision generated billions of dollars, David Shepherd banked very few of them, mostly because of his own choices, and—he'd be the first to admit—his own missteps. Now well into his eighties, he continues to develop new ways to incorporate improvisation into daily life, and still dreams of a people's theater. Moholy had been doubtful about vernacular culture's ability to survive in the technical age. "Canned music, phonographs, films and radio," he wrote, "have killed folksong, home quartets, singing choirs, market plays, commedia dell'arte productions, without canalizing the creative abilities in other positive directions." It was close. But in Chicago the human voice still cut through enough of the noise of popular culture to guarantee its continued existence.

AS THE DALEY Machine changed from a means of moving up to a tool of control, another Chicago organization quietly spread across America by standing with the little guy. At the start of 1958, thirty-nine McDonald's franchises dotted America, many owned by Rolling Green Country Club friends convinced less by the spotless Des Plaines store than by McDonald's No. 2, a franchise in Waukegan opened by a former Bible salesman. The owner, Sandy Agate, ran out of hamburger meat and buns the first day, paid off his franchise fee the first week, and within a year had a bigger house than Ray Kroc himself. Word spread. Like Daley, Kroc understood patience—until 1961, his only income came from his withering Multimixer company, yet onward he went, targeting California, the home of car culture, for expansion, though the devil-may-care attitude there conflicted with his four commandments of quality, service, cleanliness, and value (QSCV); an inspection tour revealed burritos, pizza, and chili on menus, meat cut with filler, and a frustrating lack of interest in the opportunities offered by replicating the Speedee Service System. Ray Kroc loved the regular guy, but being your own boss as a McDonald's franchise owner meant doing certain things his way. "We have found out . . . that we cannot trust some people who are nonconformists," he wrote to the McDonald brothers. "We will make conformists out of them in a hurry. . . . The organization cannot trust the individual; the individual must trust the organization."

But all organizations are not alike. Whereas Daley's Machine stood for only whatever produced the best combination of power, money, and votes, Kroc offered a fair shake to his franchise owners and suppliers, and QSCV to the burger buyer, who—Morgan Spurlock to the contrary—was never encouraged to make McDonald's his only food group. If the Machine had left service behind with Jake Arvey, Kroc had made it the foundation of his company. In fact, the deck was so stacked in everyone else's favor that as the stores spread, the McDonald's corporation was on the verge of bankruptcy. At this point Kroc's cold-eyed numbers man Harry Sonneborn took a page from the Machine's book. Ward committeemen and precinct captains provided service, but the ward and the precinct belonged to the Machine, so why not let the franchisees provide the service on McDonald's turf? Rather than eking through on their tiny share of all those hamburgers, McDonald's now focused on buying or leasing prime locations, which they rented back to the franchises. By the end of 1960, there were 228 McDonald's across America; today there are approximately 32,000 restaurants in more than one hundred countries. McDonald's remains essentially a real estate business.

A NEW MUDDY Waters hit the stage of the Newport Jazz Festival on the afternoon of July 3, 1960. England and Europe had recharged him and had done the same for Howlin' Wolf, Willie Dixon, and other bluesmen, not by stripping the cotton fields and servitude out of their music but by celebrating it as something fresh. The guitar-centered British rock bands that emerged—the Rolling Stones, the Animals, and the Yardbirds, to start— never hid the influence of Muddy as they, along with the folk revival, effectively reintroduced the blues to America in a newer, albeit whiter, form. The Chicago blues brought rock and roll to life, and now those same Chicago blues pushed rock along to something that more closely resembled the reality of the culture as a product of both races.

Muddy and the blues had survived, but Chuck Berry and Chess were on the ropes. Leonard had squeezed him hard to keep pumping out hits, even as his fans outgrew songs about teenage girls and fast cars and how stupid everything is in the world that didn't involve teenagers. Berry, now a father of three and owner of a St. Louis nightclub, got entangled with a fourteen-year-old girl from Texas named Janice Escalanti, a situation that led to his arrest on December 21, 1959, for violating the Mann Act, which in turn convinced the State of Missouri to pursue charges on the Joan Mathis case. In between the constant studio sessions that

Leonard insisted on to stockpile material, Berry faced juries in both states and in March 1960 was convicted on the Escalanti charge, though he was found not guilty in Missouri—Joan Mathis testified that she'd been a *very* willing passenger.

Chess got hit, too. The IRS announced that it would be investigating how record labels dealt with deducting gifts as business expenses—in other words, payola, the long-standing practice of paying deejays to play your records. On their way up, Leonard and Phil Chess had unashamedly schmeared palms all across America: Al Benson, for example, drove a red Lincoln given to him by Leonard, but the Old Swingmaster was sharp enough to launder the $12,000 or so he received annually through a stable of companies. Though it wasn't technically illegal, if the deejays hadn't claimed the money as income or if the labels had deducted it improperly, the IRS could come after them. The FTC and FCC climbed on board. Hearings held in January 1960 exposed much dirty laundry but resulted in little other than the decimation of Alan Freed. A business partner and personal friend to the Chess family, Freed had even slept on the couch at the place on Yates when his marriage hit the rocks, but as one of the public faces of rock and roll, the feds made him their prime target. WABC fired him for—truthfully—not signing a pledge that said he never took payola; two days later his TV gig was gone too. He would eventually plead guilty to commercial bribery charges in return for a five-hundred-dollar fine and a six-month suspended sentence. His reputation tattered, Freed died an alcoholic five years later.

Rock and Roll 1.0 was essentially finished. Leonard and Phil found themselves in the unusual position of being a step behind the black popular market. While Mahalia moved into the mainstream, black popular music was drawing more on gospel's old sense of community and identity; the Me of the blues was feeling a bit too personal in the days of Little Rock, Montgomery, and Martin Luther King. Gospel increasingly shared ownership of the We in black music with artists like Ray Charles, who'd adapted gospel energy and forms to R&B, crossover acts such as former Soul Stirrer and Wendell Phillips High alum Sam Cooke, and in 1958 the

Impressions—two kids from the Cabrini Homes named Jerry Butler and Curtis Mayfield, members of the Northern Jubilee Gospel Singers of the Traveling Souls Spiritualist Church, whose song "For Your Precious Love," cut at Universal, is considered by many the first soul recording.

Chess's neighbor on Michigan Avenue, black-owned Vee-Jay, had been on to this from its start in the early 1950s, when Vivian and James Bracken (Vee and Jay) and her brother Calvin, in two years, took their Gary record store to a building on the 2000 block of South Michigan Avenue; Leonard and Phil had moved Chess to be closer to *them*. On the strength of acts like the Spaniels ("Goodnight, Sweetheart"), the El Dorados, the Dells, Gladys Knight and the Pips, the Duke of Earl, and "The Shoop Shoop Song," Vee-Jay was on the brink of becoming the first major black-owned record label. To catch up, Leonard enlisted Harvey Fuqua of the Moonglows to help sign the baby-faced and voluptuous Etta James away from the Bihari brothers in 1959, using her as a writer and at first a background singer for Chuck Berry. Along with receptionist Minnie Riperton, big, brassy, sensuous James, a mix of Nell Carter and Beyoncé, brought a female sound to Chess. Her first hit for the label, "All I Could Do Was Cry," was intended by Berry Gordy for Aretha Franklin, but James charted it in May 1960; her signature "At Last" came at year's end.

As Muddy began his set in Newport, it was immediately clear that white America had come a long way since Mahalia held that special tutorial on clapping at Music Inn; the crowd in their wooden folding chairs at Freebody Park in Newport, probably 90 percent white, managed to clap, tap, and otherwise move their bodies in reasonable fashion to what Muddy, Otis Spann on piano, and guitarists James Cotton and Pat Hare served up. Muddy was in prime form for one of the greatest sets of his career, or at least the greatest we still can see; the United States Information Agency was filming him as a newfound national treasure. All tight and smart in his gray suit and conk, he radiated energy and playful sexuality, yet he also sounded suddenly mature after all those years of jittery, back-seat-at-the-drive-in rock and roll. Muddy couldn't help himself; his feet skipped, his right hand came up chest high, and he snapped his fingers.

He'd pulled the Coke bottle trick himself once or twice, so he got his hips going as he launched into "I've Got My Mojo Working." A few minutes in, he grabbed James Cotton and did a little foxtrot that he followed with five seconds of sly, swift, quick-stepping. Muddy was back on top.

The blues had endured by doing what they'd always done—they'd adapted to new surroundings. Chess, and Chicago, became a pilgrimage site. Willie Dixon returned, bringing along new talent from Cobra and taking over the Chess blues division as "the Mayor Daley of the Blues." The main beneficiary was Howlin' Wolf. Into the early 1960s, Dixon fed him emblematic songs like "Spoonful" and "Wang Dang Doodle." Though he'd never achieve the stardom that Muddy and B.B. King would flirt with, Wolf's band found its ultimate gut-churning sound with Hubert Sumlin up front alone on guitar, earning just enough fame and just enough money.

Willie Dixon had come back to replace Malcolm Chisholm, who left Chess in November 1959 to follow Bill Putnam to Los Angeles. Selling out his interest in his just-built Universal Recording Studios on Walton, Putnam constructed a new state-of-the-art facility, where he'd fall in with the Rat Pack and produce everything from the Beach Boys' *Pet Sounds* to all of Sinatra's Reprise work, training a generation of music producers. Putnam's absence would devastate Chicago's position in the music business; fewer big-name talents came to the city now for anything other than a few nights on tour. With the postwar wave of independent labels shaken out and its genius producer gone, Universal would still remain the prime recording location for the rise of Chicago soul and the smooth sounds of Curtis Mayfield, Jackie Wilson, and the Five Stairsteps.

Chess entered the 1960s neck and neck with Atlantic Records. While Berry was serving twenty months in federal prison, Leonard bought a small, ethnic radio station in Chicago and turned it into WVON. Marshall graduated from New Trier High School and tried a few years of college before coming home to 2120 S. Michigan to learn the family business. In 1964 the Rolling Stones made their first pilgrimage to the South Side (though Keith Richards's famous story about Muddy being forced to paint the ceiling is entirely false). As the decade progressed, Atlantic and Motown, seeded in part with Leonard's money, raced past Chess, suffering like the city as a whole from the new bicoastal culture. Marshall tried to catch up with experiments blending blues and rock, but the results were mixed, to be kind, and just when he thought his father was about to hand him the keys to the family business, Leonard and Phil sold it all in 1969. Leonard died that October, and Chess began its slow fade. By the 1970s the city's recording industry would be largely devoted to advertising jingles. Now that a major corporation owned Chess, former artists who'd had a "family" relationship with Leonard forced the books to be reopened, revealing the mess of numbers that didn't always add up, the shifting of money from one artist to another, the deals with ARC Music and casting the worst possible eye on Chess and especially Leonard, who'd shouted "motherfucker" for twenty years with more affection and respect than anger. For him, it had always been simple: "I made my money on the Negro and I want to spend it on him." The Chess brothers weren't heroes, but they weren't entirely villains. They'd lived in a uniquely Chicago way—creatively, commercially, racially, and ethically in the crossroads, the place where you go to meet new opportunities, and the devil.

The blues were enshrined as one of Chicago's cultural institutions, but as a regional specialty to be preserved rather than the mainstream force soul became in black popular music. As the city's commercial business produced Earth, Wind & Fire and Donny Hathaway, and a former WVON disk jockey named Don Cornelius debuted *Soul Train* on WCTIU-TV, the blues stuck alongside rock, a largely white form of music, in a way that could feel like assimilation when too many drunk frat boys are involved. But since the start of the Great Migration, the black Me in Chicago has always confronted the assumed black We, whether We meant Old Settlers, Communists, Strivers, or Black Muslims. Muddy, Wolf, Walter, and all their successors sang in the individual voice that helped black Chicagoans endure the Daley years as much as it helped cause them.

THE PAEPCKES AND their circle now spent much of their time amid Aspen's clouds. Still running the show at his Aspen Institute of Humanistic Studies, Walter exuded "the slightly harassed air of a patron who must also be ringmaster for a three-ring circus." Corporate executives, high-end academics, and the occasional government type reported to the gymnasium at nine a.m. for exercise, then sauna and health lectures, followed by lunch and the afternoon Great Books class. The day usually finished with a concert in the Saarinen tent. "Rebellion," said *Horizon,* "is frowned upon."

Paepcke had intended to illuminate America by creating an intellectual bonfire atop the Rockies, but the last ten years had made the light beaming from Hugh Hefner's pretend penthouse look a lot more tempting. The speakers who came these days, John Kenneth Galbraith, Adlai Stevenson, Herbert Marcuse, William Whyte, warned that Americans demanding satisfaction in the marketplace and nothing from themselves boded poorly for the nation's prospects. Paepcke and his guests had only themselves to blame. Hitching corporate money and power to high culture had seeded many good things, but democratizing the arts and knowledge was a Faustian bargain: it put them into the marketplace where the market would determine their "value." Since the days when Paepcke had first backed Moholy, art's valued power had shifted dramatically from its ability to change the world to its ability to command sales.

Paepcke's old friend Robert Maynard Hutchins had gone into the knowledge industry, with little effect. He washed out at the Ford Foundation after ladling out millions of dollars for pet projects such as Adler's Institute for Philosophical Research and its charge to make "a dialectical examination of Western humanistic thought," all the while displaying the same arrogance and unprocessed idealism he had in Hyde Park. The balance of Hutchins's life was spent amid increasing insignificance, running think tanks and funds where he supported civil rights and civil liberties in the most sanitary fashion possible, usually paying very august white men to sit in a room and discuss a designated topic, which he followed up with a report. As to actually encountering the less fortunate,

Hutchins was said to be "physically uncomfortable with people from minority groups who lacked extensive formal education." The generations of brilliant thinkers that his college produced lend the only heft to a legacy of well-paid-for words and ideas unhitched to action.

Paepcke had taken a different approach with the Institute of Humanistic Studies. A member of a vanishing species, he was a conservative Republican devoted to humanism and the upper reaches of intellectualism; he wanted his Container Corporation of America to sell boxes, but he also sincerely wanted to disseminate high culture, with energy, joy, and responsibility. Boondoggles that they may have been for many executives— even a favorable write-up in *Horizon* asked if it was "really any more than another and slightly more sophisticated manifestation of Chautauqua"— Aspen conferences maintained that Weimar flame by expressing Paepcke's appetite for life and connection to the world. It's impossible to gauge the effect of a place like Aspen on human history, and therein lies its beauty. There was no way to commodify it, no way to put a price tag or measure what it produced. In his time, Walter Paepcke had not just supported Moholy-Nagy and the Institute of Design, but he'd been one of the foremost patrons of Modernism in America, devoted to bringing art, design, and high-minded thought to the widest possible audience. The passing of Chicago's Medici on April 13, 1960, closed the era of The Third Coast.

IN CHICAGO
FOR MY FOREVER

FOUR MEN ARMED with crowbars and saws climbed over the rubble of the first floor, up the stairs to the shell of the second, trying not to be seen or heard. If anyone had been near, their clouds of breath would have given them away, but this old three-story town house a few blocks from the IIT campus stood alone, and the wrecking crew turned their heads for the right price. Richard Nickel had already photographed the building, so now this November day they were prying out balusters and pieces of ceiling that he'd bring back to his parents' house in Park Ridge. To their unhappy neighbors, it was a salvage yard, but in fact it was the world's finest collection of Louis Sullivan ornament.

Nickel directed the three; he'd first come upon them at the Lindauer House over on Wabash, IIT students cutting class to tear out ornament of which he considered himself the rightful custodian. They shared his love for Sullivan's work and were willing to work hard, so they were useful, but by now Nickel's deepest relationship was with Sullivan, trying to preserve what he could before the city destroyed all traces of the man who'd come closest to finding Chicago's "great soul." He'd tried to move ahead on the *catalogue raisonné*, but he seemed to freeze, worried that he was unqualified, though by now no one knew more about Sullivan than him. When the buildings started to fall, it was more important, and easier, to put away the manuscript and take out his crowbar. Three blocks from Mies's campus, one of the sacred spots of modern architecture, he opened the hatch of his station wagon so the boys could load in a lintel. The past year had been especially devastating—six homes or stores had either come down or been put in the path of the wrecking ball in 1958, including the one they were picking through today, the Henry Stern House at 2915 S. Prairie, once a mansion in a neighborhood of mansions, now just a hulk in a sea of open land. Two months later, it and the Lindauer House, with its three-story tower and pyramid roof, were gone. Nickel researched through much of 1959 and into 1960, as the Samuel Stern House and the expansive Babson House in Riverside came down, two of the almost six thousand structures wrecked in Chicago between September 1957 and April 1960.

The spree climaxed in January 1960, when Balaban and Katz announced plans to pull down Sullivan's Garrick Theater for a parking lot to serve the new Civic Center, in the works across the street. Built in 1890, the Garrick had never achieved the prominence in Chicago that it had elsewhere; critics compared it to the Parthenon in importance for spreading the idea of the skyscraper east. A square pillar three bays wide and seventeen stories high, buttressed halfway up on each side by another bay of windows, Sullivan had intentionally pulled it back from the edges of the lot to emphasize its height. The theater inside was a jewel: arches decorated in Sullivan's lacy geometric designs vaulted over the seats. After ten years serving its intended use as a venue for German operas, it became a stop on the vaudeville circuit, and then spun slowly downward. For a while WBKB used it as a television studio until its life now as a movie theater. Its once light-brown facade was black, further disfigured by a neon sign for the Ham n' Egger on the ground floor. Without question it needed renovation, but after the Robie House battle, tearing it down for a parking lot seemed an act of conscious vandalism. Balaban and Katz scheduled a June 1 demolition.

Heretofore a private man, Nickel made his obsession a public cause. He wrote letters, took photos, asked architects and critics like Le Corbusier, Josep Lluís Sert, Lewis Mumford, Alfred Caldwell, and Frank Lloyd Wright's widow Olga to petition Mayor Daley and to raise the $3.5 million needed to save the Garrick. The press picked up the story. Only the *Sun-Times* was fully on his side, but Nickel had created enough of a stir to make City Hall stop and think. Although Alderman Leon Despres's motion to block the wrecking permit didn't pass, it was blocked from higher up, and a hearing was scheduled to decide the Garrick's fate. A smiling Richard Nickel began picketing in front. Maybe, before it was too late, Chicago had learned to value something about itself more than money.

Explorer 1 CIRCLED the Earth. On a Saturday night at a packed Budland, the Arkestra played, wearing the strangest getups anyone had ever seen on a bandstand. Alton Abraham had purchased all the costumes from a defunct opera company, so now Sun Ra, hearkening back to his early days with Sir Oliver Bibb, put the band in sequined capes, silly hats, and puffy-sleeved shirts that had once belonged to Rhine Maidens and the townspeople of Seville. Then he wound up some toys and let them loose on the stage, whirling around and shooting sparks. This wasn't just jazz anymore—the Arkestra was creating performance art.

Between sets, Cadillac Bob pulled Sun Ra aside and told him he was "playing too far out for the people." That was it. Sun Ra prepared for departure, not from Planet Earth this time, but from Chicago. In June 1960 he brought the Arkestra into a series of marathon recording sessions that produced some forty numbers, almost all of them space-oriented, enough for four LPs over the next decade. Alton Abraham got them an autumn gig in Montreal, and the Arkestra left town for good. Decades later, after riots, moon landings, and international fame, Sun Ra would turn one night to a restless audience at the Auditorium. "Twenty years ago I was warning you of things," he shouted, "and you did not understand!"

CARL SANDBURG AND Eleanor Roosevelt came to Mayor Daley with the same request: Give Adlai one more chance. Summer of 1960, convention season again, and in the hunt for the Democratic nod along with

Hubert Humphrey, Lyndon Baines Johnson, and Stuart Symington was Daley's friend John F. Kennedy. Stevenson as usual neither stepped forward nor backed off, in hopes that a Kennedy stumble at the convention in Los Angeles would bring Daley back to his side. The mayor, now a national kingmaker, made no promises. Some of the Machine old guard weren't thrilled about how he'd thrown in with the Kennedy clan, especially with Bobby Kennedy digging around into labor and the Mob, but the Sunday before the convention, the mayor still emerged from the state caucus with 59½ out of 69 delegates declared for Kennedy, 6½ for Symington, two for Adlai, and one uncommitted.

On the floor of the year-old Los Angeles Memorial Sports Arena (soon to be the new home of the Lakers, moving from Minneapolis that fall), Daley ducked Stevenson until Arvey finally shamed him into taking his call. Adlai could only manage to say that he'd try very hard to defeat Nixon before Hizzoner shut him down. *You have no support,* he said. And then as the governor reeled, Daley knocked him out for good: *You didn't have any support in 1956 either; I made Illinois back you.* That conversation effectively ended Adlai Stevenson's career as an elected official, despite a grand and utterly pointless demonstration on his behalf the night of the roll call. With the television cameras focused on him, Stevenson smiled gamely next to Daley, who just looked away. Kennedy won but brushed aside Daley's demand for Symington as vice president. Nixon got the Republican nod at the Amphitheatre.

The decisive moment of the 1960 campaign took place September 26 in Chicago. After a day of preparation and relaxation, JFK headed over to WBBM on McClurg Court. A number of agreed-upon changes in the studio hadn't been made—the backdrop hadn't been painted dark, as Nixon's handlers had demanded, and some of the lighting had been moved around—somehow all things that favored the Democrat. Nixon blew in with virtually no prep and the coating of Lazy Shave over his five-o'clock shadow couldn't hide that he was under the weather and exhausted after giving a speech to the carpenters' union. On top of that, he'd cracked his knee getting out of the car. At eight-thirty p.m., after a cigarette commercial and an ad for Maybelline, Howard K. Smith introduced the candidates for the first televised presidential debate. Kennedy beamed forth vigorous and young, while Nixon in his light suit melted into the background, the Lazy Shave dripping down his cheeks. Kennedy spoke to the viewers; Nixon debated Kennedy, and for all the points he may or may not have won, he turned off millions of Americans.

The next week Kennedy swung through Chicago again. After a stop at Lake Meadows to praise integration before a crowd of seven thousand produced by Bill Dawson, he and Daley drove up in an open convertible to City Hall, where fifteen thousand Poles greeted the candidate before his address to the Polish-American Congress. Three years later Dawson and Adamowski would try to join forces to challenge the mayor, but the blacks and the Poles disliked each other more than they disliked Daley. Kennedy would seal the black vote—and in some ways Daley's power—by reaching out to Coretta Scott King after her husband's arrest a few weeks later in Atlanta. Kennedy's stock went through the roof in Black Chicago. From then on, Daley's connection to him helped the mayor in black wards, no matter how devastating his local policies were, even through Dr. King's failed attempt to organize on the West Side. On Election Day, Chicago poll watchers reported turnouts as high as 93 percent in some precincts, with huge pluralities in the Automatic Eleven but also in Catholic wards that had gone for Ike the last two times. Whether Kennedy won Illinois or Daley stole it for him will never be known conclusively, but Camelot was built of Chicago bricks.

GWENDOLYN BROOKS PUBLISHED her next book of poems, *The Bean Eaters*, early in 1960. Henry's friend Frank London Brown, author of *Trumbull Park*, gave it the review of a lifetime in the *Defender*, comparing its importance with black culture to Monk, Charlie Parker, Clifford Brown, and Billie Holiday all cutting an album together. "Her concern is with the ordinary," wrote Brown, "as our concern is with the ordinary. Her concern is with the baby milk, and blood, and cigarettes, and luck candles, and lonely cries on the third-floor-rear-three-rings of lonely brown girls left holding the trick bag." He begged black readers to buy the book; a few even did. In 1960, Margaret Burroughs and her husband opened the Ebony Museum of Negro History and Art, today known as the DuSable Museum, the first museum devoted exclusively to African American history and culture. After attending a conference in 1967, Brooks would turn away from mainstream publishing and give herself over to the Black Arts movement, yet always with her feet dug into the Prairie soil. "I intend," she told an interviewer, "to live in Chicago for my forever."

In 1968 she would finally write her long poem about a little girl abducted and murdered in the Mecca, that enormous symbol of Black Chicago where she'd once worked. "Sit where the light corrupts your face," starts "In the Mecca." "Mies van der Rohe retires from grace. / And the fair fables fall." It is her masterpiece. Mrs. Sallie loses track of her daughter Pepita, and the tragic search takes us room by room through the battered building and the lives in it, realizing Brooks's dream of thirty years before to "capsulize the gist of black humanity in general." A few pages later in the collection is a poem about a young boy who throws a brick through a pane of glass, a boy "whose broken window is a cry of art." "I shall create! If not a note, a hole / If not an overture, a desecration."

Mies would die in 1969; his grandson Dirk Lohan took over the firm. Brooks died in 2000, the poet laureate of Illinois since Carl Sandburg passed. Within the same acre of the Near South Side, she and Mies had both taught that a brick was another teacher.

IN JULY, BALABAN and Katz went to court to sue for their wrecking permit. Remarkably enough, the presiding judge shot it down. Nickel redoubled his efforts. He led groups of aldermen through the building; Alfred Caldwell delivered impassioned lectures; and Mayor Daley of all people suggested it become part of some sort of arts center. But while Nickel fought for the Garrick, other buildings came under attack, most notably Daniel Burnham's Great Northern Hotel, and the Republic and

Cable buildings, both by Holabird & Root and prime examples of the Chicago School. Nickel, who'd by now become the public face of preservation, met with William Hartmann in hopes of convincing SOM to renovate the Republic for its owner Home Federal Savings instead of destroying it, but the firm was more interested in making history than preserving it. Meanwhile letters of support for the Garrick arrived from around the world, yet all the talk about landmarking was just that—talk.

On November 1 the judge's decision was reversed. Chicago was bent on the future, no matter the cost to itself. Daley sited the new Circle Campus of the University of Illinois, thus demolishing in one stroke the striving Taylor Street neighborhood, while on the South Side, Saul Alinsky had started the Woodlawn Organization to block further moves by the University of Chicago to encroach on its black neighbors directly south. Planners like Gropius and Isaacs had never envisioned anything as sweeping as what the city devised for itself. On January 5, 1961, the fate of the Garrick fell into the hands of Mayor Daley, who could buy it if he chose to. But Hizzoner shrugged: nothing could be done. In Chicago, buildings are characters too, and the Garrick's last stay of execution was rejected. Daley's commissions and hearings had turned out to be exercises in visibility, like all the rest of his blue ribbon panels. The demolition could continue. Nickel organized a hasty salvage operation; bits of the frieze can be seen today outside the Second City Theatre on Wells.

In 1972 Nickel would die inside the shell of Sullivan's gutted Stock Exchange Building as it was being demolished, accidentally crushed by collapsing girders and debris. Largely through the hard work of architect John Vinci, who'd put together that I-Ball with Ellington and salvaged the Stern House with Nickel, its trading room has been reproduced inside the Art Institute. Twenty-one Louis Sullivan structures remain standing in Chicago.

A FEW WEEKS after turning his thumb down on the Garrick, Richard J. Daley, Sis, and five of the kids boarded the B&O's Capitol Limited along with the new governor, Otto Kerner, aide Matt Danaher, and a select group of aldermen. Mahalia Jackson and John Johnson were aboard too, all headed to Washington, D.C., for the inauguration, where the Daley family would sit in the presidential box and Mahalia would sing. Hef partied at Frank Sinatra's inaugural ball. Daley and Hef had their direct lines to power now. The rest of Chicago was on its own. Within ten years the factories would begin to close, and Chicago's disappearance from American consciousness would be all but complete, save for its cameo in the 1968 riots. The Magnificent Mile rose, and Towertown disappeared. The city survived, and in many ways it thrives—today it stands as one of the world's most powerful markets, competing with London, Paris, and Hong Kong, and its theater and architecture are the nation's finest, its tech business growing, its chefs renowned. Neighborhoods have been reclaimed and gentrified by the grandchildren of those who abandoned them. Just before Thanksgiving in 2008, President-elect Obama visited St. Columbanus, now a thriving black parish, though African Americans have begun to leave the city to return south, and Hispanics are now Chicago's largest minority group. Today it has the dubious honor of being only the third-most segregated city in America, after Milwaukee and New York.

But Chicago never became the city it could have been, the city it *should* have been. In the years since 1955, Chicago proper lost nearly one million residents as New York grew, and Los Angeles shot past to become the Second City of the twenty-first century. The advent of jets may have hurt, as of course did the end of the manufacturing economy, but the city had crippled itself with its cure, trading a functional democracy for the appearance of order, taxing its citizens to benefit its business elite, bleeding away its strength by turning "regular" into racism.

Nelson Algren stayed in Chicago, still painfully in love. "City that walks with her shoulder-bag banging her hip, you gave me your gutters and I gave you back gold. City I never pretended to love for something you were not, I never told you you smelled of anything but cheap cologne. I never told you you were anything but a loud old bag. Yet you're still the doll of the world and I'm proud to have slept in your tireless arms." He and

De Beauvoir kept in contact—including a long, awkward visit to Paris in 1960. But it all ended when she published her autobiography, *Force of Circumstance*, which reduced their affair to a "contingent love." His biting review in *Harper's* ended with the line "Will she ever quit talking?" He received the American Academy of Arts and Letters Award of Merit in 1974, and after a brief exile in Hackensack, moved to Sag Harbor, New York, where he died of a heart attack in 1980.

Simone was buried wearing his ring.

ACKNOWLEDGMENTS

It all starts with my dear friend and agent, Lisa Bankoff, who's always believed in me, even through the years when I wasn't all that sure myself. I'm eternally grateful to her for throwing down the challenge to write this book.

At The Penguin Press Eamon Dolan, God love him, took the initial leap of faith, and then Ginny Smith was there to catch me with deft grace and wisdom. Everything she's done has made *The Third Coast* a better book and me a better writer. And then there's Ann Godoff. For as long as I've known her, I've regarded her with an equal abundance of awe and affection and now I add gratitude. Thank you, Ann.

Thanks as well to the rest of the team at The Penguin Press: Kaitlyn Flynn, Yamil Anglada, and Victoria Klose, Karen Mayer, Barbara Campo, Amanda Dewey, Scott Moyers and Ben Platt, Hal Fessenden, and Janet Biehl. At ICM, Elizabeth Perrella and Dan Kirschen, Sloan Harris, and of course Esther Newberg and Binky Urban, who've known me since I had all my hair.

Research for *The Third Coast* took me into libraries, collections, museums, and homes across America and while I'm that kind of bookworm who loves to quietly dig through musty stacks of papers, my greatest pleasure came in meeting the people who lived the history. My deepest thanks go to those who agreed to be interviewed, especially Art and Florence Shay, Joan and Wayne F. Miller, David Shepherd, Ahmad Jamal, Robert Silvers, Hugh Hefner, Ivan Chermayeff, Len Gittleman, Nick von Hoffman, Kenneth Snelson, Marshall Chess, Ed Asner, Bernie Sahlins, Ed

Bland, Haki Madhubuti, and the late Dr. Margaret Burroughs. Spending time with them brought the period to life for me, but I'm most grateful for their mighty examples of energy and generosity. Thanks also to those who smoothed the way and opened doors: Susan Mieselas; Lisa Robinson, Patty Egan, Perry Zimel, and Charles Sherman at Quince Productions; Kellie Olisky, Diana Karaca, and Teri Thomerson at *Playboy;* Antoinette Simmons at the DuSable Museum; Nancy Hernandez of the Chicago Park District; Dave Barber at Chermayeff & Geismar; Andrew Stayman, Rose Perkins, and Cathy Compton at Third World Press, and Lynn Quayle.

That said, I really did love those months of digging through musty stacks of papers, and the following librarians and archivists were without exception crucial in some way to this book: Joy Weiner at the Archives of American Art; Paul Galloway at MoMA; Jason Escalante at Avery Library at Columbia University; Catherine Bruck and Ralph Pugh at the Paul V. Galvin Library at IIT; Debbie Vaughan and Erin Tikovitsch at the Chicago History Museum; Luke Hogan of the Daley Library Special Collection at the University of Illinois, Chicago; Joanne Wendel; Daniel Meyer at the Special Collections at University of Chicago; Stacy Hollander, Linda Dunne, and Ann-Marie Reilly at the American Folk Art Museum; Joy Kingsolver at the Spertus Institute of Jewish Studies; Mary Ann Gilbert at ProQuest; but especially Robert Norvell, who went to bat for me.

Permissions help came from Valerie Harris at the University of Illinois, Circle Campus; Brittany Patch at the Columbia Center for Oral History at Columbia University; Jenni Matz at the Archive of American Television, the place to begin any serious research into television history; Joanna Marshall at Immediate Media; MaryBeth Baker at Regnery; Mark Hyman at Wittenborn Art Books; Paul O'Connor and Edward Keegan at SOM; Susan Bean at Northern Illinois University Press; Frederick T. Courtright and Seven Stories Press; Neil Olson at Donadio & Olson; and the New Press.

My favorite cartographer, Marty Schnure, made the maps. Assembling the photo insert was made possible by a cast that starts with Paul Berlanga and Ana Brazaityte at Stephen Daiter Gallery; then goes to Jeffrey Goldstein and Anne Zakaras at Vivian Maier Photography; Erica DeGlopper,

Andrew Edlin, and Kiyoko Lerner; Brett Bonner, James Fraher, and Geary Chansley and Helen Ashford of Cache Agency; Mary Velasco at Getty; Whitney French; Lucas Blair Simpson and Corey Gaffer at Hedrich Blessing; Tomeka Jones and Kenneth Johnson at the Library of Congress; Ayana Haaruun at the *Chicago Defender;* Rena Schergen at the University of Chicago; Mary Woolever and Stephanie Coleman at the Art Institute of Chicago; Kaelan Kleber at Pace/MacGill Gallery; John Maloof, Alicia Colen at Howard Greenberg Gallery, and Martin Fuchs; Mirte Mallory, skilled custodian of her grandfather Ferenc Berko's work, at Berko Gallery; Allison Taich; Michael Boruch; and finally, Dr. Barbara Roosen and Maria Fernanda Meza of ARS, who do necessary and valuable work on behalf of artists worldwide.

Special thanks to my friend Art Shay, Wayne F. Miller, and the Harry Callahan Estate for their very kind permission and support, and to Hattula Moholy-Nagy, who not only extended herself so kindly on my behalf, but guided me to a deeper understanding of her parents.

Franz Schulze, professor emeritus at Lake Forest College; Matthew Frye Jacobson, Chairman of American Studies at Yale University; polymath writer and producer Anthony Heilbut; gospel music expert Bob Marovich; and three of the smartest people I know—Vijay Balakrishnan, Mark LaFramboise, and Andrew Arends—all read drafts and provided me with critical thoughts and corrections that vastly improved the book.

Intern Kristin Kury waded through decades of the *Chicago Tribune* and the incomparable Sophie Kimball made sharp sense of my piles of notes and references. Thanks also for some emergency research by Zoe Weinberg at Harvard and Jane Bartman at the University of Chicago.

The help I've received from my friends goes all the way back to college, when Matt Cooper lent me his copy of Arnold Hirsch's *The Making of the Second Ghetto* and I never gave it back. I owe him more than a replacement copy. A special thanks goes out to each of the following old friends and new ones I've made along this journey, for their kindness and assistance: Will Balliett and Karen Prager; Adam Weinberg and Lorraine Ferguson; Annik LaFarge; Meg Wolitzer and Richard Panek; Brian and

Sidney Urquhart; Rachel Urquhart; Ruth Pomerance and Rafael Prieto; Adriana Trigiani and Tim Stephenson; Susan Fales-Hill; Aimee Bell and David Kamp; Michael Guinzburg; Hilary Lewis; John Shostrom and Henry Ferris; Jonathan Cain, Corey Mesler, Ann Harris, Genevieve Young, and Joanne Lipmann; Victoria Phillips Geduld; Jill Kearney; Donald Evans; James Finn Garner; Adam Cohen; Deb Futter; Elizabeth Taylor; Kurt Thometz; Jon-Christian Suggs; Ward Miller; Ivan R. Dee; Deb Kogan; Will Amato; Bill Guerriero; record producer, DJ, and cultural spelunker-extraordinaire John Ciba (who also happens to be my nephew); Robert Feinstein and Jessica Elfenbein; Carl Bromley; Amy and Charles Ciba (my other nephew, whose copy of *Maxwell Street* I still have); Joe Zajdel; and Jeff Weidell.

My family came to Chicago from Poland, Germany, and Hungary in the 1920s, so we're not Old Settlers, but we worked in the city's factories and waited its tables; my mother taught in the archdiocese for some forty years and my sister ran restaurants on the seventh floor of Marshall Field's. In many ways this book is a gift to all of them, a celebration and an understanding of a great time in a great city. One night, as I pored through an old *Chicago Tribune* from February 1947 for details about Algren and De Beauvoir's torrid first weekend, my late father even made an appearance— there suddenly was Ed Dyja's face, seventeen and smiling, in an article about his starring role in Weber High School's production of *Brother Orchid*. Maybe that's what I was looking for all along . . .

I'd like to thank my children, Nick and Kaye, for enduring years of my rants about old bluesmen, politics, the bleachers at Wrigley Field, and Italian beef sandwiches. If nothing else, I hope they've learned to find passions in life. And finally there's my wife, Suzanne. From the moment I met her, I knew we'd end up together and marrying her was the single best thing I've done in my life.

NOTES

PREFACE

xxii "Having seen it, I urgently desire . . . by savages": Rudyard Kipling, *American Notes* (New York: Arno, 1974), p. 91.

xxii "the grandest, most spectacular . . . ever seen": William Cronon, *Nature's Metropolis: Chicago and the Great West* (New York: W. W. Norton, 1991), p. 97.

xxii "Here . . . was power": Louis Sullivan, *The Autobiography of an Idea* (New York: Dover Books, 1956), p. 196.

xxii mediated: Oleg Grabar, *The Mediation of Ornament* (Princeton, N.J.: Princeton University Press, 1995). I owe both the word *mediated* and the idea to Grabar.

xxiii In 1926 Chicago had put up: Carl Condit, *Chicago, 1930–70* (Chicago: University of Chicago Press, 1974), p. 3.

xxiv Teetering on bankruptcy: City of Chicago, *Chicago's Report to the People* (Chicago, 1947), p. 1.

xxiv out of 25,000 suicides: Milton Mayer, *Robert Maynard Hutchins: A Memoir* (Berkeley: University of California Press, 1993), p. 130.

xxiv "The customers seem to like it . . . food much": Byfield quoted in George Frazier, "Almost Anything Goes in Chicago," *Holiday*, May 1947.

xxiv America's biggest labor town: Randi Storch, *Red Chicago: American Communism at Its Grassroots, 1928–35* (Urbana: University of Illinois Press, 2007), pp. 7, 14, 19, passim; Studs Terkel with Sydney Lewis, *Touch and Go: A Memoir* (New York: New Press, 2007), p. 62.

xxiv In August 1931: Storch, *Red Chicago*, p. 31.

xxiv unemployment rates above 40 percent: Christopher Robert Reed, *The Chicago NAACP and the Rise of Black Professional Leadership, 1910–1966* (Bloomington: Indiana University Press, 1997), p. 75.

xxiv The CIO began unionizing: Sanford D. Horwitt, *Let Them Call Me Rebel: Saul Alinsky—His Life and Legacy* (New York: Alfred A. Knopf, 1989), p. 59 and passim.

xxiv Polo-playing department store heir: Frank Marshall Davis, *Livin' the Blues* (Madison: University of Wisconsin Press, 1992), p. 289.

xxvi By 1936 and the advent of the Works: Storch, *Red Chicago*, p. 219 and passim; Bill V. Mullen, *Popular Fronts: Chicago and African-American Cultural Politics, 1935–46* (Urbana: University of Illinois Press, 1999), passim; Lawrence P. Jackson, *The Indignant Generation: A Narrative History of African American Writers and Critics, 1934–1960* (Princeton, N.J.: Princeton University Press, 2011), pp. 55–57.

xxvi "These were the days": Margaret Taylor Burroughs, oral history interview, November 11–December 5, 1988, Archives of American Art, Smithsonian Institution.

xxvi The Illinois Writers' Project: Daniel Schulman, "Marion Perkins: A Chicago Sculptor Rediscovered," *Art Institute of Chicago Museum Studies* 24, no. 2 (1999), pp. 220, 243, 267, 271; Federal Writers Project, *The WPA Guide to Illinois* (New York: Pantheon, 1983), p. 297.

xxvi "the long isolation of the Negro": Margaret Walker, *Richard Wright: Daemonic Genius* (New York: Amistad, 1988), p. 78.

xxvii "Chicago reenacted [Harlem]": Robert Bone, "Richard Wright and the Chicago Renaissance," *Callaloo* 28 (Summer 1986), pp. 446–68; Mullen, *Popular Fronts,* passim; Walker, *Wright,* passim.

xxvii Up from Mississippi, Richard Wright: Jackson, *Indignant Generation,* p. 21; Walker, *Wright,* pp. 53–55.

xxvii "a luxurious collection of talent": Jackson, *Indignant Generation,* p. 58.

xxvii "By contrast with the raw, savage": Davis, *Livin' the Blues,* p. 130.

xxvii After the war, Davis moved to Hawaii: Barack Obama, *Dreams from My Father* (New York: Broadway, 2004), pp. 76–77.

xxvii "Beyond being regular": Nelson Algren, *Never Come Morning* (New York: Harper & Brothers, 1942), p. 133.

xxviii "Always keep neat and never drink": Kelly quoted in "Funeral of a Boss," *Life,* November 6, 1950.

xxviii a thick slice of the $20 million or so: Len O'Connor, *Clout* (New York: Avon Books, 1976), pp. 54–55.

xxix In the absence of meaningful civic coordination: Nicholas von Hoffman, interview by author.

xxix "There can be no new New York": Louis Sullivan, *Kindergarten Chats and Other Writings* (New York: Wittenborn Art Books, 1947), p. 111.

xxx Through its twenty-six train lines: Chicago Public Schools Division of Curriculum, *Chicago* (Chicago: King, 1955), p. 136.

xxxi "City of Indifference": Sullivan, *Kindergarten Chats,* p. 109.

xxxii "a fresh time": H. E. F. Donohue, *Conversations with Nelson Algren* (New York: Hill & Wang, 1963), p. 330.

xxxiv "Subtract what Chicago has given": *Chicago* (pilot issue, 1953).

PRE-1945
CHAPTER 1: THE BRICK IS ANOTHER TEACHER

3 *Hand it all back to the Indians:* Carl Condit, *Chicago, 1930–70* (Chicago: University of Chicago Press, 1974), p. 51.

4 "greatest of machines": Frank Lloyd Wright, "The Art and Craft of the Machine," in *Writings and Buildings,* ed. Edgar Kaufman

and Ben Raeburn (1974; New York: Meridian, 1995), p. 73.

4 "superficial blah or labored lip service": Frank Lloyd Wright, *Frank Lloyd Wright: An Autobiography* (1932; reprint New York: Pomegranate Press, 2005), p. 429; Columbia University, *Four Great Makers of Modern Architecture: Gropius, Le Corbusier, Mies van der Rohe, Wright* (New York: Columbia University, 1961), p. 106.

4 Gwendolyn Brooks didn't tell anyone: George E. Kent, *A Life of Gwendolyn Brooks* (Lexington: University Press of Kentucky, 1990); Gwendolyn Brooks, *Report from Part One* (Detroit: Broadside Press, 1972), p. 42.

5 Apartment life had still been a new concept: Daniel Bluestone, "Chicago's Mecca Flat Blues," *Journal of the Society of Architectural Historians* 57 (December 1998), pp. 382–403.

5 "To touch every note in the life": Brooks, *Report,* p. 189.

5 In the days of the "Old Settlers": Allen Spear, *Black Chicago: The Making of a Negro Ghetto, 1890–1920* (Chicago: University of Chicago Press, 1967), pp. 16–22.

6 By World War I the Levee was gone: Joseph Spillane, "The Making of an Underground Market: Drug Selling in Chicago, 1900–1940," *Journal of Social History* 32 (Autumn 1998), pp. 27–47; Lloyd Wendt and Herman Kogan, *Lords of the Levee: The Story of Bathhouse John and Hinky Dink* (Indianapolis: Bobbs-Merrill, 1943), passim; Spear, *Black Chicago,* pp. 25–26; St. Clair Drake and Horace Cayton, *Black Metropolis: A Study of Negro Life in a Northern City* (New York: Harcourt Brace, 1945), p. 55.

6 "Chicago . . . was to the southern Blacks of my generation": John Johnson, *Succeeding Against the Odds: The Autobiography of a Great American Businessman* (New York: Amistad, 1989), p. 57.

6 "the trials, tribulations, and tragedies": "The Mecca Flats Blues," *Chicago Tribune,* March 29, 1943.

6 "a creation of white hostility": Spear, *Black Chicago,* p. 26.

6 more restrictive covenants in place: Beryl Satter, *Family Properties: Race, Real Estate, and the Exploitation of Black Urban America* (New York: Henry Holt, 2009), p. 40.

7 **"We do not care if the barns rot down":** Richard Wright, *12 Million Black Voices* (1941; reprint New York: Thunder's Mouth Press, 1988), p. 57.

7 **Chicago's slums . . . the worst in the nation:** Harvard Graduate School of Design Alumni Association, *The Institution as a Generator of Urban Form* (Cambridge, Mass.: Harvard Graduate School of Design, 1961), pp. 27–33.

7 **"it was as if somebody had pulled a switch":** Mahalia Jackson with Evan McLeod Wylie, *Movin' On Up* (New York: Hawthorn Books, 1966), p. 51.

7 **"kitchenettes":** Drake and Cayton, *Black Metropolis*, pp. 576–77. An absolutely seminal book on Black Chicago.

7 **Rats abounded:** Arnold Hirsch, *The Making of the Second Ghetto: Race and Housing in Chicago, 1940–1960* (Cambridge, Mass.: Cambridge University Press, 1983), pp. 18–20.

7 **"The kitchenette . . . is the funnel":** Wright, *12 Million Black Voices*, p. 111.

8 **Historically, Chicago's government had lacked interest:** Carl Smith, *The Plan of Chicago: Daniel Burnham and the Remaking of the American City* (Chicago: University of Chicago, 2006), passim; Hirsch, *Making of the Second Ghetto*, passim.

9 **"jungle Negro":** "Brick Slayer Is Likened to Jungle Beast," *Chicago Tribune*, June 5, 1938.

9 **"Mr. Van der Rohe says he is sorry":** Franz Schulze, *Mies van der Rohe: A Critical Biography* (Chicago: University of Chicago Press, 1985). Schulze's, now in a second edition, is the definitive biography of Mies: Franz Schulze and Edward Windhorst, *Mies van der Rohe: A Critical Biography*, rev. ed. (Chicago: University of Chicago Press, 2012).

9 **"show that technology not only promises":** Fritz Neumeyer, *The Artless Word: Mies van der Rohe on the Building Art*, trans. Mark Jarzombek (Cambridge, Mass.: MIT Press, 1991).

10 **On his way out, Heald:** Columbia, *Four Great Makers of Modern Architecture*, p. 106.

10 **a city Mies claimed never to think:** Schulze, *Mies van der Rohe*, p. 218.

10 **Burnham's plan had addressed:** Smith, *Plan of Chicago*, pp. 35, 43.

11 **A few Paul Klees:** Werner Buch, oral history interview by Ines Dresel, © 2005, Art Institute of Chicago, p. 2, used with permission. The Art Institute's Chicago Architects Oral History Project is an invaluable record of this era and a starting point for anyone interested in the subject.

11 **"The people have more initiative":** Rolf Achilles, Kevin Harrington, and Charlotte Myhrum, *Mies van der Rohe: Architect as Educator* (Chicago: Illinois Institute of Technology, 1986), p. 54.

11 **"It was more as if God":** Gene Summers, oral history interview by Pauline A. Saliga, © 1993, Art Institute of Chicago, p. 12, used with permission.

12 **"the Chicago of Germany":** Elaine Hochman, *Architects of Fortune: Mies van der Rohe and the Third Reich* (New York: Weidenfeld & Nicolson, 1989), p. 29.

12 **"To see their city become a *Weltstadt*":** Ibid., p. 29.

12 **"genuine organic architecture":** Mies quoted in Neumeyer, *Artless Word*, p. 321.

13 **Father Romano Guardini:** Ibid., pp. 196–202.

13 **Guardini's struggles with the question:** Ibid., p. 201.

13 **the Glass Skyscraper:** Philip C. Johnson, *Mies van der Rohe* (New York: Museum of Modern Art, 1947), p. 26.

14 **"skin and bones construction":** Mies quoted ibid., p. 30.

14 **Sensible as that sounds, it also divorced the Bauhaus:** Hochman, *Architects of Fortune*, p. 83–84.

14 **Mies pursued as much business as he could:** Ibid., passim.

15 **"Mies is here. Benny held over":** Priestly quoted in Richard Pommer, David Spaeth, and Kevin Harrington, *In the Shadow of Mies: Ludwig Hilberseimer, Architect, Educator and Urban Planner* (New York: Rizzoli International, 1988), p. 9.

15 **A twenty-four-foot-square room:** Werner Blaser, *Mies van der Rohe: IIT Campus* (Basel: Birkhauser, 2002), p. 8.

15 **"with far-off country roads, soybean fields":** Mitchell Schwarzer, "Forms of the Grid," in Charles Waldheim and Katerina Ruedi Ray, eds., *Chicago Architecture: Histories, Revisions, Alternatives* (Chicago: University of Chicago Press, 2005), p. 198.

15 **Mies did not speak English regularly:** Columbia, *Four Great Makers of Modern Architecture*, p. 106.

16 **"learned menu English":** Charles Booher Genther, oral history interview by Betty J. Blum, © 2003, Art Institute of Chicago, p. 7, used with permission.

16 ***"schrecklich":*** Katharine Kuh, interview by Avis Berman, *Archives of American Art Journal* 27, no. 3 (1987), pp. 2–36.

16 **"more necropolis than metropolis":** Hilberseimer quoted in Pommer, Spaeth, and Harrington, *Shadow of Mies*, p. 17.

17 **"with a committee of the faculty":** Columbia, *Four Great Makers of Modern Architecture*, p. 107.

17 **"reluctant landlord":** "Owners Doom Mecca Flats, Slum Tenement," *Chicago Tribune*, May 23, 1950.

17 **the corner where the Mecca stands:** Phyllis Lambert, ed., *Mies in America* (New York: Harry Abrams, 2001), p. 226. Along with Schulze's biography, this lush volume is necessary for any study of Mies post-1938.

17 **anti-Communist stickers . . . racist jokes:** See, for example, Sterling Morton to Henry T. Heald, October 14, 1946, Henry T. Heald Papers, no. 1998.049, Box 13, Board of Trustees Correspondence, September 1946–47, IIT Archives, Paul Galvin Library, IIT.

17 **reputation as a glorified technical school:** Ambrose M. Richardson, oral history interview by Betty J. Blum, © 2005, Art Institute of Chicago, p. 21, used with permission.

18 **"IIT was in a slum":** Summers interview by Saliga, p. 7.

18 **"one vast slum":** Myron Goldsmith, oral history interview by Betty J. Blum, © 2001, Art Institute of Chicago, p. 48, used with permission.

18 **"Because it has been planned to wreck":** Building and Grounds Committee, December 13, 1944, Henry T. Heald Papers, no. 1998.049, Box 2, Building Program, 1941–1944, IIT Archives, Paul Galvin Library, IIT.

18 **The housing shortage may have:** Daniel Schulman, "Marion Perkins: A Chicago Sculptor Rediscovered," *Art Institute of Chicago Museum Studies* 24, no. 2 (1999).

18 **"Frenchite pastry":** Frank Lloyd Wright, *In the Cause of Architecture* (New York: McGraw-Hill, 1987).

18 **"did pretty poorly compared":** Goldsmith interview by Blum, p. 7.

18 **"Step I is an investigation":** Reginald F. Malcolmson, "A Curriculum of Ideas," *Journal of Architectural Education* 14 (Autumn 1959), pp. 41–43; Achilles, Harrington, and Myhrum, *Mies van der Rohe*, pp. 55–56.

18 **"the harmonious unfolding":** Ibid., p. 55.

18 **after their year of learning how to render:** Werner Buch, oral history interview by Ines Dresel, © 2005, Art Institute of Chicago, p. 6, used with permission.

18 **"The brick is another teacher":** Mies quoted in Neumeyer, *Artless Word*, p. 316.

19 **"through the different tiers":** Malcolmson, "Curriculum of Ideas."

19 **"He stood up front and very calmly":** Buch interview by Dresel, p. 4.

19 **Many German intellectual émigrés:** Anthony Heilbut, *Exiled in Paradise* (New York: Viking Press, 1983), p. 58.

19 **Rather than concentrate on how people used buildings:** Bertrand Goldberg, oral history interview by Betty J. Blum, © 1992, Art Institute of Chicago, p. 72, used with permission.

19 **His fixation on sunlight:** Pommer, Spaeth, and Harrington, *Shadow of Mies*, p. 11.

20 **"Students were not allowed to express":** Achilles, Harrington, and Myhrum, *Mies van der Rohe*, p. 61.

20 **"Ja, but you must be careful":** Mies quoted in Schulze, *Mies van der Rohe*, p. 233.

21 **"he came here simply because":** "Skilled German Architect Likes Freedom of U.S.," *Chicago Tribune*, March 21, 1943.

21 **"Questions of a general nature":** Mies quoted in Neumeyer, *Artless Word*, p. 246.

22 **"What does mankind need":** Mies quoted ibid., p. 204.

CHAPTER 2: WE WERE PART OF THEM

23 **"In the Mecca . . . were murder, loves":** Gwendolyn Brooks, *Report from Part One* (Detroit: Broadside Press, 1972), p. 22.

23 **"Chicago is the city":** Richard Wright, introduction to St. Clair Drake and Horace Cayton, *Black Metropolis: A Study of Negro Life in a Northern City* (New York: Harcourt Brace, 1945), p. xvii.

23 **This oldest section of the Black Belt:** Bernard C. Turner, *A View of Bronzeville* (Chicago: Highlights of Chicago Press, 2002), p. 43; Brooks, *Report from Part One*, p. 160.

24 **"We had no idea":** Ronne Hartfield, *Another Way Home: The Tangled Roots of Race in One Chicago Family* (Chicago: University of Chicago Press, 2004), p. 101.

24 **"Respectables":** Drake and Cayton, *Black Metropolis*, chaps. 19–22, covers the nuances of black class differences in great detail.

24 **"Do not loaf":** Reproduced in James R. Grossman, *Land of Hope: Chicago, Black Southerners, and the Great Migration* (Chicago: University of Chicago Press, 1989), p. 147.

25 **"the lady Paul Laurence Dunbar":** Brooks, *Report from Part One*, p. 56. The primary books on the life of Gwendolyn Brooks are her two-volume autobiography, *Report from Part One* and *Report from Part Two*; D. H. Melhem, *Gwendolyn Brooks: Poetry and the Heroic Voice* (Lexington: University Press of Kentucky, 1987), which is more of a critical biography; and George E. Kent, *A Life of Gwendolyn Brooks* (Lexington: University Press of Kentucky, 1990), which is the definitive record, written with the poet's cooperation.

25 **"freely, often on the top step":** Brooks, *Report from Part One*, p. 55.

25 **"I had not brass or sass":** Ibid., p. 38.

25 **"I was timid to the point":** Ibid., p. 57.

25 **"young radical":** Margaret Taylor Burroughs, oral history interview, November 11–December 5, 1988, Archives of American Art, Smithsonian Institution.

26 **"Hey, boy, this girl":** Burroughs quoted in Brooks, *Report from Part One*, p. 58.

26 **all integrated and politically oriented:** Margaret Walker, *Richard Wright: Daemonic Genius* (New York: Amistad, 1988), p. 80.

26 **At the Youth Council:** Kent, *Life of Brooks*, p. 47; Timothy J. Gilfoyle, "Culture Makers: Interviews with Timuel Black and Margaret Burroughs," *Chicago History* 36, no. 3 (Winter 2010).

26 **Freddie Keppard, King Oliver:** William Howland Kenney, *Chicago Jazz: A Cultural History, 1904–1930* (New York: Oxford University Press, 1993), pp. 40–43.

27 **The strip of clubs:** Ibid.; Paul Eduard Miller, ed., *Esquire's 1946 Jazz Book* (New York: A.S. Barnes, 1946). The book has a terrific map of Chicago nightlife in the 1920s and '30s.

28 **"If You See My Savior":** John Russick and Gwen Ihnat, "That's Good News! Chicago and the Birth of Gospel Music," *Chicago History* 29, no. 1 (Winter 2000), pp. 22–37.

28 **Mahalia Jackson, who'd arrived:** Jackson's three primary biographies are: her autobiography, Mahalia Jackson and Evan McLeod Wylie, *Movin' On Up* (New York: Hawthorn Books, 1966), which feels like something she signed her name to; Jules Victor Schwerin, *Got to Tell It: Mahalia Jackson, Queen of Gospel* (New York: Oxford University Press, 1994), a more cutting take; and Laurraine Goreau, *Just Mahalia, Baby* (Waco, Tex: Word Books, 1975), an almost stream-of-consciousness record of her life written with her cooperation. Anthony Heilbut's profile in *The Gospel Sound: Good News and Bad Times* (1975; New York: Limelight, 1987) and his take of her in *The Fan Who Knew Too Much* (New York: Knopf, 2012) are also useful as a view from someone not entirely taken by the Mahalia mythos. Thanks also to Bob Marovich for his insights into Chicago gospel in the 1930s.

28 **"for her hollering and getting":** Heilbut, *Gospel Sound*, p. 62.

29 **"This is the way we sing":** Goreau, *Just Mahalia*, p. 55.

29 **"established for the modern dancer":** Joyce Aschenbrenner, *Katherine Dunham: Dancing a Life* (Urbana: University of Illinois Press, 2002), p. 109.

29 **"I had it in my mind":** Goreau, *Just Mahalia*, p. 79.

30 **George Balanchine brought in Dunham:** Aschenbrenner, *Katherine Dunham*, p. 125.

30 **"how to . . . shake at the right time":** Davarian L. Baldwin, *Chicago's New Negroes: Modernity, the Great Migration, and Black Urban Life* (Chapel Hill: University of North Carolina Press, 2007), p. 182.

31 **"huge Louis Sullivan house":** Bettina Drew, *Nelson Algren: A Life on the Wild Side* (New York: Putnam, 1989), pp. 101–2.

31 **Gordon introduced his students:** Margaret Taylor Burroughs, oral history interview,

November 11–December 5, 1988, Archives of American Art, Smithsonian Institution; Daniel Schulman, "Marion Perkins: A Chicago Sculptor Rediscovered," *Art Institute of Chicago Museum Studies* 24, no. 2 (1999); Bill V. Mullen, *Popular Fronts: Chicago and African-American Cultural Politics, 1935–46* (Urbana: University of Illinois Press, 1999).

31 **"Margaret . . . *lived up from the root*":** Gwendolyn Brooks, *Report from Part One* (Detroit: Broadside Press, 1972), p. 69.

31 **"Art itself should be used as a weapon":** Burroughs oral history interview, November 11–December 5, 1988, Archives of American Art, Smithsonian Institution.

32 **Richard Wright's *Native Son:*** On this controversy, see Lawrence P. Jackson, *The Indignant Generation: A Narrative History of African American Writers and Critics, 1934–1960* (Princeton, N.J.: Princeton University Press, 2011); and Mullen, *Popular Fronts*. Walker's personal and still embittered take on him in *Daemonic Genius* makes for fascinating reading. Other crucial sources on the Chicago Black Renaissance include Margaret Walker, *This Is My Century* (Athens: University of Georgia Press, 1989); Burroughs's autobiographies; and Robert Bone, "Richard Wright and the Chicago Renaissance," *Callaloo* no. 28 (Summer 1986). Mullen, *Popular Fronts*, is probably the most comprehensive.

33 **"As young black artists":** Burroughs oral history interview, November 11–December 5, 1988, Archives of American Art, Smithsonian Institution.

33 **"You'll be raped":** Brooks, *Report from Part One*, p. 65.

33 **"in droves":** Ibid., p. 59.

33 **"If you wanted a poem":** Ibid., p. 69. The definitive edition of Brooks's poetry is *Blacks* (Chicago: Third World Press, 1987).

34 **"served cheap red wine":** Brooks, *Report from Part One*, p. 69.

34 **"tenants to move in":** Goreau, *Just Mahalia*, p. 99.

35 **"There is no race trouble in Chicago":** "Mayor Decries Fear of Race Conflict Here," *Chicago Tribune*, June 25, 1943; also quoted in St. Clair Drake, "Profiles: Chicago," *Journal of Educational Sociology* 17 (January 1944), pp. 261–71.

35 **"The race relations problem":** Mayor's Committee on Race Relations, *City Planning in Race Relations: Proceedings of the Mayor's Conference on Race Relations* (Chicago: City of Chicago, 1944).

36 **"It would be a lovely thing":** Ibid.

36 **The federal Housing Act of 1937:** D. Bradford Hunt, *Blueprint for Disaster: The Unraveling of Chicago Public Housing* (Chicago: University of Chicago Press, 2009); and Martin Meyerson and Edward C. Banfield, *Politics, Planning, and the Public Interest: The Case of Public Housing in Chicago* (Glencoe, N.Y.: Free Press, 1964), are the two seminal histories of public housing in Chicago. Arnold Hirsch, *The Making of the Second Ghetto: Race and Housing in Chicago, 1940–1960* (Cambridge, U.K.: Cambridge University Press, 1983), goes beyond them in scope. Carl Condit, *The Chicago School of Architecture* (Chicago: University of Chicago Press, 1952), p. 38, is also worth consulting.

36 **Cheap, stripped-down designs:** Hunt, *Blueprint for Disaster*, p. 47.

36 **"Hottentots":** Robert Blakely, *Earl B. Dickerson: A Voice for Freedom and Equality* (Evanston, Ill.: Northwestern University Press, 2006), p. 69.

36 **the Chicago Housing Authority (CHA):** Meyerson and Banfield, *Politics, Planning*, p. 83.

37 **"We felt it was just paradise":** Quoted in J. S. Fuerst, *When Public Housing Was Paradise: Building Community in Chicago* (Westport, Conn.: Praeger, 2003), p. 137.

37 **"an engine for upward mobility":** Ibid., p. 2.

37 **"If the grass needed cutting":** Quoted ibid., p. 77.

37 **"If I'd see a man":** Quoted ibid., p. 9.

37 **" 'Project people' was a term of pride":** Wood quoted in Studs Terkel, *Hard Times* (New York: Pantheon, 1970), p. 383.

37 **through custom and rule:** Hunt, *Blueprint for Disaster*; Fuerst, *When Public Housing Was Paradise*.

38 **"the center of a kind of left-wing cultural":** Quoted in Fuerst, *When Public Housing Was Paradise*, p. 134.

38 **Since the federal law:** Hunt, *Blueprint for Disaster*, p. 47.

38 "a personality, event, or idea": Melham, *Gwendolyn Brooks*, p. 19.

38 "Abortions will not let you forget": Brooks, *Blacks*.

39 it was Cayton who had pointed Wright: Bone, "Richard Wright and the Chicago Renaissance," pp. 446–68. Horace Cayton, *Long Old Road* (New York: Trident, 1965), is a painful telling of his tortured life.

39 "My husband and I": Brooks, *Report from Part One*, p. 72.

CHAPTER 3: WASHED UP ON A FAVORABLE SHORE

41 "along lines Bauhaus": Norma K. Stahle to László Moholy-Nagy, May 23, 1937, quoted in Terry Suhre, *Moholy-Nagy: A New Vision for Chicago* (Urbana: University of Illinois Press, 1991), p. 31.

42 "toller Brodelkessel": Walter Gropius Papers (MS Ger 208), Series III, Folder 1221, Houghton Library, Harvard University.

42 "If I didn't have to uphold": László Moholy-Nagy to Sibyl, July 16, 1937, quoted in Sibyl Moholy-Nagy, *Moholy-Nagy: Experiment in Totality* (New York: Harper & Brothers, 1950), p. 143. Sibyl's translations of her husband's letters in *Experiment in Totality*, and therefore the quotes from them herein, are expanded and poeticized versions of the German originals. Their daughter, Hattula Moholy-Nagy, cautions that her mother's book is a "widow's memoir," which means it tends to be more accurate to Sibyl's memory of him and what she wanted his legacy to be than to what the record often bears. Lloyd Engelbrecht's scholarly biography, *Moholy-Nagy: Mentor to Modernism* (Flying Trapeze Press, 2009), is factually definitive, if less emotionally powerful.

43 pronounced "schikago": László Moholy-Nagy to Sibyl, July 17, 1937, László Moholy-Nagy Papers, Archives of American Art, Smithsonian Institution.

43 "But what a lake": László Moholy-Nagy to Sibyl, July 16, 1937, quoted in Moholy-Nagy, *Experiment in Totality*, p. 144.

43 "There's something incomplete": László Moholy-Nagy to Sibyl, August 8, 1937, quoted ibid., p. 143.

43 "of a sturdy elephant": Katharine Kuh, *My Love Affair with Modern Art* (New York: Arcade, 2006), p. 79.

44 "a black hole": Schulze quoted in Sarah Whiting, "Bas-Relief Urbanism: Chicago's Figured Field," in Phyllis Lambert, ed., *Mies in America* (New York: Harry Abrams, 2001), p. 642.

44 Stationed in Galicia: Lloyd Engelbrecht, *Moholy-Nagy: Mentor to Modernism* (Cincinnati, Ohio: Flying Trapeze Press, 2009), p. 36.

44 Demobbed: Aside from Sibyl's book and the Engelbrecht bio, other starting places for Moholy in Chicago are Engelbrecht's *The Association of Arts and Industries: Background and Origins of the Bauhaus Movement in Chicago* (Ph.D. diss., University of Chicago, 1973), the definitive study of the New Bauhaus; and Suhre, *Moholy-Nagy*. Those who have added valuable information and interpretations to his life and legacy include Richard Kostelanetz, ed., *Moholy-Nagy: An Anthology* (New York: Praeger, 1970); Alain Findeli, "Moholy-Nagy's Design Pedagogy in Chicago (1937–46)," *Design Issues* 7 (Autumn 1990), pp. 4–19; Kuh, *Love Affair*; James Sloan Allen, *The Romance of Commerce and Culture* (Chicago: University of Chicago Press, 1983); and Krisztina Passuth, *Moholoy-Nagy* (New York: Thames & Hudson, 1985).

45 "Not the product": László Moholy-Nagy, *The New Vision* (New York: W. W. Norton, 1938), p. 14.

46 "The illiterate of the future": Moholy-Nagy stated and restated this idea so many times in so many ways that citing an *ur*-source seems beside the point.

46 a minor actress turned movie: Judith Paine, "Sibyl Moholy-Nagy: A Complete Life," *Archives of American Art Journal* 15, no. 4 (1975), pp. 11–16.

46 Moholy once boasted: Kuh, *Love Affair*, p. 264.

46 flimsy: Sue Ann Prince, ed., *The Old Guard and the Avant-Garde: Modernism in Chicago, 1910–1940* (Chicago: University of Chicago Press, 1990), p. 89.

46 "Moholy hater": Allen, *Romance of Commerce*, p. 56.

47 "Wanted: An American Bauhaus": Ibid., p. 48. Allen's book is central to my

understanding of Walter Paepcke and the intellectual nexus he created between Moholy, Gropius, Hutchins, and the marketplace. Also see Peter Selz's short history of the New Bauhaus and the Institute of Design in Lynne Warren, *Art in Chicago, 1945–1995* (Chicago: Museum of Contemporary Art, 1996).

47 **Rudolph Carnap had come as an émigré:** For the connections between the Vienna School and the Bauhaus, see Peter Galison, "Aufbau/Bauhaus: Logical Positivism and Architectural Modernism," *Critical Inquiry* 16 (Summer 1990), pp. 709–52. Allen, *Romance of Commerce*, picks up the thread in Chicago, via Charles Morris.

47 **"Chicago seems to me":** Author's translation, Walter Gropius Papers (MS Ger 208), Series III, Folder 1221, Houghton Library, Harvard University.

47 **"Because of Dr. Gropius' confidence":** New Bauhaus Catalog, Institute of Design Collection, Box 3, Folder 53, Richard J. Daley Library, University of Illinois at Chicago.

48 **"frenchified Yankee":** Russell Lynes, *The Tastemakers* (New York: Harper & Brothers, 1949), p. 133.

48 **"Château de Blois":** Louis Sullivan, *Kindergarten Chats and Other Writings* (New York: Wittenborn Art Books, 1947), p. 108.

48 **"absolutely corroded sight":** György Kepes, oral history interview, August 18, 1968, Archives of American Art, Smithsonian Institution.

48 **"We were among Philistines then":** Katharine Kuh, interview by Avis Berman, *Archives of American Art Journal* 27, no. 3 (1987), pp. 2–36.

48 **Eleanor Jewett:** Kuh, *Love Affair*, p. 6.

49 **C. J. Bulliet:** Sue Ann Kendall, "C. J. Bulliet: Chicago's Lonely Champion of Modernism," *Archives of American Art Journal* 26, no. 2 (1986), pp. 21–32.

49 **"The school . . . was not really":** Kepes oral history interview.

49 **"totally immersed in a program":** Nathan Lerner, "Memories of Moholy-Nagy and the New Bauhaus," in Suhre, *Moholy-Nagy*, p. 13.

50 **"art was stuff":** Nathan Lerner to Henry Holmes Smith, December 18, 1938, Institute of Design Collection, Box 7, Folder 203, Richard J. Daley Library, University of Illinois at Chicago.

50 **"Bauhaus Head Branded Flop":** *Chicago Herald Examiner*, in Walter Gropius Papers (MS Ger 208), Series III, Folder 1221, Houghton Library, Harvard University.

50 **"a first rate gangster":** Walter Gropius Papers (MS Ger 208), Series III, Folder 1221, Houghton Library, Harvard University.

51 **"Chicago is not only an unfinished canvas":** László Moholy-Nagy to Sibyl, January 5, 1939, quoted in Moholy-Nagy, *Experiment in Totality*, p. 164.

51 **"I have to manage my life":** László Moholy-Nagy to Walter Gropius, Walter Gropius Papers (MS Ger 208), Series III, Folder 1221, Houghton Library, Harvard University.

51 **"put the maximum of consciousness":** Dewey quoted in Findeli, "Moholy-Nagy's Design Pedagogy in Chicago."

52 **Moholy turned to Walter Paepcke:** Allen, *Romance of Commerce*, passim, including the quotes. For Paepcke's refusal of early entreaties, see Moholy-Nagy to Gropius, January 25, 1939, Walter Gropius Papers, Houghton Library, Harvard University.

52 **if the penniless students:** Moholy-Nagy, *Experiment in Totality*, p. 173. See also Robert J. Wolff's short description of finding the space: "About the School of Design in Chicago," Institute of Design Collection, Richard J. Daley Library, University of Illinois at Chicago.

53 **The Preliminary Course:** John Chancellor, "Institute of Design: The Rocky Road from the Bauhaus," *Chicago* 2, no. 5 (July 1955), pp. 28–35.

53 **John Cage:** Branden W. Joseph, "John Cage and the Architecture of Silence," *October* 81 (Summer 1997), pp. 80–104.

53 **"my Christ":** Unnamed student quoted in James Conrad to Henry Holmes Smith, undated, Institute of Design Collection, Box 7, Folder 203, Richard J. Daley Library, University of Illinois at Chicago.

53 **"He . . . had a million ideas":** Kuh, interview by Berman.

53 **"At the bottom of the infinite":** Filipowski quoted in Moholy-Nagy, *Experiment in Totality*, p. 176.

53 **"an electric atmosphere"**: "School of Design on Threshold of Fourth Year," *Chicago Sun,* January 3, 1942.

53 **every day in a lab coat**: David Travis and Elizabeth Siegel, eds., *Taken By Design: Photographs from the Institute of Design, 1937–1971* (Chicago: Art Institute of Chicago, 2002), p. 14.

53 **"Chicago at that time"**: Bertrand Goldberg, oral history interview by Betty J. Blum, © 1992, Art Institute of Chicago, p. 77, used with permission.

53 **a "commune" in the Stables**: Wallace Kirkland, *Recollections of a Life Photographer* (Cambridge, Mass.: Riverside Press, 1954), p. x.

53 **The Allens, at 645 N. Michigan**: Don Baum, oral history interviews, January 31 and May 13, 1986; and Miyoko Ito, oral history interview, July 20, 1978; both in Archives of American Art, Smithsonian Institution.

53 **estimated 1,500 dice girls**: Patricia Bronte, *Vittles and Vice* (Chicago: Henry Regnery, 1952), p. 15.

53 **Chicago's North Side bohemia**: Franklin Rosemont, *The Rise and Fall of the Dil Pickle* (Chicago: Charles H. Kerr, 2004), passim.

54 **"lined with cheap hotels"**: Kenneth Rexroth, *An Autobiographical Novel* (Santa Barbara, Calif.: Ross-Erickson, 1978), p. 138.

54 **"on the dry end of Pearson Street"**: Rosemont, *Rise and Fall,* p. 24.

54 **"to find Chicago's great soul"**: Bronte, *Vittles and Vice,* p. 69.

54 **"Step Down. Stoop Low"**: Slim Brundage quoted in Rosemont, *Rise and Fall,* p. 89.

54 **"the world's greatest university"**: Jacobs quoted ibid., p. 9.

55 **"We of the Dil Pickle"**: Ibid., p. 121.

55 **Rexroth's favorite, Green Mask**: Rexroth, *Autobiographical,* pp. 161–71.

55 **"a haven . . . for the broken soul"**: Stuart Brent, *The Seven Stairs* (Chicago: J. Philip O'Hara, 1962), p. 5.

55 **any sensible city planner**: Attributed to Bauer in Vernon De Mars, "Townscape and the Architect," in Coleman Woodbury, ed., *The Future of Cities and Urban Redevelopment* (Chicago: University of Chicago Press, 1953).

55 **"Art is a community matter"**: Moholy quoted in Kostelanetz, *Moholy-Nagy.*

56 **"He intended to create communities"**: Walley quoted in George J. Mavigliano, "The Chicago Design Workshop: 1939–1943," *Journal of Decorative and Propaganda Arts* 6 (Autumn 1987), pp. 34–47.

56 **"Things would get terribly gloomy"**: Chancellor, "Institute of Design."

56 **"He wears rimless glasses"**: "Moholy-Nagy Brings Life of Future—Today," *Chicago Tribune,* August 1, 1943.

56 **"painting with light"**: "Designs for a Future World—Moholy-Nagy Speaks on Art," *New York Herald Tribune,* September 14, 1941.

56 **"I think he was friendly"**: Kuh interview by Berman.

57 **"known to pull Paepcke aside"**: Allen, *Romance of Commerce,* p. 64.

57 **"I know what little interest"**: László Moholy-Nagy to Walter Paepcke, August 5, 1942, Institute of Design Collection, Box 6, Folder 183, Richard J. Daley Library, University of Illinois at Chicago.

57 **"seem to be some difficulty"**: Henry T. Heald to László Moholy-Nagy, June 22, 1942, Institute of Design Collection, Box 6, Folder 184, Richard J. Daley Library, University of Illinois at Chicago.

57 **"thoroughly disliked Moholy's"**: Kuh interview by Berman.

58 **In 1967 Mies actually "gave" the word**: Margret Kentgens-Craig, *The Bauhaus and America: First Contacts 1919–1936* (Cambridge, Mass.: MIT Press, 2001), p. 138; Mies van der Rohe to Gropius, August 18, 1967, manuscript, Ludwig Mies van der Rohe Papers, 1921–69, Library of Congress.

58 **"the definite feeling that"**: Sibyl to László Moholy-Nagy, June 8, 1942, Sibyl Moholy-Nagy Papers, Archives of American Art, Smithsonian Institution.

58 **"a total man"**: Sibyl Moholy-Nagy Papers, Archives of American Art, Smithsonian Institution. It's unclear if she actually sent these letters to her husband or if he read them, or if they just functioned as a means for Sibyl to privately blow off steam.

58 **"So, let me repeat once more"**: Walter Paepcke to László Moholy-Nagy, April 4, 1944, Institute of Design Collection, Box 6, Folder 184, Richard J. Daley Library, University of Illinois at Chicago.

CHAPTER 4: THE IDEAL WORLD OF MR. HUTCHINS

60 **its faculty and administration:** For a concise portrait of Hyde Park as an intellectual refuge, see William H. McNeill, *Hutchins' University: A Memoir of the University of Chicago, 1929–1950* (Chicago: University of Chicago Press, 1991); and Mary Ann Dzuback, *Robert M. Hutchins: Portrait of an Educator* (Chicago: University of Chicago Press, 1991), p. 80.

60 **"Living here is like living":** William Benton, quoted in Sidney Hyman, *The Lives of William Benton* (Chicago: University of Chicago Press, 1969), p. 201.

61 **"social escalator":** McNeill, *Hutchins' University*, p. 6.

61 **All this changed in 1929:** The best accounts of Hutchins's life are Dzuback, *Robert M. Hutchins*, an administrative take; McNeill, *Hutchins' University*, written from the position of a faculty member; and Milton Mayer, *Robert Maynard Hutchins: A Memoir* (Berkeley: University of California Press, 1993), an outspoken, sometimes fairly humorous, version told from Hutchins's side. Mortimer Adler, *Philosopher at Large* (New York: Macmillan, 1977), is also humorous at times but not necessarily on purpose.

62 **"that spirit of wild emotional":** Robert M. Hutchins, *The Reminiscences of Robert Maynard Hutchins* (1967), p. 43, Oral History Collection, Columbia University.

62 **"often transgressed the boundaries":** McNeill, *Hutchins' University*, p. 23.

63 **"I was an objectionable student":** Adler, *Philosopher at Large*, p. 25. In his defense, Adler was at least as damning of his own missteps as many of his worst critics, even if he wasn't sure why everyone was so angry.

63 **"explode with rage":** Ibid., p. 49.

63 **"embarrassed excitement in me":** Ibid., p. 111.

63 **"Bob confessed to me that":** Ibid., p. 128.

64 **"unfunny, ungraceful and unquiet":** Mayer, *Robert Maynard Hutchins*, pp. 106, 114.

64 **"studiously ignored":** Steven M. Avella, *This Confident Church: Catholic Leadership and Life in Chicago, 1940–1965* (Notre Dame, Ind.: University of Notre Dame Press, 1992), p. 185.

64 **Adler once compared Hyde Park:** Adler, *Philosopher at Large*, pp. 136–37.

65 **"This will be a seminary":** "What U. of Chicago Students Think About Loss of Football," *Chicago Tribune*, December 23, 1939.

65 **"The greatness of the University":** McNeill, *Hutchins' University*, p. 138.

65 **Mies made an appearance:** Kathryn Smith, "How the Robie House Was Saved," *Frank Lloyd Wright Quarterly*, 19, No. 4 (Fall 2008), pp. 4–19.

66 **"the American people [were] about":** McNeill, *Hutchins' University*, p. 100.

66 **"an instrumentality of total war":** Dzuback, *Robert M. Hutchins*, p. 216.

66 **"I didn't think they could do it":** Hutchins quoted in Mayer, *Robert Maynard Hutchins*, p. 274.

67 **"offbeat":** Robert Silvers, interview by author.

67 **"You are now members of a community":** Ibid.

67 **While Bronzeville limited IIT's future:** Dzuback, *Robert M. Hutchins*, p. 143; and Truman K. Gibson, Jr., "We Belong in Washington Park," *Chicago History* 34, no. 3 (Fall 2006), pp. 26–43.

68 **"morally offensive":** Dzuback, *Robert M. Hutchins*, p. 143.

68 **"howling mobs":** Lorraine Hansberry, *To Be Young, Gifted and Black* (New York: Signet, 1969), p. 51.

68 **"Why don't you people stay":** Gibson, "We Belong in Washington Park."

68 **"But don't ask me why":** Arnold Hirsch, *The Making of the Second Ghetto: Race and Housing in Chicago, 1940–1960* (Cambridge, U.K.: Cambridge University Press, 1983), p. 146. Hirsch's book offers an especially damning account of Hutchins in relation to race, down to some racist doggerel he once penned.

69 **Enter William Benton:** Sidney Hyman, *The Lives of William Benton* (Chicago: University of Chicago Press, 1969), veers on hagiography, but Benson's energy and accomplishments make for entertaining reading nonetheless.

69 **"a man who invented things":** Benton quoted in Studs Terkel, *Hard Times* (New York: Pantheon, 1970).

70 **passing GIs, who regarded the city:** "*Life* Sees Chicago with Serviceman," *Life,* October 19, 1942.

70 **$1.3 billion went into building:** "Chicago's Comeback," *U.S. News & World Report,* May 27, 1955.

70 **once at 40 percent, dropped to under 2:** "Employment status of the civilian noninstitutional population, 1941 to date," Bureau of Labor Statistics, U.S. Department of Labor.

PART TWO: 1945–1949
CHAPTER 5: THE CHAOS OF OUR CONCEPTIONS

75 **"All over town basements and attics":** "Apartments Wanted," *Chicago Tribune,* November 23, 1945.

76 **"Chicagoans totally ... unrepressed":** Reginald Isaacs, *Walter Gropius* (Boston: Bulfinch Press, 1991), p. 14.

77 **Earl Dickerson had sued the Palmer House:** Robert Blakely, *Earl B. Dickerson: A Voice for Freedom and Equality* (Evanston, Ill.: Northwestern University Press, 2006), p. 154. For more on Dickerson's long role in Black Chicago, see John Johnson, *Succeeding Against the Odds: The Autobiography of a Great American Businessman* (New York: Amistad, 1989), pp. 98–110.

77 **"The business people are really identified":** William Hartmann, oral history interview by Betty J. Blum, © 2003, Art Institute of Chicago, p. 18, used with permission.

77 **"our present chaotic cities ... self-contained":** Walter Gropius, *Rebuilding Our Cities* (Chicago: Paul Theobald, 1945), p. 15 and passim.

78 **"We have to go the whole hog":** Ibid., p. 26.

79 **"the chaos of our conceptions":** Ludwig Hilberseimer, *The New City* (Chicago: Paul Theobald, 1944), p. 47.

79 **"complete meals which have been":** Gropius, *Rebuilding Our Cities,* p. 27.

79 **"You start with a kitchen":** Jacques Calman Brownson, oral history interview by Betty J. Blum, © 1996, Art Institute of Chicago, p. 92, used with permission.

79 **"The idea that those in authority":** Tony Judt, *Ill Fares the Land* (New York: Penguin Press, 2010), p. 82.

80 **"forcing a re-examination":** Walter H. Blucher, "A Hospital Plans: The Michael Reese Hospital Planning Project," *Town Planning Review* 21 (January 1951), pp. 318–56.

80 **there were attempts:** Lloyd Engelbrecht, *Moholy-Nagy: Mentor to Modernism* (Cincinnati, Ohio: Flying Trapeze Press, 2009), p. 650.

80 **On July 1, 1946, at 7200 S. Eberhart:** "2,000 Surround House; Protest New Occupants," *Chicago Tribune,* July 2, 1946.

81 **Anchored to his old swivel chair:** Johnson, *Succeeding,* p. 102; Fletcher Martin and John Madigan, "The Boss of Bronzeville," *Chicago* 2, no. 4 (June 1955), pp. 22–27.

82 **"Not only for the big meetings":** Laurraine Goreau, *Just Mahalia, Baby* (Waco, Tex: Word Books, 1975), p. 61. Anthony Heilbut identified the lyrics as a play on Dorsey.

82 **"Big Bill Dawson lived a few blocks":** Ronne Hartfield, *Another Way Home: The Tangled Roots of Race in One Chicago Family* (Chicago: University of Chicago Press, 2004), p. 81.

82 **"a honeycomb of conspiracies":** Nicholas von Hoffman, *Radical: A Portrait of Saul Alinsky* (New York: Nation Books, 2010), p. 47.

82 **"Politics back then was not just":** Alvin Al Boutte quoted in Timuel Black, *Bridges of Memory* (Evanston, Ill.: Northwestern University Press, 2005), p. 272.

82 **"I make the decisions":** Dawson quoted in Blakely, *Dickerson,* p. 69.

83 **"they resent being *forced*":** St. Clair Drake, "Profiles: Chicago," *Journal of Educational Sociology* 17 (January 1944), pp. 261–71.

83 **"Those people were all Democrats":** Dawson quoted in James Q. Wilson, *Negro Politics: The Search for Leadership* (Glencoe, N.Y.: Free Press, 1960), p. 73.

83 **"In a world of negative Black images":** Johnson, *Succeeding,* p. 159.

84 **"I was a storyteller with a camera":** Wayne F. Miller, interview by author.

84 **Chicago's press, the *Defender* included:** Arnold Hirsch, *The Making of the Second Ghetto: Race and Housing in Chicago, 1940–1960* (Cambridge, U.K.: Cambridge University Press, 1983), p. 60.

85 **Jane Jacobs would later identify:** Jane Jacobs, *The Death and Life of Great*

American Cities (New York: Random House, 1961), pp. 131–32. Though Jacobs has been all but canonized by those concerned with cities, she was on the same page as Isaacs when it came to the destruction of the neighborhood. Jacobs's ideal city was the one outside her door—Greenwich Village. But all cities can't, won't, and often don't want to function that way.

85 **the archdiocese had promoted home ownership:** John T. McGreevy, *Parish Boundaries: The Catholic Encounter with Race in the Twentieth-Century Urban North* (Chicago: University of Chicago Press, 1996), p. 19.

85 **Protestants and Jews had a much lower percentage:** Philip A. Johnson, *Call Me Neighbor, Call Me Friend* (Garden City, N.Y.: Doubleday, 1965), p. 78; McGreevy, *Parish Boundaries*, p. 97.

86 **"the city's largest property owner":** Von Hoffman, *Radical*, p. 133.

86 **the nation's most progressive archdiocese:** Margery Frisbie, *An Alley in Chicago: The Life and Legacy of Monsignor John Egan* (Franklin, Wis.: Sheed & Ward, 2002), p. 31; McGreevy, *Parish Boundaries*, p. 92; Steven M. Avella, *This Confident Church: Catholic Leadership and Life in Chicago, 1940–1965* (Notre Dame, Ind.: University of Notre Dame Press, 1992), passim.

86 **Throughout the war, Bishop Sheil:** Avella, *Confident Church*, pp. 124–26.

86 **First, open housing, the right to live:** D. Bradford Hunt, *Blueprint for Disaster: The Unraveling of Chicago Public Housing* (Chicago: University of Chicago Press, 2009), pp. 104–5.

86 **whites generally believed a 15 to 20 percent:** Ibid., p. 105.

87 **sometimes on "contract":** Beryl Satter, *Family Properties: Race, Real Estate, and the Exploitation of Black Urban America* (New York: Henry Holt, 2009), goes in great depth into this practice and its devastating effect on the city and her own family. Martin Meyerson and Edward C. Banfield, *Politics, Planning, and the Public Interest: The Case of Public Housing in Chicago* (Glencoe, N.Y.: Free Press, 1964), discuss the disastrous impact of FHA policy on p. 20.

87 **"bastion . . . breached":** St. Clair Drake and Horace Cayton, *Black Metropolis: A Study of Negro Life in a Northern City* (New York: Harcourt Brace, 1945), p. 184.

87 **"a most violent though invisible":** Wood quoted in Hunt, *Blueprint for Disaster*, p. 87.

87 **"guerrilla warfare"** Hirsch, *Making of the Second Ghetto*, p. 41. On this issue, McGreevy, *Parish Boundaries*, and Satter, *Family Properties*, are also valuable.

88 **Marshall Field's still sent black shoppers:** Mamie Till-Mobley and Christopher Benson, *Death of Innocence: The Story of the Hate Crime That Changed America* (New York: Ballantine Books, 2003), p. 34.

88 **the archdiocese hoped to keep:** Avella, *Confident Church*, pp. 197–200.

89 **"The Board was not organized":** SSPB quoted in Coleman Woodbury, ed., *The Future of Cities and Urban Redevelopment* (Chicago: University of Chicago Press, 1953), p. 445.

90 **then-obscure concept of eminent domain:** "Arvey: Engineer of the New Machine," *Chicago*, July–August 1956.

90 **"the greatest Democratic ward":** Ira Berkow, *Maxwell Street: Survival in a Bazaar* (Garden City, N.Y.: Doubleday, 1977), p. 248.

90 **"It's too early to accept victory!":** "Mayor Keeps to Inner Room for Early Vote," *Chicago Tribune*, November 6, 1946.

90 **Rank and file were getting:** Mike Royko, *Boss: Richard J. Daley of Chicago* (New York: Plume, 1988), p. 55.

91 **It would have kept him:** Len O'Connor, *Clout* (New York: Avon Books, 1976), p. 57.

91 **John Fort and Letholian Waddell:** "Rocks Injure 8 in Disturbance at Vets' Home," *Chicago Tribune*, December 6, 1946; "Eight Injured in New Violence at CHA Project," *Chicago Tribune*, December 7, 1946. Hirsch, *Making of the Second Ghetto*, gives a strong account of the incident on p. 55.

91 **Kelly promised the black community:** Christopher Robert Reed, *The Chicago NAACP and the Rise of Black Professional Leadership, 1910–1966* (Bloomington: Indiana University Press, 1997), p. 147.

91 **Meanwhile the black families:** Mayerson and Banfield, *Politics, Planning*, p. 126.

91 **"all law-abiding citizens":** Hunt, *Blueprint for Disaster*, p. 81.

92 **Arvey confronted the mayor:** "Inside Story of Kelly's Fall as Party Boss,"

Chicago Tribune, December 28, 1946. See also O'Connor, *Clout;* Royko, *Boss;* and Rakove.

92 **profits and the private sector:** Hirsch, *Making of the Second Ghetto*, p. 112.

92 **"We are the government":** Wood quoted ibid., pp. 201–2.

93 **"Community Goodwill Council":** Mayerson and Banfield, *Politics, Planning*, p. 127.

93 **Thirty-five African Americans:** Hirsch, *Making of the Second Ghetto*, pp. 54–55. See also "15 Are Arrested in Housing Unit Demonstration," *Chicago Tribune*, August 15, 1947; "Police Disperse 500 Gathered At Homes Project," *Chicago Tribune*, August 16, 1947; and "1,000 Policemen Keep Order at Homes Project," *Chicago Tribune*, August 17, 1947.

93 **"It was like it was raining babies":** Bystander quoted in John Barlow Martin, "My Chicago," *Holiday*, March 1967.

93 **"know themselves what is good for them":** Isaacs quoted in Hirsch, *Making of the Second Ghetto*, p. 205.

CHAPTER 6: BELIEVERS IN THE CITY

94 **Dr. Edith Farnsworth:** Phyllis Lambert, ed., *Mies in America* (New York: Harry Abrams, 2001). Chapter 4 is especially invaluable to an understanding of Mies.

95 **"beinahe nichts":** Philip C. Johnson, *Mies van der Rohe* (New York: Museum of Modern Art, 1947).

95 **"We should attempt to bring nature":** Mies quotes in Fritz Neumeyer, *The Artless Word: Mies van der Rohe on the Building Art*, trans. Mark Jarzombek (Cambridge, Mass.: MIT Press, 1991), p. 339.

96 **she even read Guardini for him:** Franz Schulze and Edward Windhorst, *Mies van der Rohe: A Critical Biography*, rev. ed. (Chicago: University of Chicago Press, 2012).

96 **mostly rejects from the draft:** William S. Shell, *Impressions of Mies* (privately printed, 1988), p. 3.

96 **"lack of progress":** R. J. Spaeth to Ludwig Mies van der Rohe, March 12, 1945, Mies van der Rohe Archive, Architecture and Design Study Center, Museum of Modern Art.

96 **IIT approved construction:** Spaeth to Mies van der Rohe, January 16, 1946, Mies van der Rohe Archive, Architecture and Design Study Center, Museum of Modern Art.

96 **fire codes wouldn't allow:** Schulze and Windhorst, *Mies van der Rohe*, p. 226.

97 **so many talented and ambitious students:** Alfred Caldwell, oral history interview by Betty J. Blum, © 1987, Art Institute of Chicago, p. 82, used with permission.

97 **"Practically all the student body":** Reginald Malcolmson, oral history interview by Betty J. Blum, © 2004, Art Institute of Chicago, p. 42, used with permission.

97 **"We were going to rebuild the world":** Jacques Calman Brownson, oral history interview by Betty J. Blum, © 1996, Art Institute of Chicago, p. 75, used with permission.

97 **"a cult":** Reginald Malcolmson, oral history interview by Betty J. Blum, © 2004, Art Institute of Chicago, p. 42, used with permission.

97 **Alfred Caldwell:** For more on the colorful Caldwell, along with his autobiographical writings and Romantic poetry, see Dennis Domer, ed., *Alfred Caldwell: The Life and Work of a Prairie School Landscape Architect* (Baltimore: Johns Hopkins University Press, 1997).

98 **"Mies cast an aura":** Alfred Caldwell, oral history interview by Betty J. Blum, © 1987, Art Institute of Chicago, p. 83, used with permission.

98 **"Function is sweeping dirt!":** Werner Buch, oral history interview by Ines Dresel, © 2005, Art Institute of Chicago, p. 16, used with permission.

99 **"He was living, basically":** Joseph Fujikawa, oral history interview by Betty J. Blum, © 2003, Art Institute of Chicago, p. 10, used with permission.

99 **"believer in the city":** "Builder Wins Honors Here, More Elsewhere," *Chicago Daily News*, 1958, newspaper clipping, Ludwig Mies van der Rohe Papers, 1921–69, Library of Congress.

99 **cheap to build but:** Joseph Fujikawa, oral history interview by Betty J. Blum, © 2003, Art Institute of Chicago, pp. 17–19, used with permission.

99 **"It will have no outside ornamentation":** "Big Apartment Building Will Cost 1.8 Million," *Chicago Tribune*, May 4, 1947.

99 **"primitive":** Joseph Fujikawa, oral history interview by Betty J. Blum, © 2003, Art Institute of Chicago, p. 20, used with permission.

100 **"quite high-hat . . . merely a renegade":** Philip Johnson to Mies van der Rohe, June 3, 1947, manuscript, Ludwig Mies van der Rohe Papers, 1921–69, Library of Congress.

100 **Edith had volunteered:** Domer, *Alfred Caldwell*, pp. 274–75.

100 **"Much ado about":** Schulze and Windhorst, *Mies van der Rohe*, pp. 236–38.

100 **"You are the best of them all":** Ibid., p. 237.

CHAPTER 7:
A DISCOVERED BEAUTY

101 **Moholy took Claudia and Hattula:** Hattula writes about these Sunday walks (down to the piglet) in David Travis and Elizabeth Siegel, *Taken by Design: Photographs from the Institute of Design, 1937–1971* (Chicago: Art Institute of Chicago, 2002), p. 14. But most haunting are a few photos Moholy took of the girls and Sibyl in 1946, when his fate was known. These can be found in László Moholy-Nagy, *Color in Transparency* (Gottingen: Steidl, 2006), a collection of Moholy's color photographs.

101 **they'd approached Balaban and Katz:** Don Fairchild to Murrell Fischer, December 7, 1944, Institute of Design Collection, Box 1, Folder 25, Richard J. Daley Library, University of Illinois at Chicago.

101 **Every night he painted:** Sibyl Moholy-Nagy, *Moholy-Nagy: Experiment in Totality* (New York: Harper & Brothers, 1950), p. 190.

102 **It had only taken a year:** See, for example, letters from E. P. Brooks, January 10, 1945; Robert Whitelaw, July 25, 1945; and William A. Patterson, July 1945; all in Institute of Design Collection, Box 2, Folders 38, 42, 43, Richard J. Daley Library, University of Illinois at Chicago.

102 **Paepcke and Heald:** Paepcke to Heald, December 21, 1945, Institute of Design Collection, Box 2, Folder 40, Richard J. Daley Library, University of Illinois at Chicago.

102 **"Creative people don't seem to thrive":** László to Sibyl Moholy-Nagy, May 11, 1945, quoted in Moholy-Nagy, *Experiment in Totality*, p. 218. Again, the sentiment may be more accurate than the words, given Sibyl's handling of Moholy's letters.

103 **the name Harry Callahan:** There's no one standard text on Callahan, whose quiet, meditational life and long, happy marriage don't lend themselves to the curiosity of biographers. Some places to start would be Britt Salvesen, *Harry Callahan: The Photographer at Work* (New Haven, Conn.: Yale University Press, 2006); Julian Cox, *Harry Callahan: Eleanor* (Gottingen: Steidl, 2007), which features a terrific interview with Eleanor; Travis and Siegel, *Taken by Design*; and finally Harry M. Callahan, oral history interview, February 13, 1975, Archives of American Art, Smithsonian Institution.

103 **"The camera was a machine":** Harry M. Callahan, oral history interview, February 13, 1975, Archives of American Art, Smithsonian Institution.

103 **"Weeds in Snow":** Salvesen, *Callahan*, p. 27.

104 **he gave few of his thoughts:** For example, see John Szarkowski's foreword to Salvesen, *Callahan*, p. 9.

104 **"Only once in my life":** Travis and Siegel, *Taken by Design*, p. 72; Harry M. Callahan, oral history interview, February 13, 1975, Archives of American Art, Smithsonian Institution.

104 **"Oh, I only asked":** Harry M. Callahan, oral history interview, February 13, 1975, Archives of American Art, Smithsonian Institution.

105 **"Our eyes met":** Moholy-Nagy, *Experiment in Totality*, p. 234.

105 **"He knew he was dying":** Robert J. Wolff to John Thwites, December 2, 1946, Robert J. Wolff Papers, Archives of American Art, Smithsonian Institution.

105 **"I don't know about my paintings":** Moholy quoted in Wolff to Sibyl Moholy-Nagy, May 2, 1949, Robert J. Wolff Papers, Archives of American Art, Smithsonian Institution.

105 **"an unprejudiced happy child":** Gropius adapted the eulogy for the introduction to Moholy-Nagy, *Experiment in Totality*, p. viii.

105 A vocalist from the University: Minutes of the Board, Institute of Design, December 9, 1946, Institute of Design Collection, Box 1, Folder 6, Richard J. Daley Library, University of Illinois, Chicago.

106 As an artist of process and performance: Richard Kostelanetz, ed. *Moholy-Nagy: An Anthology* (New York: Praeger, 1970), p. 3.

106 for every one that he filched: Man Ray felt he'd taken too much credit for photograms, though the argument could just as easily be leveled at him. Bredendieck felt Moholy took credit for his changes to the *Vorkurs* and was bitter that he wasn't mentioned in publicity. None of this reflects well on Moholy, who didn't help his reputation as a Wizard of Oz, but egos were involved on all sides.

106 "Singleness of purpose": Kuh in the catalog for *In Memoriam László Moholy-Nagy,* Art Institute of Chicago, quoted in László Moholy-Nagy, *Color in Transparency* (Gottingen: Steidl, 2006), p. 190.

107 perfect structural design of the seal: D'Arcy Thompson, *On Growth and Form* (Cambridge, U.K.: Cambridge University Press, 1942).

107 "I manufacture space": Mies quoted in Nicholas von Hoffman, interview by author.

107 "of the leading group of Bauhaus people": Sibyl Moholy-Nagy quoted in Elaine Hochman, *Architects of Fortune: Mies van der Rohe and the Third Reich* (New York: Weidenfeld & Nicolson, 1989), p. xiv.

107 "the classics of the liberal arts": László Moholy-Nagy, *Vision in Motion* (Chicago: Paul Theobald, 1947), p. 21.

108 "discovering an interesting picture": Richard Kostelanetz, ed. *Moholy-Nagy: An Anthology,* p. 8.

108 New York School painters: Serge Guilbaut, *How New York Stole the Idea of Modern Art* (Chicago: University of Chicago Press, 1983), examines this idea in great depth.

108 Art was by its nature political: Moholy-Nagy, *Vision in Motion*, passim.

108 "It is no longer possible to praise": See Moholy's introduction to Walter Gropius, *Rebuilding Our Cities* (Chicago: Paul Theobald, 1945), p. 12. Weese is quoted in Moholy-Nagy, *Experiment in Totality*, p. 227.

Moholy liked the character of a giant centralized city, in contrast to a romanticized garden city.

109 Saul Alinsky: Sanford D. Horwitt, *Let Them Call Me Rebel: Saul Alinsky—His Life and Legacy* (New York: Alfred A. Knopf, 1989); and Nicholas von Hoffman, *Radical: A Portrait of Saul Alinsky* (New York: Nation Books, 2010). Reading these books makes Alinsky's current demonization all the more puzzling and frustrating. An equal-opportunity agitator, Alinsky was as wary of the New Deal as he was of Joseph McCarthy.

109 "The radical is that unique person": Saul Alinsky, *Reveille for Radicals* (Chicago: University of Chicago Press, 1946), p. 15.

CHAPTER 8: UNTIL MY CHANGE COMES

111 her catfish stew: Mahalia Jackson, *Mahalia Jackson Cooks Soul* (New York: Aurora, 1970).

111 "My hands . . . demonstrate what I": Studs Terkel, *Talking to Myself* (New York: Pantheon, 1977), p. 260.

111 the golden age of Chicago gospel: Bob Marovich and Anthony Heilbut, interviews by author; Nick Salvatore, *Singing in a Strange Land: C. L. Franklin, the Black Church, and the Transformation of America* (New York: Little, Brown, 2005), p. 127; Wallace D. Best, *Passionately Human, No Less Divine: Religion and Culture in Black Chicago, 1915–1952* (Princeton, N.J.: Princeton University Press, 2005), chap. 4.

111 her former pianist Ruth Jones: Jim Haskins, *Queen of the Blues: A Biography of Dinah Washington* (New York: William Morrow, 1987), p. 40.

111 You're going to be a star someday: Thomas A. Dorsey, interview by Alfred Duckett, *Black World,* July 1974.

111 The Detroit singers: Salvatore, *Singing,* p. 127.

112 to never have a doll: "Gospel Singing Queen Lonely, Sad as a Child," *Chicago Tribune,* July 31, 1955.

112 Irv Kupcinet: Kup tells his own story in Irv Kupcinet with Paul Neimark, *Kup: A Man, an Era, a City* (Chicago: Bonus Books, 1988) and Irv Kupcinet, *Kup's Chicago*

(Cleveland: World, 1962). Carol Felsenthal, "The Lost World of Kup," *Chicago,* June 2004, is required, if painfully honest, reading.

115 **Louis Terkel:** Studs Terkel, *Talking to Myself* (New York: Pantheon, 1977), and (with Sydney Lewis) *Touch and Go: A Memoir* (New York: New Press, 2007), his two autobiographies, tell many of the same stories. *Touch and Go* is better on dates and facts, but *Talking to Myself* has more charm and artistry.

114 **the Chicago Repertory Group (CRG):** Richard Christiansen, *A Theater of Our Own: A History and a Memoir of 1,001 Nights in Chicago* (Evanston, Ill.: Northwestern University Press, 2004), pp. 80–84.

114 **The Dil Pickle:** Kenneth Rexroth, *An Autobiographical Novel* (Santa Barbara, Calif.: Ross-Erickson, 1978), pp. 136–38.

114 **"theater without heroes":** Bernard Sahlins, interview by author.

114 **"farm club of the Group Theater":** Terkel, *Touch and Go,* p. 92.

114 **Langston Hughes, John Dos Passos, and Kurt Weill:** Christiansen, *Theater,* p. 82.

114 **One night during the taxi drivers' strike:** Terkel, *Talking,* pp. 119–20.

115 **"multimedia theater: It might be":** Christiansen, *Theater,* p. 79.

115 **Viola Spolin:** Janet Coleman, *The Compass* (New York: Alfred A. Knopf, 1990), p. 31.

115 **James T. Farrell's Studs Lonigan:** Terkel, *Touch and Go,* p. 104.

115 **"Villa-Lobos's 'Bachianas Brasileiras #5' ":** Ibid., p. 117.

115 **"Come in to Concord's":** *Chicago Tribune,* March 19, 1948.

116 **"There's a woman on the South Side":** Laurraine Goreau, *Just Mahalia, Baby* (Waco, Tex.: Word Books, 1975), p. 113.

116 **"So many white people":** "Mahalia Jackson," *Dayton Journal Herald,* August 8, 1963.

116 **"parishioners, bone-weary":** Terkel, *Talking,* p. 259.

CHAPTER 9: A LOCAL YOUTH IN LOVE

117 **Nelson Algren saw:** H. E. F. Donohue, *Conversations with Nelson Algren* (New York: Hill & Wang, 1963), pp. 178–83; Bettina Drew, *Nelson Algren: A Life on the Wild Side* (New York: Putnam, 1989), pp. 176–80; Simone de Beauvoir, *America Day by Day* (Berkeley: University of California Press, 1999), pp. 95–100.

118 **He'd been born in Detroit:** Drew, *Nelson Algren,* and Donohue, *Conversations,* passim.

118 **"cold, domineering and cruel":** Drew, *Nelson Algren,* p. 15.

120 **"an uneven novel written":** Nelson Algren, *Somebody in Boots* (1935; reprint New York: Thunder's Mouth Press, 1987), p. 9.

120 **"served to humanize people":** Donohue, *Conversations,* pp. 64–65.

120 **raucous theatricals:** Jack Conroy and Curt Johnson, eds., *Writers in Revolt: The Anvil Anthology 1933–1940* (New York: Lawrence Hill, 1973), p. xix.

120 **St. Stanislaus Kostka:** Richard Cahan, *They All Fall Down* (Washington, D.C.: Preservation Press, 1994), p. 29.

121 **"the Proust of the proletariat":** Wright quoted in Drew, *Nelson Algren,* p. 129.

121 **"bigger and greyer and sootier":** Algren to Richard Wright, February 12, 1941, quoted ibid., p. 132.

121 **"God has forgotten us all":** Nelson Algren, *Never Come Morning* (New York: Harper & Brothers, 1942), p. 215.

121 **"a poet of the Chicago slums":** Malcolm Cowley, "Chicago Poem," *New Republic,* May 4, 1942.

121 **"the best book to come out":** Hemingway to Evan Shipman, August 25, 1942, quoted in Drew, *Nelson Algren,* p. 143.

122 **"honestly, for honest men; for the milkman":** Algren, "Do It the Hard Way," 1943, collected in *Entrapment and Other Writings* (New York: Seven Stories Press, 2009), p. 68.

122 **"The chief thing should be to share":** Ibid., p. 70.

122 **Algren was stung:** De Beauvoir, *America Day by Day;* Donohue, *Conversations;* Drew, *Nelson Algren.* Simone's diary leaves out the fact that they ended up in bed together.

124 **a tour of the Art Institute:** "French Society Entertains for Visiting Woman Author," *Chicago Tribune,* February 24, 1947.

124 "My neighbors are going to start": Deirdre Bair, *Simone de Beauvoir: A Biography* (New York: Simon & Schuster, 1990), p. 336.

125 "local youth": Algren referred to himself as such, and De Beauvoir picked it up. See De Beauvoir to Algren, May 17, 1947, in De Beauvoir, *A Transatlantic Love Affair: Letters to Nelson Algren* (New York: New Press, 1997), p. 14.

125 "hovel, without a bathroom": Simone de Beauvoir, *Force of Circumstance* (New York: Putnam's, 1964), p. 126.

125 "the prettiest Existentialist": "Talk of the Town," *New Yorker*, February 22, 1947; also Donohue, *Conversations*, p. 266.

126 "so dissatisfied sexually that": This salacious fact and other background on De Beauvoir are primarily from Bair, *Simone de Beauvoir*, p. 171; and De Beauvoir, *Force of Circumstance*.

126 "a four months psychological contest": Trilling quoted in Bair, *Simone de Beauvoir*, p. 332.

126 "To keep the book alive": Stuart Brent, *The Seven Stairs* (Chicago: J. Philip O'Hara, 1962), p. 37.

126 "Good bye . . . I am happy": De Beauvoir to Algren, March 12, 1947, in De Beauvoir, *Transatlantic Love Affair*, p. 13.

126 "just like all the American women": De Beauvoir quoted in Bair, *Simone de Beauvoir*, p. 340.

127 "In the sad streets of Chicago": De Beauvoir to Algren, May 17, 1947, in De Beauvoir, *Transatlantic Love Affair*, p. 15.

127 "Nelson, I love you": De Beauvoir to Algren, July 23, 1947, ibid., p. 51.

128 "In the evenings especially": De Beauvoir, *America Day by Day*, p. 360.

128 These weeks together: Bair, *Simone de Beauvoir*, pp. 352–53, and Drew, *Nelson Algren*, p. 185, both paint blissful pictures of this visit. In *America Day by Day*, pp. 354–80, De Beauvoir tells it without the romance. Her insightful writings on Chicago make a mockery of Liebling's later rant (see chap. 18).

128 "It's like eating cardboard": Algren quoted in Drew, *Nelson Algren*, p. 205.

129 "Quite simply, he thought she was": Bair, *Simone de Beauvoir*, p. 353.

129 "gentle wild man": De Beauvoir quoted ibid., p. 353.

129 "loving little frog": De Beauvoir to Algren, September 26, 1947, in De Beauvoir, *Transatlantic Love Affair*, p. 67.

CHAPTER 10: LET ME DO ONE BY MYSELF

130 shtetl Jews called Czyz: Nadine Cohodas, *Spinning Blues into Gold* (New York: St. Martin's Press, 2000), is without question the definitive account of the Chess brothers and Chess Records. For the Chicago blues scene, start with Mike Rowe, *Chicago Blues: The City and the Music* (New York: Da Capo, 1975); Robert Palmer, *Deep Blues* (New York: Viking, 1981); Peter Guralnick, *Feel Like Goin' Home: Portraits in Blues and Rock 'n' Roll* (New York: Outerbridge & Dienstfrey, 1971); and Robert Gordon, *Can't Be Satisfied: The Life and Times of Muddy Waters* (Boston: Little, Brown, 2002). I have also drawn from my interview with Marshall Chess.

131 known as Drexel Square: For a fascinating brief oral history of the area, see Charles Walton, "The DuSable Hotel and the Drexel Square Area," *Jazz Institute of Chicago*, http://www.jazzinchicago.org/educates/journal/articles/dusable-hotel-and-drexel-square-area.

131 the DuSable Hotel: Charles Walton, "Bronzeville Conversation: Eddie Flagg, Manager of the DuSable Hotel," *Jazz Institute of Chicago*, http://jazzinchicago.org/educates/journal/interviews/bronzeville-conversation-eddie-flagg-manager-dusable-hotel.

131 the locals made the Macomba: Especially Eddie Chamblee and Duke Groaner. See Walton, "DuSable Hotel." Cohodas, *Spinning*, p. 30, also has details on vice at the Macomba.

131 Jazz was in chaos: Philip Ennis, *The Seventh Stream: The Emergence of Rocknroll in American Popular Music* (Hanover, N.H.: University Press of New England, 1992), p. 131.

131 "the best city in America": John Szwed, *Space Is the Place: The Lives and Times of Sun Ra* (New York: Da Capo, 1998), p. 59.

152 **"Chicagoans' attitude toward nightlife":** George Frazier, "Almost Anything Goes in Chicago," *Holiday,* May 1947.

152 **After a hiatus during:** Ennis, *Seventh Stream,* p. 7.

152 **the surprise hit "I Wonder":** Arnold Shaw, *Honkers and Shouters: The Golden Years of Rhythm & Blues* (New York: Collier Books, 1978), p. 129.

152 **dozens of labels:** Robert Pruter, *Chicago Soul* (Champaign: University of Illinois, 1992), pp. 3–8.

153 **"You'd go in and tell":** Waters quoted in Gordon, *Can't Be Satisfied,* p. 71.

153 **The old 1930s bluesmen:** Rowe, *Chicago Blues,* is the starting point, but Ted Gioia, *Delta Blues* (New York: W. W. Norton, 2008); Palmer, *Deep Blues;* Gordon, *Can't Be Satisfied;* and Guralnik, *Feel Like Goin' Home,* all cover the prewar blues scene well, as does the surprisingly good chapter in Shaw, *Honkers and Shouters.*

153 **"The bluesman is in a sense every man":** Charles Keil, *Urban Blues* (Chicago: University of Chicago Press, 1966), p. 152.

153 **"It was a very different sound":** Waters quoted in Gordon, *Can't Be Satisfied,* p. 79.

154 **"little squirrel-faced boy":** Quoted ibid., p. 85.

154 **"He had more nerve":** Quoted ibid., p. 86.

154 **Jackie Robinson had made:** Warner Saunders, "Bronzeville Memories," in Neal Samors and Michael Williams, *Chicago in the Fifties* (Chicago: Chicago's Neighborhoods, 2005), p. 10.

154 **No one knows anymore what exactly happened:** Cohodas, *Spinning,* and Palmer, *Deep Blues,* tell one story; the one in Gordon, *Can't Be Satisfied,* is slightly different. The result was the same.

154 **Its owner, Bill Putnam:** Jim Cogan and William Clark, *Temples of Sound: Inside the Great Recording Studios* (San Francisco: Chronicle Books, 2003), pp. 126–30; and Jim Cogan, "Bill Putnam," *Universal Audio WebZine* 3, no. 4 (June 2005), http://www.uaudio.com/webzine/2005/june/text/content8.html.

135 **"the Barbary Coast of the booming":** "*Life* Spends Saturday Night in Calumet City," *Life,* January 20, 1941.

135 **laff-riot emcees like Tiny Roy:** Dave Hoekstra, "Sun Ra's Calumet City," www.davehoekstra.com/travel/sun_ras_calumet_city.pdf.

135 **A tatty velvet curtain:** Szwed, *Space,* p. 59.

136 **"I've never been part of":** Sun Ra quoted ibid., p. 6. Also crucial on Sun Ra during these years is Robert L. Campbell, Christopher Trent, and Robert Pruter, "From Sonny Blount to Sun Ra: The Chicago Years," http://hubcap.clemson.edu/~campber/sunra.html.

137 **"a pool hall for the metaphysically":** Sun Ra quoted in Szwed, *Space,* p. 32.

137 **"I have never been able to think":** Quoted ibid., p. 41.

138 **After weeks of practice:** Goreau, *Just Mahalia,* pp. 114–15.

139 **Al Benson:** Adam Green, *Selling the Race* (Chicago: University of Chicago Press, 2007), p. 84.

139 **"northern being and":** Ibid., p. 87.

139 **"I talk the way the common":** "Meet Al Benson, The Wizard of Weird Words," *Chicago Tribune,* March 4, 1951.

139 **"the cultural padrone":** Green, *Selling,* p. 87.

140 **The major labels froze:** Gordon, *Can't Be Satisfied,* pp. 93–94.

140 **"Let me do one by myself":** Waters quoted in Cohodas, *Spinning,* p. 42.

140 **"What's he singing?":** Chess quoted in Palmer, *Deep Blues,* p. 159.

141 **Maxwell Street Record Company:** Gordon, *Can't Be Satisfied,* p. 94.

141 **the plan would turn the city:** South Side Planning Board. *An Opportunity for Private and Public Investment in Rebuilding Chicago* (Chicago: SSPB, 1947).

142 **"were ill-informed and they were loud":** Ronald L. Fair, *Hog Butcher,* excerpted in Richard Guzman, *Black Writing from Chicago: In the World, Not of It?* (Carbondale: Southern Illinois University Press, 2006), p. 176.

142 **the music of Me:** Craig Werner, *Higher Ground* (New York: Crown, 2004), pp. 7–10. See also Charlie Gillett, *The Sound of the City: The Rise of Rock and Roll* (New York: Pantheon, 1970), p. 155.

143 **"They'd tell me, 'Girl' ":** Jackson quoted in Don Gold, "In God She Trusts," *Ladies' Home Journal*, November 1963.

CHAPTER 11: A FRESH TIME

144 **"200 per cent English personality:** Sibyl Moholy-Nagy Papers, Archives of American Art, Smithsonian Institution.

144 **jar filled with soap bubbles:** Emily King, *Robert Brownjohn: Sex and Typography* (New York: Princeton Architectural Press, 2005), p. 21.

144 **"so gifted":** Serge Chermayeff, oral history interview by Betty J. Blum, © 2001, Art Institute of Chicago, p. 31, used with permission.

144 **she helped the Chermayeffs:** Sibyl Moholy-Nagy to Barbara Chermayeff, December 5, 1946, and the response December 6, 1946, Sibyl Moholy-Nagy Papers, Archives of American Art, Smithsonian Institution.

145 **"fuzzy-minded":** Dwight McDonald, "Author Says Wallace Has a Fuzzy Mind," *Chicago Tribune*, March 14, 1948.

146 **"fashionable":** Bertrand Goldberg, oral history interview by Betty J. Blum, © 1992, Art Institute of Chicago, p. 81, used with permission.

146 **Baldwin Kingrey:** Harry Weese, oral history interview by Betty J. Blum, © 1991, Art Institute of Chicago, pp. 74–78, used with permission; and John Brunetti, *Baldwin Kingrey: Midcentury Modern in Chicago, 1947–1957* (Chicago: Wright, 2004), passim.

146 **stayed up one night:** Serge Chermayeff, oral history interview by Betty J. Blum, © 2001, Art Institute of Chicago, p. 99, used with permission.

146 **"ahead of its time":** Brunetti, *Baldwin Kingrey,* p. 86.

146 **"We were, in a sense":** Dimmitt quoted ibid.

146 **"The people that rushed into Baldwin":** Baldwin quoted ibid., p. 120.

146 **"There is a morbid coldness in him":** Sibyl Moholy-Nagy Papers, Archives of American Art.

147 **"an old flowerpot":** Sibyl Moholy-Nagy to Robert Wolff, February 10, 1948, Robert J. Wolff Papers, Archives of American Art.

147 **"a submarine commander":** Jack Kerouac quoted repeatedly in Hugo Weber Papers, Archives of American Art.

147 **"a sort of blue-green Mephistophelian":** "Hugo Weber," George Buehr, *WFMT Perspective*, December 1961.

147 **"comprehensive anticipatory":** Fuller quoted in Joachim Krausee and Claude Lichtenstein, eds., *Your Private Sky: R. Buckminster Fuller: The Art of Design Science* (Baden: Lars Muller, 1999).

147 **"You do not have the right":** Alden Hatch, *Buckminster Fuller: At Home in the Universe* (New York: Crown, 1974), pp. 83–84.

148 **"a Merlin's cave":** Serge Chermayeff, oral history interview by Betty J. Blum, © 2001, Art Institute of Chicago, p. 34, used with permission.

148 **a full twenty-four hours:** Ivan Chermayeff, interview by author.

148 **An intrigued Mies was known:** Kenneth Snelson, interview by author.

148 **"As a strong component of modern":** Katharine Kuh, *My Love Affair with Modern Art* (New York: Arcade, 2006), p. 113.

148 **"jazzy, bumping, grinding":** Notes dated August 1964, Hugo Weber Papers, Archives of American Art.

148 **"your bebop representative":** Buckminster Fuller to John Walley, March 13, 1949, Institute of Design Collection, Box 7, Folder 216, Richard J. Daley Library, University of Illinois at Chicago.

148 **"Bucky loved jazz":** Serge Chermayeff, oral history interview by Betty J. Blum, © 2001, Art Institute of Chicago, p. 99, used with permission.

148 **cheap, high-quality heroin:** Patrick H. Hughes, Noel W. Barker, Gail A. Crawford, and Jerome H. Jaffe, "The Natural History of a Heroin Epidemic," *American Journal of Public Health* 62 (July 1972), pp. 995–1001.

149 **"In both cases a hip":** Ibid.

149 **"started getting in trouble":** Piers Jessop quoted in King, *Robert Brownjohn,* p. 24.

149 **"a wonderful tenant":** Sara Chermayeff quoted ibid. Also see Serge Chermayeff's oral history and his papers at Avery Library, Columbia University, which contain some plaintive letters written on Brownjohn's behalf.

150 Vandalism at the Art Institute: Kuh, *Love Affair*, pp. 31–32.

150 Kuh's life was shaped: Kuh, *Love Affair*, is enriched by the extensive interview she did with her editor Avis Berman. See Katharine Kuh, interview by Avis Berman, *Archives of American Art Journal* 27, no. 3 (1987), pp. 2–36.

151 "marvelous teacher": Kuh interview by Berman.

151 know them as abstract concepts: Katharine Kuh, "Seeing Is Believing," *Bulletin of the Art Institute of Chicago* 39 (April–May 1945), pp. 53–56; and Susan F. Rossen and Charlotte Moser, "Primer for Seeing: The Gallery of Art Interpretation and Katharine Kuh's Crusade for Modernism in Chicago," *Art Institute of Chicago Museum Studies* 16, no. 1 (1990), pp. 6–25, 88–90.

151 the mythic surrealism: Peter Selz, "Surrealism and the Chicago Imagists of the 1950s: A Comparison and Contrast," *Art Journal* 45 (Winter 1985), pp. 303–6.

151 "the vaporings of half-baked": Truman quoted in Naomi Sawelson-Gorse, "The Art Institute of Chicago and the Arensberg Collection," *Art Institute of Chicago Museum Studies* 19, no. 1 (1993), n63.

152 students from the School of the Art Institute: Franz Schulze, Exhibition Momentum catalog, Exhibition Momentum Papers, Archives of American Art; Franz Schulze, *Fantastic Images: Chicago Art Since 1945* (Chicago: Follett, 1972), pp. 15–18.

152 a decision that united them: Lynne Warren, *Art in Chicago, 1945–1995* (Chicago: Museum of Contemporary Art, 1996), p. 17.

152 the ID students still saw themselves: Ibid.; Exhibition Momentum papers, Archives of American Art, passim.

152 once the arts and crafts teacher: Leon Golub, "Eulogy for Herbert Greenwald," February 12, 1959, manuscript, Ludwig Mies van der Rohe Papers, 1921–69, Library of Congress.

152 but if anything the feeling was mutual: Miyoko Ito, oral history interview, July 20, 1978, Archives of American Art, Smithsonian Institution.

153 no one in Chicago had ever seen: Leon Golub, oral history interview, 1968, Archives of American Art, Smithsonian Institution.

153 a figurative, cerebral surrealism: Warren, *Art in Chicago*, p. 20; Schulze, *Fantastic Images*, pp. 14–15.

153 "Chicago art is not naive": Schulze, *Fantastic Images*, p. 8.

153 Henry Darger: My main resources for Darger are Klaus Biesenbach, *Henry Darger* (Munich: Prestel, 2009), and Darger scholar Michael Bonesteel, interview by author.

155 "felt that he had to have time": Milton Mayer, *Robert Maynard Hutchins: A Memoir* (Berkeley: University of California Press, 1993), p. 366.

155 "superficially awesome": Ibid., p. 304.

155 a staff of seventy-five: Ibid., pp. 304–5.

155 the Federal Trade Commission reprimanded: Ibid., p. 302.

156 Chicago public school system: "Education: Cleanup Man," *Time*, July 7, 1947.

156 the Paepckes had been methodically buying: James Sloan Allen, *The Romance of Commerce and Culture* (Chicago: University of Chicago Press, 1983), p. 120 and passim.

156 Hutchins liked to point out: Mayer, *Hutchins*, pp. 381–82.

157 "intellectual pride and": William H. McNeill, *Hutchins' University: A Memoir of the University of Chicago, 1929–1950* (Chicago: University of Chicago Press, 1991), p. 155.

157 "My father would visit": Binford quoted in Susie Bright, "From Tight Sweaters to the Pentagon Papers," *Susie Bright's Journal*, May 16, 2008, http://susiebright.blogs.com/susie_brights_journal_/2008/05/sally-binford-n.html.

CHAPTER 12: THE BALANCE OF POWER

159 "I'd like to talk to you": John Bartlow Martin, *Adlai Stevenson of Illinois* (Garden City, N.Y.: Doubleday, 1976), pp. 277–78; and Ira Berkow, *Maxwell Street: Survival in a Bazaar* (Garden City, N.Y.: Doubleday, 1977), p. 252.

159 "A fellow was telling me": Martin, *Stevenson of Illinois*, p. 278.

159 "Never went to Oxford": Ibid.

160 "Rabbit": Ibid., pp. 55–56.

160 He was out playing tennis: Ibid., p. 278.

161 cabinet and staff would be his: *The Reminiscences of Jacob Arvey* (1967), p. 9, Oral History Collection, Columbia University.

161 Ellen descended the stairs: Porter McKeever, *Adlai Stevenson: His Life and Legacy* (New York: William Morrow, 1989), p. 114.

162 BETTER SAFE THAN SORRY: "Arvey Workers Show Truman a Real Party," *Chicago Tribune*, October 26, 1948; Martin, *Stevenson of Illinois*, p. 344.

162 "the crackpot forces": Harry Truman, speech, *Chicago Tribune*, October 26, 1948.

162 The tide had begun to turn: Adam Green, *Selling the Race* (Chicago: University of Chicago Press, 2007), p. 64.

162 "If we've got Illinois": Berkow, *Maxwell Street*, p. 259.

163 Truman won Illinois: Porter McKeever, *Adlai Stevenson: His Life and Legacy* (New York: William Morrow, 1989), p. 126.

164 "the trouble with Mayor Kennelly": Mike Royko, *Boss: Richard J. Daley of Chicago* (New York: Plume, 1988), p. 61.

164 "require nondiscrimination in all housing": Martin Meyerson and Edward C. Banfield, *Politics, Planning, and the Public Interest: The Case of Public Housing in Chicago* (Glencoe, N.Y.: Free Press, 1964), p. 137.

164 Meanwhile, Cardinal Stritch: Steven M. Avella, *This Confident Church: Catholic Leadership and Life in Chicago, 1940–1965* (Notre Dame, Ind.: University of Notre Dame Press, 1992), pp. 201–2.

165 over 137,000 private housing units: Arnold Hirsch, *The Making of the Second Ghetto: Race and Housing in Chicago, 1940–1960* (Cambridge, U.K.: Cambridge University Press, 1983), p. 27.

165 dark brick infill of Promontory's: D. Bradford Hunt, *Blueprint for Disaster: The Unraveling of Chicago Public Housing* (Chicago: University of Chicago Press, 2009), pp. 124–25.

166 Days later at 71st and St. Lawrence: John T. McGreevy, *Parish Boundaries: The Catholic Encounter with Race in the Twentieth-Century Urban North* (Chicago: University of Chicago Press, 1996), p. 93; Avella, *Confident Church*, pp. 266–67.

166 In October the CHA submitted: Myerson and Banfield, *Politics, Planning*, chap. 5, recounts the gory details.

166 On the eighth, another mob: Jill Abrahamson, *A Neighborhood Finds Itself* (New York: Harper & Brothers, 1959), pp. 13–20; Johnson, *Call Me Neighbor, Call Me Friend*, pp. 2, 9; and McGreevy, *Parish Boundaries*, p. 94.

CHAPTER 13: THIS PROGRAM CAME TO YOU FROM CHICAGO

168 almost 81 percent of Americans with TVs: Leo Burnett, *Communications of an Advertising Man* (Chicago: Privately printed, 1961), p. 40.

168 "The world," said the new governor: Adlai Stevenson, inaugural speech, *Chicago Tribune*, January 11, 1949.

168 "big sister and girl friend" Fran Allison: *Kukla, Fran and Ollie*, telecast, February, 1950, Kukla.tv.

169 "Chicago . . . was an extraordinary, vital": Mike Wallace, interview by Steve McClellan, April 17, 1998, Archive of American Television, www.emmytvlegends.org/interviews/people/mike-wallace.

169 switch off his hearing aids: Jeff Kisseloff, *The Box: An Oral History of Television, 1920–1961* (New York: Viking Press, 1995), p. 81.

169 WBKB admitted: "Radio: Barrooms with a View," *Time*, March 24, 1947.

170 "Ah, Kukla!": Virtually every article about Tillstrom and the show features this story.

171 "the Alice who wanders": Tillstrom quoted in "Kukla's Daddy," *Television and Radio Mirror*, November 1949.

171 a long, provocative discussion about women: Richard B. Gehman, "Mr. Oliver J. Dragon . . . And Friends," *Theatre Arts*, October 1950.

171 "In less than a week": "A Puppet Gives Women and Kids Break on Video," *Chicago Tribune*, October 19, 1947.

171 "just about the best investment": Levison quoted in "Tele Replaces Sitters, Young Mother Finds," *Chicago Tribune*, September 19, 1948.

172 "It happens in the best": Kukla quoted in Lewis Gomavitz, interview by Karen

Herman, February 2, 2000, Archive of American Television, www.emmytvlegends.org/interviews/people/lewis-gomavitz.

172 the monthly *Kuklapolitan Courier:* "Fame Pursues the Kukla, Fran and Ollie Show," *Chicago Tribune,* January 23, 1949.

172 "Great . . . Let's do a parody": Tillstrom quoted in Bob Banner, interview by Henry Colman, November 5, 1999, Archive of American Television, www.emmytvlegends.org/interviews/people/bob-banner.

173 "moron kids": Ben Berquist, interview, Kukla.tv.

173 "mildly irritating": "Radio: The Chicago School," *Time,* September 11, 1950.

173 "helping to save the sanity": James Thurber, fan letter, kukla.tv/fan.html.

173 "Monsieur Josef": Tillstrom quoted in "Kukla's Daddy," *Television and Radio Mirror,* November 1949.

173 Fran, whose face was the product: "Carol Hughes, Kukla and Ollie's Real-Life Heroine," *Coronet,* October 1951.

173 "a very noisy surprise": Tillstrom quoted in "The Amazing Burr Tillstrom," *TV Forecast,* December 16, 1950.

174 An episode of *Milton Berle:* Ben Park, "She Was Poor But She Was Honest," *Chicago* pilot issue, 1953.

174 "The main thing about": "The Chicago School of Television," *Look,* March 27, 1951.

175 Mills, who'd made propaganda films: Kisseloff, *Box,* pp. 185, 187.

175 "Hello, Tiger," he'd start: Dan Petrie quoted ibid., p. 189.

175 "respectful and charming visitors": Ben Park, "She Was Poor But She Was Honest," *Chicago* pilot issue, 1953.

176 "The stars of the show": Arthur R. Railton, "They Fool You Every Night," *Popular Mechanics,* October 1951.

177 "the most beautiful girl to ever drown": Charlie Andrews in Kisseloff, *Box,* p. 186.

177 "This show came to you live": Banner interview; Kisseloff, *Box,* p. 191.

177 "a very private person": Banner interview.

177 "the farm show for city folk": "WNBQ Prepares For Key Role in Nation Wide TV," *Chicago Tribune,* May 15, 1949.

178 "a neighborhood restaurant": Studs Terkel, *Talking to Myself* (New York: Pantheon, 1977), p. 40.

178 "People were never": Studs Terkel in Kisseloff, *Box,* p. 200.

178 "It was acting, good acting": Studs Terkel with Sydney Lewis, *Touch and Go: A Memoir* (New York: New Press, 2007), p. 123.

179 "It was, of course, El Dorado": Terkel, *Talking to Myself,* p. 40.

179 "We never underestimated the audience": Terkel and Lewis, *Touch and Go,* p. 120.

179 "Radio City should be torn down": Allen quoted in "Chicago Offers Best in Video, Allen Reports," *Chicago Tribune,* December 13, 1949.

179 "After half an hour of being beat": Herbuveaux quoted in "Radio: The Chicago School," *Time,* September 11, 1950.

179 Sarah Vaughan: Rolf Malcolm, "Old Tiger," *Playboy,* November 1954.

CHAPTER 14: A CITY OF SLIGHTBROWS

180 "Highbrow, Lowbrow, Middlebrow": Russell Lynes, "Highbrow, Lowbrow, Middlebrow," *Harper's,* February 1949.

181 the Railroad Fair: "Many Engines to Be Displayed in Fair Exhibits," *Chicago Tribune,* June 24, 1949; Carl Condit, *The Chicago School of Architecture* (Chicago: University of Chicago Press, 1952), p. 196.

181 a prediction by the civil aeronautics board: "Predicts Longer Trips Will Be Made by Air in Future," *Chicago Tribune,* March 18, 1950.

181 Consultants warned the city: Carl Condit, *Chicago, 1930–70* (Chicago: University of Chicago Press, 1974), p. 259.

182 "slightbrow": "Kukla, Fran and Ollie," *Life,* May 23, 1949.

183 "You never asked me": "Studs' Place: The Opera," *Studs' Place,* http://mediaburn.org/video/studs-place-the-opera.

183 "big hitter": Ibid.

183 Dixon could get hold: Marshall Chess, interview by author.

184 "It was important in that era": John Johnson, *Succeeding Against the Odds: The Autobiography of a Great American Businessman* (New York: Amistad, 1989), p. 42.

184 For all their obvious differences: Chess interview by author.

184 "It was just 'I belongs to the'": Waters quoted in Robert Gordon, *Can't Be Satisfied: The Life and Times of Muddy Waters* (Boston: Little, Brown, 2002), p. 94.

184 "He could be an absolutely charming": Chisholm quoted in Robert Palmer, *Deep Blues* (New York: Viking, 1981), p. 163.

185 Callahan scooped up his camera bags: Wayne F. Miller, interview by author.

185 "to regulate a pleasant": Callahan quoted in Museum of Modern Art, *Harry Callahan* (New York: Museum of Modern Art, 1967), p. 6.

185 "the hunting type": "Harry Callahan, version #4," Hugo Weber Papers, Archives of American Art, Smithsonian Institution.

185 Harry *needed* Eleanor: Joan Miller, interview by author; Julian Cox, *Harry Callahan: Eleanor* (Gottingen: Steidl, 2007).

186 she became convinced she had cancer: Joan Miller, interview by author.

186 Callahan used a small alcove: Wayne F. Miller, interview by author.

186 "The school is not good": Mies van der Rohe to Henry Heald, March 5, 1949, Henry T. Heald Papers, no. 1998.049, Box 47, Institute of Design 1949–1950, IIT Archives, Paul Galvin Library, IIT.

187 the first geodesic dome: Kenneth Snelson, interview by author.

187 "getting old, tired, and worn out": Walter Paepcke to General A. Conger Goodyear, October 1, 1949, Walter P. Paepcke Papers, Box 4, Folder 3, Special Collections Research Center, University of Chicago Library.

187 "not very bright": Serge Chermayeff, oral history interview by Betty J. Blum, © 2001, Art Institute of Chicago, p. 43, used with permission.

187 the modern Goethe, Albert Schweitzer: James Sloan Allen, *The Romance of Commerce and Culture* (Chicago: University of Chicago Press, 1983), pp. 161–64.

187 "The Greatest Man in the World": "Albert Schweitzer," *Life*, October 6, 1947.

188 "has for years crusaded against": "Doesn't Like Nelson Algren," *Chicago Tribune*, March 16, 1947.

188 "campus fellows, authentic": Nelson Algren, *Who Lost an American?* (New York: Macmillan, 1963), p. 141.

188 "Wright had made us aware": Ibid., p. 142.

188 By 1948 . . . "the image": Ibid.

189 At last in early May 1948: Bettina Drew, *Nelson Algren: A Life on the Wild Side* (New York: Putnam, 1989), pp. 192–96; Deirdre Bair, *Simone de Beauvoir: A Biography* (New York: Simon & Schuster, 1990), pp. 371–78.

190 "very bad": De Beauvoir quoted in Bair, *Simone de Beauvoir,* p. 376.

190 "Oh all right": Algren quoted in Simone de Beauvoir, *Force of Circumstance* (New York: Putnam's, 1964), p. 158.

190 "One evening, we ate": Ibid., p. 159.

190 "No. Too much work": Algren quoted ibid., p. 162.

190 "as far away from everything": Algren quoted ibid., p. 166.

191 No other man would ever: De Beauvoir to Algren, August 29, 1948, in De Beauvoir, *A Transatlantic Love Affair: Letters to Nelson Algren* (New York: New Press, 1997), p. 217.

191 Sartre, though he thought the philosopher: Bettina Drew, *Nelson Algren: A Life on the Wild Side* (New York: Putnam, 1989), p. 204.

191 would fall in love: De Beauvoir quoted in Art Shay, interview by author.

191 "My ass!": Vian quoted in Bart Plantenga, "Boris Vian: Cultural Pariah, Swingin' Dilettante, or Iconoclastic Pataphysician?" *American Book Review* 21, no. 2 (January–February 2000).

191 "I never loved you": De Beauvoir to Algren, September 13, 1949, in De Beauvoir, *Transatlantic Love Affair,* p. 275.

192 "A true novelist's triumph": "Books: The Lower Depths," *Time,* September 12, 1949.

192 "This is a man writing": Ernest Hemingway, blurb provided to Doubleday.

193 Algren was certain he was: H. E. F. Donohue, *Conversations with Nelson Algren* (New York: Hill & Wang, 1963), p. 143.

194 a self-consciously important work: Haki Madhubuti, interview by author.

194 A record 1,338,761 people: "Attendance in 1948 Is 1,338,761, Art Institute Record," *Chicago Tribune,* January 11, 1949.

194 interview with local critics: Naomi Sawelson-Gorse, "The Art Institute of Chicago and the Arensberg Collection," *Art Institute of Chicago Museum Studies* 19, no. 1 (1993), not only lays out Kuh's relationships with the Arensbergs and Duchamp but also

provides a transcript of the Duchamp interview.

194 **Duchamp had pleasant connections:** Arts Club of Chicago, *The Collection 1916–1996* (Chicago: Arts Club of Chicago, 1997), pp. 15–16.

195 **paving the way for mainstream:** Sawelson-Gorse, "Art Institute of Chicago."

195 **"The gap":** Simone de Beauvoir, *America Day by Day* (Berkeley: University of California Press, 1999), p. 376.

PART THREE: 1950–1954

197 **led locally by priests:** John T. McGreevy, *Parish Boundaries: The Catholic Encounter with Race in the Twentieth-Century Urban North* (Chicago: University of Chicago Press, 1996), p. 53.

CHAPTER 15: STAND UP AND BE COUNTED

199 **Usually the Gray Wolves:** Len O'Connor, *Clout* (New York: Avon Books, 1976), p. 126.

199 **"on the road to communism":** "2 Communities Add Protest on Housing Sites," *Chicago Tribune*, February 25, 1950; Martin Meyerson and Edward C. Banfield, *Politics, Planning, and the Public Interest: The Case of Public Housing in Chicago* (Glencoe, N.Y.: Free Press, 1964), pp. 182–85.

200 **the networks established certain rules:** Erik Barnouw, *Tube of Plenty* (Oxford, U.K.: Oxford University Press, 1975), p. 130.

200 **The white suburban nuclear family:** George Lipsitz, "The Meaning of Memory: Family, Class, and Ethnicity in Early Network Television Programs," *Cultural Anthropology* 1 (November 1986), pp. 355–87.

201 **"the Doctor":** Bob Bendick quoted in Jeff Kisseloff, *The Box: An Oral History of Television, 1920–1961* (New York: Viking Press, 1995), p. 393.

201 **The long-term effects:** Lynwood King, interview by Jeff Kisseloff, November 20, 2002, Archive of American Television, www.emmytvlegends.org/interviews/people/lynwood-king; Gene Jones quoted in Kisseloff, *Box*, p. 393.

201 **"hopeless":** Mills quoted in Larry Wolters, "Television News and Views," *Chicago Tribune*, January 4, 1952.

201 **"clubbed and beaten insensible":** J. Hugh E. Davis, "Are Chi Network TV Originations Dying?" *Billboard*, April 5, 1952.

201 **elephants relieving themselves:** Mike Wallace, interview by Steve McClellan, April 17, 1998, Archive of American Television, www.emmytvlegends.org/interviews/people/mike-wallace.

202 **a special telephone:** Lewis Gomavitz, interview by Karen Herman, February 2, 2000, Archive of American Television, www.emmytvlegends.org/interviews/people/lewis-gomavitz.

202 **"cold sober":** Hugh Downs quoted in Kisseloff, *Box*, p. 195.

202 **"got inbred":** King interview by Kisseloff.

203 **"New York parochialism":** Terkel quoted in Kisseloff, *Box*, p. 203. He seems to have said or written this whenever he was discussing the blacklist and *Red Channels*.

203 **"Say you were duped":** Studs Terkel with Sydney Lewis, *Touch and Go: A Memoir* (New York: New Press, 2007), pp. 124–25; Studs Terkel, *Talking to Myself* (New York: Pantheon, 1977), p. 44.

203 **"a small-scale, intimate kind":** Jules Herbuveaux, "Pinch of Chi Aids New TV Program Recipe," *Billboard*, April 5, 1952.

203 **"with the idea of improving":** "Two Witnesses Name Score as Filmland Reds," *Chicago Tribune*, October 3, 1952.

204 **WFMT, the first all-classical:** Coleman, p. 55.

204 **"The danger of the photographic":** László Moholy-Nagy quoted in Sibyl Moholy-Nagy, *Moholy-Nagy: Experiment in Totality* (New York: Harper & Brothers, 1950), p. 28.

CHAPTER 16: LIVING SEPARATE LIVES

206 **"walk up to the terrace":** Caldwell quoted in Franz Schulze, *Mies van der Rohe: A Critical Biography* (Chicago: University of Chicago Press, 1985), p. 258.

207 **"If I would have known":** Myron Goldsmith, oral history interview by Betty J. Blum, © 2001, Art Institute of Chicago, p. 66, used with permission.

207 **Johnson often dropped by:** William S. Shell, *Impressions of Mies* (Privately printed, 1988).

207 **she countersued three months later:** "Charges Famed Architect With Fraud, Deceit," *Chicago Tribune,* October 30, 1951.

208 **the Arensbergs had double-crossed:** Naomi Sawelson-Gorse, "The Art Institute of Chicago and the Arensberg Collection," *Art Institute of Chicago Museum Studies* 19, no. 1 (1993); and Katharine Kuh, *My Love Affair with Modern Art* (New York: Arcade, 2006).

208 **the consistently progressive Arts Club:** Arts Club of Chicago, *The Collection 1916–1996* (Chicago: Arts Club of Chicago, 1997).

208 **"Anticultural Positions":** Christopher Lyon, *Nancy Spero: The Work* (Munich: Prestel, 2010), p. 24 and passim.

208 **Leon Golub and Nancy Spero:** Ibid.

209 *Harper's* **and** *Life* **both ran features:** John Bartlow Martin, "The Strangest Place in Chicago," *Harper's,* November 1950; and "The Mecca," *Life,* November 19, 1951.

209 **"Arrangements . . . made for a small":** IIT Coordinating Council Minutes, December 31, 1951, no. 1998.049, Henry T. Heald Papers, Box 56, President's Coordinating Council, 5-5-51 to 1-28-52, IIT Archives, Paul Galvin Library, IIT.

210 **an old-fashioned builder's guild:** Nathaniel Owings, *The Spaces in Between* (Boston: Houghton Mifflin, 1973), p. 66.

210 **"group design":** Ibid., p. 264.

211 **"gallery in the sky":** Sarah Whiting, "The Invisible Superblock," Skidmore, Owings & Merrill, http://www.som.com/content.cfm/the_invisible_superblock. Whiting's seminal article on the Near South Side, "Bas-Relief Urbanism: Chicago's Figured Field," reprinted in Phyllis Lambert, ed., *Mies in America* (New York: Harry Abrams, 2001), may pose a challenge to the casual reader.

211 **"It wasn't necessarily a slum":** Ambrose M. Richardson, oral history interview by Betty J. Blum, © 2005, Art Institute of Chicago, pp. 107–8, used with permission.

211 **"We were living separate lives":** Walter Netsch, oral history interview by Betty J. Blum, © 1997, Art Institute of Chicago, p. 58, used with permission.

211 **At a lunch held two years later:** Arnold Hirsch, *The Making of the Second Ghetto: Race and Housing in Chicago, 1940–1960* (Cambridge, U.K.: Cambridge University Press, 1983), p. 135; "Lake Meadows Hailed by 1,000," *Chicago Tribune,* May, 1952.

212 **"much too drastic":** Quoted in Jill Abrahamson, *A Neighborhood Finds Itself* (New York: Harper & Brothers, 1959), p. 64.

212 **"They have acquired homes":** Quoted in Hirsch, *Making of the Second Ghetto,* p. 194.

213 **"just like white people":** Barnes quoted in "Sheriff Defends Negro Family Against Crowd," *Chicago Tribune,* July 11, 1951.

213 **the world watched a race riot live:** Hirsch, *Making of the Second Ghetto,* p. 62.

213 **Photos of young white Americans:** Ibid., p. 53.

213 **"implacable hatred":** Walter White, "This Is Cicero," *Crisis,* August–September 1951.

214 **"Worried by the insecurity":** Advertisement in *Chicago Tribune,* June 15, 1949.

214 **instantly iconic:** Carl Condit, *Chicago 1930–70* (Chicago: University of Chicago Press, 1974), p. 53.

214 **"America, Americans":** Stanley Tigerman, "Mies van der Rohe: A Moral Modernist Model," *Perspecta* 22 (1986), pp. 112–35.

214 **"was between heaven":** Lilly von Schnitzler quoted in Schulze, *Mies van der Rohe,* p. 248.

214 **"Wasn't it splendid of Mies":** Cage quoted in Columbia University, *Four Great Makers of Modern Architecture: Gropius, Le Corbusier, Mies van der Rohe, Wright* (New York: Columbia University Press, 1961), p. 126.

215 **"You can't tell anybody":** Mies quoted in Jacques Calman Brownson, oral history interview by Betty J. Blum, © 1996, Art Institute of Chicago, p. 163, used with permission.

215 **producing more steel than:** "Chicago's Comeback," *U.S. News & World Report,* May 27, 1955.

215 **tilting the city grid upward:** Mitchell Schwartzer, "Forms of the Grid," in Charles Waldheim and Katerina Ruedi Ray, eds., *Chicago Architecture: Histories, Revisions, Alternatives* (Chicago: University of Chicago Press, 2005).

215 **"Technology is our fate"**: Mies quoted in "Architect Finds Beauty in 'Skin and Bones,'" *Chicago Tribune*, June 21, 1951.

215 **"His mission"**: Peter Blake, *Mies van der Rohe: Architecture and Structure* (New York: Penguin Books, 1966), p. 11.

215 **In late May 1952, *Mies v. Farnsworth:*** I am grateful to Franz Schulze for his generosity in sharing his findings on the trial, including an early look at the Farnsworth chapter of the second edition of his Mies biography.

216 **"bad in more ways"**: Farnsworth quoted in Elizabeth Gordon, "The Threat to the Next America," *House Beautiful*, April 1953.

216 **Mies got bored**: Shell, *Impressions of Mies*, p. 22.

217 **"no place to put the furniture"**: Mies quoted in Bruce John Graham, oral history interview by Betty J. Blum, © 1998, Art Institute of Chicago, p. 17, used with permission.

217 **he watched boxing**: Edward A. Duckett in Shell, *Impressions of Mies*, p. 30.

217 **"Didn't think you had it"**: Wright quoted in Julie V. Iovine, "Elizabeth Gordon, 94, Dies; Was House Beautiful Editor," *New York Times*, October 17, 2000.

217 **"In this house with its four"**: Farnsworth quoted in Joseph A. Barry, "Report on the American Battle Between Good and Bad Modern Houses," *House Beautiful*, May 1953.

217 **"The reason the Gothic church"**: Mies quoted in Shell, *Impressions of Mies*, p. 20.

218 **further spread the gospel of Mies**: Sharon Irish, *Preservation, Polemics, and Power: Carl W. Condit's The Chicago School of Architecture* (E-Technology and Culture, 2008).

219 **"Indeed, there was no thought"**: Farnsworth quoted in Joseph A. Barry, "Report on the American Battle Between Good and Bad Modern Houses," *House Beautiful*, May 1953.

219 **"All that work and what"**: Gropius quoted in Kuh, *Love Affair*, p. 80.

CHAPTER 17: NOBODY KNOWS MY NAME

220 **"Things I Like About"**: Langston Hughes, "Things I Like About Chicago I Like, And What I Don't, I Don't," *Chicago Defender*, June 25, 1949.

221 **"Phil made a wonderful"**: Quoted in James Segrest and Mark Hoffman, *Moanin' at Midnight: The Life and Times of Howlin' Wolf* (New York: Thunder's Mouth Press, 2004), p. 145.

221 **Baby Face . . . was known to hop**: Mike Rowe, *Chicago Blues: The City and the Music* (New York: Da Capo, 1975), p. 76.

221 **after their first home**: Nadine Cohodas, *Spinning Blues into Gold* (New York: St. Martin's Press, 2000), p. 56.

222 **Leonard rigged up something**: Robert Gordon, *Can't Be Satisfied: The Life and Times of Muddy Waters* (Boston: Little, Brown, 2002), p. 111.

222 **"I would argue"**: Chisholm quoted in Robert Palmer, *Deep Blues* (New York: Viking, 1981), p. 163.

223 **"Get the fuck out"**: Leonard Chess quoted ibid., p. 165.

223 **the Clean Blues versus the Dirty Blues**: Charles Keil, *Urban Blues* (Chicago: University of Chicago Press, 1966), p. 152.

223 **"where the soul of man"**: Phillips quoted in Segrest and Hoffman, *Moanin' at Midnight*, p. 83.

224 **given up Pepsi-Cola**: Peter Guralnick, *Feel Like Goin' Home: Portraits in Blues and Rock 'n' Roll* (New York: Outerbridge & Dienstfrey, 1971), p. 53.

224 **"in cahoots"**: Marshall Chess, interview by author.

224 **"I'm Ready"**: Waters quoted in Gordon, *Can't Be Satisfied*, pp. 132–33.

224 **"He was a fabulous"**: Marshall Chess, interview by author.

226 **Leonard and Phil had made a deal**: Cohodas, *Spinning*, pp. 79–80.

226 **The Mob, blessed by City Hall**: William Grimshaw, *Bitter Fruit: Black Politics and the Chicago Machine, 1931–1991* (Chicago: University of Chicago Press, 1992), p. 83.

226 **"If anybody is to profit"**: Dawson quoted in Edward Clayton, *The Negro Politician: His Success and Failure* (Chicago: Johnson, 1964), p. 83. Dawson's unique political position has made him the subject of a number of close studies, including Clayton's. Others have had much to say about him, including: James Q. Wilson, *Negro Politics: The Search*

for Leadership (Glencoe, N.Y.: Free Press, 1960); Robert Blakely, *Earl B. Dickerson: A Voice for Freedom and Equality* (Evanston, Ill.: Northwestern University Press, 2006); Grimshaw, *Bitter Fruit*; and John Johnson, *Succeeding Against the Odds: The Autobiography of a Great American Businessman* (New York: Amistad, 1989).

226 a single wheel: "Policy Wheels Still Turning Despite 'Heat,'" *Chicago Tribune*, January 7, 1951.

227 "perhaps the one most important": "Kefauver Hits Chicago as U.S. Crime Center," *Chicago Tribune*, November 13, 1950.

227 ninety-two legitimate businesses: Patricia Bronte, *Vittles and Vice* (Chicago: Henry Regnery, 1952), p. 57.

227 "the most inept man": Arvey quoted in Mike Royko, *Boss: Richard J. Daley of Chicago* (New York: Plume, 1988), p. 61.

227 "Who do you think": Dawson quoted ibid., p. 63.

227 "These people aren't going": Dawson quoted in Johnson, *Succeeding*, p. 101.

227 He slated his own candidates: Grimshaw, *Bitter Fruit*, p. 86.

228 "the fountainhead of": "Senator Calls Chicago Worst U.S. Crime Spot," *Chicago Tribune*, December 28, 1950.

228 "out-sing an angel": Langston Hughes, "Things I Like About Chicago I Like, And What I Don't, I Don't," *Chicago Defender*, June 25, 1949.

229 "She had me vomiting": Jackson quoted in Laurraine Goreau, *Just Mahalia, Baby* (Waco, Tex.: Word Books, 1975), p. 138.

229 she imagined herself: Jules Schwerin, *Got to Tell It* (New York: Oxford University Press, 1992), p. 4.

230 Music Inn: Musicinn.org.

230 "No-no, you got to clap": Jackson quoted in Goreau, *Just Mahalia*, p. 149.

230 "picking at my music": Jackson quoted ibid.

231 "When I stepped in there": Jackson quoted in Don Gold, "In God She Trusts," *Ladies' Home Journal*, November 1963.

231 "If he hadn't of kept": Jackson quoted in Goreau, *Just Mahalia*, p. 183.

231 "He want you to sign": Jackson and Terkel quoted in Studs Terkel, *Talking to Myself* (New York: Pantheon, 1977), pp. 44–45.

232 "You all got to learn how to clap": Jackson quoted in Goreau, *Just Mahalia*, pp. 189–90.

233 Little Lulu and Superman comics: John Barrow, "Here's a Picture of Emmett Till Painted by Those Who Knew Him," *Chicago Defender*, October 1, 1955.

233 leopard cape and black beret: John Corbett in "Sun Ra in Chicago: Street Priest and Father of D.I.Y. Jazz," in John Corbett, Anthony Elms, and Terry Kapsalis, curators, *Pathways to Unknown Worlds: El Saturn and Chicago's Afro-Futurist Underground 1954–1968* (Chicago: WhiteWalls, 2006), p. 6.

234 "THE NEGRO RESURRECTED": Sun Ra, "The bible was not written for negroes!!!!!!!" reprinted in John Corbett, ed., *The Wisdom of Sun Ra: Sun Ra's Polemical Broadsheets and Streetcorner Leaflets* (Chicago: WhiteWalls, 2006), p. 89.

234 "a bridge to another dimension": Szwed, *Space*, p. 109.

234 "the creators": Sun Ra, interview by Bob Rusch, *Cadence*, June 1978.

235 Elijah Muhammad: Claude Clegg, *An Original Man: The Life and Times of Elijah Muhammad* (New York: St. Martin's Press, 1997), p. 100.

235 Malcolm Little arrived: Malcolm X, as told to Alex Haley, *The Autobiography of Malcolm X* (New York: Ballantine, 1973), pp. 196–97.

235 "We will see how he does": Muhammad quoted ibid., p. 197.

235 "People have to have": Sun Ra quoted in Charles White, "The People Are the Instrument: Interview with Sun Ra," *Lightworks*, 1979.

235 how much might have been a gimmick: Edward Bland, interview by author.

CHAPTER 18: THE LONELY CROWD

237 "a good contract": Simone de Beauvoir to Nelson Algren, January 14, 1950, in De Beauvoir, *A Transatlantic Love Affair: Letters to Nelson Algren* (New York: New Press, 1997), p. 325.

237 "technical advisor": Bettina Drew, *Nelson Algren: A Life on the Wild Side* (New York: Putnam, 1989), p. 213.

237 **Garfield had screwed boxer Barney Ross:** Ira Berkow, *Maxwell Street: Survival in a Bazaar* (Garden City, N.Y.: Doubleday, 1977), p. 345.

238 **"Just because a woman":** Algren quoted in Art Shay, *Chicago's Nelson Algren* (New York: Seven Stories Press, 2007), p. xxviii.

238 **"New York is the place":** Algren quoted ibid., p. xxix.

238 **Shay went to the printer:** Art Shay, interview by author.

239 **"kind of dirty, soft custard":** De Beauvoir to Algren, September 30, 1950, in *Transatlantic Love Affair*, p. 369.

239 **"loving a woman with a broken":** Nelson Algren, *Chicago: City on the Make* (Garden City, N.Y.: Doubleday, 1951), p. 30.

239 **"An ugly, highly scented object":** "Algren Pens a Distorted, Partial Story of Chicago," *Chicago Tribune,* October 21, 1951.

240 **"Our myths are so many":** Nelson Algren, *Nonconformity* (New York: Seven Stories Press, 1992), p. 76.

240 **"his face crumpled":** De Beauvoir quoted in Deirdre Bair, *Simone de Beauvoir: A Biography* (New York: Simon & Schuster, 1990), p. 430.

240 **"What I've tried to do":** Algren quoted in Simone de Beauvoir, *Force of Circumstance* (New York: Putnam's, 1964), p. 251.

240 **A long A. J. Liebling piece:** The three pieces were "Second City: I. So Proud to Be Jammy Jammy," January 12, 1952; "Second City: II. At Her Feet the Slain Deer," January 19, 1952; and "Second City: III. The Massacree," January 26, 1952. Later that year Alfred A. Knopf published them together with a few more tablespoons of Liebling's invective as *Chicago: The Second City.*

242 **"whose inmates":** Liebling, "Second City: III. The Massacree," *New Yorker,* January 26, 1952.

242 **"determined ladies who":** Ibid.

242 **Winning the "Chicagoan of the Year":** "Hutchins Named Chicagoan of Year," *Chicago Sun-Times,* January 30, 1951.

242 **"The horrid prospect":** Hutchins quoted in Milton Mayer, *Robert Maynard Hutchins: A Memoir* (Berkeley: University of California Press, 1993), p. 399.

242 **The university had been waiting:** Jill Abrahamson, *A Neighborhood Finds Itself*

(New York: Harper & Brothers, 1959), pp. 189–94; Arnold Hirsch, *The Making of the Second Ghetto: Race and Housing in Chicago, 1940–1960* (Cambridge, U.K.: Cambridge University Press, 1983), p. 144.

243 **"acquire early in life":** David Riesman, *The Lonely Crowd* (New Haven, Conn.: Yale University Press, 1950).

244 **"Democracy":** Robert M. Hutchins, *The Great Conversation: The Substance of a Liberal Education* (Chicago: Encyclopaedia Britannica, 1952), p. xv and passim.

244 **"If you have gained":** *Saturday Review,* November 19, 1955.

CHAPTER 19: CONVENTION SUMMER

245 **"You do not invent":** One of Mies's favorite sayings, it is quoted many places, including Franz Schulze, *Mies van der Rohe: A Critical Biography* (Chicago: University of Chicago Press, 1985), p. 67.

246 **Daley was a mama's boy:** The most rounded and complete biography of Daley is Adam Cohen and Elizabeth Taylor, *American Pharaoh* (New York: Little, Brown, 2000). Len O'Connor, *Clout* (New York: Avon Books, 1976), and Mike Royko, *Boss: Richard J. Daley of Chicago* (New York: Plume, 1988), both full of great inside-baseball anecdotes and attitudes, were written in opposition to the Daley Machine.

246 **a "progressive force":** Cohen and Taylor, *American Pharaoh,* p. 65.

247 **Mob silence on his philandering:** Gay Talese, *Thy Neighbor's Wife* (Garden City, N.Y.: Doubleday, 1980), p. 83. For an opposing view, at least as to Kefauver being caught in flagrante, see William Howard Moore, "Was Estes Kefauver 'Blackmailed' During the Chicago Crime Hearings? A Historian's Perspective," *Public Historian* 4, no. 1 (Winter 1982), pp. 4–28.

247 **more than four thousand paying visitors:** "The Republican Show Gets Rolling," *Life,* July 7, 1952.

248 **"Nobody in Chicago is inclined":** "Convention City," *Life,* June 30, 1952.

248 **a pedestrian but well-located:** Carl Condit, *Chicago, 1930–70* (Chicago: University of Chicago Press, 1974), p. 33.

248 "This is exactly what we mean": Republican National Committee, *Official Report of the Proceedings of the 25th Republican National Convention* (Washington, D.C.: Republican National Committee, 1952), p. 97.

249 *anchorman:* Don Hewitt, interview by Michael Rosen, April 15, 1997, Archive of American Television, www.emmytvlegends .org/interviews/people/don-hewitt.

249 "most widely viewed": "New Leaders, New Zeal Take 'Old' Out of G.O.P.," *Life,* July 21, 1952.

249 because Red Quinlan: Studs Terkel, *Talking to Myself* (New York: Pantheon, 1977), pp. 214–16.

249 "a splendidly successful": "A Vote for Nancy," *Life,* June 30, 1952.

250 "He complained that he never": Minow quoted in John Bartlow Martin, *Adlai Stevenson of Illinois* (Garden City, N.Y.: Doubleday, 1976), p. 473.

250 *Life* published a long, fawning profile: "Adlai Stevenson," *Life,* July 21, 1952.

250 "Here on the prairies": Democratic National Committee, *Official Report of the Proceedings of the Democratic National Convention* (Washington, D.C.: Democratic National Committee, 1952), p. 8.

251 "Such strains and such spurting": Theodore H. White, *The Making of the President 1960* (New York: Atheneum, 1961), p. 227.

251 "I have been trying": Truman quoted in Martin, *Stevenson of Illinois,* p. 592.

251 "Let's talk sense": Democratic National Committee, *Official Report,* p. 550.

251 distance himself from Truman: Jeff Broadwater, *Adlai Stevenson: The Odyssey of a Cold War Liberal* (New York: Twayne, 1994), p. 117.

251 Adlai represented Burr Tillstrom: Lewis Gomavitz, interview by Karen Herman, February 2, 2000, Archive of American Television, www.emmytvlegends.org/ interviews/people/lewis-gomavitz.

252 "egghead": Alsop quoted in Broadwater, *Odyssey,* p. 125.

252 "a gaiety, a spontaneity": Martin, *Stevenson of Illinois,* p. 606.

252 "Politically speaking": McGrory quoted in Broadwater, *Odyssey,* p. 116.

252 it was all right so long: Peter Blake, *The Master Builders* (New York: W. W. Norton, 1996), p. 410.

252 "The sad part": O'Connor, *Clout,* p. 77.

CHAPTER 20: PLAYWRIGHTS AND PLAYBOYS

254 "Where you headed?": David Shepherd, "Why Compass Came to Chicago Before Cleveland," David Shepherd Papers, Box 1, Folder Publicity: 50s-60s, Special Collections Research Center, University of Chicago Library. The primary sources on the Compass Theater and Second City are Janet Coleman, *The Compass* (New York: Alfred A. Knopf, 1990), and Jeffrey Sweet, *Something Wonderful Right Away: An Oral History of the Second City and Compass Players* (New York: Avon, 1978).

255 "very mixed": Shepherd quoted in Sweet, *Something Wonderful,* p. 3.

255 In 1950 the Loop saw only: Richard Christiansen, *A Theater of Our Own: A History and a Memoir of 1,001 Nights in Chicago* (Evanston, Ill.: Northwestern University Press, 2004), p. 92.

255 many would say *because:* Bernard Sahlins, interview by author.

255 Faculty members had their tradition: "Mummery on the Midway," *Chicago,* February 1955.

256 Ed Asner, a self-professed: Ed Asner, interview by author.

256 "You had to endure": Heyward Ehrlich quoted in Coleman, *Compass,* p. 18.

256 "considered him her closest": Ibid., p. 20.

256 "effete": Asner interview by author.

256 "intense, charismatic": Sahlins interview by author.

257 "We're making games": Paul Sills and Charles L. Mee, "The Celebratory Occasion," *Tulane Drama Review* 9 (Winter 1964), pp. 167–81.

258 "lustily intrepid amateurs": Claudia Cassidy, "On the Aisle," *Chicago Tribune,* April 14, 1957.

258 "We slept in the theater": Eugene Troobnick quoted in Sweet, *Something Wonderful,* p. 190.

258 "a ballbreaker": Sahlins interview by author.

259 "Everyone was trying": Asner interview by author.

259 Bernard Sahlins: Bernard Asbell, "The Cultural Renaissance: Chapter Two," *Chicago*, September 1956; and Sahlins interview by author.

259 "Eastern mysticism about him": Asner interview by author.

259 "In a year and a half": Shepherd quoted in Christiansen, *Theater of Our Own*, p. 104.

259 "scared shitless": Asner interview by author.

259 "I would hear people": Anthony Holland quoted in Sweet, *Something Wonderful*, p. 256.

259 "the liberal-progressive theatrical": Sahlins interview by author.

260 Foxlike, Hugh Hefner stood: Hugh Hefner, interview by author; Steven Watts, *Mr. Playboy* (Hoboken, N.J.: John Wiley & Sons, 2008), p. 50; and Gay Talese, *Thy Neighbor's Wife* (Garden City, N.Y.: Doubleday, 1980), pp. 20–67.

262 "If Von Rosen could": Hefner interview by author.

262 "It brought back to me": Ibid.

262 "It just reminded me": Ibid.

262 "it was in the days": Ibid.

262 "were all rural": "Playboy: Sex on a Skyrocket," *Chicago*, October 1955, pp. 32–37.

262 "an entertainment magazine": Watts, *Mr. Playboy*, p. 62.

263 "a shirt sleeve kind of guy": Hefner interview by author.

263 "I felt I had succeeded": Ibid.

263 *Playboy* was a hit from the start: "Playboy: Sex on a Skyrocket," *Chicago*, October 1955. Another good account is Carlye Adler and Hugh Hefner, "Hugh Hefner Playboy Enterprises in 1953," *CNNMoney*, September 1, 2003, http://money.cnn.com/magazines/fsb/fsb_archive/2003/09/01/350793/index.htm.

263 "Affairs of state will be": *Playboy* 1, no. 1 (December 1953).

264 "I'm my own boss": "Playboy: Sex on a Skyrocket," *Chicago*, October 1955.

264 trying to convince his wife: Watts, *Mr. Playboy*, p. 48.

264 *Playboy* isn't very serious": "Playboy: Sex on a Skyrocket," *Chicago*, October 1955.

CHAPTER 21:
CHICAGSKY TEMP

265 "the world's largest steel and rail": "The New Chicago," *Newsweek*, August 16, 1954.

265 quarter of all the nation's electronics: Ibid.

265 "How many": Ibid.

265 *Chicagsky Temp:* Ibid.

266 rats had recently eaten: "Chicago's Shame," *Time*, June 29, 1953.

266 "Fort Dearborn": "Tomorrow's City Is on the Way," *Chicago*, September 1955.

266 "We just can't let the Loop rot away": Pirie quoted in "The New Chicago," *Newsweek*, August 16, 1954.

267 "dictated by a refusal": Kimpton quoted ibid.

268 "too much the tyrant teacher": Walter Gropius to Serge Chermayeff, March 23, 1950, Institute of Design Collection, Box 5, Folder 166, Richard J. Daley Library, University of Illinois at Chicago.

268 the FBI investigated ID students: Fitzhugh D. Dinkins, oral history interview, February 10–July 12, 1989, Archives of American Art, Smithsonian Institution.

268 "gall and bitterness": Serge Chermayeff to Walter and Elizabeth Paepcke, August 30, 1951, Institute of Design Collection, Box 5, Folder 166, Richard J. Daley Library, University of Illinois at Chicago.

269 "harryandaaron": David Travis and Elizabeth Siegel, *Taken by Design: Photographs from the Institute of Design, 1937–1971* (Chicago: Art Institute of Chicago, 2002), p. 85.

269 Richard Nickel: Two broad tellings of Nickel's life are Richard Cahan, *They All Fall Down* (Washington, D.C.: Preservation Press, 1994), and Richard Cahan and Michael Williams, *Richard Nickel's Chicago: Photographs of a Lost City* (Chicago: Cityfiles Press, 2006). Jeffrey Plank, *Aaron Siskind and Louis Sullivan: The Institute of Design Photo Section Project* (San Francisco: William Stout, 2008), goes into depth on the Sullivan project. I have also been aided in this section by Len Gittleman and Ward Miller.

270 **first major museum show for Mark Rothko:** Katharine Kuh, *My Love Affair with Modern Art* (New York: Arcade, 2006), p. 146.

270 **a new Chicago school:** Peter Selz, "Surrealism and the Chicago Imagists of the 1950s: A Comparison and Contrast," *Art Journal* 45 (Winter 1985), pp. 303–6.

270 **"one's immediate and actual":** Franz Schulze, *Fantastic Images: Chicago Art Since 1945* (Chicago: Follett, 1972), p. 23.

270 **"The Monster Roster":** Ibid., p. 6.

270 **quite taken with** *Kukla:* Simone de Beauvoir, *A Transatlantic Love Affair: Letters to Nelson Algren* (New York: New Press, 1997), p. 440.

271 **"I was first":** Algren and Stevenson quoted in Art Shay, *Chicago's Nelson Algren* (New York: Seven Stories Press, 2007), p. 38.

271 **Adlai's ex, Ellen Borden:** "A Gold Coast Relic Becomes a Home of the Arts," *Chicago*, March 1954.

271 **"Algren's dick always":** Art Shay, interview by author.

271 **"Women liked him":** Studs Terkel with Sydney Lewis, *Touch and Go: A Memoir* (New York: New Press, 2007), p. 196.

271 **"the American Prisoner":** De Beauvoir, *Transatlantic Love Affair,* p. 489.

271 **"I cannot help you":** Simone de Beauvoir to Nelson Algren, April 1953, ibid., p. 479.

271 **if you could get down on paper the life:** Shay interview by author.

272 **"I'm American, Chicago born":** Saul Bellow, *The Adventures of Augie March* (New York: Viking Press, 1953), p. 1.

273 **"Not one, not two":** Frank London Brown, *Trumbull Park* (Chicago: Henry Regnery, 1959), pp. 123–24.

273 **Mobs prowled the streets:** Arnold R. Hirsch, "Massive Resistance in the Urban North: Trumbull Park, Chicago, 1953–1966," *Journal of American History* 82, no. 2 (September 1995), pp. 522–50. This article is the single best reference on this topic.

273 **"We tell them it's fireworks":** Quoted in "When the Bombs Go Off, We Tell Them It's Fireworks," *Chicago*, August 1954.

273 **a third of all Chicago cops:** Christopher Robert Reed, *The Chicago NAACP and the Rise of Black Professional Leadership, 1910–1966* (Bloomington: Indiana University Press, 1997), p. 152.

273 **"It's an unreal world":** Alan Paton, "The Negro in America Today," *Collier's*, October 15, 1954.

274 **The situation came to a head:** Hirsch, "Massive Resistance in the Urban North."

274 **Quickly and quietly, the city:** Ibid.

274 **"That man's engine's":** Jackson quoted in Laurraine Goreau, *Just Mahalia, Baby* (Waco, Tex.: Word Books, 1975), p. 195.

275 **"not and never was":** Daley quoted in Adam Cohen and Elizabeth Taylor, *American Pharaoh* (New York: Little, Brown, 2000), p. 108.

275 **"I promised to take my kids":** Daley quoted in Mike Royko, *Boss: Richard J. Daley of Chicago* (New York: Plume, 1988), p. 87.

275 **"He was sure":** Quoted ibid.

275 **they thanked him:** Ibid., p. 88.

275 **"They gave me a fast deal":** Kennelly quoted in "Political Notes: Men v. Machine in Chicago," *Time*, March 7, 1955.

275 **"I never dreamed":** Daley quoted in "24 Years after Big Bill," *Time*, January 3, 1955.

276 **"comforting to find":** Gwendolyn Brooks, *Blacks* (Chicago: Third World Press, 1987), p. 144; Brooks, *Maud Martha* (1953; Chicago: Third World Press, 1993), p. 2.

276 **put on an Errol Garner record:** George E. Kent, *A Life of Gwendolyn Brooks* (Lexington: University Press of Kentucky, 1990), p. 148.

276 **Emmett Till didn't go:** Mamie Till-Mobley and Christopher Benson, *Death of Innocence: The Story of the Hate Crime That Changed America* (New York: Ballantine Books, 2003), p. 81.

277 **A confidential secretary:** "The Law: Trial by Jury," *Time*, October 3, 1955; U.S. Department of Commerce, Bureau of the Census, "Current Population Reports: Consumer Income," October 1955, http://www2.census.gov/prod2/popscan/p60-019.pdf.

277 **"captured something more":** Till-Mobley and Benson, *Death of Innocence*, p. 87.

PART FOUR: 1955
CHAPTER 22: A FAMILY MAN
FOR A FAMILY CITY

281 **Checks arrived from labor:** Nicholas von Hoffman, interview by author.

281 **"It is the duty":** Quoted in "The Onion Patch," *Chicago,* April 1955.

281 **Daley slammed the mayor's lack:** Adam Cohen and Elizabeth Taylor, *American Pharaoh* (New York: Little, Brown, 2000), p. 125; Mike Royko, *Boss: Richard J. Daley of Chicago* (New York: Plume, 1988), p. 94.

282 **Down to the wire:** Len O'Connor, *Clout* (New York: Avon Books, 1976), p. 113.

282 **"Chicago ain't ready":** Bauler quoted in Leon M. Despres with Kenan Heise, *Challenging the Daley Machine: A Chicago Alderman's Memoir* (Evanston, Ill.: Northwestern University Press, 2005), p. 3.

282 **"Chicago is unique":** Merriam quoted in A. J. Liebling, "Second City: III. The Massacree," *New Yorker,* January 26, 1952.

282 **"ruthless use of power":** Quoted in "Merriam Vows to Prove 'Open City' Charges," *Chicago Tribune,* April 2, 1955.

282 **"Let's talk sense":** Advertisement in *Chicago Tribune,* April 4, 1955.

283 **"New Togetherness":** Advertisement in *Chicago Tribune,* April 7, 1955.

283 **A *Sun-Times* poll:** "Daley Continues in Front After Poll at Churches," *Chicago Sun-Times,* April 4, 1955.

283 **countless dirty tricks:** Cohen and Taylor, *American Pharaoh,* p. 137; Royko, *Boss,* p. 94.

283 **she spent her days with preachers:** Laurraine Goreau, *Just Mahalia, Baby* (Waco, Tex: Word Books, 1975), p. 195.

284 **Daley's religious offensive:** "The Onion Patch," *Chicago,* May 1955.

284 **"I got 600,000, approximately":** Merriam in Milton Rakove, *We Don't Want Nobody Nobody Sent: An Oral History of the Daley Years* (Bloomington: Indiana University Press, 1979), p. 261.

284 **"They ain't found it out yet":** Bauler quoted in O'Connor, *Clout,* p. 125.

284 **throw the first pitch:** Herb Lyon, "Tower Ticker," *Chicago Tribune,* April 11, 1955.

285 **The state's home rule:** Cohen and Taylor, *American Pharaoh,* p. 144.

285 **"wrongdoing on the part":** O'Connor, *Clout,* p. 127.

285 **"not to be so inquisitive":** "Daley Calls Airline Parley to Break O'Hare Fee Delay," *Chicago Sun-Times,* May 11, 1955.

286 **"a man of inexhaustible energy":** O'Connor, *Clout,* p. 123.

286 **his secretary finally had to:** "Kup's Column," *Chicago Sun-Times,* May 16, 1955.

286 **the mayor's fifty-third birthday:** "Daley Children Come Through," *Chicago Sun-Times,* May 16, 1955.

286 **"the matadors of the Air Force":** "Thousands Thrilled by Mock Attack of Jets," *Chicago American,* May 22, 1955.

286 **Sun shining:** "I'm Glad to Be Home, Says Mayor," *Chicago Sun-Times,* May 22, 1955.

287 **the ride out:** "Kup's Column," *Chicago Sun-Times,* May 17, 1955.

287 **Though he'd bestowed:** "125,000 View Military Parade," *Chicago Sun-Times,* May 22, 1955.

288 **"Right now":** Daniel Seligman, "The Battle for Chicago," *Fortune,* June 1955.

288 **"Do you feel":** "Chicago's Comeback," *U.S. News & World Report,* May 27, 1955.

288 **"Yes," said the mayor, "I can":** Ibid.

288 **"New Breeze Is Blowing":** *Chicago Sun-Times,* May 24, 1955.

288 **"Chicago on the Move":** *Chicago Daily News,* May 24, 1955.

288 **"Chicago the Greatest?":** *Chicago American,* May 25, 1955.

288 **"Chicagoan Designs 38":** "Chicagoan Designs 38 Story, $20 Million New York Building," *Chicago Tribune,* March 30, 1955.

288 **Jules Herbuveaux noticed:** O'Connor, *Clout,* p. 131.

289 **"the pile driver has replaced":** "Chicago and Its Suburbs," *Chicago Tribune,* July 4, 1955.

289 **He made it known:** Cohen and Taylor, *American Pharaoh,* p. 155.

CHAPTER 23: THE BLUES
HAVE A BABY

290 **McDaniel had learned to play:** Nadine Cohodas, *Spinning Blues into Gold* (New York: St. Martin's Press, 2000), p. 100.

291 **"Yeah, see Leonard Chess":** Waters quoted in Chuck Berry, *The Autobiography of*

Chuck Berry (New York: Crown, 1987), p. 98. Despite his understandable tendency to tell his stories in ways that make himself look good, Berry's autobiography is exceptionally cogent and thoughtful.

291 **If Muddy had known:** Bruce Pegg, *Brown Eyed Handsome Man: The Life and Hard Times of Chuck Berry* (New York: Routledge, 2002), is more complete if not more colorful than Berry's autobiography.

294 **Marshall's bar mitzvah:** Cohodas, *Spinning*, pp. 107–9, describes possibly the greatest bar mitzvah in history.

294 **Marshall began to hang:** Marshall Chess, interview by author.

294 **cops broke up a gang fight:** "Break Up Teen-Age Gang Fight Before It Starts," *Chicago Tribune*, May 26, 1955.

294 **346 drivers had been killed:** "Highway Toll Rises as Long Holiday Ends," *Chicago Tribune*, May 31, 1955.

294 **General Motors announced:** "G.M. Directors Propose 3 to 1 Stock Split," *Chicago Tribune*, July 6, 1955.

294 **suburban Bedford Park:** "Large Marijuana Field in County to Be Destroyed," *Chicago Tribune*, June 6, 1955.

294 **eight-year-old Mary Manzo:** "Hold Suspect in Sex Killing," *Chicago Tribune*, July 8, 1955.

294 **The Shriners arrived:** "40,000 Pour into City for Shriner Fete," *Chicago Tribune*, July 11, 1955.

294 **a seven-year-old girl:** "Girl, 7, Raped by Teen-Ager on North Side," *Chicago Tribune*, July 11, 1955.

294 **Disneyland opened:** "Wonderland a Mouse Built Dawns Today," *Chicago Tribune*, July 17, 1955.

294 **Braniff plane crashed:** "22 Killed in Midway Plane Crash," *Chicago Tribune*, July 18, 1955.

295 **"spent more money":** "Production, Income Set Record Highs," *Chicago Tribune*, July 22, 1955.

295 **Mayor Daley banned watering:** "Orders Water Restrictions on South Side," *Chicago Tribune*, August 5, 1955.

295 **Someone tried to steal:** "Felon Seized in Attempt to Abduct Baby," *Chicago Tribune*, August 1, 1955.

295 **Leonard sent a touring contract:** Berry, *Autobiography*, pp. 105–7.

295 **all hands were on deck:** Cohodas, *Spinning*, p. 117.

295 **most-played, most-bought R&B record:** *Billboard*, September 3, 1955.

295 **Muddy meanwhile spent:** Robert Gordon, *Can't Be Satisfied: The Life and Times of Muddy Waters* (Boston: Little, Brown, 2002), pp. 139–40.

CHAPTER 24: AMERICAN HUNGERS

296 **"If I lost out on":** Kroc quoted in John F. Love, *McDonald's: Behind the Arches* (New York: Bantam Books, 1986), p. 47.

296 **The Greek boy:** "Golden Memories of Golden Era," *Chicago Tribune*, April 15, 2005.

296 **no carhops giving hand jobs:** Love, *McDonald's*, p. 39.

297 **Not a true fan:** Ibid., pp. 121–24; and Ray Kroc with Robert Anderson, *Grinding It Out: The Making of McDonald's* (New York: St. Martin's, 1977), pp. 76–78.

297 **Ray Kroc was fifty-two:** Love, *McDonald's*, and Kroc and Anderson, *Grinding It Out*, are the two primary biographical sources for Kroc.

297 **car registrations:** "Illinois Job Picture Bright," *Chicago Sun-Times*, May 22, 1955.

298 **commissioning the golden arches:** Alan Hess, "The Origins of McDonald's Golden Arches," *Journal of the Society of Architectural Historians* 45, no. 1 (March 1986), pp. 60–67.

298 **they gave them away:** Love, *McDonald's*, p. 23.

299 **"a small factory":** Ibid., p. 136.

299 **Kids liked the independence:** Ibid., p. 16.

299 **invention of the commodity future:** William Cronon, *Nature's Metropolis: Chicago and the Great West* (New York: W. W. Norton, 1991), chap. 3. You'd do well to read the whole book.

299 **"the hog squeal":** Upton Sinclair, *The Jungle* (New York: Doubleday, 1906), p. 41.

300 **ever speedier production:** Rick Halpern, *Down on the Killing Floor: Black and White Workers in Chicago's Packinghouses, 1904–1954* (Urbana: University of Illinois Press, 1997), p. 19.

300 **an alternative way:** Elaine Tyler May, *Homeward Bound: American Families in the Cold War Era* (New York: Basic Books, 1988), p. 22.

300 **the norm in franchising:** Love, *McDonald's*, pp. 56–62.

301 **"Some authorities consider":** "Report Lung Changes Among Cigaret Users," *Chicago Tribune*, June 3, 1955.

301 **"west of the Hudson":** Leo Burnett, *Communications of an Advertising Man* (Chicago: Privately printed, 1961), pp. 193–94 and passim.

301 **"Key clubs":** Bernard Asbell, "Unlocking the Key Clubs," *Chicago*, June 1955, pp. 28–33.

302 **"Roquefort and Ricotta":** Thomas Mario, "The Sophisticated Cheese," *Playboy*, May 1955.

302 **Charlaine's mother was not pleased:** Hugh Hefner, interview by author.

302 **Twelve-year-old Peter Gorham:** "Evanston Boy Disappears at Scout Camp," *Chicago Tribune*, July 7, 1955.

302 **another gang fight:** "Pupil Slain in Gang Battle," *Chicago Tribune*, July 2, 1955.

302 **"Actually, potential Playmates":** "*Playboy*'s Office Playmate," *Playboy*, July 1955.

303 **"an absolute sensation":** Carlye Adler and Hugh Hefner, "Hugh Hefner Playboy Enterprises in 1953," *CNNMoney*, September 1, 2003, http://money.cnn.com/magazines/fsb/fsb_archive/2003/09/01/350793/index.htm.

303 **Reverend Jack Egan:** Margery Frisbie, *An Alley in Chicago: The Life and Legacy of Monsignor John Egan* (Franklin, Wis.: Sheed & Ward, 2002), pp. 48–59.

303 **free love, a sell-out topic:** Franklin Rosemont, *The Rise and Fall of the Dil Pickle* (Chicago: Charles H. Kerr, 2004), p. 90.

303 **Chicago issued 66,000 marriage licenses:** "Statistics of Marriages, Divorces," *Chicago Tribune*, January 1, 1950.

303 **having less sex:** John D'Emilio and Estelle B. Freedman, *Intimate Matters: A History of Sexuality in America* (New York: Harper & Row, 1988), p. 268. May, *Homeward Bound*, pp. 63, 112–13, for the dangers of female sexuality.

304 **"the first nice girl":** Russell Miller, *Bunny* (New York: Signet, 1998), p. 55.

CHAPTER 25: THEATER WITHOUT HEROES

305 **"a legitimate theater director":** Ed Asner, interview by author.

305 **"come up with a startling":** Weitzel quoted in "The Town Crier," *Chicago Daily News*, May 25, 1955.

305 **"the newspaper vendor":** David Shepherd, "Plans for a Popular Theater," Box 1, Folder Publicity: 50s–60s, Special Collections Research Center, University of Chicago Library; Peter Bryan, "First Nights in a Barroom," *Chicago* 1 (January 1955).

306 **"for the sort of people":** Bertolt Brecht, *On Theatre*, trans. John Willett (London: Methuen, 1964), p. 14.

306 **"point of concentration":** Viola Spolin, *Improvisation for the Theater*, 3rd ed. (Evanston, Ill.: Northwestern University Press, 1963), p. liv; Janet Coleman, *The Compass* (New York: Alfred A. Knopf, 1990), p. 25.

307 **requiring everyone to read Riesman's book:** Ibid., p. 95.

307 **"You forget yourself":** Barbara Harris quoted in Jeffrey Sweet, *Something Wonderful Right Away: An Oral History of the Second City and Compass Players* (New York: Avon, 1978), p. 66.

307 **"not meet that one":** Ed Asner, interview by author.

307 **"These guys are culture":** Daley quoted in Coleman, *Compass*, p. 98.

307 **Bowen claimed they did it:** Sweet, *Something Wonderful*, p. 31.

308 **"People would sit out there":** Shepherd quoted in Coleman, *Compass*, p. 75.

308 **"We were articulate":** Duncan quoted in Sweet, *Something Wonderful*, p. 47. For photos of the Compass, see "Commedia dell'arte in a 55th Street Saloon," *Chicago* 2 (September 1955), pp. 60–62.

308 **"Nobody knew what":** Harris quoted in Sweet, *Something Wonderful*, p. 68.

308 **play a game of chess:** David Shepherd, interview by author.

309 **"I'd like to see neighborhoods":** Sills quoted in "Commedia dell'arte in a 55th

Street Saloon," *Chicago* 2 (September 1955), pp. 60–62.

309 **"I didn't expect it":** Shepherd quoted in Coleman, *Compass,* p. 115.

309 **"I've tried to do things":** Shepherd interview by author.

309 **"vastly superior":** Ibid.

309 **While a student:** Sweet, *Something Wonderful,* p. 145.

310 **"If you weesh":** Mike Nichols quoted ibid., p. 74.

310 **"You would literally be possessed":** Mike Nichols quoted ibid.

310 **"You had the right":** Gordon quoted ibid., p. 121.

311 **"antagonistic cooperation":** Ralph Ellison, "The Little Man at Chehaw Station," *The Collected Essays of Ralph Ellison* (New York: Modern Library, 2003), pp. 493–523.

311 **"Chicago was the best":** Darden quoted in Sweet, *Something Wonderful,* p. 96.

CHAPTER 26: WHAT KIND OF WORLD DO WE LIVE IN?

312 **Susan and Sandra Pasternak:** "500 Search Prairie for 2 Missing Girls," *Chicago Tribune,* August 9, 1955.

312 **body of Peter Gorham:** "Scout Found Shot to Death," *Chicago Tribune,* August 15, 1955.

312 **"if ever there were":** Gene O'Shea, *Unbridled Rage: A True Story of Organized Crime, Corruption and Murder in Chicago* (New York: Berkeley Books, 2005), p. 9.

312 **"kids didn't worry about the future":** Bob Polster, "The 'Perfect Place,'" in Neal Samors and Michael Williams, *Chicago in the Fifties* (Chicago: Chicago's Neighborhoods, 2005), p. 51.

312 **"I felt great anger":** Warner Saunders, "Bronzeville Memories," in ibid., p. 11.

312 **"Everybody enjoyed their civil":** Nicholas von Hoffman, *Radical: A Portrait of Saul Alinsky* (New York: Nation Books, 2010), p. 55.

313 **During the war, migrants:** Timuel Black, *Bridges of Memory* (Evanston, Ill.: Northwestern University Press, 2005), vol. 1. This two-volume oral history of Black Chicago draws a tremendous picture of Woodlawn at this time.

313 **Now the area boasted:** William Grimshaw, *Bitter Fruit: Black Politics and the Chicago Machine, 1931–1991* (Chicago: University of Chicago Press, 1992), p. 228.

313 **median income for blacks:** Adam Green, *Selling the Race* (Chicago: University of Chicago Press, 2007), p. 10.

313 **Barber Leon Cooper:** Black, *Bridges of Memory,* p. 355.

313 ***Jet* had published pictures:** "Mississippi Gunmen Take Life of Militant Negro Minister," *Jet,* May 26, 1955.

314 **"Bo," shouted Mamie:** Mamie Till-Mobley and Christopher Benson, *Death of Innocence: The Story of the Hate Crime That Changed America* (New York: Ballantine Books, 2003), p. 104.

314 **That week Senator James Eastland:** Stephen Whitfield, *A Death in the Delta: The Story of Emmett Till* (Baltimore: Johns Hopkins University Press, 1988), p. 88.

314 **"If Bo Till could get his feet":** "Mamie Bradley's Untold Story, Installment IV," *Chicago Defender,* March 6, 1956.

314 **by the end of the day:** "Protest Mississippi Shame," *Chicago Defender,* September 10, 1955.

315 **"Every black buck in the South":** William Alexander Percy, *Lanterns on the Levee* (New York: Alfred A. Knopf, 1941).

315 **if Bo hadn't been:** Whitfield, *Death in the Delta,* p. 102.

315 **Roy Bryant, the owner:** "Find Kidnaped Chicago Boy's Body in River," *Chicago Tribune,* September 1, 1955.

315 ***Jet* reporter Simeon Booker:** Simeon Booker, "My *Jet* Years, 1953–2006," *Jet,* November 13, 2006; Wil Haygood, "The Man From *Jet*," *Washington Post,* July 15, 2007.

315 **"blow his head off":** J. W. Milam in William Bradford Huie, "What's Happened to the Emmett Till Killers?" *Look,* January 1957.

315 **Chicago TV stations broke into:** Till-Mobley and Benson, *Death of Innocence,* p. 130.

315 **"Oh, God! Oh, God!":** "Mother's Tears Greet Son Who Died a Martyr," *Chicago Defender,* September 10, 1955.

316 **"I will never forget":** Till-Mobley and Benson, *Death of Innocence,* p. 132.

316 "something from outer space": "Mamie Bradley's Untold Story, Installment I," *Chicago Defender*, February 27, 1956.

316 "Let the world see": Till-Mobley and Benson, *Death of Innocence*, p. 139.

316 "a martyr and inspiration": "2,500 at Rites Here for Boy, 14, Slain in South," *Chicago Tribune*, September 4, 1955.

316 Five days later *Jet:* John Johnson, *Succeeding Against the Odds: The Autobiography of a Great American Businessman* (New York: Amistad, 1989), p. 240.

317 "There were people on the staff": Ibid.

317 "felt a deep kinship": Ali quoted in Whitfield, *Death in the Delta*, p. 94.

317 "A Good Place to Raise a Boy": "Ready For Till's Mom To Testify," *Chicago Defender*, September 24, 1955.

317 J. Edgar Hoover hinted that Daley's: Whitfield, *Death in the Delta*, p. 78.

318 "If we hadn't stopped to drink": Quoted in "The Law: Trial by Jury," *Time*, October 3, 1955.

318 A year later, Bryant and Milam: William Bradford Huie, "What's Happened to the Emmett Till Killers?" *Look*, January 1957.

318 "the first great media event": David Halberstam, *The Fifties* (New York: Villard Books, 1993), p. 437.

318 "white girls by negro": *Chicago Sun-Times*, memorandum regarding the Till murder trial, September 13, 1955, in publications. newberry.org/frontiertoheartland/items/show/123.

318 "A generation of black people": Diggs quoted in Whitfield, *Death in the Delta*, p. 145.

318 "Black Chicago, for now": Quoted in Green, *Selling the Race*, p. 201.

318 "All of Black Chicago": Ibid.

318 "Rosa Parks": Till-Mobley and Benson, *Death of Innocence*, p. 257.

319 "Anything I can do for you": Daley quoted in Laurraine Goreau, *Just Mahalia, Baby* (Waco, Tex: Word Books, 1975), p. 198.

319 speech at Trumbull Park: Adam Cohen and Elizabeth Taylor, *American Pharaoh* (New York: Little, Brown, 2000), p. 173.

320 thirteen-year-old Bobby Peterson: This narrative and the subsequent discussion of the investigation are drawn from Richard C. Lindberg and Gloria Jean Sykes, *Shattered Sense of Innocence: The 1955 Murders of Three Chicago Children* (Carbondale: Southern Illinois University Press, 2006); and Gene O'Shea, *Unbridled Rage: A True Story of Organized Crime, Corruption and Murder in Chicago* (New York: Berkeley Books, 2005). Loose ends and conspiracy theories abound in both. Lindberg and Sykes stay more focused on the boys, while O'Shea goes off more into the gruesome Horse Mafia.

321 "Mother," he cried: Lindberg and Sykes, *Shattered Sense of Innocence*, p. 56.

321 Mamie Till sent a message: "Mrs. Bradley Wires Moms of 3 Slain Chicago Boys," *Chicago Defender*, October 29, 1955.

322 his book-lined kitchenette: Robert Barry in John Corbett, Anthony Elms, and Terry Kapsalis, *Pathways to Unknown Worlds: El Saturn and Chicago's Afro-Futurist Underground 1954–1968* (Chicago: WhiteWalls, 2006), p. 125.

322 New York sax players: John Corbett, *Extended Play: Sounding Off from John Cage to Dr. Funkenstein* (Durham, N.C.: Duke University Press, 1994), p. 165.

CHAPTER 27:
WE LIKE IT THIS WAY

323 "Whenever," Algren once asked: Nelson Algren, *Who Lost an American?* (New York: Macmillan, 1963), p. 252.

323 contact with fine art actually hurt: David Travis and Elizabeth Siegel, *Taken by Design: Photographs from the Institute of Design, 1937–1971* (Chicago: Art Institute of Chicago, 2002), p. 154.

324 Doblin had Callahan and Siskind's: Ibid., p. 155.

324 "Are not the good intentions": Serge Chermayeff to Frantz Altschuler, undated, Institute of Design Collection, Box 5, Folder 165, Richard J. Daley Library, University of Illinois at Chicago.

324 Otto's brother Ingo Preminger: Foster Hirsch, *Otto Preminger: The Man Who Would Be King* (New York: Alfred A. Knopf, 2007), p. 235. Algren tells a version in his story "Otto Preminger's Strange Suspenjers" in *The Last Carousel* (1973; New York: Seven Stories Press, 1997).

325 **"downtown where nobody lives":** "The Reminiscences of Otto Preminger," 1971, p. 66, Oral History Collection, Columbia University.

325 **"How come you know":** Preminger quoted in H. E. F. Donohue, *Conversations with Nelson Algren* (New York: Hill & Wang, 1963), p. 119.

325 **"no chance of having a":** Algren quoted ibid.

325 **"While he's a wonderful writer":** "The Reminiscences of Otto Preminger," 1971, p. 66, Oral History Collection, Columbia University.

325 **"Thank you for letting me":** Preminger quoted in Donohue, *Conversations with Algren*, p. 120.

325 **"made a horse's ass out of him":** Peltz quoted in Bettina Drew, *Nelson Algren: A Life on the Wild Side* (New York: Putnam, 1989), p. 265.

325 **"He not only made it":** Goldfarb quoted ibid., p. 263.

325 **"I have no obligation":** Preminger quoted in Foster Hirsch, *Otto Preminger: The Man Who Would Be King* (New York: Alfred A. Knopf, 2007), p. 237.

326 **"sort of comical":** Algren quoted in Donohue, *Conversations with Algren*, p. 123.

327 **"Get that big black gorilla":** Quoted in Laurraine Goreau, *Just Mahalia, Baby* (Waco, Tex: Word Books, 1975), p. 197.

328 **"all the little girls":** Washington quoted ibid., p. 202; "My Love Life," *Chicago Defender,* June 19, 1956.

328 **"As mayor of Chicago":** "Daley Extends Best Holiday Wishes to All," *Chicago Tribune,* December 24, 1955.

PART FIVE: 1956–1960
CHAPTER 28: CHICAGO DYNAMIC

331 **"a high powered sports car":** "Day in Mayor Daley's Life 15 Bustling Hours," *Chicago Tribune,* June 2, 1956. Mike Royko, *Boss: Richard J. Daley of Chicago* (Chicago: Plume, 1988), begins with this trip, though a decade or so later.

331 **rarely ran more:** Lynn Williams in Milton Rakove, *We Don't Want Nobody Nobody Sent: An Oral History of the Daley Years* (Bloomington: Indiana University Press, 1979), p. 255.

331 **he made a note:** Ibid.

331 **If he grew impatient:** Nicholas von Hoffman, interview by author.

332 **"When I'm right":** Daley quoted in Peter H. Rossi and Robert A. Dentler, *The Politics of Urban Renewal: The Chicago Findings* (Glencoe, N.Y.: Free Press, 1961), p. 248.

332 **"like he just came":** Mike Bilandic in Rakove, *We Don't Want Nobody,* p. 398.

332 **"Chicago business has made up":** Owings quoted in "Predict Loop Building Boom; Industry Development Slows," *Chicago Tribune,* December 1, 1956.

332 **a virtually independent entity:** John Donald Cordwell, oral history interview by Betty J. Blum, © 2004, Art Institute of Chicago, pp. 129–31, used with permission.

333 **"American Pharoah":** Adam Cohen and Elizabeth Taylor, *American Pharaoh* (New York: Little, Brown, 2000).

333 **but somehow managed:** Royko, *Boss,* p. 75.

333 **made a billionaire of its owner:** William G. Ferris, "Who Is the Richest Man in Town?" *Chicago,* February 1955.

334 **"Good government is good":** "The Reminiscences of Jacob Arvey," 1967, p. 25, Oral History Collection, Columbia University.

334 **politics had always been:** James Q. Wilson, *Negro Politics: The Search for Leadership* (Glencoe, N.Y.: Free Press, 1960), p. 33.

334 **"probably the worst":** "A Really Good Police Force," *Life,* September 16, 1957.

334 **A small businessman:** Royko, *Boss,* p. 68.

334 **"service for favors":** Ibid.

335 **an ambiguous moral force:** John Bartlow Martin, "To Chicago, With Love," *Saturday Evening Post,* October 15, 1960.

335 **"He had a very clever":** Ralph Berkowitz in Rakove, *We Don't Want Nobody,* p. 25.

335 **"a very intelligent political program":** Richard Friedman ibid., p. 294.

335 **recorded on a card:** Leon M. Despres with Kenan Heise, *Challenging the Daley Machine: A Chicago Alderman's Memoir* (Evanston, Ill.: Northwestern University Press, 2005), p. 40.

335 **"I think patronage is":** Daley quoted by Lynn Williams in Rakove, *We Don't Want Nobody,* p. 249.

335 **"Daley is undeniably"**: Gerry Robichaud, "How Good a Mayor Is Daley?" *Chicago*, March 1956.

335 **"What's wrong with Chicago?"**: "Chicago Rises to Mighty Gem in the Prairies," *Chicago Tribune*, August 13, 1956.

336 **wedding of their son Adlai III**: Jeff Broadwater, *Adlai Stevenson: The Odyssey of a Cold War Liberal* (New York: Twayne, 1994), p. 150.

336 **"Doctor, I feel so strange!"**: Ellen Borden, "Modern Woman: A Round Table Discussion," *Chicago*, September 1955.

337 **"Go get him"**: Daley quoted in Len O'Connor, *Clout* (New York: Avon Books, 1976), p. 143.

337 **JFK and Peter Lawford**: Ira Berkow, *Maxwell Street: Survival in a Bazaar* (Garden City, N.Y.: Doubleday, 1977), p. 101.

337 **"a patsy"**: "The Reminiscences of Jacob Arvey," 1967, p. 52, Oral History Collection, Columbia University.

337 **"This is my politician"**: Stevenson quoted ibid., p. 53.

338 **"It would be an error"**: "Chicago Buildings Have Busiest Year," *Chicago Tribune*, January 2, 1957.

338 **"a finger in the right direction"**: Wright quoted in "Wright Limits Kind Words to Two Subjects," *Chicago Tribune*, October 18, 1956.

338 **"I detest seeing the boys"**: Wright quoted in "Sky City Plan No Idle Dream, Says Wright," *Chicago Tribune*, October 17, 1956.

338 **"the only Chicago mayor since"**: Wright quoted in "Wright Limits Kind Words To Two Subjects," *Chicago Tribune*, October 18, 1956.

338 **"the center of the universe"**: Eero Saarinen, "A New Architecture for a New Chicago," *Chicago Tribune*, May 13, 1956.

338 **"The moral fiber"**: Ibid.

339 **Bucking trends**: John Vinci, oral history interview by Betty J. Blum, © 2002, Art Institute of Chicago, pp. 7–8, used with permission.

339 **he usually had lunch**: Peter Blake, *The Master Builders* (New York: W. W. Norton, 1996), p. 13.

339 **"serene temple"**: Eero Saarinen, "A New Architecture for a New Chicago," *Chicago Tribune*, May 13, 1956.

339 **"A girder"**: Mies quoted in "Less Is More," *Time*, June 14, 1954.

340 **discussions were being had**: Mies tendered his official resignation in a letter to Rettaliata on December 2, 1957, but he'd been moving toward it for three years.

340 **IIT had only complaints**: See IIT to Mies van der Rohe, September 29, 1954, Mies van der Rohe Papers, Museum of Modern Art, New York.

340 **Big, approved names**: "Mayor Daley as Mister Chicago Culture," *Chicago Daily News*, March 30, 1968.

340 **Frank Lloyd Wright was one**: Kathryn Smith, "How the Robie House Was Saved," *Frank Lloyd Wright Quarterly* 19, no. 4 (Fall 2008), pp. 4–19.

341 **"sound as a nut"**: Wright quoted ibid.

341 **"Chicago Dynamic" festival**: "A Poetic Reprise for Chicago's Laureate," *Life*, November 4, 1957. The visit was also well covered in newspapers, but the most compelling document is a televised discussion between Wright and Sandberg moderated by Alastair Cooke, *The Chicago Dynamic Hour*, WTTW-TV.

341 **"We live in the time of the colossal"**: Sandburg quoted in "A Poetic Reprise for Chicago's Laureate," *Life*, November 4, 1957.

342 **"In another fifteen years"**: Wright quoted in Daniel Bluestone, "Preservation and Renewal in Post–World War II Chicago," *Journal of Architectural Education* 47, no. 4 (May 1994), pp. 210–23.

343 **"Chicago could not create"**: Schulze quoted in Carl Condit, *Chicago 1930–70* (Chicago: University of Chicago Press, 1974), p. 116.

CHAPTER 29: BETA PEOPLE FOR A BETA WORLD

344 **"Suddenly the whole"**: Gordon quoted in Janet Coleman, *The Compass* (New York: Alfred A. Knopf, 1990), p. 159.

344 **"There is no better trigger"**: Walter Benjamin, *Selected Writings*, vol. 2, *1927–1934* (Cambridge, Mass.: Harvard University Press, 1999), p. 779.

345 **"I lost control"**: David Shepherd, interview by author.

345 **"to be most loved"**: Berman quoted in Coleman, *Compass*, p. 163.

345 **"People began to"**: Gordon quoted ibid., p. 164.

345 **"went from being a potential theater"**: Gordon in Jeffrey Sweet, *Something Wonderful Right Away: An Oral History of the Second City and Compass Players* (New York: Avon, 1978), p. 115.

345 **both assert identity and opposition**: Lawrence W. Levine, *Black Culture and Black Consciousness* (Oxford, U.K.: Oxford University Press, 1977), p. 297.

346 **"In laughter as in blues"**: Ibid., p. 359.

346 **"a little like the *commedia dell' arte*"**: "dining drinking" *Playboy*, August 1956.

346 **"industrialization of gags"**: Shepherd in Sweet, *Something Wonderful*, p. 9.

346 **"Baseball is commercially"**: Paul Sills and Charles L. Mee, "The Celebratory Occasion," *Tulane Drama Review* 9 (Winter 1964), pp. 167–81.

346 **"initiate theatre of our own"**: Sahlins quoted in Bernard Asbell, "The Cultural Renaissance: Chapter Two," *Chicago*, September 1956.

346 **"If we do the right thing"**: Quoted ibid.

346 **A strong start with Geraldine**: Richard Christiansen, *A Theater of Our Own: A History and a Memoir of 1,001 Nights in Chicago* (Evanston, Ill.: Northwestern University Press, 2004), p. 109.

346 **Claudia Cassidy's acid reviews**: Claudia Cassidy, "On the Aisle," *Chicago Tribune*, April 14 and 21, 1957, in particular. Bernard Asbell, "Claudia Cassidy: The Queen of Culture and Her Reign of Terror," *Chicago* 3 (June 1956), pp. 22–29, laid out the case against her in detail.

347 **"the Worst Lysistrata"**: Cassidy quoted in Christiansen, *Theater of Our Own*, p. 109.

347 **"dramatic transactions"**: Del Close in Sweet, *Something Wonderful*, pp. 141–42.

347 **"You've ruined my dream"**: Shepherd quoted in Coleman, *Compass*, p. 220.

348 **Alton Abraham and Thmei Research**: John Szwed, *Space Is the Place: The Lives and Times of Sun Ra* (New York: Da Capo, 1998), is excellent and the two volumes edited by John Corbett are essential and great fun, but the most comprehensive examination of Sun Ra in Chicago is Robert L. Campbell, Christopher Trent, and Robert

Pruter, "From Sonny Blount to Sun Ra: The Chicago Years," http://hubcap.clemson .edu/~campber/sunra.html.

348 **"Sun Ra was another"**: Patrick quoted in Szwed, *Space*, p. 89.

349 **"I had to play"**: Sun Ra quoted in Brett Primack, "Captain Angelic: Sun Ra," *Downbeat*, May 4, 1978.

349 **"In my intergalactic"**: Sun Ra quoted in Tam Fiofori, "The Space Age Music of Sun Ra . . . 'Between Two Worlds,'" undated, Abraham Alton Collection of Sun Ra (Box 2, Folder 5), Special Collections Research Center, University of Chicago Library.

349 **"moved or spoken for years"**: Szwed, *Space*, p. 92.

350 **only Atlantic Records**: Nadine Cohodas, *Spinning Blues into Gold* (New York: St. Martin's Press, 2000), p. 121.

350 **sleeping in his car**: Bruce Pegg, *Brown Eyed Handsome Man: The Life and Hard Times of Chuck Berry* (New York: Routledge, 2002), p. 54.

350 **Marshall suddenly had a new bike**: Marshall Chess, interview by author.

350 **Aside from replacing**: For details of the renovation of 2120 South Michigan, see Cohodas, *Spinning*, pp. 138–40.

350 **they now sometimes encouraged**: Ibid., pp. 124–25.

351 **Chess had no intention**: Robert Gordon, *Can't Be Satisfied: The Life and Times of Muddy Waters* (Boston: Little, Brown, 2002), p. 146.

351 **"funk"**: Cohodas, *Spinning*, p. 142.

351 **Plopping down at a side table**: Gordon, *Can't Be Satisfied*, p. 147.

352 **"an impression of Coleridge's demon"**: Larkin quoted in James Segrest and Mark Hoffman, *Moanin' at Midnight: The Life and Times of Howlin' Wolf* (New York: Thunder's Mouth Press, 2004), p. 127.

352 **"vaguely menacing"**: Chisholm quoted ibid., p. 145.

352 **Wolf didn't let his band**: Ibid., p. 177.

352 **an outfit called Cobra**: Willie Dixon with Don Snowden, *I Am the Blues: The Willie Dixon Story* (New York: Da Capo, 1989), pp. 103–4.

352 **Ramsey Lewis and his trio**: Ronnie Reese, "The Touch," *Waxpoetics*, no. 47 (n.d.);

J. S. Fuerst, *When Public Housing Was Paradise: Building Community in Chicago* (Westport, Conn.: Praeger, 2003), p. 161; Cohodas, *Spinning,* p. 155.

352 **Ahmad Jamal:** Ahmad Jamal, interview by author.

352 **"very withdrawn, an introvert":** Ibid.

353 **"Leonard treated me":** Ibid.

353 **Gospel came to Chess:** Marshall Chess, interview by author.

353 **"the common frame of reference":** Jackson quoted in Nick Salvatore, *Singing in a Strange Land: C. L. Franklin, the Black Church, and the Transformation of America* (New York: Little, Brown, 2005), p. 192.

353 **Everyone listened, from Al Green:** Dave Hoekstra, "Aretha Franklin's Roots of Soul," *Chicago Sun-Times,* May 12, 2011.

353 **"We had Mozart, Beethoven":** Chess interview by author.

353 **"chiseled out":** Shel Silverstein, liner notes for *Gibson and Camp at the Gate of Horn,* 1961, quoted in Christopher Catania, "The Magical Backstory of Chicago's Historic Folk Venue Gate of Horn," http://christo phercatania.com/2011/01/31/ the-magical-back-story-of-chicagos -gate-of-horn.

354 **Howard Alk worked there:** Coleman, *Compass,* p. 248.

354 **"dark and hot and crowded":** Silverstein quoted in Catania, "Magical Backstory."

354 **Katie Lee:** After her career as a folksinger, Lee moved to the West and became an active environmentalist. See her website www.katydoodit.com.

354 **"The interest in folk music":** Stracke quoted in Lisa Grayson, *Biography of a Hunch: The History of Chicago's Legendary Old Town School of Folk Music* (Chicago: Old Town School of Folk Music, 1992).

CHAPTER 30: GAINING A MOON AND LOSING OURSELVES

356 **"a reader's book":** Nelson Algren, interview by Alston Anderson and Terry Southern, *Paris Review,* no. 11 (Winter 1955).

356 **"museum piece":** "Books: Who Knows?" *Time,* May 28, 1956.

356 **"more poetical and strong":** Simone de Beauvoir to Nelson Algren, July 12, 1956, in De Beauvoir, *A Transatlantic Love Affair: Letters to Nelson Algren* (New York: New Press, 1997), p. 254.

356 **"The second part":** Ibid.

357 **"Everyone is guilty of everything":** Nelson Algren, *A Walk on the Wild Side* (1956; New York: Farrar, Straus & Giroux, 1989), p. 327.

357 **"on account of becuz he":** Art Shay owns one.

357 **"she couldn't write a scene":** Algren quoted in Bettina Drew, *Nelson Algren: A Life on the Wild Side* (New York: Putnam, 1989), p. 205.

357 **"I think the lady invaded":** Art Shay, interview by author.

357 **"used to be as easy":** Ibid.

357 **"I have been trying":** Nelson Algren, *Who Lost an American?* (New York: Macmillan, 1963), p. 144.

358 **The next day the *Tribune:*** "Save Novelist from Lagoon as Ice Breaks," *Chicago Tribune,* January 1, 1957.

358 **"like a comet":** Shay interview by author.

358 **"large-hearted, funny":** Russell Banks, foreword to Algren, *Walk on the Wild Side* (1989 reprint), p. 6.

359 **"What is a Playboy":** Advertisement quoted in Steven Watts, *Mr. Playboy* (Hoboken, N.J.: John Wiley & Sons, 2008), p. 77.

359 **"see life not as a vale":** Quoted ibid.

359 **70 percent of the magazine's readers:** Ibid.

359 **"I'm very very selfish":** *The Most,* Inter Video Productions, 1963.

359 **Though he and Millie:** Watts, *Mr. Playboy,* p. 150.

359 **Only Janet Pilgrim:** Ibid.

360 **"with Eastern establishment connections":** Hugh Hefner, interview by author.

360 **"You have nothing":** Trilling quoted in Watts, *Mr. Playboy,* p. 92.

360 **"I don't want articles":** Hefner quoted ibid., p. 101.

360 **"a highly intelligent":** Victor Lownes, *The Day the Bunny Died* (Secaucus, N.J.: Lyle Stuart, 1982), p. 25.

361 **"Hefner listens to everyone":** Spectorsky quoted ibid., pp. 27–28.

361 **famously abusive:** Watts, *Mr. Playboy,* p. 96.

361 **"He likes jazz":** "Playbill," *Playboy,* June 1957.

361 **popped another Dexedrine:** Watts, *Mr. Playboy*, p. 198.

361 **"There's no right place":** Tillstrom quoted in "Television: End of the Affair," *Time*, September 9, 1957.

361 **The networks drove home:** Erik Barnouw, *Tube of Plenty* (Oxford, U.K.: Oxford University Press, 1975), p. 212.

362 **network executives claimed:** Lynn Spigel, *TV by Design: Modern Art and the Rise of Network Television* (Chicago: University of Chicago Press, 2008), p. 183.

362 **"I suspect":** Nelson Algren, "Ain't Nobody on My Side?" in *Entrapment and Other Writings* (New York: Seven Stories Press, 2009), p. 203.

CHAPTER 31: WILL SOMEBODY PLEASE LISTEN TO ME TODAY!

363 **"the most prophetic film":** Ed Bland, "Urban Classical Funk," on the film *The Cry of Jazz*, www.edblandmusic.com/TheCryofJazz.htm.

364 **Low-grade materials:** See D. Bradford Hunt, *Blueprint for Disaster: The Unraveling of Chicago Public Housing* (Chicago: University of Chicago Press, 2009), chap. 5. For more detail, see Hunt, "What Went Wrong with Public Housing in Chicago? A History of the Robert Taylor Homes," *Journal of the Illinois State Historical Society* 94, no. 1 (Spring 2001), pp. 96–123.

364 **Much of the Black Belt:** Christopher Robert Reed, *The Chicago NAACP and the Rise of Black Professional Leadership, 1910–1966* (Bloomington: Indiana University Press, 1997), pp. 181–82.

364 **Unlike Kennelly:** "The Day They Brought the Blues to the Mayor," *Chicago*, May 1955.

364 **"His approach is of":** Edward Clayton, *The Negro Politician: His Success and Failure* (Chicago: Johnson, 1964), p. 78.

364 **"ill-advised racial":** Ibid., p. 70.

364 **went after Dawson:** Reed, *Chicago NAACP*, pp. 183–88; James Q. Wilson, *Negro Politics: The Search for Leadership* (Glencoe, N.Y.: Free Press, 1960), pp. 114–15.

365 **Black Chicago's power brokers:** On the motives of the black leaders and of Daley, see Reed, *Chicago NAACP*, pp. 187–91; and

Adam Cohen and Elizabeth Taylor, *American Pharaoh* (New York: Little, Brown, 2000), pp. 205–7.

365 **Claude Holman cosponsored:** William Grimshaw, *Bitter Fruit: Black Politics and the Chicago Machine, 1931–1991* (Chicago: University of Chicago Press, 1992), pp. 108–10.

365 **City Hall held fast to its inflated:** Hunt, *Blueprint for Disaster*, p. 140.

366 **"a suburb within a city":** "Lake Meadows: A Suburb Within a City," *Ebony*, December 1960.

366 **Vivian Harsh:** "Hall Library Rates as City Culture Gem," *Chicago Tribune*, November 8, 1959.

366 **the State Department:** Robert Blakely, *Earl B. Dickerson: A Voice for Freedom and Equality* (Evanston, Ill.: Northwestern University Press, 2006), p. 182.

367 **"too brutal":** Harvard Graduate School of Design Alumni Association, *The Institution as a Generator of Urban Form* (Cambridge, Mass.: Harvard Graduate School of Design, 1961), pp. 27–33.

367 **a nonwhite population:** Peter H. Rossi and Robert A. Dentler, *The Politics of Urban Renewal: The Chicago Findings* (Glencoe, N.Y.: Free Press, 1961), p. 21.

368 **But Levi:** Arnold Hirsch, *The Making of the Second Ghetto: Race and Housing in Chicago, 1940–1960* (Cambridge, U.K.: Cambridge University Press, 1983), pp. 153–55.

368 **Levi presented:** Ibid., p. 161.

368 **"our people":** Rossi and Dentler, *Urban Renewal*, p. 161.

368 **"White and Black together":** Nichols ibid., p. 65.

368 **"so repulsed by":** Nicholas von Hoffman, *Radical: A Portrait of Saul Alinsky* (New York: Nation Books, 2010), p. 134.

369 **"the unreasoning evil":** "Warns 'Human Need' Goal of Urban Changes," *Chicago Tribune*, May 22, 1958.

369 **"smallish, invincibly likeable":** Von Hoffman, *Radical*, p. 4.

369 **after overhearing Alinsky:** Margery Frisbie, *An Alley in Chicago: The Life and Legacy of Monsignor John Egan* (Franklin, Wis.: Sheed & Ward, 2002), p. 29.

369 **1,982,030 Catholics:** "Chicago See Is Largest in Many Respects," *New World*, November 14, 1958.

369 **That August Mayor Daley:** "22 Year Plan: A New Face for Chicago!" *Chicago Tribune*, August 23, 1958.

370 **"The major moral problem":** Egan quoted in "Catholics Ask Changes in Hyde Park Plan," *Chicago Tribune*, September 24, 1958.

370 **Skeptical Jewish and Protestant:** Rossi and Dentler, *Urban Renewal*, pp. 234–36.

370 **"The people who will live":** Weinstein quoted in "Catholics Ask Changes in Hyde Park Plan," *Chicago Tribune*, September 24, 1958.

370 **Egan went on:** Von Hoffman, *Radical*, p. 137.

371 **"the worst thing I have ever seen":** Quinn quoted in Frisbie, *Alley in Chicago*, p. 115.

371 **a defensive shell:** For an overview of how poorly the city and archdiocese handled the disaster, see Daniel Greene, "Tragedy in the Parish: The Our Lady of the Angels School Fire," *Chicago History* 29, no. 3 (Spring 2001), pp. 5–19.

371 **first Leeds Triennial:** For all one could want to know about the Leeds Triennial, see http://www.leodis.net/discovery/default.asp and search for "trienniel" on the classical music page. The site also has programs from the 1958 festival and Muddy's appearance.

372 **Berry had been arrested:** Bruce Pegg, *Brown Eyed Handsome Man: The Life and Hard Times of Chuck Berry* (New York: Routledge, 2002), pp. 93–95.

372 **"Screaming Guitar and":** Quoted in Robert Gordon, *Can't Be Satisfied: The Life and Times of Muddy Waters* (Boston: Little, Brown, 2002), p. 159.

372 **kids like Eric Clapton:** Ibid., p. 163.

372 **During the Beatles':** Nadine Cohodas, *Spinning Blues into Gold* (New York: St. Martin's Press, 2000), pp. 241–42.

373 **"You'd have thought":** Jackson quoted in Don Gold, "In God She Trusts," *Ladies' Home Journal*, November 1963.

373 **who fired her longtime pianist:** Jules Schwerin, *Got to Tell It* (New York: Oxford University Press, 1992), p. 121.

373 **in the years to come she'd use her:** Taylor Branch, *Parting the Waters: America in the King Years 1954–1963* (New York: Simon & Schuster, 1988), p. 336.

373 **she'd been on the phone:** Laurraine Goreau, *Just Mahalia, Baby* (Waco, Tex: Word Books, 1975), pp. 225–26.

373 **When neighbors shot:** Ibid., p. 210.

373 **"I hadn't intended to start":** Jackson quoted in Gold, "In God She Trusts."

374 **"a most unfortunate marriage":** Ralph Ellison, "As the Spirit Moves Mahalia," in *The Collected Essays of Ralph Ellison* (New York: Modern Library, 2003), p. 254.

374 **"When I wasn't getting a dime":** Jackson quoted in Gold, "In God She Trusts."

374 **"Those humble churches":** Jackson quoted ibid. It's worth watching her performance in the documentary *Jazz on a Summer's Day*, a film that looks to have inspired the entire J. Crew catalogue.

374 **Edward R. Murrow:** Goreau, *Just Mahalia*, p. 253.

374 **Mahalia sang for the first time:** Ibid., pp. 262–63; Cassidy's review in "On the Aisle," *Chicago Tribune*, February 14, 1959.

375 **"The same birds are in":** Jackson quoted in Gold, "In God She Trusts."

375 **"all pretenses but living":** Lorraine Hansberry, *Raisin in the Sun* (New York: Vintage, 1958), p. 24.

375 **"has the fresh impact":** Claudia Cassidy, "On the Aisle," *Chicago Tribune*, February 11, 1959.

375 **a return to social realism:** Lawrence P. Jackson, *The Indignant Generation: A Narrative History of African American Writers and Critics, 1934–1960* (Princeton, N.J.: Princeton University Press, 2011), pp. 488–89.

376 **a minor cultural center:** Steven R. Carter, "Commitment amid Complexity: Lorraine Hansberry's Life in Action," *MELUS* 7 (Autumn 1980), pp. 39–53.

376 **"simply . . . a reasonably successful":** Lorraine Hansberry, *To Be Young, Gifted and Black* (New York: Signet, 1969), p. 63.

376 **Hansberry Enterprises:** Truman K. Gibson, Jr., "We Belong in Washington Park,"

Chicago History 34, no. 3 (Fall 2006), pp. 26–43.

376 **"the funnel through which":** Richard Wright, *12 Million Black Voices* (1941; reprint New York: Thunder's Mouth Press, 1988), p. 111.

376 **"a 'rich' girl":** Hansberry, *To Be Young, Gifted and Black*, p. 63.

376 **"a rebel":** Ibid.

376 **"a soap opera so corny":** Nelson Algren, *Who Lost an American?* (New York: Macmillan, 1963), p. 143.

377 **"mistaken the *oppression* of the Negro":** Hansberry, *To Be Young, Gifted and Black*, p. 211.

377 **"All travelers to my city":** Ibid., p. 45.

377 **"Will somebody please listen":** Hansberry, *Raisin in the Sun*, p. 70.

377 **"I wish to present":** Gwendolyn Brooks, *Report from Part One* (Detroit: Broadside Press, 1972), p. 189.

CHAPTER 32: THE REALM OF THE UNREAL

379 **"For better or worse":** "Mayor Daley as Mister Chicago Culture," *Chicago Daily News*, March 30, 1968.

379 **"The word 'culture' ":** Nelson Algren, *Who Lost an American?* (New York: Macmillan, 1963), p. 270.

379 **"children should be":** "Movie Censor Uses a Simple Rule of Thumb," *Chicago Tribune*, May 24, 1959.

379 **sexually aroused:** Bernard Gavzer and Norman Calhoun, "Who Censors Our Movies," *Chicago*, February 1956.

380 **funds for libraries:** "Mayor Daley as Mister Chicago Culture," *Chicago Daily News*, March 30, 1968.

380 **buy a Mark Tobey painting:** Katharine Kuh, interview by Avis Berman, *Archives of American Art Journal* 27, no. 3 (1987), pp. 2–36.

380 **"Kuh-Kuh Must Go":** Katharine Kuh, *My Love Affair with Modern Art* (New York: Arcade, 2006), p. 30.

380 **First National Bank:** Kuh interview by Berman.

380 **soaked in the Etruscans:** Christopher Lyon, *Nancy Spero: The Work* (Munich: Prestel, 2010), p. 34.

380 **a new generation:** Franz Schulze, *Fantastic Images: Chicago Art Since 1945* (Chicago: Follett, 1972), pp. 20–21.

380 **"anti-mainstream, anti-idealistic":** Ibid., p. 23.

380 **"phonily expressive" and "badly painted":** William Rubin, "New Images of Man," *Art International* 3, no. 9 (1959).

381 **Aaron Siskind, who had never really bought:** David Travis and Elizabeth Siegel, *Taken by Design: Photographs from the Institute of Design, 1937–1971* (Chicago: Art Institute of Chicago, 2002), p. 162.

381 **"I think," said Callahan later:** Callahan quoted ibid., p. 91.

381 **"I was learning photography":** Quoted ibid.

382 **"Too late now":** Darger quoted in Michael Bonesteel, "Henry Darger's Great Crusade, Crisis of Faith, and Last Judgment," in Klaus Biesenbach, *Henry Darger* (Munich: Prestel, 2009), p. 274.

382 **Vivian Maier:** I've drawn the details of Maier's life from my interview with John Maloof.

383 **Liquor kept him sociable:** Schulze, *Fantastic Images*, pp. 287–88.

383 **"Board's attitude was":** Fujikawa memo, August 5, 1958, Mies van der Rohe Archive, Architecture and Design Study Center, Museum of Modern Art, New York.

384 **"No," sniffed Mies. "I'd rather":** Mies quoted in George Danforth, oral history interview by Pauline Saliga, © 2003, Art Institute of Chicago, p. 106, used with permission.

384 **"We will not do Mies's":** Walter Netsch, oral history interview by Betty J. Blum, © 1997, Art Institute of Chicago, p. 105, used with permission.

384 **pointed his pipe:** Danforth interview by Saliga, p. 108.

384 **"Why are you here":** Alfred Caldwell, oral history interview by Betty J. Blum, © 1987, Art Institute of Chicago, p. 87, used with permission.

384 **Hilbs would not be stopped:** Ibid.

384 **"They were all yellow":** Ibid., p. 88.

384 **"too radical":** Fujikawa memo, August 5, 1958, Mies van der Rohe Archive, Architecture and Design Study Center, Museum of Modern Art, New York.

384 "in the spirit of Mies": Netsch interview by Blum, p. 107.

385 "S.O.M. took Mies's": Quoted in "The Architects from 'Skid's Row,' " *Fortune,* January 1958.

385 American Airlines flight 2: Argie Howard, *American Airlines Jet Stewardess,* american airlinesstewardess.blogspot.com.

385 Herb Greenwald fastened: "Chicago-N.Y. Air Crash," *Chicago Tribune,* February 4, 1959; "Plane Crash Brings Grief to Many Here," *Chicago Tribune,* February 5, 1959.

386 "Herb needed no hope": Ludwig Mies van der Rohe, "Eulogy for Herbert Greenwald," February 12, 1959, manuscript, Ludwig Mies van der Rohe Papers, 1921–69, Library of Congress.

386 "Squiff was," said Leon: Leon Golub, "Eulogy for Herbert Greenwald," February 12, 1959, manuscript, Ludwig Mies van der Rohe Papers, 1921–69, Library of Congress.

386 donated the Kuklapolitans: Rosemary K. Adams, "Here We Are Again: Kukla, Fran and Ollie," *Chicago History* 26, no. 3 (Fall 1997), pp. 32–51.

387 Five hundred yards off the coast of Chicago: Rosemary K. Adams, "An Unforgettable Day: Queen Elizabeth Visits Chicago," *Chicago History* (Winter 2010). The media coverage in Chicago was comprehensive, to say the least. British Pathé footage of the day can be found at www .britishpathe.com/record.php?id=35901 and 35904.

387 the list of contributors: "Adlai to Back Daley at Fund Dinner April 2," *Chicago Tribune,* March 20, 1959.

387 "Voodoo warriors from Haiti": "Chicago's Great International Trade Fair," *Chicago Tribune,* April 21, 1959.

388 "The Chicago railroad": "Trade Fair Draws 49, 702," *Chicago Tribune,* July 4, 1959.

388 "not using the Shi-cah-go": "Bring Children on Next Trip, Daley Asks," *Chicago Tribune,* July 7, 1959.

388 "the greatest reception": Quoted in "A Great City: Take the Word of a Queen," *Chicago Tribune,* July 8, 1959.

388 "proved it can do anything": Reilly quoted ibid.

389 "We can't tolerate failure": "Brundage Warns of 'City's Disgrace' If 1959 Meet Fails," *Chicago Tribune,* August 29, 1958.

389 the games were a fiasco: Earl Gustkey, "Pan Am Games Legacy: 1959," *Los Angeles Times,* August 6, 1987; "Despite All, a Delightful Show," *Sports Illustrated,* September 14, 1959.

389 "perhaps the worst-staged": Earl Gustkey, "Pan Am Games Legacy: 1959," *Los Angeles Times,* August 6, 1987.

389 "in the hilarity": Daley quoted in "Use of Sirens to Hail Sox Angers Many," *Chicago Tribune,* September 24, 1959.

390 "Hello there": *Playboy's Penthouse,* Episode 1, October 29, 1959.

390 "bring the magazine": Steven Watts, *Mr. Playboy* (Hoboken, N.J.: John Wiley & Sons, 2008), p. 160.

391 "You're not interested": *Playboy's Penthouse,* Episode 1, October 29, 1959.

391 "I kinda wish": *Playboy's Penthouse,* February 13, 1960.

391 one-third of Chicagoland's: "Mrs. Suburbia: A New Boss in America," *Chicago Tribune,* August 11, 1957.

392 "Since ancient times": Advertisement in *Playboy,* May 1957.

392 magazine ran a feature: "*Playboy*'s Penthouse Apartment," *Playboy,* September–October 1956.

392 William McFetridge: "Plan River Site Skyscraper," *Chicago Tribune,* September 15, 1959.

392 local zoning: "Deny Zoning Variation for $200,000 Home," *Chicago Tribune,* June 9, 1959.

392 the Gaslight Club: "The Lock on the Barroom Door," *Playboy,* November 1956.

393 "meeting place for": "The Playboy Club," *Playboy,* August 1960.

393 fifty thousand key holders: Watts, *Mr. Playboy,* p. 162.

393 "Well, no use to call": Algren, *Who Lost an American?,* p. 281.

393 "The stockyards stink": John Bartlow Martin, "To Chicago, With Love," *Saturday Evening Post,* October 15, 1960.

393 Elaine May's boyfriend: Sheldon Patinkin, *The Second City: Backstage at the World's*

Greatest Comedy Theater (Naperville, Ill.: SourceBooks, 2000), p. 21.

393 **long talks with Sills:** Duncan in Jeffrey Sweet, *Something Wonderful Right Away: An Oral History of the Second City and Compass Players* (New York: Avon, 1978), p. 54.

394 **"Go home":** Ibid., p. 169.

394 **The Second City:** Janet Coleman, *The Compass* (New York: Alfred A. Knopf, 1990), p. 255.

394 **the first act established:** Duncan in Sweet, *Something Wonderful*, p. 55.

394 **how guilty Chicagoans:** Paul Sills and Charles L. Mee, "The Celebratory Occasion," *Tulane Drama Review* 9 (Winter 1964), pp. 167–81.

395 **"Canned music, phonographs":** László Moholy-Nagy, *Vision in Motion* (Chicago: Paul Theobald, 1947), p. 20.

396 **The owner, Sandy Agate:** John F. Love, *McDonald's: Behind the Arches* (New York: Bantam Books, 1986), pp. 81–82.

396 **"We have found out":** Kroc quoted ibid., p. 144.

397 **Harry Sonneborn:** Ray Kroc with Robert Anderson, *Grinding It Out: The Making of McDonald's* (New York: St. Martin's, 1977), p. 109.

397 **a fourteen-year-old Apache girl:** Bruce Pegg, *Brown Eyed Handsome Man: The Life and Hard Times of Chuck Berry* (New York: Routledge, 2002), pp. 113–17.

398 **schmeared palms:** Nadine Cohodas, *Spinning Blues into Gold* (New York: St. Martin's Press, 2000), pp. 174–75.

398 **the Old Swingmaster:** Ibid., p. 179; Marshall Chess, interview by author.

398 **slept on the couch:** Chess interview by author.

399 **Jerry Butler and Curtis Mayfield:** Robert Pruter, *Chicago Soul* (Champaign: University of Illinois, 1992), p. 106.

399 **black-owned Vee-Jay:** Ibid., chap. 2. Read the whole book—it's worth it!

400 **"the Mayor Daley of the Blues":** Mike Rowe, *Chicago Blues: The City and the Music* (New York: Da Capo, 1975), p. 173.

400 **Dixon fed him:** Willie Dixon with Don Snowden, *I Am the Blues: The Willie Dixon Story* (New York: Da Capo, 1989), p. 149.

Dixon's autobiography is self-serving to an unfortunate degree.

400 **to follow Bill Putnam:** Jim Cogan and William Clark, *Temples of Sound: Inside the Great Recording Studios* (San Francisco: Chronicle Books, 2003), p. 121.

400 **Universal would still remain:** Ibid., p. 133.

400 **Keith Richards's famous story:** Chess interview by author.

400 **Atlantic and Motown, seeded in part:** Etta James with David Ritz, *Rage to Survive* (New York: Villard Press, 1995), p. 106.

401 **city's recording industry:** Cogan and Clark, *Temples of Sound*, p. 133.

401 **"I made my money on":** Chess quoted in Robert Gordon, *Can't Be Satisfied: The Life and Times of Muddy Waters* (Boston: Little, Brown, 2002), p. 222.

401 **"the slightly harassed air":** Marquis W. Childs, "The World of Walter Paepcke," *Horizon*, September 1958.

402 **"Rebellion":** Ibid.

402 **The speakers who came:** James Sloan Allen, *The Romance of Commerce and Culture* (Chicago: University of Chicago Press, 1983), p. 247.

402 **"a dialectical examination":** Milton Mayer, *Robert Maynard Hutchins: A Memoir* (Berkeley: University of California Press, 1993), p. 406.

402 **"physically uncomfortable":** Mary Ann Dzuback, *Robert M. Hutchins: Portrait of an Educator* (Chicago: University of Chicago Press, 1991), p. 266.

403 **"really any more than":** Marquis W. Childs, "The World of Walter Paepcke," *Horizon*, September 1958.

403 **The passing of Chicago's:** Allen, *Romance*, p. 283.

EPILOGUE: IN CHICAGO FOR MY FOREVER

404 **Four men armed with crowbars:** John Vinci, oral history interview by Betty J. Blum, © 2002, Art Institute of Chicago, p. 12, used with permission; Richard Cahan, *They All Fall Down* (Washington, D.C.: Preservation Press, 1994), p. 8.

404 **He'd tried to move ahead:** Cahan, *All Fall Down*, p. 83.

405 two of the almost six thousand: Ibid., p. 77.

405 critics compared it: Ibid., p. 95.

406 "playing too far out for the people": Cadillac Bob quoted in Brett Primack, "Captain Angelic: Sun Ra," *Downbeat,* May 4, 1978.

406 "Twenty years ago": Sun Ra quoted in Ray Townley, "Sun Ra," *Downbeat,* 1973.

407 Stevenson as usual: Theodore H. White, *The Making of the President 1960* (New York: Atheneum, 1961), p. 149.

407 old guard weren't thrilled: Len O'Connor, *Clout* (New York: Avon Books, 1976), p. 152.

407 *You have no support:* White, *Making,* pp. 200–201.

407 agreed-upon changes: For a deeper look at the debate, see ibid., pp. 335–44.

408 Kennedy swung through: "Crowd Cheers Kennedy at City Hall," *Chicago Tribune,* October 2, 1960.

408 Kennedy's stock went through: White, *Making,* p. 386.

408 "Her concern is": Frank London Brown, "Book Review," *Chicago Defender,* July 21, 1960.

409 "I intend," she told: Gwendolyn Brooks, *Report from Part One* (Detroit: Broadside Press, 1972), p. 136.

409 "Sit where the light corrupts": Gwendolyn Brooks, "In the Mecca," in *Blacks* (Chicago: Third World Press, 1987), p. 407.

409 "capsulize the gist": Brooks, *Report from Part One,* p. 190.

409 "whose broken window": Gwendolyn Brooks, "Boy Breaking Glass," in *Blacks,* p. 438.

409 Balaban and Katz went to court: Cahan, *All Fall Down,* p. 112.

410 Daley sited the new: Adam Cohen and Elizabeth Taylor, *American Pharaoh* (New York: Little, Brown, 2000), pp. 224–33.

410 But Hizzoner shrugged: Cahan, *All Fall Down,* p. 119; Theodore W. Hild, "The Demolition of the Garrick Theater and the Birth of the Preservation Movement in Chicago," *Illinois Historical Journal* 88, no. 2 (Summer 1995).

410 boarded the B&O's: "Kerner, Daley to Leave Today for Washington," *Chicago Tribune,* January 17, 1961.

411 "blacks have begun to leave": The Brookings Institution, *The State of Metropolitan America,* August 2011.

411 "City that walks": Nelson Algren, *Who Lost an American?* (New York: Macmillan, 1963), p. 285.

412 "contingent love": Simone de Beauvoir, *Force of Circumstance* (New York: Putnam's, 1964), p. 125.

412 "Will she ever quit talking?": Nelson Algren, "The Question of Simone de Beauvoir," *Harper's,* May 1965.

412 Simone was buried: Deirdre Bair, *Simone de Beauvoir: A Biography* (New York: Simon & Schuster, 1990), p. 615.

SOURCES

BOOKS

Abrahamson, Jill. *A Neighborhood Finds Itself.* New York: Harper & Brothers, 1959.

Achilles, Rolf, Kevin Harrington, and Charlotte Myhrum. *Mies van der Rohe: Architect as Educator.* Chicago: Illinois Institute of Technology, 1986.

Addams, Jane. *Democracy and Social Ethics.* 1902; reprint Middlesex, U.K.: Echo Library, 2006.

————. *Twenty Years at Hull House.* 1910; reprint New York: Signet, 1981.

Adler, Mortimer. *Philosopher at Large.* New York: Macmillan, 1977.

Algren, Nelson. *Somebody in Boots.* 1935; New York: Thunder's Mouth Press, 1987.

————. *Never Come Morning.* New York: Harper & Brothers, 1942.

————. *The Neon Wilderness.* Garden City, N.Y.: Doubleday, 1947.

————. *The Man with the Golden Arm.* Garden City, N.Y.: Doubleday, 1949.

————. *Chicago: City on the Make.* Garden City, N.Y.: Doubleday, 1951.

————. *A Walk on the Wild Side.* New York: Farrar, Straus & Giroux, 1956.

————. *Who Lost an American?* New York: Macmillan, 1963.

————. *The Last Carousel.* 1973; New York: Seven Stories Press, 1997.

————. *Nonconformity.* New York: Seven Stories Press, 1992.

————. *Entrapment and Other Writings.* New York: Seven Stories Press, 2009.

Alinsky, Saul. *Reveille for Radicals.* Chicago: University of Chicago Press, 1946.

————. *Rules for Radicals.* New York: Random House, 1971.

Allen, James Sloan. *The Romance of Commerce and Culture.* Chicago: University of Chicago Press, 1983.

Anderson, Margaret. *My Thirty Years War.* New York: Horizon Press, 1969.

Andrews, Wayne. *Battle for Chicago.* New York: Harcourt, Brace & Co., 1946.

————. *Architecture in Chicago and Mid-America.* Cambridge, Mass.: Athenaeum, 1968.

Apel, Dora, and Shawn Michelle Smith. *Lynching Photographs.* Berkeley: University of California Press, 2007.

Art Institute of Chicago. *Abstract and Surrealist American Art.* Chicago: Art Institute of Chicago, 1947.

————. *1945: Creativity and Crisis*. Chicago: Art Institute of Chicago, 2005.

Arts Club of Chicago. *The Collection 1916–1996*. Chicago: Arts Club of Chicago, 1997.

Aschenbrenner, Joyce. *Katherine Dunham: Dancing a Life*. Urbana: University of Illinois Press, 2002.

Avella, Steven M. *This Confident Church: Catholic Leadership and Life in Chicago, 1940–1965*. Notre Dame: University of Notre Dame Press, 1992.

Baer, Ulrich. *Spectral Evidence: The Photography of Trauma*. Cambridge, Mass.: MIT Press, 2002.

Bair, Deirdre. *Simone de Beauvoir: A Biography*. New York: Simon & Schuster, 1990.

Baldwin, Davarian L. *Chicago's New Negroes: Modernity, the Great Migration, and Black Urban Life*. Chapel Hill: University of North Carolina Press, 2007.

Barnouw, Erik. *Tube of Plenty*. Oxford, U.K.: Oxford University Press, 1975.

Barrett, James R. *Work and Community in the Jungle: Chicago's Packinghouse Workers, 1894–1922*. Urbana: University of Illinois Press, 1990.

Baum, L. Frank. *The Wonderful Wizard of Oz*. 1900; reprint New York: Alfred A. Knopf, 1992.

Bayer, Herbert, Walter Gropius, and Ise Gropius, eds. *Bauhaus 1919–1928*. 1959; reprint New York: Museum of Modern Art, 1975.

Beam, Alex. *A Great Idea at the Time*. New York: PublicAffairs, 2008.

Bego, Mark. *Aretha Franklin: The Queen of Soul*. London: Robert Hale, 1990.

Belgrad, Daniel. *The Culture of Spontaneity: Improvisation and the Arts in Postwar America*. Chicago: University of Chicago Press, 1998.

Bellow, Saul. *The Adventures of Augie March*. New York: Viking Press, 1953.

Benjamin, Walter. *The Work of Art in the Age of Its Technological Reproducibility and Other Writings on Media*. Cambridge, Mass.: Belknap Press, 2008.

————. *Selected Writings*. Vol. 2, *1927–1934*. Edited by Michael W. Jennings. Cambridge, Mass.: Harvard University Press, 1999.

Bergdoll, Barry, and Leah Dickerman. *Bauhaus 1919–1933: Workshop for Modernity*. New York: Museum of Modern Art, 2009.

Berger, Daniel, and Steve Jajkowski, eds. *Chicago Television*. Charleston, S.C.: Arcadia, 2010.

Bergren, Marie, and Virginia Norden. *See Chicago on Your Own*. Chicago: Wilcox & Follett, 1951.

Berkow, Ira. *Maxwell Street: Survival in a Bazaar*. Garden City, N.Y.: Doubleday, 1977.

Berry, Chuck. *The Autobiography of Chuck Berry*. New York: Crown, 1987.

Best, Wallace D. *Passionately Human, No Less Divine: Religion and Culture in Black Chicago, 1915–1952*. Princeton, N.J.: Princeton University Press, 2005.

Biesenbach, Klaus. *Henry Darger*. Munich: Prestel, 2009.

Black, Timuel. *Bridges of Memory*. Evanston, Ill.: Northwestern University Press, 2005.

Blake, Peter. *Mies van der Rohe: Architecture and Structure.* New York: Penguin Books, 1966.

———. *The Master Builders.* New York: W. W. Norton, 1996.

Blakely, Robert. *Earl B. Dickerson: A Voice for Freedom and Equality.* Evanston, Ill.: Northwestern University Press, 2006.

Blaser, Werner. *Mies van der Rohe: IIT Campus.* Basel: Birkhauser, 2002.

Boehm, Lisa, and Beth Krissoff. *Infamous City.* Bloomington: Indiana University Press, 2000.

Bolden, B. J. *Urban Rage in Bronzeville: Social Commentary in the Poetry of Gwendolyn Brooks, 1945–1960.* Chicago: Third World Press, 1999.

Bontemps, Arna, and Jack Conroy. *Anyplace But Here.* Columbia: University of Missouri Press, 1945.

Borchardt-Hume, Achim. *Albers and Moholy-Nagy: From the Bauhaus to the New World.* New Haven, Conn.: Yale University Press, 2006.

Boyd, Neva L. *Handbook of Games.* Chicago: H. T. FitzSimons, 1945.

Branch, Taylor. *Parting the Waters: America in the King Years 1954–1963.* New York: Simon & Schuster, 1988.

Brecht, Bertolt. *On Theatre.* Translated by John Willett. London: Methuen, 1964.

Brent, Stuart. *The Seven Stairs.* Chicago: J. Philip O'Hara, 1962.

Broadwater, Jeff. *Adlai Stevenson: The Odyssey of a Cold War Liberal.* New York: Twayne, 1994.

Bronte, Patricia. *Vittles and Vice.* Chicago: Henry Regnery, 1952.

Brookings Institution. *The State of Metropolitan America.* Washington, D.C.: The Brookings Institution, 2011.

Brooks, Gwendolyn. *Maud Martha.* 1953; Chicago: Third World Press, 1993.

———. *Report from Part One.* Detroit: Broadside Press, 1972.

———. *Blacks.* Chicago: Third World Press, 1987.

———. *Report from Part Two.* Chicago: Third World Press, 1996.

Broonzy, William, as told to Yannick Bruynoghe. *Big Bill Blues.* London: Cassell & Company Ltd., 1955.

Brown, Frank London. *Trumbull Park.* Chicago: Henry Regnery, 1959.

Brunetti, John. *Baldwin Kingrey: Midcentury Modern in Chicago, 1947–1957.* Chicago: Wright, 2004.

Burnett, Leo. *Communications of an Advertising Man.* Chicago: Privately printed, 1961.

Byrne, Jane, and Paul Simon. *My Chicago.* New York: W. W. Norton, 1992.

Cahan, Richard. *They All Fall Down.* Washington, D.C.: Preservation Press, 1994.

Cahan, Richard, and Michael Williams. *Richard Nickel's Chicago: Photographs of a Lost City.* Chicago: Cityfiles Press, 2006.

Cana Conference. *Proceedings of the Chicago Archdiocese Study Week on the Cana Conference June 28–29–30, 1949.* Chicago: Cana Conference, 1950.

Carter, Peter. *Mies van der Rohe at Work.* London: Phaidon, 1999.

Cayton, Horace. *Long Old Road.* New York: Trident, 1965.

Chicago Commission on Race Relations. *The Negro in Chicago.* Chicago: University of Chicago Press, 1922.

Chicago Housing Authority. *Low Rent Housing in Chicago.* Chicago: Chicago Housing Authority, 1947.

———. *Temporary Housing for Chicago's Veterans.* Chicago: Chicago Housing Authority, n.d.

Chicago Plan Commission. *Ten Square Miles of Chicago.* Chicago: Chicago Plan Commission, 1949.

———. *Chicago Plans.* Chicago: Chicago Plan Commission, 1950.

Chicago Public Schools Division of Curriculum. *Chicago.* Chicago: King, 1955.

Christiansen, Richard. *A Theater of Our Own: A History and a Memoir of 1,001 Nights in Chicago.* Evanston, Ill.: Northwestern University Press, 2004.

City of Chicago. *Chicago's Report to the People.* Chicago, 1947.

———. *Rehousing Residents Displaced from Public Housing Clearance Sites in Chicago, 1957–1958.* Chicago: Chicago Department of City Planning, 1958.

Clarke, Cheryl. *"After Mecca": Women Poets and the Black Arts Movement.* Piscataway, N.J.: Rutgers University Press, 2005.

Clayton, Edward. *The Negro Politician: His Success and Failure.* Chicago: Johnson, 1964.

Clegg, Claude. *An Original Man: The Life and Times of Elijah Muhammad.* New York: St. Martin's Press, 1997.

Cogan, Jim, and William Clark. *Temples of Sound: Inside the Great Recording Studios.* San Francisco: Chronicle Books, 2003.

Cohen, Adam, and Elizabeth Taylor. *American Pharaoh.* New York: Little, Brown & Co., 2000.

Cohen, Lizabeth. *Making a New Deal: Industrial Workers in Chicago, 1919–1939.* Cambridge, U.K.: Cambridge University Press, 1990.

Cohen, Rick. *Machers and Rockers: Chess Records and the Business of Rock & Roll.* New York: W. W. Norton, 2004.

Cohodas, Nadine. *Spinning Blues into Gold.* New York: St. Martin's Press, 2000.

Coleman, Janet. *The Compass.* New York: Alfred A. Knopf, 1990.

Columbia University. *Four Great Makers of Modern Architecture: Gropius, Le Corbusier, Mies van der Rohe, Wright.* New York: Columbia University Press, 1961.

Condit, Carl. *The Chicago School of Architecture.* Chicago: University of Chicago Press, 1952.

———. *Chicago, 1930–70.* Chicago: University of Chicago Press, 1974.

Conroy, Jack, and Curt Johnson, eds. *Writers in Revolt: The Anvil Anthology 1933–1940.* New York: Lawrence Hill & Co., 1973.

Corbett, John. *Extended Play: Sounding Off from John Cage to Dr. Funkenstein.* Durham, N.C.: Duke University Press, 1994.

Corbett, John, ed. *The Wisdom of Sun Ra: Sun Ra's Polemical Broadsheets and Streetcorner Leaflets.* Chicago: WhiteWalls, 2006.

Corbett, John, Anthony Elms, and Terry Kapsalis, curators. *Pathways to Unknown Worlds: El Saturn and Chicago's Afro-Futurist Underground 1954–1968*. Chicago: WhiteWalls, 2006.

Courtwright, David T. *Dark Paradise: A History of Opiate Addiction in America*. Cambridge, Mass.: Harvard University Press, 1982.

Cox, Julian. *Harry Callahan: Eleanor*. Gottingen: Steidl, 2007.

Cronon, William. *Nature's Metropolis: Chicago and the Great West*. New York: W. W. Norton, 1991.

Danz, Ernst. *The Architecture of Skidmore, Owings and Merrill, 1950–1962*. New York: Praeger, 1962.

Darling, Grace, and David Darling, eds. *Stevenson*. Chicago: Contemporary Books, 1977.

Davis, Frank Marshall. *Livin' the Blues*. Madison: University of Wisconsin Press, 1992.

———. *Black Moods*. Urbana: University of Illinois Press, 2002.

Davis, Keith, et al. *Callahan, Siskind, Sommer: At the Crossroads of American Photography*. Santa Fe, N.M.: Radius Books, 2009.

D'Emilio, John, and Estelle B. Freedman. *Intimate Matters: A History of Sexuality in America*. New York: Harper & Row, 1988.

De Beauvoir, Simone. *The Mandarins*. Cleveland: World, 1956.

———. *Force of Circumstance*. New York: Putnam's, 1964.

———. *A Transatlantic Love Affair: Letters to Nelson Algren*. New York: New Press, 1997.

———. *American Day by Day*. Berkeley: University of California Press, 1999.

Democratic National Committee. *Official Report of the Proceedings of the Democratic National Convention*. Washington, D.C.: Democratic National Committee, 1952.

Despres, Leon M., with Kenan Heise. *Challenging the Daley Machine: A Chicago Alderman's Memoir*. Evanston, Ill.: Northwestern University Press, 2005.

Dewey, John. *Art as Experience*. New York: Capricorn Books, 1958.

Dixon, Willie, with Don Snowden. *I Am the Blues: The Willie Dixon Story*. New York: Da Capo, 1989.

Domer, Dennis, ed. *Alfred Caldwell: The Life and Work of a Prairie School Landscape Architect*. Baltimore: Johns Hopkins University Press, 1997.

Donohue, H. E. F. *Conversations with Nelson Algren*. New York: Hill & Wang, 1963.

Drake, St. Clair, and Horace Cayton. *Black Metropolis: A Study of Negro Life in a Northern City*. New York: Harcourt Brace, 1945.

Drew, Bettina. *Nelson Algren: A Life on the Wild Side*. New York: Putnam, 1989.

Duis, Perry. *Chicago: Creating New Traditions*. Chicago: Chicago Historical Society, 1976.

Dzuback, Mary Ann. *Robert M. Hutchins: Portrait of an Educator*. Chicago: University of Chicago Press, 1991.

Ebert, Roger. *Life Itself: A Memoir*. New York: Grand Central, 2011.

Ehrenhalt, Alan. *The Lost City: The Forgotten Virtues of Community in America.* New York: Basic Books, 1995.

Ehrenreich, Barbara. *The Hearts of Men.* Garden City, N.Y.: Doubleday, 1983.

Ellison, Ralph. *The Collected Essays of Ralph Ellison.* New York: Modern Library, 2003.

Engelbrecht, Lloyd. *Moholy-Nagy: Mentor to Modernism.* Cincinnati, Ohio: Flying Trapeze Press, 2009.

———. *The Association of Arts and Industries: Background and Origins of the Bauhaus Movement in Chicago.* Ph.D. diss., University of Chicago, 1973, unpublished.

Ennis, Philip. *The Seventh Stream: The Emergence of Rocknroll in American Popular Music.* Hanover, N.H.: University Press of New England, 1992.

Farr, Finis. *Chicago: A Personal History of America's Most American City.* New Rochelle, N.Y.: Arlington House, 1973.

Fauset, Arthur Huff. *Black Gods of the Metropolis.* Philadelphia: University of Pennsylvania Press, 1944.

Federal Writers Project. *The WPA Guide to Illinois.* Pantheon: New York, 1983.

Fitch, James Marston. *Walter Gropius.* New York: George Braziller, 1960.

Frazier, E. Franklin. *Black Bourgeoisie.* New York: Free Press, 1957.

Frisbie, Margery. *An Alley in Chicago: The Life and Legacy of Monsignor John Egan.* Franklin, Wis.: Sheed & Ward, 2002.

Fuerst, J. S. *When Public Housing Was Paradise: Building Community in Chicago.* Westport, Conn.: Praeger, 2003.

Fuller, Buckminster, with Jerome Agel and Quentin Fiore. *I Seem to Be a Verb.* New York: Bantam Books, 1970.

Gay, Peter. *Weimar Culture: The Outsider as Insider.* New York: Harper & Row, 1968.

George, Nelson. *The Death of Rhythm & Blues.* New York: Pantheon, 1988.

Gilbert, Martin. *The First World War.* New York: Henry Holt & Co., 1994.

Gillett, Charlie. *The Sound of the City: The Rise of Rock and Roll.* New York: Pantheon, 1970.

Gingrich, Arnold. *Nothing But People.* New York: Crown, 1971.

Gioia, Ted. *Delta Blues.* New York: W. W. Norton, 2008.

Gordon, Robert. *Can't Be Satisfied: The Life and Times of Muddy Waters.* Boston: Little, Brown, 2002.

Goreau, Laurraine. *Just Mahalia, Baby.* Waco, Tex.: Word Books, 1975.

Gosnell, Harold F. *Negro Politicians: The Rise of Negro Politics in Chicago.* Chicago: University of Chicago Press, 1935.

Grabar, Oleg. *The Mediation of Ornament.* Princeton, N.J.: Princeton University Press, 1995.

Gray, Mary Lackritz. *A Guide to Chicago's Murals.* Chicago: University of Chicago Press, 2001.

Grayson, Lisa. *Biography of a Hunch: The History of Chicago's Legendary Old Town School of Folk Music.* Chicago: Old Town School of Folk Music, 1992.

Green, Adam. *Selling the Race*. Chicago: University of Chicago Press, 2007.

Grese, Robert E. *Jens Jensen: Maker of Natural Parks and Gardens*. Baltimore: Johns Hopkins University Press, 1992.

Griffin, Dick, ed. *Done in a Day*. Chicago: Swallow Press, 1977.

Grimshaw, William. *Bitter Fruit: Black Politics and the Chicago Machine, 1931–1991*. Chicago: University of Chicago Press, 1992.

Gropius, Walter. *Rebuilding Our Cities*. Chicago: Paul Theobald, 1945.

———. *The New Architecture and the Bauhaus*. Cambridge, Mass.: MIT Press, 1965.

Grossman, James R. *Land of Hope: Chicago, Black Southerners, and the Great Migration*. Chicago: University of Chicago Press, 1989.

Guide Group. *The Guide to Black Chicago*. Chicago: Guide Group, 1996.

Guilbaut, Serge. *How New York Stole the Idea of Modern Art*. Chicago: University of Chicago Press, 1983.

Guralnick, Peter. *Feel Like Goin' Home: Portraits in Blues and Rock 'n' Roll*. New York: Outerbridge & Dienstfrey, 1971.

Gussow, Adam. *Seems Like Murder Here: Southern Violence and the Blues Tradition*. Chicago: University of Chicago Press, 2002.

Guzman, Richard. *Black Writing from Chicago: In the World, Not of It*. Carbondale: Southern Illinois University Press, 2006.

Halberstam, David. *The Fifties*. New York: Villard Books, 1993.

Halpern, Rick. *Down on the Killing Floor: Black and White Workers in Chicago's Packinghouses, 1904–54*. Urbana: University of Illinois Press, 1997.

Hansberry, Lorraine. *A Raisin in the Sun*. New York: Vintage, 1958.

———. *To Be Young, Gifted and Black*. New York: Signet, 1969.

Hartfield, Ronne. *Another Way Home: The Tangled Roots of Race in One Chicago Family*. Chicago: University of Chicago Press, 2004.

Harvard Graduate School of Design Alumni Association. *The Institution as a Generator of Urban Form*. Cambridge, Mass.: Harvard Graduate School of Design, 1961.

Haskins, Jim. *Queen of the Blues: A Biography of Dinah Washington*. New York: William Morrow, 1987.

Hatch, Alden. *Buckminster Fuller: At Home in the Universe*. New York: Crown, 1974.

Hayek, F. A. *The Road to Serfdom*. Chicago: University of Chicago Press, 1944.

Hays, K. Michael, and Dana Miller. *Buckminster Fuller: Starting with the Universe*. New York: Whitney Museum of American Art, 2008.

Heilbut, Anthony. *The Gospel Sound*. 1972; New York: Limelight, 1997.

———. *Exiled in Paradise*. New York: Viking Press, 1983.

———. *The Fan Who Knew Too Much*. New York: Knopf, 2012.

Heise, Kenan. *They Speak for Themselves*. Chicago: Young Christian Workers, 1965.

Herdeg, Klaus. *The Decorated Diagram*. Cambridge, Mass.: MIT Press, 1983.

Herskovits, Melville J. *The Myth of the Negro Past.* Boston: Beacon Press, 1941.
————. *The American Negro.* Bloomington: Indiana University Press, 1964.
Hilberseimer, Ludwig. *The New City.* Chicago: Paul Theobald, 1944.
Hirsch, Arnold. *The Making of the Second Ghetto: Race and Housing in Chicago, 1940–1960.* Cambridge, U.K.: Cambridge University Press, 1983.
Hirsch, Foster. *Otto Preminger: The Man Who Would Be King.* New York: Alfred A. Knopf, 2007.
Hochman, Elaine. *Architects of Fortune: Mies van der Rohe and the Third Reich.* New York: Weidenfeld & Nicolson, 1989.
Horvath, Brooke. *Understanding Nelson Algren.* Columbia: University of South Carolina Press, 2005.
Horwitt, Sanford D. *Let Them Call Me Rebel: Saul Alinsky—His Life and Legacy.* New York: Alfred A. Knopf, 1989.
Huizinga, Johan. *Homo Ludens: A Study of the Play Element in Culture.* Boston: Beacon Press, 1955.
Hulten, Pontus, ed. *Marcel Duchamp: Work and Life.* Cambridge, Mass.: MIT Press, 1993.
Hunt, D. Bradford. *Blueprint for Disaster: The Unraveling of Chicago Public Housing.* Chicago: University of Chicago Press, 2009.
Hutchins, Robert M. *The Great Conversation: The Substance of a Liberal Education.* Chicago: Encyclopaedia Britannica, 1952.
Hyde Park–Kenwood Community Conference and South Side Planning Board, Community Appraisal Study. Chicago: HPKCC and SSPB, 1952.
Hyman, Sidney. *The Lives of William Benton.* Chicago: University of Chicago Press, 1969.
Illinois Generations. *A Traveler's Guide to African-American Heritage.* Chicago: Performance Media, 1993.
Imbiorski, Rev. Walter J., ed. *The Basic Cana Manual.* Chicago: Cana Conference of Chicago, 1963.
Isaacs, Reginald. *Walter Gropius.* Boston: Bulfinch Press, 1991.
Jackson, Lawrence P. *The Indignant Generation: A Narrative History of African American Writers and Critics, 1934–1960.* Princeton, N.J.: Princeton University Press, 2011.
Jackson, Mahalia, with Evan McLeod Wylie. *Movin' on Up.* New York: Hawthorn Books, 1966.
————. *Mahalia Jackson Cooks Soul.* New York: Aurora, 1970.
Jacobs, Jane. *The Death and Life of Great American Cities.* New York: Random House, 1961.
Jacobson, Matthew Frye. *Whiteness of a Different Color: European Immigrants and the Alchemy of Race.* Cambridge, Mass.: Harvard University Press, 1997.
————. *Special Sorrows: The Diasporic Imagination of Irish, Polish, and Jewish Immigrants in the United States.* Berkeley: University of California Press, 2002.
James, Etta, with David Ritz. *Rage to Survive.* New York: Villard Press, 1995.

Jams, George G. M. *Stolen Legacy.* Trenton: Africa World Press, 1954.

Jezer, Marty. *The Dark Ages: Life in the United States, 1945–1960.* Boston: South End Press, 1982.

Johnson, John. *Succeeding Against the Odds: The Autobiography of a Great American Businessman.* New York: Amistad, 1989.

Johnson, Philip A. *Call Me Neighbor, Call Me Friend.* Garden City, N.Y.: Doubleday, 1965.

Johnson, Philip C. *Mies van der Rohe.* New York: Museum of Modern Art, 1947.

Jones, LeRoi. *Blues People.* New York: William Morrow, 1963.

Judt, Tony. *Postwar: A History of Europe Since 1945.* New York: Penguin Press, 2005.

———. *Ill Fares the Land.* New York: Penguin Press, 2010.

Keil, Charles. *Urban Blues.* Chicago: University of Chicago Press, 1966.

Kenner, Hugh. *Bucky: A Guided Tour of Buckminster Fuller.* New York: William Morrow, 1973.

Kenney, William Howland. *Chicago Jazz: A Cultural History, 1904–1930.* New York: Oxford University Press, 1993.

Kent, George E. *A Life of Gwendolyn Brooks.* Lexington: University Press of Kentucky, 1990.

Kentgens-Craig, Margret. *The Bauhaus and America: First Contacts 1919–1936.* Cambridge, Mass.: MIT Press, 2001.

King, Emily. *Robert Brownjohn: Sex and Typography.* New York: Princeton Architectural Press, 2005.

Kipling, Rudyard. *American Notes.* 1899; reprint New York: Arno, 1974.

Kirkland, Wallace. *Recollections of a Life Photographer.* Cambridge, Mass.: Riverside Press, 1954.

Kisseloff, Jeff. *The Box: An Oral History of Television, 1920–1961.* New York: Viking Press, 1995.

Knupfer, Anne Meis. *The Chicago Black Renaissance and Women's Activism.* Urbana: University of Illinois Press, 2006.

Korth, Fred G. *The Chicago Book: Photographs.* Chicago: Fred G. Korth, 1949.

Kostelanetz, Richard, ed. *Moholy-Nagy: An Anthology.* New York: Praeger, 1970.

Krausee, Joachim, and Claude Lichtenstein, eds. *Your Private Sky: R. Buckminster Fuller: The Art of Design Science.* Baden: Lars Muller, 1999.

Kroc, Ray, with Robert Anderson. *Grinding It Out: The Making of McDonald's.* New York: St. Martin's, 1977.

Kuh, Katharine. *My Love Affair with Modern Art.* New York: Arcade, 2006.

Kupcinet, Irv. *Kup's Chicago.* Cleveland: World, 1962.

Kupcinet, Irv, with Paul Neimark. *Kup: A Man, An Era, A City.* Chicago: Bonus Books, 1988.

Lait, Jack, and Lee Mortimer. *Chicago Confidential.* New York: Crown, 1950.

Lambert, Phyllis, ed. *Mies in America.* New York: Harry Abrams, 2001.

Lambourne, Lionel. *Utopian Craftsmen*. New York: Van Nostrand Reinholt, 1980.

Le Corbusier. *Towards a New Architecture*. New York: Dover, 1986.

Lee, Martha F. *The Nation of Islam: An American Millenarian Movement*. Syracuse, N.Y.: Syracuse University Press, 1996.

Lemann, Nicholas. *The Promised Land: The Great Black Migration and How It Changed America*. New York: Alfred A. Knopf, 1991.

Levine, Lawrence W. *Black Culture and Black Consciousness*. Oxford, U.K.: Oxford University Press, 1977.

Liebling, A. J. *Chicago: The Second City*. New York: Alfred A. Knopf, 1952.

Lindberg, Richard C., and Gloria Jean Sykes. *Shattered Sense of Innocence: The 1955 Murders of Three Chicago Children*. Carbondale: Southern Illinois University Press, 2006.

Linfield, Susie. *The Cruel Radiance: Photography and Political Violence*. Chicago: University of Chicago Press, 2010.

Lock, Graham. *Blutopia*. Durham, N.C.: Duke University Press, 1999.

Lodder, Christina. *Russian Constructivism*. New Haven, Conn.: Yale University Press, 1983.

Love, John F. *McDonald's: Behind the Arches*. New York: Bantam Books, 1986.

Lowe, David. *Lost Chicago*. Boston: Houghton Mifflin, 1975.

———. *Chicago Interiors*. Chicago: Contemporary Books, 1979.

Lownes, Victor. *The Day the Bunny Died*. Secaucus, N.J.: Lyle Stuart, 1982.

Lynch, Kevin. *The Image of the City*. Cambridge, Mass.: MIT Press, 2008.

Lynes, Russell. *The Tastemakers*. New York: Harper & Brothers, 1949.

Lyon, Christopher. *Nancy Spero: The Work*. Munich: Prestel, 2010.

Macadams, Lewis. *Birth of the Cool*. New York: Free Press, 2001.

Maisel, L. Sandy, and Ira N. Forman, eds. *Jews in American Politics*. Lanham, Md.: Rowman & Littlefield, 2001.

Malcolm X, as told to Alex Haley. *The Autobiography of Malcolm X*. New York: Ballantine, 1973.

Margolin, Victor. *The Struggle for Utopia: Rodchenko, Lissitzky, Moholy-Nagy, 1917–1946*. Chicago: University of Chicago Press, 1997.

Marks, Robert W. *The Dymaxion World of Buckminster Fuller*. Carbondale: Southern Illinois University Press, 1960.

Martin, John Bartlow. *Adlai Stevenson of Illinois*. Garden City, N.Y.: Doubleday, 1976.

Mavilgiano, George J., and Richard A. Lawson. *The Federal Art Project in Illinois, 1935–1943*. Carbondale: Southern Illinois University Press, 1990.

May, Elaine Tyler. *Homeward Bound: American Families in the Cold War Era*. New York: Basic Books, 1988.

Mayer, Harold M., and Richard C. Wade. *Chicago: Growth of a Metropolis*. Chicago: University of Chicago Press, 1969.

Mayer, Milton. *Robert Maynard Hutchins: A Memoir*. Berkeley: University of California Press, 1993.

McDougal, Dennis. *The Last Mogul: Lew Wasserman, MCA, and the Hidden History of Hollywood*. New York: Da Capo Press, 2001.

McGreevy, John T. *Parish Boundaries: The Catholic Encounter with Race in the Twentieth-Century Urban North*. Chicago: University of Chicago Press, 1996.

McKeever, Porter. *Adlai Stevenson: His Life and Legacy*. New York: William Morrow, 1989.

McLuhan, Marshall, and Quentin Fiore. *The Medium Is the Massage: An Inventory of Effects*. New York: Bantam Books, 1967.

McNeill, William H. *Hutchins' University: A Memoir of the University of Chicago, 1929–1950*. Chicago: University of Chicago Press, 1991.

Melham, D. H. *Gwendolyn Brooks: Poetry and the Heroic Voice*. Lexington: University Press of Kentucky, 1987.

Merrill Hugh. *Esky: The Early Years at Esquire*. New Brunswick, N.J.: Rutgers University Press, 1995.

Metress, Christopher, ed. *The Lynching of Emmett Till: A Documentary Narrative*. Charlottesville: University of Virginia Press, 2002.

Metropolitan Housing Council. *Rebuilding Chicago's Slums*. Chicago: Metropolitan Housing Council, 1947.

Meyer, Stephen Grant. *As Long As They Don't Move Next Door: Segregation and Radical Conflict in American Neighborhoods*. Lanham, Md.: Rowman & Littlefield, 2000.

Meyerson, Martin, and Edward C. Banfield. *Politics, Planning, and the Public Interest: The Case of Public Housing in Chicago*. Glencoe, N.Y.: Free Press, 1964.

Mayor's Committee on Race Relations. *City Planning in Race Relations: Proceedings of the Mayor's Conference on Race Relations*. Chicago: City of Chicago, 1944.

Mezzrow, Mezz, and Bernard Wolfe. *Really the Blues*. New York: Random House, 1946.

Miller, Paul Eduard, ed. *Esquire's 1946 Jazz Book*. New York: A.S. Barnes, 1946.

Miller, Wayne F. *Chicago's South Side, 1946–1948*. Berkeley: University of California Press, 2000.

Moholy-Nagy, László. *The New Vision*. New York: W. W. Norton, 1938.

———. *Vision in Motion*. Chicago: Paul Theobald, 1947.

———. *Color in Transparency*. Gottingen: Steidl, 2006.

Moholy-Nagy, Sibyl. *Moholy-Nagy: Experiment in Totality*. New York: Harper & Brothers, 1950.

Morrison, Hugh. *Louis Sullivan: Prophet of Modern Architecture*. New York: W. W. Norton, 1962.

Motley, Willard. *Knock on Any Door*. New York: D. Appleton-Century, 1947.

Mullen, Bill V. *Popular Fronts: Chicago and African-American Cultural Politics, 1935–1946*. Urbana: University of Illinois Press, 1999.

Murray, Albert. *Stomping the Blues*. New York: McGraw-Hill, 1976.

Museum of Modern Art. *Harry Callahan.* New York: Museum of Modern Art, 1967.

Museum of Science and Industry. *A Guide to 150 Years of Chicago Architecture.* Chicago: Chicago Review Press, 1985.

Neiman, LeRoy. *All Told.* Guilford, Conn.: Lyons Press, 2012.

Neumeyer, Fritz. *The Artless Word: Mies van der Rohe on the Building Art.* Translated by Mark Jarzombek. Cambridge, Mass.: MIT Press, 1991.

Nickel, Richard, and Aaron Siskind, with John Vinci and Ward Miller. *The Complete Architecture of Adler & Sullivan.* Chicago: Richard Nickel Committee, 2010.

Novak, Michael. *Unmeltable Ethnics: Politics and Culture in American Life.* New Brunswick, N.J.: Transaction, 1996.

Obama, Barack. *Dreams from My Father.* New York: Broadway, 2004.

O'Connor, Len. *Clout.* New York: Avon Books, 1976.

O'Shea, Gene. *Unbridled Rage: A True Story of Organized Crime, Corruption and Murder in Chicago.* New York: Berkeley Books, 2005.

Owings, Nathaniel. *The Spaces in Between.* Boston: Houghton Mifflin, 1973.

Pacyga, Dominic A. *Polish Immigrants and Industrial Chicago: Workers on the South Side, 1880–1922.* Columbus: Ohio State University Press, 1991.

Palmer, Robert. *Deep Blues.* New York: Viking, 1981.

Passuth, Krisztina. *Moholy-Nagy.* New York: Thames & Hudson, 1985.

Patinkin, Sheldon. *The Second City: Backstage at the World's Greatest Comedy Theater.* Naperville, Ill.: SourceBooks, 2000.

Pearson, Charles T. *The Indomitable Tin Goose: The True Story of Preston Tucker and His Car.* New York: Harper & Row, 1960.

Pegg, Bruce. *Brown Eyed Handsome Man: The Life and Hard Times of Chuck Berry.* New York: Routledge, 2002.

Percy, William Alexander. *Lanterns on the Levee.* New York: Alfred A. Knopf, 1941.

Plank, Jeffrey. *Aaron Siskind and Louis Sullivan: The Institute of Design Photo Section Project.* San Francisco: William Stout, 2008.

Pommer, Richard, David Spaeth, and Kevin Harrington. *In the Shadow of Mies: Ludwig Hilberseimer, Architect, Educator and Urban Planner.* New York: Rizzoli International, 1988.

Porter, Lewis. *John Coltrane: His Life and Music.* Ann Arbor: University of Michigan Press, 1998.

Prince, Sue Ann, ed. *The Old Guard and the Avant-Garde: Modernism in Chicago, 1910–1940.* Chicago: University of Chicago Press, 1990.

Pruter, Robert. *Chicago Soul.* Champaign: University of Illinois Press, 1992.

———. *Doowop: The Chicago Scene.* Champaign: University of Illinois Press, 1996.

Puente, Moses, ed. *Conversations with Mies van der Rohe.* New York: Princeton Architectural Press, 2008.

Purdy, James. *Malcolm.* New York: Farrar, Straus & Giroux, 1959.

———. *Gertrude of Stony Island Avenue.* New York: William Morrow, 1997.

Rakove, Milton. *Don't Make No Waves; Don't Back No Losers: An Insider's Analysis of the Daley Machine.* Bloomington: Indiana University Press 1975.

—————. *We Don't Want Nobody Nobody Sent: An Oral History of the Daley Years.* Bloomington: Indiana University Press, 1979.

Reed, Christopher Robert. *The Chicago NAACP and the Rise of Black Professional Leadership, 1910–1966.* Bloomington and Indianapolis: Indiana University Press, 1997.

Reppetto, Thomas A. *Bringing Down the Mob: The War Against the American Mafia.* New York: Henry Holt, 2006.

Republican National Committee. *Official Report of the Proceedings of the 25th Republican National Convention.* Washington, D.C.: Republican National Committee, 1952.

Rexroth, Kenneth. *An Autobiographical Novel.* Santa Barbara, Calif.: Ross-Erickson, 1978.

Riesman, David. *The Lonely Crowd.* New Haven, Conn.: Yale University Press, 1950.

Rosemont, Franklin. *The Rise and Fall of the Dil Pickle.* Chicago: Charles H. Kerr, 2004.

Rossi, Peter H., and Robert A. Dentler. *The Politics of Urban Renewal: The Chicago Findings.* Glencoe, N.Y.: Free Press, 1961.

Rothwell, Fred. *Long Distance Information: Chuck Berry's Recorded Legacy.* York, U.K.: Music Mentor Books, 2001.

Rowe, Mike. *Chicago Blues: The City and the Music.* New York: Da Capo, 1975.

Royko, Mike. *Boss: Richard J. Daley of Chicago.* Chicago: Plume, 1988.

Russo, Gus. *The Outfit.* New York: Bloomsbury, 2003.

Rust, Daniel L. *Flying Across America.* Norman: University of Oklahoma Press, 2009.

Sahlins, Bernard. *Days and Nights at the Second City.* Chicago: Ivan R. Dee, 2001.

Salvatore, Nick. *Singing in a Strange Land: C. L. Franklin, the Black Church, and the Transformation of America.* New York: Little, Brown, 2005.

Salvesen, Britt. *Harry Callahan: The Photographer at Work.* New Haven, Conn.: Yale University Press, 2006.

Samors, Neal, and Michael Williams. *Chicago in the Fifties.* Chicago: Chicago's Neighborhoods, 2005.

Sandburg, Carl. *The Chicago Race Riots, July, 1919.* New York: Harcourt, Brace & Howe, 1919.

Satter, Beryl. *Family Properties: Race, Real Estate, and the Exploitation of Black Urban America.* New York: Henry Holt, 2009.

Saunders, Doris E., ed. *The Kennedy Years and the Negro.* Chicago: Johnson, 1964.

Segrest, James, and Mark Hoffman. *Moanin' at Midnight: The Life and Times of Howlin' Wolf.* New York: Thunder's Mouth Press, 2004.

Schulze, Franz. *Fantastic Images: Chicago Art Since 1945.* Chicago: Follett, 1972.

————. *Mies van der Rohe: A Critical Biography.* Chicago: University of Chicago Press, 1985.

Schulze, Franz, and Edward Windhorst. *Mies van der Rohe: A Critical Biography.* Rev. ed. Chicago: University of Chicago Press, 2012.

Schwerin, Jules. *Got to Tell It.* New York: Oxford University Press, 1992.

Seligman, Amanda I. *Block By Block: Neighborhoods and Public Policy on Chicago's West Side.* Chicago: University of Chicago Press, 2005.

Shapiro, Herbert. *White Violence and Black Response: From Reconstruction to Montgomery.* Amherst: University of Massachusetts Press, 1988.

Shaw, Arnold. *The Rockin' '50s: The Decade That Transformed the Pop Music Scene.* New York: Hawthorn Books, 1974.

————. *Honkers and Shouters: The Golden Years of Rhythm & Blues.* New York: Collier Books, 1978.

Shay, Art. *Album for an Age.* Chicago: Ivan R. Dee, 2000.

————. *Chicago's Nelson Algren.* New York: Seven Stories Press, 2007.

Shell, William S. *Impressions of Mies.* Privately printed, 1988.

Sinclair, Upton. *The Jungle.* New York: Doubleday, 1906.

Smith, Alson J. *Chicago's Left Bank.* Chicago: Henry Regnery, 1953.

Smith, Carl. *The Plan of Chicago: Daniel Burnham and the Remaking of the American City.* Chicago: University of Chicago, 2006.

Smith, Richard Norton. *The Colonel: The Life and Legend of Robert R. McCormick.* Boston: Houghton Mifflin, 1997.

Solomon, Ezra, and Zarko G. Bilbija. *Metropolitan Chicago: An Economic Analysis.* Glencoe, N.Y.: Free Press, 1959.

South Side Planning Board. *An Opportunity for Private and Public Investment in Rebuilding Chicago.* Chicago: SSPB, 1947.

Spear, Allen. *Black Chicago: The Making of a Negro Ghetto, 1890–1920.* Chicago: University of Chicago Press, 1967.

Spigel, Lynn. *TV by Design: Modern Art and the Rise of Network Television.* Chicago: University of Chicago Press, 2008.

Spolin, Viola. *Improvisation for the Theater.* 3rd ed. Evanston, Ill.: Northwestern University Press, 1963.

Stearns, Marshall W. *The Story of Jazz.* New York: Oxford University Press, 1956.

Stevenson, Adlai E., *Major Campaign Speeches of Adlai E. Stevenson, 1952.* New York: Random House, 1953.

Storch, Randi. *Red Chicago: American Communism at Its Grassroots, 1928–35.* Urbana: University of Illinois Press, 2007.

Suhre, Terry. *Moholy-Nagy: A New Vision for Chicago.* Urbana: University of Illinois Press, 1991.

Sullivan, Louis. *Kindergarten Chats and Other Writings.* New York: Wittenborn Art Books, 1947.

————. *The Autobiography of an Idea.* New York: Dover Books, 1956.

Sweet, Jeffrey. *Something Wonderful Right Away.* New York: Avon, 1978.

Szarkowski, John. *The Idea of Louis Sullivan*. Boston: Bullfinch Press, 2000.

Szwed, John. *Space Is the Place: The Lives and Times of Sun Ra*. New York: Da Capo, 1998.

Talese, Gay. *Thy Neighbor's Wife*. Garden City, N.Y.: Doubleday, 1980.

Terkel, Studs. *Division Street: America*. New York: Pantheon, 1967.

———. *Hard Times*. New York: Pantheon, 1970.

———. *Talking to Myself*. New York: Pantheon, 1977.

———. *The Good War*. New York: Pantheon, 1984.

———. *Chicago*. New York: Pantheon, 1985.

———. *Race*. New York: New Press, 1992.

Terkel, Studs, with Sydney Lewis. *Touch and Go: A Memoir*. New York: New Press, 2007.

Terkel, Studs, with Milly Hawk Daniel. *Giants of Jazz*. Rev. ed. New York: Thomas Y. Crowell, 1975.

Till-Mobley, Mamie, and Christopher Benson. *Death of Innocence: The Story of the Hate Crime that Changed America*. New York: Ballantine Books, 2003.

Thomas, William I., and Florian Znaniecki. *The Polish Peasant in Europe and America*. Urbana: University of Illinois Press, 1996.

Thompson, D'Arcy. *On Growth and Form*. Cambridge, Mass.: Cambridge University Press, 1961.

Thompson, Era Bell. *American Daughter*. Chicago: University of Chicago Press, 1945.

Thrasher, Frederic M. *The Gang*. Chicago: University of Chicago Press, 1927.

Travis, David, and Elizabeth Siegel, ed. *Taken by Design: Photographs from the Institute of Design, 1937–1971*. Chicago: Art Institute of Chicago, 2002.

Tillstrom, Burr. *Burr Tillstrom's Kuklapolitan Courier Year Book*. Chicago: Burr Tillstrom, 1951.

Turner, Bernard C. *A View of Bronzeville*. Chicago: Highlights of Chicago Press, 2002.

Twombly, Robert. *Louis Sullivan: His Life and Work*. New York: Viking, 1986.

Van Rijn, Guido. *The Truman and Eisenhower Blues: African-American Blues and Gospel Songs, 1945–1960*. London: Continuum, 2004.

Varian, Elayne H. *Hugo Weber: A Retrospective Exhibition*. New York: Finch College, 1975.

Von Eckardt, Wolf, and Sander L. Gilman. *Bertolt Brecht's Berlin*. Garden City, N.Y.: Anchor Press, 1974.

Von Hoffman, Nicholas. *Radical: A Portrait of Saul Alinsky*. New York: Nation Books, 2010.

Von Schilling, James. *The Magic Window: American Television, 1939–1953*. Binghamton, N.Y.: Haworth Press, 2003.

Waldheim, Charles, and Katerina Ruedi Ray. *Chicago Architecture: Histories, Revisions, Alternatives*. Chicago: University of Chicago Press, 2005.

Walker, Margaret. *Richard Wright: Daemonic Genius*. New York: Amistad, 1988.

———. *This Is My Century.* Athens: University of Georgia Press, 1989.

Wallach, Jennifer Jensen. *Richard Wright: From Black Boy to World Citizen.* Chicago: Ivan R. Dee, 2010.

Wankel, F. A. *Video Facilities of the Network Broadcaster at the Chicago Political Conventions.* New York: National Broadcasting Company, 1952.

Ward-Royster, Willa, as told to Toni Rose. *How I Got Over: Clara Ward and the World-Famous Ward Singers.* Philadelphia: Temple University Press, 1997.

Warren, Lynne. *Art in Chicago, 1945–1995.* Chicago: Museum of Contemporary Art, 1996.

Washington, Sylvia Hood. *Packing Them In: An Archaeology of Environmental Racism in Chicago, 1865–1954.* Lanham, Md.: Lexington Books, 2005.

Watts, Steven. *Mr. Playboy.* Hoboken, N.J.: John Wiley & Sons, 2008.

Wendt, Lloyd, and Herman Kogan. *Lords of the Levee: The Story of Bathhouse John and Hinky Dink.* Indianapolis: Bobbs-Merrill, 1943.

———. *Big Bill of Chicago.* Indianapolis: Bobbs-Merrill, 1953.

Werner, Craig Hansen. *Playing the Changes: From Afro-Modernism to the Jazz Impulse.* Urbana: University of Illinois Press, 1994.

———. *Higher Ground.* New York: Crown, 2004.

Werthamer, Shirley. *Private Planning for Urban Development.* M.A. thesis, University of Chicago, 1947, unpublished.

Wexler, Jerry, and David Ritz. *Rhythm and the Blues: A Life in American Music.* New York: Alfred A. Knopf, 1993.

White, John Franklin. *Art in Action: American Art Centers and the New Deal.* Lanham, Md.: Scarecrow Press, 1987.

White, Theodore H. *The Making of the President 1960.* New York: Atheneum, 1961.

Whitfield, Stephen. *A Death in the Delta: The Story of Emmett Till.* Baltimore: Johns Hopkins University Press, 1988.

Wilkerson, Isabel. *The Warmth of Other Suns: The Epic Story of America's Great Migration.* New York: Random House, 2010.

Williams, Raymond. *The Country and the City.* New York: Oxford University Press, 1973.

Wilson, James Q. *Negro Politics: The Search for Leadership.* Glencoe, N.Y.: Free Press, 1960.

Wingler, Hans M. *The Bauhaus.* Cambridge, Mass.: MIT Press, 1978.

Woodbury, Coleman, ed. *The Future of Cities and Urban Redevelopment.* Chicago: University of Chicago Press, 1953.

Wright, Frank Lloyd. *Frank Lloyd Wright: An Autobiography.* 1932; reprint New York: Pomegranate Press, 2005.

———. *Genius and the Mobocracy.* New York: Horizon, 1949.

———. *The Early Work of Frank Lloyd Wright.* New York: Dover, 1982.

———. *In the Cause of Architecture.* New York: McGraw-Hill, 1987.

———. *Writings and Buildings.* New York: Meridian, 1995.

Wright, Richard. *12 Million Black Voices.* 1941; reprint New York: Thunder's Mouth Press, 1988.

———. *Black Boy.* 1945; reprint New York: Harper Perennial Modern Classic, 2006.

Zukowsky, John. *Mies Reconsidered: His Career, Legacy and Disciples.* New York: Rizzoli International, 1986.

JOURNAL ARTICLES

Baraka, Amiri. *African American Review* 29 (Summer 1995).

Barrett, Paul. "Public Policy and Private Choice: Mass Transit and the Automobile in Chicago Between the Wars." *Business History Review* 49 (Winter 1975), pp. 473–97.

Barter, Judith A. "Designing for Democracy: Modernism and its Utopias," *Art Institute of Chicago Museum Studies* 27, no. 2 (2001), pp. 6–17, 105.

Blucher, Walter H. "A Hospital Plans: The Michael Reese Hospital Planning Project," *Town Planning Review* 21 (January 1951), pp. 318–56.

Bluestone, Daniel. "Preservation and Renewal in Post–World War II Chicago." *Journal of Architectural Education* 47 (May 1994), pp. 210–23.

———. "Chicago's Mecca Flat Blues." *Journal of the Society of Architectural Historians* 57 (December 1998), pp. 382–403.

Bogaert, Anthony F., Deborah A. Turkovich, and Carolyn I. Hafer. "A Content Analysis of 'Playboy' Centerfolds from 1953 Through 1990: Changes in Explicitness, Objectification, and Model's Age." *Journal of Sex Research* 30 (May 1993), pp. 135–39.

Bone, Robert. "Richard Wright and the Chicago Renaissance." *Callaloo* 28 (Summer 1986), pp. 446–68.

Breazeale, Kenon. "In Spite of Women: *Esquire* Magazine and the Construction of the Male Consumer." *Signs* 20 (Autumn 1994), pp. 1–22.

Bredendieck, Hin. "The Legacy of the Bauhaus." *Art Journal* 22 (Autumn 1962), pp. 15–21.

Brooks, H. Allen. " 'Chicago School': Metamorphosis of a Term." *Journal of the Society of Architectural Historians* 25 (May 1966), pp. 115–18.

Cappetti, Carla. "Sociology of an Existence: Richard Wright and the Chicago School." *MELUS* 12 (Summer 1985), pp. 25–43.

Carter, Steven R. "Commitment amid Complexity: Lorraine Hansberry's Life in Action." *MELUS* 7 (Autumn 1980), pp. 39–53.

Conroy, Jack. "Memories of Arna Bontemps: Friend and Collaborator." *Negro American Literature Forum* 10 (Summer 1976), pp. 53–57.

DeGraaf, John, and Alan Harris Stein. "The Guerrilla Journalist as Oral Historian: An Interview with Louis 'Studs' Terkel." *Oral History Review* 29, no. 1 (Winter–Spring 2002), pp. 87–107.

Drake, J. G. St. Clair. "Profiles: Chicago." *Journal of Educational Sociology* 17 (January 1944), pp. 261–71.

Findeli, Alain. "Moholy-Nagy's Design Pedagogy in Chicago (1937–46)." *Design Issues* 7 (Autumn 1990), pp. 4–19.

Findeli, Alain, and Charlotte Benton. "Design Education and Industry: The Laborious Beginnings of the Institute of Design in Chicago in 1944." *Journal of Design History* 4, no. 2 (1991), pp. 97–113.

Finestone, Harold. "Narcotics and Criminality." *Law and Contemporary Problems* 22 (Winter 1957), pp. 69–85.

———. "Cats, Kicks, and Color." *Social Problems* 5 (July 1957), pp. 3–13.

Fleming, John E., and Margaret T. Burroughs. "Dr. Margaret T. Burroughs: Artist, Teacher, Administrator, Writer, Political Activist, and Museum Founder." *Public Historian* 21, no. 1 (Winter 1999).

Fraterrigo, Elizabeth. "The Answer to Suburbia: Playboy's Urban Lifestyle." *Journal of Urban History* 34, no. 5 (July 2008), pp. 747–74.

Galison, Peter. "Aufbau/Bauhaus: Logical Positivism and Architectural Modernism." *Critical Inquiry* 16 (Summer 1990), pp. 709–52.

Garvey, Timothy J. "László Moholy-Nagy and Atomic Ambivalence in Postwar Chicago." *American Art* 14 (Autumn 2000), pp. 22–39.

Giles, James R., and Jerome Klinkowitz. "The Emergence of Willard Motley in Black American Literature." *Negro American Literature Forum* 6 (Summer 1972), pp. 31–34.

Gordon, Rita Werner. "The Change in the Political Alignment of Chicago's Negroes During the New Deal." *Journal of American History* 56, no. 3 (December 1969).

Gropius, Walter, and Howard Dearstyne. "The Bauhaus Contribution." *Journal of Architectural Education* 18 (June 1963), pp. 14–16.

Grunsfeld, Ernest A., and Louis Wirth. "A Plan for Metropolitan Chicago." *Town Planning Review* 25 (April 1954), pp. 5–32.

Hassell-Hughes, Sheila. "A Prophet Overheard: A Juxtapositional Reading of Gwendolyn Brooks's 'In the Mecca.'" *African-American Review* 38, no. 2 (Summer 2004).

Hess, Alan. "The Origins of McDonald's Golden Arches." *Journal of the Society of Architectural Historians* 45 (March 1986), pp. 60–67.

Hilberseimer, Ludwig. "Kasimir Malevich and the Non-Objective World." *Art Journal* 20 (Winter 1960–61), pp. 82–83.

Hild, Theodore W. "The Demolition of the Garrick Theater and the Birth of the Preservation Movement in Chicago." *Illinois Historical Journal* 88, no. 2 (Summer 1995).

Hirsch, Arnold R. "Massive Resistance in the Urban North: Trumbull Park, Chicago, 1953–1966." *Journal of American History* 82 (September 1995), pp. 522–50.

Hitchcock, Henry-Russell. "The Evolution of Wright, Mies & Le Corbusier." *Perspecta* (Summer 1952), pp. 8–15.

Hudson-Weems, Clenora. "Resurrecting Emmett Till: The Catalyst of the Modern Civil Rights Movement." *Journal of Black Studies* 29, no. 2 (November 1998).

Hughes, Patrick H., Noel W. Barker, Gail A. Crawford, and Jerome H. Jaffe. "The Natural History of a Heroin Epidemic." *American Journal of Public Health* 62, no. 7 (July 1972), pp. 995–1001.

Hunt, D. Bradford. "What Went Wrong with Public Housing in Chicago? A History of the Robert Taylor Homes." *Journal of the Illinois State Historical Society* (Spring 2001).

Huxtable, Ada Louise. "A New Plan for Chicago's South Side." *Bulletin of the Museum of Modern Art* 14 (July 1947), pp. 12–17.

Irish, Sharon. "Preservation, Polemics, and Power: Carl W. Condit's *The Chicago School of Architecture*." *E-Technology and Culture* 49, no. 1 (January 2008), pp. 202–14.

James, Willis Laurence. "The Romance of the Negro Folk Cry in America." *Phylon (1940–1956)* 16 (1st Quarter 1955), pp. 15–30.

Joseph, Branden W. "John Cage and the Architecture of Silence." *October* 81 (Summer 1997), pp. 80–104.

Kasperson, Roger E. "Toward a Geography of Urban Politics: Chicago, a Case Study." *Economic Geography* 41 (April 1965), pp. 95–107.

Kendall, Sue Ann. "C. J. Bulliet: Chicago's Lonely Champion of Modernism." *Archives of American Art Journal* 26, no. 2 (1986), pp. 21–32.

Kiang, Ying-Cheng. "The Distribution of the Ethnic Groups in Chicago, 1960." *American Journal of Sociology* 74 (November 1968), pp. 292–95.

Knupfer, Anne Meis. "African-American Designers: The Chicago Experience Then and Now." *Design Issues* 16 (Autumn 2000), pp. 84–91.

Kuh, Katharine. "Seeing Is Believing." *Bulletin of the Art Institute of Chicago* 39 (April–May 1945), pp. 53–56.

————. Interview by Avis Berman. *Archives of American Art Journal* 27, no. 3 (1987), pp. 2–36.

Lipsitz, George. "The Meaning of Memory: Family, Class, and Ethnicity in Early Network Television Programs." *Cultural Anthropology* 1 (November 1986), pp. 355–87.

Lowney, John. "A material collapse that is construction": History and Counter-Memory in Gwendolyn Brooks's 'In the Mecca.'" *MELUS* 23, no. 3 (Autumn 1998).

Malcolmson, Reginald F. "A Curriculum of Ideas." *Journal of Architectural Education* 14 (Autumn 1959), pp. 41–43.

Mavigliano, George J. "The Chicago Design Workshop: 1939–1943." *Journal of Decorative and Propaganda Arts* 6 (Autumn 1987), pp. 34–47.

Mayer, Harold M. "Urban Geography and Chicago in Retrospect." *Annals of the Association of American Geographers* 69 (March 1979), pp. 114–18.

Mies van der Rohe, Ludwig. "A Tribute to Frank Lloyd Wright." *College Art Journal* 6, no. 1 (Autumn 1946), pp. 41–42.

Miller, Ross. "Chicago Architecture After Mies." *Critical Inquiry* 6 (Winter 1979), pp. 271–89.

Moholy-Nagy, Sibyl. "The Diaspora." *Journal of the Society of Architectural Historians* 24 (March 1965), pp. 24–26.

Moore, William Howard. "Was Estes Kefauver 'Blackmailed' During the Chicago Crime Hearings? A Historian's Perspective." *Public Historian* 4, no. 1 (Winter 1982), pp. 4–28.

Paine, Judith. "Sibyl Moholy-Nagy: A Complete Life." *Archives of American Art Journal* 15, no. 4 (1975), pp. 11–16.

Parot, Joseph. "Ethnic Versus Black Metropolis: The Origins of Polish-Black Housing Tensions in Chicago." *Polish American Studies* 29, no. 1–2 (Spring–Autumn 1972).

Peretz, Henri. "The Making of Black Metropolis." *Annals of the American Academy of Political and Social Science* 595, no. 1 (September 2004), pp. 168–75.

Phelan, Andrew. "The Bauhaus and Studio Art Education." *Art Education* 34 (September 1981), pp. 6–13.

Plotkin, Wendy. " 'Hemmed In': The Struggle Against Racial Restrictive Covenants and Deed Restrictions in Post-WWII Chicago." *Journal of the Illinois State Historical Society* 94, no. 1 (Spring 2001).

Proudfoot, Malcolm J. "Chicago's Fragmented Political Structure." *Geographical Review* 47 (January 1957), pp. 106–17.

Reeder, Leo. "The Central Area of Chicago: A Re-examination of the Process of Decentralization." *Land Economics* 28, no. 4 (November 1952), pp. 369–73.

Riesman, David. "Listening to Popular Music." *American Quarterly* no. 4 (Winter 1950), pp. 359–71.

Rossen, Susan F., and Charlotte Moser. "Primer for Seeing: The Gallery of Art Interpretation and Katharine Kuh's Crusade for Modernism in Chicago." *Art Institute of Chicago Museum Studies* 16, no. 1 (1990), pp. 6–25, 88–90.

Rury, John L. "Race, Space, and the Politics of Chicago's Public Schools: Benjamin Willis and the Tragedy of Urban Education." *History of Education Quarterly* 39 (Summer 1999), pp. 117–42.

Sawelson-Gorse, Naomi. "The Art Institute of Chicago and the Arensberg Collection." *Art Institute of Chicago Museum Studies* 19, no. 1 (1993).

Schietinger, E. F. "Race and Residential Market Values in Chicago." *Land Economics* 30 (November 1954), pp. 301–8.

Schulman, Daniel. "Marion Perkins: A Chicago Sculptor Rediscovered." *Art Institute of Chicago Museum Studies* 24, no. 2 (1999), pp. 220–43, 267–71.

Selz, Peter. "Surrealism and the Chicago Imagists of the 1950s: A Comparison and Contrast." *Art Journal* 45 (Winter 1985), pp. 303–6.

Sills, Paul, and Charles L. Mee. "The Celebratory Occasion." *Tulane Drama Review* 9 (Winter 1964), pp. 167–81.

Smith, Gary. "Gwendolyn Brooks's 'A Street in Bronzeville,' The Harlem Renaissance and the Mythologies of Black Women." *MELUS* 10, no. 3 (Autumn 1983).

Spillane, Joseph. "The Making of an Underground Market: Drug Selling in Chicago, 1900–1940." *Journal of Social History* 32 (Autumn 1998), pp. 27–47.

Stavros, George. "An Interview with Gwendolyn Brooks." *Contemporary Literature* 11, no. 1 (Winter 1970).

Tigerman, Stanley. "Mies van der Rohe: A Moral Modernist Model." *Perspecta* 22 (1986), pp. 112–35.

Washington, Mary Helen. "Desegregating the 1950s: The Case of Frank London Brown." *Japanese Journal of American Studies* 10 (1999), pp. 15–32.

Wurster, Catherine Bauer. "The Social Front of Modern Architecture in the 1930s." *Journal of the Society of Architectural Historians* 24 (March 1965), pp. 48–52.

PUBLICATIONS

American Book Review
Aperture
Architectural Forum
Art & Architecture
Art Institute of Chicago Bulletin
Art International
Be-Bop and Beyond
Billboard
Black World/Negro Digest
Cadence
Casabella
Chicago
Chicago After Dark
Chicago American
Chicago Daily News
Chicago History
Chicago Sun
Chicago Sun-Times
Chicago Tribune
Chicago's Nite Life
Christian Science Monitor
Collier's
Contrary
Coronet
The Crisis

The Dallas Morning News
Dayton Ohio Journal Herald
The Defender
The Delta Review
Downbeat
Ebony
Encore
Forbes
Fortune
Frank Lloyd Wright Quarterly
Good Times: Chicago Sex-Dimensional
Harper's
Harper's Bazaar
Hiram Poetry Review
Holiday
Horizon
House Beautiful
The Illinois Entertainer
Jet
Ladies' Home Journal
The Liberator
Life
Lightworks
Look
Los Angeles Times
The New Republic
Newsweek

The New World
New York Herald Tribune
The New York Times
The New Yorker
Parade
The Paris Review
Playboy
Popular Mechanics
Print
Radio Television Mirror
The Reader
Reader's Digest
The Saturday Evening Post
The Sherman
Sports Illustrated
Telecast
Television and Radio Mirror
Theatre Arts
This Week in Chicago
Tide
Time
Time Out Chicago
Times Literary Supplement
TV Forecast
TV Guide
U.S. News & World Report
The Washington Post
Waxpoetics
The Wire

ORAL HISTORIES

COLUMBIA UNIVERSITY
ORAL HISTORY PROJECT
Jacob Arvey
Robert Hutchins
Otto Preminger

ART INSTITUTE OF CHICAGO/CHICAGO
ARCHITECTS ORAL HISTORY PROJECT
Jacques Brownson
Werner Buch
Gordon Bunshaft
Alfred Caldwell

Serge Chermayeff
John Cordwell
George Danforth
Joseph Fujikawa
Charles Booher Genther
Bertram Goldberg
Myron Goldsmith
Bruce Graham
William Hartmann
John Holabird
William Keck
Gertrude Kerbis
Reginald Malcolmson
Carter Manny
Charles Murphy
Walter Netsch
William Turk Priestly
Ambrose Richardson
A. James Speyer
Gene John Vinci Summers
John Vinci
Harry Weese

ARCHIVES OF AMERICAN ART,
SMITHSONIAN INSTITUTION
Don Baum
Margaret Burroughs
John Cage
Harry Callahan
Fitzhugh Dinkins
Richard A. Florsheim and John
    Kearney
Leon Golub
Miyoko Ito
Frederick D. Jones
György Kepes
Archibald John Motley
Gordon Parks
Arthur Siskind
Nancy Spero

ARCHIVE OF AMERICAN TELEVISION
Charlie Andrews
Bob Banner

Lewis Gomavitz
Don Hewitt
Lynwood King
Dan Petrie
Studs Terkel
Mike Wallace

INTERVIEWS BY AUTHOR

Edward Asner
Edward Bland
Michael Bonesteel
Dr. Margaret Burroughs
Ivan Chermayeff
Marshall Chess
Len Gittleman
Hugh Hefner
Ahmad Jamal
John and Lynn Kearney
Haki Madhubuti
John Maloof
Bob Marovich
Joan Miller
Ward Miller
Wayne F. Miller
Bernard Sahlins
Franz Schulze
Art Shay
David Shepherd
Robert Silvers
Kenneth Snelson
Jeffrey Sweet
Brian Urquhart
Nicholas von Hoffman

COLLECTIONS AND PAPERS

ARCHIVES OF AMERICAN ART
Gertrude Abercrombie Papers
Exhibition Momentum
Leon Golub Papers
Walter and Ise Gropius Papers

Hyde Park Art Center Records
Edward Millman Papers
László Moholy-Nagy Papers
Sibyl Moholy-Nagy Papers
Peter Pollack Papers
Hugo Weber Papers
Robert J. Wolff Papers

AVERY LIBRARY, COLUMBIA UNIVERSITY
Serge Chermayeff Papers

MUSEUM OF MODERN ART, NEW YORK
Mies van der Rohe Papers

REGENSTEIN LIBRARY, UNIVERSITY OF
CHICAGO
Alton Abraham Collection of Sun Ra
Walter Paepcke Papers
Elizabeth Paepcke Papers
David Shepherd Papers

DALEY LIBRARY, UNIVERSITY OF
ILLINOIS, CIRCLE CAMPUS
Institute of Design Collection
Metropolitan Planning Council
    Records

MUNICIPAL REFERENCE LIBRARY,
CHICAGO PUBLIC LIBRARY

LOEB DESIGN LIBRARY, HARVARD
UNIVERSITY

HOUGHTON LIBRARY, HARVARD
UNIVERSITY
Walter Gropius Papers

LIBRARY OF CONGRESS
Ludwig Mies van der Rohe Papers

PAUL GALVIN LIBRARY, IIT
Henry T. Heald Papers
Institute of Design Papers

CHICAGO HISTORY MUSEUM
Mahalia Jackson Papers

DUSABLE MUSEUM OF AFRICAN-
AMERICAN HISTORY

VIVIAN G. HARSH RESEARCH COLLEC-
TION IN AFRO-AMERICAN HISTORY
AND LITERATURE, CHICAGO PUBLIC
LIBRARY

ONLINE SOURCES

Adler, Carlye, and Hugh Hefner. "Hugh Hefner Playboy Enterprises in 1953."
CNNMoney, September 1, 2003. http://money.cnn.com/magazines/fsb/fsb
_archive/2003/09/01/350793/index.htm.

Becker, Lynn. "The Expulsion: Chicago Set to Destroy Bauhaus Modernism at
Michael Reese." *Lynn Becker.* 2009. http://www.lynnbecker.com/repeat/
reese/city_trashing_history_aGropius_at_Michael_Reese.htm.

Berger, Molly W. "Hotels." *Encyclopedia of Chicago.* www.encyclopedia.chicago
history.org/pages/603.html.

Binford, Sally. "From Tight Sweaters to the Pentagon Papers." *Susie Bright's
Journal.* May 16, 2008. http://susiebright.blogs.com/susie_brights_journal_/
2008/05/sally-binford-n.html.

"Broadcasting in Chicago, 1921–1989." www.richsamuels.com.

Callahan, Mike, and David Edwards. "The Chess Story." November 4, 2005.
http://www.bsnpubs.com/chess/chesscheck.html.

Campbell, Robert L., Christopher Trent, and Robert Pruter. "From Sonny Blount
to Sun Ra: The Chicago Years." http://hubcap.clemson.edu/~campber/sunra
.html.

Catania, Christopher. "The Magical Back Story of Chicago's Historic Folk Venue
Gate of Horn," *LiveFix*, January 31, 2011. http://christophercatania.com/2011/
01/31/the-magical-back-story-of-chicagos-gate-of-horn.

Chez Paree. http://www.parsec-santa.com/chezparee/ChezParee.html.

Chicago Sun-Times. "Memorandum Regarding Till Murder Trial," September 13,
1955. In *Frontier to Heartland,* http://publications.newberry.org/frontierto
heartland/items/show/123.

"Chuckman's Collection (Chicago Postcards)." http://chuckmancollectionvol
ume6.blogspot.com.

Cleveland, Charles B. "Col. Jack Arvey: A master politician for the Democratic
Organization." *Chicago,* November 1977. http://www.lib.niu.edu/1977/
ii771134.html.

Cogan, Jim. "Bill Putnam." *Universal Audio WebZine* 3, no. 4 (June 2005), http://
www.uaudio.com/webzine/2005/june/text/content8.html.

Corrections to The Voice of the Blues: Classic Interviews from Living Blues Magazine. http://stackhouse-bluesoterica.blogspot.com/2006/07/voice-of-blues
-muddy-waters-howlin.html.

Cooper, Simon. Interview with Marshall Chess. http://www.clashmusic.com/feature/marshall-chess.

"Dan Ryan Expressway: Historic Overview." http://www.chicagoroads.com/roads/dan-ryan.

Ed Bland . . . Urban Classical Funk. http://www.edblandmusic.com.

Encyclopedia of Chicago History. http://www.encyclopedia.chicagohistory.org/pages/700011.html.

"History." Back of the Yards Neighborhood Council. http://bync.org/?page_id=20.

Hoekstra, Dave. "Sun Ra's Calumet City." www.davehoekstra.com/travel/sun_ras_calumet_city.pdf.

"The Housing Philosophy: Can the Tugendhat Villa Be Lived In?" http://www.tugendhat.eu/en/villa-tugendhat/the-housing-philosophy.html.

Howard, Argie. *American Airlines 707 Jet Stewardess*. http://americanairlines stewardess.blogspot.com.

Independent Video Archive. Mediaburn.org.

Kaplan, Jacob. "Michael Reese Hospital." *Forgotten Chicago*. http://forgotten chicago.com/features/michael-reese-hospital.

Keith, Russell, "Design Scandal: Introduction and Method." Rev. August 4, 2008. *Kairosis*. http://kairosis.wordpress.com/article/design-scandal-introduction-13h9pp7wb34y8-10.

"Mahalia Jackson 1912–1972 Discography." http://edwin-gersbach.alpha-host.ch/Books/MJD.pdf.

"Malcolm Chisholm." *Willie Dixon's Blues Heaven*, n.d. http://www.bluesheaven.com/programs/blues-who-of-the-blues/malcolm-chisholm.

"Mapping the Stacks: A Guide to Black Chicago's Hidden Archives," Chicago Public Library. http://mts.lib.uchicago.edu.

Mobley, Mamie. Interview by Studs Terkel. http://www.studsterkel.org/race.php.

Moon, D. Thomas. "Strange Voodoo: Inside the Vaults of Chess Studios." *Blues Access*, Winter 1999. http://www.bluesaccess.com/No_36/chess.html.

Moscato, Marc. "The Tradition of Non-Tradition: The Dill Pickle Club as Catalyst for Social Change," 2009. http://marcmoscato.com/wp-content/uploads/2009/04/preview.pdf.

Music Inn: A Documentary Film. http://www.musicinnfilm.net/history/chronol ogy.html.

Music Inn Archives. Musicinn.org.

Nelson, Lynn. "Sixty-Third Street and Cottage Grove Avenue," *A Kansan in South Chicago*. http://www.kancoll.org/articles/nelson/grove.htm.

Otwell, Andrew. "Moholy-Nagy and Chicago," 1997. *Louis Sauer Architect*. http://louissauer.wordpress.com/2010/01/06/artfunctio.

Pruter, Robert, and Robert L. Campbell. "The Legendary Parkway Label." http://hubcap.clemson.edu/~campber/parkway.html.

"Romano Guardini." http://romanoguardini.blogspot.com.

Shapiro, Sydney H. "Ner Tamid Congregation and Its History." http://www.sh
.org/nt/nt_history.html.

Snelson, Kenneth, to R. Motro. *International Journal of Space Structures,* November 1990. http://www.grunch.net/snelson/rmoto.html. Also http://www.ken
nethsnelson.net/biography.

South Side Community Art Center Collection. http://southsidecommunityartcen
ter.com/sscac_artcollection/index.html.

"Story Urban Renewal and the Role of the Hyde Park–Kenwood Community
Conference Therein." *Hyde Park–Kenwood Community Conference.* http://
www.hydepark.org/historicpres/HPKCCstoryurbren.htm.

United States Department of Commerce, Bureau of the Census. "Current Population Reports: Consumer Income, October 1955." http://www2.census.gov/
prod2/popscan/p60-019.pdf.

University of Chicago. Centennial Catalogues. "Lawrence A. Kimpton, 1910–
1977." *Presidents of the University of Chicago.* http://www.lib.uchicago.edu/e/
spcl/centcat/pres/presch06_01.html.

———. Department of Sociology. "East 63rd Street,1930s." *Social Scientists Map
Chicago,* University of Chicago Library. http://www.lib.uchicago.edu/e/su/
maps/chisoc/G4104-C6-2W9Q4-1930z-U5.html.

———. Department of Sociology. "Ethnic Change, Hyde Park, 1950–1956,"
Social Scientists Map Chicago, University of Chicago Library. http://www.lib
.uchicago.edu/e/su/maps/chisoc/G4104-C6-2H9E11-1956-T3.html.

———. News Office. "Improv Comedy's 50th Anniversary to be Celebrated
Where It All Began: The University of Chicago," June 16, 2005. http://www
-news.uchicago.edu/releases/05/050616.compass.shtml

University of Illinois at Chicago. Office of the Historian. "Permanent Campus
Site Selection, 1958–1963." University of Illinois at Chicago. http://www.uic
.edu/depts/uichistory/permanentcampus.html.

Walton, Charles. "Bronzeville Conversation: Eddie Flagg, Manager of the DuSable
Hotel." *Jazz Institute of Chicago.* http://jazzinchicago.org/educates/journal/
interviews/bronzeville-conversation-eddie-flagg-manager-dusable-hotel.

———. "The DuSable Hotel and the Drexel Square Area." *Jazz Institute of Chicago.* http://www.jazzinchicago.org/educates/journal/articles/
dusable-hotel-and-drexel-square-area.

Whitaker, Hugh Stephen. "A Case Study in Southern Justice: The Emmett Till
Case." Master's thesis, Florida State University, 1963, unpublished. http://etd
.lib.fsu.edu/theses/available/etd-05272004-140932/unrestricted/whitaker
_thesis.pdf.

Whiting, Sarah. "The Invisible Superblock." Skidmore, Owings & Merrill LLP,
no date. http://www.som.com/content.cfm/the_invisible_superblock.

Witter, David. *Newcity.* "This Particular Patch: Nelson Algren's Indiana Getaway,"
n.d., http://summer.newcity.com/2009/05/19/this-particular-patch-nelson
-algrens-indiana-getaway/.

INDEX

CREDITS

Charlie Andrews Interview, Archive of American Television, interviewed by Henry Colman on October 20, 1998. Visit www.emmytvlegends.org/interviews/people/charlie-andrews for more information.

Bob Banner Interview, Archive of American Television, interviewed by Henry Colman on November 5, 1999. Visit www.emmytvlegends.org/interviews/people/bob-banner for more information.

Jacques Calman Brownson, oral history interview by Betty J. Blum, © 1996, Art Institute of Chicago, used with permission.

Werner Buch, oral history interview by Ines Dresel, © 2005, Art Institute of Chicago, used with permission.

Alfred Caldwell, oral history interview by Betty J. Blum, © 1987, Art Institute of Chicago, used with permission.

Serge Chermayeff, oral history interview by Betty J. Blum, © 2001, Art Institute of Chicago, used with permission.

John Donald Cordwell, oral history interview by Betty J. Blum, © 2004, Art Institute of Chicago, used with permission.

George Danforth, oral history interview by Pauline Saliga, © 2003, Art Institute of Chicago, used with permission.

Joseph Fujikawa, oral history interviewed by Betty J. Blum, © 2003, Art Institute of Chicago, used with permission

Charles Booher Genther, oral history interview by Betty J.Blum, © 2003, Art Institute of Chicago, used with permission.

Bertrand Goldberg, oral history interview by Betty J. Blum, © 1992, Art Institute of Chicago, used with permission.

Myron Goldsmith, oral history interview by Betty J. Blum, © 2001, Art Institute of Chicago, used with permission.

Lewis Gomavitz Interview, Archive of American Television, interviewed by Karen Herman on February 2, 2000. Visit www.emmytvlegends.org/interviews/people/lewis-gomavitz for more information.

Bruce John Graham, oral history interview by Betty J. Blum, © 1998, Art Institute of Chicago, used with permission.

William Hartmann, oral history interview by Betty J. Blum, © 2003, Art Institute of Chicago, used with permission

Don Hewitt Interview, Archive of American Television, interviewed by Michael Rosen on April 15, 1997. Visit www.emmytvlegends.org/interviews/people/don-hewitt for more information.

Lynwood King Interview, Archive of American Television, interviewed by Jeff Kisseloff on November 20, 2002. Visit www.emmytvlegends.org/interviews/people/lynwood-king for more information.

Reginald Malcolmson, oral history interview by Betty J. Blum, © 2004, Art Institute of Chicago, used with permission.

Walter Netsch, oral history interview by Betty J. Blum, © 1997, Art Institute of Chicago, used with permission.

Daniel Petrie Interview, Archive of American Television, interviewed by Michael Rosen on February 28, 2001. Visit www.emmytvlegends.org/interviews/people/daniel-petrie for more information.

Ambrose M. Richardson, oral history interview by Betty J. Blum, © 2005, Art Institute of Chicago, used with permission.

Gene Summers, oral history interview by Pauline A. Saliga, © 1993, Art Institute of Chicago, used with permission.

Studs Terkel Interview, Archive of American Television, interviewed by Karen Herman on July 19, 1999. Visit www.emmytvlegends.org/interviews/people/studs-terkel for more information.

John Vinci, oral history interview by Betty J. Blum, © 2002, Art Institute of Chicago, used with permission.

Mike Wallace Interview, Archive of American Television, interviewed by Steve McClellan on April 17, 1998. Visit www.emmytvlegends.org/interviews/people/mike-wallace for more information.

Harry Weese, oral history interview by Betty J. Blum, © 1991, Art Institute of Chicago, used with permission.